Managerial Economics

Managerial Economics

Ivan Png

BLACKWELL
Publishers

Blackwell Publishers Inc.
350 Main Street
Malden, MA
02148

Blackwell Publishers Ltd.
108 Cowley Road
Oxford OX4 1JF
UK

Library of Congress Cataloging-in-Publication Data

Png, Ivan
  Managerial economics / Ivan Png.
    p.   cm.
  Includes index.
  ISBN 1-55786-927-8 (hc)
  1. Managerial economics. I. Title.
HD30.22.P62   1997   97-12043
658.15—dc21   CIP

British Library of Congress Cataloging-in-Publication Data

Manufactured in the USA.

For my parents and three Cs: CW, CY, and CH

Preface

Managerial economics is the science of directing costly resources to achieve managerial objectives. This book presents tools and concepts from managerial economics that practicing managers use. The book is aimed at business students as well as practitioners. Accordingly, it is deliberately written in a simple and accessible style. There is a minimum of technical jargon, complicated figures, and high-brow mathematics. The emphasis is on simple, practical ideas.

The book starts with the very basics. It presumes no prior knowledge of economics and only very elementary mathematics. As the orientation and content of this book differs substantially from traditional economics texts, it will also challenge readers with some background in economics.

Managerial economics is unique in integrating the various functions of management. In addition to presenting the essentials of managerial economics, this book includes many links to other management functions. Some examples are accounting (activity-based costing and statistical cost analysis), finance (takeover strategies), human resource management (incentives and organization), and marketing (brand extensions, promotion, and pricing). Fans of the World Wide Web may like to think of these links as jump points to other management functions.

In addition to the managerial focus, two features are worth emphasizing. First, the same principles of managerial economics apply in Africa, Asia, the Pacific, and Europe as in North and South America. Reflecting that unity, the book includes examples and cases from throughout the world. Second, the book uses examples from both consumer and industrial markets. The reasons are simple: A customer is as likely to be another business as a human being and likewise for suppliers.

For most readers, this may be their only formal book on economics. Accordingly, the book omits sophisticated theories and models, such as indifference curves and production functions, which are more useful in advanced economics courses. Further, the book recognizes that many topics traditionally covered by managerial economics textbooks are now the domain of other basic management courses. Accordingly, the book omits linear programming, present-value analysis, and capital budgeting.

Regarding language, this book refers to *businesses* rather than *firms*. Realistically, many firms are involved in a wide range of businesses. In economics, the usual unit of analysis is a business, industry, or market rather than a firm. Also, the book refers to *buyers* and *sellers* rather than *consumers* and *firms*, since in most real markets, the demand and supply do not neatly divide among households and businesses. To cite just one example, in the market for telecommunications, the demand side consists of businesses and households.

Finally, some comments on how to use this book are in order. Managerial economics is a practical science. Just as no one has learned swimming or tennis simply by watching a professional, no one can learn managerial economics merely by reading this book. Every chapter of this book includes a set of review and discussion questions. The review questions are to help the reader check and reinforce the chapter material. It is essential that new-found skills be practiced on the review questions. The discussion questions are intended to challenge, provoke, and stretch. They will be useful for class and group discussions.

Some chapters include suggestions for further reading. These are practical references for the typical reader, rather than academic journal articles intended for Ph.D. economists.

Some chapters include mathematical supplements. These provide reinforcement to the text using algebra and calculus. The supplements will benefit students with a mathematics background.

Managerial economics is a science that is driven by data. Accordingly, the text and discussion questions frequently refer to actual data and the end of the book includes an appendix that lists many useful sources of data.

Organization

This book is organized in three parts. Following the Introduction, Part I presents the framework of perfectly competitive markets. Chapters 2–6 are the basic starting point of managerial economics. These are presented at a very gradual pace, accessible to readers with no prior background in economics.

The book moves faster in Parts II and III. These are relatively self-contained, so the reader may skip Part II and go directly to Part III. Part II broadens the perspective to situations of market power, while Part III focuses on the issues of management in imperfect markets. Chapter 14 on regulation is the only chapter in Part III that depends on understanding Part II.

A complete course in managerial economics would cover the entire book. If time is limited, a shorter course might consist of Chapters 1–6, followed by either Chapters 7–10, emphasizing market power, or Chapters 11–13, focusing on managing in imperfect markets.

Updates

In the spirit of continuous improvement, I will maintain a Web page containing updates and corrections to the book. The URL is http://www.iscs.nus.edu.sg/~ipng.

Suggestions for improvement are most welcome. The Web page includes a feedback form.

Acknowledgments

First, I must acknowledge my deep gratitude to the reviewers: George Bittling-mayer (University of California, Davis), Margaret Capen (East Carolina University), Mike Granfield (University of California, Riverside), Bob Hansen (Dartmouth College), Douglas Lamdin (University of Maryland, Baltimore County), Lawrence Martin (Michigan State University), Mark Schupack (Brown University), and Mark Zupan (University of Southern California). With great patience, they encouraged and helped me nurture a rough sketch into a complete manuscript.

Next, I wish to thank various individuals, companies, and organizations that provided information and assistance. They include Pinelopi Koujianou Goldberg (Princeton University); Fred Kwan (Hong Kong University of Science and Technology); Lin Chu-chia (National Chengchi University); Frank Mathewson (University of Toronto); Robert Metcalfe, Gloria Pei, Jania Rosen, Fernando Salas, Tao Zhigang, and Wu Changqi (Hong Kong University of Science and Technology); the Australian Competition and Consumer Commission; Cisco Systems, Inc.; the Coalition for Vehicle Choice; the Commission of India, Hong Kong; Echo Bay Mines, Inc.; the office of the European Commission in Hong Kong; Honda Motor Company; the Hong Kong government; National Mutual Ltd., Hong Kong; the Prudential Insurance Company of America, Inc.; the Southern California Rapid Transit District; and Telstra Ltd. Digital Equipment Corporation's Altavista web search service deserves special mention as the starting point of the search for many of the examples in this book.

Finally, I wish to thank the Hong Kong University of Science and Technology, National University of Singapore, and University of California, Los Angeles, the team at Blackwell Publishers (Al Bruckner, Rolf Janke, Lisa McLaughlin, and Mary Riso), compositor Brian Smith and indexer Carol Noble, my economics teachers (Roger Witcomb, Oliver Hart, Mitch Polinsky, and John Roberts), and my family for their support and encouragement.

About the Author

Ivan Png is a Professor of Information Systems at the National University of Singapore. He graduated with a BA with First Class Honours in Economics from Cambridge University (1978) and a PhD from the Graduate School of Business, Stanford (1985).

Mr Png has previously taught at the Anderson School, University of California, Los Angeles (Assistant Professor, 1985–90, Associate Professor 1990–95, Professor 1995–96). He was also a visitor at the Hong Kong University of Science & Technology from 1993–96.

Mr Png received the Outstanding Teaching Award from UCLA's MBA Program for Fully Employed Students, Class of '91. His research has been published in leading scholarly journals including the *American Economic Review, Economic Journal, Journal of Political Economy, Management Science, Marketing Science,* and the *RAND Journal of Economics.* Mr Png is an Associate Editor of the *Journal of Industrial Economics.*

Brief Contents

Contents

Part II   Market Power

7 Costs 216

8 Monopoly 250

9 *Pricing Policy* 289

10 *Strategic Thinking* 331

13 *Incentives and Organization 441*

14 *Regulation 473*

Chapter 1

Introduction to Managerial Economics

1 Typical Issues

In April 1995, the financial services group Dean Witter, Discover & Co. adopted a shareholder rights plan that created one right for every outstanding common share.[1] If any party acquired 15% or more of the group's common shares, the rights could be activated and exercised to buy additional shares of the group at a 50% discount to their value. The party whose acquisition activated the rights, however, would not be allowed to exercise its rights. How does Dean Witter, Discover's shareholder rights plan affect the likelihood of a hostile takeover?

The Walt Disney Company manages theme parks throughout the world, including Disneyland in California, Disney World in Florida, Tokyo Disneyland, and Euro-Disney near Paris. These parks attract thousands of visitors a day. In addition to spending money within the theme park, the visitors patronize nearby shops, hotels, restaurants, and transport services. In the late 1980s, the Walt Disney Company planned a large program of investments to upgrade Disneyland. Before commencing the investments, the company purchased much of the property around the theme park, including the Disneyland Hotel. Why did the company buy the surrounding property before upgrading the theme park?

A personal computer's internal (read-write) memory handles the complex calculations for graphics and spreadsheets. During the summer of 1988, the management of Apple Computer anticipated a shortage of memory chips and

---

[1] In February 1997, Dean Witter, Discover announced that it would merge with the investment bank Morgan Stanley.

Figure 1.1 The price of oil

Source: International Energy Statistics Sourcebook, 4th ed. (Tulsa: PennWell Publishing Company, 1994), p. 164.

Between 1973 and 1974, the price of Saudi Arabian light crude spiked up by 450% from $2.41 to $10.84 per barrel.

bought several hundred million dollars of 1-megabit chips at an average cost of $38. To recoup this cost, Apple's management raised prices across the entire Macintosh line. By January 1989, however, shortages in the memory chip market eased, with the average cost falling to $23. Apple, nonetheless, maintained the prices of its computers. Was this a correct decision?

The Limits to Growth, one of the 1970s' most influential books, predicted that the world would run out of gold by 1983, silver by 1988, and oil by 2003.[2] The publication of the book coincided with a sharp increase in the prices of oil and other minerals (see Figure 1.1). *The Limits to Growth* sparked an intense

---

[2] Donella H. Meadows, Dennis L. Meadows, Jorgen Randers, and William W. Behrens III, *The Limits to Growth* (New York: Universe Books, 1972), pp. 56-60, Table 4.

debate among policymakers around the world. Some experts, citing the sharp price increases, called for urgent government regulation to avert catastrophe. By contrast, however, most economists were relatively sanguine and argued that the price increases were a good sign. Why were the economists right?

Elena is three months' pregnant. Both she and her husband, Frank, work as systems analysts in the same company. The company offers such couples the choice of eight weeks' paid paternity or maternity leave—either the father or the mother may take the leave but not both. If Elena takes the leave, how will this affect the distribution of child-care responsibilities between Frank and her in the future?

Managerial economics is the science of directing costly resources to achieve managerial objectives. Wherever resources are costly, a manager can make more effective decisions by applying the discipline of managerial economics. It does not matter whether the setting is a business, nonprofit organization, or home. In all of these settings, managers must deal with costly or limited resources.

> Managerial economics is the science of directing costly resources to achieve managerial objectives.

For instance, in the introductory examples, finance directors must bear the cost of financial resources, marketing managers have responsibility for the cost of what they sell, governments must set energy policy with respect to finite stocks of oil and gas, and parents have to balance career and family demands within the 24 hours of a day. In all of these examples, an understanding of managerial economics will enable more effective decisions.

Here, we shall present the framework of managerial economics and indicate how it can be applied to the introductory examples. For detailed answers, we must wait until the concepts of managerial economics are fully developed in later chapters.

Managerial economics consists of three branches: competitive markets, market power, and imperfect markets. This book is organized in three parts, one part for each branch. Before discussing these three branches, let us first develop some preliminary background.

2 Preliminaries

To appreciate when and how to apply managerial economics, we should understand the scope and methodology of the discipline. We also need to understand several basic analytical concepts that are used throughout the three branches of managerial economics. This preliminary background is a necessary first step toward mastering the discipline.

Scope

Regarding the scope of managerial economics, we should distinguish the science from **microeconomics** and **macroeconomics**. Microeconomics is the study of individual economic behavior where resources are costly. It addresses

Microeconomics is the study of individual economic behavior where resources are costly.

issues such as how consumers respond to changes in prices and income and how businesses decide on employment and sales. Microeconomics also extends to such issues as how voters choose between political parties and how governments should set taxes. Managerial economics has a more limited scope—it is the application of microeconomics to managerial issues.

Macroeconomics is the study of aggregate economic variables.

By contrast with microeconomics, the field of macroeconomics focuses on aggregate economic variables. Macroeconomics addresses such issues as how a cut in interest rates will affect the inflation rate and how a depreciation of the U.S. dollar will affect unemployment, exports, and imports. While it is certainly true that the whole economy is made up of individual consumers and businesses, the study of macroeconomics often considers economic aggregates directly rather than as the aggregation of individual consumers and businesses. This is the key distinction between the fields of macroeconomics and microeconomics.

Some issues span both macroeconomics and microeconomics. For instance, energy is such an important part of the economy that changes in the price of energy have both macroeconomic and microeconomic effects. If the price of oil were to rise by 10%, it would trigger increases in other prices and hence generate price inflation, which is a macroeconomic effect. The increase in the price of oil would also have microeconomic effects; for instance, power stations might switch to other fuels, drivers might cut back on using their cars, and oil producers might open up new fields.

Methodology

Having defined the scope of managerial economics, let us now consider its methodology. The fundamental premise of managerial economics is that individuals share common motivations that lead them to behave systematically in making economic choices. This means that a person who faces the same choices at two different times will behave in the same way at both times.

An **economic model** is a concise description of behavior and outcomes.

If economic behavior is systematic, then it can be studied. Managerial economics proceeds by constructing models of economic behavior. An **economic model** is a concise description of behavior and outcomes. By design, the model omits considerable information, so as to focus on a few key variables. In this regard, economic models are like maps: A map with too much detail is confusing rather than helpful. Imagine driving around Toronto with a map that included every pothole on the street. The map could not fit into the car! To be useful, a map must be less than completely realistic.

Economic models are like maps in another way. Different maps of Toronto serve different purposes: street maps for drivers, guides to main attractions for tourists, and charts of underground utility lines for builders. Likewise, there may be different economic models of the same situation, each of them focusing on a different issue.

Models are constructed by inductive reasoning. For instance, inductive reasoning suggests that the demand for new software increases with the amount that the publisher spends on advertising. We can build a model in which the demand for a product depends on advertising expenditure. The model should then be tested with actual empirical data. If the tests support the model, it can be accepted; otherwise, it should be revised.

Marginal vis-à-vis Average

In managerial economics, many analyses resolve to a balance between the marginal values of two variables. Accordingly, it is important to understand the concept of a **marginal value**. Generally, the marginal value of a variable is the change in the variable associated with a unit increase in a driver. By contrast, the **average value** of a variable is the total value of the variable divided by the total quantity of a driver.

> The **marginal value** of a variable is the change in the variable associated with a unit increase in a driver.

What is a *driver*? To explain, consider the following example. Alan and Hilda are clerks at the Luna Store. The store pays each clerk $10 per hour for a basic eight-hour day, $15 per hour for overtime of up to four hours, and $20 for overtime exceeding four hours a day. Suppose that Alan works 10 hours a day. Then he earns $10 per hour for eight hours and $15 per hour for two hours of overtime, which adds up to a total of ($10 × 8) + ($15 × 2) = $110.

> The **average value** of a variable is the total value of the variable divided by the total quantity of a driver.

With respect to Alan's pay, the driver is the number of hours worked. Hence, Alan's marginal pay is the amount that he could earn by working one additional hour. His marginal pay is $15 per hour. By contrast, Alan's average pay is his total pay divided by the total number of hours worked, which is $110/10 = $11 per hour. The marginal pay exceeds the average pay because the store pays higher rates for additional hours beyond the basic eight. Since the marginal pay is the pay for an additional hour of overtime, it is higher than the average pay.

Note that the marginal and average pay depend on the number of hours worked. Suppose that Hilda works 14 hours a day. She earns $10 per hour for eight hours, $15 per hour for the first four hours of overtime, and $20 per hour for the fifth and sixth hours of overtime, which sums to ($10 × 8) + ($15 × 4) + ($20 × 2) = $180. Her marginal pay is $20 per hour, while her average pay is $180/14 = $12.86 per hour. Hilda's marginal pay exceeds Alan's because she works four hours longer, which puts her into the $20 per hour overtime bracket.

Generally, the marginal value of a variable may be less than, equal to, or greater than the average value. The relation between the marginal and average values depends on whether the marginal value is decreasing, constant, or increasing with respect to the driver.

Stock vis-à-vis Flow

Another important distinction in managerial economics is that between **stocks** and **flows**. A stock is the quantity at a specific point in time. By contrast, a flow is the change in a stock over some period of time. While stocks are measured in units of the item, flows are measured in units per time period.

> A **stock** is the quantity of a given item at a specific point in time.

Every manager must understand the distinction between stocks and flows. A balance sheet represents the financial status of a business at a specific point in time, hence the items on a balance sheet—assets and liabilities—are stocks. By contrast, the income statement reports changes in the financial status of a business. The items in an income statement—receipts and expenses—are flows. An annual income statement reports flows over a year, while a quarterly income statement reports flows over three months.

Let us illustrate the distinction between stocks and flows with several other examples. In the Luna Store, the number of clerks on the May 1 payroll is a stock, while the number of hours that Alan works each day is a flow. Apple Computer's inventory of 1-megabit memory chips on January 1, 1989, is a stock, while the company's consumption of chips in January 1989 is a flow. The world's oil reserves at the beginning of the current year is a stock. This stock may be measured in billions of barrels. By contrast, the world's current production of oil is a flow. This flow may be measured in millions of barrels per day.

Other Things Equal

The third basic concept in managerial economics is the device of holding **other things equal**. At any one time, the environment of business may be changing in several different ways. It would be difficult to analyze the implications of all the various changes together. The difficulty is compounded if the separate changes have conflicting effects. An alternative approach is to simplify the problem by analyzing each change separately, holding other things equal. Having analyzed the separate effects, we can then put them together for the complete picture.

For instance, a silver mine may be confronted with an increase in the price of electricity, a drop in the price of silver, and a change in labor laws, all on the same day. How should the mine adjust its production? The most practical way to address this question is to consider each change separately, holding "other things equal." Having understood each of the separate effects, the next step is to assemble them to get the complete picture.

Either explicitly or implicitly, almost every piece of managerial economics analysis holds other things equal. This usage is so close to being universal that we will not explicitly state the proviso. Nevertheless, it is always important to bear the proviso in mind when applying the results of some analysis to a practical managerial issue.

3 *Markets*

One basic concept of managerial economics—the market—is so fundamental that it appears in the names of each branch of the discipline. A **market** consists of the buyers and sellers that communicate with one another for voluntary exchange. In this sense, a market is not limited to any physical structure or particular location. The market extends as far as there are buyers or sellers who can communicate and trade at relatively low cost.

Consider, for instance, the market for cotton. This extends beyond the New York Cotton Exchange to growers in the Carolinas and textile manufacturers in East Asia. If the price on the Cotton Exchange increases, then that price increase will affect Carolina growers and Asian textile manufacturers. Likewise, if the demand for cotton in Asia increases, this will be reflected in the price on the Cotton Exchange.

In markets for consumer products, the buyers are households and sellers are businesses. In markets for industrial products, both buyers and sellers are businesses. Finally, in markets for human resources, buyers are businesses and sellers are households.

By contrast with a market, an **industry** is made up of the businesses engaged in the production or delivery of the same or similar items. For instance, the consumer electronics industry consists of all consumer electronics manufacturers, and the semiconductor industry consists of all semiconductor manufacturers. Members of an industry can be buyers in one market and sellers in another. The consumer electronics industry is a buyer in the semiconductor market and a seller in the consumer electronics market.

An **industry** consists of the businesses engaged in the production or delivery of the same or similar items.

Competitive Markets

The global silver market includes many competing producers and thousands of buyers. How should a mine respond to an increase in the price of electricity, a drop in the price of silver, or a change in labor laws? How will these changes affect buyers? The basic starting point of managerial economics is the model of competitive markets. This applies to markets with many buyers and many sellers. The market for silver is an example of a competitive market. In a competitive market, buyers provide the demand and sellers provide the supply. Accordingly, the model is also called the *demand-supply model*.

The model describes the systematic effect of changes in prices and other economic variables on buyers and sellers. Further, the model describes the interaction of these choices. In the silver mine example, the model can describe how the mine should adjust prices when the price of electricity increases, the price of silver drops, and labor laws change, all on the same day. These changes affect all silver mines. Hence, the model also describes the interaction among the adjustments of the various mines and how these affect buyers.

Part I of this book presents the model of competitive markets. It begins with the demand side, considering how buyers respond to changes in prices and income (Chapter 2). Next, we develop a set of quantitative methods that support precise estimates of changes in economic behavior (Chapter 3). Then, we look at the supply side of the market, considering how sellers respond to changes in the prices of products and inputs (Chapter 4). We bring demand and supply together and analyze their interaction in Chapter 5, then show that the outcome of market competition is efficient (Chapter 6).

Using the model of competitive markets, we can explain why most economists disagreed with *The Limits to Growth* and considered that the sharp increases in the prices of minerals were a good sign. In the case of oil, price increases encouraged users of oil to conserve, hence reducing the quantity demanded. The price increases also stimulated producers of oil to expand production and increase the quantity supplied. The reduction in quantity demanded coupled with the increase in quantity supplied led to the shortages being resolved. Indeed, more than 20 years after the publication of *The Limits to Growth*, there is no indication of the catastrophic shortages that the authors so confidently predicted.

The Catastrophe That Failed to Happen

Consistent with the economists' view, there was no disaster: None of *The Limits to Growth*'s predictions has even come close to being borne out. Far from presaging disaster, the rapid increases in mineral prices were a critical step in the process by which resource markets adjusted to increasing consumption and diminishing stocks. On the demand side, higher prices encouraged users to conserve, switch to other sources of energy, and use alternative materials. For instance, Figure 1.2 shows that, between 1973 and 1994, the fuel efficiency of American passenger cars increased by 60% from 13.3 to 21.5 miles per gallon.

On the supply side, higher prices also stimulated mineral producers to seek out new sources of supply and encouraged businesses to develop new energy sources and alternative materials. For instance, Figure 1.3 shows that, between 1973 and 1994, the world's proven reserves of oil increased by 50% from 666 to 999 billion barrels.

Market Power

Market power is the ability to influence market conditions.

In a competitive market, an individual manager may have little freedom of action. Key variables such as prices, scale of operations, and input mix may be determined by market forces. The role of a manager is simply to follow the market and survive. Not all markets, however, have so many buyers and sellers to qualify as competitive. **Market power** is the ability to influence market conditions. A seller with market power will have relatively more freedom to choose suppliers, set prices, and use advertising to influence demand.

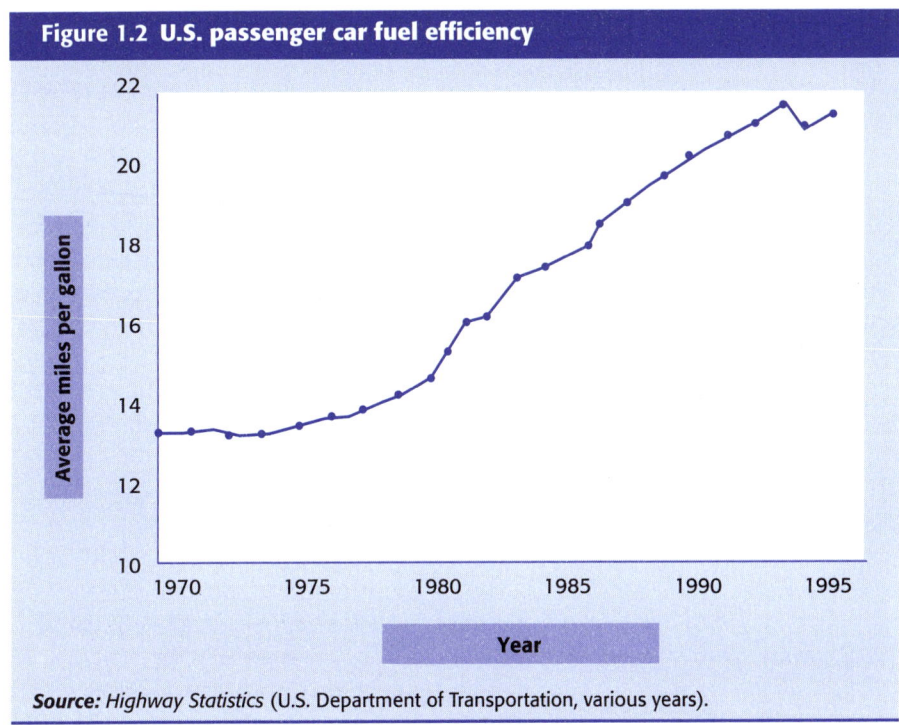

Figure 1.2 U.S. passenger car fuel efficiency

Source: Highway Statistics (U.S. Department of Transportation, various years).

Following the rise in the price of oil, American passenger car fuel efficiency increased by 60% from 13.3 to 21.5 miles per gallon between 1973 and 1994.

Businesses with market power need to manage their costs. For instance, until recently, Apple Computer was the only manufacturer of personal computers based on its proprietary user-friendly operating system. Apple certainly had the power to influence market conditions. Given the large inventory of memory chips purchased at $39 each in the summer of 1988, management had to decide what was the relevant cost when the market cost had fallen to $23.

In addition to managing costs, businesses with market power need to manage their demand. Three key tools in managing demand are price, advertising, and policy toward competitors. What price maximizes profit? A lower price boosts sales, while a higher price brings in higher margins. A similar issue arises in determining advertising expenditure. With regard to competitors, what are the benefits of cooperation?

Part II of this book addresses all of these issues. We begin by analyzing costs (Chapter 7), then consider management in the extreme case of market power, where there is only one seller (Chapter 8). Next, we discuss pricing policy (Chapter 9) and strategic thinking (Chapter 10).

We apply the cost analysis to Apple Computer's situation in January 1989 and explain how the company could have determined the relevant cost of its

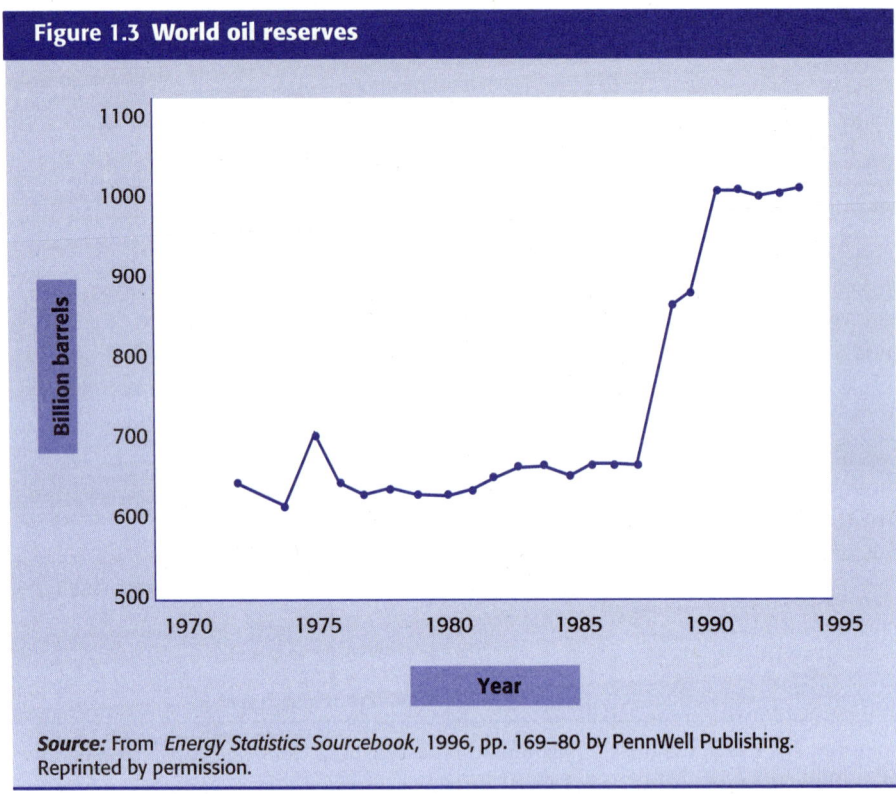

Figure 1.3 World oil reserves

Source: From *Energy Statistics Sourcebook*, 1996, pp. 169–80 by PennWell Publishing. Reprinted by permission.

Following the rise in the price of oil, the world's proven reserves of oil increased by 50% from 666 to 999 billion barrels between 1973 and 1994.

memory chips. We apply the strategic framework to analyze the impact of Dean Witter, Discover's shareholder rights plan and show that it will diminish the likelihood of a hostile takeover. We also apply the strategic framework to the decision as to whether Elena or Frank should take leave to care for their new baby and show that the person who takes the leave is more likely to become the primary caregiver in the extended future.

Imperfect Markets

In an **imperfect market,** choices of one party affect other parties directly rather than passing through a market or one party has better information than others.

Businesses with market power have relatively more freedom of action than those in competitive markets. Managers will also have relatively more freedom of action in markets that are subject to imperfections. A market may be imperfect in two ways: where the choices of one party affect other parties directly rather than passing through a market and where one party has better information than others. The challenge for managers operating in **imperfect markets** is to resolve the imperfection and, so, enable the cost-effective provision of their products.

In the late 1980s, the Walt Disney Company decided to embark on a large program of investments to upgrade Disneyland. These investments in new attractions would have directly benefited nearby businesses such as motels, restaurants, souvenir stores, and transportation services. There was no market through which the Disney Company could charge these businesses for the benefits. Accordingly, the market for Disney's investments in upgrading was imperfect.

As another example, consider the market for residential mortgages. Applicants for mortgages have better knowledge of their ability and willingness to repay than potential lenders. In this case, the market is imperfect owing to differences in information. The challenge for lenders is how to resolve the informational differences so that they can provide loans in a cost-effective way.

Managers of businesses with market power or operating in imperfect markets need to think strategically. For instance, a residential mortgage lender may require all loan applicants to pay for a credit check, with the lender refunding the cost if the credit check is favorable. The lender might reason that bad borrowers would not be willing to pay for a credit check because they would fail the check. Good borrowers, however, would pay for the check because they would get their money back from the lender. Hence, the credit check requirement will screen out the bad borrowers. This is an example of strategic thinking in an imperfect market.

Differences in information can cause a market to be imperfect. The same imperfection can arise within an organization, where some members have better information than others. Accordingly, another issue is how to structure incentives and organization.

Part III of this book addresses all of these issues. We begin by considering the sources of market imperfections (Chapters 11 and 12), then the appropriate structure of incentives and organization (Chapter 13). Finally, we consider how government regulation can resolve market imperfections (Chapter 14).

We apply this analysis to explain how the Walt Disney Company could have resolved the market imperfection it faced. Its solution was to purchase the surrounding property, thus ensuring that it would capture relatively more of the benefits from new attractions.

4 *Global Principles*

We have mentioned that a market extends as far as there are buyers or sellers who can communicate and trade at relatively low cost. Owing to relatively high costs of communication and trade, some markets are local. Examples include grocery retailing, housing, and live entertainment. The price in one local market will be independent of prices in other local markets. For instance, an increase in the price of apartments in New York City does not affect the housing market in Houston.

By contrast, some markets are global because the costs of communication and trade are relatively low. Examples include financial services, minerals, and shipping. In the case of an item with a global market, the price in one place will move together with the prices elsewhere. For instance, when the price of silver increases in London, the price will also rise in Tokyo.

We emphasize that, whether a market is local or global, the same managerial economics principles apply. For instance, when the price of fresh vegetables in Britain increases, consumers will switch to frozen vegetables. The same will be true in Japan, the United States, and any other place. An airline with market power in France will use that power to raise prices above the competitive level. The same will be true all over the world. A mortgage lender in Australia will act strategically to resolve the difference in information vis-à-vis borrowers. Again, the same will be true all over the world. Throughout this book, we shall give examples from different parts of the world to reiterate that managerial economics applies globally.

A related point is that the costs of communication and trade have systematically fallen over time. This trend has caused many markets to become relatively more integrated across geographical boundaries. For instance, Canadian insurers sell life insurance and mutual funds in Asia, Israeli growers ship fresh flowers by air to Europe, and U.S.-based callback services offer cheap international telephone calls throughout the world.

As a result of the trend toward integration, managers need to pay increasing attention to markets in other places. Some markets may be similar, while others are different. In all cases, managers must not allow their planning to be limited by traditional geographical boundaries.

Global Sourcing

Global integration means not only the opportunity to sell in new markets but also the opportunity to secure supplies from new sources. Foreign sources may provide cheaper skilled labor, specialized resources, or superior quality. These advantages allow a manufacturer to reduce production costs and improve quality.

Intel Corporation, well known for its line of microprocessors for IBM-compatible personal computers, is the world's leading semiconductor manufacturer. Each year, the company bestows its Intel Preferred Quality Supplier Award on suppliers that have provided world-class products and service. The recipients of the 1995 awards included two Japanese, one British, and two American companies.

5 *Summary*

Managerial economics is the science of directing costly resources to achieve managerial objectives. It consists of three branches: competitive markets, market power, and imperfect markets. A market consists of buyers and sellers that communicate with each other for voluntary exchange. Whether a market is local or global, the same managerial economics principles apply.

A seller with market power will have freedom to choose suppliers, set prices, and use advertising to influence demand. A market is imperfect when the choices of one party affect other parties directly rather than through prices or when one party has better information than others.

For effective management, it is important to distinguish marginal from average values and stocks from flows. Managerial economics applies models that are necessarily less than completely realistic. Typically, a model focuses on one issue, holding other things equal.

Key Concepts

managerial economics	average value	industry
microeconomics	stock	market power
macroeconomics	flow	imperfect market
economic model	other things equal	
marginal value	market	

Review Questions

1. Using relevant examples, explain the distinction between macroeconomics and microeconomics.

2. "Managerial economics uses less than completely realistic models." Is this necessarily bad?

3. Kokusai Denshin Denwa (KDD) is Japan's leading provider of international telephone services. In November 1995, KDD's standard rate for calls from Japan to Singapore was ¥360 (yen) for the first minute and ¥210 for each subsequent minute. Yoko makes a five-minute call.
   a. What is the average price per minute of Yoko's call?
   b. What is the price of Yoko's marginal minute?

4. Which of the following are stocks and which are flows?
   a. Monthly usage of laser printer toner cartridges.
   b. Number of technicians on the payroll as of January 1.
   c. Number of workstations in inventory as of July 31.

5. Explain the difference between
   a. The market for electricity.
   b. The electricity industry.

6. True or false?
   a. In every market, all the buyers are consumers.
   b. In every market, all the sellers are businesses.

7. Which of the following manufacturers has relatively more market power?
   a. Intel, which accounts for more than 50% of worldwide production of microprocessors for IBM-compatible personal computers.
   b. Compro, which has less than a 1% share of the global market for IBM-compatible personal computers.

8. Managers operating in an imperfect market must (choose a or b)
   a. Set high prices to make up for the imperfection.
   b. Act strategically to resolve the imperfection.

9. Which of the following are consequences of the falling costs of international communication and trade?
   a. Buyers can obtain products from a wider range of suppliers.
   b. Sellers can market their products to a wider set of customers.

10. Explain the distinctions among the three branches of managerial economics.

Discussion Questions

1. In a battle now underway, Major-General Maria has deployed the 100th and 101st Brigades in front, while holding the 102nd Brigade in reserve. General Maria judges that the enemy will withdraw in another 12 hours. The commanders of both forward brigades have requested General Maria to send reinforcement. They have given predictions of enemy kills over the next 12 hours (see Table 1.1). To impress the press, the Army headquarters has ordered General Maria to maximize the "body count" of enemy soldiers killed.
   a. What will be the marginal increase in body count if General Maria sends the reserve brigade to reinforce the (i) 100th Brigade? (ii) 101st Brigade?
   b. Which brigade will score the higher body count with the reinforcement of the reserve brigade?
   c. Where should General Maria send the reserve brigade?

Table 1.1 Deploying the reserve brigade		
	Enemy Body Count	
Unit	*No Reinforcement*	*Reinforcement with Reserve Brigade*
100th Brigade	200	350
101st Brigade	400	500

2. Refer to the financial statements of any publicly listed company. Taking any page at random, identify which of the financial data are stocks and which are flows.

3. Referring to the definition of a *market*, consider whether the following groups of buyers and sellers are part of the corresponding market.
   a. After Iraq invaded Kuwait in August 1990, the United Nations banned Iraq from exporting oil to the rest of the world. During the ban, was Iraq part of the world market for oil?
   b. Prisoners cannot freely work outside the jail. Do prisoners belong to the national labor market?

4. Using data from relevant sources, graph
   a. Passenger car fuel efficiency,
   b. World oil reserves, and
   c. The price of oil,
   from 1970 to the most recent year. Comment on the relation among a, b, and c.

5. Bombay, an island on the west coast of India, has been the country's leading commercial and financial center for many years. The constraint of land may limit the city's future development. Critics complain that housing and office space in Bombay is now more expensive than in London. Consider the effect of increasing housing and office prices on
   a. Development of taller buildings.
   b. Conversion of land from industrial to residential and commercial use.
   c. Relocation of poorer residents to cheaper areas.
   d. Filling in the sea to provide land for construction of new buildings.

6. Consider the market for life insurance. Applicants for insurance have better knowledge of their health and lifestyles than potential insurers.
   a. In this market, who are the buyers and who are the sellers?
   b. Explain why this market is imperfect.
   c. Suppose that an insurer requires all applicants to pay for a medical examination, with the insurer refunding the cost if the applicant passes the examination. (i) Will unhealthy applicants be willing to pay for the examination? (ii) What about healthy applicants?

Part I

Competitive Markets

Chapter 2

Demand

1 Introduction

Hoover, based in Merthyr Tydfil, is a major British manufacturer of household appliances including vacuum cleaners and washing machines. In Autumn 1992, Hoover's management launched a special promotion offering two free air tickets to any customer who purchased an appliance at a price of £100 (British pounds) or more. The tickets were valid for round-trip travel to continental Europe or the United States. Each ticket was worth over £200. How could Hoover's promotion be expected to affect its sales of appliances?

The National Football League (NFL) controls major league American football teams such as the Chicago Bears and the San Francisco 49ers. NFL teams play a series of home and away games during the regular season. The teams derive revenue from sales of tickets and concession items such as food, beverages, and souvenirs at live games. They also earn substantial income from television broadcasting, but this is limited to away games. Should the owners of NFL teams allow live broadcasting of home games?

An American's average income is over $20,000 a year. By contrast, with an average income of less than $1000 a year, the people of India are among the world's poorest. Yet, in 1991, they purchased over 80,000 air conditioners at a retail price of about $600 per unit. How could anyone afford these appliances?

Starting from scratch in the early 1980s, the United States' mobile phone industry is projected to reach 60 million subscribers by the year 2000. Typically, mobile phone operators set a two-part pricing scheme, consisting of a basic monthly fee covering a specified quantity of airtime plus a rate for additional minutes. How should a mobile phone operator determine the basic monthly charge?

To address these questions—the effect of Hoover's promotion on its appliance sales, whether to allow live broadcasting of home football games, who in India can afford air conditioners, and how a mobile phone operator can determine the basic monthly charge—this chapter develops an analysis of consumer and business demand.

We begin with the demand curve of an individual buyer. This shows the quantity of the item that an individual will purchase as a function of its price. Next, we consider how demand depends on other factors, including income, the prices of other products, and advertising. Then, we extend from the demand of an individual to the demand curve of the entire market. With the model of demand, businesses can identify factors that affect the demand for their products, and how to influence that demand. In particular, we can apply the model to analyze how Hoover's promotion would affect its appliance sales, whether team owners should allow live broadcasting of home games, and who in India can afford air conditioners.

We then consider three important aspects of demand. The first is how changes in demand are dependent on time. The second is that the demand curve also shows the maximum amount of money that the buyer is willing to pay for each unit of the item. Using this information, a seller can determine the maximum that a buyer is willing to pay for any specified quantity. We can apply this analysis to show how a mobile phone operator can determine its basic monthly charge. Finally, we highlight the important differences between consumer and business demand.

2 *Individual Demand*

To understand how a price cut will affect sales, we need to know how the cut in price will affect the purchases of the individual buyers and, generally, how an individual's purchases depend on the price of an item. The **individual demand curve** provides this information: It is a graph that shows the quantity that one buyer will purchase at every possible price.

We shall present the concept of a demand curve with reference to an individual consumer. The principles underlying the demand curve for a business buyer are quite similar. Hence, this section focuses on consumer demand, and a later section highlights the important differences for business demand.

The **individual demand curve** is a graph showing the quantity that one buyer will purchase at every possible price.

Construction

The basic issue is how to determine an individual's demand curve. Let us address the issue by considering Joy's demand for movies. We must ask Joy a series of questions that elicit her responses to changes in price, while holding other things equal.

We first ask, "Other things equal, how many movies would you attend a month at a price of $10 per movie?" Suppose that Joy's answer is, "None." We must add the proviso of "other things equal" because Joy's decision may depend on other factors, such as her income and the price of popcorn in the movie theater. When constructing Joy's demand curve for movies, we focus on the effect of changes in the price of movies and hold all other factors constant.

We then pose similar questions to Joy for other possible prices for a movie: $7.50, $5, $2.50, and 0. For each of these prices, Joy will tell us how many movies she would attend a month. We can tabulate this information as shown in Table 2.1. This table represents Joy's demand for movies.

Next we graph the information from Table 2.1 as shown in Figure 2.1. We represent the price of movies on the vertical axis and the quantity in movies a month on the horizontal axis. At a price of $10, Joy says that she would go to no movies, so we mark the point where the price is $10 and quantity of movies is 0. Continuing with the information from Table 2.1, we mark every pair of price and quantity that Joy reports. Joining these points, we then have Joy's demand curve for movies. This is the stepped curve drawn in bold.

The demand curve in Figure 2.1 shows, for every possible price, the quantity of movies that Joy will attend. Knowing Joy's demand curve, a movie theater can predict how Joy will respond to changes in its price. For instance, if presently, the theater charges $5 per movie, Joy goes to two movies a month. If the theater reduces its price to $2.50 per movie, it knows that Joy will increase her consumption to four movies a month. By contrast, if the theater raises its price to $7.50 per movie, Joy would cut back to one movie a month.

The demand curve in Figure 2.1 is a series of steps. Later in this chapter, we will present demand curves that are smooth. The principles of demand curves are the same whether the curves are stepped or smooth.

Table 2.1 Individual demand	
Price ($ per movie)	**Quantity (Movies a month)**
10.00	0
7.50	1
5.00	2
2.50	4
0.00	7

Figure 2.1 Individual demand curve

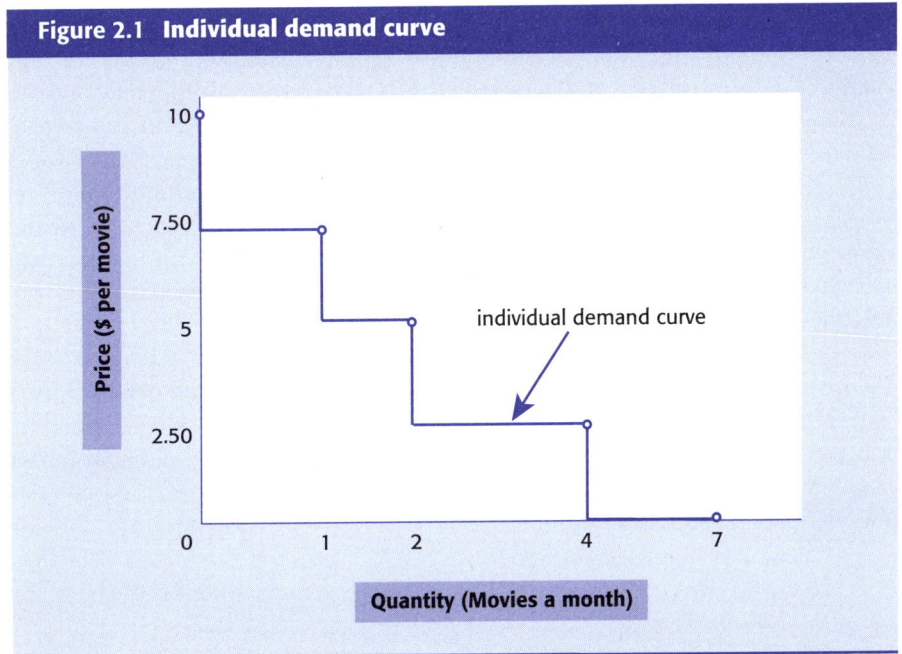

The individual demand curve shows, for every possible price, the quantity of movies that Joy will attend. It also shows how much Joy would be willing to pay for various quantities.

Slope

The individual demand curve shows the quantity that the buyer will purchase at every possible price. Let us now consider the individual demand curve from another perspective.

Referring to Joy's demand curve in Figure 2.1, we can use the curve to determine how much Joy would be willing to pay for various quantities of movies. Specifically, the curve shows that she is willing to pay $7.50 per movie for one movie a month. Further, it shows that Joy is willing to pay $5 per movie for two movies a month, and $2.50 per movie for four movies a month.

Generally, if the number of movies is larger, the price that Joy is willing to pay is lower. Equivalently, at a lower price, Joy is willing to buy a larger quantity (specifically, go to more movies). These two related properties of a demand curve reflect the principle of diminishing **marginal benefit**.

Any item that a consumer is willing to buy must provide some benefit, which may be psychic or monetary. We measure the benefit in monetary

The **marginal benefit** is the benefit provided by an additional unit of the item.

terms as we are interested in goods and services that are bought and sold. The *marginal benefit* is the benefit provided by an additional unit of the item. The marginal benefit of the first movie is the benefit from one movie a month. Similarly, the marginal benefit of the second movie is the additional benefit from seeing a second movie each month.

By the principle of *diminishing marginal benefit,* each additional unit of consumption or usage provides less benefit than the preceding unit. In Joy's case, this means that the marginal benefit of the second movie is less than the marginal benefit of the first movie, the marginal benefit of the third movie is less than the marginal benefit of the second movie, and so on.

Accordingly, the price that an individual is willing to pay will decrease with the quantity purchased. In terms of a graph, this means that the demand curve will slope downward. This is a general property of all demand curves: the lower the price, the larger will be the quantity demanded. Hence, demand curves slope downward. The fundamental reason for this downward slope is diminishing marginal benefit.

Progress check

Progress Check 2A   Suppose that a movie theater is presently charging $7.50 per movie. By how much must the theater cut its price for Joy to increase her consumption by three movies a month?

Preferences

Our procedure for constructing a demand curve relies completely on the consumer's individual preferences. The individual decides how much he or she wants to buy at each possible price. The demand curve then displays information in a graphical way.

There are two implications of this approach. First, the demand curve will change with changes in the consumer's preferences. As a person grows older, her or his demand for rock videos and junk food will decline, while the demand for adult contemporary compact discs and meals in stylish restaurants will increase.

Second, different consumers may have different preferences and hence different demand curves. One consumer may like red meat while another is a vegetarian. We get the demand curve for each consumer from her or his individual responses to the questions regarding the quantity she or he would buy at each possible price.

Quantity Demanded at a Negative Price: Hoover's Free Flight Promotion

In Autumn 1992, the British home appliance manufacturer, Hoover, offered two free air travel tickets to every customer who purchased an appliance with a price of £100 or more. Each ticket was valid for round-trip travel to continental Europe or the United States. The market value of a pair of tickets exceeded £400.

For a £100 appliance, Hoover's effective price was $£(100 - 400) = -£300$ pounds; that is, the company was *paying* each customer £300 to take an appliance. As might be expected, huge numbers of consumers were willing to buy Hoover appliances on those terms. The promotion attracted over 100,000 customers.

Hoover's management, however, had not anticipated this response. It had to establish a special 250-person task force to deal with the flight bookings and set aside £48 million to cover the cost of over 200,000 free flights. William Foust, president of Hoover Europe, and two other senior executives were dismissed for their role in the promotion.

At the time of the promotion, Hoover was owned by the American appliance manufacturer Maytag. In May 1995, Maytag sold Hoover to an Italian home appliances group for £106 million.

Source: "Hoover 'Free Flights' Scheme Costs 48 Million Pounds," *Financial Times* (April 21, 1994), p. 7; "Hoover Sold after Free Flights Fiasco," *The Times* (May 31, 1995).

3 *Demand and Income*

We have mentioned that Joy's demand for movies may depend on other factors in addition to the price of such movies. For instance, if she gets a raise, she might spend more on movies. Her demand for movies will also depend on the price of alternative forms of entertainment such as video rentals.

The individual demand curve shows explicitly how the quantity that a person buys depends on the price of the item. The demand curve, however, does not explicitly display the effect of changes in income and other factors that affect demand. How do changes in these other factors affect an individual's demand curve? In this section, we focus on the effect of changes in the buyer's income and consider the impact of other factors in the next section.

Income Changes

Let us consider the effect of changes in income on demand in the context of Joy's demand for movies. Suppose that Joy's income is presently $30,000 a year.

Table 2.1 and Figure 2.1 represent Joy's demand curve for movies when her income is $30,000 a year.

We then ask Joy a series of questions. These questions probe the effect of changes in income as well as price: "Suppose that your income were $25,000 a year. Other things equal, how many movies would you buy a month at a price of $10 per movie?" We then pose the same question with other possible prices—$7.50, $5, $2.50, and 0—and tabulate the information.

Suppose that Table 2.2 represents Joy's answers. We also represent this information in Figure 2.2, with the price of movies on the vertical axis and number of movies a month on the horizontal axis. Marking the pairs of prices and quantities, and joining the points, we have Joy's demand curve with an income of $25,000 a year. We can see that Joy's demand curve for movies with a $25,000 income lies to the left of her demand curve with a $30,000 income. At every price, Joy's quantity demanded with a $25,000 income is less than or equal to her quantity demanded with a $30,000 income.

Change in Price vis-à-vis Income

The effect of a change in income on the demand curve is very different from that of a change in price. Recall that an individual demand curve shows the quantity that the person will buy for every possible price, other things equal. Referring to Figure 2.1, if the price of movies drops from $7.50 to $5 per movie, while Joy's income remains unchanged at $30,000 a year, we can trace Joy's response by moving along her demand curve from the $7.50 level to the $5 level.

Suppose, however, that Joy's income drops from $30,000 to $25,000 a year. This change in income will affect her purchases of movies at all price levels—$10, $7.50, $5, $2.50, and 0. Accordingly, the drop in income will shift her entire demand curve. Figure 2.2 shows that, when Joy's income drops from $30,000 to $25,000 a year, her entire demand curve for movies shifts toward the left.

Table 2.2 Individual demand with lower income

Price ($ per movie)	Quantity (Movies a month)
10.00	0
7.50	0
5.00	1
2.50	2
0.00	7

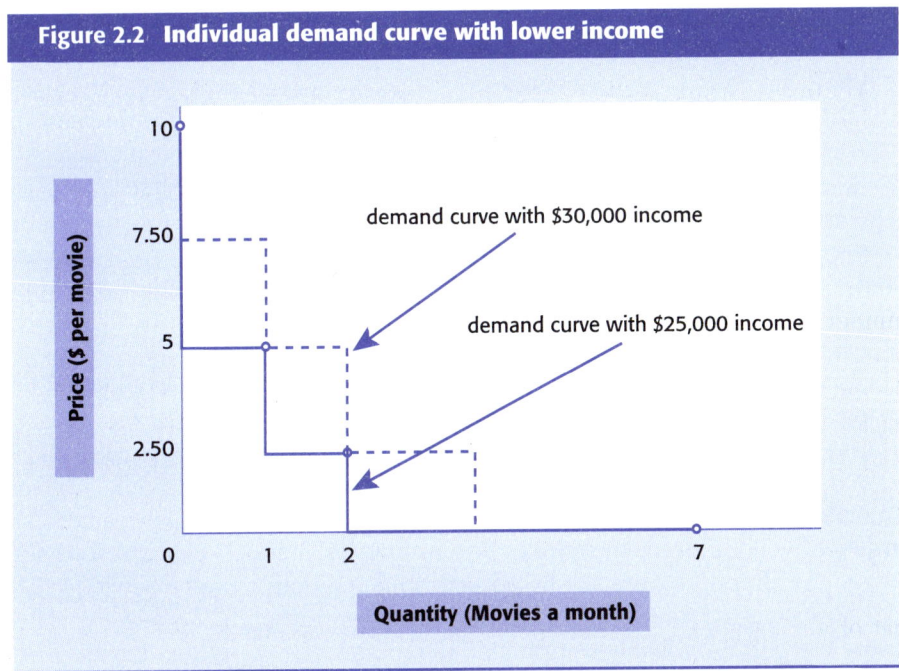

Figure 2.2 Individual demand curve with lower income

As Joy's income falls from $30,000 to $25,000, her entire demand curve shifts toward the left.

Let us understand the difference between a change in price and a change in income from another perspective. On Figure 2.2, at the $5 level, we can mark two quantities: a quantity of two movies a month when Joy's income is $30,000, and another quantity of one movie a month when Joy's income is $25,000. Can we join these points to form a demand curve? The answer is definitely "no," because each point corresponds to a different income. A demand curve shows how a buyer's purchases depend on changes in the price of some item, holding income and all other factors unchanged. Accordingly, for each of the points that we have marked, there is a separate demand curve.

In general, a change in the price of an item will cause a movement along the demand curve for that item. By contrast, a change in income or any factor other than the price of the item will cause a shift in the entire demand curve.

Normal vis-à-vis Inferior Products

When Joy's income drops from $30,000 to $25,000 a year, her demand for movies shifts to the left. As Joy's income falls, her demand for movies also falls. By contrast, if her income were to rise, her demand would increase.

Let us compare Joy's demand for movies in general with her demand for afternoon matinees. Many movie theaters offer afternoon matinees at a cheaper price than their regular evening showings. If Joy's income falls, it is quite possible that she will substitute cheaper forms of entertainment for more expensive ones. In particular, the drop in her income may lead to an increase in her demand for afternoon matinees.

By contrast, when Joy's income increases, we can expect her to switch away from cheaper forms of entertainment and toward more expensive alternatives. So, as her income rises, Joy's demand for afternoon matinees will fall.

Goods and services can be categorized according to the effect of changes in income on demand. If the demand for an item increases as the buyer's income increases, while the demand falls as the buyer's income falls, then the item is considered a **normal product**. Equivalently, the demand for a normal product is positively related to changes in buyer's income.

By contrast, the demand for an **inferior product** is negatively related to changes in buyer's income. This means that the demand falls as the buyer's income increases, while the demand increases as the buyer's income falls.

We can apply this classification to Joy. For her, movies in general are a normal product, while afternoon matinees are an inferior product. Generally, broad categories of products tend to be normal, while particular products within the categories may be inferior. Consider, for instance, transportation services. The entire category is probably a normal product: the higher a person's income, the more he or she tends to spend on transportation. Public transportation, however, may be an inferior product: With a higher income, the typical commuter switches from public transport to a private car.

Consumer electronics provide another example of the difference in the effect of changes in income on the demand for a category as compared with the effect on the demand for a specific product. While consumer electronics as a category is a normal product, particular products such as black-and-white TVs may be inferior.

The distinction between normal and inferior products is important for business strategy. When the economy is growing and incomes are rising, the demand for normal products will rise, while the demand for inferior products will fall. By contrast, when the economy is in recession and incomes are falling, the demand for normal products will fall, while the demand for inferior products will rise.

The normal-inferior product distinction is also important for international business. The demand for normal products is relatively higher in richer countries, while the demand for inferior products is relatively higher in poorer countries. For instance, in developed countries, relatively more people commute to work by car than bicycle. The reverse is true in very poor countries.

For a **normal product**, demand is positively related to changes in buyer's income.

For an **inferior product**, demand is negatively related to changes in buyer's income.

Progress check

Progress Check 2B Draw a curve to represent an individual consumer's demand for black-and-white TVs. (1) Explain why it slopes downward. (2) How will a drop in the consumer's income affect the demand curve?

4 *Other Factors in Demand*

The individual demand for an item may depend on other factors in addition to the price of the item and the buyer's income. The other factors include the prices of related products, advertising, season, weather, and location. In this section, we focus on the prices of related products and advertising. The principles for the other factors are similar, hence we do not analyze each one of them explicitly.

Complements and Substitutes

Assume that Joy always eats popcorn when she goes to the movies. How will an increase in the price of popcorn affect Joy's demand for movies? Recall that Joy's demand curve for movies shows the quantity that she will purchase for every possible price of a movie, other things equal. A change in the price is represented by a movement along the demand curve. By contrast, a change in any other factor such as the price of popcorn will affect Joy's purchases of movies at all prices of movies. Hence, it will cause a shift in the entire demand curve.

Suppose that, presently, the price of popcorn is $1. Figure 2.1 represents Joy's demand curve for movies when the price of popcorn is $1.

We next construct Joy's demand when the price of popcorn is $1.50. To do so, we ask Joy a series of questions to probe the effect of changes in the prices of both popcorn and movies: "Suppose that the price of popcorn is $1.50. Other things equal, how many movies would you attend a month at a price of $10 per movie?"

By repeating this question for all other prices of movies and marking the pairs of prices and quantities on a graph, we can obtain Joy's demand curve when the price of popcorn is $1.50. Figure 2.3 shows this demand curve: When the price of popcorn is higher, the demand curve for movies is further to the left.

In general, related products can be classified as either **complements** or **substitutes** according to the effect of a price increase in one product on the demand for the other. Two products are *complements* if an increase in the price of one causes the demand for the other to fall. By contrast, two products are *substitutes* if an increase in the price of one causes the demand for the other to increase.

In Joy's case, popcorn and movies are complements. The more movies that she sees, the more popcorn she will want. Hence, if the price of popcorn is higher, the price of the overall movie experience will be higher, and she will go to fewer movies.

How will an increase in the price of video rentals affect Joy's demand for movies? Instead of seeing a movie, Joy could watch a rented video. Accordingly, these two products are substitutes. If there is an increase in the price of video rentals, Joy's demand for movies will increase.

Two products are **complements** if an increase in the price of one causes a fall in the demand for the other.

Two products are **substitutes** if an increase in the price of one causes an increase in the demand for the other.

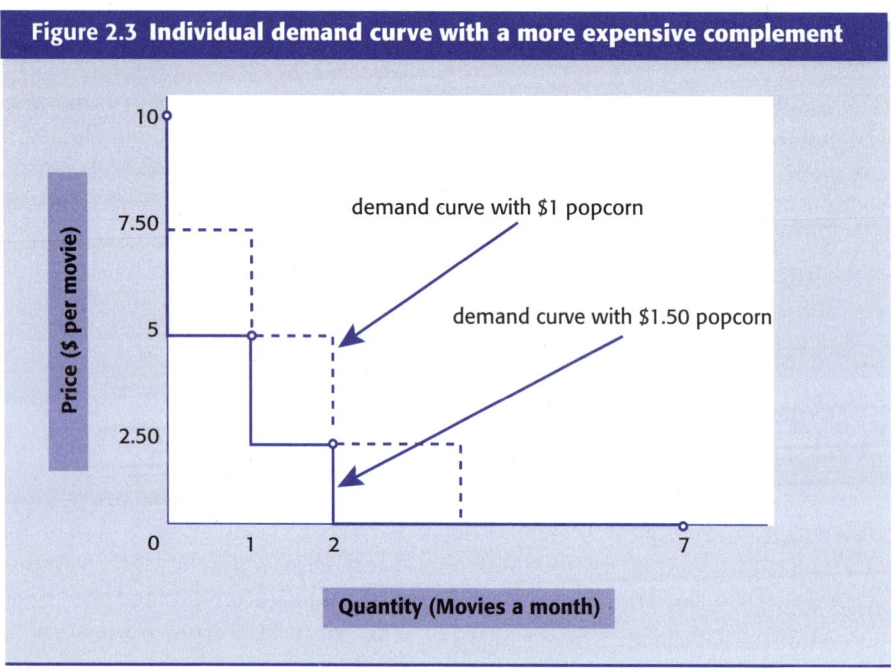

Figure 2.3 Individual demand curve with a more expensive complement

As the price of popcorn increases, Joy's entire demand curve shifts toward the left.

Generally, a demand curve will shift to the left if there is either an increase in the price of a complement or a fall in the price of a substitute. By contrast, a demand curve will shift to the right if there is either a fall in the price of a complement or an increase in the price of a substitute.

To appreciate the business implications of complements and substitutes, let us consider the components of a personal computer. The basic components include the microprocessor, the memory, and the disk drive. Computer users need all three components; hence, these are complements. This means that when the price of memory or disk drives falls, the demand for microprocessors will rise, which increases the sales and profits of microprocessor manufacturers.

By contrast, a computer can generate sound through either a card or a chip; hence, sound cards and chips are substitutes. A drop in the price of sound cards will reduce the demand for sound chips, which cuts the sales and profits of manufacturers of sound chips. An increase in the price of sound cards will raise the sales and profits of chip manufacturers.

Progress check

Progress Check 2C   Referring to Figure 2.3, how will a fall in the price of video rentals affect the original demand curve?

TV Football

National Football League teams derive income from gate and concession receipts at live games as well as from TV broadcasting. Fans can enjoy football both at live games and on TV. Should the owners of NFL teams allow live broadcasting of home games?

Let us first consider the relationship between live broadcasting of away games and the demand to attend home games. Live broadcasting of away games entertains fans when their home team is playing away and stimulates popular support for the home team and interest in attendance at home games. Accordingly, live broadcasting of away games and attendance at home games are complements.

Live broadcasting of home games, however, may draw fans away from attending the game in person. To this extent, the two products are substitutes. On the other hand, live broadcasting of home games also stimulates popular support for the home team and hence attendance at home games. To this extent, the two products are complements. Whether NFL team owners should allow live broadcasting of home games depends on the balance among these effects.

Advertising

Advertising expenditure is another factor in demand. For instance, Joy's demand for movies may depend on advertising by the theater. Advertising may be informative as well as persuasive. Informative advertising communicates information to potential buyers and sellers. For instance, movie theaters list the movies that they are showing and their show times in the daily newspapers. These listings inform potential customers.

Persuasive advertising aims to influence consumer choice. Manufacturers of cigarettes and cosmetics, for instance, use commercials to retain the loyalty of existing consumers and attract others to switch brands. Marketers may also use persuasive advertising to promote new products.

Generally, an increase in advertising expenditure, whether informative or persuasive, will increase demand. Conversely, a reduction in advertising expenditure will cause demand to fall. The effect of advertising expenditure on demand may be subject to a diminishing marginal product, which means that each additional dollar spent on advertising has a relatively smaller effect on demand. (We will elaborate on the concept of a diminishing marginal product in Chapter 4.)

The effect of advertising on a consumer's demand depends on the medium. TV commercials during football games will have more effect on male consumers, while those during cartoons will have relatively more effect on children. Print advertisements in women's magazines will have more effect on female consumers, while those in car magazines will have relatively more effect on auto enthusiasts.

Durable Goods

Durable goods, such as automobiles, home appliances, and machinery, provide a stream of services over an extended period of time. In addition to price, income, the prices of complements and substitutes, and advertising, three factors are particularly significant in the demand for durable goods. They are expectations about future prices and incomes, interest rates, and the price of used models.

By the very nature of durable goods, buyers have some discretion over the timing of purchase. Hence, the demand for durables depends significantly on buyer expectations about future prices and incomes. For instance, a consumer who is pessimistic about his future income may postpone replacing his car. A consumer who expects automobile manufacturers to cut prices at the end of the model year may delay a purchase until the price is cut.

In addition, many buyers need to finance their purchases of durable goods. Accordingly, the demand for durables depends significantly on interest rates. If interest rates are low, then the cost of buying a car or home will be lower; hence,

Used Cars

The American consumer's demand for used cars has been growing fast for several reasons. One reason is the increasing price of new cars. Between 1984 and 1994, the average price of a new car rose by 70% from $11,500 to $19,500, while average incomes and consumer prices increased by only 40%.

Another reason for the growth in demand for used cars is the improving quality. Auto manufacturers have steadily improved the quality of their products. Between 1976 and 1990, the proportion of six-year-old vehicles damaged by rust dropped from 90% to 6%. Consequently, used cars have become relatively more attractive.

A negative factor in the demand for used cars is financing. Most financial institutions charge an interest rate 2 percentage points higher on loans for used cars than for new cars. With improvements in the quality of used cars and the shift of middle-income consumers toward used cars, some financial institutions are beginning to offer more favorable rates on loans for used cars. This trend will further shift consumer demand toward used cars and away from new cars.

Source: "America's New Darling: The Used Car," *Asian Wall Street Journal*, (November 2, 1994), p. 2.

the demand for these durables will be higher. By contrast, if interest rates are high, then the cost of buying a durable will be higher and the demand will be lower.

Finally, an important factor in the demand for "big-ticket" durable goods such as automobiles and machinery is the price of used models. Used cars are a substitute for new automobiles and, likewise, used machinery is a substitute for new equipment. A higher price for used cars affects the demand for new cars in two ways. First, the higher price makes the used car less attractive; hence, it increases the demand for a new car. Second, the higher price signals a higher resale value and so will encourage consumers to purchase new cars.

5 *Market Demand*

Businesses that deal with many different customers may determine their strategy on the basis of the entire market rather than individual customers. Such businesses need to understand the demand of the entire market. The **market demand curve** is a graph that shows the quantity that all buyers will purchase at every possible price. The analysis of a market demand curve is essentially similar to that for an individual demand curve, hence we need only highlight the key points in the following discussion.

The **market demand curve** is a graph showing the quantity that all buyers will purchase at every possible price.

Construction

To construct the market demand for an item, we must interview all the potential consumers and ask each person the quantity that he or she would buy at every possible price. For each price, we then add the reported individual quantities to get the quantity that the market as a whole will demand.

Let us apply this procedure to construct the market demand for movies. Suppose that there are only three potential viewers: Joy, Max, and Lucas. We ask each of them, "Other things equal, how many movies would you attend a month at a price of $10 per movie?" Table 2.3 reports their answers. The market quantity demanded is 0.

Table 2.3 Market demand

Price ($ per movie)	Quantity (Movies a month)			
	Joy	Max	Lucas	Market
10.00	0	0	0	0
7.50	1	0	0	1
5.00	2	1	0	3
2.50	4	2	3	9
0.00	7	6	4	17

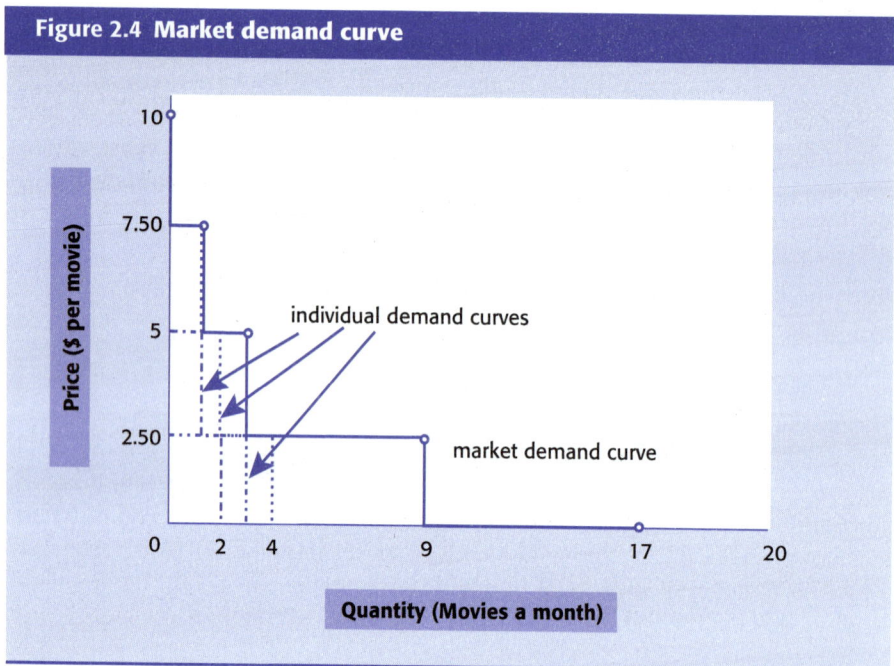

Figure 2.4 Market demand curve

The market demand curve is the horizontal summation of the individual demand curves. At every price, the market quantity demanded is the sum of the individual quantities demanded.

We then repeat these questions for other possible prices: $7.50, $5, $2.50, and 0 per movie. At each price, we add the reported individual quantities to get the market quantity demanded. For instance, at a price of $5, Joy would go to two movies, Max would go to one movie, and Lucas would go to none; hence, the market quantity demanded is 2 + 1 + 0 = 3 movies.

We represent the market demand on a graph, with the price of movies on the vertical axis and quantity on the horizontal axis, in Figure 2.4. Joining the pairs of prices and quantities, we have the market demand for movies. This market demand curve is in bold.

To do a **horizontal summation**, add the demand curves in the horizontal direction.

Another procedure for constructing a market demand curve is as the **horizontal summation** of the individual demand curves. On Figure 2.4, we draw the individual demand curves of the three potential consumers: Joy, Max, and Lucas. *Horizontal summation* means that we add the curves in the horizontal direction. The individual demand curves show the number of movies that each of the three consumers will buy at every possible price. So, at every price, we add the quantities that the three consumers buy to arrive at the quantity that the market will buy.

Since the individual demand curves slope downward, the market demand curve also slopes downward. The fundamental reason is that all consumers get diminishing marginal benefit; hence, at a lower price, the market as a whole will buy a larger quantity.

The market demand curve in Figure 2.4 has kinks where the quantity demanded rises in response to reductions in the price. As the number of consumers increases, the market demand curve will increase. Graphically, it will move further up and to the right. As the demand increases, we must reduce the scale of the figure and the kinks will gradually diminish in significance. Eventually, with a large number of consumers, the market demand curve will be an almost smooth curve. In the remaining chapters, we focus on smooth market demand curves.

Piracy and the Demand for Software

The Software Publishers Association represents America's major publishers of personal computer software. The association estimated that, in 1993, a total of 25.7 million copies of software were pirated, while the average cost of a legitimate package was $61. Multiplying these two numbers, the association found that publishers lost $1.568 billion to piracy.

Pirated software costs almost nothing. Is it reasonable to assume that users of pirated software would buy 25.7 million packages if they had to pay $61 for each unit? For a valid estimate of the losses of software publishers, the association ought to estimate the market demand curve of people using pirated software. Using this demand curve, the association can then estimate the quantity that these users would buy at a price of $61. That quantity multiplied by $61 would be a more accurate (and smaller) estimate of the revenues that software publishers lose to piracy.

Source: Software Publishers Association, *Report on Global Software Piracy*, (Washington, DC: Software Publishers Association, 1994), p. 33.

Other Factors

Like individual demand, the market demand depends on other factors, including buyers' incomes, the prices of related products, and advertising. The market demand curve for an item shows explicitly only the effect of price on the quantity that the market wishes to buy. So, a change in the price of the item will cause a movement along the market demand curve from one point to another on the same curve.

By contrast, the market demand curve does not explicitly show other factors, such as incomes, the prices of related products, and advertising. Accordingly, changes in these factors will shift the entire market demand curve. In the math supplement to this chapter, we use algebra to explain how changes in the various factors affect a special type of smooth demand curve: a straight-line demand curve.

The directions of the effects of changes in the other factors on the market demand curve are similar to those for the individual demand curve. We will not repeat the discussion here. Instead, we focus on the key differences. An important application of demand analysis is to compare market demands in different countries. In each country, the market demand will depend on incomes as well as other factors. Let us discuss how to measure incomes in different countries.

Generally, there are two ways of measuring the income of an entire country: the gross national product (GNP) and the gross domestic product (GDP). Broadly, the GNP and GDP measure the total amount produced in a country for a given year. Since employers must pay workers, landlords, and lenders, the total value of production is also the total income of the country. The GNP is the GDP plus net income from foreign sources; hence, the two measures are closely related.

The average income of the residents of some country may be estimated by dividing either the GNP or the GDP by the population, which yields the GNP and GDP per capita, respectively. This can be converted into U.S. dollars by using the relevant exchange rate between the domestic currency and the U.S. dollar.

Income Distribution

Market researchers frequently take a shortcut when assessing market demand. Instead of considering the demand of all individual consumers and adding these individual demands, a common simplification is to estimate the demand for an individual with average income and multiply that by the number of buyers.

This simple approach ignores the distribution of income; that is, whether consumers have very similar or very disparate incomes. The distribution of income may have an important effect on the demand for particular items.

For instance, suppose that Northland and Southland have identical national incomes of $29.8 billion and populations of 1 million. In both countries, the average per capita income is $29,800. In Northland, 1% of the people earn $100,000 a year, while the other 99% earn $20,000 a year; in Southland, everyone has an equal income. Northland may have a substantial demand for cosmetic surgery, luxury cars, and designer clothing. By contrast, there will be no demand for these items in Southland.

Generally, the more uneven is the distribution of income, the more important it is to consider the actual distribution of income and not merely the average income when estimating market demand.

Progress check **Progress Check 2D** Referring to Figure 2.4, show how an increase in the price of a complement would affect the market demand.

Who Buys Air Conditioners in India?

With an average income of less than $1000 a year, the people of India are among the poorest in the world. How could they afford to buy over 80,000 units of $600 air conditioners? The answer to this question is that some people earn much more than the average income.

In India, income is less evenly distributed than in major developed countries such as the United States. Less than 5% of Indian urban households own an air conditioner. This pattern corresponds very well to the upper-income bracket. India's National Council of Applied Economic Research classifies about 4% of urban households as "high income," with incomes exceeding $3,360 a year.

Source: "A Fresh Look at India," *McKinsey Quarterly*, no. 2 (1993), pp. 29–44.

Market Structure

We have analyzed how the individual demand curves of the various buyers can be horizontally summed to yield the market demand curve. The market quantity will be provided by one or more sellers. Hence, the market demand must be divided among the various sellers, each of whom faces its individual demand curve. Figure 2.5 depicts how the demands of individual buyers add up to the market demand and how the market demand divides into the demands facing individual sellers.

As Figure 2.5 shows, the concept of an individual demand curve has two possible meanings: the individual demand curve of a buyer or the individual demand curve faced by a seller. It is important to maintain a clear distinction between the two meanings.

In Chapters 3 and 4, we discuss in detail a seller's individual demand curve. Meanwhile, let us consider a question that managers frequently pose, "What is the demand for my product?" Our analysis of demand shows that this question has no answer. The answer can only be, "It depends." The quantity demanded

Figure 2.5 Market structure

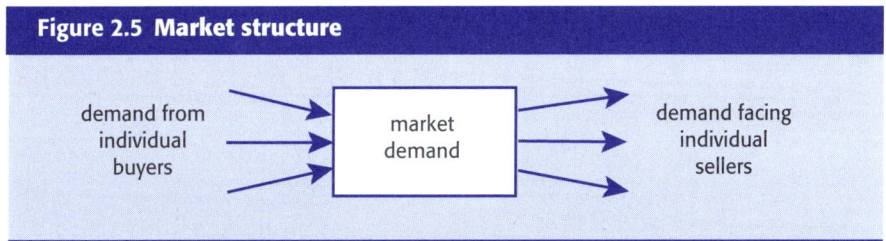

Demands from individual buyers add up to the market demand. The market demand divides into the demands facing individual sellers.

depends on the selling price, buyers' incomes, the prices of related products, and other factors. Only when these variables are specified is it possible to gauge the quantity of demand.

6 *Buyer Surplus*

An individual buyer's demand curve shows the quantity that the buyer will purchase at every possible price. We now consider the buyer's demand curve from another perspective, which is to show the maximum amount that a buyer is willing to pay for each unit of the item. This perspective is important for business strategy as it shows how a seller can calculate the maximum price that the buyer can be charged for a given purchase.

Benefit

Recall that the marginal benefit is the benefit provided by an additional unit of an item. It can be measured as the maximum amount of money that the buyer is willing to pay for that unit. To illustrate, consider Joy's demand curve for movies, reproduced in Figure 2.6. This shows that Joy is willing to pay $7.50 for the first movie; hence, her marginal benefit from one movie is $7.50. Similarly,

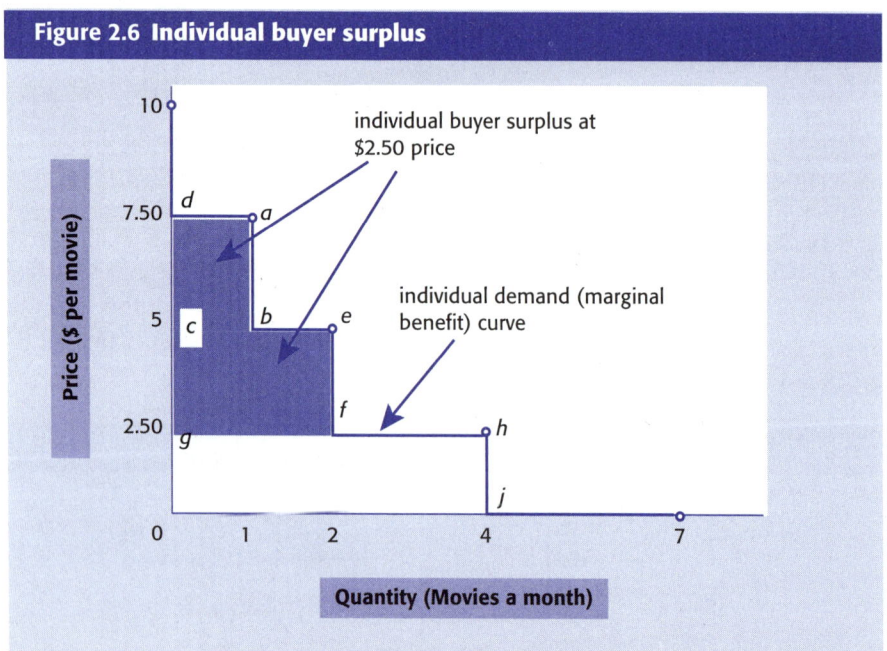

Figure 2.6 Individual buyer surplus

The individual buyer surplus is the buyer's total benefit from some quantity of purchases less the actual expenditure. At a price of $2.50, Joy's buyer surplus is the shaded area *gfebad* between the demand curve and the $2.50 line.

Joy is willing to pay $5 for the second movie; hence, her marginal benefit from the second movie is $5, and so on.

In effect, Joy's demand curve is also her marginal benefit curve. This perspective also implies that the demand curve slopes downward. By the principle of diminishing marginal benefit, each additional movie gives less benefit than the one before. Hence, Joy's marginal benefit curve will slope downward. Since the marginal benefit curve is identical with Joy's demand curve, this means that Joy's demand curve will slope downward.

We have just seen how the demand curve shows the marginal benefit from each unit that a buyer purchases. Using this information, we can then calculate the buyer's **total benefit**, which is the benefit yielded by all the units that the buyer purchases. The total benefit is the marginal benefit from the first unit plus the marginal benefit from the second unit, and so on, up to and including marginal benefit from the last unit that the buyer purchases.

> The **total benefit** is the benefit yielded by all the units that the buyer purchases.

A buyer's total benefit from some quantity of purchases is the maximum that the buyer is willing to pay for that quantity. Graphically, the total benefit is represented by the area under the buyer's demand curve up to and including the last unit purchased. Let us apply this concept to calculate Joy's total benefit from four movies a month. This is the area under her demand curve up to and including four movies a month. In Figure 2.6, this is $7.50 + $5 + ($2.50 × 2) = $17.50. Hence, the maximum that Joy would be willing to pay for four movies a month is $17.50.

Benefit vis-à-vis Price

Suppose that the price of a movie is $2.50. Then Joy goes to four movies a month. As already calculated, her total benefit would be $17.50. Joy, however, needs to pay only $2.50 × 4 = $10, which is substantially less than her total benefit. The difference between a buyer's total benefit from some quantity of purchases and the actual expenditure is called the **buyer surplus**. At a price of $2.50 per movie, Joy's buyer surplus is $17.50 – $10 = $7.50.

> The **buyer surplus** is the difference between a buyer's total benefit from some quantity of purchases and her or his actual expenditure.

Referring to Figure 2.6, Joy's total benefit from four movies a month is represented by the area 0jhfebad under her demand (marginal benefit) curve up to and including four movies a month. At a price of $2.50, her expenditure on four movies a month is represented by the area 0jhg under the $2.50 line up to and including four movies a month. Joy's buyer surplus is the difference between these two areas, that is, the area gfebad between her demand curve and the $2.50 line.[1]

Generally, provided that purchases are voluntary, a buyer must get some surplus; otherwise, he or she will not buy. Hence, the maximum that a seller can charge is the buyer's total benefit. If a seller tries to charge more, then the buyer will walk away.

---

[1] Changes in prices can affect a buyer's real income, hence shift the individual demand curve. Strictly, the buyer surplus must be measured from a demand curve that is adjusted for changes in real income. For simplicity, we ignore this detail.

Progress check

Progress Check 2E   Suppose that the price of movies is $5. In Figure 2.6, mark Joy's buyer surplus at that price.

Price Changes

Referring to Joy's demand for movies, suppose that the price is $5 and Joy goes to two movies a month. Her buyer surplus is area *cbad*. Now suppose that the price drops to $2.50. Then Joy will raise her attendance from two to four movies a month. Her buyer surplus will increase by area *gfec*. The increase in buyer surplus can be attributed to two effects—she gets the two original movies at a lower price, and she goes to more movies.

Generally, a buyer gains from a price reduction in two ways. First, he or she gets a lower price on the quantity that the buyer would have purchased at the original higher price. Second, he or she can buy more, gaining buyer surplus on each of the additional purchases. The extent of the second effect depends on the buyer's response to the price reduction. The greater the increase in purchases, the larger will be the buyer's gain from the price reduction.

Similarly, a buyer loses from a price increase in two ways—the buyer must pay a higher price, and he or she will buy less.

Package Deals: Soaking up the Buyer Surplus

A seller that has complete flexibility over pricing maximizes its profit by charging each buyer just a little less than his or her total benefit. Suppose, for instance, that Figure 2.7 describes Jania's demand for mobile telephone calls. If the mobile telephone service charges a price of 50 cents per minute, Jania will make 30 minutes of calls a month. The service would earn a revenue of $30 \times$ 50 cents = $15. Jania would get buyer surplus of $0.5 \times 30 \times 150$ cents = $22.50.

Jania's total benefit from 30 minutes of calls a month is the area under her demand curve from 0 to 30 minutes, or $30 \times 0.5(200 + 50) = \$37.50$. Suppose that the mobile telephone service offers Jania a package deal of 30 minutes of calls at $37 with no other alternative. The package deal will give Jania a buyer surplus of $37.50 − $37 = 50 cents. Since there is no other alternative, Jania will buy this package. The service will earn $37 in revenue, which is more than double the revenue from the 50-cent pricing policy. The package deal enables the service to soak up almost all of Jania's buyer surplus.

Package deals are a widespread practice in the telecommunications industry. Mobile telephone services typically set a two-part pricing scheme consisting of a basic monthly fee covering a specified quantity of airtime plus a rate for additional minutes. The basic monthly fee is essentially a package deal. We study package deals and other pricing schemes in Chapter 9, "Pricing Policy."

Figure 2.7 Package deal

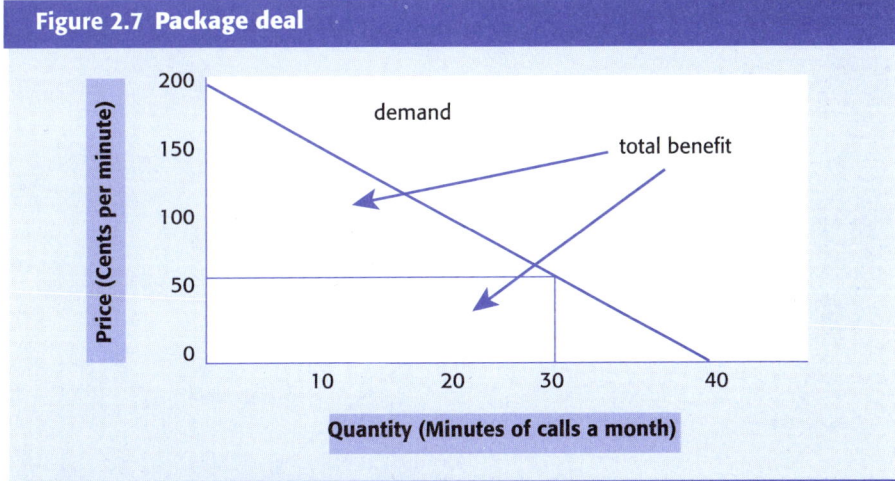

Jania will buy a package deal of 30 minutes of calls for any price not exceeding her total benefit of $37.50.

Price Promotions: The More You Buy, the More You Save?

Students at the University of California, Los Angeles, enjoy several privileges. One is a good education at a low price. Another is California's unbeatable weather, and a third is discounted movie tickets. Suppose that Alan buys 12 tickets a year at $4 rather than the full price of $7. By how much does he gain from the discount scheme?

One answer is that Alan "saves" $7 − $4 = $3 on each ticket, which adds to a total of $3 × 12 = $36. This answer, however, implicitly assumes that Alan would buy 12 tickets a year whether the price is $4 or $7.

For the correct answer, we apply the concept of buyer surplus. Figure 2.8 represents Alan's demand curve for movies. At the $7 full price, Alan would buy six tickets a year and get the buyer surplus of the shaded area *bac*. By contrast, at the discount price of $4, Alan buys 12 tickets a year and gets the buyer surplus of the shaded area *bac* plus the area *deab*.

Thus, the discount scheme increases Alan's buyer surplus by the area *deab*. This represents $7 − $4 × 0.5(6 + 12) = $27, which is Alan's gain from the discount scheme.

We can analyze this $27 gain in two parts. First, Alan can buy six tickets (the number that he would have bought at the full $7 price) at a lower price. He gains $7 − $4 = $3 on each of these six tickets, or a total of $3 × 6 = $18. Second, the discount scheme induces Alan to increase his purchases to 12 tickets a year. Alan will get some buyer surplus on each of the additional tickets. In Figure 2.8, the buyer surplus on the seventh through twelfth tickets is 0.5 × $(7 − 4) × 6 = $9.

Figure 2.8 Value of discount movie tickets

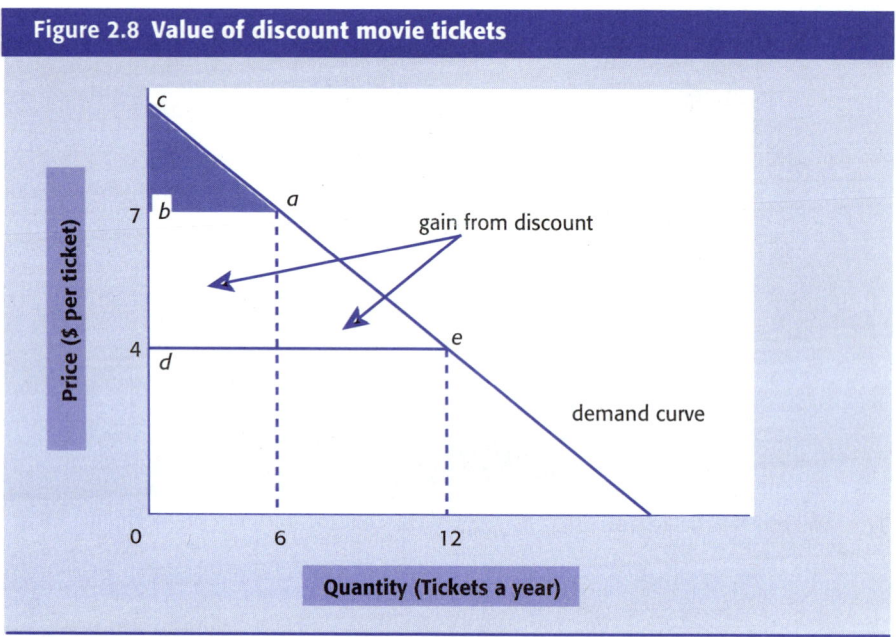

The reduction in the price of movie tickets from $7 to $4 increases Alan's buyer surplus by the area *deab*.

Market Buyer Surplus

We have introduced the concept of buyer surplus for individual buyers. To see how the concept applies at the market level, let us consider the market demand for movies reproduced in Figure 2.9. At a price of $2.50, the market quantity demanded is nine movies. The market's total benefit is the area under the market demand curve up to and including nine movies. By contrast, the market's expenditure for nine movies is the area under the $2.50 line up to and including nine movies a month.

The total benefit exceeds the expenditure; that is, the market as a whole is not paying the maximum that it would be willing to pay for that quantity of purchases. The difference is the market buyer surplus. Graphically, it is the area between the market demand curve and the $2.50 line.

Recall that the buyer surplus of an individual consumer at the price of $2.50 is the area between his or her demand curve and the $2.50 line. The sum of these areas for all the individual consumers is the area between the market demand curve and the $2.50 line. Hence, the market buyer surplus is equal to the sum of the individual buyer surpluses.

The principles underlying the market buyer surplus are the same as those for the individual buyer surplus. When the market price rises, the market buyer surplus drops as buyers suffer from the higher price and cut their purchases. By

Figure 2.9 Market buyer surplus

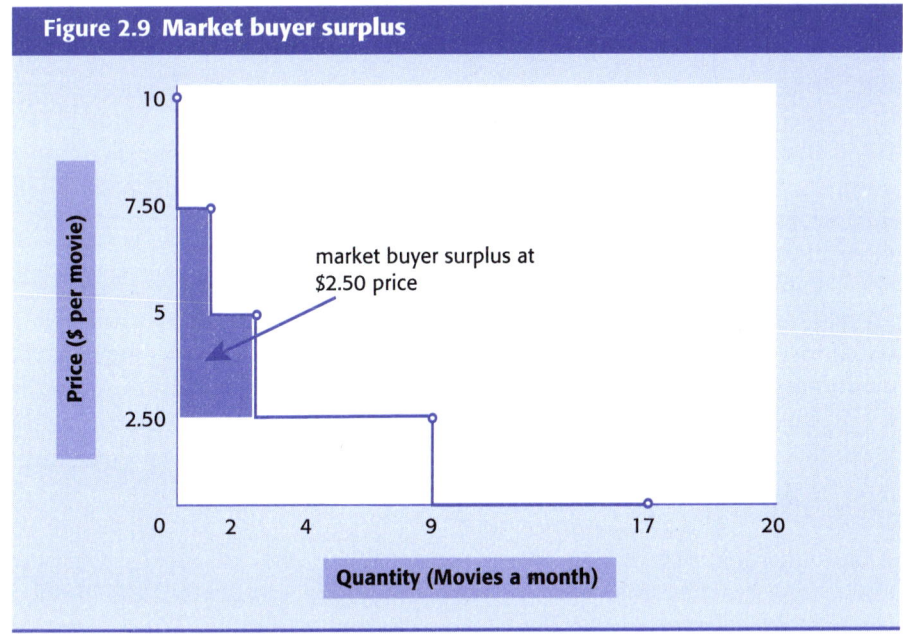

At a price of $2.50, the market buyer surplus is the shaded area between the market demand curve and the $2.50 line.

contrast, when the market price falls, the market buyer surplus increases as buyers enjoy the lower price and expand their purchases.

The concept of market buyer surplus will be useful in analyzing the impact of price changes on the market as a whole and in developing pricing policies to maximize a seller's profit.

7 Business Demand

We have introduced the concepts of individual and market demand through the example of movies. Movies are a consumer good. By contrast, some items are purchased only by businesses. Examples include TV commercials, heavy trucks, machine tools, and human resources. Some items, such as gasoline and telephone calls, are purchased by both consumers and businesses.

Accordingly, it is important to understand the principles of business demand. In many ways, these principles are similar to those underlying consumer demand. Therefore, in discussing business demand, we will briefly highlight the similarities and then focus on the important differences.

Inputs

Consumers buy goods and services for final consumption or usage. By contrast, businesses do not purchase goods and services for their own sake but to use them as inputs in the production of other goods and services. We will make a detailed analysis of business operations in Chapter 4. Here, we will review only the essentials necessary to understand the business demand for inputs.

For convenience, the inputs purchased by a business can be classified into raw materials, energy, labor, and capital. Businesses use these inputs to produce outputs for sale to consumers or other businesses. For example, a steel mill manufactures steel bars and sheets for sale to automakers and construction companies.

The inputs may be substitutes or complements. Consider, for instance, an express delivery service. Its trucks and drivers are complements: A truck without a driver is quite useless, as is a driver without a truck. Other inputs may be substitutes. For example, the service may use machines or workers to sort packages. Similarly, operations such as loading and packing could be performed by machine or manually.

Demand

A business produces items for sale to consumers or other businesses. The business earns revenues from sales. By raising the quantity of inputs, the business can produce a larger output and hence a change in revenue. Accordingly, the business can measure its marginal benefit from an input as the increase in revenue arising from an additional unit of the input.

We suppose that, when the quantity of an input is larger, each additional unit of the input will generate a smaller increase in revenue. This means that the input provides a diminishing marginal benefit to the business.

Using the marginal benefit of an input, we can construct the individual demand curve of a business. This shows the quantity of the input that the business will purchase at every possible price. A business should buy an input up to the quantity that its marginal benefit from the input exactly balances the price.

To see why, consider the demand for labor of a delivery service. Figure 2.10 represents the marginal benefit of labor to the service. Let the wage be $10 per worker hour. The quantity of labor that balances the marginal benefit with the wage is 1000 worker hours a month. Suppose that the service buys only 900 worker hours. Then, the marginal benefit will exceed the wage. By increasing the quantity of the input, the business will increase revenue by more than the wage, hence it will raise profit by the shaded area *bac*. Similarly, we can show that, if the service purchases 1100 worker hours, it can increase profit by reducing the input.

We have shown that a business should buy an input up to the quantity at which its marginal benefit from the input exactly balances the price. Generally, the input provides diminishing marginal benefit. Hence, when the price is lower, the business will buy a larger quantity, and conversely, when the price is higher, the business will buy a smaller quantity. Thus, as shown in Figure 2.10, the demand curve for the input slopes downward.

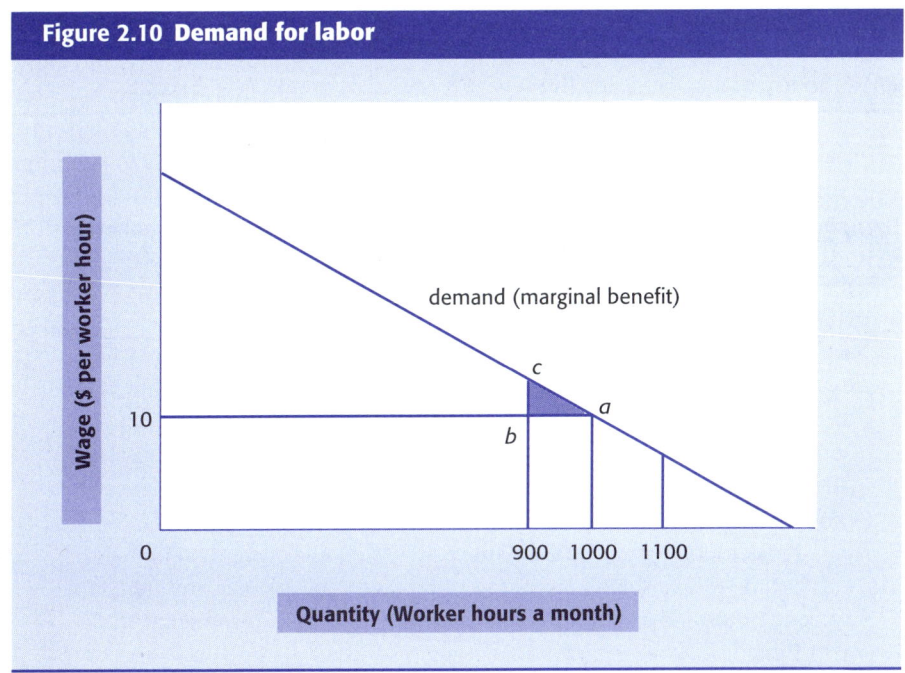

Figure 2.10 Demand for labor

A business will buy 1000 worker hours of labor a month, at which quantity, its marginal benefit equals the $10 wage. If it buys only 900 worker hours, then, by raising the quantity of labor, it can increase profit by the shaded area *bac.*

Factors in Demand

A change in the price of an input is represented by a movement along the demand curve. By contrast, changes in other factors will lead to a shift of the entire demand curve. A major factor in consumer demand is income. Business demand does not depend on income but rather on the quantity of the output. If the output is larger, then the business will increase its demand for inputs. This is a shift of the entire demand curve because the increase occurs at all prices. If, however, the output is lower, then the demand for inputs will be lower.

The demand of a business for an input also depends on the prices of complements and substitutes in the production of the output. For instance, delivery trucks and drivers are complements, hence an increase in the drivers' wages will reduce the demand for trucks.

As we have outlined, business demand is derived from calculations of marginal benefit. On the whole, purchasing decisions of businesses are relatively less subject to impulse buying than those of consumers. Hence, advertising plays a smaller role in business demand, and there is relatively more informative than persuasive advertising.

Progress check   **Progress Check 2F**   Referring to Figure 2.10, suppose that the service buys 1100 worker hours of labor. How can the service increase its profit?

Automated Teller Machines

One of the major services provided by a retail bank is dispensing cash to customers. Traditionally, the service was performed by tellers operating within the bank office. As wages rose, the service became increasingly costly. This provided the motivation for banks to substitute labor with capital through automated teller machines (ATMs). Customers can withdraw cash from an ATM, and bank tellers can devote their time to tasks that require relatively more human attention.

Banks found that ATMs were more accurate and secure than human tellers. Further, ATMs allowed banks to extend their service outside of traditional banking hours and also to remote locations. In this case, technology enabled a cost saving as well as an improvement in service.

8 *Summary*

A demand curve shows the quantity demanded as a function of price, other things equal. Generally, the demand curve slopes downward. Changes in price are represented by movements along the demand curve; changes in other factors, such as income, the prices of related products, and advertising, are represented by shifts of the entire demand curve. The market demand curve is the horizontal summation of the individual demand curves of the various buyers.

Buyer surplus is the difference between a buyer's total benefit from some quantity of purchases and his or her actual expenditure. Changes in price affect buyer surplus through the price changes themselves as well as through changes in the quantity demanded.

Key Concepts

individual demand curve	complement	total benefit
marginal benefit	substitute	buyer surplus
normal product	market demand curve	
inferior product	horizontal summation	

Further Reading

For the behavior of consumer and business buyers, see Philip Kotler's classic, *Marketing Management*, 8th ed. (Englewood Cliffs, NJ: Prentice Hall, 1994), Chapters 7 and 8.

Robert S. Pindyck and Daniel L. Rubinfeld present an economic analysis of demand using the model of indifference curves in *Microeconomics*, 3d ed. (Englewood Cliffs, NJ: Prentice Hall, 1994), Chapters 3 and 4.

Review Questions

1. Define each of the following terms and give an example to illustrate your definition:
   a. Substitute.
   b. Complement.
   c. Normal product.
   d. Inferior product.

2. Name a good or service that you bought recently. Would you have bought less of the item if the price had been lower? Explain why or why not.

3. The female condom protects women against both pregnancy and sexually transmitted diseases such as AIDS. Some claim that the female condom will liberate women of the 1990s in the way that the pill liberated women of the 1960s. How will the introduction of this product affect each of the following:
   a. The demand for male condoms.
   b. The demand for lingerie.

4. Manufacturers of soft drinks like Coke and Pepsi can use either corn syrup or sugar to sweeten their beverages. Owing to federal restrictions against imports, sugar is relatively more expensive in the United States than in the rest of the world. Comparing U.S. with foreign soft drink manufacturers, which do you expect to use relatively more sugar and less corn syrup?

5. Consider the following price changes. For each change, state whether it will cause a movement along the demand curve for corn syrup or a shift of the entire curve.
   a. An increase in the price of sugar.
   b. An increase in the price of corn syrup.
   c. An increase in the production of Pepsi Cola.

6. Microcomputers record data permanently on hard and flexible disks. You are a major supplier of hard disks to the microcomputer industry. Recently, you cut the wholesale price of your 2-gigabyte hard disk by 10% from $150 to $135. Your sales manager is planning to push the new price with the theme of "save $15 on every disk that you buy." Does this
   a. Overstate,
   b. State exactly,
   c. Understate,
   the benefit to your customers?

7. Suppose that there is a general increase in incomes. Compare the effect of this increase on the demand faced by the following two chains:
   a. Marriott, a four-star hotel chain with properties throughout the world.
   b. Motel 6, a chain of low-price motels.

8. You are exporting European products to South Africa. Real per capita income in South Africa is 88% lower than in Britain. Consider the several pairs of products that follow. For each pair, identify the product for which it is more important to know South Africa's distribution of income when estimating demand (choose a or b).

   For writing instruments,
   a. Bic disposable ballpoint pens.
   b. Mont Blanc fountain pens.

   For watches,
   a. Rolex watches.
   b. Generic Swiss watches.

9. Which of the following are important factors in the demand for new homes?
    a. Interest rates.
    b. Household incomes.
    c. Expectations of future home prices.
    d. The current price of building materials.

10. Explain how a long-distance telecommunications carrier can use the concept of buyer surplus to price a 1-hour package of long-distance calls.

Discussion Questions

1. Using data from 93 countries compiled by the World Resources Institute, *The Economist* estimated a relationship between the literacy rate of women and the number of births per woman (fertility rate). When the literacy rate is 0%, the fertility rate is 8 per woman; and when the literacy rate is 100%, the birth rate is 2.5 per woman ("Population: Battle of the Bulge," *The Economist* [September 3, 1994], pp. 19–21).
    a. Construct a diagram with literacy rate on the vertical axis and fertility rate on the horizontal axis. Mark the two points that the *The Economist* estimated. Join the two points with a straight line.
    b. Perhaps the largest cost of having a baby is the time that the mother must invest during pregnancy and when rearing the child. For a woman with a higher level of education, is the value of this time higher or lower?
    c. Returning to your diagram, mark "cost of child" on the vertical axis. Does your diagram have any relation to a demand curve? Please explain.

2. Compile the following data for any two countries: (i) gross national product (GNP) or gross domestic product (GDP) and (ii) population. State the sources of your data.
    a. Use the above information to compare average income per capita in the two countries.
    b. Compare the demand for (i) a normal product and (ii) an inferior product in the two countries.

3. In the following situations, explain how an increase in hotel room rates will affect the demand curve for airline travel.
    a. Mohamed, of Jeddah, Saudi Arabia, plans to take all three generations of his family to Italy for a vacation. They will fly by Saudia Airlines from Jeddah to Rome. Mohamed has reserved three rooms in a Rome hotel for one week.
    b. Anne, a London-based merchant banker, is taking the early morning flight to Warsaw, Poland, for a business meeting. If her meeting lasts less than three hours, she will be able to catch the last flight back to London; otherwise, she must spend the night in a Warsaw hotel.

4. A disposable camera consists of a simple lens and a roll of film built into a cardboard box. It can be used only once: Having finished the film, the consumer sends the entire camera to a photo finisher. Kodak and Fuji introduced disposable cameras to the U.S. market in 1987. Sales grew rapidly to 5 million units in 1989, to 9 million in 1990, and 15 million in 1991. By comparison, total film sales, including disposable cameras, were 706 million units in 1990 and 710 million in 1991

("For Cardboard Cameras, Sales Picture Enlarges and Seems Brighter than Ever," *Wall Street Journal* [February 11, 1992], p. B1).

    a. How would the introduction of disposable cameras affect the sales of film for conventional (nondisposable) cameras?

    b. Based on the preceding data, Photo Marketing Association International's director of Marketing Research, Barry Harland, inferred that, if disposable cameras had not been available, total film sales would have dropped between 1990 and 1991. Do you agree?

5. Refer to a recent issue of a women's magazine such as *Cosmopolitan*, *Elle*, or *Vogue*. Take any 50 pages at random.

    a. Count the number of pages of advertisements for (i) men's, (ii) women's, and (iii) gender-neutral products.

    b. Why are men's products advertised in a women's magazine?

6. Color TVs are more expensive than black-and-white TVs. In 1989, American purchases of black-and-white TVs were 13 per thousand persons, while purchases of color TVs were 88 per thousand persons. By contrast, Canadian purchases of black-and-white TVs were 6 per thousand persons, while purchases of color TVs were 63 per thousand persons (*International Marketing Data and Statistics*, 17th ed. [London: Euromonitor, 1993], pp. 167 and 457).

    a. Compare the total purchases of TVs (color plus black and white) per thousand persons in Canada and the United States.

    b. How does the availability and quality of TV programming affect the demand for TVs? Use these factors to explain the difference in (a).

    c. Compare the ratio of purchases of color to black and white TVs in Canada and the United States.

    d. How does the distribution of income affect the demand for color relative to black-and-white TVs? Apply this factor to explain the difference in (c).

7. This question applies the techniques introduced in the math supplement. Suppose that the market demand for car rentals is represented by the equation

$$D = 50 - p + 0.2Y, \qquad (2.1)$$

where D is the quantity demanded in rentals a month, p is the price in dollars per rental, and Y is the average consumer's income in thousands of dollars a year. Assume that $Y = 50$.

    a. Draw the market demand curve. Show the effect of a cut in price, from $p = 30$ to $p = 20$.

    b. Show the effect on demand of an increase in income from $Y = 50$ to $Y = 60$.

8. The price of Chanel perfume is around $200 per fluid ounce, while the price of Arrowhead bottled water is $1 per gallon. Hilda buys 2 fluid ounces of Chanel and 10 gallons of bottled water a month.

    a. Using relevant demand curves, illustrate Hilda's choices. Illustrate how the following changes will affect Hilda's demand for Chanel perfume: (i) a price increase to $220 per fluid ounce, and (ii) a cut in the price of another of Hilda's favorite perfumes.

    b. Hilda spends more money each month on perfume than bottled water. Does this necessarily mean that perfume gives her more total benefit than water? Use appropriate demand curves to address this question.

9. This question applies the techniques introduced in the math supplement. Suppose that a typical household's demand for long-distance calls is represented by the equation

$$D = 200 - 4p + 0.4Y, \qquad (2.2)$$

where D is the quantity demanded in minutes a month, p is the price of calls in cents per minute, and Y is the household's income in thousands of dollars a year. Assume that $Y = 100$.

a. Draw the household's demand curve.

b. How many minutes will the household buy at a price of 25 cents a minute?

c. What is the maximum lump sum that a long-distance carrier can charge the household for a package of 140 minutes of calls?

10. Suppose that Moonshine Electronics manufactures semiconductors in the Netherlands. Manufacturing begins with fabrication of semiconductor wafers, which is a very capital-intensive process. The next stage is to cut the wafers and package the product for sale to customers. Cutting and packaging is relatively labor intensive. Moonshine is planning to shift the cutting-and-packaging process to a new factory in India, where wages are lower. By doing so, Moonshine will be able to reduce the cost of its semiconductors and gain a larger share of the international market.

a. How will Moonshine's plan to shift production affect its demand for production workers in the Netherlands?

b. How will a fall in Indian wages affect Moonshine's demand for production workers in the Netherlands?

c. How will a fall in Indian wages affect Moonshine's demand for sales personnel in the Netherlands?

Math Supplement

Individual Demand Curve

Using a little mathematics, we can reinforce our understanding of the individual demand curve, especially the effect of changes in price vis-à-vis other factors. Let the individual's demand for some item be represented by the equation

$$D = 30 - 2p + 0.04Y + 4s, \qquad (2.3)$$

where D is the quantity demanded in units a year, p is the price of the item in dollars per unit, Y is the buyer's income in thousands of dollars a year, and s is the value of another factor.

This demand curve is a straight line. To explain, suppose that $Y = 100$ and $s = 0.5$. Then, substituting in (2.3),

$$D = 30 - 2p + 4 + 2 = 36 - 2p. \qquad (2.4)$$

Differentiating (2.4) with respect to price

$$\frac{dD}{dp} = -2, \qquad (2.5)$$

which means that the demand equation has a constant slope, or equivalently, that the demand curve is a straight line.

To sketch the demand curve, we consider two points on the curve. First, when the price $p = 0$, the quantity demanded $D = 36$. Next, if $D = 0$, $p = 36/2 = 18$.

Marking and joining these two points on Figure 2.11, we have the buyer's demand curve.

As shown in Figure 2.11, the demand curve is drawn with price on the vertical axis and quantity on the horizontal axis. Hence, the slope of the demand curve is the derivative of price with respect to quantity. From the demand equation, we can obtain the derivative of quantity with respect to price, which is –2. Inverting this, we find that the derivative of price with respect to quantity, or the slope, is –0.5.

The demand curve can be used to illustrate the effect of a change in price. By (2.4), when the price $p = 9$, the quantity demanded $D = 36 - (2 \times 9) = 18$. When the price is higher, $p = 10$, the quantity demanded $D = 36 - (2 \times 10) = 16$. We represent this change by a movement along the demand curve from the point where $p = 9$ and $D = 18$ to the point where $p = 10$ and $D = 16$.

This demand curve can be used to illustrate the effect of a change in income. Recall that, originally, the buyer's income was $Y = 100$. Suppose that the buyer's income rises to $Y = 150$. The other factor remains $s = 0.5$. Then, by (2.3), the demand curve becomes

$$D = 30 - 2p + 6 + 2 = 38 - 2p. \qquad (2.6)$$

In this case, when the price $p = 0$, the quantity demanded $D = 38$, while if the quantity demanded

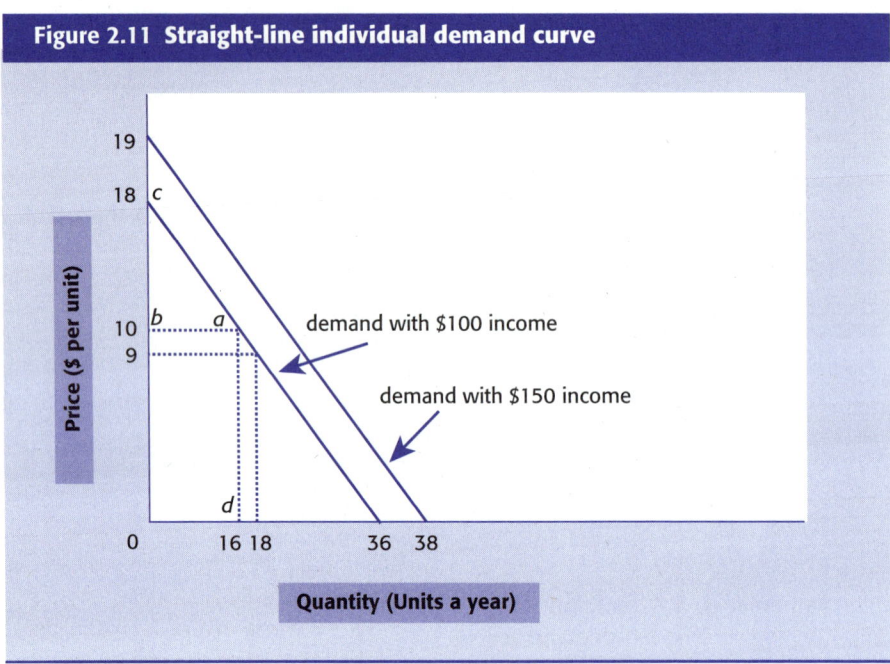

Figure 2.11 Straight-line individual demand curve

$D = 0$, the price $p = 38/2 = 19$. Marking and joining these two points on Figure 2.11, we have the demand curve with the income of $Y = 150$. This is a straight line that lies to the right of the demand curve with the income of $Y = 100$. By contrast to a change in price, the change in income is represented by a shift of the entire demand curve.

Recall that s is the value of another factor in demand. Originally, $s = 0.5$. Suppose that the other factor increases to $s = 0.6$, while income remains $Y = 100$. Then, by (2.3), the demand curve becomes

$$D = 30{-}2p + 4 + 2.4 = 36.4{-}2p. \qquad (2.7)$$

Accordingly, the change in the other factor is also represented by a shift of the entire demand curve. This other factor could be the price of a related product, advertising expenditure, season, weather, or location. A change in any of these factors would shift the entire demand curve.

With the equation of the demand curve, we can calculate the total benefit and buyer's surplus.

Recall the demand curve, with $Y = 100$ and $s = 0.5$ was

$$D = 36{-}2p. \qquad (2.8)$$

At the price $p = 10$, the buyer purchases quantity $D = 16$. The buyer's total benefit is represented by trapezium $0dac$, while the buyer's expenditure is represented by rectangle $0dab$. Hence, at the price $p = 10$, the buyer's surplus is represented by the triangle bac. The area of this triangle is $1/2 \times \$(18{-}10) \times 16 = \$64$.

Market Demand Curve

Using a mathematical approach, it is very simple to see the relation between individual and market demand curves. Suppose that the market for some item has two buyers, Alan and Jania. Alan's demand for the item is

$$D_a = 18{-}2p + 0.02Y_a, \qquad (2.9)$$

while Jania's demand is

$$D_j = 42 - 3p + 0.01Y_j. \tag{2.10}$$

To draw the curves, suppose that $Y_a = 100$ and $Y_j = 300$. Then

$$D_a = 20 - 2p, \text{ and} \tag{2.11}$$
$$D_j = 45 - 3p. \tag{2.12}$$

We draw these curves in Figure 2.12.

Notice that Jania's quantity demanded is 0 for prices above 15, while Alan's quantity demanded is 0 for prices above 10. By horizontal summation, the market demand curve has two segments. The upper segment covers prices between 10 and 15, where

the market quantity demanded $D = D_j = 45 - 3p$. The lower segment covers prices of 10 or less, where the market quantity demanded $D = D_a + D_j = 65 - 5p$. We draw the market demand curve in Figure 2.12.

We can check this market demand curve for the price $p = 5$. With $p = 5$, the individual quantities demanded are $D_a = 20 - 10 = 10$, and $D_j = 45 - 15 = 30$; hence, $D_a + D_j = 40$. This is exactly the quantity from the market demand curve in Figure 2.12.

Just as for an individual demand curve, a price change is represented by a movement along the market demand curve, while a change in income or any factor is represented by a shift of the entire demand curve.

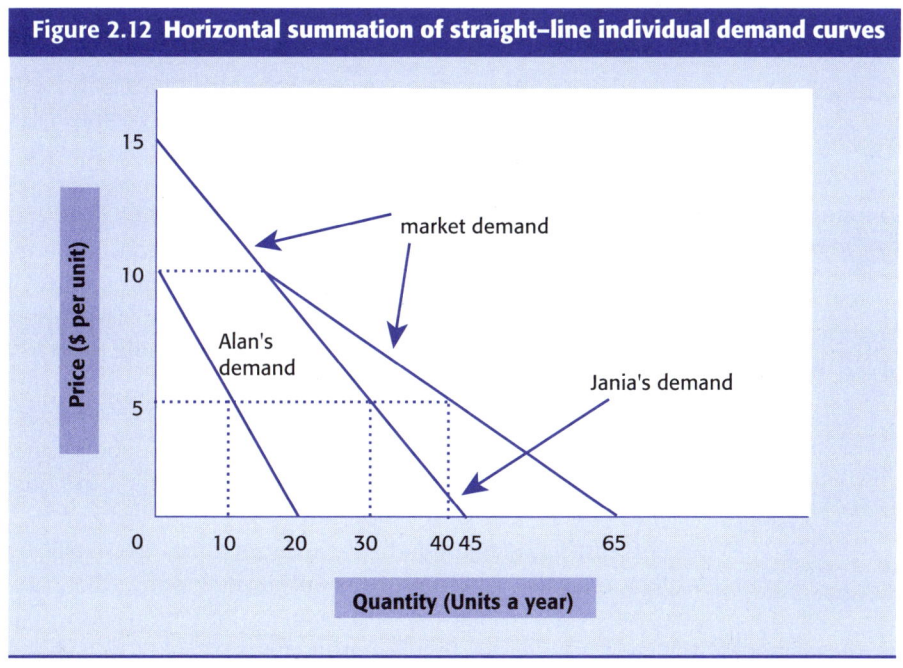

Figure 2.12 Horizontal summation of straight–line individual demand curves

Chapter 3

Quantitative Demand Analysis

1 Introduction

Whenever managers are asked to raise prices, their most frequent worry is, "But my sales would drop!" Since demand curves slope downward, it certainly is true that a higher price will reduce sales. The real issue is the extent to which the sales will fall in response to the change in price; that is, how sensitive are buyers to price changes. What is the answer to this question?

Automobile manufacturers are always concerned about the effect of price increases on sales. Suppose that, if Chevrolet raises the price of its Chevette by $100, then sales would fall by 5000 units a year. Similarly, suppose that, if Honda raises the price of its Civic by $100, then sales would drop by 3000 units a year. Are buyers of Chevettes more or less price sensitive than buyers of Civics? One answer is that they are less price sensitive: 3000 is less than 5000. But, this is not comparing like with like. We need some way of comparing price sensitivity that does not depend on the units with which we measure quantities and prices.

When forecasting demand, industry analysts must often deal with changes in several factors at the same time. For instance, suppose that, presently, the price of cigarettes is $1 a pack and sales are 1.5 billion packs a month. If the price of cigarettes increases by 5% and incomes rise by 3%, what will be the effect on cigarette sales? In particular, will sales rise or fall? Consider the changes in price and income separately. The price increase should reduce quantity demanded. Assuming that cigarettes are a normal product, a rise in real incomes will increase demand. So, the two changes affect the demand for cigarettes in different directions. What we need is some way of comparing the relative impact of the two changes.

To address these questions, we develop the concept of *elasticity*. The **elasticity of demand** measures the responsiveness of demand to changes in an underlying factor, such as the price of the product, income, the prices of related products, or advertising. There is an elasticity corresponding to every factor that affects demand.

Elasticity of demand is the responsiveness of demand to changes in an underlying factor.

The *own-price elasticity of demand* measures the responsiveness of the quantity demanded to changes in the price of the item. With the own-price elasticity, a manager can tell the extent to which buyers will respond to a price increase. Moreover, the own-price elasticity provides a simple way to compare the price sensitivity of demands for different products such as Chevrolet Chevettes and Honda Civics.

We will show how elasticities can be used to forecast the effect of single as well as multiple changes in the factors underlying demand. Accordingly, a tobacco industry analyst can use elasticities to consider how changes in both price and income will affect the demand for cigarettes. We will also discuss how elasticities depend on the time available for adjustment. Finally, we consider the data and statistical methods to use in estimating elasticities.

In this chapter, we present elasticities in the context of demand. The same analysis applies to the supply side of a market as well. In Chapter 4, we discuss the factors underlying supply and its corresponding elasticities.

2 *Own-Price Elasticity*

To address the issue of whether to raise price, we need a measure of buyers' sensitivity to price changes. The **own-price elasticity** of demand provides this information. By definition, the own-price elasticity of demand is the percentage by which the quantity demanded will change if the price of the item rises by 1%, other things equal. Equivalently, the own-price elasticity is the ratio,

The **own-price elasticity** of demand is the percentage by which the quantity demanded will change if the price of the item rises by 1%.

$$\frac{\text{percentage change in quantity demanded}}{\text{percentage change in price}}$$

or

$$\frac{\text{proportionate change in quantity demanded}}{\text{proportionate change in price}}.$$

Understanding the own-price elasticity of demand is fundamental to management of a business. Indeed, this concept is so basic that it is often called simply the *price elasticity* or *demand elasticity*. In Chapter 2, we distinguished the demand curve of an individual buyer, the market demand curve, and the demand curve faced by an individual seller. Every demand curve has a corresponding own-price elasticity. Before discussing how to apply this concept, let us first consider how it can be calculated.

Construction

Generally, there are two ways of deriving the own-price elasticity of demand.
One is the **arc approach,** in which we collect records of a price change and the
corresponding change in quantity demanded. Then we calculate the own-price
elasticity as the ratio of the proportionate (percentage) change in quantity
demanded to the proportionate (percentage) change in price.

To illustrate, Figure 3.1 represents the demand for cigarettes. Presently,
the price of cigarettes is $1 a pack and quantity demanded is 1.5 billion packs a
month. According to Figure 3.1, if the price rises to $1.10 per pack, the quan-
tity demanded would drop to 1.44 billion packs.

The proportionate change in quantity demanded is the change in quantity
demanded divided by the average quantity demanded. Since the change in
quantity demanded is 1.44 – 1.5 = –0.06 billion packs and the average quantity
demanded is 0.5 × (1.44 + 1.5) = 1.47 billion packs, the proportionate change in
quantity demanded is –0.06/1.47 = –0.041.

Similarly, the proportionate change in price is the change in price divided
by the average price. The change in price is $1.10 – $1 = $0.10 per pack, while

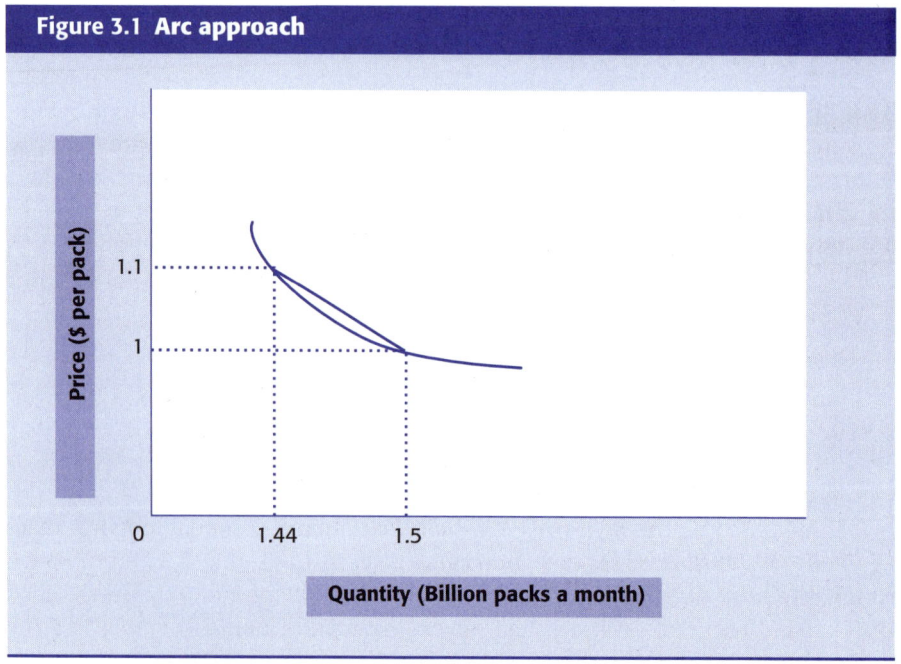

Figure 3.1 Arc approach

By the arc approach, the own-price elasticity of the demand for cigarettes is the
proportionate change in quantity demanded divided by the proportionate change in
price = (–0.041)/0.095 = –0.432.

the average price is $0.5 \times (1.10 + 1) = \$1.05$ per pack. Hence, the proportionate change in price is $0.1/1.05 = 0.095$.

By the arc approach, the own-price elasticity of the demand for cigarettes is the proportionate change in quantity demanded divided by the proportionate change in price, or $(-0.041)/0.095 = -0.432$. Equivalently, in this example, the percentage change in quantity demanded was -4.1%, while the percentage change in price was 9.5%; hence, the own-price elasticity is $-4.1/9.5 = -0.432$.

An alternative way of calculating the own-price elasticity of demand is the **point approach**, which sets up a mathematical equation with quantity demanded as a function of the price and other variables. The own-price elasticity can then be derived from the coefficient of price in this equation. We illustrate this procedure later in the chapter.

*The **point approach** calculates own-price elasticity from a mathematical equation, in which the quantity demanded is a function of the price and other variables.*

The point approach calculates the elasticity at a specific point on the demand curve. By contrast, the arc approach calculates the elasticity between two points on the demand curve. In principle, as we consider shorter and shorter arcs, the estimate from the arc approach will tend to the point estimate. Thus, for an infinitesimally short arc, the arc and point approaches will provide identical numbers for the elasticity.

The arc and point approaches are the two ways of calculating the elasticity of demand with respect to all the factors that affect demand.

Properties

The cigarette example illustrates several properties of the own-price elasticity of demand. First, as discussed in Chapter 2, demand curves generally slope downward: If the price of an item rises, the quantity demanded will fall. Hence, the own-price elasticity will be a negative number. For ease of interpretation, some analysts report own-price elasticities as an absolute value, that is, without the negative sign. Accordingly, when applying the concept, it is very important to bear in mind that the own-price elasticity is a negative number.

Second, the own-price elasticity is a pure number, independent of units of measure. In our example, we measured the quantity demanded of cigarettes in packs per month. The percentage change in quantity demanded, however, is the change in quantity demanded divided by the average quantity demanded. It is a pure number that does not depend on any units of measure: The percentage change will be the same whether we measure quantity demanded in packs or individual cigarettes.

Likewise, the percentage change in price is a pure number. Since the own-price elasticity is the percentage change in quantity demanded divided by the percentage change in price, it is also a pure number. Thus, the own-price elasticity of demand provides a handy way of characterizing price sensitivity that does not depend on units of measure.

Third, recall that the own-price elasticity is the ratio

$$\frac{\text{percentage change in quantity demanded}}{\text{percentage change in price}}$$

If a very large percentage change in price causes no change in quantity demanded, then the elasticity will be 0. By contrast, if an infinitesimal percentage change in price causes a large change in quantity demanded, then the elasticity will be negative infinity. Accordingly, the own-price elasticity ranges from 0 to negative infinity.

The demand is price **elastic** if a 1% increase in price leads to more than a 1% drop in the quantity demanded.

Table 3.1 reports the own-price elasticities of the market demand for several product categories, while Table 3.2 reports the own-price elasticities of the demand for individual sellers of several products. We say that the demand for an item is price **elastic** or *elastic with respect to price* if a 1% increase in price leads to more than a 1% drop in quantity demanded. Equivalently, demand is

Table 3.1 Own-price elasticities of market demand

Product	Market	Own-Price Elasticity	Source (see References)
Automobiles			
Domestic compacts	U.S.	−3.4	Koujianou-Goldberg (1995)
Foreign compacts	U.S.	−4.0	Koujianou-Goldberg (1995)
Domestic intermediates	U.S.	−4.2	Koujianou-Goldberg (1995)
Foreign intermediates	U.S.	−5.2	Koujianou-Goldberg (1995)
Consumer products			
Cigarettes	U.S.	−0.2, −0.4	Becker et al. (1994) Tegene (1991)
Liquor	U.S.	−0.2	Baltagi & Griffin (1995)
Utilities			
Electricity (residential)	Quebec	−0.7	Bernard et al. (1996)
Telephone service	Spain	−0.1	Garin Munoz (1996)
Water (residential)	U.S.	−0.2, −0.3	Williams & Suh (1986)
Water (industrial)	U.S.	−0.7, −1.0	Williams & Suh (1986)

Table 3.2 Own-price elasticities of individual seller demand

Product	Seller	Own-Price Elasticity	Source (See References)
Automobiles			
Chevette	Chevrolet	−3.2	Koujianou-Goldberg (1995)
Civic	Honda	−3.4	Koujianou-Goldberg (1995)
Escort	Ford	−3.4	Koujianou-Goldberg (1995)
Century	Buick	−4.8	Koujianou-Goldberg (1995)
Fleetwood	Cadillac	−0.9	Koujianou-Goldberg (1995)
Ferrari	Ferrari	−1	Koujianou-Goldberg (1995)
Consumer Products			
Breakfast cereal	Columbus, OH supermarkets	−0.6, −0.7	Jones et al. (1996)
Gasoline	Boston, MA stations	−3, −8.4	Png & Reitman (1994)

price elastic if a price increase causes a proportionately larger drop in quantity demanded.

We say that demand is price **inelastic** or *inelastic with respect to price* if a 1% price increase causes less than a 1% drop in quantity demanded. An alternative definition is that demand is price inelastic if a price increase causes a proportionately smaller drop in quantity demanded.

From Table 3.1, the own-price elasticity of the market demand for domestic compacts is −3.4. This means that a 1% price increase will reduce the quantity demanded by 3.4%. So, the demand for domestic compacts is elastic. The own-price elasticity of the market demand for foreign-made compacts is −4.0. This indicates the demand for foreign compacts is more elastic than the demand for domestic makes.

By contrast, the own-price elasticity of the market demand for liquor is −0.2. This means that a 1% increase in the price of liquor will reduce the quantity demanded by 0.2%. The demand for liquor is inelastic.

> The demand is price **inelastic** if a 1% increase in price leads to less than a 1% drop in the quantity demanded.

Progress Check 3A   Referring to Table 3.1, is the United States' residential demand for water relatively more or less elastic than the industrial demand?

Progress check

Intuitive Factors

Managers can consider several intuitive factors to gauge whether demand will be relatively more elastic or inelastic. The first factor is the availability of direct or indirect substitutes. The fewer substitutes available, the less elastic will be the demand. People who are dependent on alcoholic drinks or cigarettes feel that they cannot do without them; hence, the demand for these products is relatively inelastic. For the image-conscious teenager, sporting a pair of the "in" athletic shoes is the only way to gain peer acceptance, so teenage demand for the shoes is very inelastic.

In many countries, the Post Office has a legally established monopoly over carriage of letters. Hence, there are no direct substitutes for Post Office letter service. Indirect substitutes, however, are popping up all over the world. With the spread of electronic mail and fax machines, the demand for Post Office letter service is becoming relatively more elastic.

By considering the availability of substitutes, we can conclude that the demand for a product category will be relatively less elastic than the demand for specific products within the category. The reason is that there are fewer substitutes for the category than for specific products. Consider, for instance, the demand for cigarettes compared with the demand for a particular brand. The particular brand has many more substitutes than the category as a whole. Accordingly, the demand for the brand will tend to be more elastic than the demand for the category. This means that, if cigarette manufacturers can raise prices collectively by 10%, their sales will fall by a smaller percentage than if only one manufacturer increases its price by 10%.

Another factor that affects the own-price elasticity of demand is the buyer's prior commitments. A person who has bought an automobile becomes a captive customer for spare parts. Automobile manufacturers understand this very well. Accordingly, they set relatively higher prices on spare parts than on new cars. The same applies as well in the software business. Once users have invested time and effort to learn one program, they become captive customers for future upgrades. Whenever there is such a commitment, demand is less elastic.

A third factor that affects the own-price elasticity of demand is the cost relative to the benefit from searching for better prices. Buyers have limited time to spend on searching for better prices, so they focus attention on items that account for relatively larger expenditures. Families with toddlers, for instance, spend more time economizing on diapers than Q-tips. Similarly, office managers focus attention on copying paper rather than paper clips. Marketing practitioners have given the name *low involvement* to products that get relatively little attention from buyers.

The balance between the cost and benefit of economizing also depends on a possible split between the person who incurs the cost of economizing and the person who benefits. Almost everyone who has driven a damaged car to a body repair shop has been asked the question, "Are you covered by insurance?" Experienced repair managers know that car owners who are covered by insurance care less about price. In this example, the car owner gets the benefit of the repair work, while the insurer pays most or all the costs. A car owner who bargains over the repairs must spend his or her own time, while the insurer will get most of the saving.

Buyer Price Sensitivity: Chevette vis-à-vis Civic

Chevrolet and Honda cater to the subcompact segment of the automobile market with their Chevette and Civic models, respectively. A consistent way of comparing the price sensitivity of Chevette vis-à-vis Civic buyers is to use the own-price elasticities of the demands.

The own-price elasticities of the demands for Chevettes and Civics have been estimated to be −3.2 and −3.4, respectively. These elasticities indicate that Chevette buyers are relatively less sensitive to price than Civic buyers. For a 1% increase in price, Chevette buyers reduce purchases by 3.2% as compared with 3.4% for Civic buyers. The demand for Chevettes is relatively less elastic than the demand for Civics.

Source: Pinelopi Koujianou-Goldberg, "Product Differentiation and Oligopoly in International Markets: the Case of the U.S. Automobile Industry," *Econometrica* 63, no. 4 (July 1995), pp. 891–951.

Shared Costs: Frequent Flyer Programs

Whenever there is a split between the person who pays and the person who chooses the product, the demand will be less elastic. In 1981, American Airlines established its AAdvantage program for frequent flyers. This program records each member's travel on American Airlines and awards free flights according to the number of miles that the member accumulates. The AAdvantage program does not give mileage credit for travel on competing airlines such as United or Delta, hence it provides members with a strong incentive to concentrate travel on American Airlines.

The AAdvantage program is especially attractive to travelers, such as business executives, who fly at the expense of others. Such travelers are relatively less price sensitive than those who pay for their own tickets. The AAdvantage program gives them an incentive to choose American Airlines even if the fare is higher. Among customers who fly at the expense of others, the program makes demand relatively less elastic. AAdvantage was a brilliant marketing strategy, and all of American's competitors soon established their own frequent flyer programs.

Elasticity and Slope

When comparing the demands for different products or even quantities demanded of the same product at different prices, it is important to remember that these comparisons are relative. The reason is that the own-price elasticity describes the shape of only one portion of the demand curve. A change in price, by moving from one part of a demand curve to another part, may lead to a change in own-price elasticity.

Let us show this by considering the demand curve for cars in Figure 3.2. This demand curve is a straight line. Suppose that, initially, the price is $7,000 per car and the quantity demanded is 22,000 cars a month. When the price increases to $8000, the quantity demanded falls to 20,000 cars. The proportionate change in quantity demanded is –2,000/21,000 = –0.1, while the proportionate change in price is 1000/7500 = 0.13. Hence, by the arc approach, the own-price elasticity is –0.1/0.13 = –0.8.

Now, suppose that the price increases from $8000 to $9000; then the quantity demanded falls from 20,000 to 18,000 cars. The proportionate change in

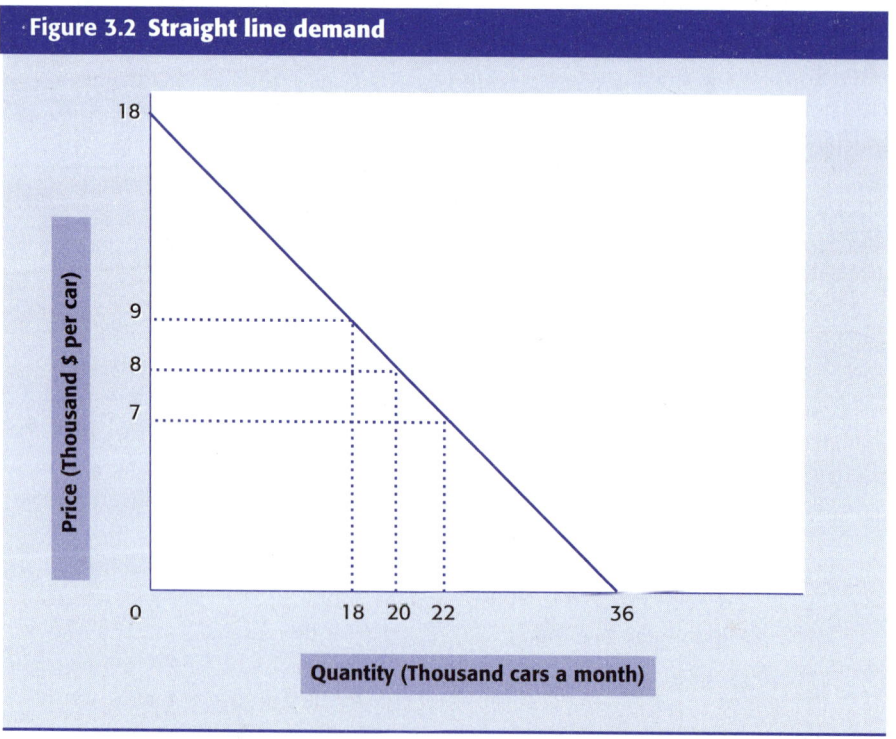

Figure 3.2 Straight line demand

Price (Thousand $ per car)

Quantity (Thousand cars a month)

By the arc approach, the own-price elasticity at a price of $7000 is –0.1/0.13 = –0.8, and the own-price elasticity at a price of $8000 is –0.11/0.12 = –0.9.

quantity demanded is now –2,000/19,000 = –0.11, while the proportionate change in price is 1000/8500 = 0.12. Hence, by the arc approach, the own-price elasticity is –0.11/0.12 = –0.9. Thus, the demand curve in Figure 3.2 is inelastic at both prices of $8000 and $7000. It is relatively more elastic at the price of $8000 per car than at a price of $7000.

Generally, whether the demand curve is a straight line or curved, the own-price elasticity can vary with changes in the price of the item. In the case of a straight line demand curve, the demand becomes more elastic at higher prices. For demand curves with other shapes, the demand may become less elastic at higher prices.

Another point worth noting is that the own-price elasticity can also vary with changes in any of the other factors that affect demand. Recall that the own-price elasticity is the percentage by which the quantity demanded will change if the price of the item rises by 1%. If there are changes in any of the other factors that affect demand, then the demand curve will shift; hence, the own-price elasticity may also change.

A frequently asked question is the relation between own-price elasticity and the slope of the demand curve. In the math supplement, we show that the own-price elasticity is related to the slope, the price, and the quantity demanded. Thus, other things equal, where the demand curve is steeper, the demand is less elastic, and where the demand curve is less steep, the demand is more elastic. It is very important to stress that the price and quantity demanded are the "other things equal." To illustrate, let us consider again the straight line demand curve in Figure 3.2. The slope of this curve is the rate of change of price for changes in the quantity demanded. The slope is –18/36 = –0.5. The demand curve is a straight-line; hence, it has the same slope throughout.

By contrast, as we have already shown, the own-price elasticity is –0.8 at a price of $7000, and –0.9 at a price of $8000. Generally, the own-price elasticity varies throughout the length of a straight-line demand curve.

If the own-price elasticity varies throughout the demand curve, while the slope is the same everywhere, what explains the difference? The answer is the price and quantity demanded. Even though the slope remains constant, the changes in price and quantity demanded along the demand curve mean that the own-price elasticity will vary. Thus, the own-price elasticity and slope are related but are not equivalent.

Progress Check 3B   Referring to Figure 3.2, suppose that the price increases from $11,000 to $12,000. Calculate the own-price elasticity of demand using the arc approach.

Progress check

3 *Forecasting Quantity Demanded and Expenditure*

The own-price elasticity of demand can be applied to forecast the effect of price changes on quantity demanded and buyer expenditure. Expenditure is related to the quantity demanded, since expenditure equals the quantity demanded multiplied by the price. The own-price elasticity can be applied at the level of an entire market as well as for individual sellers. From the stand-point of an individual seller, the quantity demanded is sales, while buyer expen-diture is revenue. Hence, using the own-price elasticity of demand, the seller can forecast the effect of price changes on sales and revenue.

Quantity Demanded

Let us first consider how to use the own-price elasticity of demand to forecast the effect of price changes on the quantity demanded. Refer, for instance, to the demand for automobiles at a price of $7000 in Figure 3.2. How will a 10% increase in price affect the quantity of cars that buyers demand?

We have already calculated the own-price elasticity of demand at the $7000 price to be –0.8. By definition, the own-price elasticity is the percentage by which the quantity demanded will change if the price rises by 1%. Hence, if the price of cars increases by 10%, then the quantity demanded will change by –0.8 × 10 = –8%; that is, the quantity demanded will fall by 8%.

To forecast the change in quantity demanded in terms of the number of cars, we should multiply the percentage change of –8% by the quantity demanded before the price change. By this method, the change in quantity demanded is –0.08 × 22,000, that is, a drop of 1,760 cars. (In this calculation, we used the equality, 8% = 0.08.) The new quantity demanded would be 22,000 – 1,760 = 20,240 cars a month.

We can also use the elasticity method to estimate the effect of a reduction in the price on quantity demanded. Referring to Figure 3.2, suppose, for instance, that the price of cars is initially $7000 and then drops by 5%. The quantity demanded will change by –0.8 × (–5) = 4%; that is, it will increase by 4%. This example shows that it is important to keep track of the signs of the own-price elasticity and the price change.

Expenditure

Let us next see how to use the own-price elasticity of demand to estimate the effect of changes in price on buyer expenditure. Buyer expenditure equals the quantity demanded multiplied by the price. Hence, a change in price will affect expenditure through the price itself as well as through the related effect on quantity demanded. Generally, the percentage change in the expenditure is equal to the percentage change in the price plus the percentage change in the quantity demanded. (We prove this result in the math supplement.)

Consider the effect of an increase in price. By itself, the price increase will tend to raise the expenditure. The price increase, however, will reduce the quantity that buyers demand and so tend to reduce the expenditure. Hence, the net effect on expenditure depends on which effect is relatively larger.

This is where the concept of own-price elasticity is useful. Recall that demand is elastic with respect to price if an increase in price causes a proportionately larger fall in quantity demanded, while demand is inelastic if a price increase causes a proportionately smaller fall in quantity demanded. The own-price elasticity enables us to compare the relative magnitude of changes in price and quantity demanded.

If demand is price elastic, then the drop in the quantity demanded will be proportionately larger than the increase in price; hence, the price increase will reduce expenditure. If, however, demand is price inelastic, the drop in quantity demanded will be proportionately smaller than the increase in price; hence, the price increase will increase expenditure.

Generally, if demand is price elastic, a price increase will reduce expenditure while a price reduction will increase expenditure. By contrast, if demand is price inelastic, a price increase will increase expenditure while a price reduction will reduce expenditure.

In the introduction to this chapter, we recounted a manager's most common concern when asked to raise price: "But my sales would drop!" We claimed that the real issue is how sensitive buyers are to price changes. A manager ought to be thinking about the own-price elasticity of demand.

To explain, consider the demand facing an individual seller and suppose that the demand is price inelastic at the current price. What if the seller raises price? Then, since demand is price inelastic, the price increase will lead to a proportionately smaller reduction in the quantity demanded. The buyer's expenditure will increase, which means that the seller's revenue will increase. Meanwhile, owing to the reduction in quantity demanded, the seller can reduce production, cutting its costs. Since revenues will be higher and costs will be lower, the seller's profits definitely will be higher. Accordingly, if demand is price inelastic, a seller can increase profit by raising price.

This discussion shows that, under the right conditions, a price increase can raise profits even though it may cause sales to drop. Therefore, when setting the price for an item, managers ought to focus on the own-price elasticity of demand. Generally, the price should be raised until the demand becomes price elastic. We will develop this idea further in Chapter 9 on "Pricing Policy."

> ## *Pricing Breakfast Cereals*
>
> Eugene Jones and Barry W. Mustiful of Ohio State University studied the demand for breakfast cereals at six outlets of a national supermarket chain in the Columbus, Ohio, metropolitan area. They found that the demand was inelastic with respect to price: The own-price elasticity of demand for the top 10 brands was −0.7, while the elasticity for private label cereal was −0.6.
>
> We have shown that, where demand is price inelastic, a seller can increase profits by raising price. The supermarket chain could have increased its profits by raising the prices of both branded and private label breakfast cereals at its Columbus area stores.
>
> *Source:* Eugene Jones and Barry W. Mustiful, "Purchasing Behaviour of Higher- and Lower-Income Shoppers: A Look at Breakfast Cereals," *Applied Economics* 28, no. 1 (January 1996), pp. 131–7.

Accuracy

We have used the own-price elasticity of demand to forecast that, in Figure 3.2, if the price of cars rises by 10% from $7000, then the quantity demanded would drop to 20,240 cars a month. We can calculate the effect of the price increase in another way—directly from the demand curve. After a 10% increase, the new price would be $7700. From the demand curve, the quantity demanded at that price would be 20,600 cars a month.

What explains the discrepancy between the quantities of 20,240 and 20,600? The reason for the discrepancy is that, as we have emphasized previously, the own-price elasticity may vary along a demand curve. Accordingly, the forecast using the own-price elasticity will not be as precise as a forecast directly from the demand curve. The same applies to forecasting changes in expenditure with the own-price elasticity.

Generally, the error in a forecast based on the own-price elasticity will be larger for larger changes in the price and the other factors that affect demand. Elasticities do not provide as much information as the entire demand curve. In many cases, however, managers do not know the entire demand curve. Their information is limited to the quantity demanded around the current values of the factors that affect the demand.

For many business decisions, however, managers do not need to know the full demand curve. The manufacturer of a luxury car, for instance, would never consider cutting the price to the level of a subcompact. So, it need not know the quantity demanded at such a low price. Likewise, the manufacturer of a subcompact would never consider raising the price to the level of a luxury car. Hence, the elasticities often provide sufficient information for business decisions.

4 *Other Elasticities*

In addition to price, the demand for an item also depends on buyers' incomes, the prices of related products, and advertising, among other factors. Changes in any of these factors will lead to a shift in the demand curve. There is an elasticity to measure the responsiveness of demand to changes in each factor. Managers can use these elasticities to forecast the effect of changes in these factors. In particular, the elasticities can be used to forecast the effect of changes in multiple factors that occur at the same time.

The analyses of elasticities of demand with respect to income, the prices of related products, and advertising are very similar. Accordingly, we will focus on the elasticity of demand with respect to income and discuss only the key differences for the other elasticities.

Income Elasticity

The **income elasticity** of demand measures the sensitivity of demand to changes in buyers' incomes. By definition, the *income elasticity of demand* is the percentage by which the demand will change if the buyer's income rises by 1%, other things equal. In this case, the price of the item is one of the other things that must remain unchanged. Equivalently, the income elasticity is the ratio

$$\frac{\text{percentage change in demand}}{\text{percentage change in income}}$$

or

$$\frac{\text{proportionate change in demand}}{\text{proportionate change in income}}$$

The income elasticity may be calculated using either the arc or point approach. (Since the demand curve diagram does not explicitly show income, we cannot draw a picture of the arc approach for calculating income elasticity.) For an infinitesimally small change in income, the arc estimate equals the point elasticity. Like the own-price elasticity, the income elasticity of demand varies with changes in the price and any other factor that affects demand.

By definition, the income elasticity is a ratio of two proportionate changes; hence, it is a pure number and independent of units of measure. In the case of a normal product, if income rises, the demand will rise, so the income elasticity will be positive. By contrast, for an inferior product, if income rises, demand will fall, so the income elasticity will be negative. So, depending on whether the product is normal or inferior, the income elasticity can be either positive or

The **income elasticity** of demand is the percentage by which the demand will change if the buyer's income rises by 1%.

Table 3.3 Income elasticities of market demand

Product	Market	Income Elasticity	Source (see References)
Consumer products			
Cigarettes	U.S.	0.1	Tegene (1991)
Liquor	U.S.	0.2	Baltagi & Griffin (1995)
Food	U.S.	0.8	Baye et al. (1992)
Clothing	U.S.	1	Baye et al. (1992)
Newspapers	U.S.	0.9	Bucklin et al. (1989)
Utilities			
Electricity (residential)	Quebec	0.1	Bernard et al. (1996)
Telephone service	Spain	0.5	Garin Munoz (1996)

negative. Hence, it is important to note the sign of the income elasticity. Income elasticity can range from negative infinity to positive infinity.

We say that demand is *income elastic* or *elastic with respect to income* if a 1% income increase causes more than a 1% change in demand. Demand is said to be *income inelastic* or *inelastic with respect to income* if a 1% income increase causes less than a 1% change in demand.

The demand for necessities tends to be relatively less income elastic than the demand for discretionary items. Consider, for instance, the demand for food as compared with restaurant meals. Eating in a restaurant is more of a discretionary item. Accordingly, we expect the demand for food to be relatively less income elastic than the demand for restaurant meals.

Table 3.3 reports the income elasticities of the market demand for various items. In the United States, the demand for cigarettes and liquor hardly changes with income, while, in Quebec, the residential demand for electricity is also extremely inelastic with respect to income.

We can apply the income elasticity of demand to forecast the effect of changes in income on demand and expenditure. Suppose that, presently, the price of cigarettes is $1 per pack, the quantity demanded is 1.5 billion packs a month, and the income elasticity of demand is 0.1. How will a 3% increase in income affect the demand?

By definition, the income elasticity of demand is the percentage by which the demand will change if the buyer's income rises by 1%, other things equal. In the present case, the income rises by 3%; hence, the percentage change in demand will be $0.1 \times 3 = 0.3\%$; that is, demand will increase by 0.3%. Since the initial quantity was 1.5 billion packs, the increase in quantity is 0.003×1.5 billion = 4.5 million packs. Provided that the price remains at $1 per pack, this increase in demand will mean an increase in expenditure of $4.5 million.

A major difference between income and some of the other variables that affect demand such as price and advertising is that, generally, sellers have no control over buyers' incomes. While a seller can set price and advertising, it must take buyers' incomes as a given. Accordingly, we do not study how a seller should determine buyers' incomes.

Progress Check 3C   Referring to Table 3.3, is the demand for liquor relatively more or less income elastic than the demand for cigarettes?

Progress check

Cross-Price Elasticity

Just as the income elasticity of demand measures the sensitivity of demand to changes in income, the **cross-price elasticity** measures the sensitivity of demand to changes in the prices of related products. By definition, *the cross-price elasticity of demand* with respect to another item is the percentage by which the demand will change if the price of the other item rises by 1%, other things equal. In this case, the (own) price of the item is one of the other things that must remain unchanged.

The **cross-price elasticity** of demand is the percentage by which the demand will change if the price of another item rises by 1%.

If two products are substitutes, an increase in the price of one will increase the demand for the other, so the cross-price elasticity will be positive. By contrast, if two products are complements, an increase in the price of one will reduce demand for the other; hence, the cross-price elasticity will be negative. The cross-price elasticity can range from negative infinity to positive infinity.

We say that demand is *elastic with respect to the price of another item* if a 1% increase in the price of the other item causes more than a 1% change in demand. Demand is said to be *inelastic with respect to the price of another item* if a 1% price increase in the other item causes less than a 1% change in demand. Generally, the more two items are substitutable, the higher their cross-price elasticity will be. Table 3.4 reports the cross-price elasticities of the demand for various items.

Advertising Elasticity

The **advertising elasticity** measures the sensitivity of demand to changes in the sellers' advertising expenditure. By definition, the *advertising elasticity of demand* is the percentage by which the demand will change if the sellers' advertising expenditure rises by 1%, other things equal. In this case, the (own) price of the item is one of the other things that must remain unchanged.

The **advertising elasticity** of demand is the percentage by which the demand will change if the seller's advertising expenditure rises by 1%.

Table 3.4 Cross-price elasticities of market-demand

Products	Market	Cross Price Elasticity	Source (see References)
Consumer products			
Clothing/food	U.S.	0.1	Baye & Beil (1994)
Gasoline at competing stations	Boston, MA	1.2	Png & Reitman (1994)
Utilities			
Electricity/gas (residential)	Quebec	0.1	Bernard et al. (1996)
Electricity/oil (residential)	Quebec	0.0	Bernard et al. (1996)
Bus/subway	London	0.0, 0.5	Gilbert & Jalilian (1991)

Switched Access vis-à-vis Leased Circuits in Long-Distance Service

In the United States, long-distance telecommunication carriers spend billions every year to gain access to customers through the networks of local telephone companies. A carrier such as American Telephone and Telegraph (AT&T) or MCI Communications can gain access to customers through either the regular switch of a local telephone company ("switched access") or a dedicated leased circuit. From the viewpoint of a long-distance carrier, switched access and leased circuits are substitutes in the delivery of long-distance telecommunications services.

A study of the demand of AT&T and other long-distance carriers found that the cross-price elasticity of AT&T's demand for switched access with respect to the price of leased circuits was 0.07, while the cross-price elasticity of the other carriers' demand was 0.34. This indicates that the other long-distance carriers could substitute leased circuits for switched access relatively more easily than AT&T.

Source: Steve G. Parsons and Michael R. Ward, "Factor Substitution in Long-Distance Telecommunications," *Southern Economic Journal* 62, no. 2 (October 1995), pp. 405–10.

Table 3.5 reports the advertising elasticities of the demand for several consumer product categories. The advertising elasticity for beer is 0, which means that a 1% increase in advertising expenditure will not change the demand for beer. The advertising elasticity for cigarettes is 0.04, which means that a 1% increase in advertising expenditure will increase the demand for cigarettes by 0.04%.

Table 3.5 Advertising elasticities of market demand

Product	Market	Advertising Elasticity	Source (see References)
Beer	U.S.	0.0	Franke & Wilcox (1987)
Wine	U.S.	0.08	Franke & Wilcox (1987)
Cigarettes	U.S.	0.04	Tegene (1991)
Clothing	U.S.	0.01	Baye et al. (1992)
Recreation	U.S.	0.08	Baye et al. (1992)

Given these small elasticities, it may seem surprising that beer and cigarette manufacturers spend so much on advertising. Note that the advertising elasticities reported in Table 3.5 pertain to market demand. Most advertising, however, is undertaken by individual sellers to promote their own business. By drawing buyers away from competitors, advertising has a much stronger effect on the sales of an individual seller than on the market demand. Accordingly, the advertising elasticity of the demand faced by an individual seller tends to be larger than the advertising elasticity of the market demand.

Forecasting the Effects of Multiple Factors

The business environment will often change in conflicting ways. For instance, the prices of substitutes may rise, but the prices of complements may rise as well. The only way to discern the net effect of factors pushing in different directions is to use the elasticities with respect to each of the variables.

To illustrate, consider the introductory question of the effect on cigarette demand if, starting from a price of $1 per pack and quantity of 1.5 billion packs a month, the price increases by 5% and income rises by 3%. We have shown how to apply the own-price elasticity to forecast the effect of a change in price on quantity demanded and similarly to apply the income elasticity to forecast the effect of a change in income on demand. To calculate the net effect of the increases in both price and income, we simply add the changes due to each of the factors.

Suppose that the own-price elasticity of the demand for cigarettes is –0.4. Then, a 5% increase in price would change quantity demanded by $-0.4 \times 5 =$ –2%. We have already calculated that a 3% increase in income would increase demand by 0.3%. Therefore, the net effect of the increases in price and income is to change demand by $-2 + 0.3 = -1.7\%$. Originally, the quantity demanded of cigarette services was 1.5 billion packs. After the increases in price and income, the quantity demanded will be 1.475 billion packs.

We can use similar techniques to forecast the effects of changes in other factors, such as the prices of related products and advertising expenditures. Generally, the percentage change in demand due to changes in multiple factors is the sum of the percentage changes due to each separate factor.

5 *Adjustment Time*

We have analyzed the elasticities of demand with respect to changes in price, income, the prices of related products, and advertising expenditures. We have discussed the intuitive factors that underly these elasticities. In addition, another factor affects all elasticities: the time available for buyers to adjust.

The **short run** is a time horizon within which a buyer cannot adjust at least one item of consumption or usage.

With regard to adjustment time, it is important to distinguish the **short run** from the **long run**. The short run is a time horizon within which a buyer cannot adjust at least one item of consumption or usage. By contrast, the long run is a time horizon long enough for buyers to adjust all items of consumption or usage.

The **long run** is a time horizon long enough for buyers to adjust all items of consumption or usage.

To illustrate the distinction, consider how Max commutes into Chicago. He does not have a car, so he takes the train. To switch from the train to a car, he needs time to buy or lease a car. Accordingly, with regard to Max's choice of transportation mode, a short run is any period of time shorter than that which he needs to get a car. A long run is any period of time longer than that which he needs to get a car.

We shall now discuss the effect of adjustment time on the elasticities of demand, and how the effect depends on whether the item is durable or nondurable.

Nondurables

Consider an everyday item like commuter train services. Suppose that one Monday morning, the local railway operator announces a permanent 10% increase in fares. Many commuters may have already made plans for that day, so the response to the higher fare may be quite weak on that day. Over time, however, the response will be stronger: As more commuters acquire cars, the demand for the railway service will drop.

Generally, for nondurable items, the longer the time that buyers have to adjust, the bigger will be the response to a price change. Accordingly, the demand for such items will be more elastic in the long run than in the short run. This applies to all nondurable items, including both goods and services.

Figure 3.3 illustrates the short- and long-run demand for a nondurable item. Suppose that the current price is $5 and quantity demanded is 1.5 million units. If the price drops to $4.50, the quantity demanded will rise to 1.6 million units in the short run and 1.75 million units in the long run.

Figure 3.3 Short- and long-run demand for a non-durable item

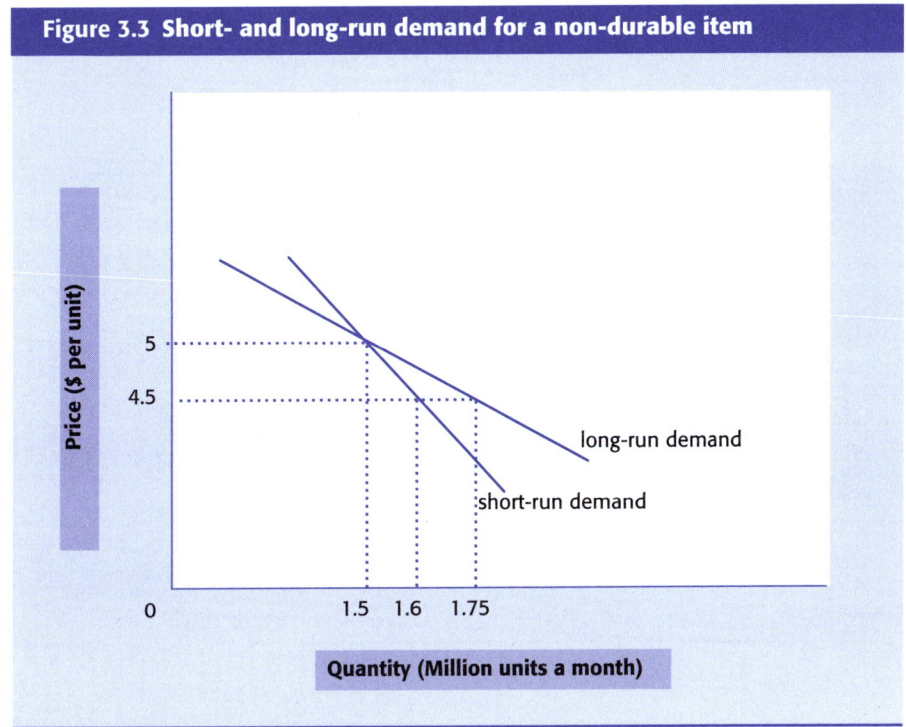

If the price drops from $5 to $4.50, the quantity demanded will rise to 1.6 million units in the short run and 1.75 million units in the long run.

Table 3.6 reports the short- and long-run own-price elasticities of market demand for several nondurables. Consistent with our analysis, the demand for these items is relatively more elastic in the long run than in the short run.

Two nondurable goods worth highlighting are alcohol and tobacco. To the extent that consumption of these items is addictive, the demand will be relatively inelastic. The effect of price changes on the quantity demanded will work through discouraging new people from taking up smoking and drinking. Accordingly, the demand for alcohol and tobacco will be relatively more elastic in the long run.

Durables

The effect of adjustment time on the demand for durable items such as automobiles and foreign travel is somewhat different. As for nondurables, buyers need time to adjust, which leads demand to be relatively more elastic in the long run. However, a countervailing effect leads demand to be relatively more

Table 3.6 Short- vis-à-vis long-run elasticities

Product	Demand Factor	Market	Short-Run Elasticity	Long-Run Elasticity	Source (see References)
Nondurables					
Cigarettes	Price	U.S.	−0.2, −0.4	−3.3	Becker et al. (1994) Tegene (1991)
Liquor	Price	U.S. Canada	−0.2	−1.8	Baltagi & Griffin (1995) Johnson & Oksanen (1977)
Gasoline	Price Income	U.S. U.S.	−0.1 0	−0.5 0.3	Pindyck & Rubinfeld (1995) Pindyck & Rubinfeld (1995)
Bus	Price	London	−0.8	−1.3	Gilbert & Jalilian (1991)
Subway	Price	London	−0.4	−0.7	Gilbert & Jalilian (1991)
Railway	Price	Philadelphia	−0.5	−1.8	Voith (1987)
Durables					
Automobiles	Price Income	U.S. U.S.	−0.2 3	−0.5 1.4	Pindyck & Rubinfeld (1995) Pindyck & Rubinfeld (1995)

elastic in the short run. This countervailing effect is especially strong for changes in income.

Consider, for instance, the demand for cars. Most drivers buy cars at intervals of several years. Suppose that there is a drop in incomes. Then, drivers will plan to keep their cars longer. Some drivers, who were just about to replace their cars, will keep their cars longer. So, the drop in incomes will cause purchases to dry up until sufficient time passes that these drivers want to replace their cars at the new lower income. By contrast, in the long run, the effect on sales will be more muted: Eventually, all drivers will replace their cars but less frequently. Thus, the drop in income will cause demand to fall more sharply in the short run than in the long run.

Similarly, if income rises, drivers will replace their cars more frequently. Some drivers will find that they want to replace their cars immediately, causing a boom in purchases. This boom, however, will last only as long as it takes all such drivers to adjust to their new replacement frequency. Thus, the increase in income will tend to cause demand to increase more sharply in the short run than in the long run.

Accordingly, for durable items, the difference between short- and long-run elasticities of demand depends on a balance between the need for time to adjust and the replacement frequency effect. Adjustment time has a similar effect on the own-price and other elasticities of the demand for durable items.

Referring to Table 3.6, we see that, for automobiles, the demand is more price elastic in the long run than the short run, indicating that the need for time to adjust outweighs the replacement frequency effect. By contrast, the demand for automobiles is more income elastic in the short run than the long run, suggesting that the replacement frequency effect is relatively stronger for changes in income.

Forecasting Demand

In the preceding section, we showed how short-run elasticities can be used to forecast the effect of multiple (short-run) changes in the factors that affect demand. We can apply the same method to forecast the effect of long-run changes, using long-run elasticities in place of short-run elasticities.

Progress Check 3D   Draw a figure, analogous to Figure 3.3, showing the short- and long-run demand for a durable.

Progress check

Gasoline Prices and the Demand for V6 Automobiles

The real price of gasoline fell continuously through the early 1980s. In principle, this should have increased the demand for cars and persuaded drivers to switch from smaller to larger cars as well as from diesel-powered to sportier gasoline-powered cars. The immediate effect on consumer choice, however, was quite limited. When oil prices first began to fall, drivers did not adjust their expectations of future oil prices and did not change their auto-buying patterns.

In line with consumer purchases, General Motors, the United States' largest automobile manufacturer, continued to focus production on smaller and diesel-powered cars. When, however, lower oil prices persisted into the mid-1980s, consumers did adjust their long-term expectations. They switched en masse back to large cars with powerful, sporty, gasoline engines.

When the adjustment came, General Motors was caught with excess inventories of four-cylinder (relative to six-cylinder) cars as well as too many diesel-engine automobiles. The auto manufacturer had overlooked the difference between the short- and long-run cross-price elasticities between the demand for automobiles and the price of gasoline.

Source: Speech given by Vince Barabba, executive director, General Motors, at UCLA, February 5, 1987.

6 *Estimating Elasticities*[1]

We have seen how elasticities can be applied to forecast changes in demand and expenditure for entire markets as well as individual products. Tables 3.1 to 3.6 present various elasticities of demand. As we have emphasized, an elasticity can change with a change in any one of the factors that affect demand. Further, to the extent that businesses sell different products or cater to different buyers, they will face different demand curves; hence, they will also face different elasticities. Accordingly, managers may not be able to rely on "off-the-shelf" estimates of elasticities.

Suppose, for instance, that the management of the Moonlight Lube chain would like to know the sensitivity of the demand for its auto lubrication service to changes in price and advertising. In this section, we outline the data and statistical techniques that can be used to estimate the elasticities of demand. We focus on an intuitive explanation of the basic concepts. For a detailed presentation, the reader should consult the Further Reading section at the end of the chapter.

Data

Generally, there are two sources of data. One is records of past experience, including published statistics as well as private records. The other source of data is surveys and experiments specifically designed to discover buyers' preferences. An experiment conducted with genuine buyers making actual purchases is said to be done on a *test market*.

The data from past experience or surveys and experiments can be collected in two ways. One way is to focus on a particular group of buyers and observe how their demand changes as the factors affecting demand vary over time. For instance, using this method, Moonlight Lube could compile year-by-year records of sales, prices, and advertising expenditures. This type of data is called a **time series,** as it records changes over time.

A **time series** is a record of changes over time in one market.

The other way of collecting data is to compare the quantities purchased in markets with different values of the factors affecting demand. Using this method, Moonlight Lube would collect records of sales, prices, and advertising expenditures in each of its markets. This type of data is called a **cross section,** because it records all the data at one time.

A **cross section** is a record of data at one time over several markets.

Just as time series or cross-section data can be compiled from records of past experience, the same applies to surveys and experiments. For instance, a program of test marketing can be designed to yield either time series or cross-section data.

---

[1]This section is more advanced. It may be omitted without loss of continuity.

Conjoint Analysis: Determining Buyer Preferences

Bank Luna is considering whether to offer an express teller service that guarantees no waiting for a charge of up to 50 cents. The bank's marketing department has selected a random sample of customers to determine how much they would pay for such a service. Presently, the average waiting time is 5 minutes.

The marketing department can apply the technique of conjoint analysis. This is a market research technique to determine buyers' preferences among various product attributes by asking them to rank alternative combinations of the attributes.

In Bank Luna's case, there are two relevant attributes: price and waiting time. Suppose that the price for express service can be limited to 25 or 50 cents. Combined with the price of nothing for regular teller service, the price can take three possible values—none, 25, and 50 cents. The waiting time can take two possible values: none and 5 minutes. A full factorial design would ask each sample customer to rate the $3 \times 2 = 6$ combinations in Table 3.7. The results can then be analyzed using multiple regression (explained later) or other statistical techniques.

Conjoint analysis is especially useful for evaluating new products or new markets. In these cases, past experience is of limited help, and so, experiments and surveys are the main way to collect relevant data.

Table 3.7 Conjoint analysis

Alternative									
Price (cents)	Waiting Time (minutes)	Least Desirable				Most Desirable			
0	0	1	2	3	4	5	6	7
25	5	1	2	3	4	5	6	7
50	0	1	2	3	4	5	6	7
0	5	1	2	3	4	5	6	7
25	0	1	2	3	4	5	6	7
50	5	1	2	3	4	5	6	7

(Please rate each of the following alternatives by circling a rating of 1 to 7)

Specification

Moonlight Lube would like to estimate the own-price and advertising elasticities of the demand for its auto lube service. Suppose that it selected 15 outlets as test markets and, in each market, set different levels of price and advertising expenditure for one week and recorded the corresponding sales.

As Chapter 2 suggests, however, the demand for Moonlight's lube service may depend on other factors. To obtain accurate estimates of elasticities, it is important to specify all the factors that have a significant effect on demand and the mathematical relationship between demand and the various factors.

The **dependent variable** is the variable whose changes are to be explained.

The mathematical relationship can be specified in a number of ways. In a relationship, the **dependent variable** is that whose changes are to be explained, while an **independent variable** is a factor affecting the dependent variable. A common specification is a linear equation in which the dependent variable is equal to a constant plus the weighted sum of the independent variables.

An **independent variable** is a factor affecting the dependent variable.

In the case of a Moonlight outlet, the other factors affecting demand may include the number of cars in the area, and the price of competing lube services. Many factors, however, can safely be ignored. These include the weather, the prices of groceries, and the number of schoolchildren in the area. Table 3.8 records the test market data.

As for the mathematical form, the following is a linear equation relating the demand for lube service with four independent variables:

$$D = b_0 + b_1 \times p + b_2 \times N + b_3 \times A + b_4 \times c + u \qquad (3.1)$$

where D represents the quantity demanded; p, the price of lube service; N, the number of cars; A, the advertising expenditure; and c, the average price at competing lube services. In equation (3.1), b_0 is a constant, while $b_1, ..., b_4$ are the coefficients of quantity demanded, the price of lube service, the number of cars, and the average competing price, respectively. The variable u represents the collective effect of other factors.

Multiple Regression

Referring to Table 3.8, we see variations in all the independent variables among the 15 test markets. To estimate the own-price elasticity of the demand for lube service, we need some way to isolate the effect of price on quantity demanded from the effects of the other variables; we need a similar procedure for estimating the advertising elasticity of demand.

Multiple regression is a statistical technique to estimate the separate effect of each independent variable on the dependent variable.

The statistical technique of **multiple regression** can estimate the separate effect of each independent variable on the dependent variable. Essentially, multiple regression operationalizes the "other things equal" condition needed to estimate an elasticity.

Multiple regression aims to determine values for the constant and the coefficients. To explain the technique, we denote the estimates for the constant and the coefficients by $\hat{b}_0$, $\hat{b}_1$, $\hat{b}_2$, $\hat{b}_3$, and $\hat{b}_4$. Using these values and the corre-

Table 3.8 Test market data

Market	Quantity	Price ($)	Number of Cars (thousands)	Advertising Spending ($)	Average Competing Price ($)
1	86	30	22.00	500	20
2	87	35	23.00	550	29
3	93	28	23.40	430	31
4	92	25	23.00	400	35
5	86	30	23.60	500	29
6	93	20	24.00	400	30
7	88	29	24.10	300	35
8	89	31	24.50	450	28
9	88	35	25.00	430	25
10	93	29	25.60	500	30
11	87	35	26.00	400	29
12	89	40	26.00	570	31
13	88	47	26.70	520	35
14	82	34	27.30	300	29
15	93	35	28.00	450	35
Average	88.93	32.20	24.81	446.67	30.07

sponding records of p, N, A, and c, we can calculate the *predicted value* of the dependent variable,

$$\hat{b}_0 + (\hat{b}_1 \times p) + (\hat{b}_2 \times N) + (\hat{b}_3 \times A) + (\hat{b}_4 \times c), \qquad (3.2)$$

for each test market.

The predicted value may diverge from the actual quantity demanded, D, for the corresponding market. Let us call this difference the *residual*; that is, the residual is the actual value of the dependent variable, D, minus the predicted value:

$$D - [\hat{b}_0 + (\hat{b}_1 \times p) + (\hat{b}_2 \times N) + (\hat{b}_3 \times A) + (\hat{b}_4 \times c)]. \qquad (3.3)$$

Figure 3.4 presents a simplified version of the demand for lube service with only one independent variable, the price. The straight line represents the predicted values of the demand, using the estimated constant and coefficient. We also mark the actual values for several markets. In markets 1 and 8, the actual quantity exceeds the predicted value, hence the residuals are positive. By contrast, in markets 2 and 5, the actual quantity is less than the predicted value, so the residuals are negative.

Ideally, the estimates of the constant and the coefficients will be such that every predicted value equals the corresponding actual value. Then, all the residuals will be 0. Referring to Figure 3.4, this would mean that every point would lie along the straight line.

Realistically, however, it is not likely that all the residuals will be 0. This leads to the question of what is the best way to determine the constant and estimates, and the line in Figure 3.4. The most common approach is called the *method of least squares*. This is based on the view that positive residuals are equivalent to negative residuals and that large residuals are disproportionately bad.

The method of least squares seeks a set of estimates for the constant and the coefficients to minimize the sum of the squares of the residuals. Since equally large positive and negative residuals have identical squares, the method treats them identically. By squaring the residuals, the method gives relatively greater weight to large residuals. Least-squares multiple regression analysis is available in common spreadsheet programs as well as specialized statistical packages.

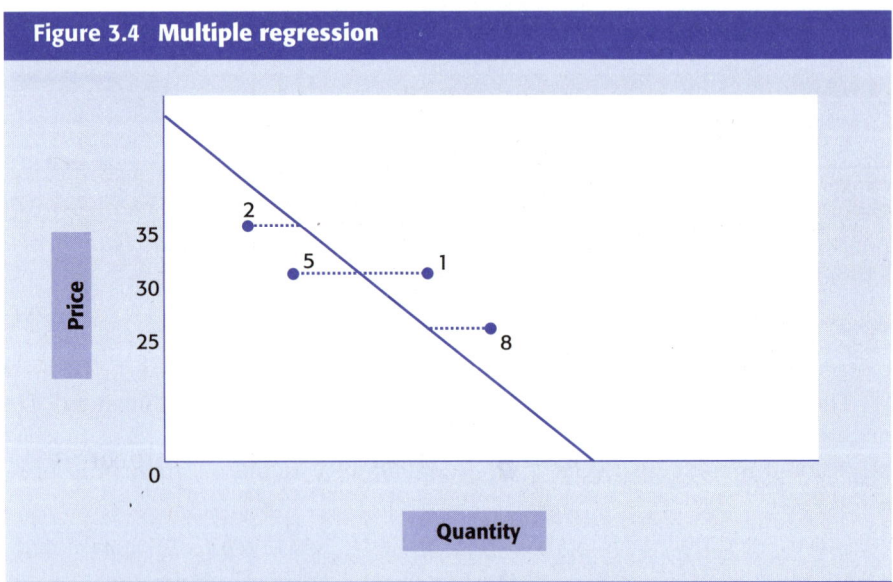

Figure 3.4   Multiple regression

In years 1 and 8, the actual quantity exceeds the predicted value, hence the residuals are positive; in years 2 and 5, the actual quantity is less than the predicted value, so the residuals are negative.

Interpretation

By applying least-squares multiple regression to estimate the equation for the lube service demand, we obtain the results in Table 3.9. The estimates of the constant and coefficients are $b_0 = 63.48$, $b_1 = -0.48$, $b_2 = 0.65$, $b_3 = 0.03$, and $b_4 = 0.42$.

Using these estimates, we can calculate the elasticities of demand. In equation (3.1), the coefficient of price, b_1, is the rate of change of the quantity demanded with respect to changes in price. From Table 3.9, the estimate of this rate of change, $\hat{b}_1 = -0.48$. The math supplement shows that the own-price elasticity is this rate of change multiplied by price and divided by quantity. From Table 3.8, the average price is \$32.20 and the average quantity is 88.93. Hence, the own-price elasticity at the average price and quantity is

$$-0.48 \times 32.20/88.93 = -0.17. \tag{3.4}$$

We can use the same approach to calculate the elasticity of demand with respect to advertising and other independent variables.

Next, we use this example to discuss how to evaluate the significance of least-squares multiple regression results. The estimates of the constant and coefficients depend on the particular sample of observations in Table 3.8. With another sample, we would obtain somewhat different estimates. By repeating the regression

Table 3.9 Multiple regression results

Regression statistics				
R-square		0.65		
Standard error		2.29		
Number of observations		15		
F-statistic		4.68		
Significance		0.02		

Independent Variable	Coefficient	Standard Error	t-Statistic	Significance
Constant	63.48	11.60	5.47	0.001
Price	−0.48	0.14	−3.31	0.008
Number of cars	0.65	0.51	1.28	0.242
Advertising spending	0.03	0.01	2.85	0.022
Competing price	0.42	0.17	2.53	0.036

many times with different samples, we will obtain many sets of estimates. Using the probability distributions of these estimates, we can calculate measures to assess the significance of the regression estimates.

The F-statistic measures the overall significance of the independent variables. The statistic is computed on the assumption that there is no relationship between the dependent variable and the set of independent variables, meaning that the constant and coefficients are all 0. The F-statistic ranges from 0 to infinity.

Using the probability distributions of these estimates, we can calculate the probability of obtaining any particular value for the F-statistic if the constant and coefficients are all 0. If this probability falls below a specific benchmark, then we say that the regression estimates are statistically significant. The conventional benchmarks are 1% and 5%.

From Table 3.9, the F-statistic is 4.68 and the significance is 0.02 = 2%, which meets the 5% benchmark. We can be fairly confident that the regression estimates are statistically significant.

Related to the F-statistic is R-squared. This statistic uses the squared residuals to measure the extent to which the independent variables account for the variation of the dependent variable. R-squared ranges from 0 to 1. An R-squared value of 1 means that all the residuals are exactly 0, or equivalently, that every predicted value is exactly equal to the corresponding actual value. By contrast, an R-squared value of 0 means that the independent variables account for none of the variation in the dependent variable.

From Table 3.9, R-squared is 0.65. This means that the the regression equation accounts for 65% of the variation of the dependent variable. This is a reasonably large part of the variation.

The F-statistic and R-squared are ways to evaluate the independent variables as a group. By contrast, we use the t-statistic to evaluate the significance of a particular independent variable. Specifically, the t-statistic is the estimated value of the coefficient divided by the standard error. The standard error measures the dispersion of the estimate of the coefficient.

The t-statistic will be negative or positive according to the sign of the estimated coefficient. It ranges from negative to positive infinity. Using the probability distribution of the estimate, we can calculate the probability of obtaining any particular value for the t-statistic if the coefficient is 0. If this probability falls below a specific benchmark, then the estimated coefficient is statistically significant. The conventional benchmarks are 1% and 5%.

In Table 3.9, the t-statistic for the price of lube service is –3.31 and the significance is 0.008 = 0.8%, which meets both the 1% and 5% benchmarks. The t-statistic for advertising spending is 2.85 and the significance is 0.022 = 2.2%, which meets the 5% benchmark. By contrast, the t-statistic for the number of cars is 1.28 and the significance is 0.242 = 24.2%, which does not meet even the 5% benchmark. Accordingly, we infer that the price of lube service and advertising spending have significant effects on the demand for lube service, but the effect of the number of cars is questionable.

The Demand for Gasoline at a Service Station

A multiple regression study of the demand for gasoline at individual Boston-area service stations found that the elasticity of demand with respect to the price of gasoline was −3.3.

Customers of service stations, however, pay two prices: one in money to the seller and another in the form of waiting time. Estimates of demand must take into account the customers' sensitivity to waiting. If a station raises its price by 1%, its customers must pay 1% more in money. But this tends to reduce customer purchases. Given the station's fueling capacity, the reduction in purchases will reduce waiting times, which tends to increase the quantity demanded.

Accordingly, the estimated "price elasticity" of −3.3 combines the responsiveness to an increase in price alone together with the responsiveness to a reduction in waiting time. After adjusting for the effect on waiting time, Png and Reitman estimate that the own-price elasticity ranged between −6.3 and −8.4.

Other businesses that serve randomly arriving customers from a fixed capacity include banks, hospitals, and supermarkets. In estimating the own-price elasticity of demand at any such business, an analyst must take care to adjust for the effect of price changes on waiting times.

Source: I.P.L. Png and David Reitman, "Service Time Competition," *RAND Journal of Economics* 25, no. 4 (Winter 1994), pp. 619–34.

7 Summary

The elasticity of demand measures the responsiveness of demand to changes in a factor that affects demand. Elasticities can be estimated for price, income, prices of related products, and advertising expenditures. The own-price elasticity can be used to forecast the effects of price changes on quantity demanded and buyer expenditure. Elasticities can be used to forecast the effects on demand of simultaneous changes in multiple factors. All elasticities vary with adjustment time. Elasticities can be estimated from records of past experience or test markets by the technique of multiple regression.

Key Concepts

elasticity of demand	income elasticity	cross section
own-price elasticity	cross-price elasticity	dependent variable
arc approach	advertising elasticity	independent variable
point approach	short run	multiple regression
elastic	long run	
inelastic	time series	

Further Reading

H.F. Houthakker and Lester B. Taylor report comprehensive estimates of U.S. consumer demand in *Consumer Demand in the United States: Analyses and Projections*, 2d ed. (Cambridge, MA: Harvard University Press, 1970). For a simple introduction to the estimation of demand, refer to Chapter 4 of Robert E. McCormick's *Managerial Economics* (Englewood Cliffs, NJ: Prentice Hall, 1993). Peter

Kennedy covers the details of econometrics, which is the application of statistical techniques to economic issues, in *A Guide to Econometrics* (Cambridge, MA: MIT Press, 1992). Paul R. Messinger reviews the techniques of market research in Chapter 11 of the *Marketing Paradigm* (Cincinnati: South-Western College Publishing, 1995).

Review Questions

1. For each of the comparisons that follow, choose the product or situation where the demand is relatively more elastic (choose a or b).

    For a campus bookstore,
    a. Textbooks. The campus bookstore stocks all texts required for business school courses. Off-campus bookstores may not carry the titles or may not have sufficient stock.
    b. Fiction. The campus bookstore also sells novels. Students, however, can easily find novels in other bookstores and even supermarkets.

    For consumer products,
    a. Toilet paper is a product for which most people have a somewhat set demand. Rarely do they cut toilet paper from the budget when trying to save money.
    b. Music CDs are more of a discretionary item in the household budget.

    For downtown restaurants,
    a. Weekday lunch. Office workers have a limited time for lunch. Instead of patronizing nearby restaurants, their main alternatives are to bring their own lunch or buy from delivery services.
    b. Weekend meals. Meals on the weekend are more flexible: Everyone has more time and people are willing to travel longer distances to eat.

2. Consider a service that you buy frequently.
    a. Suppose that the price was 5% lower and all other factors do not change. How much more would you buy each year?
    b. Using this information, calculate the own-price elasticity of your demand.
    c. Explain why the own-price elasticity of demand is negative.

3. Suppose that the own-price elasticity of the demand for food is -0.7 and that, as a result of a nationwide drought, the price of food rises by 10%. Will this cause expenditure on food to rise or fall?

4. Consider a good that you buy frequently.
   a. Suppose that your income was 10% higher and all other factors do not change. How much more would you buy each year?
   b. Using this information, calculate the income elasticity of your demand.
   c. Is the good an inferior product or normal product for you?

5. True or false?
   a. The income elasticity of demand can be estimated by either the arc approach or the point approach.
   b. Changes in the price of an item will affect the income elasticity of demand.

6. Manufacturers such as Dunlop and Goodyear use both natural and synthetic rubber to produce tires. If the elasticity of the demand for natural rubber with respect to changes in the price of synthetic rubber is negative, then the two types of rubber are (choose a or b):
   a. Substitutes.
   b. Complements.

7. Suppose that the advertising elasticity of the demand for one brand of cigarettes is 1.3. If the manufacturer raises advertising expenditure by 5%, by how much will the demand change?

8. Explain why the advertising elasticity of the market demand for beer may be smaller than the advertising elasticity of the demand for one particular brand.

9. Consider the effect of changes in fares on the quantity demanded of taxi services. Do you expect demand to be more elastic with respect to fare changes in the short run or the long run?

10. This question applies the analysis presented in the section on estimating elasticities. Explain the difference between cross-section and time series data.

Discussion Questions

1. In 1978, Texas Instruments (TI) introduced Speak and Spell, a new educational toy aimed at teaching young children to spell in an entertaining way. TI's market research indicated the vast majority of target customers were not willing to pay more than $50. At $49.99, many felt that the toy was reasonably priced, but above $50, the number of people who would buy the toy was drastically lower.
   a. Draw the demand curve for Speak and Spell with an appropriate kink at $50.
   b. On which side of the $50 kink is the demand more price elastic?

2. In 1981, American foreign travel expenditure was $10.04 billion in 1982 dollars. Suppose that the price elasticity of foreign travel expenditure is –1.77 and the elasticity with respect to changes in private consumption expenditure is 3.09. Between 1981 and 1982, the price index (in 1982 dollars) of foreign travel fell from 1.8 to 1.0, while private consumption expenditure rose from $2024 billion to $2051 billion in 1982 dollars (*National Income and Product Accounts of the United States*, 1986).
   a. How would a devaluation of foreign currencies such as the French franc against the U.S. dollar affect the price index of foreign travel?
   b. Estimate the effect of the changes in price and private consumption expenditure on foreign travel expenditure.
   c. Given the fall in the price index, how much of a reduction in private consumption expenditure would have caused American expenditure on foreign travel to remain unchanged?

3. This question applies techniques introduced in the math supplement to Chapter 2. Suppose that Moonshine Car Rentals faces a demand represented by the equation

$$D = 30 - p + 0.4Y, \qquad (3.5)$$

where D is the quantity demanded in rentals a month, p is the price in dollars per rental, and Y is the average consumer's income in thousands of dollars a year. Use the arc approach in the following calculations.

a. Suppose that income $Y = 100$ and Moonshine raises the price from $p = 30$ to $p = 35$. Calculate the own-price elasticity of demand.

b. Suppose that income $Y = 110$ and Moonshine raises the price from $p = 30$ to $p = 35$. Calculate the own-price elasticity of demand.

c. Suppose that the price $p = 30$ and that income rises from $Y = 100$ to $Y = 110$. Calculate the income elasticity of demand.

d. Suppose that the price $p = 35$ and that income rises from $Y = 100$ to $Y = 110$. Calculate the income elasticity of demand.

4. A study of the demand for water among commercial users such as apartment buildings, hotels, and offices reported that the own-price elasticity was −0.36, the elasticity with respect to the number of commercial establishments was 0.99, and the elasticity with respect to the average summer temperature was 0.02 (Williams & Suh, 1986).

a. Intuitively, would an increase in the number of commercial establishments increase or reduce the demand for water? Is the estimated elasticity consistent with your explanation?

b. Intuitively, would a rise in the average summer temperature increase or reduce the demand for water? Is the estimated elasticity consistent with your explanation?

c. By considering the own-price elasticity of demand, explain how the water company could increase its profit.

5. A study of the demand for gasoline at Boston-area service stations reported that the elasticity with respect to price (combining the pure price effect with the effect on waiting times) was −3.3, the elasticity with respect to station fueling capacity was 0.7, and the elasticity with respect to the average price at nearby stations was 1.2 (Png & Reitman, 1984).

a. Explain why the elasticity with respect to the average price at nearby stations is a positive number.

b. Suppose that, at Al's station, price is 2% higher and fueling capacity is 3% higher than at Amy's station. What will be the difference in quantity demanded between the two stations?

c. If Amy raises capacity from 6 to 7 fueling places, by how much could she increase price without affecting sales?

6. Electric power producers have a choice of several fuels, including oil, natural gas, coal, and uranium. Once an electric power plant has been built, however, the scope to switch fuels may be very limited. Since power plants last for 30 years or more, producers must consider the relative prices of the alternative fuels well into the future when choosing a generating plant.

a. Do you expect the cross-price elasticity between the demand for oil-fired power plants and the price of oil to be positive or negative?

b. Will the cross-price elasticity between the demand for oil-fired power plants and the price of coal be positive or negative?

c. Compare the short with the long-run own-price elasticity of the demand for oil-fired power plants.

7. Table 3.6 presents the short- and long-run elasticities of the demand for automobiles in

the United States. Suppose that the price of cars rises by 5% while per capita income rises by 3%. What will be the effect on purchases of cars in the (a) short run and (b) long run?

8. According to a study of U.S. cigarette sales between 1955 and 1985, when the price of cigarettes was 1% higher, consumption would be 0.4% lower in the short run and 0.75% lower in the long run (Becker et al., 1994).
   a. Calculate the short- and long-run own-price elasticities of the demand for cigarettes.
   b. Is demand more or less elastic in the long run than in the short run? Explain your answer.
   c. If the government were to impose a tax that raised the price of cigarettes by 5%, would total consumer expenditure on cigarettes rise or fall in the short run? What about in the long run?

9. This question applies the analysis presented in the section on estimating elasticities. Suppose that the government has just announced a revision to the data in Table 3.8. The new data increases the number of cars in markets 11–15 by 10%. All other data remain valid.
   a. Use multiple regression to estimate the demand with (i) the original data and (ii) the revised data.
   b. Calculate the new estimates for the elasticities with respect to price, number of cars, and advertising expenditure at the average values of quantity, price, number of cars, and advertising expenditure.

10. An Australian telecommunications carrier wants to estimate the own-price elasticity of the demand for international calls to the United States. It has collected annual records of international calls and prices. In each of the following groups, choose the one factor that you would also consider in the regression equation. Explain your reasoning.
   a. Consumer characteristics: (i) average per capita income, (ii) average age.
   b. Complements: (i) number of telephone lines, (ii) number of mobile telephone subscribers.
   c. Prices of related items: (i) price of electricity, (ii) postage rate from Australia to the United States.

References

Badi H. Baltagi and James M. Griffin. 1995. "A Dynamic Demand Model for Liquor: The Case for Pooling." *Review of Economics and Statistics* 77, no. 3 (August): pp. 545–54.

Michael R. Baye and Richard O. Beil. 1994. *Managerial Economics and Business Strategy.* Burr Ridge, IL: Irwin.

———, Dennis W. Jansen, and Jae-Woo Lee. 1992. "Advertising Effects in Complete Demand Systems." *Applied Economics* 24, no. 10: pp. 1087–96.

Gary Becker, Michael Grossman, and Kevin Murphy. 1994. "An Empirical Analysis of Cigarette Addiction." *American Economic Review* 84 (June): p. 396.

Jean-Thomas Bernard, Denis Bolduc, and Donald Belanger. 1996. "Quebec Residential Electricity Demand: A Microeconometric Approach." *Canadian Journal of Economics* 29, no. 1 (February): pp. 92–113.

Randolph E. Bucklin, Richard E. Caves, and Andrew W. Lo. 1989. "Games of Survival in the U.S. Newspaper Industry." *Applied Economics* 21, no. 5 (May): pp. 631–49.

George R. Franke and Gary B. Wilcox. 1987. "Alcoholic Beverage Advertising and Consumption in the United States." *Journal of Advertising* 16, no. 3: pp. 22–30.

Teresa Garin Munoz. 1996. "Demand for National Telephone Traffic in Spain from 1985–1989: An Econometric Study Using Provincial Panel Data." *Information Economics and Policy* 8, no. 1 (March): pp. 51–73.

Christopher Gilbert and Hossein Jalilian. 1991. "The Demand for Travel and for Travelcards on London Regional Transport." *Journal of Transport Economics and Policy* 25, no. 1 (January): pp. 3–29.

James A. Johnson and Ernest H. Oksanen. 1977. "Estimation of Demand for Alcoholic Beverages in Canada from Pooled Time Series and Cross Sections." *Review of Economics and Statistics* 59 (February): pp. 113–18.

Eugene Jones and Barry W. Mustiful. 1996. "Purchasing Behaviour of Higher- and Lower-Income Shoppers: A Look at Breakfast Cereals." *Applied Economics* 28, no. 1 (January): pp. 131–7.

Pinelopi Koujianou-Goldberg. 1995. "Product Differentiation and Oligopoly in International Markets: The Case of the U.S. Automobile Industry." *Econometrica* 63, no. 4 (July): pp. 891–951.

National Income and Product Accounts of the United States. 1986.

Robert S. Pindyck and Daniel L. Rubinfeld. 1995. *Microeconomics*, 3d ed., p. 37. Englewood Cliffs, NJ: Prentice Hall.

I.P.L. Png and David Reitman. 1994. "Service Time Competition." *RAND Journal of Economics* 25, no. 4 (Winter): pp. 619–34.

Abebayehu Tegene. 1991. "Kalman Filter and the Demand for Cigarettes." *Applied Economics* 23: pp. 1175–82.

Richard Voith. 1987. "Commuter Rail Ridership: The Long and Short Haul," *Business Review,* Federal Reserve Bank of Philadelphia (November–December): pp. 13–23.

Martin Williams and Byung Suh. 1986. "The Demand for Urban Water by Customer Class." *Applied Economics* 18: pp. 1275–89.

Chapter 3

Math Supplement

Own-Price Elasticity

By definition, the own-price elasticity of demand is the proportionate change in quantity demanded divided by the proportionate change in price. Let Q represent the quantity demanded; dQ, the change in quantity demanded; p, the price; and dp, the change in price. Then dQ/Q is the proportionate change in quantity demanded, while dp/p is the proportionate change in price. Thus, in algebraic terms, the own-price elasticity is

$$e_p = \frac{dQ/Q}{dp/p} = \frac{p}{Q}\frac{dQ}{dp}. \qquad (3.6)$$

Using this definition, we can study the relationship between the own-price elasticity and the slope of the demand curve. Rearrange the definition of the own-price elasticity as follows:

$$e_p = \frac{p}{Q}\Big/\frac{dp}{dQ}. \qquad (3.7)$$

The variable dp/dQ is the change in price divided by the change in quantity demanded, that is, the slope of the demand curve. So, by (3.7), the own-price elasticity is (p/Q) divided by the slope of the demand curve. Clearly, the own-price elasticity and slope are related but are not the same.

Changes in Price

Let us now show how to use the definition in (3.6) to forecast changes in quantity demanded and buyer expenditure as a function of the own-price elasticity, percentage change in price, and the quantity demanded. Rearranging the definition in (3.6),

$$\frac{dQ}{dQ} = e_p \times \frac{dp}{p}. \qquad (3.8)$$

This says that the proportionate change in quantity demanded is the own-price elasticity multiplied by the proportionate change in price.

Let %Q represent the percentage change in quantity demanded and %p represent the percentage change in price. Then %$Q = 100 \times dQ/Q$, and %$p = 100 \times dp/p$. Multiplying both sides of (3.8) by 100 and substituting, we have

$$\%Q = e_p \times \%p, \qquad (3.9)$$

which says that the percentage change in the quantity demanded is the own-price elasticity multiplied by the percentage change in the price.

To forecast changes in buyer's expenditure, note that the buyer's expenditure is the price multiplied by the quantity demanded,

$$E = p \times Q. \qquad (3.10)$$

Taking the total derivative,

$$dE = (dp \times Q) + (dQ \times p). \qquad (3.11)$$

Dividing both sides of this equation by $E = p \times Q$, we have

$$\frac{dE}{E} = \frac{dp}{p} + \frac{dQ}{Q}. \qquad (3.12)$$

Let %E represent the percentage change in expenditure, hence %$E = 100 \times dE/E$.

Multiplying both sides of (3.12) by 100 and substituting, we have

$$\%E = \%p + \%Q, \qquad (3.13)$$

which says that the percentage change in expenditure is the percentage change in price plus the percentage change in quantity demanded.

From equation (3.9), the percentage change in quantity demanded is the own-price elasticity multiplied by the percentage change in price. Substituting in equation (3.13), we have a formula for the percentage change in expenditure in terms of the own-price elasticity and the percentage change in price:

$$\%E = \%p \times (1 + e_p). \qquad (3.14)$$

If demand is elastic, so that $e_p < -1$, then $1 + e_p < 0$. So, an increase in price %$p > 0$ will cause %$E < 0$, meaning a drop in expenditure, while a fall in price %$p < 0$ will cause %$E > 0$, which is an increase in expenditure.

Similarly, if demand is inelastic, so that $e_p > -1$, then $1 + e_p > 0$. In this case, an increase in price %$p > 0$ will cause %$E > 0$, while a fall in price %$p < 0$ will cause %$E < 0$.

Changes in Multiple Variables

Generally, the analysis of income, cross-price, and advertising elasticities is similar to that for the own-price elasticity, so there is no need to repeat the analysis. Here, we will focus on showing how to use the elasticities to forecast the effect of multiple changes in the factors that affect demand.

Let Y, Z, and A represent income, the price of a related item, and advertising expenditures, respectively. Then, supposing that demand is a function of the price of the item itself, income, the price of a related item, and advertising expenditures, we have

$$Q = Q(p, Y, Z, A). \qquad (3.15)$$

By definition, the income elasticity is

$$e_y = \frac{dQ/Q}{dY/Y} = \frac{Y}{Q}\frac{dQ}{dY}; \qquad (3.16)$$

the cross-price elasticity with respect to a related item,

$$e_z = \frac{dQ/Q}{dZ/Z} = \frac{Z}{Q}\frac{dQ}{dZ}; \qquad (3.17)$$

and the elasticity with respect to advertising expenditure,

$$e_a = \frac{dQ/Q}{dA/A} = \frac{A}{Q}\frac{dQ}{dA}. \qquad (3.18)$$

Taking the total derivative of equation (3.15),

$$dQ = \frac{dQ}{dp}dp + \frac{dQ}{dY}dY + \frac{dQ}{dZ}dZ + \frac{dQ}{dA}dA. \qquad (3.19)$$

Dividing throughout by Q,

$$\frac{dQ}{Q} = \frac{1}{Q}\frac{dQ}{dp}dp + \frac{1}{Q}\frac{dQ}{dY}dY + \frac{1}{Q}\frac{dQ}{dZ}dZ + \frac{1}{Q}\frac{dQ}{dA}dA. \qquad (3.20)$$

Consider the term on the left-hand side of equation (3.20). Multiplying by 100, it becomes the percentage change in quantity. Next, consider the first term on the right-hand side. Multiplying the term by $100p$ and dividing by p, it becomes

$$100 \times \frac{p}{Q}\frac{dQ}{dp}\frac{dp}{p} = 100 \times e_p\frac{dp}{p} = e_p\%p, \qquad (3.21)$$

that is, the own-price elasticity multiplied by the percentage change in price.

Similarly, each of the other terms on the right-hand side of equation (3.20) simplifies to the product of an elasticity and the percentage change in the corresponding factor. Accordingly, equation (3.20) simplifies to

$$\%Q = e_p\ \%p + e_y\ \%Y + e_z\ \%Z + e_a\ \%A. \quad (3.22)$$

This says that the percentage change in demand due to changes in multiple factors is the sum of the percentage changes due to each factor separately.

Chapter 4

Supply

1 *Introduction*

Dynamic random access memory (DRAM) chips are an essential component of personal computers as well as mobile telecommunications equipment. In 1995, a surge in demand led DRAM manufacturers to expand production. Supply increased so much that the market price of 16-megabit DRAMs fell by over 50% within the first six months of 1996. At the time, Fujitsu Limited was building a factory in Durham, England, to produce 16-megabit DRAMs. How should Fujitsu respond to the drop in price?

The gold mine on Lihir Island, off the northeast coast of Papua, New Guinea, is one of the world's 15 largest. In October 1995, the owners of Lihir Gold launched an initial public offering of shares to raise $450 million for the development of the mine. The prospectus for the share offering included projections of the mine's profits in 1999. With the price of gold at $400 per ounce, the projected profit was $52 million; whereas, if the price was 12.5% higher, at $450 per ounce, the projected profit was 46% higher, at $76 million. Why would a 12.5% increase in the price of gold raise Lihir Gold's projected profit by 46%?

An employer that needs a worker to put in longer hours must pay an overtime rate that is 50–100% higher than the regular wage. Why is the overtime rate so much higher than the regular wage? Why is it not enough to pay the regular wage for the additional hours?

To address these questions—how Fujitsu should respond to the drop in the market price of 16-megabit DRAMs, why a 12.5% increase in the price of gold would raise Lihir Gold's projected profit by 46%, and why overtime rates for workers are so much higher than regular wages—we need to understand how a seller determines the quantity that it will supply.

In this chapter, we first consider the relation between costs and the production rate and how a business will adjust its production rate to changes in the price of its output. We also analyze whether an enterprise should continue in business. This provides the foundation for the concepts of the individual supply curve and seller surplus, which are the seller-side counterparts to the demand curve and buyer surplus. Applying this analysis, we explain why a 12.5% increase in the price of gold would raise Lihir Gold's projected profit by 46%.

Then, we compare supply in the short run, when businesses are restricted in the extent to which they can adjust inputs, with supply in the long run, when businesses can freely adjust all inputs. Using this long-run analysis, we can explain how Fujitsu should respond to the drop in the market price of 16-megabit DRAMs.

Next, extending from the individual seller to the market, we examine the market supply curve and market seller surplus. Following this, we introduce elasticities of supply, which measure the responsiveness of quantity supplied to changes in various factors. Finally, we highlight the special aspects of supply in human resource markets. We then explain why overtime rates for workers are so much higher than regular wages.

2 *Short-Run Costs*

Two key decisions of a business, whether to continue in operation and the rate at which to operate, both depend on the length of the time horizon. In Chapter 3, we introduced the concepts of short run and long run in relation to buyers. The same concepts apply to sellers as well. A **short run** is a time horizon in which a seller cannot adjust at least one input. In the short run, the business must work within the constraints of past commitments such as employment contracts and investment in facilities and equipment. Over time, however, these commitments expire. A **long run** is a time horizon long enough for sellers to adjust all inputs.

> The **short run** is a time horizon within which a seller cannot adjust at least one input.

The difference between the short run and long run depends on the circumstances. For instance, if a building contractor has just engaged 100 workers on a 12-month contract, then the employment of these workers cannot be adjusted until the expiration of the contract. Hence, the contractor's short run is at least 12 months long. By contrast, a contractor that has hired workers on a daily basis could adjust its workforce every day. Similarly, a contractor who has purchased construction equipment has committed to a relatively longer horizon than one who has rented the equipment on a weekly contract.

> The **long run** is a time horizon long enough for sellers to adjust all inputs.

In this and the next section, we focus on short-run business decisions; we consider long-run behavior in the fourth section.

Fixed vis-à-vis Variable Costs

To determine its production rate, a business needs to know the cost of delivering an additional unit of product. To decide whether to continue in operation, a business needs to know how shutting down will affect its costs. An important factor in both decisions is the distinction between fixed and variable costs. The **fixed cost** is the cost of inputs that do not change with the production rate. By contrast, the **variable cost** is the cost of inputs that change with the production rate.

Let us consider the distinction between fixed and variable costs in the context of Luna Farm, which produces eggs. Like those of most businesses, Luna's financial and accounting records do not classify expenses into fixed and variable. Rather, the records organize expenses according to the type of input: rent, wages, and payments for supplies. By interviewing Luna's management, we can learn the costs required for alternative short-run production rates. Table 4.1 presents this information.

To distinguish between fixed and variable costs, a business must analyze how each category of expense varies with changes in the scale of operations. Referring to Table 4.1, we can perform this analysis for Luna. Luna cannot adjust the size of its facility, so the rent does not vary with the production rate. The rent is $2000 whether Luna produces nothing or 9000 dozen eggs a week; hence, it is a fixed cost. Wages vary with the production rate, but even when Luna produces no eggs, it incurs wages of $200. Hence, the wages include a fixed component of $200, while the remainder is variable. Finally, the cost of supplies is completely variable.

In Table 4.2, we assign Luna's expenses—rent, wages, and cost of supplies—into the two categories of fixed costs and variable costs. As the production rate increases from nothing to 9000 dozen eggs a week, the fixed cost is

Table 4.1 Short-run weekly expenses

Weekly Production Rate	Rent	Wages	Cost of Supplies	Total
0	$2000	$200	$0	$2200
1000	$2000	$529	$100	$2629
2000	$2000	$836	$200	$3036
3000	$2000	$1216	$300	$3516
4000	$2000	$1697	$400	$4097
5000	$2000	$2293	$500	$4793
6000	$2000	$3015	$600	$5615
7000	$2000	$3870	$700	$6570
8000	$2000	$4862	$800	$7662
9000	$2000	$5996	$900	$8896

Table 4.2 Analysis of short-run costs

Weekly Production Rate	Fixed Cost	Variable Cost	Total Cost	Marginal Cost	Average Fixed Cost	Average Variable Cost	Average Cost
0	$2200	$0	$2200				
1000	$2200	$429	$2629	$0.43	$2.20	$0.43	$2.63
2000	$2200	$836	$3036	$0.41	$1.10	$0.42	$1.52
3000	$2200	$1316	$3516	$0.48	$0.73	$0.44	$1.17
4000	$2200	$1897	$4097	$0.58	$0.55	$0.47	$1.02
5000	$2200	$2593	$4793	$0.70	$0.44	$0.52	$0.96
6000	$2200	$3415	$5615	$0.82	$0.37	$0.57	$0.94
7000	$2200	$4370	$6570	$0.95	$0.31	$0.62	$0.94
8000	$2200	$5462	$7662	$1.09	$0.28	$0.68	$0.96
9000	$2200	$6696	$8896	$1.23	$0.24	$0.74	$0.99

always $2200. By contrast, the variable cost increases from nothing for no production to $6696 for 9000 dozen eggs a week.

Total cost is the sum of fixed cost and variable cost. Algebraically, if we represent total cost by C, fixed cost by F, and variable cost by V, then

$$C = F + V. \qquad (4.1)$$

Total cost is the sum of the fixed and variable costs.

Provided that there are some variable costs, then total cost will increase with operations. In Luna's case, referring to Table 4.2, the total cost is $2200 for no production, and rises to $8896 for production of 9000 dozen eggs a week.

It is helpful to illustrate the concepts of total, fixed, and variable costs. In Figure 4.1, the vertical axis represents cost, while the horizontal axis represents the scale of operations. We draw a curve representing variable cost. The total cost curve is the variable cost curve, shifted up everywhere by the amount of the fixed cost. In particular, the fixed cost is represented by the height of the total cost curve at the zero production rate.

By analyzing its costs as fixed and variable, the management of a business can understand which cost elements will be affected by changes in the scale of operations. The distinction between fixed and variable costs is important whether the business is growing or shrinking. For instance, suppose that management is planning to downsize to reduce costs. Downsizing will have no effect on fixed costs and will only reduce the variable costs. Hence, in a business with large fixed costs, downsizing may have relatively little effect on costs.

Figure 4.1 Short-run total cost

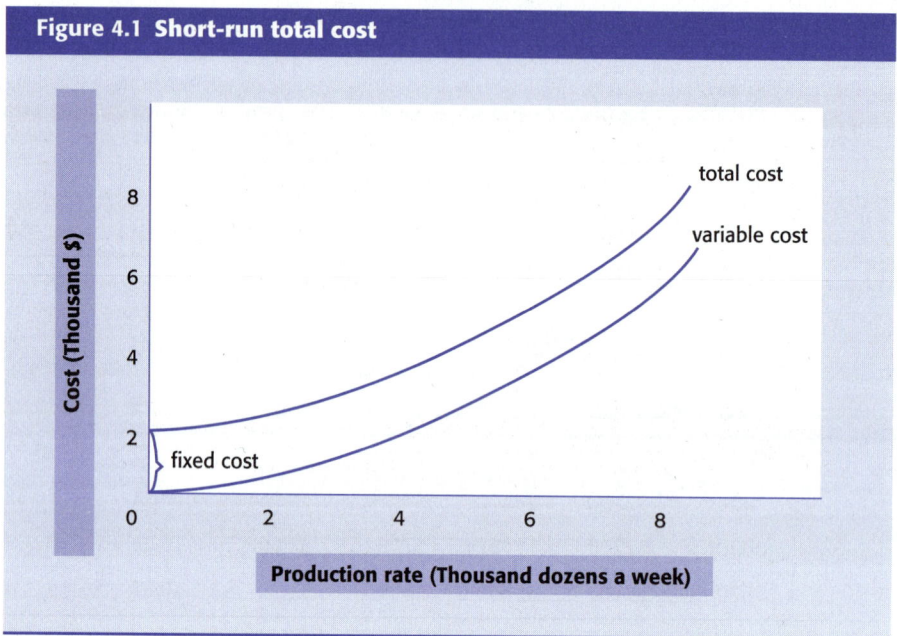

The total cost curve is the variable cost curve shifted up by the amount of the fixed cost.

Progress check **Progress Check 4A** In Figure 4.1, if the fixed cost were higher, how would that affect the total and variable cost curves?

Marginal Cost

The **marginal cost** is the change in total cost due to the production of an additional unit.

To determine the scale at which it should operate, a business needs to know the cost of making an additional unit of product. Then, the business can see whether selling the additional unit will add to or subtract from its total profit. The change in total cost due to the production of an additional unit is the **marginal cost**. The marginal cost can be derived from the analysis of fixed and variable costs.

Let us derive the marginal cost in the case of the Luna Farm. Referring to Table 4.2, as the production rate increases from none to 1000 dozen eggs a week, the total cost increases from \$2200 to \$2629. The increment \$2629 – \$2200 = \$429 is the additional cost of producing the 1000 dozen eggs. Hence, the marginal cost is \$429/1000 = 43 cents per dozen.

Notice that, as the production rate increases from none to 1000 dozen a week, the fixed cost remains unchanged; only the variable cost increases.

Hence, we also can calculate the marginal cost from the increase in variable cost. Using this approach, as the production rate increases from none to 1000 dozen eggs a week, the variable cost increases from $0 to $429. Therefore, the marginal cost is $429/1000 = 43 cents per dozen.

Similarly, as the production rate increases from 1000 to 2000 dozen eggs a week, the variable cost increases from $429 to $836. The marginal cost is now $407 for 1000 dozen eggs, or 41 cents per dozen. With each increase in the production rate, the marginal cost increases, reaching $1.23 at the rate of 9000 dozen eggs a week. In Luna's case, each additional dozen requires more variable cost than the one before. We display this information in Table 4.2.

Average Cost

The marginal cost is the cost of producing an additional unit. A related concept is **average cost**, which is the total cost divided by the production rate. The average cost is also called the *unit cost*. Given the scale of operations, the average cost reflects the cost of producing a typical unit.

The average cost (unit cost) is the total cost divided by the production rate.

Let us derive the average cost in the case of the Luna Farm. Referring to Table 4.2, we can obtain the average cost as total cost divided by the production rate. At 1000 dozen eggs a week, the average cost is $2629/1000 = $2.63, while at 2000 dozen a week, the average cost is $3036/2000 = $1.52. The average cost continues to fall with increases in the production rate until it reaches a minimum of 94 cents at 6000–7000 dozen a week. Thereafter, it increases with the production rate. At 9000 dozen a week, the average cost is 99 cents.

To understand why the average cost first drops with increases in the production rate and then rises, recall that the total cost is the sum of the fixed cost and the variable cost:

$$C = F + V. \tag{4.2}$$

If q represents the production rate, then dividing throughout by q, we have

$$\frac{C}{q} = \frac{F}{q} + \frac{V}{q}. \tag{4.3}$$

In words, the average cost is the average fixed cost plus the average variable cost. The average fixed cost is fixed cost divided by the production rate. So, if the production rate is higher, the fixed cost will be spread over more units; hence, the average fixed cost will be lower. This factor causes the average cost to fall with increases in the production rate.

The other element in average cost is the average variable cost, which is the variable cost divided by the production rate. In the short run, at least one input is fixed; hence, to raise the production rate, the business must combine increasing quantities of the variable inputs with an unchanged quantity of the fixed input.

The **marginal product** is the increase in output arising from an additional unit of the input.

The increase in output arising from an additional unit of an input is called the **marginal product** from that input. At low production rates, there is a mismatch between the variable inputs and the fixed input. Owing to the mismatch, the marginal product is low and the average variable cost is high. With a higher production rate, the variable inputs match the fixed input relatively better, and the average variable cost is lower.

As more of the variable inputs are added in combination with the fixed input, there will be a mismatch again. Eventually, there will be a *diminishing marginal product* from the variable inputs. This means that the marginal product becomes smaller with each increase in the quantity of the variable input. With a diminishing marginal product from the variable inputs, the average variable cost will increase with the production rate.

In Luna's case, Table 4.2 shows that the average variable cost first drops from 43 cents to 42 cents as the production increases from 1000 to 2000 dozen eggs a week. Then, the average variable cost rises from 42 cents to 74 cents as the production increases from 2000 to 9000 dozen a week.

Recall that the average cost is the average fixed cost plus the average variable cost. While the average fixed cost falls with the production rate, the average variable cost falls and then increases. Accordingly, where the average variable cost is increasing, the relationship between the average cost and the production rate depends on the balance between the declining average fixed cost and the increasing average variable cost.

If the fixed cost is not too large and the average variable cost increases sufficiently, the average cost will first decline with the production rate and then increase. As Table 4.2 shows, this is the case for Luna.

In Figure 4.2, we graph the marginal, average, and average variable costs against the production rate. The marginal cost curve falls from 43 cents at 1000 dozen a week, to reach a minimum of 41 cents at 2000 dozen a week, and rises thereafter. The average variable cost curve falls from 43 cents at 1000 dozen a week, to a minimum of 42 cents at 2000 dozen a week, and then rises. Similarly, the average cost curve falls from $2.63 at 1000 dozen a week, to a minimum of 94 cents at 6000–7000 dozen a week, and then rises. The graphs of the marginal, average variable, and average cost curves are each shaped like the letter *U*.

Progress check

Progress Check 4B In Figure 4.2, if the fixed cost were lower, how would that affect the marginal, average variable, and average cost curves?

Figure 4.2 Short-run marginal, average variable, and average costs

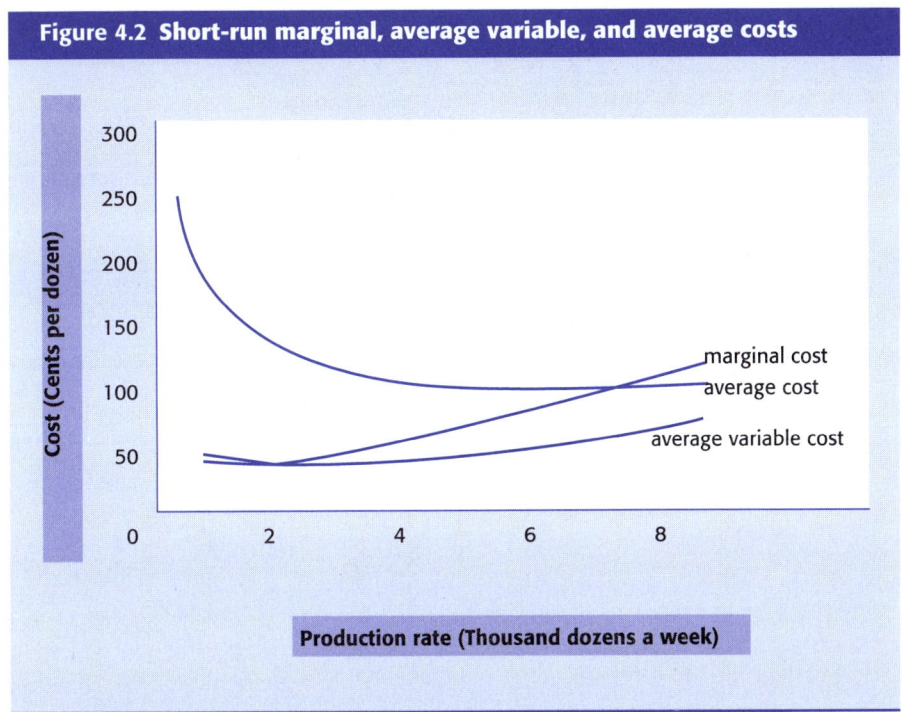

The marginal, average variable, and average cost curves are U-shaped: The curves decrease at low production rates, reach a minimum, and then increase for higher production rates.

Technology

In the preceding analysis, we derived the information about costs by asking the seller for the cost of producing at various rates. Accordingly, at every production level, the total, average, and marginal cost depend on the seller's individual operating technology.

There are two implications of this approach. First, the curves will change with adjustments in the seller's technology. For instance, a seller that discovers a technology involving a lower fixed cost will lower its average cost curve. A seller that uses a technology with a lower variable cost will lower its average, average variable, and marginal cost curves.

Second, different sellers may have different technologies and, hence, different cost curves. They may differ in the structure of fixed vis-à-vis variable costs. Some may have better technologies and hence lower costs than others.

Fixed vis-à-vis Variable Labor Cost: DAF Trucks

By contrast with the United States, it is very difficult for businesses in many Western European countries to lay off workers for economic reasons. Accordingly, labor can become a fixed cost for a very long horizon. As the example of DAF Trucks shows, some European businesses try to reduce fixed costs by substituting temporary workers for permanent employees.

DAF Trucks NV is one of Europe's largest truck manufacturers. It was established in 1993 to take over production in Belgium and the Netherlands from DAF NV, which had collapsed under pressure from a falling European demand for trucks.

DAF Trucks retained only 2500 of its predecessor's 13,300 workforce. Within two years, by late 1995, growth in demand had enabled the new organization to increase daily production to 70 trucks. It expanded employment to a permanent workforce of 3500 plus 2200 temporary workers.

Although the company planned to step up production further to 80–85 trucks a day, DAF Trucks chairman Cor Baan cautioned, "Flexibility is the key word for the market…. The old levels of employment will never come back[.]" DAF Trucks gears its permanent workforce of 3500 to a production rate of 60 trucks, while the company meets additional demand through temporary workers. In this way, it can limit its fixed labor cost and avoid excess labor during economic downturns.

Source: "DAF Is Back on the Road," *International Herald Tribune*, (September 20, 1995), p. 15.

3 *Short-Run Individual Supply*

Costs are one dimension of the short-run decisions whether to continue in operation and how much to produce. The other side to these decisions is revenue. We now consider the revenues of a business.

In analyzing revenues, we shall assume that the business aims to maximize profit. Realistically, of course, managers may pursue a number of objectives in addition to maximizing profit. We maintain the assumption of profit maximization because it is enough to account for a wide variety of common business practices and provides a foundation for a useful model of market competition.

Further, we assume that the business is so small relative to the market that it can sell as much as it would like at the going market price. We need this assumption to construct individual and market supply, which are the counterparts to individual and market demand. In Chapter 5, we explain the need to assume that the business can sell as much as it would like at the going market price.

Production Rate

Supposing that the price of eggs is 70 cents a dozen, how much should Luna produce? Generally, the profit of a business is its total revenue less its total cost, and in turn, **total revenue** is the price multiplied by sales.

In Table 4.3, we show Luna's cost and revenue at different production rates, with the assumption that the price is 70 cents. For instance, if sales are 1000 dozen a week, then Luna's total revenue will be $0.70 × 1000 = $700. If sales are 2000 dozen a week, then Luna's total revenue will be $0.70 × 2000 = $1400. Similarly, we can calculate the total revenue at other production rates. From Table 4.3, the highest profit is a *loss* of $1293, which comes from producing at a rate of 5000 dozen a week. (Later, we will explain why it makes sense for Luna to produce "at a loss.")

We can derive a general rule for the profit-maximizing production rate by illustrating cost and revenue with a diagram. In Figure 4.3, we draw the cost curves from Figure 4.1, adding a line to represent Luna's total revenue at a price of 70 cents. The line rises at a rate of $700 for every increase of 1000 dozen in the production rate. Equivalently, the slope of the line is 0.70. For instance, one point on the total revenue line is at a production rate of 4000 dozen and revenue of $0.70 × 4000 = $2800.

The **total revenue** of a business is the price of its product multiplied by the number of units sold.

Table 4.3 Short-run profit

Weekly Production Rate	Variable Cost	Total Cost	Total Revenue	Profit	Marginal Cost	Marginal Revenue
0	$0	$2200	0	−$2200		
1000	$429	$2629	$700	−$1929	$0.43	$0.70
2000	$836	$3036	$1400	−$1636	$0.41	$0.70
3000	$1316	$3516	$2100	−$1416	$0.48	$0.70
4000	$1897	$4097	$2800	−$1297	$0.58	$0.70
5000	$2593	$4793	$3500	−$1293	$0.70	$0.70
6000	$3415	$5615	$4200	−$1415	$0.82	$0.70
7000	$4370	$6570	$4900	−$1670	$0.95	$0.70
8000	$5462	$7662	$5600	−$2062	$1.09	$0.70
9000	$6696	$8896	$6300	−$2596	$1.23	$0.70

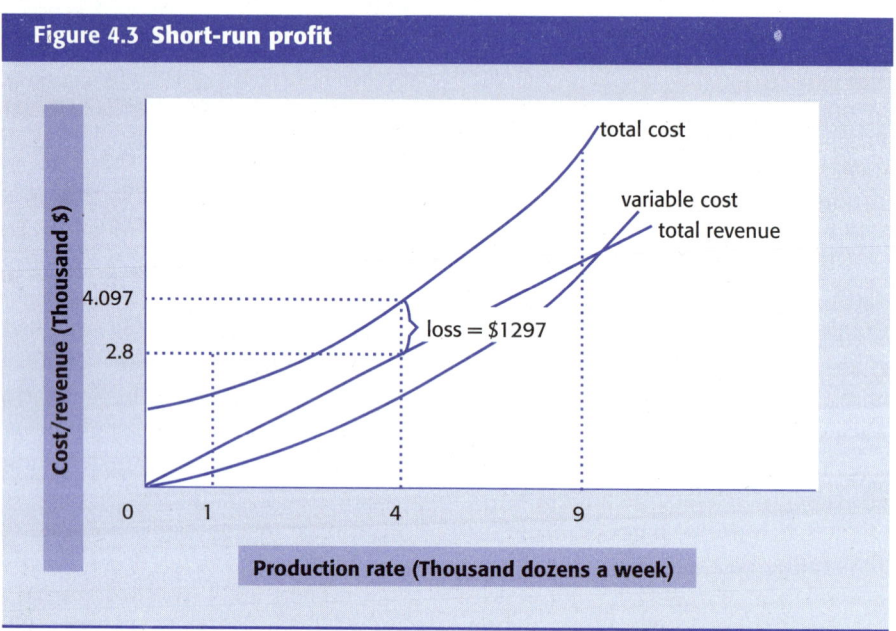

Figure 4.3 Short-run profit

At a production rate of 4000 dozen, the total revenue is $2800 and the total cost is $4097; hence, the vertical difference between revenue and cost is a loss of $1297. Marginal revenue is represented by the slope of the total revenue line, while marginal cost is represented by the slope of the total cost curve.

Using Figure 4.3, we can measure the difference between the total revenue and the total cost at any production rate. In the figure, the vertical difference between the total revenue line and the total cost curve represents the profit. For instance, at a production rate of 4000 dozen a week, the height of the total revenue line is $2800, while the height of the total cost curve is $4097. Hence, the vertical difference is a loss of $1297.

Generally, to maximize profit, a business should produce at that rate where its marginal revenue equals its marginal cost. The **marginal revenue** is the change in total revenue arising from selling an additional unit.

To explain the rule for maximizing profit, consider Figure 4.3. Graphically, the marginal revenue is represented by the slope of the total revenue line. Similarly, since marginal cost is the change in total cost due to the production of an additional unit, the marginal cost is represented by the slope of the total cost curve.

At a production rate such as 1000 dozen a week, the total revenue line climbs faster than the total cost curve, or equivalently, the marginal revenue exceeds the marginal cost. Then, an increase in production will raise the profit. Wherever the marginal revenue exceeds the marginal cost, Luna can raise profit by increasing production.

The **marginal revenue** is the change in total revenue arising from selling an additional unit.

By contrast, at a production rate of 9000 dozen a week, the total revenue climbs more slowly than the total cost curve, or equivalently, the marginal revenue is less than the marginal cost. Then, a reduction in production will increase profit. Wherever the marginal revenue is less than the marginal cost, Luna can raise profit by reducing production.

Thus, Luna will maximize profit at the production rate where its marginal revenue equals marginal cost. At that point, the total revenue line and the total cost curve climb at exactly the same rate. Hence, a small change in production (either increase or reduction) will affect both total revenue and total cost to the same extent. Accordingly, it is not possible to increase profit any further.

We can use another approach to explain why a business maximizes profit by balancing marginal revenue and marginal cost. By definition, the marginal revenue is the change in total revenue arising from selling an additional unit. For a business that can sell as much as it would like at the market price, the change in total revenue arising from selling an additional unit is exactly equal to the price. Hence, the marginal revenue equals the price of the output.

In Figure 4.4, we draw the marginal and average cost curves from Figure 4.2 and also include the marginal revenue line. The marginal revenue line also represents the price. Where the price exceeds the marginal cost, Luna can increase profit by raising production. By contrast, where the price is less than

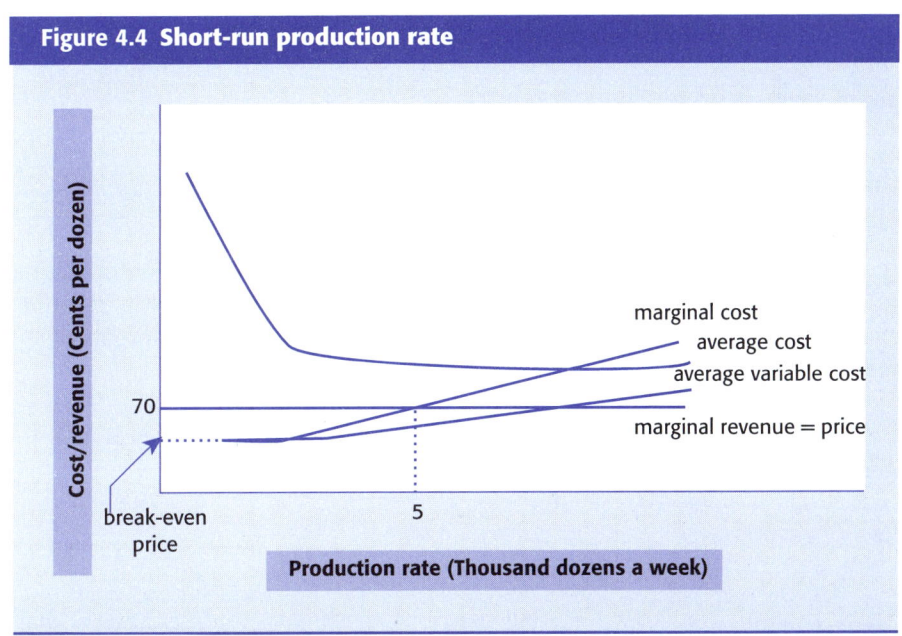

Figure 4.4 Short-run production rate

Given the price of 70 cents, the seller maximizes profits by producing at the rate of 5000 dozen a week, where marginal cost equals the price.

the marginal cost, Luna can increase profit by cutting production. Therefore, Luna will maximize profit by producing at 5000 dozen a week, a rate at which its marginal cost just balances the price.

Breakeven

Our discussion of the profit-maximizing production rate assumed that the business is continuing in operation. To decide whether to continue production, the business needs to compare the profit from continuing in production with the profit from shutting down. We shall see that the key factor in this comparison is the composition of fixed vis-à-vis variable costs.

Suppose that a business continues production. Let the revenue from the profit-maximizing production rate be R, while the fixed cost is F and the variable cost is V. Then, the maximum profit is $R - F - V$.

A **sunk cost** is a cost that has been committed and cannot be avoided.

Now suppose that the business shuts down. Clearly, this will reduce its total revenue to 0. How will the shutdown affect its costs? We assume that the entire fixed cost, F, of the business is also **sunk** in the short run. A cost is *sunk* if it has been committed and cannot be avoided. The opposite of sunk is avoidable.

By assumption, the entire fixed cost, F, is also sunk. This means that, even if the business shuts down, it must still pay the fixed cost, F. In contrast to the fixed cost, the variable cost is avoidable. Hence, if the business shuts down, it need not pay anything in variable cost. Thus, if it shuts down, the profit will be the zero revenue minus the fixed cost, that is, $-F$.

The business should continue in production if the maximum profit from continuing in production is at least as large as the profit from shutting down. Algebraically, this condition is

$$R - V - F \geq -F, \tag{4.4}$$

which simplifies to

$$R \geq V. \tag{4.5}$$

Because the fixed cost is sunk, it drops out of the condition for continuing in production. The business should continue in production so long as its revenue covers the variable cost. Equivalently, the business breaks even where its revenue covers the variable cost.

Recall that revenue is the price multiplied by sales, $R = p \times q$. We can divide the break-even condition throughout by sales (or the production rate) to obtain

$$p \geq \frac{V}{q}. \tag{4.6}$$

Hence an equivalent way of stating the short-run break-even condition is that the price must cover the average variable cost.

To summarize, in the short run, a business maximizes profit by producing at the rate where the marginal cost equals the price, provided that the price covers the average variable cost. Otherwise, it should shut down.

Let us apply the short-run break-even analysis to Luna Farm. Suppose that Luna continues production. Then, from Table 4.3, by producing at a rate of 5000 dozen eggs a week, Luna will operate at a loss of $1293. By assumption, Luna's entire $2200 fixed cost is also sunk, while if Luna shuts down, it need not pay anything in variable cost. Thus, if Luna shuts down, its profit will be the zero revenue minus the $2200 fixed cost, that is, a loss of $2200. Clearly, Luna is better off continuing in production.

Another way to make this decision simply ignores the fixed cost. Table 4.3 shows the variable cost and total revenue. If Luna produces 5000 dozen a week, it will earn a total revenue of $3500, while its variable cost would be $2593. Since the revenue exceeds the variable cost, Luna should continue in production. Thus, we have explained why it makes sense for Luna to produce "at a loss"—the reason is the "loss" includes a sunk cost that should be ignored.

Individual Supply Curve

Using the rule for profit-maximizing production, we can determine how much a business should produce at other prices for its output. This is the information needed to construct a seller's individual supply curve. The **individual supply curve** is a graph showing the quantity that one seller should supply at every possible price.

> The **individual supply curve** is a graph showing the quantity that one seller should supply at every possible price.

For every possible price of its output, a business should produce at the rate that balances its marginal cost with the price, provided that the price covers the average variable cost. Referring to Figure 4.4, if the price is 80 cents rather than 70 cents a dozen, Luna should expand production to the rate where the new price equals the marginal cost.

Indeed, by varying the price, we can trace out the quantity that Luna should supply at every possible price and, hence, construct Luna's individual supply curve. In fact, the individual supply curve is identical with the portion of the seller's marginal cost curve that lies above the average variable cost curve.

Just as the marginal cost curve, the individual supply curve slopes upward. If the seller is to expand production, then it will incur a higher marginal cost. Hence, the seller should expand production only if it receives a higher price. Accordingly, the individual supply curve slopes upward. Further, the slope of the supply curve is identical to the slope of the marginal cost curve.

The individual supply curve shows how a seller should adjust its production in response to changes in the price of its output. Hence, a change in the output price will be represented by a movement along the supply curve.

Demand for Inputs

We can now explain in detail how to obtain an individual seller's demand for inputs. We have derived the seller's marginal cost from its total cost, which in turn was derived from the estimates of the expenses on rent, wages, and other supplies needed at various production rates. These estimates depend on the prices of the various inputs.

Suppose, for instance, that Table 4.1 assumes a wage of $10 per hour. The calculations in Tables 4.2 and 4.3 and Figures 4.3 and 4.4 are based on a wage of $10 per hour. What if the wage is $9 per hour? Then, we must go back to adjust Tables 4.1–4.3 and Figures 4.3–4.4 using the new wage rate.

Intuitively, as we show in Figure 4.5, the marginal cost curve will shift downward. The profit-maximizing production rate increases from 5000 to 5600 dozen. From the new production rate of 5600 dozen, we can go back to determine the corresponding quantity of the labor input. With a higher production, the quantity of labor demanded will also be higher.

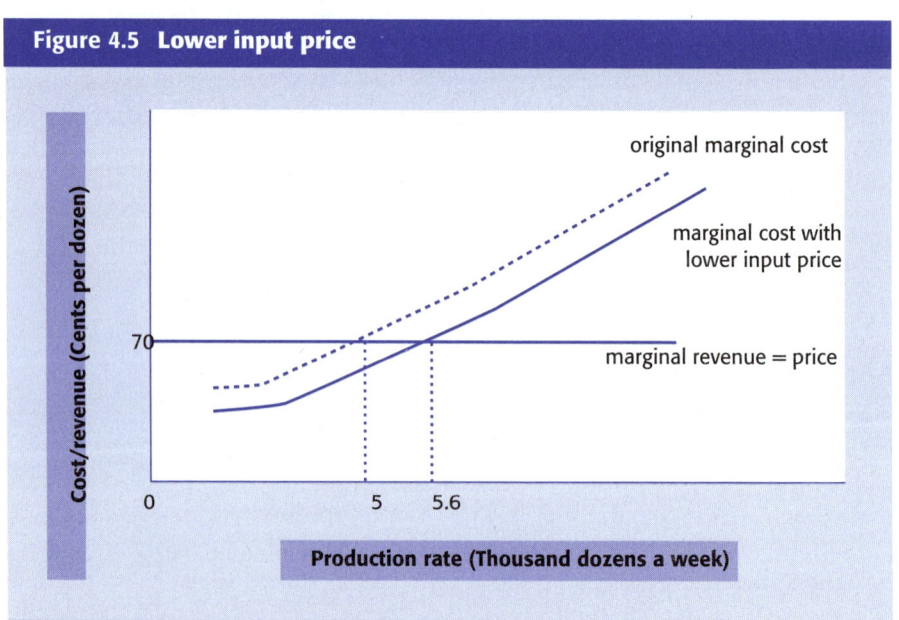

Figure 4.5 Lower input price

With a lower input price, the marginal cost curve will shift downward; hence, the seller will increase the production rate from 5000 to 5600 dozen.

By varying the wage rate, we can determine the quantity demanded of labor at every possible wage rate. This will allow us to construct the individual seller's demand for labor. As we have just shown, the quantity demanded will be higher at a lower wage; hence, the demand curve will slope downward. The same method can be used to derive the individual seller's demand for every other input.

Organizing Production at Multiple Facilities

Echo Bay Mines has gold mines at Lupin in Canada as well as Cove in Nevada. How should it organize production at the two mines? Assuming that it can sell as much as it would like at the market price, Echo Bay Mines could simply direct each mine to produce at a rate balancing the price of gold with its marginal cost.

Another, more general approach applies even to sellers that are large enough to affect the market price. These should organize production so as to equalize the marginal cost at every facility. By doing so, the seller will minimize its companywide production cost.

To explain this rule, suppose that Echo's marginal cost at Lupin is $370 per ounce, while its marginal cost at Cove is $350 per ounce. If Echo reduced production at Lupin by one ounce and increased production at Cove by one ounce, it could reduce total cost by $370 − $350 = $20. These adjustments would not affect the total production of the entire company. Generally, if the two mines have different marginal costs of production, the company can always reduce costs by switching production between the mines.

Therefore, to minimize the companywide cost of production, a seller should organize production so as to equalize the marginal cost at every facility.

4 *Long-Run Individual Supply*

In the short run, a business must work within the constraints of past commitments such as employment contracts and investment in facilities and equipment. Over time, however, contracts expire and investments wear out. With sufficient time, all inputs become avoidable. A long-run planning horizon is a time frame far enough into the future that all inputs can be freely adjusted. Then the business will have complete flexibility in deciding on inputs and production.

How should a business make two key decisions—whether to continue in operation and how much to produce—in the long run? To address these issues, we first analyze the long-run costs and then look at the revenue.

Long-Run Costs

Let us analyze long-run costs in the context of Luna Farm. We ask the management to estimate the costs of producing at various rates when all inputs are avoidable. Suppose that Table 4.4 presents the expenses classified into rent, wages, and cost of supplies.

In the long run, Luna can vary the size of its facility. The rent is $250 at zero production and increases to $2500 for production of 9000 dozen eggs a week. Similarly, the wages are $200 at zero production and rise to $5289 at a production rate of 9000. The cost of supplies rises from nothing for zero production to $900 at a production rate of 9000.

As this example shows, in the long run, the business may incur some cost even at production levels close to zero. For instance, it may not be possible to build an egg-producing facility smaller than some minimum size. The $250 is the rent associated with a facility of the minimum size. Similarly, Luna's owner must work at least 20 hours a week. At a wage of $10 per hour, the minimum labor cost is $10 \times 20 = $200 a week. Extracting the relevant information from Table 4.4, we can compile the long-run marginal and average costs in Table 4.5. We draw the long-run marginal and average costs in Figure 4.6.

Table 4.4 Long-run weekly expenses

Weekly Production Rate	Rent	Wages	Cost of Supplies	Total
0	$250	$200	$0	$450
1000	$500	$279	$100	$879
2000	$750	$461	$200	$1411
3000	$1000	$757	$300	$2057
4000	$1250	$1176	$400	$2826
5000	$1500	$1722	$500	$3722
6000	$1750	$2403	$600	$4753
7000	$2000	$3221	$700	$5921
8000	$2250	$4182	$800	$7232
9000	$2500	$5289	$900	$8689

Table 4.5 Analysis of long-run costs

Weekly Production Rate	Total Cost	Marginal Cost	Average Cost
0	$450		
1000	$879	$0.43	$0.88
2000	$1411	$0.53	$0.71
3000	$2057	$0.65	$0.69
4000	$2826	$0.77	$0.71
5000	$3722	$0.90	$0.74
6000	$4753	$1.03	$0.79
7000	$5921	$1.17	$0.85
8000	$7232	$1.31	$0.90
9000	$8689	$1.46	$0.97

Figure 4.6 Long-run production rate

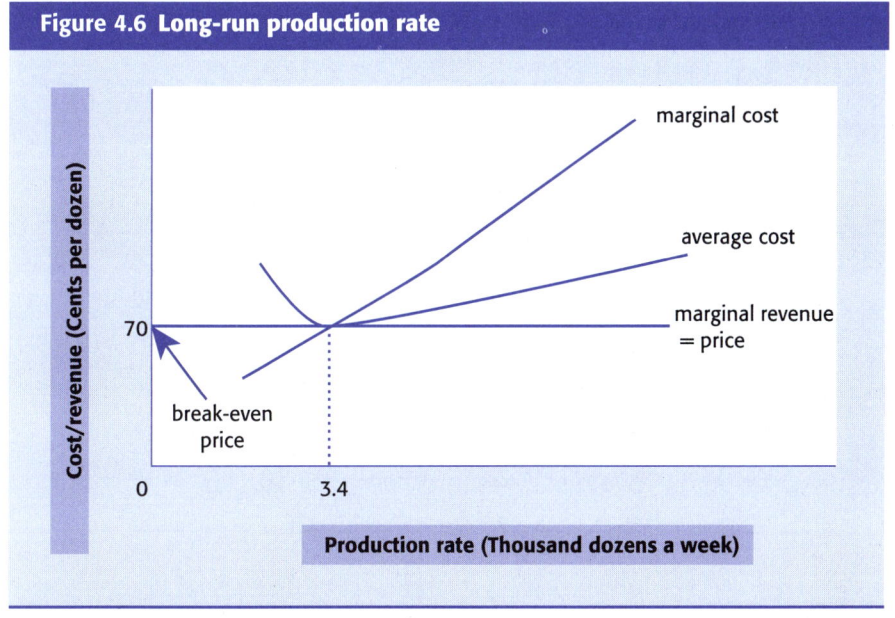

Given a price of 70 cents, the seller maximizes profits by producing 3400 dozen, where the long-run marginal cost equals the price.

Comparing the short-run and long-run average cost curves, we see that the long-run average cost curve is lower and has a gentler slope. The reason is that, in the long run, the seller has more flexibility in adjusting inputs to changes in the production rate. Accordingly, it can produce at a relatively lower cost than in the short run, when one or more inputs cannot be changed.

Production Rate

Let us now consider how much the business should produce in the long run. We can apply the general rule derived for short-run production: To maximize profit, a business should produce at that rate where its marginal cost equals the price of its output. In the long run, however, we use the long-run marginal cost.

The reasoning for this rule is the same as before. Where the price exceeds the long-run marginal cost, the seller can increase profit by raising production. By contrast, where the price is less than the long-run marginal cost, the seller can increase profit by cutting production. Thus, the seller will maximize profit by producing at the rate such that its long-run marginal cost just equals the price.

For the Luna Farm, Table 4.6 shows the long-run cost, revenue, and profit. The profit column shows that profit reaches a maximum at a production rate of

Table 4.6 Long-run profit

Weekly Production Rate	Total Cost	Total Revenue	Profit	Marginal Cost	Marginal Revenue
0	$450	0	−$450		
1000	$879	$700	−$179	$0.43	$0.70
2000	$1411	$1400	−$11	$0.53	$0.70
3000	$2057	$2100	$43	$0.65	$0.70
4000	$2826	$2800	−$26	$0.77	$0.70
5000	$3722	$3500	−$222	$0.90	$0.70
6000	$4753	$4200	−$553	$1.03	$0.70
7000	$5921	$4900	−$1021	$1.17	$0.70
8000	$7232	$5600	−$1632	$1.31	$0.70
9000	$8689	$6300	−$2389	$1.46	$0.70

3400. The marginal cost at a production rate of 3400 is 70 cents. Since the price is 70 cents, this confirms that the production rate of 3400 maximizes profit.

Breakeven

We next analyze the break-even condition under which a business should continue in long-run production. Combining this with the profit-maximizing production rate, we can derive the long-run individual supply curve.

In the long run, a business should continue in production if the maximum profit from continuing in production is at least as large as the profit from shutting down. In the long run, all costs are avoidable; hence, if the business shuts down, it will incur no costs and so its profit from shutting down is nothing.

Let $(R - C)$ represent the maximum profit from continuing in production. Then the business should continue in production if

$$R - C \geq 0, \tag{4.7}$$

which simplifies to

$$R \geq C. \tag{4.8}$$

This break-even condition says that the business should continue in production so long as total revenue covers total cost.

Since total revenue is price multiplied by sales, $R = p \times q$, we can divide the break-even condition throughout by sales (or the production rate) to obtain

$$p \geq \frac{C}{q}. \tag{4.9}$$

An equivalent way of stating the long-run break-even condition is that the price must cover the average cost.

Referring to Table 4.5, Luna's lowest average cost is 69 cents. It attains this cost at a production rate of 3000. Hence, if the price of eggs falls below 69 cents, then Luna should go out of business.

Individual Supply Curve

A seller maximizes profits by producing at the rate where its long-run marginal cost equals the price of the output. By varying the price, we can determine the quantity that the seller will supply at every possible price. We have also shown that the seller should remain in business only if the price covers its average cost. Thus, the seller's long-run individual supply curve is that part of its long-run marginal cost curve, which lies above its average cost curve.

Progress check

Progress Check 4D Referring to Table 4.5, if the market price of eggs is $1.31, how much should Luna produce and what will be its profit?

When to Produce Oil

In the oil industry, production is the process of extracting crude oil from the ground. The cost of producing oil in the United States is relatively low in Alaska but much higher in the lower 48 states. The decision of high-cost producers whether to produce can be quite sensitive to changes in the price of crude oil.

Figure 4.7 shows year-by-year percentage changes in the price of West Texas Intermediate crude and the number of active drilling rigs in Canada and the United States between 1983 and 1993. From 1983–1989, the change in the number of active rigs tended to lag behind the change in the oil price. Then, from 1990 onward, the change in the number of active rigs followed the change in the oil price very closely.

Fujitsu's New Factory in Durham, England

Between January and June 1996, the market price of 16-megabit DRAMs fell by over 50%. The drop in price led Samsung Electronics, the world's largest DRAM manufacturer, to announce that it would cut production from 14 to 12 million units a month. Number two, NEC Corporation, announced a cut in production from 11 to 9 million units a month. Evidently, Samsung and NEC had decided that the price of 16-megabit DRAMs did not cover the average variable cost.

With a factory in Durham, England, under construction to produce 16-megabit DRAMs, Fujitsu had to make a different calculation. Fujitsu would have to consider whether the future price of 16-megabit DRAMs would cover the average cost, ignoring the costs that were already sunk. The company decided to delay commencing production. Kazunari Shirai, president of Fujitsu's electronic devices group, explained that production "will be put on hold to watch the market situation."

Sources: "Toshiba Cites Price Concerns for Cuts in Chip Output," *Straits Times* (June 12, 1996), p. 37; "Fujitsu Lowers DRAM Output Estimates," *Asian Wall Street Journal* (June 11, 1996), p. 11.

Figure 4.7 Oil price and drilling rigs

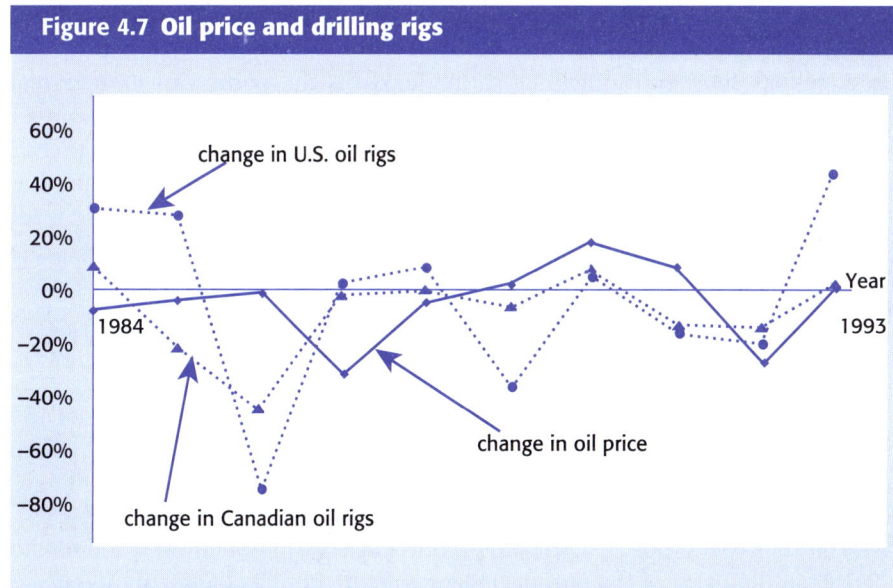

From 1983 to 1989, the change in the number of active rigs tended to lag behind the change in the oil price. Then, from 1990 onward, the change in the number of active rigs followed the change in the oil price very closely.

5 *Market Supply*

If the price of eggs is 70 cents a dozen, how much will be produced by the market as a whole? To address this question, we need to know the market supply curve of eggs. The **market supply curve** of an item is a graph showing the quantity that the market will supply at every possible price. At any particular price, the quantity that the market will supply is the sum of the quantities supplied by each individual seller.

The market supply is the counterpart to the market demand, which we introduced in Chapter 2. Together, supply and demand constitute a market. We first analyze the short-run market supply, and then consider the long-run supply.

Short Run

To construct the market supply, we can draw an analogy from our analysis of market demand. Recall that the market demand curve is the horizontal sum of the individual demand curves. Similarly, the market supply curve is the horizontal sum of the individual supply curves. At any particular price, each seller's individual supply curve shows the quantity that seller will supply. The sum of these quantities is the quantity supplied by the market as a whole. By varying

*The **market supply curve** is a graph showing the quantity that the market will supply at every possible price.*

the price, we can get the information needed to construct the market supply curve.

A seller's short-run individual supply curve is the portion of its marginal cost curve that lies above its average variable cost curve. Hence, the market supply curve begins with the seller that has the lowest average variable cost. The market supply curve then gradually blends in sellers with higher average variable cost.

In Figure 4.8, we assume that there are just two producers of eggs: Luna Farm and Venus Farm. We draw the individual supply curves of the two producers and sum these horizontally to obtain the market supply curve. This shows that, at a price of 70 cents, the market as a whole will supply 5,000 + 8,000 = 13,000 dozen a week.

Our analysis of individual supply showed that the higher the price of the output, the more the seller will wish to produce. Since each seller will produce more, the market as a whole will also produce a larger quantity. Accordingly, the market supply curve slopes upward.

The market supply curve shows how market production responds to changes in the price of the output. Hence, the effect of a change in the output price is represented by a movement along the supply curve. Suppose, for

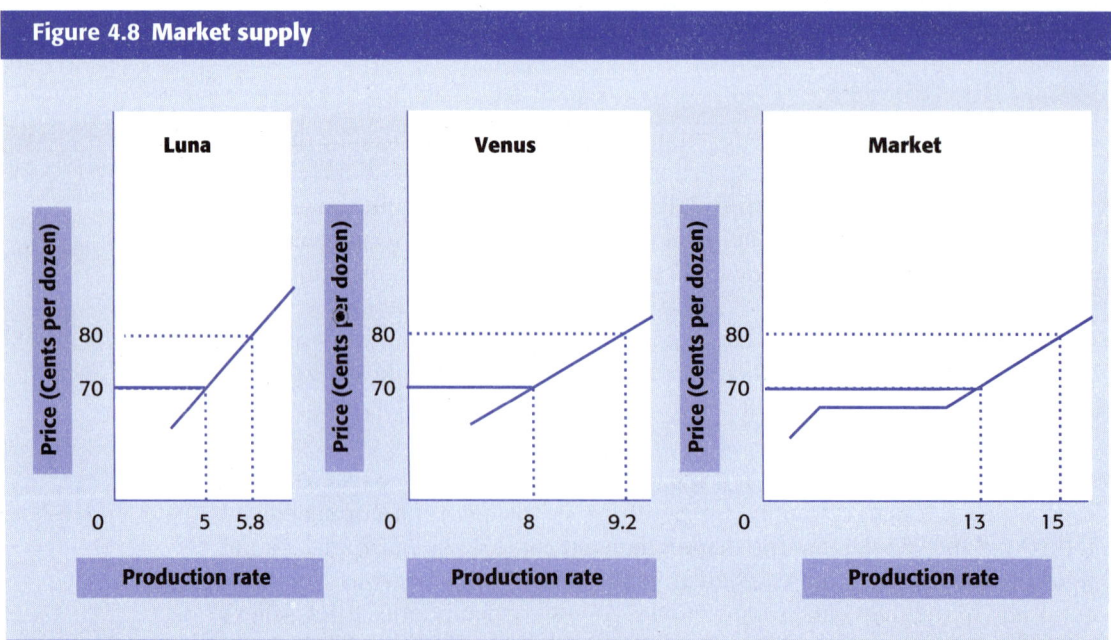

Figure 4.8 Market supply

The market supply curve is the horizontal summation of the individual supply curves. At a price of 70 cents per dozen, the market quantity supplied is 5,000 + 8,000 = 13,000 dozen. At a price of 80 cents per dozen, the market quantity supplied is 5,800 + 9,200 = 15,000 dozen.

instance, that the price of eggs rises from 70 to 80 cents per dozen. Then, referring to the market supply curve in Figure 4.8, the market quantity supplied increases from 13,000 to 15,000.

The supply of an individual seller depends on the prices of all inputs, including labor, equipment, and supplies. A change in an input price will affect the seller's marginal cost at all production levels. The change will shift the entire marginal cost curve and hence the entire individual supply curve.

Since the market supply curve is the horizontal summation of the various individual supply curves, the change in the input price will also shift the entire market supply curve. Specifically, an increase in the price of an input will shift the market supply up, while a reduction in an input price will shift the market supply down.

We can apply this analysis to predict how an increase in the price of animal feed would affect the market supply of eggs. The higher price of feed will raise each seller's marginal cost of production and shift its individual supply curve up. Hence, the market supply curve will shift up.

In general, a change in the price of the output is represented by a movement along the market supply curve, while a change in the price of any input will cause a shift of the entire market supply curve.

Progress Check 4E In Figure 4.8, show how a fall in the price of animal feed would affect the market supply of eggs.

Progress check

Long Run

Many of the principles of long-run market supply are similar to those underlying short-run supply. Accordingly, for brevity, we will focus on the special aspects of long-run supply. In the long run, every business will have complete flexibility in deciding on inputs and production. This flexibility implies that existing sellers can leave the industry, and new sellers can enter. The freedom of entry and exit is a key difference between the short run and long run.

We have shown that, for a seller to break even in the long run, its total revenue must cover its total cost. If a seller's total revenue does not cover the total cost, then the seller should leave the industry. Hence, the seller's individual supply will reduce to zero. This departure will reduce the market supply, hence raise the market price and the profits of the other sellers. Sellers that cannot cover their total costs will continue to leave the industry until all the remaining sellers break even.

By contrast, an industry where businesses can make profits will attract new entrants. Each of the new entrants will contribute its individual supply and so add to the market supply. The increase in the market supply will push down the market price and hence reduce the profit of all the existing sellers. If the existing sellers continue making profits, new entrants will continue to enter the industry until all the sellers just break even.

Accordingly, in the long run, when there is a change in the market price, the quantity supplied will adjust in two ways: First, all existing sellers will adjust their quantities supplied along their individual supply curves, and second, some sellers may enter or leave the market.

Let us apply this analysis to understand how producers of eggs will respond to an increase in the market price from 70 to 80 cents. Referring to Figure 4.9, when the price rises from 70 to 80 cents, the short-run quantity supplied will increase from 13,000 to 15,000. Further, the price increase will raise the profits of the existing producers.

Over time, however, the higher profits will attract new producers to enter the industry. The new entrants will add to the market supply; hence, in the long run, the quantity supplied will increase from 13,000 to 20,000. As this example

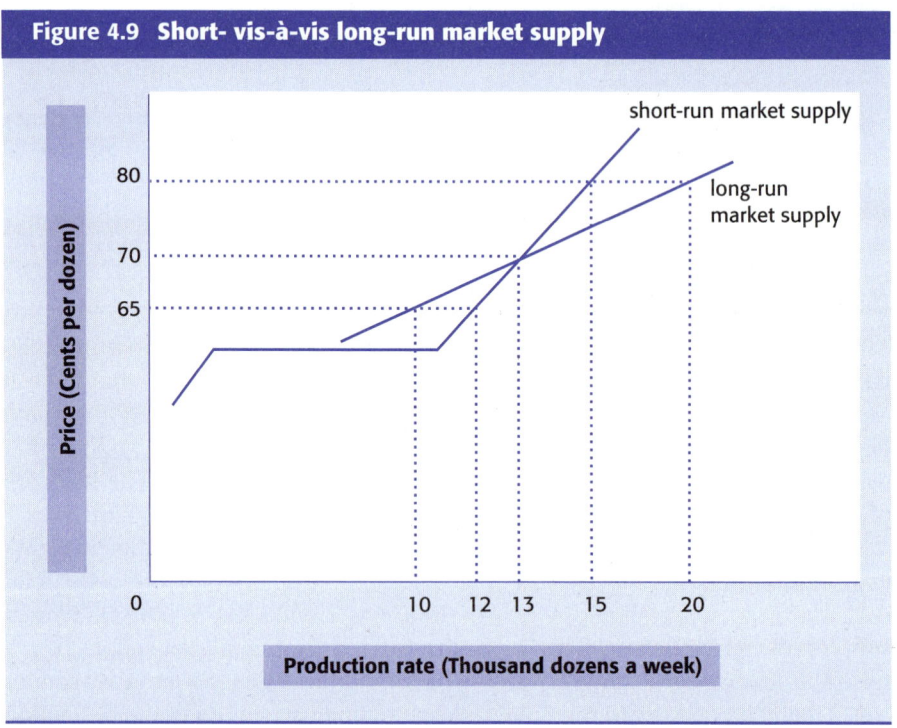

Figure 4.9   Short- vis-à-vis long-run market supply

If the price rises from 70 to 80 cents per dozen, the quantity supplied will increase from 13,000 to 15,000 in the short run and to 20,000 in the long run. If the price falls from 70 to 65 cents per dozen, the quantity supplied will fall from 13,000 to 12,000 in the short run and to 10,000 in the long run.

shows, for a given increase in price, the long-run market supply slopes more gently than the short-run market supply.

How will producers respond to a fall in the market price from 70 to 65 cents? Referring to Figure 4.9, when the price drops from 70 to 65 cents, the short-run quantity supplied will drop from 13,000 to 12,000. In the short run, a business will continue to produce so long as the price covers its average variable cost.

Over time, however, producers for whom the price is below average cost will leave the industry. The departures will reduce the market supply. So, in the long run, the quantity supplied will drop relatively more, from 13,000 to, say, 10,000. This example shows that, for a price reduction, the long-run market supply slopes more gently than the short-run market supply.

Accordingly, for any change in price, the long-run market supply slopes more gently than the short-run market supply. Using terminology that we will introduce later in the chapter, we say that the long-run market supply is *more elastic* than the short-run supply.

Properties

While the short-run market supply generally slopes upward, the long-run market supply may be flat. In the long run, new businesses can enter and existing businesses can leave. Specifically, in the long run, the quantity supplied can expand through replication of existing businesses. The increase in production will raise the demand for inputs. Provided that there is no change in input prices, the cost of the production supplied by the new entrants should be the same as the cost of production supplied by the existing businesses. Then, the long-run supply will be completely flat.

If, however, the increased demand for inputs results in higher input prices, then the cost of supplying the increased production will be higher. Hence, the long-run supply will slope upward.

There is another reason why the long-run market supply may slope upward. The resources available to the various suppliers may vary in quality. New entrants may not be able to replicate the resources of existing suppliers; hence, the new entrants must incur higher costs. This is especially true of resource-based markets such as minerals and agriculture. Resource differences also are signficant in markets where location plays an important role. For instance, in air transportation, suppliers with access to more convenient airports will have relatively lower costs.

The long-run market supply curve shows the quantity that the market will supply at every possible price. Hence, the effect of a change in the output price is represented by a movement along the market supply curve. By contrast, a change in wage or any factor other than the price of the output will cause a shift of the entire market supply curve.

⊚6 *Seller Surplus*

We derived the individual supply curve by asking a seller how much it would supply at every possible price. Another way to interpret the supply curve is to view it as showing the minimum price that the seller will accept for each unit of production. Using this approach, we can explain how a seller benefits or suffers from changes in the price of its output, and why a seller's profit varies relatively more than the price of its output.

Price vis-à-vis Marginal Cost

The **seller surplus** is the difference between a seller's revenue from some production rate and the minimum amount necessary to induce the seller to produce that quantity.

In the case of Luna, referring to Figure 4.10, the marginal cost of producing 1000 dozen eggs a month is 43 cents. This is the minimum price that Luna will accept for the first 1000 dozen. At a market price of 70 cents, however, Luna receives 70 cents for each unit of production. The difference of $(0.70 − 0.43) × 1000 = $270 is a surplus for the seller. Generally, the **seller surplus** is the dif-

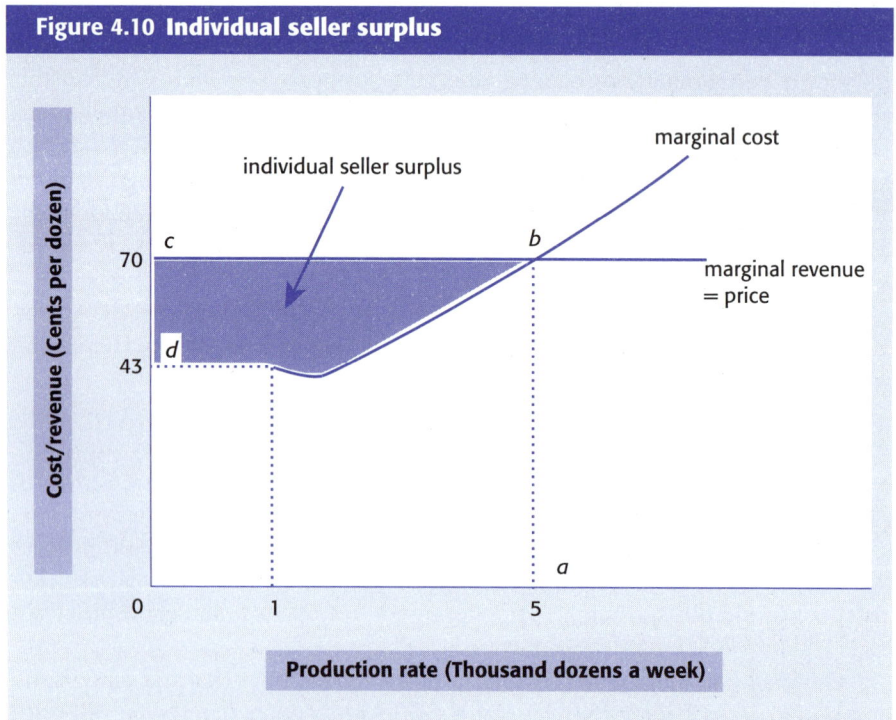

Figure 4.10 Individual seller surplus

The marginal cost of producing 1000 dozen eggs is 43 cents per dozen. At a price of 70 cents per dozen, the seller receives a surplus of $(0.70 − 0.43) x 1000 = $270 for that production. At the 70 cent price, the seller will produce 5000 dozen a week. The individual seller surplus is the shaded area *dbc* between the price line and the marginal cost curve.

ference between a seller's revenue from some quantity of production and the minimum amount necessary to induce the seller to produce that quantity. Luna receives a seller surplus on all production up to the marginal unit.

We will show that the short-run seller surplus can also be defined as the difference between the seller's revenue from some production rate and the variable cost. The minimum amount sufficient to induce a seller to deliver some production rate is the minimum that it requires for each unit up to the specified quantity. The minimum that a seller requires for each unit is the marginal cost. Hence, the minimum amount sufficient to induce a seller to deliver some production rate is the sum of the marginal costs for each unit up to the specified quantity.

The sum of the marginal costs for each unit up to some specified quantity is the variable cost. Accordingly, in the short run, the minimum amount necessary to induce a seller to deliver some production is the variable cost. Graphically, this is the area under the marginal cost curve up to the specified production rate. Thus, the seller surplus is the difference between the seller's revenue from some production rate and the variable cost, or $R - V$.

To illustrate, let us consider Luna's seller surplus at the price of 70 cents. Referring to Figure 4.10, the revenue is represented by the area of the rectangle 0abc under the price line up to the quantity of 5000. The variable cost can be represented by the area 0abd under Luna's marginal cost curve up to 5000 dozen a month. The shaded area dbc between the price line and the marginal cost curve represents the seller surplus.

In the short run, a seller breaks even where total revenue covers the variable cost; hence, the seller surplus is equal to total revenue less variable cost. In the long run, however, total revenue must cover total cost for the seller to break even. Hence, the long-run seller surplus is equal to total revenue less total cost.

Purchasing

Suppose that Speedy Foods is a large dairy manufacturer. It buys eggs as an input into manufacturing confectionery and ice cream. Presently, Speedy pays 70 cents per dozen to suppliers such as Luna Farm. We have shown that the 70-cent price gives Luna the area dbc in seller surplus.

Speedy can use the analysis of seller surplus to reduce the cost of its purchases and hence raise its own profit. Referring to Figure 4.10, the minimum amount of money necessary to induce Luna to sell 5000 dozen eggs a month is the area 0abd under Luna's marginal cost curve. Speedy should offer Luna a lump sum equal to area 0abd plus $1 to supply a bulk order of 5000 dozen eggs. This amount of money leaves Luna with $1 of seller surplus and is just enough to induce Luna to supply the order. Through the bulk order, Speedy saves an amount represented by area dbc less $1.

The foregoing example illustrates how a buyer can apply the concept of seller surplus to reduce the cost of its purchases. The buyer should design a bulk order that extracts the seller surplus and pay the seller the minimum amount of money necessary to induce production of the desired quantity of output. Essentially, the buyer is purchasing up the seller's marginal cost curve.

Profit/Price Variation

Let us now analyze how a seller benefits or suffers from changes in the price of its output. Generally, a change in the price of the output will affect a seller's profit in two ways. The price change will affect the seller's revenue at the original production rate. Further, the price change will induce the seller to adjust production. We can illustrate these effects with the Luna example. Our example will also explain why a seller's profit varies relatively more than the price of its output.

Recall from Table 4.2 that, when the price of eggs is 70 cents per dozen, Luna maximizes short-run profit by producing 5000 dozen. If the price is 80 cents, however, Luna should increase production up to 5800 dozen a week, where its marginal cost is 80 cents. The price increase raises Luna's profit in two ways: First, Luna gets 10 cents more for the original 5000 production, and second, Luna expands production to 5800 dozen, thus earning some additional profit.

In this example, the price of eggs increases by 10/70 = 14%. For each of the 5000 dozen that it produced at the original price of 70 cents, Luna was making different amounts of profit. In Figure 4.10, however, we can see that the profit on each unit of production would definitely be less than 70 cents. Accordingly, a 10-cent price increase would raise the profit on each unit of production by more than 10/70 = 14%. In addition, at the higher price of 80 cents, Luna chooses to expand production to 5800 dozen, further increasing its profit. Hence, the 14% price increase raises Luna's profit by more than 14%.

Suppose instead that the price of eggs drops by 10 cents or 14% to 60 cents a dozen. Then, in Table 4.2, Luna should cut production to 4200 dozen a week, where its marginal cost is 60 cents. This would reduce Luna's profit in two ways: First, Luna would get 10 cents less for every unit that it produces, and second, Luna will cut production by 800 dozen. By the same reasoning that we used to consider the effect of a price increase on Luna's profit, we can show that the 14% cut in the price of eggs would reduce Luna's profit by more than 14%.

Generally, a change in the price of the output will affect the seller surplus by changing the revenue at the original production rate and inducing the seller to adjust production.

Progress check

Progress Check 4F In Figure 4.10, shade the area representing the increase in seller surplus arising from an increase in the price of eggs from 70 to 90 cents.

Profit/Price Variation: Lihir Gold

In October 1995, the owners of the Lihir gold mine launched an initial public offering of shares. The prospectus for Lihir Gold's offering projected the mine's profit in 1999 to be $52 million if the price of gold turned out to be $400 per ounce, while the projected profit was $24 million or 46% higher if the price of gold turned out to be just $50, or 12.5%, higher.

These projections are consistent with the general principle that a seller's profit varies relatively more than the price of its output. Lihir Gold's prospectus also included a production forecast of 584,000 ounces a year. At this production rate, a $50 increase in the price of gold would change revenues by $50 × 584,000 = $29.2 million. This calculation, however, does not take into account increases in production, royalties, and taxes. The company projected that a $50 price increase would raise profit by $24 million.

Source: "Lihir Sparks a Gold Rush with Hot Stock Offering," *Asian Wall Street Journal* (September 12, 1995), p. 13.

Market Seller Surplus

The seller surplus for an individual is the difference between its revenue from some production rate and the minimum amount necessary for it to produce that quantity. The seller surplus for the whole market is the sum of the individual seller surpluses. It is the difference between the market revenue from some production rate and the minimum amount necessary for the market to produce that quantity. Graphically, the market seller surplus is represented by the area between the price line and the market supply curve. This concept applies in both the short run and the long run.

Figure 4.11 shows a short-run market supply curve. For example, at a price of 70 cents, the short-run market seller surplus is represented by the shaded area between the price line and the short-run market supply curve.

We have mentioned previously that, in the long run, the market supply curve may be flat. In this case, there will be no market seller surplus. If, however, the long-run market supply curve slopes upward, then there will be some market seller surplus.

To whom the long-run surplus accrues depends on the reason why the long-run market supply curve slopes upward. If the long-run supply slopes upward because an increase in production raises the price of some input, then

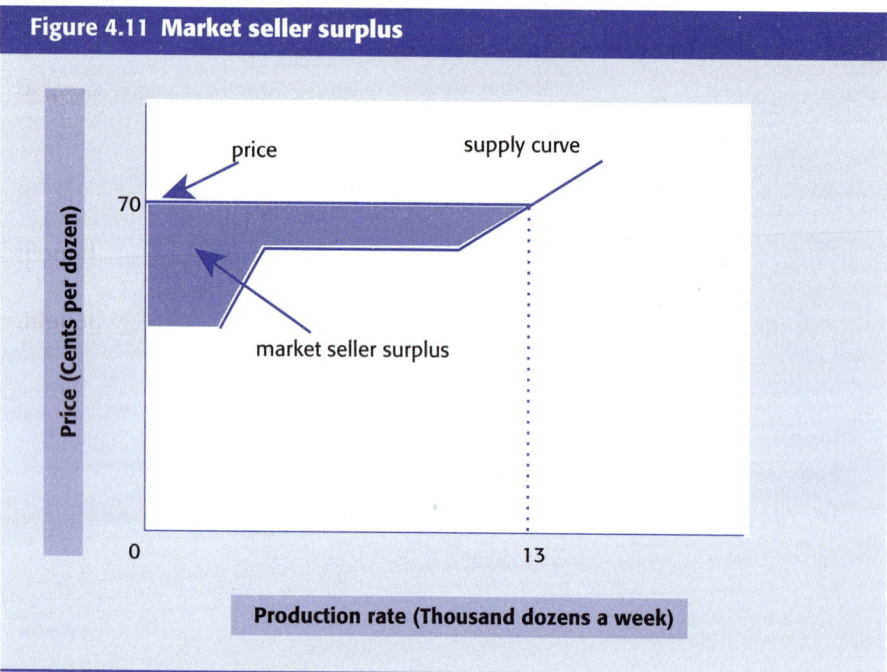

Figure 4.11 Market seller surplus

At a price of 70 cents, the market seller surplus is the shaded area between the price line and the market supply curve.

the seller surplus accrues to the suppliers of that input. If the long-run supply slopes upward because sellers have heterogeneous resources, then the seller surplus accrues to those who own the superior resources.

7 *Labor Supply*

So far, we have discussed supply in the context of businesses that sell goods and services. In human resource markets, however, the sellers are individual persons. The principles of human supply are similar to those underlying business supply. Accordingly, for brevity, we will focus on the special aspects of supply by individual persons.

Marginal Cost of Labor

The basis of individual supply by a business is maximization of profit. The business supplies the production rate where its marginal cost equals the market price. As we now explain, the individual supply of services by a person has a different basis.

A person's time is limited to $24 \times 7 = 168$ hours a week. The person must divide this time between labor and leisure, where *leisure* means any use of time that does not produce income. Hence, leisure includes time devoted to sleep as well as shopping and sport. Leisure is a consumer good. We suppose that, like other consumer goods, leisure provides diminishing marginal benefit. (At this point, the reader may wish to review the second section of Chapter 2 on diminishing marginal benefit.)

In Figure 4.12, we draw a curve representing a person's marginal benefit from leisure. The horizontal axis represents time, while the vertical axis represents the marginal benefit. By the principle of diminishing marginal benefit, the marginal benefit of leisure starts high and declines with increasing leisure time.

Owing to the constraint of 168 hours a week, if a person spends more time on labor, there will be less time for leisure. Conversely, if a person spends less

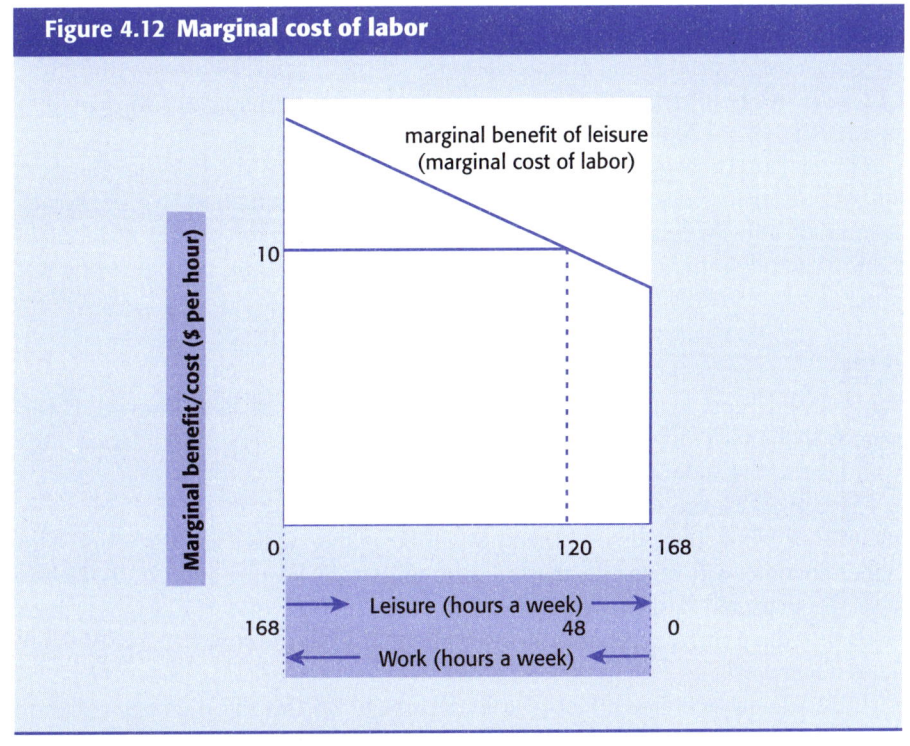

Figure 4.12 Marginal cost of labor

The marginal benefit of leisure declines with increasing leisure time; hence, the marginal cost of labor increases with the hours of labor. Given a wage of $10 per hour, the individual chooses 48 hours of work, or 120 hours of leisure.

time on labor, there will be more time for leisure. Referring to Figure 4.12, the quantity 0 hours of leisure is equivalent to 168 hours of labor, while the quantity 168 hours of leisure is equivalent to 0 hours of labor.

Accordingly, in Figure 4.12, we can interpret the curve for the marginal benefit from leisure as the marginal cost of labor by viewing the horizontal axis from right to left. Viewed this way, the marginal cost of labor begins from a low level for 0 hours of labor and rises with increases in the hours of labor. Essentially, the diminishing marginal benefit from leisure time translates into an increasing marginal cost of labor.

Supply

The procedure for constructing a person's individual supply curve of labor is similar to that for constructing a business' individual supply curve of output. Suppose that the person can choose to supply any quantity of labor at the market wage of $10 per hour. In Figure 4.12, we draw a horizontal line representing the market wage of $10 per hour.

Then, the person maximizes net benefit by choosing the quantity of labor where the marginal cost of labor equals the wage. The reasoning is the same as for why a business maximizes profit by choosing the production rate where the marginal cost of production equals the price of the output. Referring to Figure 4.12, if the wage is $10 per hour, the individual chooses 48 hours of work, which means 168–48 = 120 hours of leisure.

By varying the wage, we can determine the quantity of labor that the person will supply at every possible wage. With this information, we construct the person's individual supply curve of labor. The market supply of labor is the horizontal summation of the individual curves of all the people supplying labor.

Slope

The marginal cost of labor increases with the quantity of labor; hence, if the wage is higher, an individual will tend to supply a larger quantity of labor. This would cause the individual supply curve to slope upward.

However, Figure 4.12 does not show a countervailing effect: For any given quantity of labor, the person's income will be higher with a higher wage. The higher income will raise the marginal benefit from leisure and, equivalently, raise the marginal cost of work. Owing to this "income effect," a higher wage tends to reduce the quantity of labor supplied, making the supply curve of labor slope downward.

Accordingly, the net effect of a higher wage on the the quantity of labor that a person will supply depends on the balance of the two effects: the increasing marginal cost of labor and the income effect. This balance determines whether the supply of labor will slope upward at all wage levels.

Paying for Overtime

Typically, employers must pay workers 50–100% more than the regular wage rate for overtime work. Let us understand why employers must pay such a large premium for overtime work.

A worker's marginal cost of labor increases with the quantity supplied. The typical employer, however, does not allow its workers to choose any quantity of labor for some specified wage rate. Instead, the employer purchases a bulk order of 40 hours a week. Through the bulk order, the employer can extract some of the worker's seller surplus.

The regular wage rate reflects the worker's average cost of labor for 40 hours a week. The average cost of 40 hours of labor will be less than the marginal cost of the 40th hour, to an extent that depends on the steepness of the worker's marginal cost of labor.

If the employer wants to purchase overtime of an additional 5 hours of labor, it must pay the worker's marginal cost for the 41st-45th hours. As we have already explained, depending on the steepness of the worker's marginal cost of labor, the marginal cost of these hours may be substantially more than the regular wage. This explains why overtime rates are 50–100% higher than the regular wage.

8 *Elasticity of Supply*

Consider a typical issue for an industry analyst: If the price of gasoline and wages increases by 5 and 10%, respectively, what would be the effect on the short-run supply of gasoline by oil refineries? The analyst could answer this question with the market supply curve. In practice, however, analysts seldom have sufficient information to construct the entire market supply curve.

Another way of responding to the question applies the **elasticities of supply**, which measure the responsiveness of supply to changes in underlying factors such as the prices of the item and inputs. The elasticities of supply are the supply-side counterparts to the elasticities of demand, which we introduced in Chapter 3.

The **elasticity of supply** is the responsiveness of supply to changes in an underlying factor.

There is an elasticity corresponding to every factor that affects supply. Further, the elasticity can be estimated for individual supply curves as well as the market supply.

Price Elasticity

The **price elasticity of supply** measures the responsiveness of the quantity supplied to changes in the price of the item. The price elasticity of individual

The **price elasticity of supply** is the percentage by which the quantity supplied will change if the price of the item rises by 1%.

supply reveals how a seller will respond to a price change. Moreover, the price elasticity provides a simple way to compare the price sensitivity of sellers providing different items.

By definition, the price elasticity of supply is the percentage by which the quantity supplied will change if the price of the item rises by 1%, other things equal. Equivalently, the price elasticity is the ratio

$$\frac{\text{percentage change in quantity supplied}}{\text{percentage change in price}}$$

or

$$\frac{\text{proportionate change in quantity supplied}}{\text{proportionate change in price}}.$$

We can estimate the price elasticity of supply by either the arc or point approach. Let us apply the arc approach to calculate the price elasticity of Luna's short-run supply of eggs. Referring to Figure 4.13, at a price of 70 cents, Luna produces 5000 dozen. If the price increases to 80 cents, Luna would increase production to 5800 dozen.

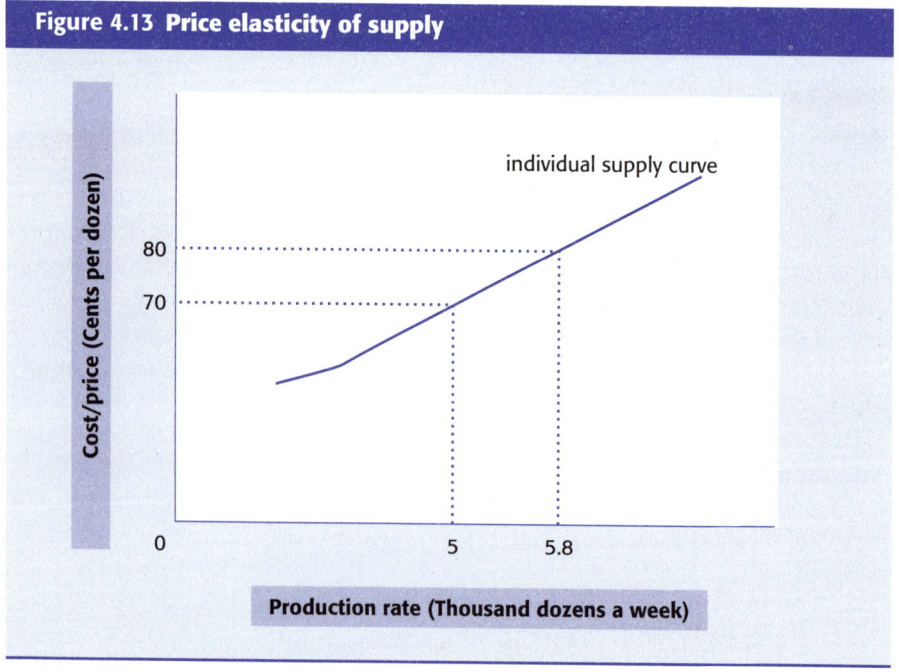

Figure 4.13 Price elasticity of supply

individual supply curve

Cost/price (Cents per dozen)

80

70

0   5   5.8

Production rate (Thousand dozens a week)

The proportionate change in quantity supplied is 15%, while the proportionate change in price is 13%. Hence, the price elasticity of supply is 0.15/0.13 = 1.15.

The proportionate change in quantity supplied is the change in quantity supplied divided by the average quantity supplied. The change in quantity supplied is 5800 – 5000 = 800 dozen a year, and the average quantity supplied is (5800 + 5000)/2 = 5400 dozen a year; hence the proportionate change in quantity supplied is 800/5400 = 0.15 = 15%.

Similarly, the proportionate change in price is the change in price divided by the average price. The change in price is 80 – 70 = 10 cents, while the average price is (70 + 80)/2 = 75 cents. Hence, the proportionate change in price is 10/75 = 0.13 = 13%. Accordingly, the price elasticity of Luna's short-run supply is 0.15/0.13 = 1.15.

Properties

The price elasticity of supply is a pure number that does not depend on any units of measure. Generally, the individual supply curves of businesses selling goods and services slope upward. Hence, the price elasticity of supply is a positive number that ranges from 0 to infinity.

If the price elasticity is less than 1, then a 1% increase in price will lead to less than a 1% increase in quantity supplied. In this case, the supply is inelastic. By contrast, if the price elasticity is more than 1, then a 1% increase in price will lead to more than a 1% increase in quantity supplied. Then, the supply is elastic.

In the case of human beings selling labor, the price of the service is the wage; hence, we measure sensitivity by the wage elasticity of supply. As mentioned in the preceding section, the supply curve of labor may slope downward at some wage levels. Then, the wage elasticity is negative.

From a managerial standpoint, the price elasticity is a handy way of characterizing the sensitivity of sellers to changes in price without worrying about choosing appropriate units of measure. For instance, a human resource manager may want to know whether unionized workers are more or less sensitive to changes in wages than nonunion workers. The manager can address this question by comparing the wage elasticities of the two groups.

When comparing the supplies of different items or even quantities supplied of the same item at different prices, it is important to remember that these comparisons are relative, because the price elasticity may vary along the same supply curve. A change in price, by moving from one point on a supply curve to another, may lead to a change in the price elasticity. Similarly, a change in any of the factors that affect supply may affect the price elasticity.

Intuitive Factors

The price elasticity of supply depends on the extent of capacity relative to current production. For instance, a seller that has considerable excess capacity will step up production in response to even a small increase in price. In this case,

Table 4.7 Price elasticities of supply

Product	Time Horizon	Price Elasticity	Source
Automobiles			
Distillate (heating oil)	Short run	1.57	Considine (1992)
Gasoline	Short run	1.61	Considine (1992)
Pork	Long run	0.23	Holt & Skold (1989)
Tobacco	Long run	7.00	Fulginiti & Perrin (1993)

Sources: Timothy J. Considine, "A Short-Run Model of Petroleum Product Supply," *Energy Journal* 13, no. 2 (1992): pp. 61–91.
Lilyan Fulginiti and Richard Perrin, "The Theory and Measurement of Producer Response Under Quotas," *Review of Economics and Statistics* 75, no. 1 (February 1993): pp. 97–105.
Matthew T. Holt and Karl D. Skold, "Dynamic Elasticities and Flexibilities in a Quarterly Model of the U.S. Pork Sector," *Applied Economics* 21, no. 12 (December 1989): pp. 1683–1700.

the individual supply will be relatively elastic. On the other hand, if capacity is tight, the seller may not increase production very much even if the price rises substantially. Hence, when capacity is tight, the individual supply will be relatively inelastic. Capacity utilization affects the elasticity of both individual and market supply.

The price elasticity of supply also depends on time. In the short run, some inputs may be costly or impossible to change. Consequently, the marginal cost of production is very steep. For instance, a factory wishing to step up production immediately may have to engage the workforce on overtime. Since overtime rates are 50–100% higher than regular wage rates, the marginal cost of overtime work is relatively high. With sufficient time, however, the factory could hire more workers at the regular wage. Accordingly, in the long run, the marginal cost of production will slope more gently.

Generally, the long-run supply is relatively more elastic than the short-run supply. This applies to both individual and market supply. Table 4.7 presents the price elasticities of the market supply for several products in the United States.

Forecasting Changes in Production and Revenue

We can use the price elasticity of supply to calculate the effect of changes in price on production and revenue for an individual seller as well as the entire market. A change in price will affect revenue both directly and also through changing the sales or quantity supplied. Generally, the percentage change in revenue is the percentage change in price plus the percentage change in sales or quantity supplied.

To illustrate, let us calculate how a 5% increase in the price of eggs will affect Luna's production and revenue. Earlier, we estimated that the price elasticity of Luna's short-run supply was 1.15. The price elasticity of supply is the percentage by which the quantity supplied will change if the price rises by 1%. Hence, if the price of eggs increases by 5%, the quantity supplied will change by $1.15 \times 5 = 5.8\%$; that is, the quantity supplied will increase by 5.8%.

The percentage change in revenue is the percentage change in price plus the percentage change in sales or quantity supplied. Hence, for Luna, the percentage change in revenue is $5 + 5.8 = 10.8\%$.

Progress Check 4G Referring to Figure 4.13, suppose that, if the price were 90 cents per dozen, Luna would supply 6500 dozen. Calculate the price elasticity of supply for an increase in price from 80 to 90 cents.

Progress check

Gasoline Supply

Using the relevant elasticities of supply, we can address the issue of how changes in the price of gasoline and wages would affect the short-run supply of gasoline by oil refineries. The price elasticity of gasoline supply has been estimated to be 1.61, while the elasticity of gasoline supply with respect to wages has been estimated to be −0.05.

Hence, a 5% increase in the price of gasoline would change quantity supplied by $1.61 \times 5 = 8\%$, while a 10% increase in the wage would change supply by $-0.05 \times 10 = -0.5\%$. Thus, the net effect of both changes is to change the quantity of gasoline supplied by $8 - 0.5 = 7.5\%$.

9 Summary

A small seller, which cannot affect the market price, maximizes profit by producing at a rate where its marginal cost equals the price. In the short run, at least one input cannot be adjusted. The business breaks even when total revenue covers variable cost. In the long run, the business can adjust all inputs and leave or enter the industry. It breaks even when total revenue covers total cost.

The supply curve shows the quantity supplied as a function of price, other things equal. A change in price is represented by a movement along the supply curve to a new quantity. Changes in other factors such as wages and the prices of other inputs are represented by shifts of the entire supply curve.

Seller surplus is the difference between revenue from some production rate and the minimum amount necessary to induce the seller to produce that quantity. Elasticities of supply measure the responsiveness of supply to changes in underlying factors that affect supply.

Key concepts

short run	average (unit) cost	market supply curve
long run	marginal product	seller surplus
fixed cost	marginal revenue	elasticity of supply
variable cost	total revenue	price elasticity of supply
total cost	sunk cost	
marginal cost	individual supply curve	

Further Reading

For the role of individual persons in supplying labor and savings, refer to Chapter 5, "The Household as Supplier," of the book by Michael Katz and Harvey Rosen, *Microeconomics*, 2d ed., (Homewood, IL: Irwin, 1994).

Review Questions

1. Explain the distinction between the short run and long run. How is this related to the distinction between fixed and variable costs?

2. Comment on the following statement: "It costs our factory an average of $2 to produce a piece of clothing. If you ask me how much it would cost to step up the production rate, I would say $2 per piece."

3. Presently, Mercury Oil is producing 2000 barrels of crude oil a day. The price is $15 per barrel. Its marginal cost is $20 per barrel. How can Mercury increase its profit?

4. Does the following analysis under- or overestimate the change in profit? Presently, the price of eggs is 60 cents per dozen. Sharon's farm is producing 10,000 dozen eggs a month with a profit of $2,000. If the price of eggs rises to 70 cents a dozen, Sharon's profit will rise by $1000.

5. Luna Metals uses substantial quantities of diesel fuel to power excavators and dump trucks in its silver mine. How will the following changes affect Luna's average and marginal cost curves?
    a.   An increase in the price of diesel fuel.
    b.   A drop in the price of silver.
    c.   A cut in the wages of workers.

6. Consider the market supply curve of new apartments. For each of the following changes, identify whether the change will cause a movement along the curve or a shift of the entire curve.
    a.   An increase in the price of new apartments.
    b.   An increase in the price of building materials.
    c.   A cut in the wages of construction workers.

7. How can a buyer use the concept of seller surplus to reduce the cost of its purchases?

8. True or false?
   a. When capacity is tight, a seller's supply will be relatively more elastic.
   b. Except for labor, the price elasticity of supply is always positive.

9. Consult a friend who works part-time, say, in the college bookstore or cafeteria.
   a. Suppose that wages are 5% higher. How many more hours would your friend work each year?

   b. Using this information, calculate the wage elasticity of your friend's supply.

10. Consider the price elasticity of the market supply of taxi service. Do you expect supply to be relatively more elastic with respect to fare changes
    a. In the long run?
    b. In the short run?

Discussion Questions

1. Production of injection-molded plastic toys begins with the design and production of a mold. Then the raw material is prepared in molten form and injected into the mold. When the molten plastic cools, the basic molded toy is ready. To finish the toy, the manufacturer attaches other components.
   a. Which of the following costs are fixed and which are variable: (i) production of the mold, (ii) raw material, and (iii) other components?
   b. In a short-run planning horizon, which of the costs in (a) must the manufacturer cover to remain in business?

2. A typical bank's sources of funds include savings deposits, certificates of deposit (CDs), and checking (demand) deposits.
   a. Obtain the current interest rates on savings and checking accounts and CDs from a local bank. Suppose that the bank incurs an additional 1% cost to administer checking accounts. There are no additional administrative costs for savings accounts and CDs. List the three sources of funds in ascending order of annual cost per dollar of funds.
   b. Suppose that the bank has equal amounts of savings and checking depos-

   its and CDs. Compare its average cost of funds with its marginal cost of funds.

3. Table 4.1 shows the weekly expenses of the Luna Farm. Suppose that wages are 5% higher, increasing the cost of labor by 5%.
   a. By recalculating Tables 4.1 and 4.2, explain how the increase in wages will affect the (i) average variable cost and (ii) average cost.
   b. Luna's management claims that it needs a 5% higher price to make up for the wage increase. Assess whether this claim is valid in the (i) short run and (ii) long run.

4. Jupiter Oil produces crude oil from two fields, one in the north and another in the south. Table 4.8 reports the total costs at the two fields for various rates of production.
   a. To produce a total of 5000 barrels per day in the cheapest way, how much should the company produce from the northern field and how much from the southern field?
   b. At the production rates that you give for (a), what is the cost of the last thousand barrels from the northern and the southern fields?

Production Rate (Barrels/day)	Total Cost from:	
	Northern Field	Southern Field
1000	$5,000	$8,000
2000	$11,000	$16,000
3000	$18,000	$24,000
4000	$26,000	$32,000
5000	$35,000	$40,000

Table 4.8 Jupiter Oil

5. Venus Ltd. was finalizing plans for a brick factory. The variable and fixed costs would have been identical to those of Sol Inc.'s existing brick factory. The only difference between the two companies was that Sol had already incurred the fixed cost of its plant, while Venus had not. Then, an industry analyst forecast that the price of bricks would fall by 20% and remain at that level for two years. Sol announced that it would continue production. By contrast, Venus suspended all investment plans.

   a. For a business that can sell as much as it would like at the market price, explain the short-run break-even condition.

   b. For a business that can sell as much as it would like at the market price, explain the long-run break-even condition.

   c. Suppose that the new price is less than Venus' average cost but higher than Sol's average variable cost. Explain why the two companies came to different decisions.

6. This question applies the techniques presented in the math supplement. Let the market supply for aluminium be represented by the equation

   $$S = p - 0.5z - 2,$$

   where S is the quantity supplied in tons a year, p is the price of the aluminium in dollars per ton, and z is the price of electricity.

   a. Suppose that that $z = 5$. Sketch the supply curve.

   b. Illustrate the effect of a change in the price of aluminium from $p = 20$ to $p = 16$.

   c. Illustrate the effect of a change in the price of electricity from $z = 5$ to $z = 2$.

7. Oil exploration is the process of locating oil-producing fields, while production is the process of removing crude oil from the ground. In 1984, Pennzoil Co. entered into an agreement to acquire 1.008 billion barrels of Getty Oil's reserves for $3.4 billion. Shortly after, however, Getty accepted a higher offer from Texaco, Inc. Pennzoil then sued Texaco for interference with contract. Pennzoil claimed that its damages were 1.008 billion barrels times $10.87, which had been its average exploration cost, less the proposed acquisition cost of $3.4 billion. The price of West Texas Intermediate Crude was $30 per barrel in 1984. (*Texaco, Inc. v. Pennzoil, Co.*, Court of Appeals, First District, Houston, 729 S.W. 2d, p. 768)

a. Suppose that the future price of oil is $30 per barrel, while the production cost from the Getty fields is a constant $5, $10, or $15 per barrel. In each case, what is the profit from producing 1.008 barrels of oil? (Ignore the fact that the profit will be received in the future.)

b. For each case, deduct $3.4 billion from your profit in (a).

c. Which is a more accurate way to estimate Pennzoil's damages, the approach in (b) or that used by Pennzoil?

8. Compile two series of data, one for the price of physical gold and another for an index of gold mining shares, on a monthly basis for the most recent 10-year period. Convert the two series into comparable indexes by rebasing both series to 100 at the beginning of the period.

a. Graph the two series against time.

b. Compare the volatility of the two series.

c. Explain the difference in the volatility.

9. Several studies have estimated the wage elasticity of the market supply of labor among women to be 0.2.

a. By what percentage must wage rates increase for women to supply 10% more labor?

b. By what percentage would that wage increase affect employers' total wage bill for women workers?

10. Suppose that a study of the ocean tanker industry shows that, when tanker rates are 5% higher, the market quantity supplied is 1% higher in the short run and 25% higher in the long run.

a. Calculate the short- and long-run price elasticities of supply.

b. Is demand more or less elastic in the long run than in the short run? Explain your answer.

c. If tanker rates were to fall by 5%, what would be the effect on industry revenues in the (i) short run and (ii) long run?

Chapter 4

Math Supplement

Production Decision

Let us prove that, for a business that can sell as much as it would like at the market price, the profit-maximizing production rate is the one where marginal revenue equals marginal cost. Let q be the rate or scale of production. We express total cost, $C(q)$, as a function of the production rate, q. Let F and $V(q)$ represent fixed and variable costs, respectively. Since the fixed cost does not vary with production, F is not a function of q. Then, total costs

$$C(q) = F + V(q). \tag{4.10}$$

Let p be the price of the product, and $P(q)$ and $R(q)$ represent profit and total revenue, respectively. Profit equals total revenue less total cost:

$$P(q) = R(q) - C(q). \tag{4.11}$$

Now, total revenue is price multiplied by sales (that is, the production rate), $R(q) = pq$; hence,

$$P(q) = pq - C(q). \tag{4.12}$$

To find the profit-maximizing production rate, we differentiate profits with respect to the production rate and set the derivative equal to 0:

$$p - \frac{dC(q)}{dq} = 0. \tag{4.13}$$

Hence, to maximize profits, the business must produce at a rate such that

$$p = \frac{dC(q)}{dq}. \tag{4.14}$$

The right-hand side of condition (4.14) is the derivative of total cost, which is the marginal cost. Hence, the condition states that the business maximizes profit where the price of the product just balances the marginal cost.

Finally, by differentiating the equation (4.10) for fixed and variable costs, we find that marginal cost is just the rate of change of the variable cost:

$$\frac{dC(q)}{dq} = \frac{dV(q)}{dq}. \tag{4.15}$$

Market Supply Curve

Using algebra, we can reinforce our understanding of the market supply curve and especially the effect of changes in price vis-à-vis other factors. Let the market supply for some item be represented by the equation

$$S = p - 0.5z - 3, \tag{4.16}$$

where S is the quantity supplied in units a year, p is the price of the item in dollars per unit, and z is the price of an input.

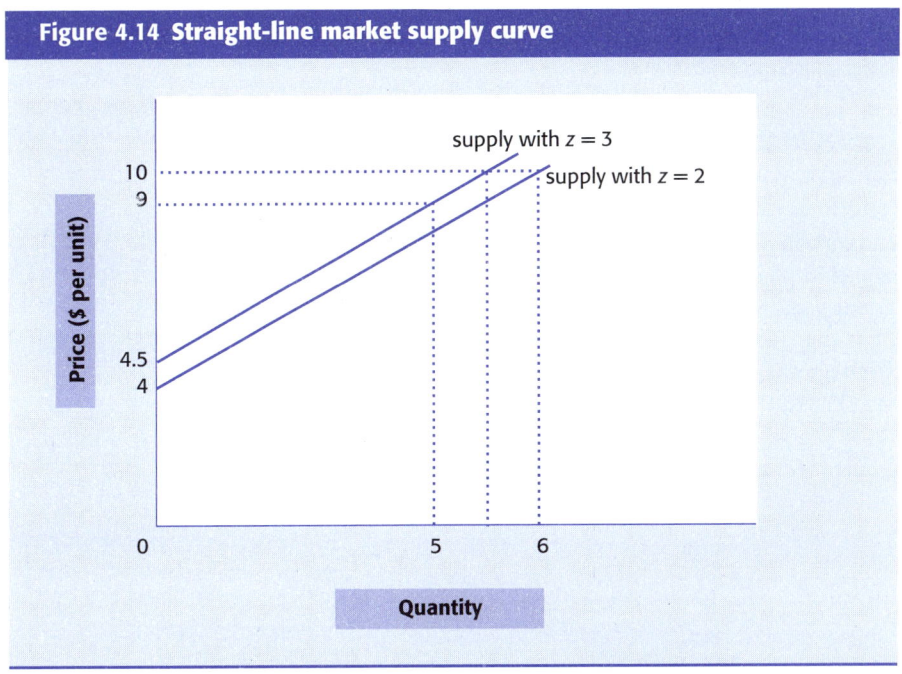

Figure 4.14 Straight-line market supply curve

This supply curve is a straight line. To explain, suppose that $z = 2$. Then, substituting in equation (4.16),

$$S = p - 1 - 3 = p - 4. \qquad (4.17)$$

Differentiating (4.17) with respect to price,

$$\frac{dS}{dp} = 1 \qquad (4.18)$$

which means that the supply equation has a constant slope, or equivalently, that the supply curve is a straight line.

To sketch the supply curve, we consider two points on the curve. First, when the price $p = 10$, the quantity supplied $S = 10 - 4 = 6$. Next, if the quantity supplied is $S = 0$, the price $p = 4$. Marking and joining the two points $p = 10$, $s = 6$ and $p = 4$, $s = 0$ on Figure 4.14, we have the market supply curve.

We can use the supply curve to illustrate the effect of a change in price. For instance, when the price $p = 9$, the quantity supplied $S = 9 - 4 = 5$.

When the price is higher, $p = 10$, the quantity supplied $S = 10 - 4 = 6$. We represent this change by a movement along the supply curve from the point at which $p = 9$ and $S = 5$ to the point at which $p = 10$ and $S = 6$.

The market supply curve in (4.16) can also illustrate the effect of a change in the price of an input. Recall that, originally, the price of the input was $z = 2$. Suppose that the price rises to $z = 3$. Then, referring to (4.16), the supply curve would become

$$S = p - 1.5 - 3 = p - 4.5 . \qquad (4.19)$$

In this case, when the price $p = 10$, the quantity supplied $S = 5.5$; if the quantity supplied $S = 0$, the price $p = 4.5$. Marking and joining these two points on Figure 4.14, we have the supply curve with the input price of $z = 3$. This is a straight line that lies to the left of the supply curve with the input price of $z = 2$. By contrast to a change in price, the change in the input price is represented by a shift of the entire supply curve.

Generally, a change in any factor other than the price of the item is represented by a shift of the entire market supply curve.

Forecasting Quantity Supplied

Using mathematics, we can derive a general formula with which to calculate changes in quantity supplied as a function of the price elasticity and percentage changes in price. Let S represent the average quantity supplied; $\%S$, the percentage change in the quantity supplied; p, the average price; and $\%p$, the percentage change in price. Then, by definition, the price elasticity of supply is

$$s_p = \frac{\%S}{\%p}. \qquad (4.20)$$

We can rearrange the price elasticity as follows:

$$\%S = s_p\, \%p, \qquad (4.21)$$

which says that the percentage change in quantity supplied is the price elasticity multiplied by the percentage change in price.

If there are multiple changes in the factors affecting the quantity supplied, then the net percentage effect on quantity supplied is the sum of the separate effects. Each separate effect is the corresponding elasticity multiplied by the percentage change in the factor.

Competitive Markets

1 Introduction

Bulk carriers carry American exports of grain to markets in China, India, and Russia. The supply of dry bulk cargo service is international and includes American, Asian, and European shipping lines. A shipping line's major variable costs are fuel and labor, while a major fixed cost is the investment in the vessels. Suppose that the cost of fuel drops by 15%. How will this affect the price of bulk cargo service? In particular, will the price of bulk cargo service fall by 15% as well? What will be the effect on the quantity of bulk cargo service?

Suppose that a severe drought has devastated India's production of wheat, leading the government to order emergency purchases of grain from the United States. The additional exports will increase the demand for bulk cargo service to India. How will this affect the price and quantity of bulk cargo service?

Consumer goods manufacturers sell their products through retailers, including supermarkets and grocery stores. Manufacturers charge a wholesale price to retailers, who in turn charge a retail price to consumers. Manufacturers frequently complain that, when they reduce wholesale prices, their retailers do not reduce retail prices by the same amount: The retailers take bigger margins instead of passing on the full reduction to consumers. Some consultants believe that the cause of the problem is a lack of competition among retailers and claim that, if retailing was competitive, then retailers would pass on the full amount of reductions in the wholesale price. Do you agree?

A major issue for manufacturers of industrial products such as cement is whether their prices should include the costs of shipment to the customer. Under one approach, the manufacturer sets an "ex-works" price and leaves the customer to pay the freight. Under an alternative approach, the manufacturer pays the freight and sets an inclusive price. How would the market for cement be affected if manufacturers switched from pricing inclusive of freight to ex-works pricing?

We have posed several questions—how a 15% drop in the cost of fuel and a drought in India will affect the price and quantity of dry bulk cargo service, whether a lack of competition explains why retailers do not pass on the full amount of wholesale price reductions, and how a switch from pricing inclusive of freight to ex-works pricing would affect the market for cement. To answer each of these questions, we must understand demand, supply, and the interaction between the two sides of the market.

At first glance, the need to understand both demand and supply may seem surprising. The drop in the cost of fuel affects the supply of bulk cargo service but not the demand. The Indian drought affects the demand for bulk cargo service but not the supply. Yet, as we shall see, in both of these cases, we cannot get a complete answer unless we consider both sides of the market. The same applies to many other managerial issues: Although the initial change affects only one side of a market, it is necessary to consider the interaction with the other side to obtain a sensible and complete picture.

In this chapter, we combine our earlier analyses of demand and supply to understand how they interact in competitive markets. The central concept is that of market equilibrium. Applying this concept, we can understand the short- and long-run effects of changes in demand and supply. Further, we show how the relevant elasticities of demand and supply can be used to calculate the precise changes. Within this framework, we can explain the effects of a 15% drop in the cost of fuel and a drought in India on the price and quantity of dry bulk cargo service. We show also that a lack of competition cannot explain why retailers do not pass on the full amount of wholesale price reductions.

Finally, we consider the distinction between paying a price and bearing that amount. Within this framework, we show that a switch from from pricing inclusive of freight to ex-works pricing would have no effect on the market for cement.

The demand-supply framework is the core of managerial economics. It can be applied to address business issues in a wide range of markets, including both goods and services, consumer as well as industrial products, and items sold in domestic and international markets. Accordingly, it is important to understand this framework very well.

2 *Perfect Competition*

In the preceding chapters, we developed the concepts of demand and supply. Recall that a market demand curve shows, for every possible price, the quantity that all buyers will purchase. When deriving a demand curve, we implicitly assume that every buyer can purchase as much as he or she would like at the going price and that all buyers pay the same price. Similarly, when deriving a market supply curve, we implicitly assume that every seller can deliver as much as he or she would like at the going price and that all sellers receive the same price.

Let us now make explicit the assumptions underlying the concepts of demand and supply. Generally, demand-supply analysis applies to markets in which competition is very keen in the sense of the following five conditions: the product is homogeneous; there are many buyers, each of whom purchases a quantity that is small relative to the market; there are many sellers, each of whom supplies a quantity that is small relative to the market; new buyers and sellers can enter freely, and existing buyers and sellers can exit freely; and all buyers and all sellers have equal information about market conditions.

Collectively, these five conditions define **perfect competition**. The adjective *perfect* is not intended in a normative sense. A more appropriate name for *perfect competition* would be *extreme competition*. The term *perfect competition*, however, has been universally adopted, hence we follow the established usage.

In principle, the concepts of demand and supply curves are valid only in a perfectly competitive market. In practice, however, the demand-supply framework can be applied even to markets that do not perfectly meet the five conditions. When applying the framework in such markets, we must check how the implications of the analysis might be sensitive to the particular conditions.

We shall treat the terms *perfect competition* and *demand-supply framework* as synonymous. Let us now review the five conditions for perfect competition.

A market is said to be in **perfect competition** if

1. Its products are homogeneous.
2. It includes many buyers, each purchasing a small quantity.
3. It includes many sellers, each supplying a small quantity.
4. Buyers and sellers can enter and exit freely.
5. All buyers and all sellers have equal information.

Homogeneous Product

Competition in a market where products are differentiated is not as keen as that in a market where products are homogeneous. Gold is a homogeneous commodity. Gold mined in North America is a perfect substitute for gold from Australia, Brazil, South Africa, or any other part of the world. If Echo Bay Mines, a North American gold producer, tries to sell its gold at even 1% above the prevailing world market price, absolutely no one would buy. By the same token, if Echo Bay Mines offered its gold at 1% less than the market price, it would be swamped with more orders than it could meet. The price of gold from any source is exactly the same.

Let us contrast gold with mineral water. Mineral water is not homogeneous. Water from different sources has a different chemical composition and hence different taste and therapeutic effect. Even mineral waters that are chemically identical need not be homogeneous. For instance, two waters from nearby sources may be chemically identical but differentiated through brand marketing.

Owing to the chemical and marketing differentiation, Evian can raise its price by 1% without worrying that all its consumers would switch to other brands. Likewise, if Evian reduced its price by 1%, its sales would increase but not so much as to exhaust production capacity. The same is true for other manufacturers of mineral water. Consequently, there is no uniform price for mineral water: Different manufacturers may charge different prices. In general, competition among manufacturers of mineral water is relatively weaker than competition among gold mines.

Many Buyers Purchasing Small Quantities

The second condition for perfect competition is that there are many buyers, each of whom purchases a quantity that is small relative to the market. In such a market, no buyer can get a lower price than others; hence, all buyers face the same price. This means that all buyers compete on the same level playing field.

To illustrate this condition, let us compare the market for gold with that for uranium. There are countless buyers of gold, ranging from Indian villagers to Paris jewelers. The purchases of each buyer are very small relative to the world stock. No one buys enough to get an especially low price. Rather, every buyer pays the same world price.

Market power is the power of a buyer or seller to influence market conditions.

By contrast, buyers in the market for uranium are relatively few. Some buyers, such as the defense organizations of the nuclear powers, are so big that they can get lower prices. A buyer or seller that can influence market conditions is said to have **market power**. In a market where some buyers have market power, different buyers pay different prices: The buyers with market power get lower prices. The buyers do not compete on a level playing field.

Let us now see why we must have the second condition to construct a market demand curve. A market demand curve shows, for every possible price, the total quantity that buyers will purchase. Suppose that all buyers are small buyers. Then, for every possible price, the quantity that buyers collectively will buy is the sum of the quantities that each individual buyer will purchase at that price. By considering all possible prices, we can construct a market demand curve.

Suppose, however, some buyers have market power and get lower prices. Then, different buyers pay different prices. Moreover, a buyer with market power can affect the price that it pays. A buyer with market power cannot answer the question, "How much would you buy, assuming that you could buy as much as you would like at the going price?" Such a buyer cannot answer this question because it can affect the going price. Thus, when some buyers have market power, it is not possible to construct a market demand curve.

Many Sellers Supplying Small Quantities

The third condition for perfect competition is that there are many sellers, each of whom supplies a quantity that is small relative to the market. The logic for this condition is similar to that for requiring many small buyers. In a market where there are many sellers, all of whom are small, no seller has market power. This means that no seller can get a higher price than others; hence, they all face the same price. All sellers compete on the same level playing field. The condition that there are many sellers supplying small quantities also is necessary to construct a market supply curve.

We can illustrate this condition by comparing the markets for silver and platinum. There are many producers of silver throughout the world, in North and South America, Africa, Asia, and Australia. None of these has market power. By contrast, three South African companies and Russia dominate the world production of platinum. Each of these four producers has substantial market power. Accordingly, the market for silver is much more competitive than that for platinum.

Free Entry and Exit

The fourth condition for perfect competition is that new buyers and sellers can enter freely, and existing buyers and sellers can exit freely. In particular, this means that no technological, legal, or regulatory barriers constrain entry or exit. To explain this condition, let us focus on free entry by new sellers and free exit by existing sellers. The logic for free entry and exit among buyers is quite similar.

Consider a market with free entry and exit. As we saw in Chapter 4 on market supply, if the market price rises above a seller's average cost, then new sellers will be attracted to enter. This will add to the market supply and bring down the price. Hence, with free entry and exit, the market price cannot stay above a seller's average cost for very long. The market will be very competitive.

To illustrate, let us contrast the market for Internet service in Singapore and Hong Kong. Both territories are highly urbanized with well-educated populations. Hong Kong has about twice as many people as Singapore. Hong Kong, however, has almost 20 times as many Internet service providers. The explanation for the difference is government regulation of licenses for Internet service providers. Hong Kong issues licenses much more liberally than Singapore. Consequently, Hong Kong has proportionately more providers of Internet service, and the degree of competition among them is much keener than in Singapore.

The degree of competition also depends on barriers to exit. Suppose that an Internet service provider must pay the government a compensation fee to cease service. It must consider this exit cost when deciding whether to enter the market. Therefore, the higher such exit costs, the less likely new providers are to enter the market; hence, the less competitive the market will be.

Equal Information

The fifth condition for perfect competition is that all buyers and all sellers have equal information about market conditions such as prices, available substitutes, and technology. With equally distributed information, every seller or buyer will be subject to intense competition. If, for instance, a new supplier offers a key input at a lower price, then, immediately, every producer will get the same lower price. No seller can enjoy the privilege of secret information.

Photocopying service is a mature industry. Information about market conditions is widely and evenly available among buyers as well as sellers. As a result, the market is extremely competitive.

By contrast, information is not equally distributed in the market for medical services. Patients rely on their doctors for advice about their health problems and recommended treatment. In this market, sellers (doctors) have better information than buyers (patients). There may be differences in information on the supply side as well as between the two sides of the market. Doctors who attend continuing education and read the latest journals may have better information than others. Better-informed doctors may offer more effective advice and treatment than less well-informed doctors.

Markets where there are differences in information among buyers, or among sellers, or between buyers and sellers are not as competitive as those where all buyers and all sellers have equal information.

Progress check

Progress Check 5A Explain why it is possible to construct a market supply curve only if there are many sellers, each of whom supplies a quantity that is small relative to the market.

Regulatory Barriers to Competition: The Japanese Beer Market

With annual consumption of 7 billion liters (1.5 billion gallons), the market for beer in Japan is one of the world's largest. Compared with other markets, there is little physical differentiation: "Japan's beers all taste pretty much the same. Whether your glass contains Kirin, Suntory, Sapporo, or Asahi, you would be hard pressed to distinguish" ("Japan Rolls out the Barrels," *Asian Business* [September 1994], p. 72).

At the time of writing, however, the market was far from competitive. The four domestic manufacturers controlled over a 95% share. The reason was government regulation. Breweries must have a license from the Ministry of Finance. Until 1994, the ministry would issue licenses only for production of a minimum of 2 million liters a year. Retail stores also must have a ministry license to sell alcohol. The ministry limited licenses to small family-owned stores that tended to stick with the big four brewers.

The ministry's regulations on breweries prevented the entry of new domestic brewers. Further the restrictions on retail sales hampered foreign brewers that could offer beer at half the Japanese price.

In April 1994, the ministry lowered the threshold for brewery licenses to production of 60,000 liters a year. This led to the rapid entry of numerous specialty breweries. In addition, the ministry also liberalized the regulations on retail sales of alcohol. In 1997, the ministry will freely permit any store larger than 10,000 square meters (107,600 square feet) to sell beer. This will further open the market to competition from domestic as well as foreign brewers.

Source: "Only Here for the Biru," The Economist (May 14, 1994), pp. 69–71.

3 Market Equilibrium

We have reviewed the five conditions for perfect competition. If a market meets these conditions, we can validly apply the concepts of demand and supply. We now introduce the concept of market equilibrium, which unifies demand and supply. **Market equilibrium** is the price at which the quantity demanded equals the quantity supplied. The concept of equilibrium is the basis for all analyses of how changes in demand or supply affect market prices and quantities.

Market equilibrium is the price at which the quantity demanded equals the quantity supplied.

Demand and Supply

To illustrate the concept of equilibrium, consider the market for bulk cargo service. Shippers generate the demand, and shipping lines provide the supply.

Suppose that this market meets the five conditions for perfect competition. Using a graph, we mark the price of bulk cargo service in dollars per ton-mile on the vertical axis and the quantity of bulk cargo service in millions of ton-miles a year on the horizontal axis. (One ton-mile represents the carriage of one ton over a distance of one mile.) Then, we draw the demand for and the supply of bulk cargo service.

As emphasized in Chapter 2, the demand curve slopes downward. From Chapter 4, we know that, depending on the circumstances, the supply curve is flat or slopes upward. In this case, we suppose that the the supply curve slopes upward. In Figure 5.1, consider the point at which the demand and the supply curves cross. That point represents the market equilibrium: the price at which the quantity demanded just balances the quantity supplied.

Suppose that the equilibrium in the market for bulk cargo service is at a price of $20 per ton-mile and quantity of 10 million ton-miles a year. Referring to Figure 5.1, the demand curve shows that, at the price of $20, buyers want to purchase a total of 10 million ton-miles a year. The supply curve in Figure 5.1 shows that, at the price of $20, sellers want to supply a total of 10 million ton-miles a year. The quantity that buyers want to purchase exactly balances the quantity that sellers want to supply.

Figure 5.1 Market equilibrium

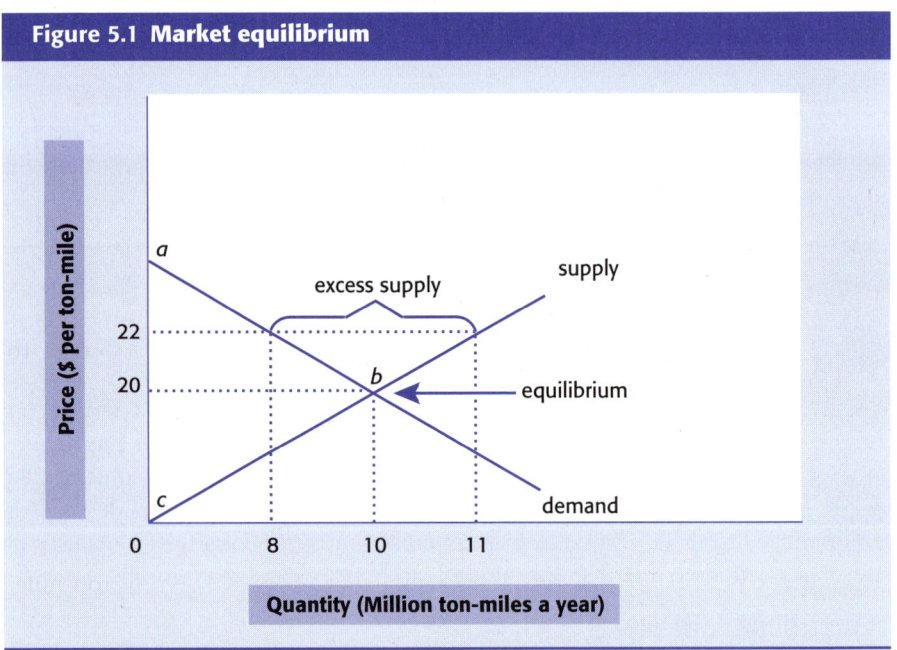

At the price of $20 per ton-mile, the quantity demanded is 10 million ton-miles a year and the quantity supplied is the same. When the price is $22 per ton-mile, the quantity supplied exceeds the quantity demanded by 3 million ton-miles a year.

At the market equilibrium, there is no tendency for price, purchases, or sales to change. The price will not tend to change because the quantity demanded of 10 million ton-miles just balances the quantity supplied of 10 million ton-miles. Purchases will not tend to change because, at the price of $20, buyers (shippers) maximize benefits less expenditure by purchasing 10 million ton-miles. Further, sales will not tend to change because, at the price of $20, sellers (shipping lines) maximize profits by supplying 10 million ton-miles.

Excess Supply

What happens when the market is not in equilibrium? Then, generally, the market price will tend to change in such a way as to restore equilibrium. For instance, suppose that the market price is $2 above equilibrium, at $22 per ton-mile. Then, referring to the demand curve in Figure 5.1, buyers would cut back purchases to 8 million ton-miles a year. The supply curve in Figure 5.1 shows that, at a price of $22, sellers would supply more, specifically 11 million ton-miles a year.

Hence, at a price of $22 per ton-mile, the quantity supplied would exceed the quantity demanded by 11 − 8 = 3 million ton-miles a year. In more colorful terms, there would be too many ships chasing too few customers. We give the name **excess supply** to the amount by which the quantity supplied exceeds the quantity demanded. So, at a price of $22, there would be an excess supply of 3 million ton-miles a year. In a situation of excess supply, the market price will tend to fall. Shipping lines would compete to clear their extra capacity and the market price would drop back toward the equilibrium level of $20.

> The **excess supply** is the amount by which the quantity supplied exceeds the quantity demanded.

From Figure 5.1, it is clear that, if the price were even higher, at $25 per ton-mile, the excess supply would be even larger than the excess supply at a price of $22. Generally, the higher is the price above the equilibrium level, the larger will be the excess supply.

Excess Demand

Another way in which the market can be out of equilibrium is when the price is below the equilibrium level. In this case, the market price will tend to rise. To illustrate, suppose that in the market for bulk cargo service, the price is $18 dollars per ton-mile. Further, suppose that, at the price of $18, buyers would purchase 12 million ton-miles a year, and sellers would supply 9 million ton-miles a year. Then, the quantity demanded would exceed the quantity supplied by 12 − 9 = 3 million ton-miles a year.

We give the name **excess demand** to the amount by which the quantity demanded exceeds the quantity supplied. Hence, at a price of $18 per ton-mile, there would be excess demand of 3 million ton-miles a year. Faced with this excess demand, buyers would compete for the limited capacity and the market price would rise toward the equilibrium level of $20. Generally, the lower is the price below the equilibrium level, the larger will be the excess demand.

> The **excess demand** is the amount by which the quantity demanded exceeds the quantity supplied.

Progress check
Progress Check 5B In Figure 5.1, illustrate the excess demand if the price is $16 per ton-mile. Mark the quantities demanded and supplied.

Significance of Equilibrium

We focus on equilibrium for two reasons. First, as we have seen, if a market is not in equilibrium, either buyers or sellers will push the market toward equilibrium. Second, by comparing equilibria, we can achieve a firm understanding of a wide range of questions like, "If the price of a related product, the cost of inputs, or government policy were different, how would that affect the market for my product?" To address such questions, we compare the market equilibrium under the original circumstances to the equilibrium under the new set of parameters. When prices are quite flexible, the market will adjust to the new equilibrium fairly quickly, so comparing equilibria is a fairly accurate method of analysis.

As earlier chapters have emphasized, the demand side of a market may consist of either people or businesses, and similarly, the supply side may consist of either people or businesses. The concept of market equilibrium is the same whether buyers are people or businesses and whether sellers are people or businesses. The market equilibrium is the price at which the quantity demanded just balances the quantity supplied.

For a market to be in equilibrium, both the quantity demanded and the quantity supplied must be the result of voluntary choices by buyers and sellers, respectively. As we shall see in Chapter 6, if buyers are restricted to a particular quantity that they would not voluntarily demand, then the market will not be in equilibrium. Similarly, if sellers are restricted to a particular quantity that they would not voluntarily supply, then the market will not be in equilibrium.

In practice, very few markets exactly satisfy the five conditions for perfect competition. This means that demand-supply analysis does not precisely apply. Nevertheless, we can still apply this method of analysis: Many of the managerial implications are the same even if a market is not perfectly competitive. However, we must be careful to check the implications against the conditions that the market does not satisfy.

4 *Supply Shift*

In general, changes in economic variables such as the prices of inputs or changes in government policies will cause shifts in demand, supply, or both. Even if the change superficially appears to affect only one side of the market, it is essential to analyze the effects on the other side as well. As we shall soon see, an analysis that ignores the other side of the market could be seriously misleading.

In this section, we consider the effect of a change that shifts the supply curve. Specifically, the introduction to this chapter asked how a 15% drop in the cost of fuel would affect the price of bulk cargo service. Let us apply the demand-supply framework to address this question.

Since the question concerns the price of bulk cargo service, we focus on this market. We need to start from the equilibrium before the change in fuel cost. Suppose that, before the change in fuel cost, the price of cargo service was $20 per ton-mile and the quantity purchased was 10 million ton-miles a year.

Equilibrium Change

Fuel is a major input into the supply of cargo service. The supply curve of cargo service does not explicitly show the cost of fuel. Accordingly, any change in the cost of fuel will shift the entire supply curve. Suppose that, before the change in fuel cost, the average fuel cost of cargo service were $4 per ton-mile. Now, the cost of fuel drops by 15% or 60 cents per ton-mile. This would cause the entire supply curve of bulk cargo service to shift downward by 60 cents per ton-mile. We represent this shift in Figure 5.2.

The entire supply curve shifts down because the reduction in fuel cost affects sellers' marginal costs whatever the quantity that they supply. Another way of looking at the impact of the change in fuel cost is that it shifts the supply curve to the right: At every possible price, sellers want to supply more.

The change in fuel cost, however, does not affect the demand for cargo service. Referring to Figure 5.2, the new supply curve crosses the unchanged

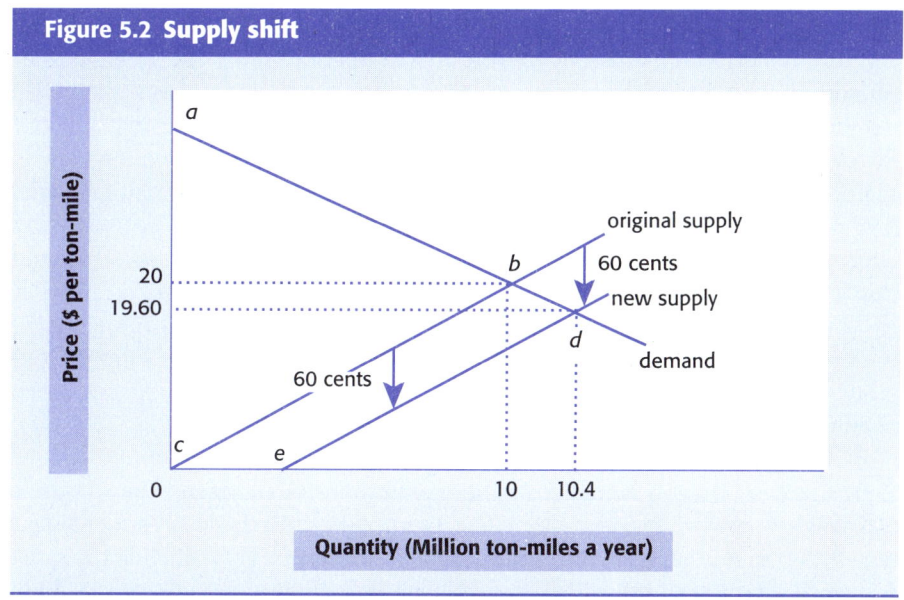

Figure 5.2 Supply shift

When the cost of fuel drops 60 cents per ton-mile, the entire supply curve shifts downward by 60 cents. At the new equilibrium, the price is $19.60 per ton-mile and the quantity is 10.4 million ton-miles a year.

demand curve at a new equilibrium point d, where the price is $19.60 per ton-mile. The fall in price from $20 to $19.60 increases the quantity demanded from 10 to 10.4 million ton-miles a year. On the new supply curve, at the price of $19.60, the quantity supplied is 10.4 million ton-miles a year. The price of $19.60 is the new market equilibrium.

Price Elasticities

In the example of the bulk cargo market, when the supply curve shifted down by 60 cents, the equilibrium price fell by only 40 cents. Generally, a downward or upward shift in the supply curve will change the equilibrium price by no more than the amount of the supply shift. What determines the extent of the change in price? We shall show that the change in the equilibrium price depends on the price elasticities of demand and supply.

Consider Figure 5.3(a), which depicts an extremely inelastic demand. This means that buyers are completely insensitive to the price: They purchase the same quantity regardless of the price. Accordingly, when the supply curve shifts, the buyers do not change their behavior—they continue to purchase exactly the same quantity. In Figure 5.3(a), when the supply curve shifts down by 60 cents, the equilibrium price drops by exactly 60 cents to $19.40 per ton-mile.

Regarding the market demand curve, the other extreme is an extremely elastic demand, as depicted in Figure 5.3(b). This means that buyers are extremely sensitive to price. When the supply curve shifts, the buyers soak up all the additional quantity supplied. Consequently, the equilibrium price does not change at all. In Figure 5.3(b), when the supply shifts down by 60 cents, the equilibrium price remains unchanged at $20 per ton-mile. The new equilibrium quantity is 10.6 million.

Realistically, however, the market demand probably is somewhat but not extremely sensitive to price. If there is an increase in supply, some buyers will switch from other forms of transport to bulk cargo service, while existing buyers may purchase more. Hence, when the supply curve shifts down, the price will fall but by less than the downward shift. Likewise, if the supply curve should shift up, the market price will rise but by less than the upward shift.

By comparing Figures 5.3(a) and (b), we can see the relationship between the price elasticity of demand and the price response to a shift in supply. Generally, if the demand is more elastic, then the change in the equilibrium price resulting from a shift in supply will be smaller.

Let us next see how the change in the equilibrium price depends on the price elasticity of supply. Figure 5.3(c) depicts an extremely inelastic supply. This means that sellers are completely insensitive to the price: They provide the same quantity regardless of the price. In particular, if their costs change, they will not change the quantity supplied. Referring to Figure 5.3(c) for the bulk cargo market, shipping lines supply 10 million ton-miles a year whatever the market price. Consequently, the change in fuel cost does not change the equilibrium price.

Figure 5.3 Price elasticities of demand and supply

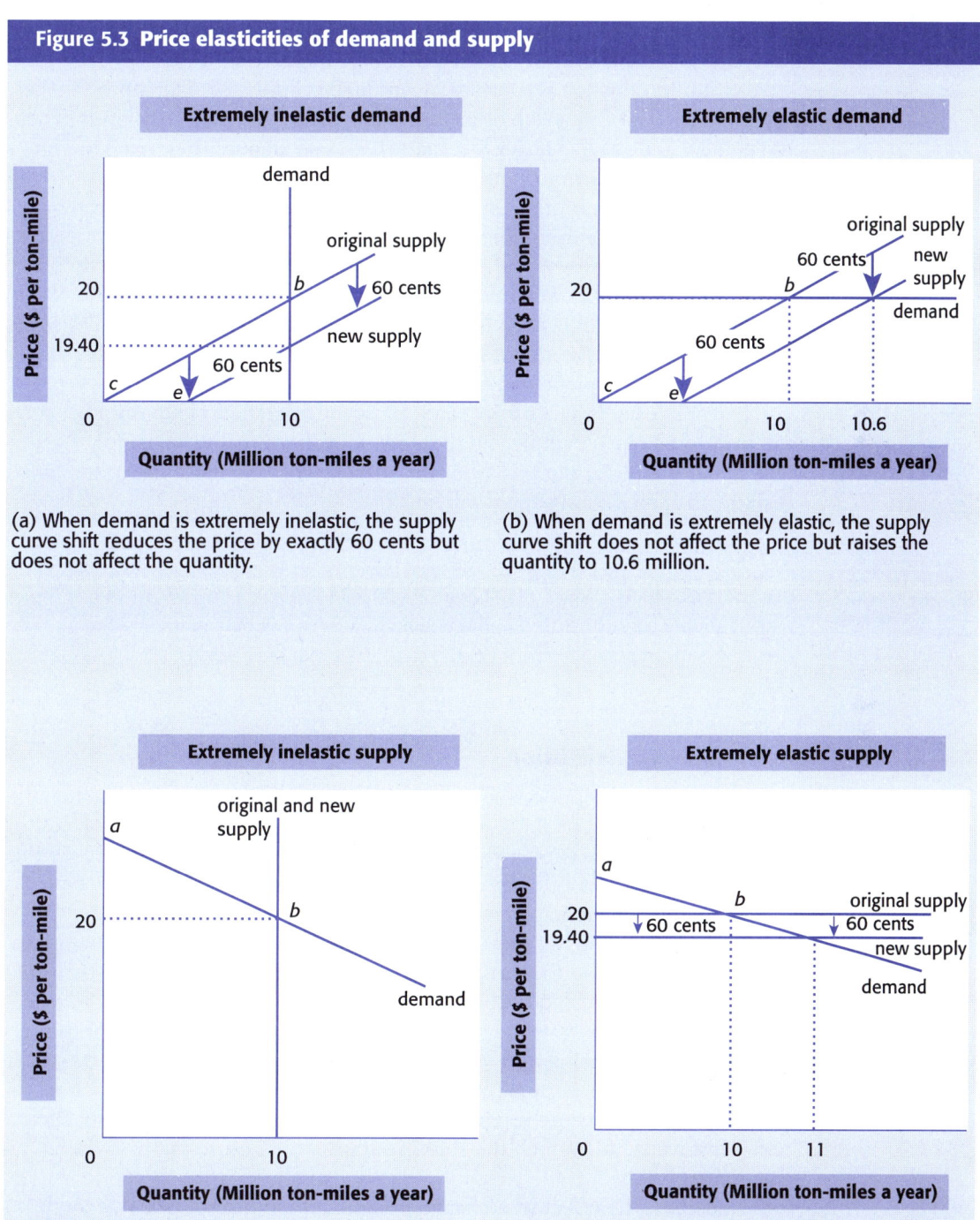

(a) When demand is extremely inelastic, the supply curve shift reduces the price by exactly 60 cents but does not affect the quantity.

(b) When demand is extremely elastic, the supply curve shift does not affect the price but raises the quantity to 10.6 million.

(c) When supply is extremely inelastic, the supply curve does not shift.

(d) When supply is extremely elastic, the supply curve shift reduces the price by exactly 60 cents and raises the quantity to 11 million.

Regarding the market supply curve, the other extreme is an extremely elastic supply, as depicted in Figure 5.3(d). This means that, essentially, the marginal cost of production is constant. Accordingly, if the cost of an input changes, the marginal cost changes by the same amount at all production levels. Then, the equilibrium price changes by exactly the same amount. Referring to Figure 5.3(d) for the bulk cargo market, when the supply curve shifts down by 60 cents, the equilibrium price drops by exactly 60 cents per ton-mile. The quantity rises to 11 million ton-miles a year.

Realistically, however, the supply of bulk cargo service is sensitive to price: To supply more service requires more capacity and, so, higher costs. An elastic supply means that sellers can increase service with some increase in costs. So, when the supply curve shifts down, the price will fall. Likewise, if the supply curve should shift up, the market price will rise.

By comparing Figures 5.3(c) and (d), we can see the relationship between the price elasticity of supply and the price response to a shift in supply. Generally, if the supply is more elastic, then the change in the equilibrium price resulting from a shift in supply will be larger.

Progress check   **Progress Check 5C** Which of (1) and (2) is true? For a given downward shift of the market supply curve, the drop in the equilibrium price will be larger if (1) the demand is more price elastic or (2) the supply is more price elastic.

Common Misconception

A common misconception is that, if sellers' costs fall by some amount, then the market price will fall by the same amount. For instance, a change in the cost of fuel affects only the supply side of the bulk cargo service market. Does this mean that, if the cost of cargo service drops by 60 cents, then the price would fall by the same amount?

Such simple thinking overlooks the impact of the shift in supply on buyers. If they are insensitive to price, then they will not buy more; hence, the price will drop by the entire 60 cents. If, however, they are very sensitive to price, then the shift in supply would result in no change to the equilibrium price.

The simple thinking also overlooks the price sensitivity of sellers. If sellers are insensitive to price, then the drop in cost will not induce them to sell more; hence, the price of cargo service will not change at all. If, however, sellers are very sensitive to price, then the shift in supply would cause the price to fall by the entire 60 cents.

Generally, the effect of a change in costs on the market price depends on the price elasticities of both demand and supply. This point is reinforced by the accompanying cases on French exports and retail competition.

Progress Check 5D In Figure 5.2, show how an 80 cent drop in the cost of fuel would affect the supply curve and the equilibrium price.

Progress check

The Demand for French Products: Foie Gras vis-à-vis Butter

France's agricultural exports include foie gras and butter. The supplies of French products to world markets depend on the exchange rate between the French franc and other world currencies, such as the U.S. dollar. If the franc becomes more expensive, the cost of providing French products to world markets and the supply curves will be higher. If, however, the franc becomes cheaper, then the supply curves will be lower.

Suppose that the franc becomes 10% more expensive, causing the supply curves of French foie gras and butter to shift up by 10%. How will these shifts affect the prices of foie gras and butter on world markets?

There are few substitutes for French foie gras; hence, the demand is relatively inelastic. The upward shift of the supply curve will result in a relatively large increase in the world price. By contrast with foie gras, butter is a relatively homogeneous product. There are many close substitutes for French butter, so that the demand is relatively elastic. Accordingly, the upward supply shift curve will result in a relatively small increase in the world price.

Retail Competition and Wholesale Price Cuts

A frequent complaint among consumer goods manufacturers is that, when they reduce wholesale prices, their retailers do not reduce retail prices by the same amount. The retailers take bigger margins instead of passing on the full reduction to consumers. Some consultants believe that the cause of the problem is a lack of competition among retailers and claim that, if retailing were competitive, retailers would pass on the full amount of reductions in the wholesale price.

Let us apply the demand-supply framework to study this argument. Consider, for instance, the retail market for tissues. In this market, consumers generate the demand, while retailers provide the supply. We make the extreme assumption that the market is perfectly competitive. Figure 5.4 represents the demand and supply. The equilibrium is a price of $15 per carton and quantity of 200 million cartons a year.

Figure 5.4 Wholesale price cut

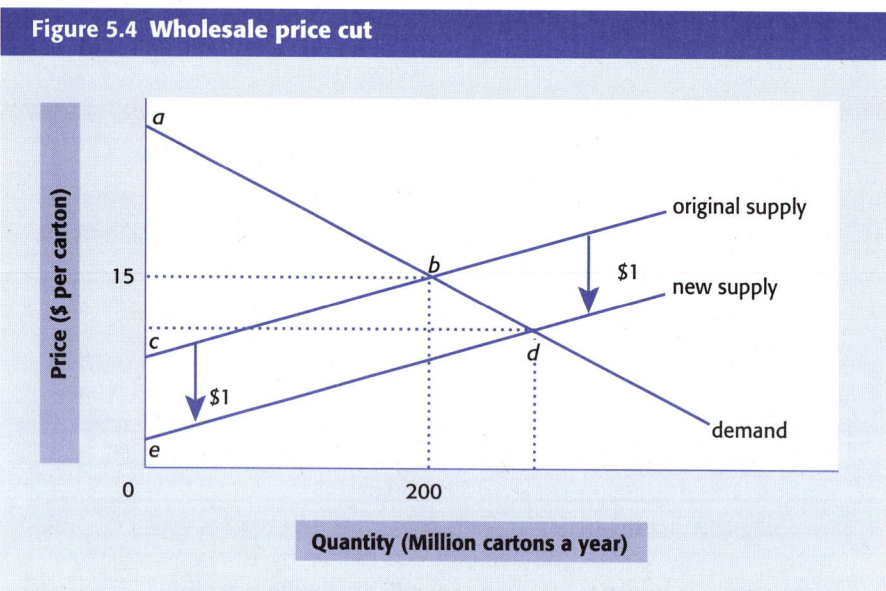

A $1 cut in the wholesale price shifts down the retail supply curve by $1 and results in a lower retail price and larger quantity.

Now suppose that tissue manufacturers reduce the wholesale price by $1 a carton. In the retail market, this will reduce the cost of supplying tissues by $1 at all quantities. Hence, the supply curve will shift down by $1.

Does the market price fall by $1? Only if either the market demand is extremely inelastic or the market supply is extremely elastic. In all other cases, the market price will fall by less than $1.

Recall that we assumed that the retail market was perfectly competitive. And yet we found that, in most cases, the retail price will fall by less than $1 when manufacturers reduce the wholesale price by $1. Accordingly, the reason why retailers absorb part of a cut in wholesale prices is not a lack of competition. The explanation lies in the price elasticities of retail demand and supply.

5 *Demand Shift*

In the case of the market for bulk cargo service, we saw that, to understand the impact of a shift in supply, we had to consider the interaction between supply and demand. Our next application begins with a change that shifts demand. To get a complete understanding of the final outcome, however, it is necessary to consider the supply side as well.

Figure 5.5 Demand shift

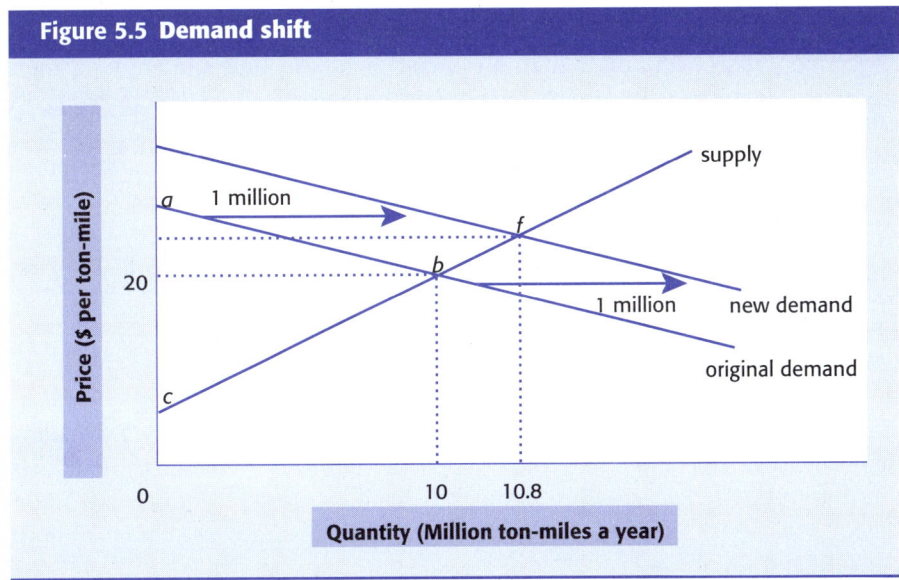

A 1-million ton-mile increase in demand shifts the demand curve to the right and results in a higher price and larger quantity.

Equilibrium Change

The introduction asked how an increase in Indian purchases of American grain would affect the price and quantity of bulk cargo service. Figure 5.5 shows the original equilibrium at point b, with a price of $20 and quantity of 10 million ton-miles a year. Suppose that the increase in Indian purchases increases the demand by 1 million ton-miles at all price levels. Accordingly, in Figure 5.5, the entire demand curve shifts to the right by 1 million ton-miles. The increase in Indian grain purchases, however, does not affect the supply of bulk cargo service. So, the supply curve does not change.

From Figure 5.5, we see that the new demand curve crosses the unchanged supply curve at a new market equilibrium (point f). The new equilibrium has a higher price and a larger quantity of bulk cargo service. By how much will the price rise and by how much will the quantity of new bulk cargo service increase? The answer depends on the price elasticities of both demand and supply.

Since the analysis is very similar to that for a shift in supply, we leave the details to the following progress check.

Progress Check 5E Using Figure 5.5 as a basis, construct a series of four figures to show the effect of the increase in the demand for cargo service on the market price when (a) demand is extremely inelastic, (b) demand is extremely elastic, (c) supply is extremely inelastic, and (d) supply is extremely elastic.

Progress check

Common Misconception

A common misconception is that, if demand increases by some amount, then the market quantity will increase by the same amount. For instance, a change in Indian grain purchases affects only the demand side of the bulk cargo service market. Hence, it is easy to think that, if the demand increases by 1 million ton-miles, then the market equilibrium quantity would increase by the same amount.

This simple thinking overlooks the impact of the shift in demand on sellers: Specifically, what is the marginal cost of providing additional bulk cargo service? The simple thinking also overlooks the price-sensitivity of buyers: How much are they willing to pay for additional service?

Generally, as shown in the answer to Progress Check 5E, the change in market equilibrium resulting from a shift in demand depends on the price elasticities of both demand and supply. When the demand increases by 1 million ton-miles, the market equilibrium quantity would increase by between 0 and 1 million ton-miles. The precise change depends on the price elasticities of both demand and supply.

Demand and Supply on Valentine's Day

People buy greeting cards and roses throughout the year. As Valentine's Day approaches, however, cards and roses become necessities. The demand for both products jumps. Applying demand-supply analysis, we expect the prices of both products to rise. The price of roses, however, always increases much more sharply than the price of greeting cards. Why?

We can explain this disparity by considering the price elasticities of supply in the two markets. The supply of greeting cards on Valentine's Day is much more elastic than the supply of roses. Greeting cards can be stored, so manufacturers can easily step up production and prepare larger stocks ahead of Valentine's Day. This means that the supply of cards is relatively elastic; hence, an increase in demand has little effect on price.

By contrast, roses are perishable. Only roses maturing around Valentine's Day will be suitable for that day. It is relatively costly to increase the quantity supplied on Valentine's Day. This means that the supply is relatively inelastic, and consequently, the increase in demand causes the price to increase sharply.

Source: B. Peter Pashigian, "Demand and Supply on Valentine's Day," in *Price Theory and Applications* (New York: McGraw-Hill, 1995), p. 19.

Demand, Supply, and the Price of Aluminium

Aluminium is a lightweight yet strong material that resists corrosion. It is also an excellent conductor of heat and electricity. The main uses of aluminium are in the construction of aircraft, military equipment, buildings, and home appliances as well as beverage and food containers.

Aluminium is smelted by an electrolytic process from the metal alumina, which is an oxide of aluminium found mainly in deposits of bauxite. The smelting process uses electric power very intensively. Since electricity is costly to transport, smelting tends to be concentrated near sources of cheap electricity. Major aluminium producers include Australia, Canada, the European Union, Norway, Russia, and the United States. The Russian smelters at Bratsk and Krasnoyarsk, with annual capacities of 810,000 and 750,000 tons, respectively, are among the world's largest.

Until 1990, most Russian aluminium was used to produce aircraft and military equipment for the Soviet Union. Beginning in 1991, however, the Russian aluminium industry entered a slide to the brink of disaster. First, the Soviet Union broke up into a number of independent republics. Then, Russia, the largest surviving republic, cut defense spending by 80%. Further, the Russian government dissolved its aluminium marketing organization.

David Ruben, a London metals trader, saw the opportunity to use the Russian production capacity. He arranged for three smelters, including those at Bratsk and Krasnoyarsk, to smelt raw alumina for a "tolling fee." He then exported the finished aluminium to the world market. As a result of these arrangements, Russia's aluminium exports surged from 300,000 tons in 1990 to 1.6 million tons in 1993. This increase in supply coincided with a worldwide economic slowdown. The world price of aluminium plunged below $1200 a ton (see Figure 5.6).

In February 1994, representatives of major aluminium producing countries met in Brussels and agreed to restrain production. Meanwhile, a strong U.S. economic recovery increased the demand for aluminium. As a result, the price of aluminium climbed back above $1500 a ton by the end of 1994.

Source: "Aluminium Prices May Cool Down Due to Industry, Political Factors," *Asian Wall Street Journal* (December 19, 1994), p. 21; "Russian Aluminium: King of the Castle?" *The Economist* (January 21, 1995), pp. 66–7.

6 *Calculating Equilibrium Changes*[1]

In the preceding sections, we have seen how to apply demand-supply analysis to analyze the effect of changes in demand or supply on the market equilibrium.

---

[1]This section is more advanced. It may be omitted without loss of continuity.

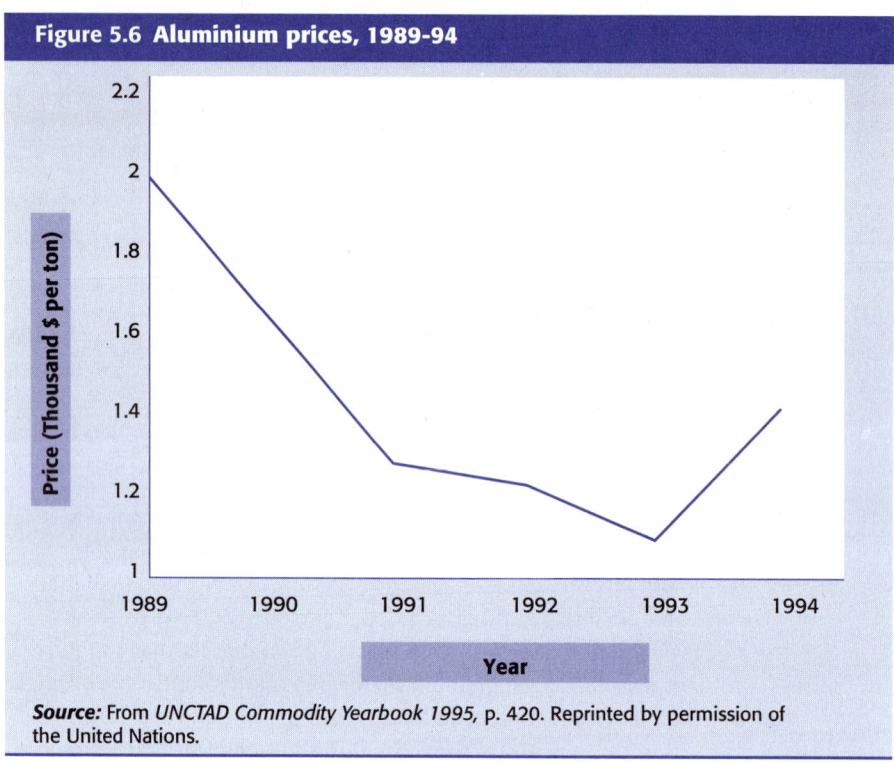

Figure 5.6 Aluminium prices, 1989-94

Source: From *UNCTAD Commodity Yearbook 1995,* p. 420. Reprinted by permission of the United Nations.

An increase in Russian exports and a worldwide economic slowdown caused the price of aluminium to fall from 1990 to 1993. An international agreement to restrain production and a strong U.S. economic recovery lifted the price in 1994.

We emphasized that the effect depends on the elasticities of demand and supply.

To obtain a precise estimate of the effect of the supply shift on the market price and quantity, we need to know either the entire demand and supply curves or the relevant elasticities. As we explained in Chapters 3 and 4, information on elasticities is often more readily available than the entire demand and supply curves. Accordingly, it is important to understand how we can use the elasticities to calculate the effects of shifts in demand and supply on the market price and quantity.

Essentially, we combine the techniques presented in Chapters 3 and 4. Chapter 3 showed how to use elasticities of demand to calculate changes in demand. Chapter 4 showed how to use elasticities of supply to calculate changes in supply. Now we must combine these methods to calculate changes in the market equilibrium.

Using Elasticities

Suppose, for instance, that we would like to know how a 5% increase in the cost of fuel would affect the price of bulk cargo service. Referring to Figure 5.7, in the original equilibrium at point b, the price is $20 per ton-mile and the quantity is 10 million ton-miles. Suppose that the price elasticity of demand is –2, the price elasticity of supply is 1, and the elasticity of supply with respect to the cost of fuel is –0.4.

After the reduction in supply, the market will move to a new equilibrium at point g. Between the original and new equilibria, there will be changes in the market price and quantity demanded. Let %p represent the percentage change in the price. Since the price elasticity of demand is –2, the percentage change in the quantity demanded due to the change in price will be $-2 \times \%p$.

On the supply side of the market, two variables change. First, the quantity supplied will change with the change in the price. Since the price elasticity of supply is 1, the percentage change in the quantity supplied due to the change in price will be $1 \times \%p$. Second, the quantity supplied will change with the 5% increase in the cost of fuel. Since the elasticity of supply with respect to the cost of fuel is –0.4, the percentage change in the quantity supplied due to the change in the cost of fuel will be $-0.4 \times 5 = -2$. Hence, the percentage change in the quantity supplied due to the changes in the price and fuel cost will be $1 \times \%p - 2$.

Referring to Figure 5.7, when the market moves from the original equilibrium at point b to the new equilibrium at point g, the quantities demanded and supplied will change. In the original equilibrium, the quantity demanded equals the quantity supplied. Likewise, in the new equilibrium, the quantity demanded equals the quantity supplied. Accordingly, between the two equilibria, the change in the quantity demanded must equal the change in the quantity supplied.

This implies that the percentage change in the quantity demanded equals the percentage change in the quantity supplied. Since the percentage change in the quantity demanded is $-2 \times \%p$ and the percentage change in the quantity supplied is $1 \times \%p - 2$, the equality means that

$$-2 \times \%p = \%p - 2, \tag{5.1}$$

or %$p = 0.67$. This means that the new price will be 0.67% higher. Now, in the original equilibrium, the price $p = 20$. Hence, in the new equilibrium, the price will be $20 \times 1.0067 = \$20.13$.

Since the percentage change in the quantity demanded is $-2 \times \%p$, it will be $-2 \times 0.67 = -1.34$; that is, a reduction of 1.34%. In the original equilibrium, the quantity was 10 million ton-miles; hence, in the new equilibrium, the quantity will be $10 \times 0.9866 = 9.866$ million ton-miles. Using the elasticities of demand and supply, we have calculated the new equilibrium (point g on Figure 5.7).

Figure 5.7 Supply reduction

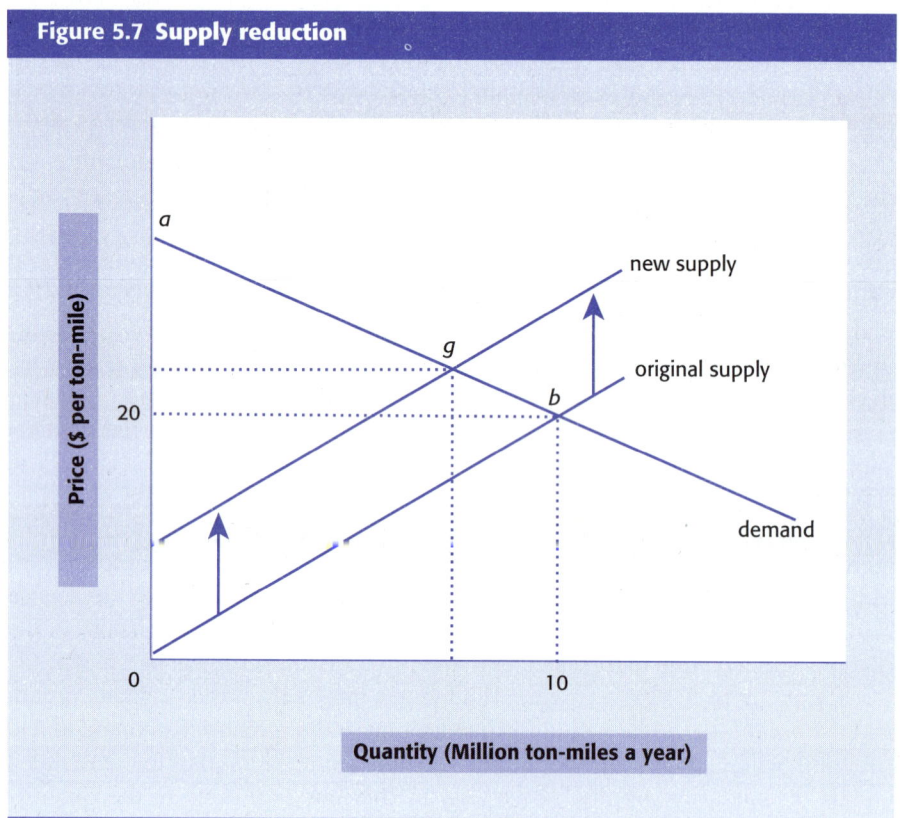

An increase in costs shifts up the supply curve and results in a higher price and smaller quantity.

To calculate changes in the market equilibrium,

1. Calculate the percentage in the quantity demanded.
2. Calculate the percentage change in the quantity supplied.
3. Equate these percentage changes to solve for the percentage change in price.
4. Calculate the percentage change in quantity.

Formula

Generally, the procedure for calculating the changes in the market equilibrium price and quantity is as follows. First, calculate the percentage change in quantity demanded due to changes in the price and other variables. Next, calculate the percentage change in quantity supplied due to changes in the price and other variables. Then, equate the percentage changes in quantity demanded and quantity supplied and solve for the percentage change in price. Finally, use the percentage change in price to calculate the percentage change in quantity. This procedure can be used to make precise estimates of the effects of changes in a variable that affects demand or supply or simultaneous changes in multiple variables.

Progress Check 5F Starting from the equilibrium with a price of $20 per ton-mile and quantity of 10 million, calculate the effect of a 10% reduction in the cost of fuel on the price and quantity of bulk cargo service.

Increasing Demand and the Market for Gasoline

Suppose that the price of gasoline is presently 95 cents per gallon and sales are 500 million gallons a week. How will a 3% increase in household income affect the price and sales of gasoline? Referring to Figure 5.8, the increase in household income will cause the demand for gasoline to shift to the right. The increase in household income, however, will not affect the supply of gasoline. Accordingly, there will be a new market equilibrium with higher price and quantity.

To calculate the new equilibrium using the procedure just given, we need the relevant elasticities. Previous research provides the following estimates. The price elasticity of the demand for gasoline is −0.14, while the income elasticity is 0.48.[1] Further, the price elasticity of the supply of gasoline is 0.62.[2]

The first step is to calculate the percentage change in the quantity demanded. Let %p represent the percentage change in price. Then, the percentage change in the quantity demanded due to the change in price will be −0.14 × %p. The percentage change in the quantity

demanded due to the increase in income will be 0.48 × 3 = 1.44. Hence, the percentage change in the quantity demanded due to the changes in price and income will be −0.14 × %p + 1.44.

The next step is to calculate the percentage change in the quantity supplied. The percentage change in the quantity supplied due to the change in price will be 0.62 × %p.

The third step is to equate the percentage changes in quantity demanded and quantity supplied. This implies that

$$-0.14 \times \%p + 1.44 = 0.62 \times \%p.$$

Solving this equation, we have

$$1.44 = (0.62 + 0.14) \times \%p,$$

which implies that the percentage change in price, %p = 1.44/0.76 = 1.89, which is approximately 1.9%. Hence, the 3% increase in household income results in the market price rising by 1.9%. Since the original price is 95 cents per gallon, the new price will be 95 × (1.019) = 96.8 cents.

The fourth step is to use the percentage change in price to calculate the percentage change in quantity. In this case, the equilibrium quantity will increase by a proportion of 0.62 × 1.9 = 1.178, or approximately 1.2%. Since the original quantity is 500 million gallons a week, the new quantity will be 500 × (1.012) = 506 million gallons.

[1] H.F. Houthakker and Lester B. Taylor, *Consumer Demand in the United States: Analyses and Projections*, 2d ed. (Cambridge, MA: Harvard University Press, 1970).
[2] Timothy J. Considine, "A Short Run Model of Petroleum Product Supply," *Energy Journal* 13, no. 2 (1992): pp. 61–91.

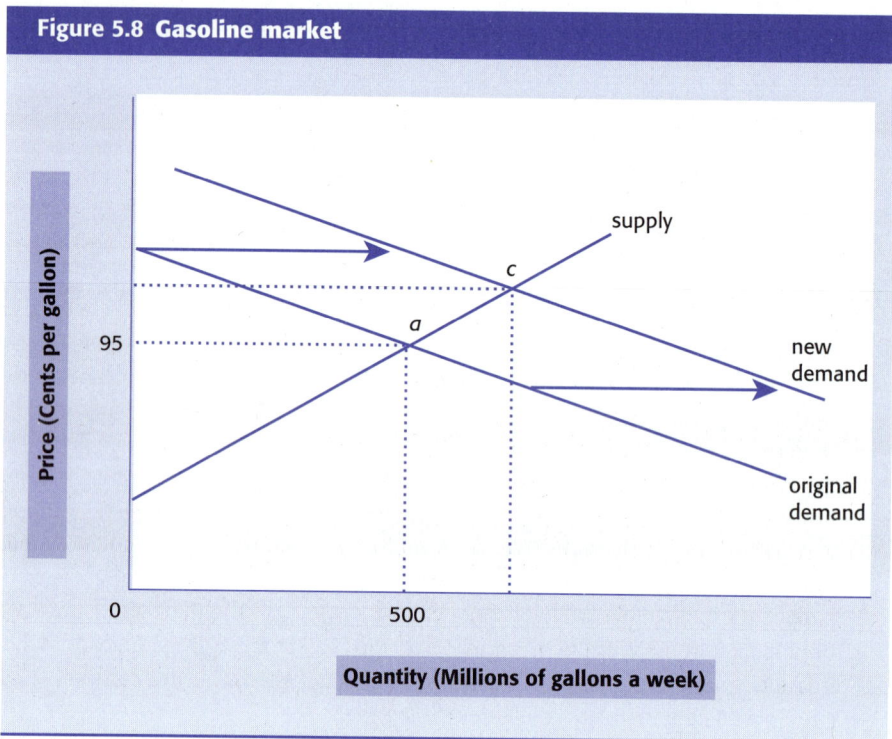

Figure 5.8 Gasoline market

An increase in household income shifts the demand curve to the right and results in a higher price of gasoline and larger quantity.

7 *Short- vis-à-vis Long-Run Effects*

Earlier, we studied the effects of shifts in demand and supply on the market equilibrium. An important factor in the size of these effects is the time horizon. Specifically, the elasticities of demand and supply vary with the time horizon. Accordingly, shifts in demand and supply may have different short-run and long-run effects. We now consider the differences between the short- and long-run effects of shifts in demand and supply.

We start from a market that is in short- and long-run equilibrium. Generally, in equilibrium, each individual buyer purchases the quantity where her or his marginal benefit equals the price, and each individual seller provides the quantity where its marginal cost equals the price. Figure 5.9 represents the interactions among individual buyers and sellers in a market equilibrium.

The market demand curve is the horizontal summation of the individual demand curves, and the market supply curve is the horizontal summation of the individual supply curves. At the equilibrium price, the market demand curve crosses the market supply curve. The price then signals to each buyer how much

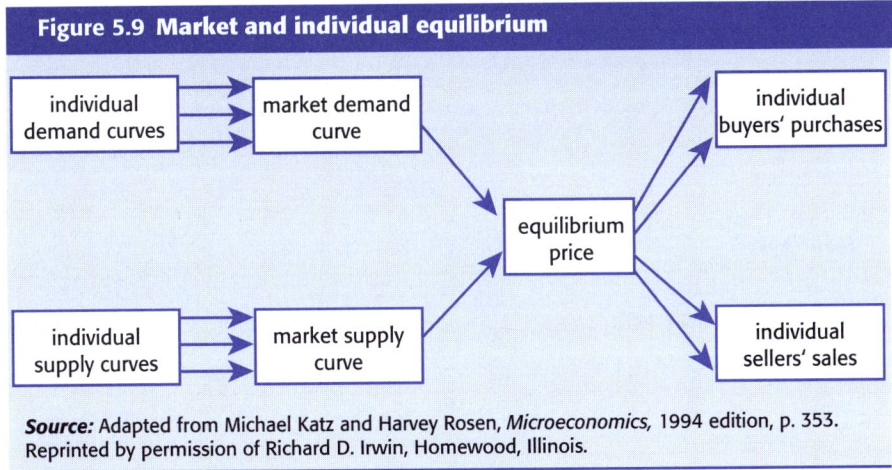

Figure 5.9 Market and individual equilibrium

individual demand curves → market demand curve → equilibrium price → individual buyers' purchases

individual supply curves → market supply curve → equilibrium price → individual sellers' sales

Source: Adapted from Michael Katz and Harvey Rosen, *Microeconomics*, 1994 edition, p. 353. Reprinted by permission of Richard D. Irwin, Homewood, Illinois.

The individual demands add up to market demand, and individual supplies add up to market supply. The equilibrium price signals to each buyer how much to purchase and to each seller how much to provide.

to purchase and to each seller how much to provide. Figure 5.9 applies to both short- and long-run equilibria.

Suppose that, originally, the market for bulk cargo service is in short- and long-run equilibrium, with a price of $20 per ton-mile and quantity of 10 million ton-miles. Let us now analyze the short-run vis-à-vis long-run effects of an increase in demand by 1 million ton-miles.

Short-Run Equilibrium

Figure 5.10 depicts the **short-run market equilibrium** at a price of $20 per ton-mile. Figure 5.10(a) shows the cost and demand curves of an individual seller. The short-run supply curve of any individual seller is that portion of its short-run marginal cost curve that lies above its short-run average variable cost curve.

By the assumption of perfect competition, each seller supplies a quantity that is small relative to the market. Equivalently, it has a small market share. Hence, the demand facing the seller is extremely elastic at the $20 market price. In the short run, the seller maximizes profit by operating at the point where its short-run marginal cost equals the market price. In Figure 5.10(a), the profit-maximizing scale of short run operations is 100,000 ton-miles a year.

Figure 5.10(b) shows the short-run market equilibrium at point *a*. At the $20 equilibrium price, the short-run market demand curve crosses the short-run market supply curve. The short-run market demand curve is the horizontal summation of the short-run individual demand curves. Similarly, the short-run market supply curve is the horizontal summation of the short-run individual supply curves.

Short-run market equilibrium is the price at which the short-run quantity demanded equals the short-run quantity supplied.

Figure 5.10 Short-run market equilibrium

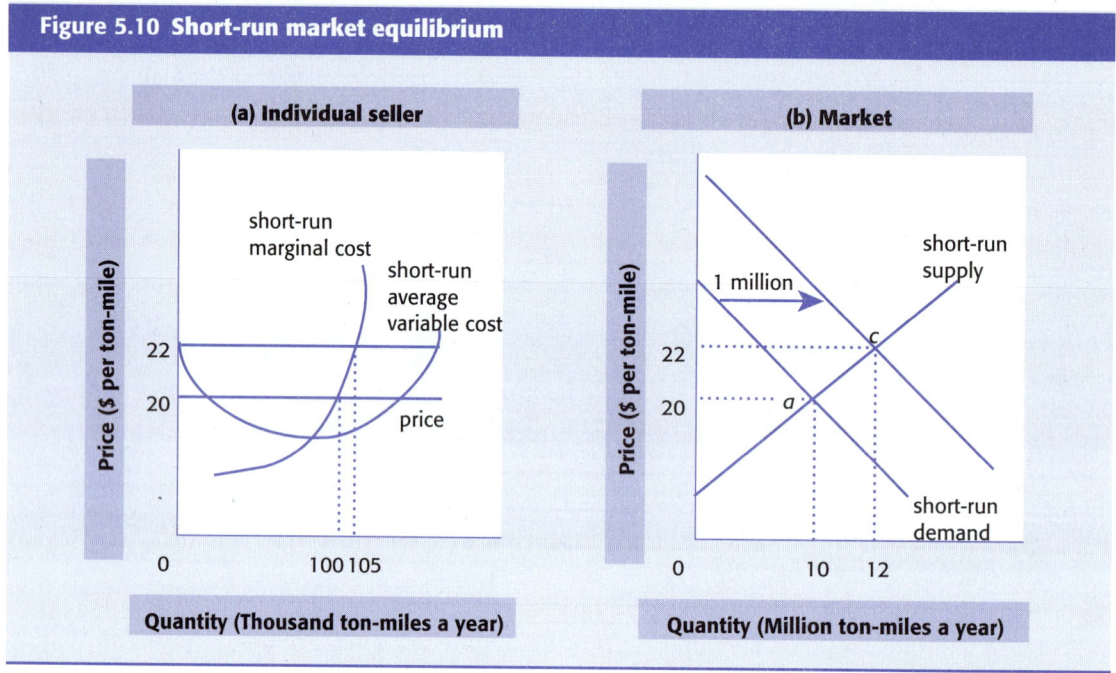

(a) An individual seller operates at 100,000 ton-miles a year, where the short-run marginal cost equals the market price.

(b) The market is in equilibrium at a price of $20, where the short-run demand crosses the short-run supply.

Long-Run Equilibrium

Long-run market equilibrium is the price at which the long-run quantity demanded equals the long-run quantity supplied.

Figure 5.11 depicts the **long-run market equilibrium** at a price of $20 per ton-mile. Figure 5.11(a) shows the cost and demand curves of an individual seller. The long-run supply curve of any individual seller is that portion of its long-run marginal cost curve that lies above its long run average cost curve. As each seller has a small market share, it faces a demand that is extremely elastic at the $20 market price. In the long run, it maximizes profit by operating at the point where its long-run marginal cost equals the market price. By Figure 5.11(a), the profit-maximizing scale of long-run operations is 100,000 ton-miles a year.

Figure 5.11(b) shows the long-run market equilibrium at point *a*. At the $20 equilibrium price, the long-run market demand curve crosses the long-run market supply curve. The long-run market demand curve is the horizontal summation of the long-run individual demand curves. Similarly, the long-run market supply curve is the horizontal summation of the long-run individual supply curves.

From Chapter 4, we know that the long-run market supply curve may be flat or slope upward. It slopes upward if an increase in the demand for the inputs of

Figure 5.11 Long-run market equilibrium

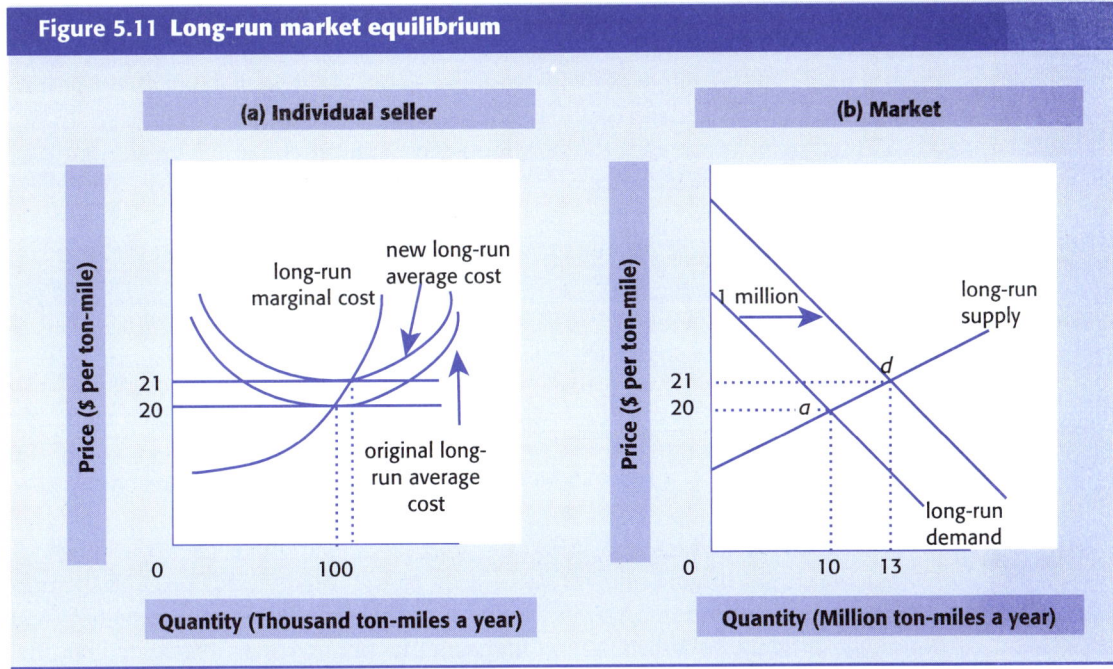

(a) Individual seller

(b) Market

(a) An individual seller operates at 100,000 ton-miles a year, where the long-run marginal cost equals the market price.

(b) The market is in equilibrium at price of $20, where the long-run demand crosses the long-run supply.

bulk cargo service will lead to higher prices for those inputs or if different providers of bulk cargo service have access to resources with different cost.

Demand Increase

Starting from the short- and long-run equilibria, we suppose that the demand curve shifts to the right by 1 million ton-miles. For simplicity, we assume that the short- and long-run demand curves are the same.

Let us first consider the new short-run equilibrium. Referring to Figure 5.10(b), the shift in demand will move the short-run market equilibrium to point *c*, with a higher price of $22. At the same time, referring to Figure 5.10(a), every seller expands its operations to the scale of 105,000 ton-miles, where its short-run marginal cost equals the new market price of $22. This means operating service capacity more intensively; for instance, by delaying routine maintenance on ships and postponing annual vacations for crews.

Generally, the extent to which a seller expands its operations depends on the slope of its short-run marginal cost curve. If the short-run marginal cost curve is steep, then the price increase will not lead the seller to expand operations by very much. By contrast, if the short-run marginal cost curve is gentle, then the price increase will induce a large expansion of operations. The steepness of the short-run marginal cost curve depends on such factors as the availability of excess production capacity and the cost of overtime relative to standard wage rates.

Let us next consider the new long-run equilibrium. In a long-run horizon, there is enough planning time for all costs to become avoidable, for new sellers to enter the market, and for existing sellers to leave. Accordingly, as we have shown in Chapter 4, the market supply tends to be more elastic in the long run than in the short run.

With regard to the bulk cargo market, the increase in demand raises the market price and hence each seller's profits. Over the long run, this will induce existing sellers to expand capacity and enlist additional crew members and also will attract new sellers to enter the market. The industry will expand along the long-run market supply curve. To the extent that the expansion will increase the prices of inputs or attract sellers with relatively less favorable resources, the long-run market supply will slope upward.

Referring to Figure 5.11(b), the shift in demand will move the long-run market equilibrium to point d with a price of $21. Figure 5.11(a) shows the new long-run equilibrium for an individual seller. Although the price is higher than in the original equilibrium, the higher input prices result in higher marginal and average cost curves. Accordingly, in the new long-run equilibrium, each individual seller just breaks even. No other sellers will wish to enter the industry, and no seller will wish to leave.

Figure 5.12 depicts both the short- and long-run market equilibria. The original equilibrium is point b, the new short-run equilibrium is point c, and the new long-run equilibrium is point d. The price in the new long-run equilibrium is lower than in the new short-run equilibrium but higher than in the original equilibrium. The quantity in the new long-run equilibrium is higher than in the new short-run equilibrium, which in turn is higher than in the original equilibrium. The basic reason for these differences is that the supply is more elastic in the long run than the short run.

In the new long-run equilibrium, there will be more sellers than in the new short-run equilibrium or the original equilibrium. The higher price attracts new sellers to enter and supports a larger number of sellers; hence, a larger industry.

Progress check

Progress Check 5G Suppose that the demand for bulk cargo service increases by 2 million ton-miles. Use Figure 5.12 to illustrate the short- and long-run effects on the market equilibrium.

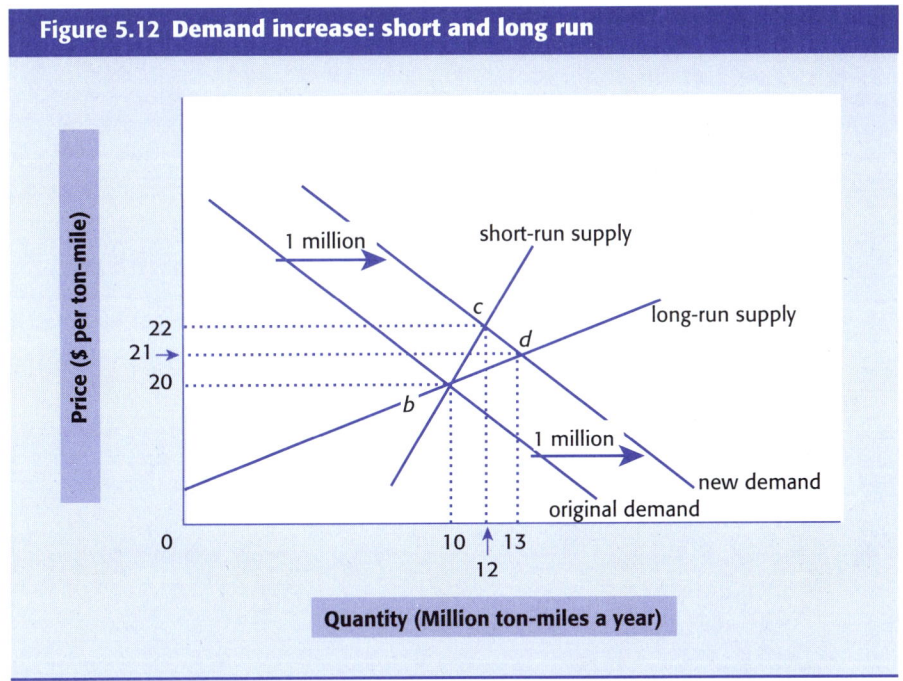

Figure 5.12 Demand increase: short and long run

Following an increase in demand, the new short-run equilibrium is at point *c* and the new long-run equilibrium is at point *d*. The price rises more in the short run than the long run. The quantity increases less in the short run than the long run.

Demand Reduction

We have considered the short- and long-run impacts of an increase in demand. We can apply the same approach to study the effects of a fall in demand. Figure 5.13 illustrates a 1 million ton-mile reduction in the demand for bulk cargo service. The original equilibrium is at point *b*.

The reduction in demand will move the short-run market equilibrium to point *e*, with a lower price of $17. Those sellers whose average variable cost exceeds the price will shut down. In the bulk cargo market, this means laying up their ships. Those sellers for whom the price covers their average variable cost will continue in business. Each will cut back operations to the scale where its short-run marginal cost equals the new market price of $17.

The extent of the cutback depends on two factors. One factor is the extent of sunk costs. If a seller has many prior commitments, most costs are sunk. It will continue to produce so long as the price covers its average variable cost. In this case, the price reduction will lead to a relatively minor cutback in operations. Generally, in an industry involving substantial sunk costs, the reduction in demand will translate into a relatively large drop in price and a small reduction in quantity.

Figure 5.13 Demand reduction: short and long run

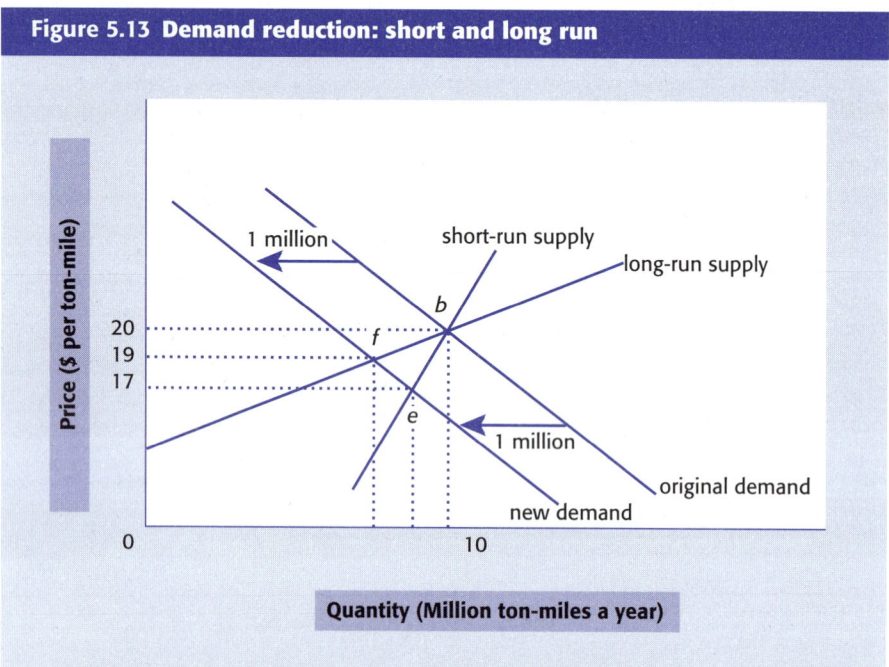

Following a reduction in demand, the new short-run equilibrium is at point *e* and the new long-run equilibrium is at point *f*. The price falls further in the short run than the long run. The quantity drops less in the short run than the long run.

The second factor is the slope of the seller's short-run marginal cost curve. If the short-run marginal cost curve is steep, then the price reduction will lead the seller to cut back operations substantially. By contrast, if the short-run marginal cost curve is gentle, then the price reduction will have a relatively smaller impact.

In the long run, there is enough planning time for all costs to become avoidable, for new sellers to enter the market, and for existing sellers to leave. Referring to Figure 5.13, the shift in demand will move the long-run market equilibrium to point *f* with a price of $19. For some sellers, the long-run price is below their average total cost. These will exit the industry, which means selling off all ships and equipment and dismissing all workers. The entire industry will contract along the long-run market supply curve. In the new long-run equilibrium, there will be a smaller number of sellers and each will exactly break even with average total cost equal to the market price.

Referring to Figure 5.13, the price in the new long-run equilibrium is higher than in the new short-run equilibrium but lower than in the original equilibrium. Further, the quantity in the new long-run equilibrium is less than in the new short-run equilibrium, which in turn is less than in the original equilibrium. The basic reason for these differences is that the market supply is more elastic in the long run than the short run.

General Principles

Our analysis of the short- and long-run effects of shifts in the demand illustrates two general points. First, in response to shifts in demand, the market price will be more volatile in the short run than the long run. Specifically, if there is an increase in demand, the market price will increase more in the short run than in the long run. By contrast, if there is a reduction in demand, then the market price will fall more in the short run than in the long run.

Second, in response to shifts in demand, there is a greater change in the market quantity over the long run than in the short run. If there is an increase in demand, the quantity will increase more in the long run than in the short run. Likewise, if there is a reduction in demand, the quantity will drop more in the long run than the short run.

The distinction between the short run and long run is that, in the short run, some costs are sunk. Accordingly, the disparity between the short run and long run is relatively sharper in industries where operations involve substantial sunk costs. In such industries, the price will be relatively volatile, as the market adjusts to shifts in demand. When demand increases, the short-run price will exceed the long-run price. When, however, there is a fall in demand, the short-run price will be less than the long-run price

Further, in industries with substantial sunk costs, the adjustment of production will be concentrated in the long run. Owing to the substantial sunk costs, relatively little adjustment can be made in the short run.

By contrast, in industries where sunk costs are minor, the adjustment to shifts in demand will be relatively smoother. The market price will be relatively less volatile. The adjustment of production will be spread through the short run and long run.

Like the elasticity of the market supply, the elasticity of the market demand depends on the time horizon. Recall from Chapter 3 that, depending on the nature of the item, the long-run demand may be more or less elastic than the short-run demand. Just as we analyzed the short- and long-run effects of shifts in demand, we can apply the same approach to consider the short- and long-run effects of shifts in supply.

Previously, we applied the elasticities of demand and supply to calculate the precise effects of shifts in demand or supply. Here, we need note only that we should use short-run elasticities to estimate the short-run impact of shifts in demand and supply and long-run elasticities to estimate the long-run impact. In both cases, the procedure is exactly the same as presented previously. The only difference is whether we apply short- or long-run elasticities.

8 *Receipts vis-à-vis Incidence*

The introduction asked how the market for cement would be affected if manufacturers switched from pricing inclusive of freight to ex-works pricing. The difference between freight inclusive and ex-works pricing is a common issue in industrial markets. Let us apply the demand-supply framework to compare these two approaches to pricing. We will find that freight inclusive vis-à-vis ex-works pricing is a particular application of a general issue in competitive markets. The general issue is the distinction between paying a price and bearing that amount.

Freight Inclusive Pricing

The **cost and freight (CF) price** includes the cost of delivery to the buyer.

We begin by considering the market with freight inclusive pricing. A price that includes freight is called **cost and freight,** abbreviated CF. In the market for cement, the buyers are building contractors and the sellers are cement manufacturers. Suppose that all manufacturers set CF prices that include a freight cost of 25 cents. The market price is $1.50 per pound, at which price, the buyers purchase 1 million pounds a year. Figure 5.14 illustrates the market equilibrium at point *a*.

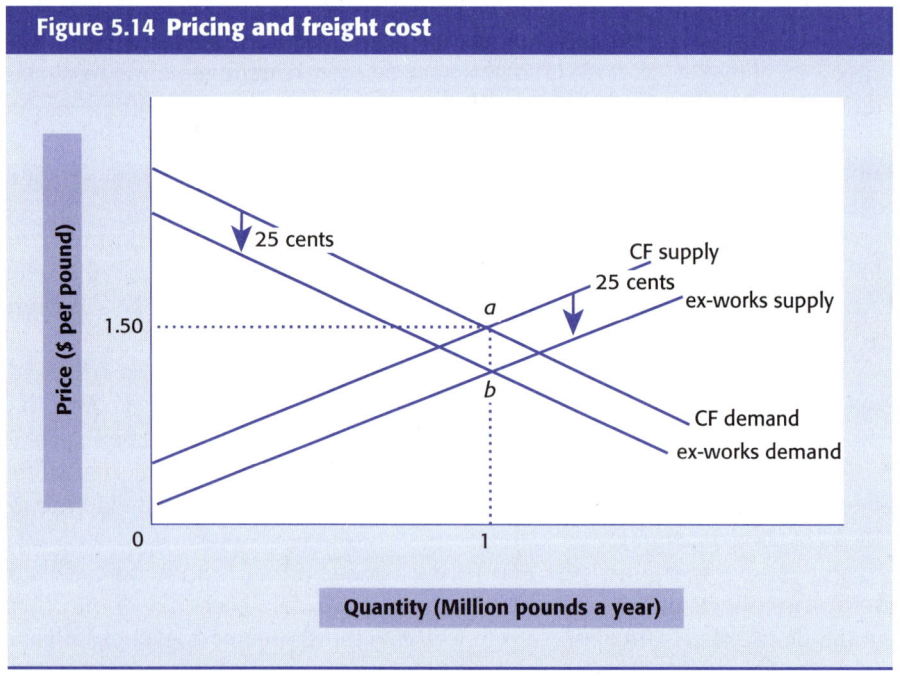

Figure 5.14 Pricing and freight cost

If all manufacturers switch to ex-works pricing, the supply curve shifts down by 25 cents and the demand curve also shifts down by 25 cents. The equilibrium quantity remains unchanged at 1 million pounds.

Ex-Works Pricing

Next, suppose that all manufacturers switch to ex-works pricing. An **ex-works price** does not include the freight cost: it literally means "the price at the gate to the works." Since the manufacturers no longer incur the 25-cent freight cost, the switch will shift the entire supply curve of cement down by 25 cents. In Figure 5.14, the entire supply curve shifts down because each manufacturer's marginal cost of supplying cement is reduced whatever the quantity that it actually supplies.

The switch to ex-works pricing also affects the market demand. With ex-works pricing, each buyer must pay 25 cents a pound to obtain the cement. In Figure 5.14, this can be represented by shifting the entire retail demand curve down by 25 cents. To explain this shift, recall that the market demand curve is the horizontal sum of the individual demand curves. In turn, each buyer's demand curve shows the amount that the consumer is willing to pay for each pound of cement. Since each buyer must pay 25 cents in freight for every pound, the buyer's willingness to pay will be 25 cents lower at all quantities. This means that the entire demand curve will shift down by 25 cents.

There is another way to confirm that the switch to ex-works pricing will shift down the demand curve. Consider the buyer of the 1 millionth pound. By the original demand curve, that buyer would be willing to pay exactly $1.50 for that pound. If, however, the buyer must incur a 25-cent freight cost, it will now be willing to pay $1.50 – $0.25 = $1.25 for the 1 millionth pound. The same 25 cent reduction in willingness to pay applies to all the inframarginal units as well. Hence, the entire demand curve shifts down by 25 cents.

In Figure 5.14, the new demand and supply curves cross at point *b*. Relative to the original equilibrium at point *a*, the price is lower. The new demand curve is the original demand curve shifted down by 25 cents. Likewise, the new supply curve is the original supply curve shifted down by 25 cents. Hence, the new equilibrium point *b* must be vertically below the original equilibrium point *a*, and the vertical distance *ab* must be 25 cents.

Thus, in the new equilibrium, each buyer pays $1.25 to the seller and $0.25 in freight, making a "total price" of $1.25 + $0.25 = $1.50, which is exactly the price under freight-inclusive pricing. Further, the quantity of sales is exactly the same in the old and new equilibria. Generally, the price and sales are the same whether the sellers do or do not include the freight cost in their prices.

Incidence

When demand or supply shift, the consequent change in the price for a buyer or seller is called the **incidence** on that party. In the cement example, when manufacturers switch from freight-inclusive to ex-works pricing, the market price drops by 25 cents to $1.25; hence, the net effect on buyers is zero. This shows that, although the switch in pricing method requires buyers to "pay" the

The ex-works price does not include the cost of delivery to the buyer.

Incidence is the change in the price for a buyer or seller resulting from a shift in demand or supply.

freight cost, there is no net effect after we consider adjustments in both demand and supply.

Equivalently, whether manufacturers set prices that do or do not include the freight cost, the incidence is the same. The incidence does not depend on which side—buyer or seller—initially pays the freight cost.

In fact, the incidence of the freight cost depends only on the price elasticities of demand and supply. This analysis reflects common sense. If sellers pay the freight cost, the buyers would be willing to pay a higher price. By contrast, buyers that must pay the freight cost would insist on paying less to sellers.

The distinction between receiving or paying an amount of money and the incidence of the receipt or payment is a very fundamental economic concept. We have applied this distinction in the context of industrial pricing. The distinction is also important for understanding the effect of brokerage fees and government taxes.

Using demand-supply analysis, it can be shown that, regardless of whether buyers or sellers pay brokerage fees, the market price and quantity will be the same. Similarly, demand-supply analysis can show that, regardless of whether a tax initially is imposed on buyers or sellers, the market price and quantity will be the same. The incidence of brokerage fees and taxes depends only on the price elasticities of demand and supply.

Progress check

Progress Check 5H Using Figure 5.14 as a basis, construct a series of four figures to compare the market equilibria with freight-inclusive pricing and ex-works pricing when (a) demand is extremely inelastic, (b) demand is extremely elastic, (c) supply is extremely inelastic, and (d) supply is extremely elastic.

Promoting Retail Sales: Cents-off Coupons

Some consumer marketing consultants suggest that cents-off coupons are more effective in lowering retail prices than cuts in wholesale prices. According to this suggestion, manufacturers should distribute coupons widely. Then, when consumers make purchases, they can redeem the coupons and get the full price reduction. This argument, however, overlooks the possibility that retailers will raise their prices when consumers use coupons. So, are coupons more effective than direct cuts in wholesale prices?

To address this question, we consider the retail market for Luna shampoo, where consumers provide the demand and competitive grocery stores provide the supply. Figure 5.15 illustrates the market equilibrium at point *s*, with a price of $4 per bottle and quantity of 500,000 bottles a year.

First, we suppose that Luna cuts the wholesale price of its shampoo by 25 cents. In the retail market, this wholesale price cut will shift the supply curve down by 25 cents. The entire supply curve shifts down because the wholesale price cut affects retailers' marginal costs of supplying Luna shampoo at all quantities. The cut in the wholesale price does not affect the retail demand. At the new equilibrium (point t), the price is lower and the quantity of sales is higher. Suppose that the price is $3.80 and the quantity is 550,000 bottles a year.

Next, suppose that, instead of cutting the wholesale price, Luna maintains the wholesale price, while distributing 25-cent coupons to all consumers. Supposing that every consumer uses a coupon for every bottle purchased, the effective price of a bottle of shampoo would become the retail price less 25 cents. Since the consumer will be cashing in a 25-cent coupon for every bottle,

the consumer's willingness to pay will be 25 cents higher at all purchase levels. This means that each consumer's and hence the market demand curve will shift up by 25 cents.

The coupons, however, do not affect the supply curve. Referring to Figure 5.15, the new demand curve crosses the original supply curve at point u. Relative to the original equilibrium, the price is higher, and the quantity of sales is higher.

In Figure 5.15, compare the triangle vsu with the triangle swt. Line sv represents a 25-cent upward shift of the demand curve, and line sw represents a 25-cent downward shift of the supply curve. Accordingly, lines sv and sw are of equal length.

Curve st is a segment of the original demand curve, and curve vu is the same segment shifted up by 25 cents. Further, curve su is a segment of the original supply curve, and curve wt is the same segment shifted down by

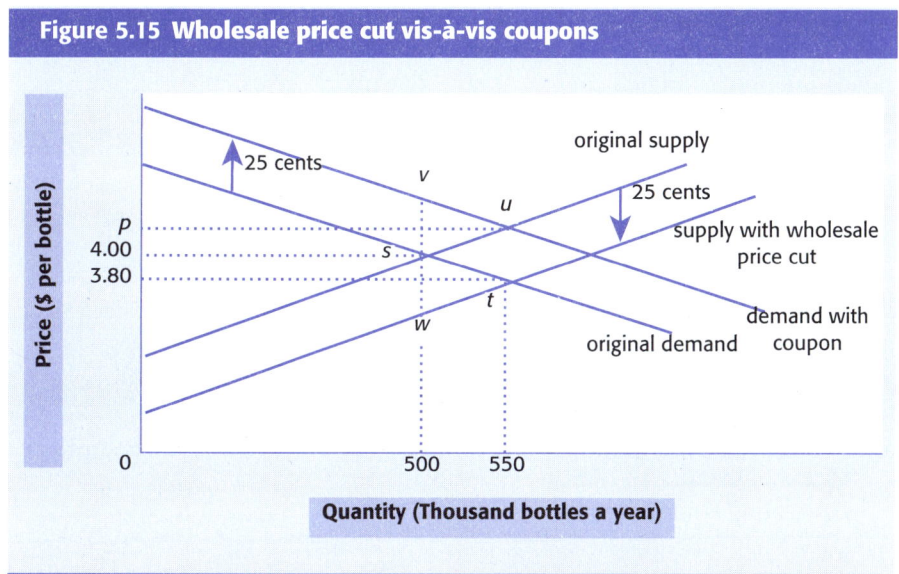

Figure 5.15 Wholesale price cut vis-à-vis coupons

If the wholesale price is cut by 25 cents, the retail supply curve shifts down by 25 cents and the quantity increases to 550,000 bottles. If every consumer uses a 25-cent coupon, the retail demand curve shifts up by 25 cents and the quantity increases to 550,000 bottles. In both cases, the effective retail price and sales are the same.

25 cents. Accordingly, the triangles *vsu* and *swt* must be identical. This means that the point *u* must be vertically above the point *t* and the vertical distance *tu* must be 25 cents. Since the quantity at point *t* is 550,000 bottles, the quantity at point *u* also is 550,000 bottles.

Since the price at point *t* is $3.80, the price at point *u* must be $3.80 + 0.25 = $4.05. This is the retail price with coupons. Hence, the effective price to consumers is $4.05 − 0.25 = $3.80. The effective price with a coupon is identical to the price when Luna directly cuts the wholesale price by 25 cents. This means that, in the new equilibrium, the price and sales are the same whether Luna cuts the wholesale price or all consumers use coupons.

Assuming that all consumers use coupons, there is no difference between coupons and a direct cut in the wholesale price. Hence, there must be a different reason for using coupons. In Chapter 9, we explain how coupons can be used to discriminate between consumers with different willingness to pay for a product.

9 *Summary*

How will a 15% drop in the price of fuel affect the price of bulk cargo service? Questions such as this one are commonplace. The answers, however, are not so simple. To understand the complete effect of a shift in demand or supply, it is necessary to consider both sides of the market. Generally, the effect of any change in demand or supply depends on the elasticities of both demand and supply.

The time horizon is a key factor affecting elasticities of demand and supply. Prices are more volatile and quantity adjustment takes relatively longer in industries where production involves substantial sunk costs.

Finally, it is important to distinguish a receipt or payment from incidence. A payment or receipt can be shifted from one to the other side of the market. Incidence is fundamental and depends only on the elasticities of demand and supply.

Key concepts

perfect competition	short-run market equilibrium
market power	long-run market equilibrium
market equilibrium	cost and freight price
excess supply	ex-works price
excess demand	incidence
calculating equilibrium change	

Further Reading

Useful references on the economics of competitive markets include Michael L. Katz and Harvey Rosen, *Microeconomics*, 2d ed. (Homewood, IL: Irwin, 1994), Chapter 10, and Steven E. Landsburg, *Price Theory and Applications*, 3d ed. (St. Paul, MN: West Publishing, 1995), Chapter 7.

Review Questions

1. Several pairs of markets follow. For each comparison, which market better fits the model of perfect competition at the retail level (choose a or b)? Explain your answers.

   For entertainment,
   a. Cable television.
   b. Video rentals.

   For energy,
   a. Electric power.
   b. Gasoline.

   For investments,
   a. Publicly listed shares.
   b. Antiques.

2. True or false? If some sellers have market power, then it is not possible to construct a supply curve. Explain your answer.

3. If the market price exceeds the equilibrium price, there will be (choose a or b)
   a. Excess demand.
   b. Excess supply.

   Explain your answer.

4. How would each of the following changes affect the market for new apartments?
   a. An increase in the price of building materials.
   b. A cut in the wages of construction workers.
   c. A cut in mortgage rates.
   d. An increase in household incomes.
   e. An increase in the price of food.

5. Under what circumstances would an increase in household incomes have the least effect on the market price of new apartments? Please state conditions in terms of the price elasticities of demand and supply.

6. Suppose that wages in the hotel industry are rising at the rate of 3% a year. Which determines the effect of an increase in wages on hotel room rates?
   a. Price elasticity of demand.
   b. Price elasticity of supply.
   c. Both (a) and (b).

7. In the section on calculating equilibrium changes, we showed that a 3% increase in household income would cause the market price of gasoline to rise by 1.9%. Suppose that the price elasticity of supply were 0.8 rather than 0.62. How would the 3% increase in income affect the market price?

8. Consider the effect of a cut in mortgage rates on the price of new housing. Compare the short-run changes in price and quantity with the long-run changes.

9. True or false? Prices will be relatively less volatile in industries with substantial sunk costs. Explain your answer.

10. Suppose that disposable diaper manufacturers cut their wholesale price by 50 cents a package. Consider the retail market. Explain the difference between receipt and incidence of the wholesale price cut for retailers.

Discussion Questions

1. This question applies the techniques for solving equilibrium explained in the math supplement. Let p and w represent the price of new construction (in dollars per square foot) and a laborer's wage (in dollars per hour), respectively. Further, let the demand for new construction be represented by the equation

$$D = 40 - p, \qquad (5.2)$$

and the supply be represented by the equation

$$S = 5 + 1.5\,p - w. \qquad (5.3)$$

All quantities are in millions of square feet a year.

a. Suppose that, initially, $w = 5$. Calculate the market equilibrium price and quantity.

b. Next, suppose that a laborer's wage increases to 7. Calculate the new market equilibrium price and quantity. Does the price of new construction increase by the same proportion as the increase in the wage?

2. Until 1979, almost all the oil exported from the Middle East was shipped by tanker through the Persian Gulf. When war broke out between Iraq and Iran, both countries launched attacks on gulf shipping. By February 1988, an estimated 308 tankers had been hit, of which 53 were total losses. The war also damaged oil production facilities. Consequently, between 1979 and 1988, Iraq's oil exports fell from 3 to 2.7 million barrels/day (bpd), while Iran's oil exports fell from 5.3 to 2.5 million bpd. To sustain its European exports, Iraq built pipelines to carry oil to the Red Sea and the eastern Mediterranean (Michael Westlake, "Less Oil in Troubled Waters," *Far Eastern Economic Review* [October 20, 1988]).

a. Using an appropriate supply-demand diagram, illustrate the effect of (i) the production cut and (ii) the new pipelines on the market for tanker services.

b. How would air and naval attacks on gulf shipping affect the market for tanker services?

c. The net effect of the production cuts, construction of pipelines, and military action was to increase the lease rates for tanker services. Using the supply-demand diagram, illustrate the net effect.

3. The price of housing is a major issue in Hong Kong. Many blame speculators for wide swings in housing prices. To cool speculation in the housing market, the Hong Kong gov-

ernment has prohibited banks from lending more than 70% of the value of new homes.

a. How do the following factors affect the demand for housing: (i) rising incomes, (ii) population growth, and (iii) trend away from multigenerational households to single-generation households?

b. Is the supply of housing more elastic in the short run or in the long run?

c. How would the government's mortgage restrictions affect the rate of new construction, housing prices, and the housing stock in (i) the short-run and (ii) the long-run?

4. Samsung of Korea is the world's leading manufacturer of dynamic random access memory (DRAM) semiconductors. Other DRAM manufacturers include American, European, and Korean companies. Recently, several Taiwanese consortiums announced plans to build DRAM factories as well.

a. Is the DRAM market becoming more or less competitive?

b. Global demand for DRAMs rises every year. Which of the following situations is better for Samsung: (i) that the worldwide industry is operating close to capacity with very full order books or (ii) that the industry is wallowing in excess capacity due to the entry of the Taiwanese manufacturers. Explain your answer.

5. Japan is one of the world's leading exporters of consumer electronics. A major problem for Japanese consumer electronics manufacturers has been the steady appreciation of the yen against the U.S. dollar. This means that the yen is becoming progressively more expensive in terms of the U.S. dollar.

a. Explain how the appreciation of the yen from ¥150 per U.S. dollar to ¥100 per U.S. dollar affects the wholesale cost of supplying Japanese consumer electronics to the United States.

b. Suppose that the Japanese yen rises by one-third against the U.S. dollar. Which of the following are plausible explanations of why the U.S. retail price of Japanese-made CD players will rise by less than one-third: (i) the wholesale cost accounts for only part of retailers' costs, (ii) American retail demand for Japanese-made CD players is inelastic, (iii) American retail supply of Japanese-made CD players is inelastic?

c. How will a one-third appreciation of the yen affect the price and sales of Korean CD players in the United States?

6. Consider any fresh fruit or vegetable grown in the United States.

a. Using suitable demand and supply curves, explain how you expect the price of the item to vary over the four seasons of the year.

b. Next, consider heating oil. Using suitable demand and supply curves, explain how you expect the price of heating oil to vary through the seasons.

c. Compile two time series of monthly prices: one for the fruit or vegetable that you are considering and another for heating oil over the same 36-month period. Compare the seasonal variation in the two series.

7. Suppose that Campbell's is planning to cut the wholesale price of its tomato juice. Consider the retail market where supermarkets and grocery stores sell tomato juice and consumers buy the product. Under what circumstances would the wholesale price cut have the least effect on the retail price? Please state conditions in terms of the price elasticities of retail demand and supply.

8. Manufacturers of paper products are major buyers of wastepaper. They use a combination of wood pulp and wastepaper to produce paper products. The supply of wastepaper comes from households and businesses. An issue in environmental policy is the effectiveness of price incentives in encouraging recycling of wastepaper. The price elasticity of the demand for wastepaper has been estimated to be 0.07, while the price elasticity of the supply has been estimated to be 0 (John A. Edgren and Kemper W. Moreland, "An Econometric Analysis of Paper and Wastepaper Markets," *Resources and Energy* 11 [1989]: pp. 299–319).

a. Consider a government policy that reduces the price of wastepaper to manufacturers by 5%. How will this affect the quantity demanded?

b. Consider a government policy that increases the price of wastepaper to sellers by 5%. How will this affect the quantity supplied?

c. Are price incentives an effective way of increasing the recycling of wastepaper?

9. This question applies the techniques presented in the section on calculating equilibrium change. The elasticities of the demand for gasoline with respect to price and income are –0.14 and 0.48, respectively. The elasticities of the supply with respect to price and labor wages are 0.62 and 0.05, respectively. Suppose that the price of gasoline is $1 per gallon and sales are 400 million gallons a year. What will be the effect on the market price and quantity

a. If income rises by 4%.

b. If wages rise by 10%.

c. If both changes (a) and (b) occur.

10. Typical real-estate broker: "In California, the seller always pays the broker's commission, so, buyers get brokerage services free."

MBA: "If the custom were for the buyer to pay the commission, then would sellers be getting brokerage services free?"

Real-estate broker, clearly losing patience: "That is a purely hypothetical scenario, but if that situation were to arise, yes, I guess you're right."

a. Assume that each seller pays a brokers' commission of $18,000. Then, the supply of houses includes the cost of brokerage. Illustrate the market equilibrium with a price of $310,000 per house and sale of 200,000 houses a year.

b. Now suppose that buyers rather than sellers pay the $18,000 commission.

Using your figure, illustrate the following: (i) shift the supply curve down by $18,000 since sellers do not pay the commission, and (ii) shift the demand curve up by $18,000 since buyers now pay the commission.

c. Compare the market equilibria of (a) and (b) in terms of (i) the net price received by sellers and (ii) the net price paid by buyers. (Net prices are net of brokerage commission, if any.)

Math Supplement

Market Equilibrium

Earlier, we used graphs to analyze the equilibrium in the market for bulk cargo service. To reinforce our understanding, we now derive the market equilibrium using algebraic methods. Let p and f represent the price of bulk cargo service and the cost of fuel, respectively. Further, let the demand for bulk cargo service be represented by the equation

$$D = 30 - p, \qquad (5.4)$$

and the supply be represented by the equation

$$S = 4 + 0.5\,p - f. \qquad (5.5)$$

Suppose that, initially, $f = 4$. Then, the supply equation simplifies to

$$S = 0.5\,p. \qquad (5.6)$$

Before calculating the equilibrium, it is useful to graph the equilibrium. From the demand equation, when $D = 0$, $p = 30$, and when $p = 0$, $D = 30$. This gives us two points on the demand curve. Moreover, differentiating the demand equation with respect to price,

$$\frac{dD}{dp} = -1 \qquad (5.7)$$

which means that the demand equation has a constant slope, or equivalently, that the demand curve is a straight line. This is enough information to draw the demand curve.

Similarly, we can draw the supply curve. From the supply equation, when $S = 0$, $p = 0$, and when $p = 20$, $S = 10$. Further, by differentiating the supply equation with respect to price, we can show that the supply curve is also a straight line. This completes Figure 5.1.

In market equilibrium, the quantity demanded equals the quantity supplied, that is,

$$D = S. \qquad (5.8)$$

Substituting from (5.4) and (5.6), this means

$$30 - p = 0.5p, \qquad (5.9)$$

which implies that

$$p = 20 \qquad (5.10)$$

and, hence, that

$$D = S = 10. \qquad (5.11)$$

Therefore, as depicted in Figure 5.1, the market equilibrium occurs at a price of \$20 per ton-mile and quantity of 10 million ton-miles.

Demand and Supply Shifts

We can also use an algebraic method to analyze the impact of shifts in demand or supply. Consider, for instance, the effect of a 15% drop in the cost of fuel. As the original cost is 4, the 15% drop will reduce the cost to $4 \times 0.85 = 3.40$. Substituting $f = 3.40$ in the supply equation, (5.5)

$$S = 4 + 0.5p - 3.40 = 0.60 + 0.5p. \qquad (5.12)$$

In market equilibrium, the quantity demanded equals the quantity supplied: that is,

$$D = S. \qquad (5.13)$$

Substituting from (5.4) and (5.6), this means

$$30 - p = 0.60 + 0.5p, \qquad (5.14)$$

which implies that

$$p = 19.60 \qquad (5.15)$$

and, hence, that

$$D = S = 10.4. \qquad (5.16)$$

Therefore, as depicted in Figure 5.2, the new market equilibrium occurs at a price of $19.60 per ton-mile and quantity of 10.4 million ton-miles.

Using Elasticities

Next, we derive the procedure for estimating the effect of changes in variables that affect demand or supply on the market equilibrium. We will refer to the gasoline example. Let the price of gasoline be p and household income be Y.

Suppose that the demand for gasoline depends only on price and income. We can then write the demand as a function:

$$D(p, Y). \qquad (5.17)$$

On the supply side, suppose that the supply of gasoline depends on the price of gasoline. So, we can write the supply as a function:

$$S(p). \qquad (5.18)$$

Initially, in equilibrium, demand and supply must balance:

$$D(p, Y) = S(p). \qquad (5.19)$$

Now suppose that household income increases, which causes the market equilibrium to shift. Let us compare the equilibrium before and after the change. In moving from the initial to the final equilibrium, the percentage change in quantity demanded, $\%D$, must balance the percentage change in quantity supplied, $\%S$:

$$\%D = \%S. \qquad (5.20)$$

Let the elasticities of demand with respect to price and income be e_p and e_y, respectively, and the elasticity of supply with respect to price be s_p. Then, from Chapter 3, the percentage change in quantity demanded

$$\%D = (e_p \times \%p) + (e_y \times \%Y), \qquad (5.21)$$

where $\%p$ is the percentage change in price and $\%Y$ is the percentage change in income.

Similarly, the percentage change in quantity supplied

$$\%S = (s_p \times \%p). \qquad (5.22)$$

By (5.20), these percentage changes must be equal, hence we have

$$(e_p \times \%p) + (e_y \times \%Y) = (s_p \times \%p). \qquad (5.23)$$

Solving this equation, we can obtain the percentage change in price and hence the percentage change in quantity.

This same procedure applies when demand depends on more than two variables and supply depends on more than one variable. The approach is exactly the same: We must work out the percentage changes in demand and supply, then equate these changes and solve for the percentage change in the price, and hence the percentage change in quantity.

Chapter 6

Economic Efficiency

1 Introduction

The 1917 Bolshevik Revolution established the world's first communist government in the Soviet Union. During and after World War II, communism spread through Eastern Europe and Asia. Under a communist system, the government owns all property including factories, farms, housing, and mines, and every citizen is a government employee. The government directs and manages economic activity through central planning rather than a market system.

In 1978, some 60 years after the Bolshevik Revolution, Chinese leader Deng Xiao Ping replaced communist central planning in favor of "socialism with Chinese characteristics." This Chinese brand of socialism bore several hallmarks of a market system, including private property and competitive markets. Then, in just two years, between 1989 and 1990, almost all the communist governments in Eastern Europe gave way to democracy and the market system. Why did China and most of Eastern Europe abandon central planning in favor of market systems?

In August 1992, Hurricane Andrew struck south Florida, causing $30 billion of damage and one of America's most devastating civil disasters in recent times. Rebuilding in the aftermath of Hurricane Andrew, communities in south Florida needed building supplies, construction equipment and tools, and labor, all in substantial quantities. Who told Weyerhauser to produce more lumber? Who ordered hundreds of laborers to the area?

Table 6.1 shows that, in 1994, International Business Machines (IBM) was the world's seventh largest manufacturer of integrated circuits. The largest was Intel, which is a called a *merchant*, because it sells the bulk of its production to

Table 6.1 **Integrated circuit manufacturers, 1994**	
Company	**Sales of Integrated Circuits ($ million)**
Intel	9850
NEC	7855
Toshiba	6580
Motorola	5846
Hitachi	5730
Texas Instruments	5500
Samsung	4365
IBM	4050

Source: Standard and Poor's industry surveys, *Electronics* (August 3, 1995), pp. E27–8.

other manufacturers. By contrast, most of IBM's production is used internally. IBM produces integrated circuits in various factories and supplies these to multiple downstream manufacturing facilities. How should IBM organize production and delivery of integrated circuits?

Governments all over the world depend on tax revenues to support public services such as national defense, administration of justice, and public health. Some taxes are levied on consumers, others on businesses, and some are levied on both. For instance, the United States government imposes an airport tax on airlines for every passenger that they carry. By contrast, many Asian governments collect the airport tax from the passenger. What difference would it make if the U.S. government switched to the Asian system?

We have posed four questions: Why did China abandon central planning, who organized the reconstruction of south Florida after Hurricane Andrew, how should IBM organize production and delivery of integrated circuits, and what would be the effects of a switch to collecting an airport tax from passengers rather than airlines? In this chapter, we develop the concept of economic efficiency to address such questions.

A firm understanding of economic efficiency is important to every manager because it provides the intellectual foundation for the market system. We show that market prices allocate scarce resources in an economically efficient way. This efficiency is the reason why Deng Xiao Ping switched China from central planning to a market system. The analysis also explains how market prices marshaled the resources needed to rebuild south Florida in the aftermath of Hurricane Andrew.

The same concept of economic efficiency is also fundamental in management for two reasons. First, it provides a guide to managing resources within an organization. For instance, we explain how IBM can use the concept to organize production and internal use of components.

Second, it provides a guide to opportunities for profit. Whenever the allocation of resources is not economically efficient, there is a way to make money by resolving the inefficiency. This is a simple yet very powerful rule. In this chapter, we focus on the concept of economic efficiency. Later, in Chapters 9, 11, and 12 on pricing, externalities, and asymmetric information, we apply the rule extensively to identify opportunities for profit in different contexts.

Finally, in this chapter, we apply the concept of economic efficiency to assess the various ways by which governments intervene in competitive markets. In particular, we consider the effects of ceilings and floors on market prices. Further, we analyze taxes and explain that a switch to collecting an airport tax from passengers rather than airlines will have *no* effect on the air travel market.

2 *Conditions for Economic Efficiency*

Before discussing economic efficiency, we must define this concept. An allocation of resources is **economically efficient** if no reallocation of resources can make one person better off without making another person worse off. In this definition, persons may be human beings or businesses.

To appreciate the concept of economic efficiency, let us consider an allocation of resources that is not economically efficient. Then, by some reallocation of resources, it is possible to make one person better off without making another person worse off. Clearly, the original allocation of resources is undesirable. Accordingly, it seems very reasonable to aim for economic efficiency in the allocation of resources.

An allocation of resources is **economically efficient** if no reallocation of resources can make one person better off without making another person worse off.

Sufficient Conditions

The concept of economic efficiency seems very reasonable. The definition, however, is difficult to apply in practice. It is easier to consider economic efficiency in terms of three sufficient conditions that are based on users' benefits and suppliers' costs.

An allocation of resources is economically efficient if, for every item,

1. All users achieve the same marginal benefit.

2. All suppliers operate at the same marginal cost.

3. Every user's marginal benefit is equal to every supplier's marginal cost.

For economic efficiency, every product and resource—consumer as well as industrial, goods as well as services, and domestic as well as imported—must satisfy these conditions.

Let us review these three conditions in the context of Russian passenger airlines operating under central planning.

- *Equal marginal benefit.* The first condition for economic effiency is that all users receive the same marginal benefit. Consider two people in the city of Novosibirsk, Siberia. Mikhail, a senior Communist party official, can take any number of flights anywhere in Russia free of charge. Raisa works in a factory and, every year, pays one month's wages for a flight to visit her family in Moscow. In this example, Mikhail will fly so much that the marginal flight provides almost no benefit. By contrast, Raisa's annual flight is worth at least one month's wages. If the Russian government reallocated a flight from Mikhail to Raisa, Mikhail's loss would be less than Raisa's gain, so society as a whole would be better off. This shows that an allocation of resources is economically efficient only if all users of a product achieve the same marginal benefit.

- *Equal marginal cost.* The second condition for efficiency is that all suppliers of an item must be operating at the same marginal cost. Suppose that the Central Planning Bureau has designated two airlines, Narodny Airways and Siberia Airlines, to serve the Novosibirsk–Moscow route. Owing to higher fuel efficiency and better allocation of personnel, however, Siberia Airlines' marginal cost on the route is 10% lower than that of Narodny Airways. In this case, society as a whole could reduce the cost of airline travel while maintaining the number of flights if Siberia Airlines were to expand its services and Narodny Airways were to shrink. This shows that an allocation of resources is economically efficient only if all suppliers operate at the same marginal cost.

- *Marginal benefit equals marginal cost.* The final condition for efficiency ties together users and suppliers: For a resource allocation to be economically efficient, the users' marginal benefit must balance the suppliers' marginal cost. Suppose that, in accordance with a Russian government policy of encouraging migration to Siberia, the Central Planning Bureau allocated more aircraft, fuel, and human resources to the two airlines and ordered them to increase service. To fill the extra seats, the Central Planning Bureau had to distribute free airline tickets to all factories in the Novosibirsk area. Not all the free tickets were used, which indicates that, for some passengers, the marginal benefit of flying was 0.

Under these circumstances, the marginal benefit of flying to passengers will be lower than the airlines' marginal cost. Since marginal benefit is less than marginal cost, society overall could benefit by reducing the number of flights. The cut in service will reduce the (marginal) benefit by less than it reduces the (marginal) cost. The difference between the marginal cost and the marginal benefit is a gain to society. Likewise, if the marginal benefit from some product exceeds the marginal cost of providing it, society should increase provision of that item. Accordingly, an allocation of resouces is economically efficient only if users' marginal benefit balances suppliers' marginal cost.

Philosophical Basis

We have presented the concept of economic efficiency. Let us review two aspects of this concept. The first is the distinction between economic efficiency and technical efficiency. **Technical efficiency** means providing an item at the minimum possible cost. Technical efficiency alone, however, does not imply that scarce resources are being well used. For instance, an airline may be providing service at the minimum possible cost. These, however, may be flights that no one wants. The concept of economic efficiency extends beyond technical efficiency. For economic efficiency, the quantity of the item must be such that the marginal benefit equals the marginal cost.

Technical efficiency is the provision of an item at the minimum possible cost.

The other important aspect of the concept of economic efficiency is that it assesses resource allocations in terms of each individual user's evaluation of the benefit. So, for instance, if Siberian residents like to fly and do not like to take the train, the concept takes these preferences as a given. By contrast, under communism, the central planners may disregard individual preferences and instead, impose their own view of what people should or should not consume. For instance, the Central Planning Bureau may dictate that Siberian workers should travel by train rather than plane or that only senior Communist party officials should be allowed to fly.

Progress Check 6A Referring to the market for oil, explain the difference between economic efficiency and technical efficiency.

Progress check

Internal Organization

Let us now see how to apply the same concept of economic efficiency within an organization. Suppose that Moonlight Paper has paper mills and forests in various locations. Paper is produced from wood pulp. Since Moonlight has multiple paper mills and forests, it must decide how to organize production at the various forests and delivery of wood to the various mills.

The concept of economic efficiency provides a guide to how Moonlight should use its scarce resources. Production will be efficient if all users achieve the same marginal benefit, all suppliers operate at the same marginal cost, and every user's marginal benefit balances every supplier's marginal cost.

Let us explain these three conditions in the context of Moonlight's production and delivery of wood. In this case, the users are the paper mills and the suppliers are the forests. The first condition for efficiency is that all users receive the same marginal benefit. This means that each of the company's paper mills must get the same profit from an additional ton of wood. If one mill could get more profit than another, the company should switch some supplies of wood to the mill that gets the higher profit. Then, the company's overall profit will be higher.

The second condition for efficiency is that all suppliers of an item must be operating at the same marginal cost. If one forest can produce wood at a lower marginal cost than another, then the company should direct the lower-cost forest to produce more and the higher-cost forest to produce less. This would increase the company's overall profit.

The final condition for efficiency is that the marginal benefit must balance the marginal cost. If the marginal benefit of wood to the paper mills is less than the marginal cost of producing wood, then the company should cut back production. The reduction in cost would be greater than the reduction in benefit, so overall profit would rise. By contrast, if the marginal benefit of wood is greater than the marginal cost, then the company should increase production. The company will maximize profit when the marginal benefit equals the marginal cost.

The concept of economic efficiency is very useful. It provides a guide to making the best use of scarce resources within individual organizations as well as across entire economies.

3 *Adam Smith's Invisible Hand*

"He intends only his own gain, and he is ... led by an invisible hand to promote an end which was no part of his intention" (Adam Smith, *The Wealth of Nations*, Book 4, first published in 1776).

The **invisible hand** that guides multiple buyers and sellers, acting independently and selfishly, to channel scarce resources into economically efficient uses, is the market price.

Although published over 200 years ago, Adam Smith's insight is no less valid today. In a competitive market, buyers and sellers, all acting independently and selfishly, will channel scarce resources into economically efficient uses. The **invisible hand** that guides the multitude of buyers and sellers is the market price. This invisible hand is a simple and practical way of achieving economic efficiency.

Competitive Market

Suppose that Russia privatizes airline travel and, as a result, the Novosibirsk–Moscow route becomes a perfectly competitive market. Let us see how the invisible hand will work in this market. Demand comes from individual persons and supply from airlines. Figure 6.1 shows the market equilibrium with a price of 100,000 rubles and quantity of 20,000 seats a year.

On the demand side, as we explained in Chapter 2, each person will buy enough to balance his or her marginal benefit with the price of travel, and this is

Figure 6.1 Air travel market

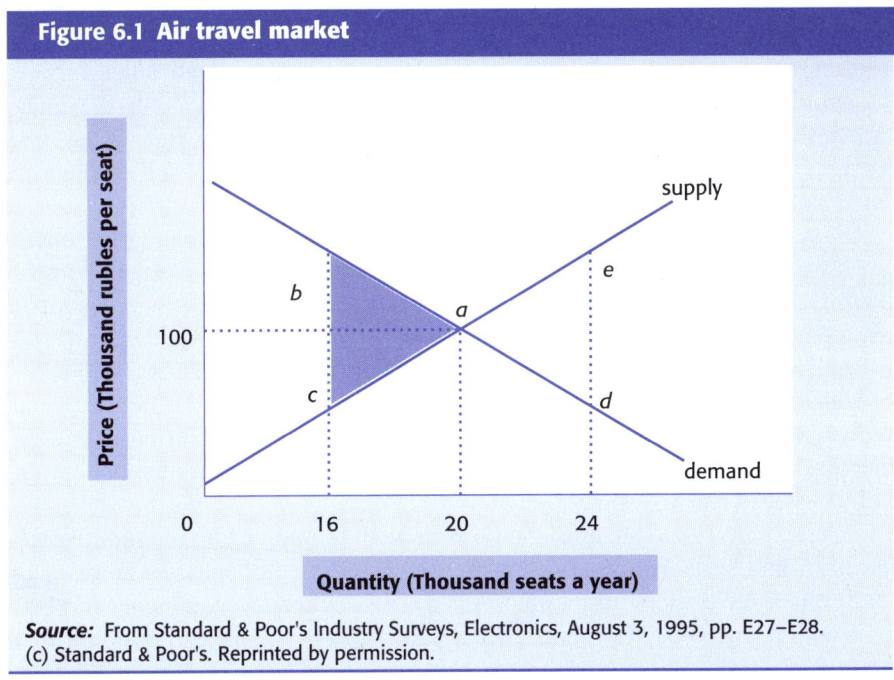

Source: From Standard & Poor's Industry Surveys, Electronics, August 3, 1995, pp. E27–E28. (c) Standard & Poor's. Reprinted by permission.

In equilibrium, the demand crosses the supply at a price of 100,000 rubles. Each consumer purchases up to the quantity where marginal benefit is 100,000 rubles. Each provider supplies the quantity where marginal cost is 100,000 rubles.

true for every buyer. In a perfectly competitive market, all buyers face the same price; hence, their respective marginal benefits will be equal. This is the first condition for economic efficiency. Note that, in deciding on his or her purchases, every individual is acting selfishly—no one is thinking about economic efficiency.

What about the airlines? On the supply side, as we explained in Chapter 4, each airline will expand up to the point where the marginal cost of a larger scale of operations just balances the price. This scale of operations maximizes profit. Again, in a perfectly competitive market, all airlines face the same price. Thus, with each airline selfishly maximizing profits, every airline will be operating at the same marginal cost. This is the second condition for economic efficiency.

We have seen that all buyers balance marginal benefit with price and all airlines balance marginal cost with price. But, in a market equilibrium, all buyers and all airlines face the same price. Therefore, marginal benefit and marginal cost must balance. This is the third condition for economic efficiency. So, a perfectly competitive market satisfies all three requirements for economic efficiency.

This example illustrates the power of Adam Smith's "invisible hand." The market price guides multiple buyers and sellers, all acting independently and selfishly, to achieve economic efficiency.

Maximum Buyer and Seller Surplus

In discussing markets, we have used the concepts of buyer and seller surplus extensively. Let us now show that economic efficiency is equivalent to maximizing the sum of market buyer surplus and market seller surplus. Recall that economic efficiency is defined by three conditions. Let us relate each of them to buyer and seller surplus.

First, if not all users achieve the same marginal benefit, then market buyer surplus could be increased by reallocating some quantity from users with lower marginal benefit to users with higher marginal benefit. Second, if not all suppliers operate at the same marginal cost, market seller surplus could be increased if suppliers with lower marginal cost produced more and suppliers with higher marginal cost produced less. Third, if not every user's marginal benefit is equal to every supplier's marginal cost, the sum of buyer and seller surplus could be increased by reducing production if marginal cost exceeds marginal benefit or, if otherwise, by raising production.

Accordingly, economic efficiency is equivalent to maximizing the sum of market buyer and seller surplus. Moreover, since perfect competition achieves economic efficiency, it also must maximize the sum of market buyer and seller surplus.

To illustrate, consider the market for air travel in Figure 6.1. Suppose that the quantity produced is 16,000 seats a year, which is less than the equilibrium quantity of 20,000. Then, by increasing the quantity to the equilibrium quantity, the sum of market buyer and seller surplus will increase by the shaded area *bca*. Likewise, if the quantity of air travel is 24,000 seats a year, which exceeds the equilibrium quantity of 20,000, then a reduction to the equilibrium quantity will increase the market buyer and seller surplus by the area *ade*. These arguments demonstrate that, with perfect competition, the market equilibrium maximizes the sum of market buyer and seller surplus.

Market System

Adam Smith's invisible hand is the market price. A price performs two roles. First, it communicates all the necessary information: The price tells buyers how much to purchase and tells sellers how much to supply. Second, it provides a concrete incentive for each buyer to purchase the quantity that balances marginal benefit with the market price: By purchasing this quantity, the buyer achieves the maximum net benefit. Similarly, the price provides a concrete incentive for every seller to supply the quantity that balances marginal cost with the market price: By supplying this quantity, the seller maximizes its profit.

*The **market** or **price** system is the economic system in which resources are allocated through the independent decisions of buyers and sellers, guided by freely moving prices.*

We give the name of **market system** or **price system** to an economic system in which resources are allocated through the independent decisions of buyers and sellers, guided by freely moving prices. The alternative names, *market system or price system*, recognize the key role of prices in markets. The role of the invisible hand in achieving economic efficiency is the intellectual foundation of the market system.

By contrast with a market system, under central planning, the Central Planning Bureau must collect information about each buyer's marginal benefit and each seller's marginal cost. Then the bureau must calculate the economically efficient purchases and sales. Finally, the bureau must persuade each buyer to purchase the efficient quantity and each seller to supply the efficient quantity.

Let us note just one difficulty for the Central Planning Bureau in collecting the required information and implementing the planned quantities. Suppose that the managers and staff of some factory decide to reduce their workload. The factory could report that it lacks sufficient personnel so that the central planning bureau would allocate more funds and workers. With the additional resources, the managers and staff of that factory will have an easier time. Indeed, one of the key problems with a centrally planned system is that work incentives are very weak. Under communism, workers receive the same wages whether they work hard or slack off.

The invisible hand explains why China and Eastern Europe abandoned central planning. Prior to World War II, East and West Germany were a single country with the same income throughout the nation. When Germany was defeated in 1945, it was divided into a Western part that adopted a market system, and an Eastern part that came under Communist central planning. After 50 years of central planning, East Germany had fallen far behind West Germany. It reunited with the West to regain an equal standard of living. The example of East and West Germany clearly proved the superiority of a market system in allocating resources. By switching to a market system, China and Eastern Europe hoped to replicate the economic success of West Germany and other market economies.

The invisible hand also explains why economists have disagreed with the predictions of many distinguished scientists regarding global resources. In Chapter 1 of this book, we recounted the warnings published in *The Limits to Growth* that world supplies of mercury, silver, tin, and zinc would be exhausted before 1995. In 1970, Stanford University professor Paul Ehrlich predicted that crude oil, natural gas, and uranium would run out by the year 2000. These very precise predictions have either been proven utterly wrong or very soon will be.

During the early 1970s, the prices of oil and many other minerals rose sharply. Many "experts" proclaimed that the sharp price increases were the harbinger of impending disaster. Far from presaging the end of the world, these rapid price increases were a critical step in the process by which resource markets were adjusting to increasing demand and diminishing supply. On the demand side, higher prices encouraged users to conserve, switch to other sources of energy, and use alternative materials. On the supply side, higher prices stimulated mineral producers to seek out new sources of supply, while encouraging businesses to develop new energy sources and alternative materials. The invisible hand has proven itself very effective in managing nonrenewable resources.

The introduction to this chapter asked who organized the reconstruction of south Florida in the wake of Hurricane Andrew. The simple answer is, "no one." The invisible hand organized building supplies, construction equipment, and labor. The increase in south Florida lumber prices signaled manufacturers such as Weyerhauser to step up production. Likewise, increases in wages attracted construction workers to south Florida. At the time, many people criticized local builders and suppliers for price gouging. Yet, it was exactly this "price gouging" that helped to resolve shortages of construction materials and labor that arose when south Florida began to rebuild.

Progress check

Progress Check 6B Some agricultural experts forecast that China's continuing economic and population growth will lead to severe shortages of grain. Explain how the invisible hand can help.

The Invisible Hand in the Electromagnetic Spectrum: Licenses for Personal Communications Services

The Federal Communications Commission (FCC) regulates telecommunications and broadcasting in the United States. As the electromagnetic spectrum is limited, one of the FCC's major responsibilities is to allocate licenses to use frequencies for wireless telecommunications and broadcasting. Until 1994, the FCC assigned licenses by administrative fiat. Administrative law judges held hearings to decide which of the many applicants deserved the limited number of licenses. When this method proved too time consuming, the FCC turned to allocating licenses by lottery. Some lotteries attracted over 500,000 applications!

In August 1993, with a view to developing a new source of revenue, Congress mandated the FCC to award licenses by competitive auction. The FCC adopted an auction procedure suggested by Stanford University professors Paul Milgrom and Robert Wilson and University of Texas (Austin) professor Preston McAfee. In July 1994, the auction for narrowband Personal Communications Services (PCS) licenses raised $617 million, while in March 1995, the auction for broadband PCS licenses raised $7.7 billion.

There are two major differences between allocation by administrative fiat and by auction. One, as emphasized by Congress, is revenue. The other is that the auction will be much more likely to assign licenses to the applicants with the highest marginal benefit. Those applicants will be willing to pay the highest bids.

When there is a limited number of items, it is economically efficient to allocate the items to the users with the highest marginal benefit. The auction will be more likely than administrative fiat to allocate licenses in an economically efficient way.

Source: Peter C. Cramton, "Money out of Thin Air: The Nationwide Narrowband PCS Auction," *Journal of Economics and Management Strategy 4*, (1995) pp. 267–343.

4 *Decentralized Management*

We have shown that the concept of economic efficiency can guide the best use of scarce resources within individual organizations as well as across whole economies. An entire economy can apply the invisible hand to achieve economic efficiency. Let us now see how an individual organization can also apply the invisible hand.

Internal Market

Recall that Moonlight Paper needs to organize production and delivery of wood. Suppose that there is a competitive market for the wood used to make paper. One approach is central planning: The company headquarters can collect information about production costs and revenues from all the various forests and mills, and then decide how much each forest should produce and deliver to each mill.

An alternative for Moonlight is to decentralize management of wood production in the following way. Moonlight should direct the managers of every forest to maximize profit and sell wood at the market price, whether to the company's own paper mills or outside buyers. Similarly, Moonlight should direct every mill to maximize profit and allow mills the freedom to buy wood from any supplier, whether it be one of the company's own forests or an outside source.

Under the decentralized policy, if one of Moonlight's forests sells wood to one of Moonlight's mills, the forest must charge the market price. As this sale is a transfer within the same organization, the corresponding price is called a **transfer price**. Moonlight should set the transfer price for wood equal to the market price.

With the the decentralized policy, each paper mill will buy wood up to the point that its marginal benefit balances the market price. Since all mills face the same market price, their marginal benefits will be equal. Similarly, each forest will produce up to the point that its marginal cost balances the market price. As all forests face the same market price, their marginal costs will be equal. Since the mills and the forests face the same market price, marginal benefit will be equal to marginal cost. Thus, the decentralized policy achieves the three conditions for economic efficiency within the same organization. Essentially, by decentralizing wood production, Moonlight is establishing an internal market that is integrated with the external market.

> A **transfer price** is the price charged for the sale of an item within the same organization.

Implementation

The Moonlight example illustrates two general rules that an organization should follow when decentralizing control over an internal resource. First, if there is a competitive market for the item, the transfer price should be set equal to the market price. If there is no competitive market for the item, then the appropriate transfer price is more complicated. The reader should refer to the Further Reading section at the end of this chapter for a source of such information.

Outsourcing is the purchase of services or supplies from external sources.

The second general rule of decentralized management is that producing units should be allowed to sell the product to outside buyers and consuming units should be allowed to buy the product from external sources. Purchase of services or supplies from external sources is described as **outsourcing**.

To explain why the right of outsourcing is crucial, suppose that Moonlight required all mills to buy wood only from the company's own forests. Then, the forests would have market power, and as we show in Chapter 8 they would charge a price above the competitive market level. As a result, the mills would no longer purchase the economically efficient quantity of wood. A similar argument shows why it is necessary to allow producing units to sell the product to outside buyers.

Any organization that uses resources or products for which there are competitive markets can apply decentralization to achieve internal economic efficiency. For example, financial institutions can apply decentralization to manage the internal use of funds, oil companies can apply the technique to manage production and use of crude oil, and auto manufacturers can apply it to manage production and use of components.

The introduction to this chapter asked how IBM, the world's seventh largest manufacturer of integrated circuits, should organize production and delivery of these components. The answer is that IBM should decentralize the management of those integrated circuits for which there are competitive markets. This will ensure that production and delivery are economically efficient.

Progress check

Progress Check 6C Bank Luna has two divisions, corporate lending and consumer lending. Both divisions draw funds from a central treasury. Explain how the bank can use decentralization to ensure efficient use of the funds.

Half an Invisible Hand: Pricing Supplies at the Anderson School

In 1989, University of California's (Los Angeles) (UCLA) Anderson Graduate School of Management adopted a pricing system to encourage members of the faculty and staff to economize on services and supplies. The dean's office allocated a budget for services and supplies to each academic department. In turn, the dean's office charged each department for telephone calls, photocopying paper, and other services and supplies. For administrative convenience, the dean's office excluded some basic items from the new pricing system. One of the omitted items was bond paper.

The new system was very effective in cutting the school's consumption of photocopying paper. At the same time, however, there was a significant jump in the use of bond paper and breakdown of photocopying machines. The reason soon became very obvious: Because the pricing system excluded bond paper, secretaries throughout the Anderson School had switched to feeding bond paper into their photocopying machines.

5 *Capital Markets*

For economic efficiency, the marginal benefit must balance the marginal cost in all markets, including those for capital. In a market system, there are markets for shares, bonds, and loans. These markets extend beyond these organized exchanges like the New York and London Stock Exchanges to banks, other financial intermediaries, insurance companies, and individual investors.

Allocation of Capital

A **capital market** comprises buyers and sellers of investment funds in communication with one another for voluntary exchange. Capital markets channel funds from individuals and institutions with surplus funds to those in need of funds. Owing to the central role of capital markets, another name for a market system is the *capitalist* system.

By contrast with a market system, under central planning, the government owns all property and there are no capital markets. Instead, the Central Planning Bureau allocates funds for investments. Traditional Marxist principles emphasized heavy industries such as coal mining, rail transportation, chemicals, and steel. Accordingly, the Communist governments of Eastern Europe and China directed resources toward heavy industry and away from agriculture and light industry.

For instance, in the 1950s, China's economy was predominantly agricultural and the country had relatively little capital. Nevertheless, the government depressed interest rates and the prices of raw materials to subsidize the development of heavy industries such as chemicals and steel. Following Deng Xiao Ping's "Four Modernizations," however, the Chinese government relaxed the emphasis on heavy industry and also encouraged private investment. The result was a boom in agriculture, light manufacturing such as toys and clothing, and services such as entertainment and travel.

We are not saying that heavy industries such as chemicals and steel are necessarily bad or that light manufacturing is necessarily good. Rather, we mean that there should be a balance between heavy industry and other sectors and that this balance should depend on the country's economic resources. For instance, Germany, one of the world's leading market economies, has the world's three largest chemical manufacturers and a substantial steel industry. It makes sense that a rich country like Germany should focus on capital-intensive businesses. By contrast, China, which has relatively more human resources, should focus on labor-intensive production. To achieve an economically efficient balance, it is best to leave the balancing process to the invisible hand.

An economy that employs central planners instead of the invisible hand runs the risk of resources being misallocated. The central planners may not be able to get all the information necessary to manage the economy, they may not be able to persuade all individuals to comply with central directives, or they may even deliberately direct resources in an inefficient way.

*A **capital market** comprises buyers and sellers of investment funds in communication with one another for voluntary exchange.*

Progress check

Progress Check 6D At one time, the Soviet Union produced more steel than the United States. The Communist government hailed this as a great achievement and proof of the Soviet Union's economic success. Do you agree?

Bankruptcy

As we have just stressed, in a market system, investment funds are channeled through capital markets. In capital markets, the supply side includes lenders as well as investors in shares and bonds. Lenders and investors devote considerable effort to assessing potential borrowers and investments. Lenders want to know potential borrowers' ability to repay. Investors want to know how much profit they can expect. Since no one can perfectly predict the future, some lenders and investors will make mistakes. A market system provides for this possibility through the institution of bankruptcy.

Bankruptcy is a set of legal provisions that take effect when an entity (person, partnership, or company) cannot meet its obligations to lenders. Bankruptcy is a distinctive feature of a market system.

Let us see how bankruptcy works. Suppose that Sol Trucking is overstaffed relative to its fleet, so its costs are higher than those competing carriers. Then society would be better off with Sol's human and physical resources reallocated toward the lower-cost carriers. Society could get the same amount of service at lower cost. In a market system, Sol will accumulate losses and, eventually, reach a point where it cannot pay its bills. At that point, Sol's lenders may institute bankruptcy proceedings to close the carrier and recover their loans.

We should emphasize that, when Sol goes bankrupt, nothing will necessarily be destroyed. For instance, Sol's trucks may be sold to other carriers and Sol's personnel will find employment elsewhere. Indeed, these movements are necessary steps in the process of reallocating Sol's human and physical resources to more effective management.

Although employees in weak businesses live in fear of bankruptcy, we contend that, from a social standpoint, the institution of bankruptcy is good. The institution of bankruptcy helps to improve the allocation of resources. Indeed, one of the conditions for a market to be perfectly competitive is that there be no barriers to exit. The institution of bankruptcy facilitates exit and hence helps to make a market more competitive.

By contrast, in a centrally planned economy, the government supports all enterprises, whether they make profits or losses: The institution of bankruptcy does not exist. Consequently, there is no pressure to reallocate resources from inefficient to efficient uses.

> **Bankruptcy** is a set of legal provisions that take effect when an entity cannot meet its obligations to lenders.

The Aftermath of Bankruptcy: Barings PLC

Barings PLC, the 233-year-old British investment bank, collapsed on the weekend of February 26, 1995. Management disclosed that Barings' Singapore futures trading business had amassed losses of £827 million. These losses far exceeded Barings' equity capital of £325 million. Britain's central bank, the Bank of England, tried to arrange a rescue. When this attempt failed, Barings was forced into administration, which is a form of bankruptcy in the British legal system.

Some of Barings' businesses, however, were deemed to be very sound. Only 10 days later, on March 6, Internationale Nederlanden Groep NV (ING), a Dutch financial services group, purchased Barings' asset-management, banking, and securities subsidiaries. ING quickly injected £660 million of new capital, which allowed these businesses to resume normal operations.

ING, however, stopped short of buying Barings PLC, the publicly listed holding company; neither did it assume responsibility for the holding company's debt and preferred shares. Barings' ordinary shares became worthless.

ING retained most of Barings' asset-management, banking, and securities personnel. To dissuade key Barings personnel from quitting, ING even provided £95 million to pay bonuses for 1994. The new owners dismissed just two dozen senior executives, whom it held responsible for the collapse. Peter Baring and Andrew Tuckey, respectively chairman and deputy chairman of Barings, were among those who resigned or were fired.

Sources: "Gone Dutch," *The Economist* (March 11, 1995), p. 89; "ING Baring Unit Is Denied Deals by U.K. Firms," *Asian Wall Street Journal* (March 20, 1995), p. 1; "ING Drops Axe on 21 at Barings," *South China Morning Post* (May 2, 1995), Business, p. 12.

No Way Out: Business in India

Although India encourages private enterprise, the government restricts some rights to which businesses in other countries are accustomed. Under Indian labor laws, a business must get official permission to dismiss workers or shut down. For fear of powerful labor unions, however, the government is rarely willing to grant such permission.

This means that, even when business prospects are poor, investors cannot shut down and instead must accumulate losses until they have exhausted their entire capital. For example, in the center of Bombay, a large number of old textile mills occupy some of the most expensive real estate in the world. An economically efficient solution would be to relocate the mills to areas with cheaper land and cheaper labor, then to redevelop their present sites for commercial or residential use. Without government permission, however, the mills cannot move, and they continue to creak along.

Not only do India's labor laws prevent reallocation of resources, they also deter new investment. In a system where investors lack the option of shutting down, the risk of making an investment is higher and hence the supply of new investment is smaller.

Sources: "How to Keep Investors Out," *The Economist* (June 11, 1994), p. 27; "The Most Expensive Slum in the World," *The Economist* (May 6, 1995), pp. 29–30.

6 *Price Ceilings*

We have discussed two extreme models of economic management: central planning and the market system. Even within a market system, however, the government may choose to intervene with the market outcome. The intervention may take the form of controls on prices or taxes. Let us now analyze the effects of government intervention in a market system.

Rent Control

Housing is considered a necessity, and so, it attracts considerable government attention. The supply of housing tends to be fairly inelastic especially in the short run. When rising incomes and population growth cause demand to increase, the result is rapid increases in rents and a shortage of "affordable" housing.

One response to rising rents is rent control. Rent control, so the argument goes, makes housing more affordable and protects poor tenants from rapacious landlords. In reality, does rent control relieve shortages of affordable housing? Who benefits from rent control and who loses?

New York and Los Angeles are just two of the many American cities that regulate residential rents. Supposing that New York's apartment market were perfectly competitive, let us apply demand-supply analysis to learn the effects of New York's rent control. First, we draw the demand for residential rental units and then the supply of rental units in Figure 6.2. Suppose that the equilibrium is at point *b*, with a rental of $1000 per month and 300,000 units rented.

A **price ceiling** is an upper limit to the price that sellers can charge and buyers can pay.

Rent control is a **price ceiling:** It sets an upper limit to the rent that landlords can charge and renters can pay. If the limit exceeds the free-market equilibrium rent, then the rent control is irrelevant. The rent control bites only when the limit falls below the free-market equilibrium rent.

Suppose that the typical controlled rent is 10% below the free-market equilibrium. To illustrate this, on Figure 6.2, we mark the point $900 on the monthly rent axis and draw a horizontal line outward. This $900 line first crosses the supply curve, showing that landlords will supply 290,000 units at $900 per month. Then the $900 line crosses the demand curve, showing that renters will demand 310,000 units at $900 per month.

At a rent of $900 per month, quantity demanded exceeds quantity supplied by 310,000 – 290,000 = 20,000 units per month. There is an excess demand of 20,000 units per month. So, far from alleviating the shortage of affordable housing, rent control exacerbates the problem by stimulating demand and discouraging supply. The result is that the number of renters seeking housing exceeds available quantity. In general, whenever the government sets a price ceiling below the free-market equilibrium, there will be excess demand.

Figure 6.2 Rent control

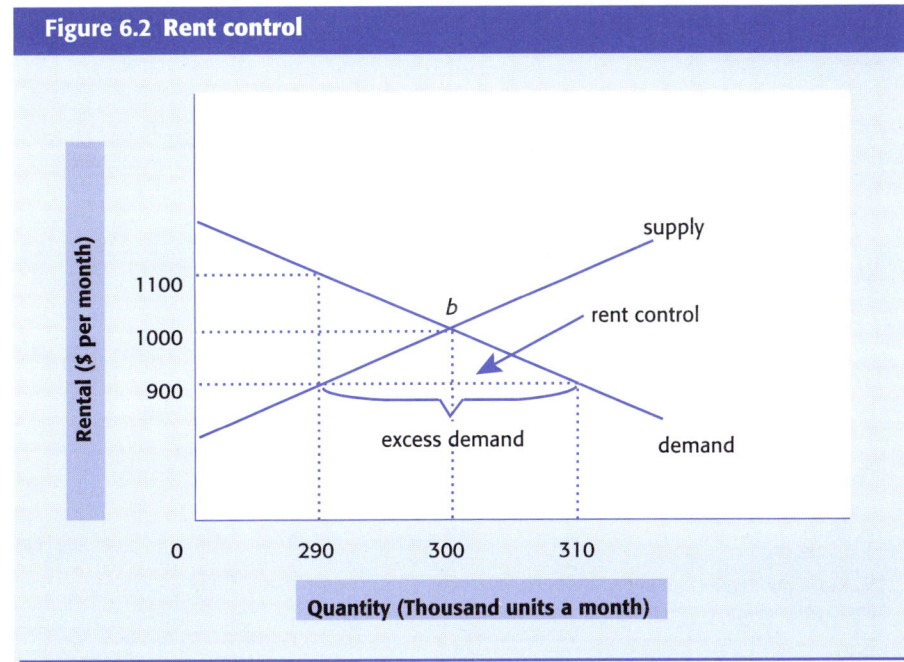

The rent control of $900 per month results in excess demand of 20,000 units.

What determines the degree of shortage? In our example, a 10% reduction in rent from $1000 to $900 per month caused landlords to reduce quantity supplied by 3.33% from 300,000 to 290,000 units per month. So, the price elasticity of supply at a rent of $1000 was 3.33/10 = 0.33.

Suppose, instead, that the price elasticity of supply had been 0.5. Then the 10% reduction in rent would have caused landlords to change quantity supplied by 0.5 × (–10)%; that is, reduce it by 5%. This means that the number of units available at a $900 per month rent would be 0.95 × 300,000 = 285,000 units. Generally, the more elastic is the supply, the greater will be the shortage. Similarly, the more elastic is the demand, the greater the shortage that rent controls will create.

The amount of excess demand (or shortage) also depends on the controlled rent. The higher the controlled rent, the more units landlords will supply and the fewer units renters will demand; hence, the excess demand will be smaller. In particular, if the control is set at or above the free-market equilibrium rate of $1000 per month, there will be no excess demand.

Whenever there is a shift in demand or supply, buyers and sellers will be concerned about the effects on price and sales. From Chapter 5, we know that

Figure 6.3 Buyer surplus

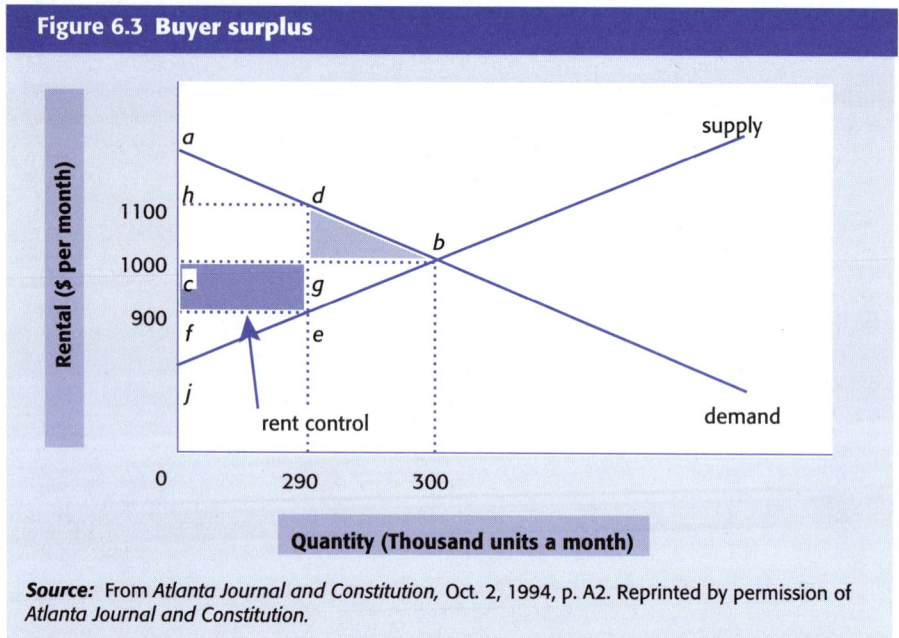

Source: From *Atlanta Journal and Constitution,* Oct. 2, 1994, p. A2. Reprinted by permission of *Atlanta Journal and Constitution.*

The rent control increases buyer surplus by the area *cfeg* as some tenants get units for $100 a month lower rent. The rent control reduces buyer surplus by the area *dgb* because some renters who are willing to pay $1000 per month cannot get housing.

the effects depend on the elasticities of demand and supply. We have just shown the same is true when the government sets a price ceiling.

Gains and Losses

When the government sets a price ceiling, an important concern is the costs and benefits to buyers and sellers. For instance, in the case of rent control, who gains and who loses? We can apply the concepts of buyer and seller surplus to address these questions.

First, consider renters. Referring to Figure 6.3, at the free-market equilibrium rate of $1000 per month, buyer surplus is the area *acb* under the demand curve down to the $1000 level. With rent control, the rent drops to $900 per month but only 290,000 units are available. So, the buyer surplus is now the area *afed* under the demand curve down to the rental of $900 per month and limited by the quantity of 290,000 units per month.

Thus, as a result of rent control, buyer surplus increases by the shaded area *cfeg* as some tenants get units for $100 a month less than before. On the other hand, buyer surplus falls by shaded area *dgb* as some renters who are willing to pay $1000 per month cannot get housing. Our analysis indicates that some renters benefit from rent control, while others lose. The gains may outweigh the

Figure 6.4 Seller surplus

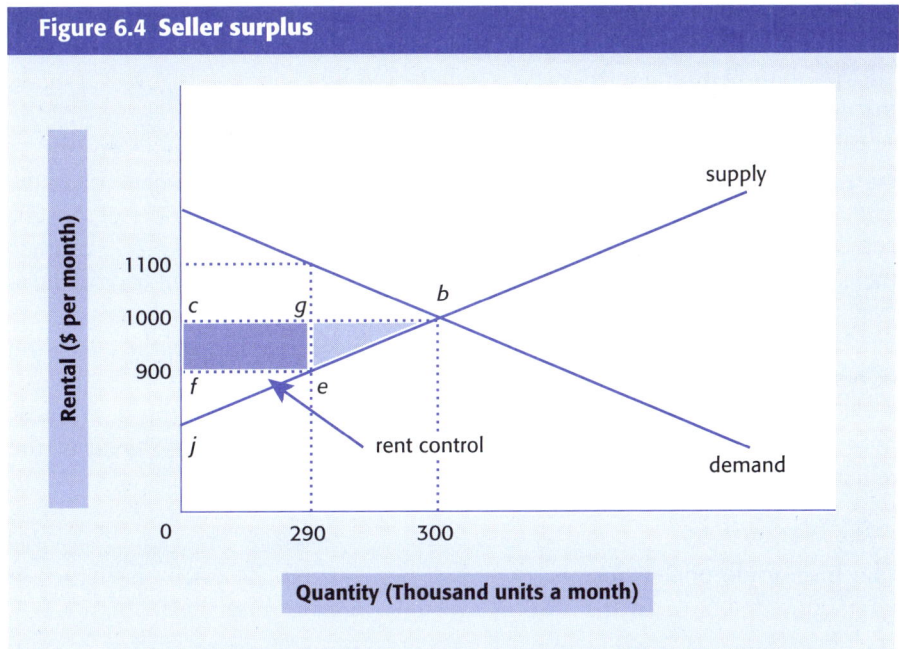

The rent control reduces seller surplus by the shaded area *geb* as some landlords withdraw from the market and by the shaded area *cfeg* as other landlords who continue in business receive $100 less rent.

losses or they may be smaller than the losses. In general, we cannot say whether buyer surplus will rise or drop on a net basis.

The picture on the supply side is much simpler. Referring to Figure 6.4, at the free-market equilibrium, seller surplus is the area *cjb* above the supply curve up to the $1000 level. With rent control, the rent drops to $900 per month and landlords cut back quantity supplied to 290,000 units. Seller surplus now is the area *fje* above the supply curve up to the $900 level. Hence, seller surplus clearly falls: Some landlords withdraw from the market (shaded area *geb*) and landlords who continue in business receive $100 less rent (shaded area *cfeg*). So, seller surplus unequivocally falls.

Deadweight Loss

The buyer surplus increases by the shaded area *cfeg* and falls by the shaded area *dgb*. So, part of the landlords' loss, the shaded area *cfeg*, is the tenants' gain: The reduction in rent for the units that continue in the market is a pure transfer from landlords to tenants. Part of the landlords' loss, the shaded area *geb*, however, is a complete loss in the sense that it does not show up as a gain to renters.

This difference is called a **deadweight loss.** A *deadweight loss* is any loss of buyer surplus or seller surplus that is not transferred to another party. Buyer

A **deadweight loss** is any loss of buyer or seller surplus that is not transferred to another party.

surplus falls by the shaded area *dgb*. This loss does not accrue to any other party; hence, it is also a deadweight loss. Accordingly, the total deadweight loss arising from the rent control is the shaded areas *dgb* and *geb*. Figure 6.5 shows the deadweight loss.

Generally, a deadweight loss arises whenever sellers are willing to provide an item at a price that buyers are willing to pay and that provision does not occur. In the case of the rent control, Figure 6.5 shows that, between the quantities of 290,000 and 300,000, landlords are willing to rent 10,000 units at a marginal cost lower than the corresponding marginal benefit to renters. As a result of the rent control, however, these units are not provided. Accordingly, there is a deadweight loss.

When the marginal benefit is not equal to the marginal cost, the allocation of resources violates the third condition for economic efficiency. This suggests another way to calculate the deadweight loss: It is the sum of the differences between the buyers' marginal benefits and the sellers' marginal costs for all the units that are not provided.

Price Elasticities

The magnitude of the deadweight losses depends on the price elasticities of demand and supply. In the case of the rent control, referring to Figure 6.5,

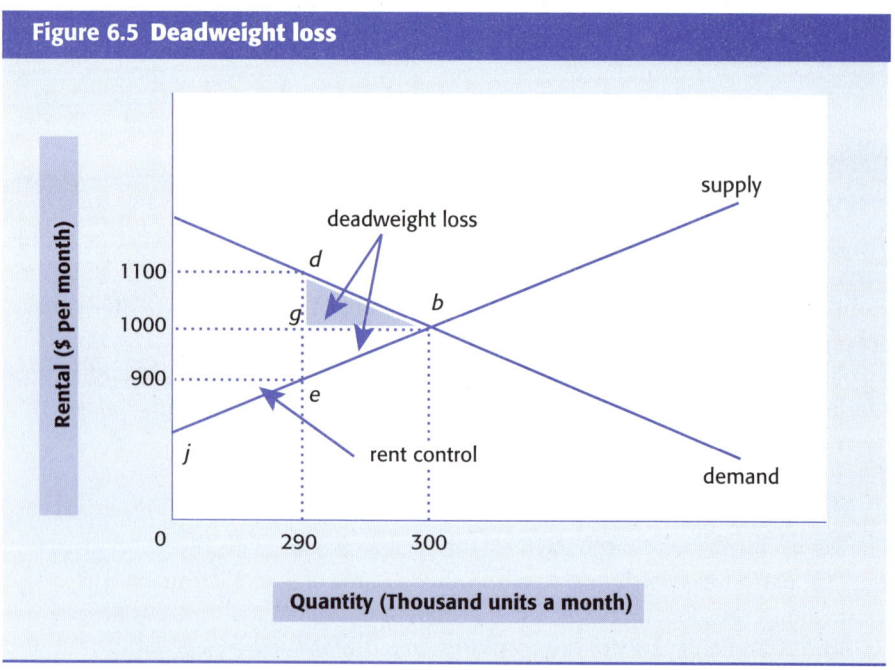

Figure 6.5 Deadweight loss

Rent control causes a deadweight loss of the shaded areas *dgb* and *geb*. The more inelastic demand is, the larger the area *dbg* will be. The more elastic supply is, the larger the area *geb* will be.

given that the quantity supplied falls to 290,000 units, area *dgb* will be larger the more inelastic is demand. Intuitively, the less sensitive renters are to rent increases, the greater will be the pain that they will suffer from having fewer units to rent.

Similarly, the more elastic the supply, the greater will be the cut in quantity supplied resulting from the 10% rent cut. The bigger the cut in quantity supplied, the larger will be area *geb*. Intuitively, the more sensitive are landlords to a cut in rent, the more units they will take off the market; hence, fewer units will be there for renters.

The rent control example highlights a general point: The deadweight losses will be relatively larger when demand is more inelastic or supply is more elastic. Deadweight losses arise whenever sellers are willing to provide an item at a price buyers are willing to pay and that provision does not occur. Deadweight losses are a serious cost of government interference with a competitive market.

Progress Check 6E In Figure 6.5, mark the deadweight loss with a rent control of $800 per month. Shade the areas representing the changes in buyer and seller surplus.

Progress check

Circumventing Rent Control: Obituary Pages and Key Money

Generally, when a market is out of free-market equilibrium, the marginal benefit is not equal to the marginal cost. Then, there is an opportunity to make a profit by resolving the economic inefficiency. In the case of rent control, landlords and renters resort to a number of creative mechanisms. Some New Yorkers regularly scan newspaper obituary pages to spot rent-controlled units that might become available. These activities are deadweight losses, as the costs incurred in such activities do not accrue as a benefit to another party.

Another way of circumventing rent control is "key money." The owner or holder of a lease on a rent-controlled unit may charge a hefty nonrefundable fee to change the locks on the unit. Key money is a pure transfer from tenants to landlords, so it is not a deadweight loss. To the extent that renters can indirectly pay more than the regulated rent, the quantity of units supplied will be increased. Key money is an illicit way of pushing the rent, and hence the quantity of units supplied to the free market equilibrium. To the extent that key money is effective in increasing the number of apartments for rent, it reduces the deadweight loss.

Price Ceilings and the Profitability of China's State-owned Enterprises

Shanghai Petrochemical is listed on the Hong Kong and New York Stock Exchanges. In 1993, the company was among the first of China's state-owned enterprises to be restructured and listed on international exchanges. The following year, securities analysts applauded when the company announced its annual results. The company had achieved a 73% increase in profit to 1.78 billion yuan.

A closer look at the company, however, provided a different picture. In 1994, Shanghai Petrochemical was able to raise prices of synthetic fibers by 30–35%, as the Chinese government relaxed restrictions on the prices of chemicals.

Crude oil accounted for almost half of Shanghai Petrochemical's costs. The Chinese government supplied Shanghai Petrochemical with 4.5 million metric tons of crude at a government-controlled price of 689 yuan. Compared with the free-market price of 1100 yuan, this was an implicit subsidy of 1.85 billion yuan. When this subsidy was deducted from the company's reported profit of 1.78 billion yuan, the financial picture did not look so rosy after all. In fact, the company's profitability depended critically on continued government support.

Shanghai Petrochemical's use of oil was not economically efficient. It was using oil at a price 35% below the market price that other manufacturers had to pay. Hence, the allocation of oil did not meet the equal marginal benefit condition for economic efficiency.

Source: I.P.L. Png and Changqi Wu, "A Tale of Two Companies," *Far Eastern Economic Review* (October 12, 1995), p. 39.

7 Price Floors

A **price floor** is a lower limit to the price that sellers can charge and buyers can pay.

Rent control is an example of a price ceiling. Another way by which governments intervene in markets is to set a floor below the market price. A **price floor** is a lower limit to the price that sellers can charge and buyers can pay. A minimum wage is a price floor in the labor market. In the United States, the federal government stipulates a minimum wage that applies throughout the country. As Table 6.2 shows, individual states may set minimum wages above the federal minimum. Some Asian and many European countries also set minimum wages.

Table 6.2 **State minimum wages, 1994**	
State	**Minimum Wage ($ per hour)**
Hawaii	5.25
District of Columbia	5.25
New Jersey	5.05
Washington	4.90
Alaska	4.75
Oregon	4.75
Iowa	4.65
Rhode Island	4.45
Connecticut	4.27

Source: Atlanta Journal and Constitution (October 2, 1994), p. A2.

Minimum Wage

How does a minimum wage affect wages, earnings, and employment? We use demand-supply analysis to address these questions. We will see that, under some conditions, a minimum wage can reduce the total earnings of workers.

Suppose that the market for labor is perfectly competitive. In Figure 6.6, we mark the wage rate on the vertical axis and quantity of labor on the horizontal axis. Then we draw employers' demand for labor and workers' supply of labor. Suppose that the equilibrium is at point b, with a wage is $4.00 per hour and that, at that wage, employment is 3 billion worker-hours a week.

To have any effect, the minimum wage must exceed the free-market equilibrium. Suppose that the minimum wage is $4.20 per hour, which is 5% above the equilibrium wage. The higher the wage rate, the less labor employers will want to hire. Suppose that the elasticity of labor demand with respect to the wage is –0.6. Then, the rise in the wage to $4.20 per hour will change the quantity demanded of labor by $-0.6 \times 5 = -3\%$; that is, reduce it by 3%. Hence, referring to Figure 6.6, at the wage of $4.20 per hour, the quantity of labor demanded would be 2.91 billion worker-hours.

A higher wage, however, increases the quantity supplied as more people enter the labor force and part-timers switch to full-time work. Suppose that the elasticity of labor supply with respect to the wage is 0.2. Then, the 5% wage increase will increase the quantity of labor supplied by $0.2 \times 5 = 1\%$. Hence,

Figure 6.6 Minimum wage

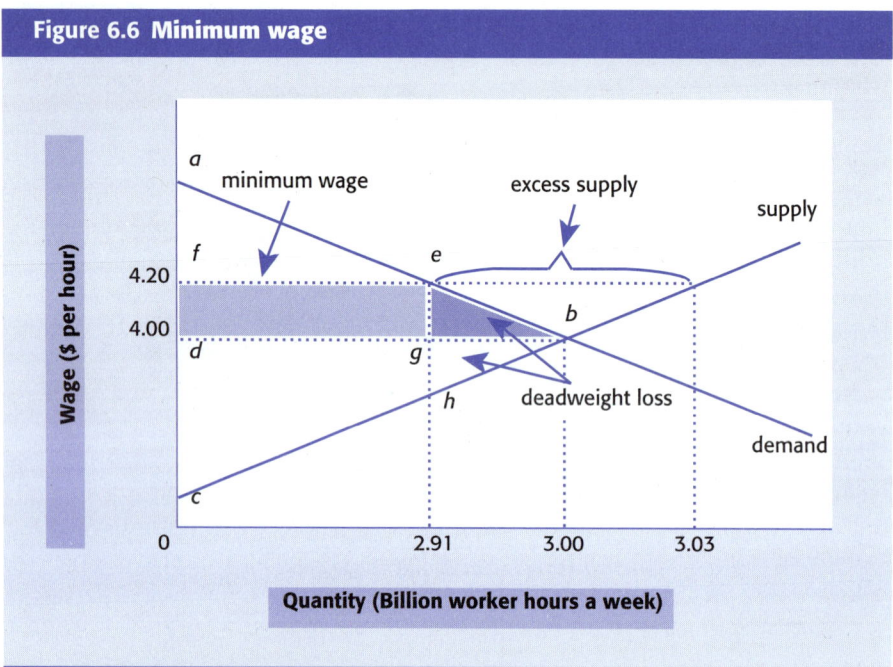

The minimum wage of $4.20 results in excess supply of 120 million worker-hours a week and deadweight loss equal to area *egb* and *ghb*.

referring to Figure 6.6, at the wage of $4.20 per hour, the quantity supplied of labor is 3.03 billion worker-hours. The result of the minimum wage is excess supply of 3.03 – 2.91 = 0.12 billion worker-hours or 120 million worker-hours.

Compared with the free-market equilibrium, the wage is higher but total employment is lower. Let us consider the impact on total earnings. Total earnings equal the wage multiplied by number of hours worked. With a free market, total earnings are 4.00 × 3.0 = $12 billion a week. With the $4.20 minimum wage, total earnings are 4.20 × 2.91 = $12.22 billion, which is $220 million higher than the free-market equilibrium.

Suppose, however, that the demand for labor is more elastic. Specifically, suppose that the wage elasticity is –1.2. Then, the 5% increase in the minimum wage will cause the quantity demanded of labor to fall by 1.2 × 5 = 6%. With a 6% reduction, the quantity demanded of labor will become 2.82 billion worker-hours a week. Then, total earnings with the minimum wage would be $4.20 × 2.82 = $11.844 billion a week. As calculated previously, with a free market, total earnings are $12 billion a week. Hence, the minimum wage reduces total earnings by $12 – 11.844 = $0.156 billion or $156 million a week.

This example shows that whether a minimum wage raises or reduces total earnings depends on the wage elasticity of demand for labor. The more elastic is the demand for labor, the more likely is it that a minimum wage will reduce total earnings. By contrast, if the demand for labor is inelastic, a minimum wage will increase total earnings.

Gains and Losses

Let us also consider the costs and benefits of the minimum wage in terms of buyer and seller surplus. In the labor market, the buyers are businesses and the sellers are people. Referring to Figure 6.6, at the free-market equilibrium, the buyer surplus is area *adb*. With the minimum wage, the buyer surplus becomes the area *afe*. Hence, the minimum wage reduces buyer surplus by the shaded area *fdge* and the shaded area *egb*.

At the free market equilibrium, the seller surplus is area *dcb*. With the minimum wage, the seller surplus becomes the area under the wage of $4.20 and above the supply curve up to the quantity that employers demand, that is, 2.91 billion hours a week. This area is *fche*. Hence, as a result of the minimum wage, the seller surplus falls by the area *ghb*, as some workers lose employment, and increases by the area *fdge*, as those workers who retain employment gain a higher wage.

Accordingly, the minimum wage may increase or reduce seller surplus, depending on whether area *fdge* is greater or smaller than area *ghb*. Essentially, the less elastic the demand for labor, the more likely it is that the minimum wage will increase seller surplus.

Part of the buyers' loss of surplus (shaded area *fdge*) accrues to sellers in the form of a higher wage. The other part (shaded area *egb*), is a deadweight loss. There is also deadweight loss (shaded area *ghb*) on the seller side. The total deadweight loss is the areas *egb* and *ghb*.

Intuitively, the deadweight loss arises because workers willing to provide labor at a wage of $4.00, which buyers are willing to pay, cannot provide that labor. Hence, another way to calculate the deadweight loss is the sum of the differences between the buyers' marginal benefits and the sellers' marginal costs for all the work that is not provided.

Progress Check 6F In Figure 6.6, mark the deadweight loss with a minimum wage of $4.50 per hour. Compare it with the the deadweight loss at the $4.20 minimum.

Progress check

Heterogeneous Labor

So far, we have treated all labor as homogeneous and, hence, traded in a single market. Realistically, there are many different grades of labor. The equilibrium wage for skilled labor is much higher than the legal minimum, so the minimum wage does not have a significant direct effect on the market for skilled labor.

There may be an indirect effect, however. By raising the cost of low-skilled labor, the minimum wage encourages employers to substitute away from low-skilled labor toward more automated operations. This will increase the demand for skilled labor. Thus, while an increase in the minimum wage will reduce employment of low-skilled labor, it may increase the employment of skilled labor.

In most countries, a relatively larger proportion of skilled workers join unions. Accordingly, unions tend to represent the interests of skilled workers. Our explanation of the effect of a minimum wage on the demand for skilled labor explains why unions often favor increases in the minimum wage, even though their members earn far more than the minimum.

8 *Taxes*

In addition to controls on prices, another way by which governments often intervene in markets is through taxes. The introduction to this chapter asked about the effects of a switch to collecting an airport tax from passengers rather than airlines. To address this question, we must first understand the impact of taxes on a market.

Let us apply the demand-supply framework to investigate the effect of taxes on market price and quantity. Specifically, suppose that the U.S. government levies a $10 tax on international airline tickets. How would this affect the market for air travel between Chicago and London?

Buyer's vis-à-vis Seller's Price

We assume that the market is perfectly competitive. The demand comes from business and leisure travelers, while American and foreign airlines provide the supply. Since this market is subject to a tax, it is necessary to make one change to the usual demand-supply analysis. We must distinguish the price that buyers pay (buyer's price) from the price that sellers receive (seller's price). The seller's price is the buyer's price minus the amount of the tax.

We draw the demand and supply curves in Figure 6.7. Suppose that, initially, there is no tax on airline tickets and the equilibrium is at point b, with a price of $800. Since there is no tax, $800 is the buyer's price as well as the seller's price. At the price of $800, airlines sell 920,000 tickets a year.

Now the federal government requires airlines to pay a tax of $10 on each ticket. This raises the marginal cost of delivering economy class air travel between Chicago and London by $10. Note that the same $10 applies, regardless of the number of tickets that the airlines sell. Accordingly, the $10 tax increases the airlines' marginal cost at all quantities of tickets. Graphically, in Figure 6.7, we represent the tax by shifting the entire supply curve up by $10.

Figure 6.7 Airline travel tax

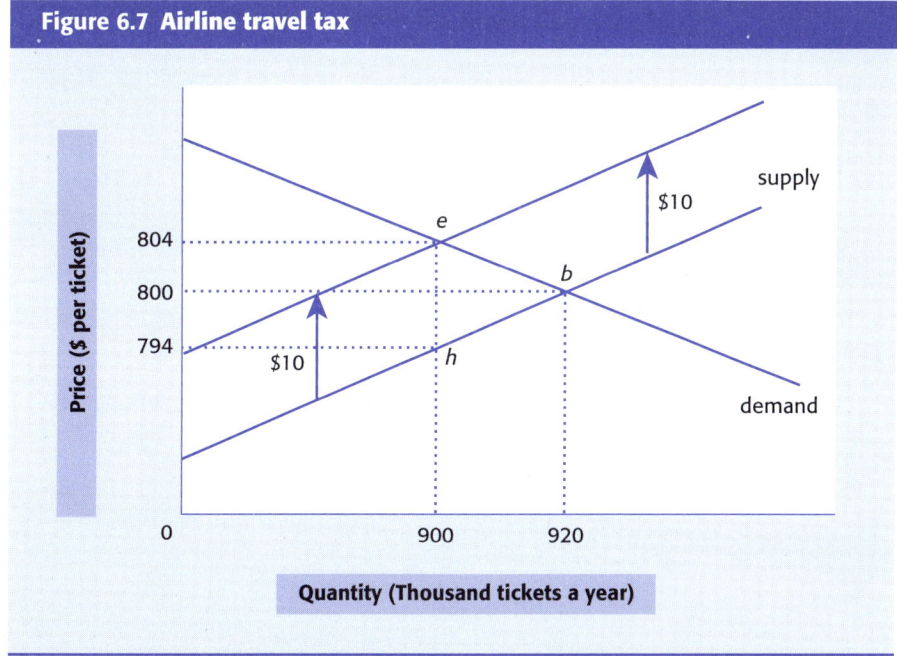

The tax of $10 per ticket raises the marginal cost of supplying air travel, increases the buyer's price to $804, and reduces the quantity to 900,000 tickets a year.

As a result of the tax, there will be a new equilibrium at point *e*, with a price of $804 and quantity of 900,000 tickets a year. The price is higher and the quantity of travel is smaller. Now that there is a tax, the buyer's price differs from the seller's price. The buyer's price is $804, while the seller's price is the buyer's price less the $10 tax, or $794. In the new equilibrium, the seller's price of $794 is lower than the original seller's price with no tax, which was $800.

Incidence

What determines the extent to which the buyer's price increases, the seller's price falls, and the quantity falls? In general, the effect on prices and quantity depends on the price elasticities of demand and supply. With moderate demand and supply elasticities, the buyer's price will rise by less than the amount of the tax, the seller's price will drop by less than the amount of the tax, and the quantity will fall by some amount.

Referring to Figure 6.8, the buyer's price rises to $804, the seller's price falls to $794, and the quantity falls to 900,000 tickets. Recall from Chapter 5 that *incidence* is the change in the price for buyer or seller resulting from shift in demand or supply or some other condition. In the same way, tax experts use

Figure 6.8 Gains and losses from tax

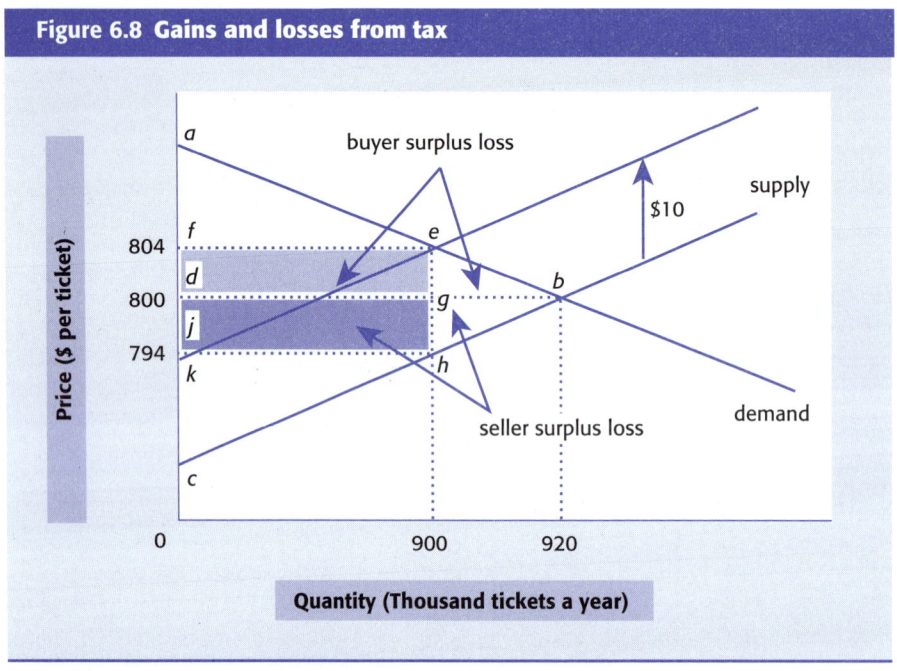

The tax reduces buyer surplus by the shaded area *egb* because travelers make fewer trips the shaded area *fdge* because travelers must pay $4 more. The tax also reduces seller surplus by the shaded area *ghb* because airlines sell fewer tickets and by the shaded area *djhg* because they receive $6 less for each ticket.

Tax incidence describes the actual burden of a tax in terms of the change in either the price or buyer/seller surplus.

incidence to describe the actual burden of a tax. In our example, the change in the buyer's price is $804 – $800 = $4, hence, the incidence on the demand side is $4. The change in the seller's price is $800 – $794 = $6, so the incidence on the supply side is $6.

Another way of looking at incidence is to consider the effect on buyer and seller surplus. Before the tax, the buyer surplus was area *adb*, and after the tax, the buyer surplus is area *afe*. Accordingly, the tax affects the buyer surplus in two ways. First, it reduces the buyer surplus by the shaded area *egb* because travelers make fewer trips. Second, it reduces the buyer surplus by the shaded area *fdge* because they must pay $4 more for each trip that they do make.

Before the tax, the seller surplus was area *dcb*, and after the tax, the seller surplus is area *fke*. By geometry, area *fke* is exactly equal to area *jch*. So, effectively, the tax affects the seller surplus by the difference between areas *dcb* and *jch*. This means that the tax affects the seller surplus in two ways. First, it reduces the seller surplus by the shaded area *ghb* because airlines sell fewer tickets. Second, it also reduces the seller surplus by the shaded area *djhg* because they receive $6 less for each ticket that they do sell.

Part of the loss of buyer and seller surplus, the shaded areas *fdge* and *djhg*, accrue to the government as tax revenue. These areas represent a sum of $10 × 900,000 = $9 million. The remaining part of the buyer and seller loss, the areas *egb* and *ghb*, do not accrue to the government. They are a deadweight loss.

Recall that the effect of tax on price and quantity depends on the price elasticities of demand and supply. Accordingly, the effect of a tax on the buyer and seller surplus also depends on these elasticities. If travelers are so insensitive to price that they would rather accept higher prices than cut back on flying, then demand will be extremely inelastic. In this case, the tax reduces the buyer surplus but does not affect the seller surplus and causes no deadweight loss. The incidence of the tax falls completely on the buyers.

By contrast, if airlines are so insensitive to price that they would rather accept lower prices than cut back on sales, then supply is extremely inelastic. In this case, the tax reduces the seller surplus but does not affect the buyer surplus and causes no deadweight loss. The incidence of the tax falls completely on the sellers.

Progress Check 6G In Figure 6.8, draw in a more inelastic demand curve. How does this affect the incidence of tax on travelers relative to airlines?

Progress check

The Ideal Tax?

From a social standpoint, the cost of raising revenue through taxes is the resulting deadweight loss. The ideal tax is one that causes no deadweight loss. Generally, the deadweight loss from a tax will be smaller if the demand and the supply are less elastic. Accordingly, governments should focus taxes on items for which either demand or supply is relatively inelastic.

The supply of land is quite inelastic. If there is a fall in the price of land, the quantity supplied will not fall by very much. Over the long term, the supply may be somewhat elastic as landowners reduce investments in drainage and protection against erosion. But, relative to most other items, the supply of land is quite inelastic. Accordingly, a tax on land ownership would be a relatively efficient way to raise revenue.

Collecting Taxes

We are now ready to address the introductory question of the effects of a switch to collecting an airport tax from passengers rather than airlines. This is just one specific case of the general issue of whether a tax should be imposed on the buyers or the sellers.

Obviously, there may be differences in administrative costs and perhaps psychological differences between collecting the tax from passengers rather than airlines. For instance, since there are relatively fewer airlines than passengers, it may be less costly to collect the tax from airlines.

Aside from administrative and psychological differences, however, we claim that the effect of a tax will be the same, whether it is collected from the buyers or the sellers. To explain this point, let us consider again the effect of a $10 tax on the market for economy class air travel between Chicago and London. Figure 6.7 showed the U.S. practice, which is to collect the tax from airlines. The $10 tax raised the buyer's price to $804, reduced the seller's price to $794, and reduced travel to 900,000 tickets. By contrast with the U.S., many Asian governments collect air travel taxes from travelers.

Suppose that the U.S. government were to adopt the Asian method of collecting the tax from travelers. Then, flying from Chicago to London would mean paying a price to an airline and the $10 tax to the government. The $10 tax reduces travelers' willingness to pay airlines at all quantities of tickets. Graphically, in Figure 6.9, we represent the tax by shifting the entire demand curve down by $10. As a result of the tax, the equilibrium shifts from the original point b to a new point t: Both the seller's price and the quantity of tickets drop.

Now compare triangle ehb in Figure 6.7 with triangle utb in Figure 6.9. Point b is common to both triangles, both lines eh and ut represent $10, both be and bu are segments of the original demand curve, and both hb and tb are segments of the original supply curve. So, the two triangles must be identical. This means the new buyer's price, the seller's price, and the quantity of tickets are the same whether the government collects the tax from the airlines or travelers.

To reiterate, regardless of who pays the tax, the outcome is identical. Our demand-supply analysis simply reflects common sense. If airlines pay the tax, the increase in costs will lead them to charge higher prices to the extent that airlines are not willing to accept lower prices and travelers are willing to absorb higher prices. By contrast, if passengers pay the tax, they would pay less in price to airlines to the extent that airlines are willing to accept lower prices and travelers are not willing to bear higher prices.

We have shown that the incidence on passengers relative to airlines does not depend on which side pays the tax. Incidence depends only on the price elasticities of demand and supply. Generally, the effect of a tax will be the same, whether it is collected from the buyers or the sellers.

Figure 6.9 Collecting the air travel tax from passengers

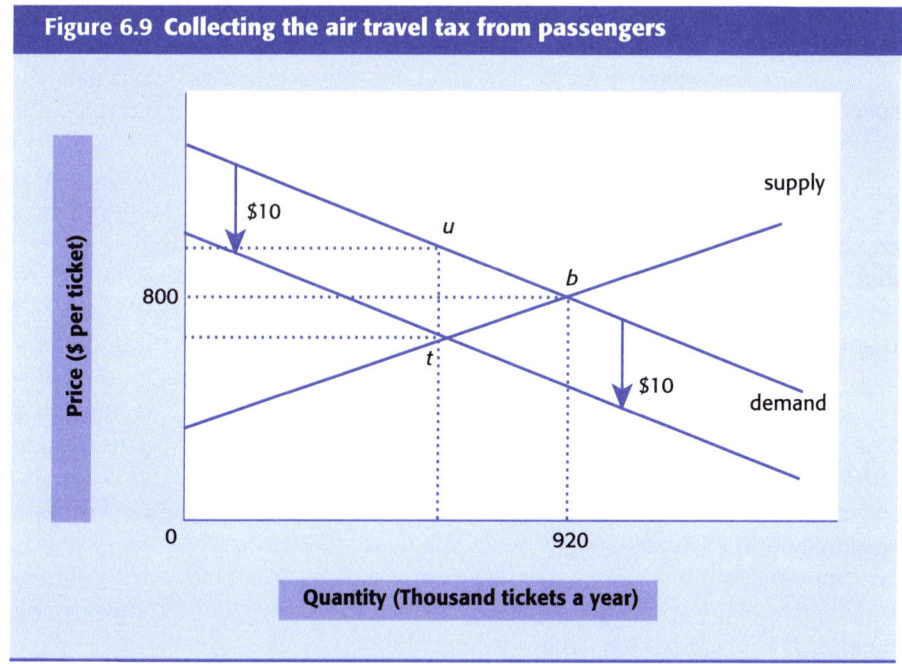

The $10 tax reduces travelers' willingness to pay. The new buyer's price, the seller's price, and the quantity of tickets are the same whether the government collects the tax from airlines or travelers.

9 *Fairness*

Under perfect competition, the invisible hand allocates resources in an economically efficient way. Although the competitive outcome is efficient, it need not be very just or fair. An example is the situation of physically or mentally handicapped people. With free competition in the labor market, wages for handicapped people would probably be very low. Prices may be so low that handicapped people may not be able to maintain a standard of living that other members of society would consider acceptable.

Likewise, with free competition in housing markets, many people may not be able to afford housing of a standard that others consider decent. By contrast, market forces may generate high or even astronomical wealth for owners of scarce resources such as real property in the Ginza district of Tokyo.

Income Tax

In analyzing demand, we argued that, generally, all goods and services provide a diminishing marginal benefit. The more that a person consumes, the less benefit each additional unit will provide. If income also provides a diminishing marginal benefit, then if society transfers a dollar from a wealthy person to an impoverished person, the wealthy person's loss will be less than the poor person's gain. To the extent that this is valid, there is a justification for taxing the rich and redistributing the proceeds to the poor.

As we have just seen, however, all taxes generate deadweight losses. The only exceptions are where either the demand or the supply of the item being taxed is extremely inelastic. In deciding on a program of redistribution, society should carefully balance the impact on income distribution against the deadweight losses.

In comparing the value of one dollar to a rich person with the value of that dollar to a poor person, we are making a value judgment. A society that is willing to make such judgments may also consider making judgments about the value of one form of consumption relative to another. We have mentioned redistributing income from rich people to poorer people. What if a poor person consumes all his income on alcohol. Should society continue to make welfare payments to him? Society might be willing to say that alcohol is a less desirable form of consumption than basic necessities such as food and shelter. These arguments point to providing help in kind, say, free meals, cheap housing, and subsidized education, rather than cash transfers.

Price Controls

Earlier in this chapter, we showed that rent control does not alleviate shortages of affordable housing. What then does rent control accomplish? Recall that, by reducing the market price, rent control transfers some surplus from landlords to tenants. Accordingly, it redistributes income from landlords to tenants.

As shown earlier, rent control results in a deadweight loss, the extent of which depends on the price elasticities of demand and supply. The deadweight loss is the cost of the redistribution. If supply is inelastic—that is, not sensitive to changes in rent—then the deadweight loss will be small and the redistribution will be very effective. Almost all the seller surplus that landlords lose will accrue to renters. If, however, supply is elastic, then redistribution will be less effective: A substantial part of the landlords' loss will be a deadweight loss that does not benefit renters. Obviously, the extent of redistribution also depends on the degree to which landlords and renters circumvent the rent controls.

As an empirical matter, some landlords are poor people. For instance, some people buy property as an investment to support themselves in their old age. By the time that these people have retired and are living on their rental income, they may be relatively poor, especially compared to tenants who are still working. For instance, the actress Mia Farrow had a huge rent-controlled flat in a prime area overlooking Central Park in New York City. Accordingly, redistributing income from landlords to tenants does not exactly equate with redistributing income from the rich to the poor.

Invisible Hand versus Social Policy: Hong Kong Public Housing

In Hong Kong, the Housing Authority provides subsidized rental housing to over 650,000 low-income families. Owing to the subsidy, there is a huge demand for these units. In 1994, over 16,000 families were on the waiting list for public rental housing. Once the authority allocates a unit, the tenant can occupy the unit at a subsidized rental for an unlimited time.

An estimated 13% of tenants have become wealthy enough to afford private housing, which is better furnished and more comfortable than public housing. The Housing Authority's rents, however, are so low that these tenants retain their public housing units. Some provide their units to relatives, while others use their units as storage space.

The benefit that people derive from public housing units used as storage space is probably much smaller than the benefit that the same units could provide to people on the waiting list. If the Housing Authority could reassign these units, the loss to those using apartments as storage space would be less than the gain to those moving off the waiting list.

The Housing Authority's dilemma is how to identify the people who derive relatively low benefit from public housing and how to effect the reassignment. If the Housing Authority were to circulate a notice asking all those that own private apartments to voluntarily vacate their public units, how many would own up?

Suppose, instead that the Housing Authority were to allow every tenant to sub-lease her or his unit. Then, a market for public housing units would arise immediately. A family using a public housing unit as storage space would surely make a profit by renting that unit to another family as a residence and using part of the proceeds to rent storage space in a warehouse. The invisible hand would resolve the problems of identifying the people who derive relatively low benefit from public housing and reallocating the units.

Why does the Housing Authority not harness the invisible hand? It probably would be politically unacceptable to give such a valuable right so explicitly to people who already own private property. Using the invisible hand would be attacked as giving money to the rich.

Source: Hong Kong Housing Authority, *Annual Report, 1993–94*, pp. 114–5, and press release, October 8, 1994.

10 *Summary*

The central idea in this chapter was Adam Smith's invisible hand. Free-market competition will ensure that the allocation of resources is economically efficient.

Although the buyers and sellers act selfishly, the net outcome is at least as good as the best efforts of the most enlightened and well-informed central planner. This applies to markets for goods and services as well as capital.

The same principle applies within an organization. Through decentralization, management can achieve efficient use of scarce internal resources. This means charging a transfer price for items produced and consumed within the organization.

Government policies such as price ceilings, price floors, and taxes cause deadweight losses and impede economic efficiency. The extent of these deadweight losses depends on the price elasticities of demand and supply. There will be no deadweight loss if either the demand or the supply is extremely inelastic.

Key Concepts

economically efficient	transfer price	price ceiling
technical efficiency	outsourcing	deadweight loss
invisible hand	capital market	price floor
market or price system	bankruptcy	tax incidence

Further Reading

Steven E. Landsburg provides a detailed analysis of market efficiency in Chapter 9, "Knowledge and Information," of *Price Theory and Applications*, 3d ed. (St. Paul, MN: West Publishing, 1995). For a comprehensive study of transfer pricing, refer to Chapter 25 of Charles Horngren, George Foster, and Srikant Datar's *Cost Accounting: A Managerial Emphasis*, 8th ed. (Englewood Cliffs, NJ: Prentice Hall, 1994).

Review Questions

1. In 1987, Soviet leader Mikhail Gorbachev complained that children were kicking bread in games of football. Consider this observation in terms of the conditions for economic efficiency.

2. The external auditor of the local school system has found that some schools are paying 20% more for the same cleaning services than other schools in the same area. Which condition of economic efficiency is being violated?

3. Consider a competitive labor market. Explain how the invisible hand ensures that the allocation of labor is economically efficient.

4. Using relevant examples, explain the concept of a transfer price.

5. Super Pied is considering where to establish a new rubber shoe factory. The cost of the equipment is $10 million. Super Pied will produce for two years. If the demand is insufficient, it will shut down and move the equipment to another country. Country A has an effective bankruptcy law, while country B does not allow factories to shut down. Which country has higher barriers to exit?

6. Using relevant examples, explain the differences between
   a. A price floor.
   b. A price ceiling.

7. Explain why deadweight losses from rent controls will be larger
   a. If demand is more inelastic.
   b. If supply is more elastic.

8. Suppose that the government is planning to raise the minimum wage. Considering each of the following pairs, will the increase in the minimum wage have a greater effect on employment in (a) or (b)?
   For services,
   a. Lawyers.
   b. Janitors.

For manufacturing,
   a. Rubber shoes.
   b. Disposable diapers.

9. In the United States, the federal income tax applies to all earned income exceeding a specific threshold. Does the income tax affect economic efficiency in the labor market? If so, explain how.

10. The market for telephones is competitive. Since telephones are almost a necessity, demand is very inelastic. By contrast, supply from factories in China, Taiwan, and elsewhere in Asia is very elastic. Suppose that the government were to impose a tax on telephones. How much will this affect a manufacturer of telephones?

Discussion Questions

1. Luna Mining operates silver mines in Colorado and Peru. Until recently, corporate headquarters set production targets for each mine based on average production costs. Then, on the recommendation of a management consultant, the company changed its production policy. Under the new policy, each mine must aim to maximize profits given the prevailing price of silver.
   a. Under Luna Mining's old production policy, which condition(s) for economic efficiency might not be satisfied?
   b. Does the new production policy improve economic efficiency?
   c. Explain the role of price under the new policy.

2. Tickets to popular musical and sporting events, like the U2 world tour and the Superbowl, often sell out. Devoted fans must either spend long hours waiting in line for a limited supply of tickets or pay a premium price to scalpers or touts. Scalpers and touts buy tickets to resell.

   a. When tickets sell out, which condition(s) for economic efficiency might not be satisfied?
   b. Do scalpers and touts improve economic efficiency?

3. For many years, the American Telephone and Telegraph Company (AT&T) had a monopoly over long-distance telecommunication. In many areas, AT&T also provided local telephone service through Bell operating companies (BOCs). In January 1984, under the terms of a court decree, AT&T divested its BOCs. At the time, AT&T's principal competitor in long-distance was MCI.

   The newly independent BOCs asked all their subscribers to select a long-distance carrier. Millions of subscribers, however, did not bother to express a preference. A major issue for the FCC was what to do with these "silent" subscribers ("Auction

Long-Distance Service for the Undecided," *Wall Street Journal* [May 29, 1985], p. 28).

a. *A Default Plan.* One theory proposed to the FCC was that those subscribers who did not bother to express a preference were implicitly choosing the incumbent carrier, AT&T. Which long-distance carrier does this proposal favor?

b. *A Market Share Plan.* Another proposal to the FCC was to consider the choices of the subscribers who did exercise a preference and then to allocate the "silent" subscribers in the same proportions among the various carriers. Would MCI prefer the default plan or the market share plan?

c. *An Auction Plan.* A third suggestion was for the FCC to require that long-distance carriers bid for the rights to serve the "silent" subscribers in an auction. Compare this proposal with the Default Plan and the Market Share Plan in terms of economic efficiency.

4. The Federal Deposit Insurance Corporation (FDIC) insures deposits at most major American banks. The FDIC has always been concerned about the domino effect of a major bank run on the rest of the banking system. In 1984, Continental Illinois National Bank, one of America's largest banks at the time, reported that it was in difficulty, with losses estimated at $1.5 billion. To avert a bank run, the FDIC arranged to rescue Continental Illinois. This rescue signaled the FDIC's "too large to fail" policy, which means that the FDIC would not allow large banks to go bankrupt ("Continental Bank's Pilots Say They're Above the Credit Clouds," *Wall Street Journal* [April 3, 1990], p. A25).

a. In a competitive capital market, what is the function of bankruptcy?

b. How does the FDIC's "too large to fail" policy affect the allocation of financial resources across large vis-à-vis small banks?

5. Consider a company that manages a network of hospitals across several counties in one state. Household incomes and the cost of living are higher in urban than rural areas. The company, however, has set the same prices for pharmaceuticals and services in all of its hospitals. It has also paid the same salaries for doctors, nurses, and other professional staff throughout the state.

a. Management has noticed that there are long waiting lists for treatment at its urban hospitals. Can you explain this problem?

b. The company has had great difficulty in recruiting professional staff for its urban hospitals. Can you explain this problem?

c. What advice would you give to management?

6. In 1994, one-quarter of all British workers were engaged in part-time employment. The European Union proposed to require that part-time workers receive similar benefits to full-time workers. This would mean better redundancy pay and maternity benefits for many part-time workers. Britain's employment minister Michael Portillo vetoed the proposal ("European Summit: The Black Cloud," *Economist* [December 10, 1994], pp. 45–6).

a. A disproportionate number of part-time workers are young people and women. How would the proposed directive affect them?

b. In 1993, the European Union unemployment rate was almost 10% among the general population and almost 20% among workers aged below age 25. How would the proposed directive affect these rates?

c. Explain why British trade unions supported the European Union proposal.

7. In Singapore, the Ministry of Communications regulates taxi services through licensing and control over fares. In 1985–86, the ministry noticed that, at prevailing fares, there were long lines for taxis. The ministry decided to raise taxi fares to the equilibrium level.
   a. Assuming that all rides are identical, illustrate the fare increase on an appropriate demand-supply diagram. Identify the effects on the buyer and seller surpluses.
   b. In estimating the supply curve, the ministry did not appreciate that about one-third of all holders of taxi licenses were inactive or semiactive. How would the increase in fares affect this group of licensees? What would be the effect of this mistake on the estimate of the impact on the seller surplus as compared with the original estimate given in (a)?
   c. Unfortunately, the increase in fares coincided with the onset of Singapore's severest economic recession in two decades. On your diagram, show how the economic downturn would affect the market for taxi rides.

8. Throughout the world, governments target cigarettes and alcohol for especially high taxes. Let us consider the arguments in favor of these so-called sin taxes.
   a. Suppose that the demand for alcohol is relatively inelastic compared with the demand for other products. Compare the deadweight loss resulting from a tax on alcohol compared with a tax on other products.
   b. Suppose that the demand for alcohol is relatively elastic. How would a tax on alcohol affect consumption?

9. In Switzerland, the federal government levies a social security tax, partly on employers and partly on employees. Employers and employees pay equal percentages of the employee's salary in tax.
   a. Using relevant demand-supply analysis, explain the effect of the social security tax on wages, employment, and the buyer and seller surpluses.
   b. Suppose that the government changed its policy and decided to collect the entire tax from employees. How would this new policy benefit employers?

10. The West African country of Nigeria is a major producer and exporter of oil. The Nigerian government subsidizes domestic gasoline sales. At the time of writing, the retail price was about 45 U.S. cents per gallon.
    a. A tax can be represented by shifting up the supply curve. How would you represent a subsidy?
    b. Using a relevant demand-supply diagram, explain the effect of a subsidy on retail price and sales.
    c. Do you expect Nigerians to have bigger or smaller cars relative to residents of another country with a similar income but no subsidy on gasoline?

Part II

Market Power

Chapter 7

Costs

1 Introduction

Chicago, New York, and Toronto each have populations exceeding a million. Despite their size, each of these cities has only two or three general circulation daily newspapers. Los Angeles has only one general circulation daily. Why do large North American cities not have more general circulation dailies? Moreover, in some cities with morning and afternoon papers, the same company produces both papers. Why does one company produce both papers?

Dynamic random access memory (DRAM) chips make up the internal (read-write) memories of personal computers. In the Summer of 1988, Apple Computer offered its Macintosh II personal computer with internal memory consisting of between 4 and 32 units of 1-megabit DRAMs. Anticipating a future shortage, Apple bought several hundred million dollars of 1-megabit DRAMs at an average of $38 per chip. By January 1989, however, the shortage of DRAMs eased and the market price dropped to $23. For purposes of pricing Macintoshes in January 1989, what should Apple deem to be the cost of a 1-megabit DRAM from its inventory?

Direct costs are those that can be identified with a particular product or job relatively easily. Those costs that cannot be easily identified with a particular product or job are indirect costs. In a typical tractor repair business, the direct costs of a job include labor and major parts but not grease and screws. If management required, however, the mechanics could track their use of grease and screws on every repair job. Then, why does the tractor repair business count grease and screws as indirect rather than direct costs?

For many important business decisions—including pricing, deciding whether to outsource, assessing performance, and planning investments—managers must have accurate information about costs. In Chapter 4, we introduced the concepts of fixed, variable, marginal, and average costs. Now, we build on this foundation and present three basic principles to guide managers in understanding business costs.

The first principle is to consider how costs depend on the scale and scope of the business. The scale refers to the production rate, while the scope means the variety of different products. This principle can guide managers on the issues of whether to operate on a small scale or a large scale and whether to offer many products or focus on a single item. The effect of scale on production costs can explain why many large North American cities have only one or two general-circulation daily newspapers. The effect of scope on production costs can explain why, in some cities, a single company produces both the morning and afternoon newspapers.

The second principle is relevance: Managers should consider only relevant costs and ignore all others. To identify what costs are relevant, a manager needs to consider the alternative courses of action. This approach will reveal costs not shown in accounting statements, called *opportunity costs*. It also shows that some expenses that are recorded in accounting statements are not relevant. Applying the principle of relevance, Apple Computer could have determined the cost of 1-megabit DRAMs for pricing Macintoshes.

The third principle is balance: In analyzing costs, managers should aim for a degree of accuracy that balances the marginal benefit and the marginal cost of accurate costing. The principle of balance explains why the tractor-repair business does not track use of grease and screws but rather includes them in indirect costs.

2 *Economies of Scale*

A fundamental issue for any business is whether to operate on a small scale or large scale. Large-scale production means mass marketing and relatively low pricing; by contrast, small-scale production is associated with niche marketing and relatively high pricing. Here, we shall analyze how costs depend on the scale or rate of production. (We shall treat the *scale* and *rate* of production as synonymous.) It is important, however, to note that the decision on scale also depends on market demand and competition. We will analyze these factors in Chapters 8 and 10.

To understand how costs depend on the scale of production, let us recall the distinction between the fixed and variable costs introduced in Chapter 4. The *fixed cost* is the cost of inputs that do not change with the production rate. The *variable cost* is the cost of inputs that change with the production rate.

In Chapter 4, we introduced fixed and variable costs in a short-run planning horizon. The same distinction applies in the long run as well and explains how costs depend on the scale of production.

Fixed vis-à-vis Variable Costs in the Long Run

To illustrate the distinction between long-run fixed and variable costs, let us consider the production of an old-fashioned newspaper, the *Daily Globe*. The production process begins when the typesetting department receives the text ("copy") of the forthcoming edition from the editorial and the advertising departments. The typesetters compose the copy in type, which are metal pieces with raised shapes. The type is then mounted on electric-powered printing presses. Once the type has been set, the presses can be switched on and fed a continuous flow of newsprint and ink to produce the printed product.

We ask the management of the *Daily Globe* to estimate the daily expenses required for production rates up to 90,000 copies a day. Table 7.1 reports this information in the four categories of labor, printing press, ink and paper, and electric power. For simplicity, we ignore other costs.

Consider each category of expense. The cost of labor is $5000, and does not vary with the size of the print run. The labor required to produce the paper is the same whether the newspaper plans to print 10,000 or 90,000 copies a day. Accordingly, the labor is a fixed cost of newspaper production.

Next, the cost of the printing press ranges from $1000 with no production up to $5500 at a production rate of 90,000. The cost of the press includes a fixed cost of $1000. The remainder is a variable cost.

Table 7.1 Daily expenses

Daily Production (thousands)	Labor	Printing Press	Ink and Paper	Electric Power	Total
0	$5,000	$1,000	$0	$200	$6,200
10	$5,000	$1,500	$1,200	$300	$8,000
20	$5,000	$2,000	$2,400	$400	$9,800
30	$5,000	$2,500	$3,600	$500	$11,600
40	$5,000	$3,000	$4,800	$600	$13,400
50	$5,000	$3,500	$6,000	$700	$15,200
60	$5,000	$4,000	$7,200	$800	$17,000
70	$5,000	$4,500	$8,400	$900	$18,800
80	$5,000	$5,000	$9,600	$1,000	$20,600
90	$5,000	$5,500	$10,800	$1,100	$22,400

Table 7.2 Analysis of fixed or variable costs

Daily Production (thousands)	Fixed Cost	Variable Cost	Total Cost	Marginal Cost	Average Fixed Cost	Average Variable Cost	Average Cost
0	$6,200	$0	$6,200				
10	$6,200	$1,800	$8,000	$0.18	$0.62	$0.18	$0.80
20	$6,200	$3,600	$9,800	$0.18	$0.31	$0.18	$0.49
30	$6,200	$5,400	$11,600	$0.18	$0.21	$0.18	$0.39
40	$6,200	$7,200	$13,400	$0.18	$0.16	$0.18	$0.34
50	$6,200	$9,000	$15,200	$0.18	$0.12	$0.18	$0.30
60	$6,200	$10,800	$17,000	$0.18	$0.10	$0.18	$0.28
70	$6,200	$12,600	$18,800	$0.18	$0.09	$0.18	$0.27
80	$6,200	$14,400	$20,600	$0.18	$0.08	$0.18	$0.26
90	$6,200	$16,200	$22,400	$0.18	$0.07	$0.18	$0.25

The cost of ink and paper is nothing with no production; hence, this item is completely variable. For a print run of 10,000 copies, the cost of ink and paper is $1200, while for a run of 20,000 copies, the cost is $2400. The cost of ink and paper is proportional to the production rate.

The cost of electricity is also partly fixed and partly variable. There is a $200 cost of power for lighting which does not vary with the production rate. It is a fixed cost. By contrast, the cost of powering the presses is variable. It increases by $100 for every 10,000 copy increase in the production rate.

In Table 7.2, we assign the costs of newspaper production—labor, printing press, ink and paper, and electric power—into the two categories of fixed and variable costs. There is a fixed cost of $6200. A substantial fixed cost is a fact in producing a newspaper. The industry has given the name *first copy cost* to the fixed cost. It is the cost of producing just one copy a day.

By contrast, as the print run increases from 0 to 90,000 copies a day, the variable cost rises from nothing to $16,200. By distinguishing between fixed and variable costs, the management of a business can understand which cost elements will be affected by changes in the scale of production.

Marginal and Average Costs

Applying the analysis of fixed vis-à-vis variable costs, we can see how costs depend on the scale of production. In Chapter 4, we also introduced the concepts of marginal and average costs. Recall that the marginal cost is the change in total cost due to the production of an additional unit. The average (or unit) cost is the total cost divided by the production rate or scale.

Let us study the marginal and average costs of production of the *Daily Globe*. Referring to Table 7.2, as the print run increases from 0 to 90,000 copies a day, the total cost of production increases from $6,200 to $22,400.

The marginal cost of the first 10,000 copies is $8000 − $6200 = $1800, or $1,800/10,000 = 18 cents per copy. The marginal cost is constant at 18 cents at all scales of production. From Chapter 4, we know that the marginal cost equals the rate of change of the variable cost. For the *Daily Globe*, the average variable cost remains constant at 18 cents per copy. Hence, the marginal cost is also constant at 18 cents per copy.

Dividing total cost by the scale of production, we can obtain the average cost. The average cost drops from 80 cents at a scale of 10,000 copies a day to 25 cents at 90,000 copies a day. To understand why the average cost decreases with the scale of production, recall that the average cost is the average fixed cost plus the average variable cost. The average fixed cost is the fixed cost divided by the production scale. With a larger scale of production, the fixed cost will be spread over more units of production and the average fixed cost will be lower.

The average variable cost is constant at 18 cents per copy. Therefore, the average cost declines as the scale of production increases. In Figure 7.1, we graph the marginal, average variable, and average costs against the scale of production. The marginal and average variable cost curves are identical and flat. The average cost curve slopes downward.

Economies of scale (increasing returns to scale) means that the average cost decreases with the scale of production.

A business for which the average cost decreases with the scale of production is said to exhibit **economies of scale** or *increasing returns to scale*. With economies of scale, the marginal cost will be lower than the average cost. Since the marginal unit of production costs less than the average, any increase in production will reduce the average. Therefore, the average cost curve slopes downward.

Intuitive Factors

Scale economies arise from two possible sources. One is significant fixed inputs, that is, those that can support any scale of production. Then, at a larger scale, the cost of the fixed inputs will be spread over more units of production, so that the average fixed cost will be lower. If the average variable cost is constant or does not increase very much with the scale of production, then the average cost will fall with the scale. Newspaper production illustrates economies of scale arising from substantial fixed inputs.

Any business with a strong element of composition, design, or invention has significant fixed inputs. For instance, the cost of designing and developing a

Figure 7.1 Economies of scale

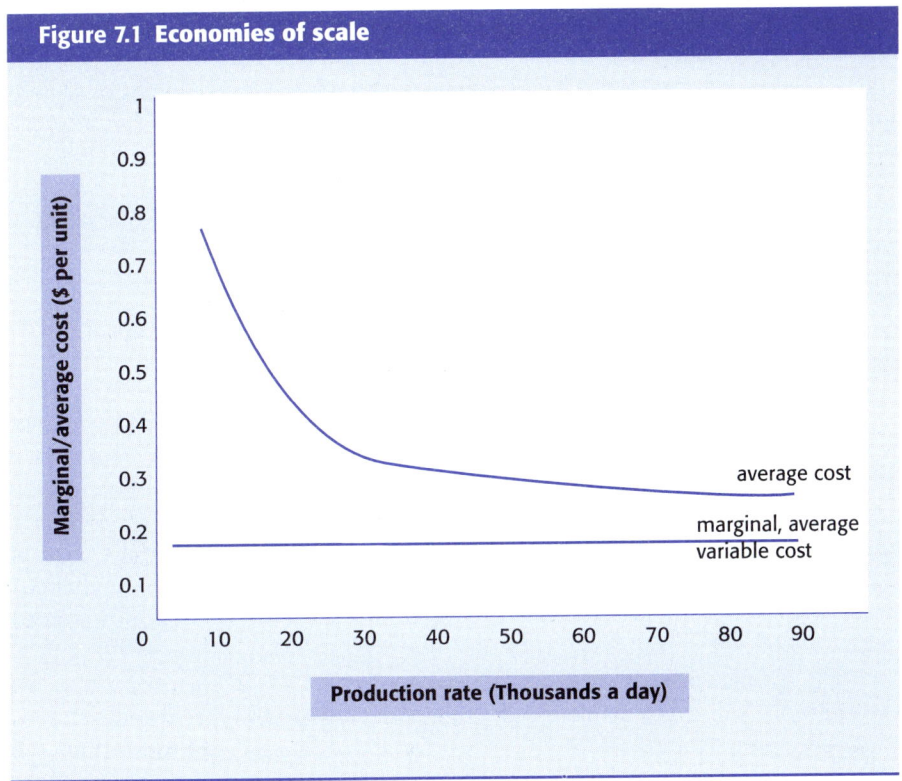

The marginal and average variable costs are identical and do not change with the scale of production. The average cost decreases with the scale of production.

new pharmaceutical is fixed. Regardless of the production rate, the design and development cost will remain the same. Similarly, the cost of preparing the computer code for a software package is fixed. It is the same whether the publisher distributes 1 million copies or only 1. Accordingly, there are strong economies of scale in these businesses. Indeed, for pharmaceuticals and software, the marginal production cost is tiny compared with the average cost.

The other reason for scale economies is if the average variable cost falls with the scale of production. Generally, an increase in scale may increase or reduce the average variable cost. Whether the average variable cost increases or falls depends on the particular technology of the business.

For example, a distributor of gas needs a pipeline to transport its product. The transmission capacity of a pipeline depends on its cross-sectional area, which increases with the square of the radius of the cross section. By contrast, the amount of material required to build the pipeline depends on the circumference of the pipeline, which increases with the radius of the cross section.

Accordingly, a 10% increase in the transmission capacity of the pipeline requires less than 10% additional materials. In this case, the average variable cost falls with the scale of operations. This factor tends to generate economies of scale in pipeline operations.

Progress check

Progress Check 7A Using the data in Table 7.2, draw the average fixed cost in Figure 7.1.

Diseconomies of Scale

Diseconomies of scale (decreasing returns to scale) means that the average cost increases with the scale of production.

A business where the average cost increases with the scale of production is said to exhibit **diseconomies of scale** or *decreasing returns to scale*. A business will have diseconomies of scale if the fixed cost is not significant and the variable cost rises more than proportionately with the scale of production.

To illustrate diseconomies of scale, let us consider Sharon's hair-dressing salon. The salon does not involve a significant fixed cost. The main variable cost is labor. Sharon estimates that the cost of labor rises more than proportionately with the scale of production.

The average cost is the average fixed cost plus the average variable cost. For Sharon's salon, the average cost initially decreases with the scale because of the decreasing average fixed cost. Since the variable cost rises more than proportionately with the scale of production, the average variable cost is increasing. Hence, there is a scale where the decreasing average fixed cost is outweighed by the increasing average variable cost. Then, the average cost reaches a minimum and rises with further increases in the scale. The average cost curve is shaped like the letter U. As we explained in Chapters 4 and 5, the average cost curve of a perfectly competitive business is U-shaped.

Strategic Implications

The relation between average cost and the scale of production influences the structure of the industry. If there are economies of scale, a business operating on a relatively large scale will achieve a lower average cost than smaller-scale competitors. Large-scale production means mass marketing and relatively low pricing. An industry where individual suppliers have economies of scale tends to be concentrated, with a few suppliers serving the entire market. In Chapter 8, we analyze the extreme case of a monopoly, where there is only one supplier.

By contrast, in a business with diseconomies of scale, the management should aim at a relatively small scale. Small-scale production is associated with niche marketing and relatively high pricing. Industries where individual suppliers have diseconomies of scale tend to be fragmented. The extreme case is the model of perfect competition in Chapter 5, where there are many sellers, none of whom can influence the market demand.

Economies of Scale in Telecommunication

Two major elements in the cost of a telecommunication transmission link are the labor for installation and maintenance and the basic components. Neither of these costs varies much with the transmission capacity; hence, they are largely fixed costs. The cost of the transmission cable, however, is variable.

Owing to the substantial fixed costs, there are economies of scale in providing transmission links. A line with a capacity of 1.536 million bits per second (Mbps) carries 24 times more data than a 64-thousand-bits-per-second (kbps) line. The cost of the 1.536-Mbps line, however, is much less than 24 times the cost of the 64-kbps line.

The prices charged by telecommunications carriers reflect the economies of scale. In January 1995, Singapore Telecom charged 71,300 Singapore dollars a month for a 1.536-Mbps line to the United States, as compared with 8,500 dollars for a 64-kbps line. On the basis of 1 bit per second, the prices were $71,300/$1,536,000 = 4.6 cents for the bigger-capacity line, and $8,500/64,000 = 13.3 cents for the smaller line.

The disparity in unit prices has given rise to a demand for machines called *multiplexers*, which combine transmissions at low rates into higher rates to take advantage of the lower unit price available on large-capacity lines.

Source: Peter G.W. Keen and J. Michael Cummins, *Networks in Action* (Belmont, CA: Wadsworth Publishing Co, 1994), pp. 207–9; Singapore Telecom, International Leased Circuit Tariffs, January 1, 1995.

Technology and Economies of Scale: Processing Credit Card Transactions

Changes in technology can affect the extent of scale economies. Consider, for instance, the processing of credit card transactions. Credit cards are issued by businesses ranging from banks and credit unions to oil companies and department stores. In the past, every transaction made with a credit card was processed manually.

Automation, however, has changed the processing of credit card transactions into a production-line operation. Automated processing requires significant fixed investments in computer systems. Consequently, the processing of credit card transactions is now a business with economies of scale. It is no longer cost-efficient for each issuer of credit cards to process its own transactions on a small scale.

The efficient scale of processing exceeds the volume of transactions at many individual credit card issuers. As a result, several specialized firms have arisen to process the credit card transactions of issuers. Indeed, over 50% of American banks now outsource their processing of credit card transactions

Source: "Banks and Technology," *The Economist* (October 3, 1992), p. 22.

3 *Economies of Scope*

Economies of scope means that the average cost of production is lower with joint than with separate production.

Diseconomies of scope means that the average cost of production is higher with joint than with separate production.

A fundamental strategic issue for any business is whether to offer many different products or focus on a single item. The answer to this question depends in part on the relation between average costs and the scope of production. There are **economies of scope** across two products if the average cost of production is lower when two products are produced together than when they are produced separately. Conversely, there are **diseconomies of scope** across two products if the average cost of production is higher when two products are produced together.

Joint Cost

Let us consider how costs depend on the scope of production through the following example. Suppose that the management of the *Daily Globe* is considering whether to launch an afternoon paper, the *Afternoon Globe*. Table 7.3 shows three categories of expenses required to produce the *Daily Globe* and the *Afternoon Globe*, assuming a print run of 50,000 copies a day for each paper.

If the two newspapers are printed in separate facilities, then the total production cost is $15,200 a day for each paper. Dividing by the print run of 50,000 copies a day, the average cost of each paper is 30 cents per copy. If, however, both newspapers are printed in the same facility, then the total cost of producing the two newspapers is $26,900. Dividing by the print run of 50,000 + 50,000 = 100,000 copies a day, the average cost of each paper is 27 cents per copy. The cost of producing both newspapers in the same facility is 10% lower than if they were produced separately.

What explains the difference in cost? The key is that the same printing press can be used in the night to print the morning paper, and in the late morning to print the afternoon paper. To produce the *Daily Globe* by itself, the publisher must spend $3500 a day on the printing press. Likewise, to produce the *Afternoon Globe* by itself, the publisher must spend $3500 a day on the printing

Table 7.3 Expenses for two products

Organization	Daily Production (thousands)	Labor	Printing Press	Ink, Paper, Electric Power	Total Cost	Average Cost
Separate production						
Daily Globe	50	$5,000	$3,500	$6,700	$15,200	$0.30
Afternoon Globe	50	$5,000	$3,500	$6,700	$15,200	$0.30
Combined production	100	$10,000	$3,500	$13,400	$26,900	$0.27

press. To produce both newspapers from the same facility, however, the publisher spends $3500 only once.

The expense of the printing press is a **joint cost** of the morning and afternoon newspapers. The *joint cost* is the cost of inputs that do not change with the scope of production. Economies of scope arise wherever there are significant joint costs.

*The **joint cost** is the cost of inputs that do not change with the scope of production.*

Strategic Implications

Where two products are linked by economies of scope, it will be relatively cheaper to produce the products together. Then, a supplier of both items can achieve relatively lower average costs than competitors that specialize in one or the other product. Subject to conditions of market demand and competition, the management should offer both products. Multiproduct suppliers dominate industries with economies of scope.

Telecommunication and broadcasting provide an important example of scope economies. Fixed-line telephone service requires a wire network connecting all potential subscribers. Similarly, cable television requires a wire network connecting all potential subscribers. In this case, the cost of building and maintaining the network is a significant joint cost. Consequently, there are very substantial economies of scope across the telephone and television businesses. Combined providers of telephone and television service can deliver the products at relatively lower cost than specialized services. Hence, telephone companies and cable television services are expanding into each other's businesses.

Economies of scope in advertising and promotion are essential for the strategy of *brand extension* in marketing. When Kimberly-Clark spends $1 to advertise Kleenex, it is promoting the sales of every product carrying the Kleenex brand. Accordingly, the expenditure on advertising a brand is a joint cost of marketing all the products marked with the brand. This joint cost gives rise to economies of scope in advertising and promotion. Through a brand extension, the owner of an established brand can introduce new products at relatively lower cost than a competitor with no established brand.

Economies of scope also underlie the strategic concept of *core competence*. A *core competence* is generalized expertise in the design, production, and marketing of products based on common or closely related technologies. For instance, a manufacturer with a core competence in small liquid crystal displays can apply this as a basis for manufacturing pocket calculators as well as digital watches. It can produce these items at a relatively lower cost than a specialized competitor. Essentially, a core competence is a joint cost that gives rise to economies of scope.[1]

---

[1] This discussion in based on Paul Milgrom and John Roberts, *Economics, Organization, and Management* (Englewood Cliffs, NJ: Prentice Hall, 1992), pp. 107–9.

Economies of Scale and Scope in Newspapers

Many large North American cities have only one, two, or three general-circulation daily newspapers. This observation can be explained by the significant economies of scale in the newspaper business. Industries where producers have economies of scale tend to be dominated by a few large-scale businesses.

Another feature of the North American newspaper business is that, in some cities, a single publisher produces both morning and afternoon newspapers. This is consistent with significant economies of scope. One publisher can produce morning and afternoon newspapers at relatively lower cost than two specialized publishers.

Diseconomies of Scope

There are diseconomies of scope across two products if the average cost of production is higher when the two items are produced together than when they are produced separately. Diseconomies of scope arise where joint costs are not significant and making one product increases the cost of making the other in the same facility.

To illustrate diseconomies of scope, consider two retail businesses: basic clothing and fast food. Both cater to a similar mix of customers looking for good value. Why then does some entrepreneur not sell clothing together with fast food?

Such a combined business would probably encounter diseconomies of scope. There is no significant joint cost between the two products. Further, people consuming fast food might wander over to the clothing section and spill food and drinks on the merchandise. So, the fast food service increases the cost of selling clothing in the same facility. Given these difficulties, it would be less costly to sell the two products in separate facilities.

Where diseconomies of scope prevail, it will be relatively cheaper to produce the various items separately. Hence, specialized producers can achieve relatively lower average costs than competitors that combine production. In such circumstances, the management should aim for a narrow scope and focus on one product.

Progress check   **Progress Check 7B** Referring to Table 7.3, suppose that, with combined production, the expenses on the printing press would be $7000 a day. Are there economies or diseconomies of scope?

Economies of Scale and Scope in Gold Mining

Echo Bay Mines Limited owns the Cove open-pit mine in Nevada. The company exploits economies of both scale and scope in operating the mine. Given the fixed cost of keeping the mining pit free from water, it is relatively cheaper to blast rock at a high rate. In 1994, the blasting rate was 160,000 tons a day.

The rock is removed from the pit and separated into three categories. The high-grade ore-bearing rock is ground in a mill, after which the metal is extracted by a physical or chemical process. The low-grade ore-bearing rock is collected in a large heap on an impermeable pad and leached with a solvent to dissolve the metal. Finally, the unusable rock is dumped on a waste pile.

The rock contains both gold and silver. Removing the rock from the pit is a joint cost of producing gold and silver. Instead of dumping the silver-bearing rock on the waste pile, the company recovers the silver as well as the gold. In 1994, Cove produced 10.4 million ounces of silver as well as 359,400 ounces of gold.

Source: Echo Bay Mines Ltd., *1994 Annual Report*, pp. 13–15, and letter dated May 24, 1995.

4 Relevance I: Opportunity Cost

We have seen how business costs depend on economies of scale and scope. To actually determine the extent of scale and scope economies, we must know how to measure costs. Analyses of costs usually begin with the accounting statements. These, however, do not always provide the information appropriate for effective business decisions. It is often necessary to look beyond the conventional accounting statements.

Here, we present a key principle to guide managers in measuring costs. That principle is **relevance:** Managers should consider only relevant costs and ignore all others. There is no simple definition of which costs are relevant. Which costs are relevant depends on the alternative courses of action for the decision at hand.

*Principle of **relevance**: managers should consider only relevant costs.*

Alternative Courses of Action

The following example shows how an analysis of the alternative courses of action will uncover relevant costs that conventional accounting statements leave out. Suppose that, in 1960, Eleanor Williams bought a warehouse in an industrial area that has since been transformed into a tourist zone. Eleanor paid

Table 7.4 **Conventional income statement**	
Revenue	$700,000
Expenses	$220,000
Profit	$480,000

$300,000 for the warehouse, using $200,000 of her own money and a bank loan of $100,000. She has since repaid the loan in full.

Table 7.4 presents the most recent income statement for her warehouse. Eleanor's annual sales revenue is $700,000, her cash outlays are $220,000, hence her profit is $480,000. She is making a return on sales of 480/700 = 69%. Eleanor's warehouse business seems to be doing very well.

We contend, however, that this assessment of performance overlooks some significant costs of Eleanor's warehouse business. To evaluate Eleanor's business, we should investigate her alternative courses of action. Since the area has become a tourist zone, an obvious alternative is to redevelop the warehouse into a tourist facility such as a shopping center or entertainment complex.

Suppose that a developer were willing to buy the warehouse for $2 million. If Eleanor sells the warehouse, she could invest the proceeds in government bonds and get a secure income of, say, 8% a year, which works out to $2 million $\times 0.08$ = $160,000. Moreover, Eleanor could then work elsewhere for a salary of, say, $400,000. Thus, if Eleanor were to sell the warehouse, she could earn $560,000 a year. This is more than she earns from continuing in the warehouse business. So, if Eleanor considers the alternative of selling the warehouse, she will soon see that this is better than continuing in business.

This example highlights a major deficiency of the conventional income statement: It does not present the revenues and costs of the alternative courses of action. In Table 7.5, we present an expanded income statement that explicitly shows the revenues and costs of Eleanor's two alternatives. It is then very clear that Eleanor should sell the warehouse.

Table 7.5 **Income statement showing alternatives, I**		
	Continue Warehouse Operations	**Shutdown**
Revenue	$700,000	$560,000
Expenses	$220,000	$0
Profit	$480,000	$560,000

Opportunity Cost Defined

By continuing in the warehouse business, Eleanor foregoes the opportunity to earn $560,000 a year. The **opportunity cost** of the current course of action is the net revenue from the best alternative course of action. In Eleanor's case, the opportunity cost of continuing in the warehouse business is $560,000 a year.

The **opportunity cost** is the net revenue from the best alternative course of action.

We can apply the concept of opportunity cost to present the revenues and costs of continuing in the warehouse business in another way. This includes opportunity costs among the costs of the business. Table 7.6 presents a single income statement, in which costs include both the cash outlays and the opportunity cost. The cost of $780,000 consists of $220,000 in outlays plus $560,000 in opportunity cost.

Using the opportunity cost approach, we find that Eleanor is incurring a loss of $80,000 a year; hence, she should get out of the warehouse business. This approach leads to the same decision as in Table 7.5, where we explicitly show the two alternative courses of action.

Uncovering Relevant Costs

Thus, there are two ways to uncover relevant costs: explicitly consider the alternative courses of action or use the concept of opportunity cost. When applied correctly, both approaches lead to the same business decision.

In Eleanor's case, there was one alternative to the existing course of action. Where there is more than one alternative, the explicit approach still works well. The opportunity cost approach, however, becomes more complicated: We must first identify the best of the alternatives and then charge the net revenues from that alternative as an opportunity cost of the existing course of action.

Conventional methods of cost accounting focus on the cash outlays associated with the course of action that management has adopted. This means that they do not consider the revenues and costs of alternative courses of action; hence, they ignore costs that are relevant but do not involve cash outlays. One reason for these omissions is that alternative courses of action and opportunity costs change with the circumstances and hence are more difficult to measure and verify. Conventional methods of cost accounting focus on easily verifiable costs. Accordingly, they overlook opportunity costs.

Table 7.6 Income statement reporting opportunity costs	
Revenue	$700,000
Cost	$780,000
Profit	−$80,000

Progress check

Progress Check 7C Suppose that government bonds pay an interest rate of 3% a year. Revise Tables 7.5 and 7.6. Should Eleanor continue in the warehouse business?

Opportunity Cost: A Downtown Department Store

The main store of the Wing On chain is one of the few department stores in Hong Kong's central district. The store occupies 25,000 square feet on the ground floor and 64,000 square feet on three other floors of the Wing On Centre. The tenants of street-level floors of other nearby buildings include banks, fast-food chains, and jewelers. In 1993, the Wing On department stores reported revenues of HK$2,236 million, costs of HK$2,210 million, and a profit of HK$26 million.

At the time, the market rent for retail space around the Wing On Centre was HK$100–150 per square foot for ground floors and HK$30–50 for other floors. Let us use this data to estimate the opportunity cost of the premises used by

Wing On's main store. To be conservative, we use the lower figures of HK$100 and HK$30 a month. Then, on an annual basis, the opportunity cost of the ground-floor space was HK$(25,000 × 100 × 12) = HK$30 million, while the opportunity cost of the other floors was HK$(64,000 × 30 × 12) = HK$23 million. The total opportunity cost was HK$53 million a year.

To evaluate the performance of its department stores, the Wing On Group should take account of the HK$53 million a year income that it could earn by leasing space to other tenants such as banks and fast-food chains.

Source: Wing On Group, *1993 Annual Report*, pp. 25–6.

Opportunity Cost of Investment: The American Steel Industry

In the early 1980s, Japanese, Korean, and South American steel producers stepped up exports to the American market. The pressure of these imports forced down the prices of steel in the U.S. market. At a conference of American Iron and Steel Institute, senior steel industry executives explained that they needed new technology and production facilities to compete effectively with imported steel. They lamented, however, that imports had cut their profits so

low that they lacked sufficient retained earnings to fund new investments.

To analyze this complaint, let us first ask a basic question: How do completely new businesses, such as the many biotechnology ventures that sprang up in the 1980s, finance themselves? Certainly, not by retaining part of their profits—because new start-ups have no profits at all. The answer is that start-ups are financed through new capital and borrowing.

Why could American steel companies not issue new shares or borrow funds? Presumably because outside investors were reluctant to buy new shares or to lend. If outside investors were reluctant to commit funds to steel projects, should existing shareholders be any more willing? Retained earnings are profits that companies do not distribute to shareholders. The steel executives were talking as if retained earnings had no cost: Hence, it would be worth investing retained earnings in projects that generate very small profits.

This kind of thinking arises because conventional accounting does not show the relevant cost of using retained earnings. Of course, retained earnings have alternative uses; hence, they have an opportunity cost. The opportunity cost is the return that shareholders could get from other investments bearing similar risk. For effective investment decisions, managers should consider all relevant costs. Managers who treat retained earnings as costless may be losing money for their shareholders.

Free Lunch: Picasso versus Rockefeller

The following story is apocryphal. Nelson Rockefeller (a member of the wealthy New York family that controlled the Chase Manhattan Bank) and the famous European artist Pablo Picasso had lunch at the Four Seasons restaurant in New York City. At the end of a fine meal, Picasso reached for the bill, "Let me pay. I'll write a personal check, draw a few squiggles, and sign it. The manager won't ever cash it. She will display it as a work of art. And we'll have a free lunch."

Rockefeller would not agree. "No, allow me to write a personal check. Remember, this is New York City. Here, our Rockefeller name is as good as gold. The manager won't cash my check. She can use it just like money and our lunch will be free."

Who was right? Picasso or Rockefeller? The correct answer to the puzzle is that neither Picasso nor Rockefeller was right. By drawing a few squiggles, Picasso was adding to the world's stock of his works. The increase in the supply would reduce the price that he could get for future works. Picasso would not get a free lunch—he was bartering a picture for a lunch.

Rockefeller was also wrong. Each check that he wrote added to his stock of debts and, ultimately, reduced his creditworthiness. He could not create an unlimited number of checks. So, by creating a check, Rockefeller was exchanging a lunch for a reduction in his creditworthiness. In believing that they could get a free lunch, both Pablo Picasso and Nelson Rockefeller overlooked opportunity cost.

Source: Frank Rabinovitch, personal communication, 1984.

5 *Relevance II: Sunk Costs*

For effective business decisions, managers should take account of all relevant costs. We have just seen that, because conventional accounting methods do not present alternative courses of action, they may fail to reveal important relevant costs. We shall next consider situations where some of the costs reported in conventional accounting statements are not relevant, and should be ignored.

In Chapter 4, we introduced the concept of a sunk cost, which is a cost that has been committed and so cannot be avoided. Since sunk costs cannot be avoided, they are not relevant to business decisions. As with opportunity costs, the easiest way to identify sunk costs is to consider the alternative courses of action.

Alternative Courses of Action

The following example shows how an analysis of the alternative courses of action will identify sunk costs in a conventional accounting statement. Suppose that Sol Athletic is about to launch a line of new athletic shoes. Some months ago, management prepared an advertising campaign and booked space in *Road Runner* magazine and the *Daily Globe* newspaper. The total budget for the new advertisements was $310,000.

Sol forecast that the advertisements would generate sales of 20,000 units. The unit contribution margin, which is price less average variable cost, would be $20. Hence the contribution margin, which is revenue less variable cost, would be $20 × 20,000 = $400,000. Thus, the new product would yield a profit of $400,000 − $310,000 = $90,000.

Recently, however, one of Sol's major competitors also launched a new product. Sol now estimates that its own launch will generate sales of only 15,000 units. The unit contribution margin would still be $20; hence, the contribution margin would only be $20 × 15,000 = $300,000. This seems to be less than the cost of the advertisements. Should Sol cancel the launch?

To address this question, we should carefully lay out the revenues and costs associated with the alternative courses of action. Table 7.7 shows the required information.

Supposing that Sol continues with the launch, the contribution margin would be $300,000. Sol must pay $50,000 to a graphic arts consultant for art-

Table 7.7 Income statement showing alternatives, II

	Continue Product Launch	Cancel Launch
Contribution margin	$300,000	$0
Graphic arts consultant fee	$50,000	$50,000
Road Runner charge	$60,000	$30,000
Daily Globe charge	$200,000	$20,000
Profit	($10,000)	($100,000)

work, $60,000 to *Road Runner* magazine, and $200,000 to the *Daily Globe*. The total advertising cost would be $310,000, hence Sol's profit would be –$10,000.

By contrast, if Sol cancels the launch, the contribution margin would be $0. Even if it cancels the launch, Sol must still pay something to the graphic arts consultant, the magazine, and newspaper. Table 7.7 shows the amounts that Sol must pay in the event of cancellation. Hence, if Sol decides to cancel the launch, the total advertising cost would be $100,000; thus, its profit would be—$100,000.

By this analysis, Sol should continue with the product launch. Continuation yields a loss of $10,000, which is less than the loss of $100,000 from cancellation.

Avoidable Costs

By canceling the launch, Sol does not save the entire advertising budget of $310,000. Some expenses already have been committed and are now sunk. Sol can correctly decide whether or not to continue the launch by using a single income statement that omits sunk costs and includes only avoidable costs.

Table 7.8 presents this information. The contribution margin is $300,000. Note that Table 7.8 presents costs rather than expenses. The total (avoidable) cost of the advertising plan is $210,000. If Sol continues with the launch, it will earn a profit of $90,000. Accordingly, the correct decision is to continue with the launch.

Strategic Implications

Generally, managers should ignore sunk costs and consider only avoidable costs. Sunk costs, once incurred, are not relevant for pricing, investment, or any other business decision. Managers who consider sunk costs may stumble into serious mistakes.

From a prospective viewpoint, managers should be very careful before committing to costs that will become sunk, since such commitments cannot be reversed. In Chapter 10, we discuss how businesses can exploit investments in sunk costs as a way to strategically influence the behavior of competitors.

We have shown two ways of dealing with sunk costs: explicitly consider the alternative courses of action or remove all sunk costs from the income

Table 7.8 Income statement omitting sunk costs	
Contribution margin	$300,000
Graphic arts cost	$0
Road Runner cost	$30,000
Daily Globe cost	$180,000
Profit	$90,000

statement. When applied correctly, both approaches lead to the same business decision.

In Sol's case, there was one alternative to the existing course of action. Where there is more than one alternative, the explicit approach still works well. The sunk cost approach, however, becomes more complicated. Which costs are sunk depends on the alternative at hand. Accordingly, it is easier to consider the alternative courses of action explicitly.

Conventional methods of cost accounting focus on the cash outlays associated with the course of action that management has adopted. These methods report all costs that involve cash outlays, even sunk costs. To make effective business decisions, managers must look beyond conventional accounting statements to consider only relevant costs. This means ignoring sunk costs.

Commitments and the Planning Horizon

To identify sunk costs, managers should consider two factors: past commitments and the planning horizon. Suppose that Sol Athletic has engaged an advertising agency on a retainer basis with a minimum monthly fee. The contract requires six months' notice of termination. Then, from the current standpoint, the advertising agency's minimum fee is sunk for a six-month planning horizon but not for the seventh and following months.

If Sol's commitment had been different, the sunk cost picture would also be different. Suppose that the contract provided for only three months' notice of termination. Then, from the current standpoint, the advertising agency's minimum fee is sunk for only the next three months. For planning beyond the fourth month, the fee is avoidable.

This example also illustrates how the extent to which a cost is sunk depends on the planning horizon. Generally, the longer the planning horizon, the more time there will be for past commitments to unwind and hence the greater will be management's freedom of action.

In Chapter 4, we distinguished between short-run and long-run planning horizons. The short run is a time horizon in which at least one input cannot be adjusted. By contrast, the long run is a time horizon long enough that all inputs can be freely adjusted. Consequently, in a short-run planning horizon, there will be some sunk costs, while in a long-run horizon, there will be no sunk costs.

Progress check   **Progress Check 7D** Suppose that Sol has made no commitments to the suppliers of artwork or advertising space. Revise Tables 7.7 and 7.8. Should Sol cancel the launch?

Apple Computer's 1-Megabit DRAMs

Apple Computer manufactures the Macintosh line of personal computers. During the first half of 1988, the company's sales of high-end Macintosh machines equipped with larger memory had been unexpectedly strong. By the summer, management had become concerned about the company's stocks of 1-megabit DRAMs. Moreover, Apple's DRAM suppliers were falling behind in their deliveries and, in the words of its chairman and chief executive officer, John Sculley, "We also thought that 1-megabit chips supplies would get even tighter towards the end of the year."

Consequently, Apple bought several hundred million dollars' worth of 1-megabit DRAMs, at an average cost of $38 per chip. This was significantly higher than the cost earlier in the year. To recoup the higher cost of memory, management raised prices across the entire Macintosh line. The company based the differential in price between machines with larger memory and those with smaller memory on the DRAM cost of $38.

By January 1989, however, shortages in the DRAM market eased and the price dropped to $23. This exposed a problem with Apple's pricing. Computer resellers such as Computerland undercut Apple's high-end machines by adding memory and hard disks from third-party sources to basic Macintosh computers. Moreover, resellers enjoyed higher margins on third-party components than Apple Computer products.

Apple's sales of high-end Macintoshes collapsed and millions of excess DRAMs accumulated in inventory. Consequently, Apple's gross margin fell from 51.5% in the third quarter of 1988 to 46.2% in the second quarter of 1989. For a company with quarterly sales of $1.25 billion, each 1% of gross margin amounted to $12.5 million.

What went wrong at Apple? In January 1989, the historical cost of each 1-megabit DRAM was $38, but the market value was only $23. By then, the $15 difference was a sunk cost. Apple's management should have faced the fact that anyone could buy DRAMs at $23; hence, the relevant cost of Apple's DRAMs, new or old, was $23.

Apple's management, however, did not follow this principle. It maintained prices for the entire Macintosh line based on a cost of $38 per DRAM. Apple's high-end Macintosh computers were too expensive relative to the basic machines. Consequently, sales of the high-end machines collapsed, and the company's quarterly profit slumped.

Source: "Apple Slips as Result of Hoarding Chips," *Wall Street Journal* (January 30, 1989), p. A6; Apple Computer, *1989 Annual Report*, pp. 19–20.

Sunk vis-à-vis Fixed Costs

In popular as well as professional discussion, the term *fixed cost* is often used in two different senses: a cost that cannot be avoided once incurred (what we call *sunk cost*) and the cost of inputs that do not change with the production rate (what we call *fixed cost*).

For the sake of clarity, we distinguish these two meanings with two different terms. It is important to understand this distinction very clearly because the two types of costs have very different implications for business decisions. Managers should ignore sunk costs that have been incurred, as these cannot be avoided. By contrast, the presence of fixed costs in the long run tends to give rise to economies of scale, and so management should aim to operate on a large scale.

Some fixed costs become sunk once incurred. For instance, suppose that the soles of Sol Athletic's jogging shoes are made of molded rubber. For each size of shoe, Sol Athletic must have at least one pair of molds (left and right). So, the cost of designing the molds is a fixed cost. Moreover, once the molds have been designed, the cost has been committed and cannot be avoided. Hence, the design cost is a sunk cost, once incurred.

Not all sunk costs, however, are fixed in the sense of supporting any scale of operations. Having designed the molds, Sol must manufacture one set of molds to begin production of shoes. The cost of making the molds is sunk, once incurred. If the demand for the shoes is sufficiently high, Sol might have to invest in a second production line. Then it will need a second set of molds, which requires an additional investment. So, the cost of making molds is not a fixed cost. Rather, it depends on the scale of operations.

Likewise, not all fixed costs become sunk when incurred. For instance, Sol must have at least one production operator on each production line. Accordingly, the wage of a production operator is a fixed cost of making a particular model of shoes. If, however, the demand for that model of shoes should fall, Sol can close the line and shift the operator to another model. Thus, the production operator's wage need not be sunk.

Figure 7.2 illustrates a basic approach to analyzing costs. First, we divide costs into sunk and avoidable. This division depends on past commitments and the current planning horizon. Managers should ignore all costs that are sunk for the

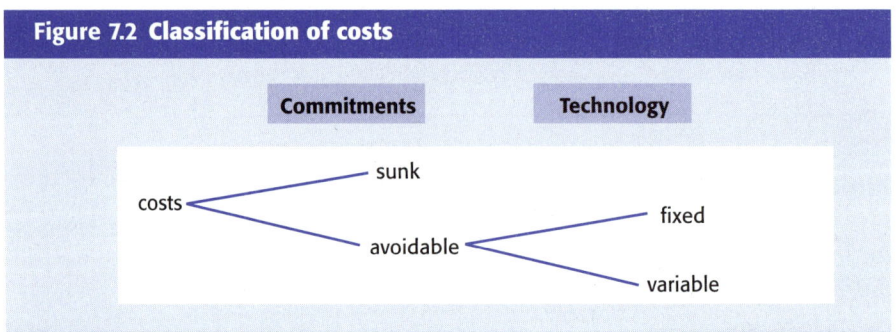

Figure 7.2 Classification of costs

The division of costs into sunk and avoidable depends on past commitments and the current planning horizon. The division of avoidable costs into variable and fixed elements depends on the technology of the business.

planning horizon at hand. Next, we can analyze avoidable costs into variable and fixed elements. This division depends on the technology of the business. The presence of substantial long-run fixed costs gives rise to economies of scale. Then, management should aim to operate on a relatively large scale.

Sunk Costs in American Automobile Manufacturing

During the 1980s, America's big three domestic automakers—Chrysler, Ford, and General Motors—steadily lost sales to Japanese competitors. Honda, Nissan, and Toyota began by exporting cars from Japan. Later, to secure their share of the American and Canadian markets, all three established "transplant" factories in North America.

What explains the success of Japanese car manufacturers in the North American market? One theory is special advantages such as an undervalued exchange rate for the yen and a more disciplined labor force. This theory, however, does not account for the success of the transplant factories, which are located within North America and use domestic labor.

Another theory is that American automakers must pay for the medical benefits and pensions of a large number of retired workers. "With one retiree for every active worker, Chrysler must put $5 in its pension fund for every hour its current employees work." According to this reasoning, Japanese transplant factories do not have retirees to support; hence, they have much lower costs.

Let us scrutinize this argument. The retirees whom the American auto makers are supporting have *already retired.* Whether Chrysler manufactures 100,000 or 300,000 cars a year, it must support the same number of existing retirees. If Chrysler manages to sell so many cars that it must recruit a thousand more workers, the company will not have to add a thousand more retirees. The cost of supporting the retirees is sunk: It is not relevant for current production or pricing decisions. Accordingly, this cost does not justify the big three's failure to be competitive with Japanese transplant factories.

Source: "Detroit and the UAW: Sink or Swim Together," *The Economist* (September 1, 1990), pp. 62–3.

6 Balance

Applying the principle of relevance, we have seen how to look beyond conventional accounting statements to obtain a more accurate picture of business costs. Accuracy in measuring costs, however, is not an absolute standard. Rather, management must decide how much to invest in measuring costs and hence the degree of accuracy.

The third principle of cost analysis, **balance,** provides a guide to accuracy. Managers should aim for a balance between the marginal benefit and the marginal cost of accurate costing. The principle of balance applies throughout cost

Principle of **balance**: managers should balance the marginal benefit and marginal cost of accurate costing analysis. For instance, how far should managers go to distinguish between fixed and variable costs? The answer is this: to the point where the marginal benefit equals the marginal cost of accurate costing. This implies that management may ignore some very small fixed expenses and add them to the variable expenses.

To illustrate the principle of balance, let us consider two specific issues in cost analysis: distinguishing direct from indirect costs and allocating indirect costs.

Direct vis-à-vis Indirect Costs

A **direct cost** is a cost that can be relatively easily identified with a particular product or job.

An **indirect (overhead) cost** is a cost that cannot be easily identified with a particular product or job.

Direct costs are those that can be relatively easily identified with a particular product or job. Examples of direct costs are production-line labor and material inputs. Not all costs, however, can be easily identified with a particular product or job. Those costs that cannot be easily identified are **indirect costs** (also called *overhead* costs).

No rigid distinction is made between direct and indirect costs. Rather, the distinction depends on the benefit relative to the effort required to identify an item of cost. For instance, in the business of repairing tractors, direct costs include mechanics' labor and major parts but not grease and screws. If management required them to do so, repair mechanics could track their usage of grease and screws, in which case, grease and screws could be measured as direct costs.

Management, however, does not require repair mechanics to track use of grease and screws because the marginal cost of such tracking outweighs the marginal benefit. As this example shows, the distinction between direct and indirect costs depends on the balance between the marginal benefit and the marginal cost of accuracy.

This example also shows that the distinction between direct and indirect costs is not the same as that between variable and fixed costs. If the mechanics repair one more tractor, they will use more grease and screws. Accordingly, grease and screws are a variable cost. Generally, direct costs may be variable or fixed, and similarly, indirect costs may be variable or fixed.

Allocating Indirect Costs

We have just seen how to apply the principle of balance to the distinction between direct and indirect costs. Managers should apply the same principle when allocating indirect costs.

Many businesses, whether in manufacturing or services, produce multiple products. In a multiproduct business where indirect costs represent a significant proportion of total costs, an important issue is how to allocate the indirect costs among the various products. For pricing and other business decisions, it is vital to allocate indirect costs in a reasonable way.

Consider the following example. Suppose that Luna Machining produces two models of cast-iron pulleys for the elevator industry, the A-510 and the

A-530. To set prices, management would like to know the cost of each model, including direct costs as well as relevant indirect costs.

Currently, Luna Machining produces 20 units of the A-510 and 60 units of the A-530 each week. Using specialized equipment, Luna's workers machine cast-iron pieces to produce high-quality pulleys. Both the A-510 and the A-530 require 5 hours of direct labor at an average cost of $15 per hour. Both products require material inputs of $10.20 per unit and take the same amount of machine time, at a cost of $6.80 per unit.

For simplicity, we suppose that the only indirect cost is a Shipping Section, whose annual expenses are $50,000, consisting of $48,000 in wages and $2000 in telephone and fax charges. So, the issue is how to allocate the cost of the Shipping Section between the two products.

Activity-based costing   We apply the method of activity-based costing to allocate the indirect costs. The first step is to identify the expenses and activities of the Shipping Section. By interviewing the shipping supervisor, we learn that the section spends most of its time on two activities: processing shipments and dealing with customer inquiries. The main expenses are wages and telephone and fax charges. Table 7.9 presents the expenses.

We must then learn how the expense categories are divided among the activities. The shipping supervisor estimates that the section spends 62.5% of its time on shipments and 37.5% on customer service. Taking the total of $48,000 in wages, we then allocate $48,000 × 0.625 = $30,000 to shipments and the balance of $18,000 to customer service. The supervisor believes that all the telephone and fax charges are associated with customer inquiries.

We compile this information in columns 3 and 4 of Table 7.9. The total cost of shipments is $30,000, while the total cost of servicing customer inquiries is $18,000 + $2,000 = $20,000.

The next step is to learn the relationship between the two products and the activities of the Shipping Section. Continuing the interview, we learn that the A-510 requires 500 shipments a year while the A-530 requires 800 shipments a

Table 7.9 Analyzing expenses and activities

Item	Expenses	Activity Shipments	Customer Inquiries	Allocation Method
Wages	$48,000	$30,000	$18,000	Worker-hours
Telephone and fax	$2,000	$0	$2,000	Identified
Total	$50,000	$30,000	$20,000	

Table 7.10 Allocating expenses to activities		
	Activity	
	Shipments	**Customer Inquiries**
A-510	500	1000
A-530	800	1600
Total activity	1300	2600
Annual expenses	$30,000	$20,000
Weekly expenses	$600	$400
Allocation: A-510	$231	$154
Allocation: A-530	$369	$246

year. Further, the A-510 involves 1000 customer service inquiries a year, while the A-530 involves 1600 inquiries a year. We compile this information in the top part of Table 7.10.

From Table 7.9, the total cost of shipments is $30,000. Assuming 50 working weeks a year, this is equivalent to $30,000/50 = $600 a week. We then allocate this $600 weekly cost in proportion to the shipments of the two products. For the A-510, the allocated shipment cost is $600 × (500/1300) = $231, while for the A-530, the allocated shipment cost is $600 − $231 = $369.

Also from Table 7.9, the cost of customer service is $20,000 a year, or $20,000/50 = $400 a week. We then allocate this weekly $400 cost in proportion to the number of inquiries for the two products. For the A-510, the allocated inquiries cost is $400 × (1000/2600) = $154, while for the A-530, the allocated shipment cost is $400 − $154 = $246. With these calculations, we complete the lower part of Table 7.10.

Finally, in Table 7.11, we combine the information on direct costs with the allocations of indirect costs. The calculations show, as we might intuitively expect, that the A-510, which is a low-volume product, has a higher average cost than the A-530, the high-volume product.

Intuitively, shipping involves some fixed costs. It does not cost three times as much to support the A-530 as the A-510. So, the higher-volume product has a lower average cost.

Activity-based costing consists of identifying the activities undertaken by the group incurring indirect costs, investigating how the various products drive these indirect activities, allocating the costs of the activities among the products, and combining the allocated indirect costs with the direct costs.

To summarize, the procedure in **activity-based costing** is to first identify the activities that are undertaken by the group incurring indirect costs. The next step is to systematically investigate how the various products drive the indirect activities, and, accordingly, to allocate the costs of the activities among the products. The final step is to combine the allocated indirect costs with the direct costs.

Table 7.11 Allocated costs

Model	Weekly Output	Direct Labor	Direct Materials	Machine Time	Ship-ments	Customer Inquires	Total Cost	Average Cost
A-510	20	$1500	$204	$136	$231	$154	$2225	$111
A-530	60	$4500	$612	$408	$369	$246	$6135	$102

In conventional methods of cost accounting, the indirect costs are allocated in proportion to direct costs. Conventional methods ignore the possibility that there are fixed elements in the way that indirect activities support the various products. The result is a tendency to overstate the costs of high-volume products and understate the costs of low-volume products.

Notice that, in compiling Table 7.10, we implicitly assumed that the costs of the shipments and dealing with customer inquiries were proportionate. Should management consider whether there are fixed elements in these activities? The answer depends on the balance between the marginal benefit and the marginal cost of accuracy.

Progress Check 7E Referring to Tables 7.10 and 7.11, suppose that the A-530 product requires 1500 shipments and 3000 customer inquiries a year. Under this assumption, compare the average cost of the two products.

Progress check

Activity-Based Costing at Harris Semiconductor

In 1989, the Harris Corporation acquired General Electric's semiconductor business. The business, however, did not perform well. A year after the acquisition, Harris wrote off $72.9 million in restructuring expenses. The following year, Harris semiconductor sector reported a loss of $75.5 million, which led to management being replaced.

Phillip Farmer, the new president of the semiconductor sector, discovered that the company had no accurate information on costs. Semiconductor manufacturing involves relatively small direct costs. Harris produced a wide spectrum of products, ranging from basic memories to specialized chips. The company should have paid close attention to the allocation of indirect costs.

Farmer introduced activity-based costing. The new system revealed that margins on logic and memory chips were low, while specialized chips for automobiles and medical equipment were much more profitable. By laying off 2,400 of 11,500 employees, including more than a third of middle management, and by refocusing sales on the higher-margin products, Farmer restored the semiconductor business to profit by the middle of 1992.

Source: "Harris Finally Digests Big Semiconductor Acquisition," *Wall Street Journal* (October 13, 1992), p. B6.

7 *Statistical Methods*[2]

We have presented three principles to guide managers in analyzing business costs. While these principles are very clear, in practice, managers are often confronted with a mass of disparate information. Under these circumstances, it helps to use statistical methods, specifically, multiple regression, to understand the data. These methods are also useful in making forecasts about costs.

Multiple regression can help in many analyses of costs, including researching the relationship between costs and the scale and scope of production and also understanding how indirect costs depend on various indirect activities. (At this point, it may be useful to review Chapter 3 on Quantitative Demand Analysis.)

Multiple Regression

In the following example, we show how to use multiple regression analysis to investigate the extent of fixed costs and economies of scale. Suppose that, from past experience, the management of Mercury Elevator has identified four major factors in the direct manufacturing cost of an elevator system: the rated capacity and speed, the distance through which the elevator travels, and the number of landings.

To support its pricing, Mercury would like to understand how its direct cost depends on the four factors. It would also like to know whether there are significant fixed elements in the direct cost. Fixed costs would give rise to economies of scale in production.

We can use multiple regression to address these questions. First, we collect data on the direct cost and the corresponding characteristics for some recent projects (see Table 7.12).

In the multiple regression analysis, we specify direct cost as the dependent variable and four independent variables: capacity (in thousand kilograms), speed (in meters per second), travel (in meters), and number of landings. Table 7.13 reports the results of the analysis.

Referring to Table 7.13, the F-statistic is 27.79, and the probability that all the coefficients are 0 is 0.00. Accordingly, we can be very confident that the regression equation is statistically valid. The R-squared is 0.95; hence, the equation explains a very high percentage of the variation of the cost.

The intercept is –5.51, which is negative. The probability that the intercept is 0 is 0.41. If there is a fixed direct cost in manufacturing, then the direct cost would be positive even with all the independent variables being equal to 0. Hence, the fixed cost would be reflected in the intercept. We find, however, that the intercept is negative and not statistically significant. This suggests that there are no significant fixed elements in manufacturing.

---

[2]This section is more advanced. It may be omitted without loss of continuity.

Table 7.12 Elevator manufacturing costs

Direct Cost (thousand $)	Capacity (thousand kg)	Speed (m/s)	Travel (m)	Landings
65	1.60	1.6	21.0	2
63	0.71	1.6	47.5	8
64	0.85	1.6	47.5	8
39	1.00	0.6	15.0	6
59	0.90	1.0	45.2	9
50	0.90	1.0	28.6	6
56	0.90	1.6	60.9	6
35	0.80	1.0	6.9	2
58	0.54	1.0	40.6	15
45	0.54	1.0	40.7	8
68	0.82	1.0	43.8	16

Table 7.13 Multiple regression analysis estimates

Regression statistics:

R-square	0.95
Standard error	3.23
Number of observations	11
F-statistic	27.79
Significance	0.00

Independent Variable	Coefficient	Standard Error	t-Statistic	Significance
Intercept	−5.51	6.16	−0.89	0.41
Capacity	21.20	4.77	4.44	0.00
Speed	19.63	4.80	4.09	0.01
Travel	0.04	0.12	0.35	0.74
Landings	2.19	0.36	6.12	0.00

The coefficients for capacity, speed, and landings are positive. The probability that each of these coefficients is 0 is less than 0.05. Hence, we can be very confident that these variables are significant factors in the direct cost of manufacturing an elevator.

The coefficient for travel is positive, but the probability that this coefficient is 0 is 0.74. This suggests that, contrary to management's belief, the distance of travel is not a significant factor in the direct manufacturing cost.

Forecasting

A multiple regression equation can be used to forecast the dependent variable when the independent variables take different values. For this, we need a statistically significant multiple regression equation that explains a high percentage of the variation of the dependent variable.

Referring to Table 7.13, the equation for Mercury Elevator meets these conditions. Management can use the equation to forecast the cost of any future project. For instance, suppose that a client has requested a quotation for a system with the following characteristics: capacity of 1000 kilograms, speed of 1.0 meter per second, travel of 20 meters, and four landings. Then, the estimated cost (in thousands of dollars) would be

$$-5.51 + (21.20 \times 1) + (19.63 \times 1) + (0.04 \times 20) + (2.19 \times 4) = 44.88,$$

$$\text{or } \$44{,}880. \tag{7.1}$$

Other Applications

We have just seen how multiple regression can be used to research the presence of fixed costs. Managers can also apply multiple regression to investigate the presence of joint costs across two products. To research this question, we need data about average costs when different quantities of the two products are produced together and when they are produced separately.

In this case, there will be two regression equations, one for each of the two products. In each regression equation, the dependent variable should be the average cost and there should be three independent variables: the quantities of the two products and an indicator that takes the value of 1 where the two products are produced together and the value of 0 where the two products are produced separately. If there are joint costs, then the coefficient of the indicator should be negative and statistically significant.

Previously, we discussed how to use activity-based costing in allocating indirect costs. We implicitly assumed that we could proportionately allocate each indirect activity to the various products. If this is not reasonable, then managers can use multiple regression to allocate the costs of each indirect activity. There should be one equation for each indirect activity, in which the dependent variable is the cost of the indirect activity and the independent variables are the quantities of the various products. The regression coefficients will then show how to allocate the cost of the indirect activity to the various products and whether the activity involves a fixed cost.

8 Summary

Conventional accounting statements do not always provide all the information on costs necessary for effective business decisions. Managers should use the principles presented in this chapter to develop accurate information about costs. They should consider how costs depend on scale and scope. They should consider only relevant costs, bearing in mind that accounting statements overlook opportunity costs, while including sunk costs. Finally, managers should balance the marginal benefit and the marginal cost of accuracy in costing.

Key concepts

economies of scale	joint cost	direct cost
diseconomies of scale	relevance	indirect (overhead) cost
economies of scope	opportunity cost	activity-based costing
diseconomies of scope	balance	

Further Reading

For a general introduction to cost accounting, refer to Charles Horngren, George Foster, and Srikant Datar's *Cost Accounting: A Managerial Emphasis*, 8th ed. (Englewood Cliffs, NJ: Prentice Hall, 1994). Chapters 2, 3, 10, 11, and 14 are especially closely related to the concepts presented here. C.K. Prahalad and Gary Hamel launched the concept of core competence in "The Core Competence of the Corporation," *Harvard Business Review* 68, no. 3 (May–June 1990): pp. 79–91.

Review Questions

1. Define each of the following terms and give an example to illustrate your definition:
   a. Variable cost.
   b. Fixed cost.
   c. Economy of scale.
   d. Joint cost.
   e. Economy of scope.

2. Generation of electric power involves significant short-run fixed costs. Owing to the entry of several independent power producers, the demand for Southern Power's electricity has dropped. Management has reduced production. How will this cutback affect Southern Power's average fixed costs?

3. We list several pairs of situations. For each comparison, identify the situation for which economies of scale are more significant (choose a or b).
   For automobiles
   a. Rolls Royce, which makes cars by hand.
   b. Mercedes Benz, which uses a highly automated manufacturing process.

For restaurants,

a. Tre Stagioni, which has a permanent staff of two chefs and five waiters.

b. Campus Deli, which relies mainly on part-time workers, hired on a monthly basis.

4. Family medicine practice involves relatively little equipment. The most significant cost is human resources. To treat twice as many patients, a clinic probably will need twice as many doctors, nurses, and other professional staff. Does this business have economies of scale?

5. Banks and insurers both need distribution networks to sell products and serve their customers. An office that takes deposits and makes loans can just as easily sell insurance policies. In France, many banks sell life insurance. Is the combination of banking and insurance, called *bancassurance*, a result of economies of scale or scope?

6. Hindus must not eat beef, while Moslem people must not consume pork. A restaurant catering to both Hindu and Moslem customers must have two separate facilities and staffs: one for preparing Hindu food and another for preparing Moslem meals. Are there economies or diseconomies of scope across the Hindu and Moslem restaurant businesses?

Discussion Questions

1. A commercial passenger jet must be operated by a pilot and co-pilot. Aircraft designed to fly over large expanses of water also require a third officer. Many jets have cargo bays in their "bellies," under the passenger seating areas. Consider each of the following costs. Identify which are joint costs of the passenger and belly cargo services, which are fixed costs of passenger service, and which are both.

7. For which of the following businesses are sunk labor costs more significant (choose a or b)?

a. A Japanese conglomerate that guarantees lifetime employment.

b. A U.S. manufacturer that employs workers at will, which means that workers can be dismissed without cause.

8. Consider the costs of offering freight transport service between Munich and Stuttgart. In which of the following situations are sunk costs relatively largest?

a. The railway company owns the tracks.

b. The railway company pays another company to use the track on a long-term contract.

c. The truck operator pays tolls to use the highway as and when necessary.

9. Venus Machine Tools has automated production to the point that direct labor and materials accounts for less than 20% of the production cost. Explain why Venus should not allocate indirect costs in proportion to direct labor and materials.

10. Explain how the principle of balance applies to

a. The distinction between direct and indirect costs.

b. The distinction between fixed and variable costs.

a. *Cockpit personnel.* All jets, large and small, require a pilot and co-pilot. Belly cargo service requires no additional officers in the cockpit.

b. *Airport landing fees.* Some airports charge landing fees by weight of the aircraft, while others levy a fixed fee, regardless of weight.

c. *Fuel.* Larger aircraft and those carrying heavier loads consume relatively more fuel.

2. Elevators generally break down at random times and for different reasons. Elevator maintenance contractors must have trained service personnel to provide routine and emergency service. Pluto Elevator has 300 service personnel to maintain 4000 elevators.

   a. Suppose that Pluto has received a contract to maintain an additional 1000 elevators. Do you expect that Pluto will need 25% more service personnel? Why or why not?

   b. Does the example in (a) illustrate economies of scale or scope?

   c. Escalators and elevators use quite different technology and parts. But many clients buy the two products, escalators and elevators, together. Are there any economies of scope in supplying escalators and elevators together?

3. Integrated steel mills produce steel in large quantities from iron ore and coking coal. Their multistep process can take weeks to produce the finished product. Integrated mills produce steel cheaply only on a large scale. By contrast, mini-mills use electric furnaces to convert scrap steel into finished steel products. The process takes minutes and requires relatively less labor ("Big Steel Is Threatened," *Wall Street Journal* [February 2, 1993], p. A1).

   a. Suppose that the supply of scrap steel has been increasing. How would this affect the price of scrap steel and the average cost of production at a mini-mill?

   b. Suppose that the supplies of iron ore and coking coal have been falling. How would this affect the prices of iron ore and coking coal and the average cost of production at an integrated mill?

   c. Under the conditions in (a) and (b), explain why mini-mills are taking away market share from integrated steel producers.

4. Mercury Electric imports Taiwanese and Japanese room air-conditioners for sale in Kuwait. In 1993, Mercury Electric bought a shipment of 1000 Japanese air-conditioners

for $200,000 and another 1000 air-conditioners from Taiwan for $180,000.

   a. Between 1993 and 1994, the yen appreciated by 10%. For purposes of pricing, what is the relevant cost of the air-conditioners in 1994?

   b. Between 1993 and 1994, the New Taiwan dollar depreciated by 2%. For purposes of pricing, what is the relevant cost of the Taiwanese machines?

   c. Use the examples in (a) and (b) to explain the concepts of opportunity cost and sunk cost.

5. Under the international Multi-Fiber Agreement, international trade in clothing is governed by bilateral quotas awarded on a country-to-country basis. Until 1987, the Singapore government gave export quotas to manufacturers according to their past export record. A recipient was permitted to subcontract the manufacturing of the items to be exported under its quota. The Hong Kong government also gives quota allocations to certain selected manufacturers. It allows recipients to sell quotas on a secondary market.

   a. Suppose that Venus Fashion (Singapore) Limited has an export quota for men's clothing. Consider Venus's internal manufacturing cost relative to that of a subcontractor. Under what circumstances will Venus choose to subcontract manufacturing?

   b. Suppose that Venus Fashion (Hong Kong) Limited has an export quota for men's clothing. Consider Venus's internal manufacturing cost relative to that of other manufacturers. Under what circumstances will Venus choose to sell its quota on the secondary market?

   c. If the Singapore government were to adopt the Hong Kong resale system, what would be the effect on the quantities of clothing produced internally by quota recipients?

6. The costs of developing a new civil jetliner can run as high as $1 billion. In the early 1980s, the Dutch aircraft manufacturer Fokker began development of two new models, the Fokker 50 and Fokker 100. Around the same time, however, several other aircraft manufacturers introduced new models aimed at similar market segments. By 1984, having incurred heavy development costs, Fokker verged on bankruptcy and appealed to the Dutch government for help. The company was the Netherland's only aerospace manufacturer and a major employer. The government faced a difficult decision. In a commercial decision whether to rescue the company, which of the following factors are relevant?
   a. Anticipated sales.
   b. Production costs.
   c. Tooling costs already incurred.
   d. Development costs.
   Explain your answers.

7. In the early 1980s, the Singapore government made substantial loans to finance a petrochemical plant. Unfortunately, the plant opened during a period of worldwide excess capacity in basic petrochemicals, so it incurred large losses. The government then helped by converting some of its loans to equity. This substantially cut the plant's annual interest expenses. By contrast with debt, equity involves no annual charge; hence, the debt-equity conversion reduced the plant's recorded losses.
   a. If the plant had to record an annual charge for an "expected dividend" on equity, would the debt-equity conversion have been so successful in reducing the plant's losses?
   b. From a business standpoint, would you impute a charge for an expected dividend on equity when evaluating the performance of a business?

8. In 1979, before the outbreak of the Iraq-Iran war, almost all Middle East oil exports were shipped by tanker through the Persian Gulf. The huge volume of exports led to the introduction of very-large and ultralarge crude carriers. As a result of the war, however, Iraq's exports fell from a prewar level of 3 million barrels/day (bpd) to 2.7 million bpd in July 1988. Likewise, Iran's exports fell from 5.3 million bpd prewar to 2.5 million bpd in July 1988.

   Both Iraq and Iran attacked gulf shipping by air and sea. The International Association of Independent Tanker Owners estimated that, by February 1988, a total of 308 tankers had been hit, of which 53 were total losses. To sustain its exports to Europe, Iraq built pipelines to the Red Sea and the eastern Mediterranean.

   When the Iraq-Iran war ended, the *Far Eastern Economic Review* posed the issue, "The war's end, if permanent, leaves many uncertainties—its effect on secondhand tanker values for instance, and consequent effects on new buildings in yards around the world" (Michael Westlake, "Less Oil in Troubled Waters," *Far Eastern Economic Review* [October 20, 1988]).
   a. How would the end of the war affect the cost of conveying a barrel of crude from Iraq to the eastern Mediterranean by pipeline?
   b. How would the end of the war affect the cost of conveying the same barrel of crude from Iraq to the eastern Mediterranean by tanker?
   c. Which method of transportation involves a larger proportion of sunk costs, once incurred: pipelines or tankers?
   d. Do you expect tankers to recapture a dominant share of the Iraqi export market from the pipelines?

9. Major law firms organize their lawyers into functional practices, such as corporate law, litigation, real estate, and tax. One of the major indirect expenses of a law firm is the library. Explain how you would allocate the expenses of a library among the functional practices.

10. Suppose that Mercury Elevator has just discovered a mistake in the data of Table 7.12. In the first column, every entry for cost should be $14,000 higher. All other data remain valid.

a. Estimate the cost equation with the original data (before the revision of the first column).

b. Estimate the cost equation with the revised data. Does production involve substantial fixed elements?

c. Using the revised estimates in (b), calculate the cost of a system with the following characteristics: capacity of 1000 kilograms, speed of 1.0 meter per second, travel of 20 meters, and four landings.

Chapter 8

Monopoly

1 Introduction

The owner of a patented invention has an exclusive right for a specified period of time. Glaxo Wellcome PLC owns the patent to zidovudine (AZT). At the time of writing, AZT was one of the leading treatments for AIDS-related conditions. AZT blocks the enzyme that stimulates HIV (the AIDS virus) to proliferate. The drug can mean the difference between life and death for HIV-infected people. Does this imply, as claimed by *The Economist*, that, "Once its products were approved, a big drug firm such as Glaxo could sell them at almost whatever price it wanted"?

Eurostar operates the only high-speed passenger through train service between the centers of London and Paris. Other rail services must connect with ferries to cross the English Channel, which separates Britain from the European continent. For travel between London and Paris, Eurostar is faster than airlines as well as other train services. One of Eurostar's major costs is the interest on bank loans. If Eurostar renegotiates these loans, so reducing the average cost of service, should the company cut its fares by the same amount?

In the United States, the sport of professional baseball is controlled by the major leagues. In the spring of 1976, the owners of the major league baseball teams signed a new collective bargaining agreement that allowed free agency for players with over six years' experience. How could free agency be expected to affect the salaries of baseball players?

To address these questions, we must understand the behavior of buyers or sellers that have the power to influence market conditions. A buyer or seller that can influence market conditions is said to have *market power*. A buyer with market power can influence market supply, in particular, the price and quantity supplied. A seller with market power can influence market demand, in particular, the price and quantity demanded.

For simplicity, we will focus on markets in which there is either just one seller or one buyer. If there is only one seller in a market, that seller is called a **monopoly**. If there is only one buyer in a market, that buyer is called a **monopsony**. Monopoly and monopsony are extreme cases: At the opposite extreme lies perfect competition, where there are numerous buyers and sellers, all of whom are small relative to the market. The knowledge of these extremes helps us to understand the intermediate case where there are several buyers or sellers who are large enough to influence market conditions.

We begin by discussing the sources of market power. Then, we analyze how a profit-maximizing monopoly sets its price and scale of production. This allows us to show how the monopoly should adjust price and production in response to changes in demand and costs. Applying this analysis, we can address the issue of whether Glaxo can sell its drugs at "almost whatever price it wants." We can also consider how Eurostar should adjust price if it succeeds in renegotiating its loans and reducing its interest costs.

Next, we consider how much a monopoly should spend on advertising. Then, we compare prices, production rates, and profits under a monopoly with perfect competition. This explains how competing sellers can benefit by restricting competition among themselves through cartels or horizontal integration.

Finally, we focus on monopsony and analyze how a monopsony that maximizes net benefit will set its price and scale of purchases. Applying this analysis, we can explain how free agency would affect the salaries of American baseball players.

> A **monopoly** is the only seller in a market.

> A **monopsony** is the only buyer in a market.

2 *Sources of Market Power*

Before analyzing how monopolies and monopsonies use market power, we first review the sources of this power. To understand the reasons for a monopoly, we need to ask why other sellers do not enter the market to compete for the business. Generally, the sources of market power are the barriers that deter or prevent entry by other competing sellers. Similarly, the sources of market power for a monopsony are the barriers that deter entry of competing buyers.

Monopoly

Unique Resource   One barrier to entry by competing sellers is access to unique human resources. All team sports regulate the number and roles of players. For instance, football teams are limited to one quarterback and soccer teams to one goalkeeper. A football manager cannot field two quarterbacks nor can a soccer team have two goalkeepers. Under such circumstances, it is not possible to substitute quantity for quality.

Similarly, directors of performing arts such as movies, music, and theater cannot substitute quantity for quality. Imagine *Pulp Fiction* with Uma Thurman, John Travolta, and Bruce Willis replaced by randomly chosen extras from Central Casting. In sport and performing arts, the next-best performer or athlete is a poor substitute for a superstar. Accordingly, the superstar will have substantial market power and earnings that are disproportionate to performance.

By contrast, in many occupations, it is possible to substitute quantity for quality. For instance, a building contractor can replace a superfast bricklayer with two relatively slow bricklayers. Similarly, a restaurant can substitute two slow dishwashers for a single fast one. In occupations such as bricklaying and dishwashing, superior performers have relatively little market power and their earnings will tend to be proportionate to performance.

Another reason why competing sellers cannot enter is that they may be unable to get access to a unique physical or natural resource. Eurostar has exclusive right to use the Eurotunnel, which allows it to offer much faster service than regular trains. Competing rail operators must transfer their passengers to ferries for the channel crossing. In this case, exclusive access to a physical resource—the Eurotunnel—is the source of market power.

The platinum industry provides an example of natural resources giving rise to market power. Platinum is a relatively inert corrosion-resistant metal with a high electrical resistance that has relatively few substitutes. Anglo-American Corporation, a South African conglomerate, owns over 75% of the world's reserves of platinum. Anglo-American is an example where ownership of a natural resource is the source of market power.

The Value of a Star

In the 1995–96 season, Patrick Ewing of the New York Knicks earned $18.7 million, making him the highest paid player in the American basketball league. Ewing's salary was almost double that of the next highest paid player, Clyde Drexler of the Houston Rockets, who earned $9.8 million.

As shown in Table 8.1, the difference in salaries was more muted for players further down the rankings. The difference in salaries between the second and third highest paid players, Drexler and David Robinson of the San Antonio Spurs was 27%. From the fifth highest paid player down, all but one of the salary differences were less than 5%.

Table 8.1 Basketball player salaries, 1995–96

	Player	Team	Salary (millions $)	Difference over Next Player (%)
1	Patrick Ewing	New York Knicks	18,724	91
2	Clyde Drexler	Houston Rockets	9,810	27
3	David Robinson	San Antonio Spurs	7,700	10
4	Chris Webber	Washington Bullets	7,000	2
5	Joe Dumars	Detroit Pistons	6,881	1
6	Danny Manning	Phoenix Suns	6,833	6
7	A.C. Green	Phoenix Suns	6,473	14
8	Shaquille O'Neal	Orlando Magic	5,700	4
9	Derrick Coleman	Philadelphia 76ers	5,476	3
10	Sean Elliott	San Antonio Spurs	5,333	1
11	Hakeem Olajuwon	Houston Rockets	5,305	1
12	Anfernee Hardaway	Orlando Magic	5,230	2
13	James Worthy	Los Angeles Lakers	5,150	3
14	Detlef Schrempf	Seattle Supersonics	5,000	4
15	Sam Bowie	Los Angeles Lakers	4,800	1
16	Charles Barkley	Phoenix Suns	4,760	1
17	Brad Daugherty	Cleveland Cavaliers	4,700	1
18	Danny Ferry	Cleveland Cavaliers	4,643	2
19	Alonzo Mourning	Miami Heat	4,560	1
20	Tom Gugliotta	Minnesota Timberw.	4,500	0
21	C. Weatherspoon	Philadelphia 76ers	4,500	4
22	Shawn Bradley	New Jersey Nets	4,320	1
23	Larry Johnson	Charlotte Hornets	4,295	1
24	Brian Shaw	Orlando Magic	4,250	2
25	John Williams	Phoenix Suns	4,151	

Source: *Dallas Morning News* (December 24, 1995).

Intellectual Property   A second source of market power is control over intellectual property; that is, property over inventions or expressions. To encourage research and development of new products and processes, most governments award patents for new inventions. A patent gives the owner an exclusive right to the invention for a specified period of time. Thus, the owner of a patent has a monopoly over the invention. Glaxo Wellcome, for instance, owns the patent to AZT; hence, it has a monopoly over the drug.

Another form of intellectual property is a copyright. A copyright establishes property in published expressions, including computer software and engineering drawings. Microsoft, for example, has the copyright over Office 97, so it is illegal for another person to copy or manufacture the Office 97 operating system. The copyright to Office 97 gives Microsoft a monopoly over the software. In Chapter 11, we discuss the economics of patents and copyrights in greater detail.

Economies of Scale and Scope   A third source of market power is economies of scale or scope, as discussed in Chapter 7. Electricity distribution illustrates economies of scale. This service requires an extensive network of cables leading from generating stations to the various users, including factories, residences, and offices. To have two competing distributors of electricity would mean duplication of the cable network. So, in electricity distribution, one provider can achieve lower costs than multiple providers. Hence, the industry will tend to be dominated by a single provider.

Cable television and local telephone service illustrate economies of scope. Both services depend on a network of cables from the service provider to the individual subscribers. Owing to economies of scope, a combined provider of television and telephone service can achieve lower average costs than specialized providers. Consequently, these industries will tend to be dominated by a single provider.

Regulation   A fourth source of market power is government regulation. In businesses where economies of scale or scope are strong, the government may decide to award an exclusive franchise to one provider. By deliberately prohibiting competition, the government hopes to avoid duplication and, so, reduce the cost of the service. Examples of businesses in which governments award exclusive franchises include local telephone service, and distribution of electricity and natural gas.

The government itself may also keep a monopoly over specific activities for reasons of national interest. For instance, almost all national governments have monopolies over defense and issuance of currency. In the United States, the Department of Defense monopolizes military services, and the Federal Reserve Board has a monopoly over the issuance of currency notes and coins.

The U.S. Federal Reserve System: A Monopoly Money Machine

In 1913, the U.S. Congress established the Federal Reserve System. The system consists of 12 Federal Reserve Banks, which have the exclusive right to issue currency notes. As of December 1994, $381 billion worth of U.S. currency were in public circulation.

Considering that currency notes are merely high-quality printed paper, it is not surprising that the Federal Reserve's monopoly is extremely profitable. Table 8.2 shows that, in 1994, the Federal Reserve Banks earned $19.12 billion on sales of $20.91 billion—a performance that would be the envy of any business.

Although the Federal Reserve System has a monopoly within the United States, it has no such privilege overseas. International business can be transacted in any currency. Despite competition from other currencies, the greenback has held up very well in international transactions. It has been estimated that up to 80% of Federal Reserve notes circulate outside the United States. There was even $600 million in Vietnam at a time when that country did not have diplomatic relations with the United States.

Source: Board of Governors of the Federal Reserve System, *1994 Annual Report*, pp. 300–1; "The Case of the Missing Currency," *Journal of Economic Perspectives* 7, no. 4 (Fall 1993): pp. 175–84; "Hanoi Dictates Currency Clamp," *South China Morning Post* (August 10, 1994), Business, p. 10.

Table 8.2 U.S. Federal Reserve Banks, income and expenses, 1994

Current income	
Federal securities	19,247
Others	1,664
Total	20,911
Current expenses	2,006
Net income	19,115

Note: All amounts in millions of dollars.

Source: Board of Governors of the Federal Reserve Systems, *Annual Report, 1994,* pp. 310–3.

Product Differentiation   Finally, a seller may be able to establish market power by differentiating itself from competitors. Sellers can differentiate their products through advertising, promotion, product design, and location. Coca Cola provides an excellent example of product differentiation. There are many competing colas in the retail market. To differentiate its product, Coca Cola has made intensive investments in its brand.

In retailing, an important dimension by which sellers can differentiate themselves is location. Retailers know well that consumer demand varies with location. In city centers, fast-food restaurants try to locate on streets with heavy pedestrian traffic. Gasoline stations prefer to locate at busy intersections.

Monopsony

So far, we have been discussing why a seller may be a monopoly or, more generally, have market power. These same factors explain why a buyer may have market power. There is one additional reason for the presence of a monopsony: the existence of a monopoly. A seller that has a monopoly over some good or service is also likely to have market power over the inputs into that item. For instance, a monopoly electricity distributor will have market power over suppliers of electricity meters and high-voltage switch-gear. The monopoly electricity distributor will probably be a monopsony in the market for the services of power engineers.

When AT&T had a near–monopoly over local telecommunications in the United States, it was also the dominant buyer of terminal equipment. Indeed, AT&T established a subsidiary, Western Electric, to manufacture terminal equipment for itself.

Defense provides another example. We have mentioned that national governments monopolize defense. By this monopoly, the government will have market power over suppliers of military equipment and supplies, as well as the services of military personnel.

Individual vis-à-vis Market Demand Elasticities

Generally, the products of an entire market have fewer close substitutes than the product of an individual seller. Accordingly, the individual seller's demand will tend to be more elastic than the market demand. At one extreme, if the market is perfectly competitive, the individual seller's demand will be extremely elastic. At the other extreme, if the market is a monopoly, the individual seller's demand will be the same as the market demand; hence, it will have the same price elasticity as the market demand.

Table 8.3 reports the price elasticities of demand for representative individual businesses as compared with their respective markets. In food and apparel, a typical business faces a demand that is almost four times more elastic than the corresponding market demand. By contrast, in paper and petroleum, the individual demand is only slightly more elastic than the market demand. These data suggest that American manufacturers of paper and petroleum have relatively more market power than manufacturers of food and apparel.

Table 8.3 Market and individual demand elasticities

| | Price Elasticity of Demand | |
Industry	Market	Individual Business
Food	−1.0	−3.8
Textiles	−1.5	−4.7
Apparel	−1.1	−4.1
Paper	−1.5	−1.7
Printing and publishing	−1.8	−3.2
Petroleum	−1.5	−1.7
Rubber	−1.8	−2.3
Leather	−1.2	−2.3

Source: Matthew D. Shapiro, "Measuring Market Power in U.S. Industry," National Bureau of Economic Research, Working Paper No. 2312, 1987.

3 *Monopoly Pricing*

Having reviewed the sources of market power, let us now consider how a seller can use market power. Suppose that Solar Pharmaceutical has just received a patent for a new drug, Gamma-1, that cures bone-marrow cancer. How should Solar set the price for this drug? The essence of market power is that the seller faces a demand curve that slopes downward. Solar Pharmaceutical, being a monopoly, faces the market demand curve. Unlike a perfectly competitive seller, a monopoly has to consider how its sales will affect the market price.

Given the market demand curve, a monopoly can either set the price and let the market determine how much it will buy, or decide how much to sell and let the market determine the price at which it is willing to buy that quantity. If the monopoly tries to set both the price and sales, the price and the sales may be inconsistent in the sense that, at that price, the market wants to buy more or less than the quantity the monopoly is selling. In terms of a graph, inconsistency means that the monopoly is choosing a combination of price and sales off the demand curve. Accordingly, a monopoly can set either the price or sales but not both.

Suppose that Solar decides to set the price and let the market determine the quantity of sales. A preliminary issue is Solar's objective. We shall assume that Solar aims to maximize profit, which is revenue less cost. This assumption, although not completely realistic, is enough for us to understand a monopoly's pricing strategy and several other practices as well. So, assuming that Solar aims to maximize profit, we must ask how Solar's price affects its revenue and cost.

Revenue

First, let us look at the relationship between price and revenue. Table 8.4 shows the demand for Gamma-1: Specifically, the second column shows, for every price, the quantity of Gamma-1 that Solar expects to sell. We see that the quantity demanded increases by 200,000 units for every $10 reduction in price. Using this information, we can then calculate Solar's *total revenue* for every price, which is price multiplied by sales. From the total revenue, we can then

Table 8.4 Monopoly revenue, cost, and profit

Price ($)	Sales	Total Revenue ($)	Marginal Revenue ($)	Total Cost ($)	Marginal Cost ($)	Profit ($)
200	0.0	0		50		−50
190	0.2	38	190	52	10	−14
180	0.4	72	170	56	20	16
170	0.6	102	150	62	30	40
160	0.8	128	130	70	40	58
150	1.0	150	110	80	50	70
140	1.2	168	90	92	60	76
130	1.4	182	70	106	70	76
120	1.6	192	50	122	80	70
110	1.8	198	30	140	90	58
100	2.0	200	10	160	100	40
90	2.2	198	−10	182	110	16

Note: Sales, total revenue, total cost, and profit in millions of dollars.

calculate *marginal revenue,* which is the change in total revenue arising from selling an additional unit.

To sell additional units, Solar Pharmaceutical must reduce its price. So, when increasing sales by one unit, Solar will gain revenue from selling the additional (or marginal) unit, but it will lose revenue on the **inframarginal units**. The *inframarginal* units are those other than the marginal unit. Solar would have sold the inframarginal units without reducing the price.

Inframarginal units are those other than the marginal unit.

For example, referring to Table 8.4, to increase sales from 200,000 to 400,000 units, Solar must reduce the price from $190 to $180. Hence, Solar will gain revenue of $180 × 200,000 = $36 million on the additional units, but lose $(190 − 180) × 200,000 = $2 million on the inframarginal 200,000 units that it could have sold at $190. Thus, Solar's revenue for the additional 200,000 units is $36 − $2 = $34 million, which means that marginal revenue is $170 per unit.

In general, the marginal revenue from selling an additional unit will be less than the price of that unit. The reason, as we have explained, is that the marginal revenue is the price of the marginal unit minus the loss of revenue on the inframarginal units.

The difference between the price and the marginal revenue depends on the price elasticity of demand. If demand is very elastic, then the seller need not reduce the price very much to increase sales; hence, the marginal revenue will be close to the price. If, however, demand is very inelastic, then the seller must reduce the price substantially to increase sales; so, the marginal revenue will be much lower than the price.

We should also emphasize that the marginal revenue can be negative, if the loss of revenue on the inframarginal units exceeds the gain on the marginal unit. Table 8.4 shows that, if Solar cut the price from $100 to $90, sales would increase from 2.0 to 2.2 million units. The change in revenue, however, is −$2 million for the additional 200,000 units, which means that marginal revenue is −$10 per unit.

Progress Check 8A If demand is extremely elastic, what will be the difference between the price and the marginal revenue?

Progress check

Costs

We have considered the relation between price and revenue. The other side to profit is cost. Table 8.4 also shows data for Solar Pharmaceutical's production costs. It reports only avoidable costs and omits sunk costs. From the total cost at a zero production scale, we can infer that production requires a fixed cost of $50 million.

Total cost increases with the scale of production. Table 8.4 shows Solar's marginal cost, which is the change in total cost due to the production of an additional unit. The change in total cost arises from change in the variable cost.

Profit-Maximizing Price

With information on both revenue and cost, we can calculate Solar's profit. Profit is total revenue less total (fixed and variable) cost. The last column of Table 8.4 reports profit at every quantity of sales. Looking down the column, we see that Solar's maximum profit is $76 million. It achieves this profit with a price of $130 and sales of 1.4 million units.

In addition to calculating the profit from all possible prices or quantities of sales, the profit-maximizing scale of production can be identified in another way: Determine the scale at which the marginal revenue balances the marginal cost. At the price of $130, Solar's sales are 1.4 million units. The marginal revenue is $80 per unit. The marginal cost is also $80 per unit. So, at the profit-maximizing quantity, the marginal revenue equals the marginal cost.

This suggests a general rule: To maximize profit, a monopoly should produce at a scale where its marginal revenue balances its marginal cost. This rule applies to any seller and not only a monopoly. It can be expressed in another way. The **contribution margin** is the total revenue less the variable cost. If the seller sells an additional unit, then its contribution margin will change by the difference between the marginal revenue and the marginal cost. Hence, a seller maximizes profit by operating at a scale where the sale of an additional unit will result in no change to the contribution margin.

The **contribution margin** is the total revenue less variable cost.

Let us illustrate the profit-maximizing price and production scale with a diagram. Figure 8.1 shows Solar Pharmaceutical's demand, marginal revenue, and marginal cost curves. The demand curve shows, for every price, the quantity that the market will buy. Equivalently, it shows, for every quantity of purchases (on the horizontal axis), the maximum price (on the vertical axis) that the market will pay for that quantity.

The marginal revenue curve shows, for every quantity (on the horizontal axis), the marginal revenue (on the vertical axis). As we have explained, for every quantity, the marginal revenue is less than the price. Accordingly, at all quantities, the marginal revenue curve lies below the demand curve.

The marginal revenue and marginal cost curves cross at the quantity of 1.4 million units. From the demand curve, we see that the price at that quantity is $130. This is the profit-maximizing price.

Let us understand why a seller maximizes profit at a production scale where marginal revenue balances marginal cost. Suppose that Solar produces at a scale, such as 1.2 million units, where the marginal revenue exceeds the marginal cost.

Figure 8.1 Monopoly production rate

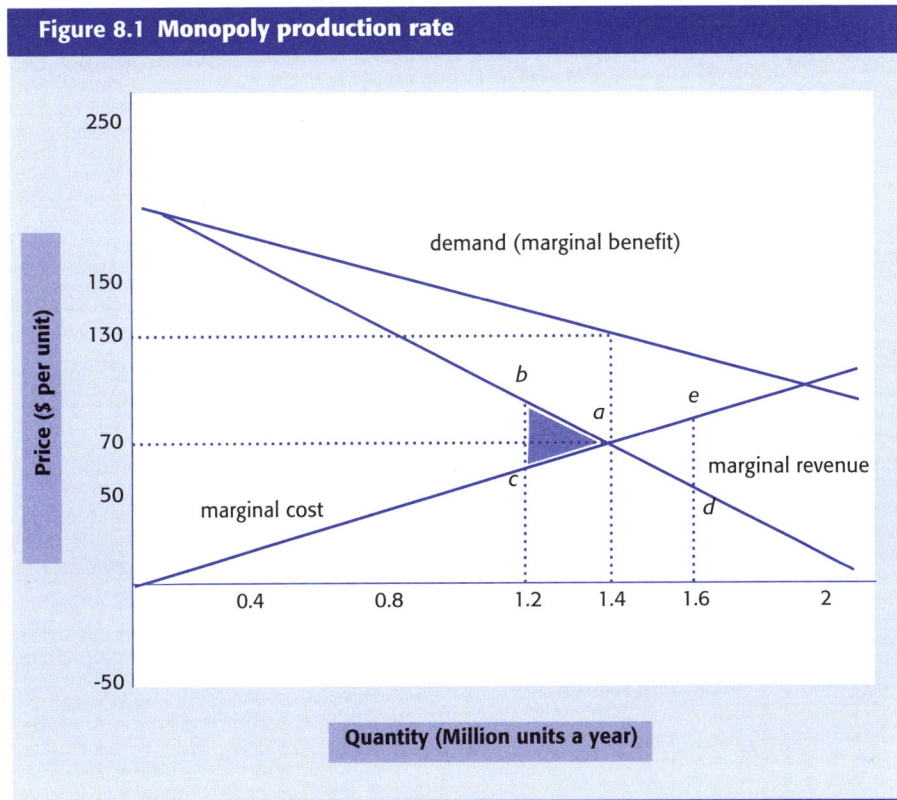

The marginal revenue and marginal cost curves cross at the quantity of 1.4 million units. Reading from the demand curve, the profit-maximizing price is $130. The demand curve also shows the marginal benefit. At 1.4 million units, the marginal benefit exceeds the marginal cost.

Then, if Solar increases production by 200,000 units, its revenue will increase by more than its cost; indeed, it will increase its profit by the area shaded *bca*.

By contrast, suppose that Solar produces at a scale such as 1.6 million units, where the marginal revenue is less than the marginal cost. Then, if Solar cuts production by 200,000 units, its revenue will fall by less than its cost; hence it will increase its profit by the area *ade*. Generally, a seller will maximize profit if it produces at a scale where its marginal revenue balances its marginal cost.

Progress Check 8B Suppose that, at the current scale of production, Solar's marginal revenue is less than its marginal cost. How should management adjust its price?

Progress check

Life-and-Death Monopoly: Glaxo Wellcome and the Pricing of AZT

Glaxo Wellcome PLC owns the patent to AZT. At the time of writing, the anti-viral drug AZT was the leading treatment for AIDS-related conditions. AZT blocks the enzyme that stimulates the HIV virus to proliferate. While the drug does not cure AIDS, it may relieve symptoms and prolong remission.

For many people, Glaxo's drug means the difference between life and death. Even well-informed analysts have been confused into thinking that such a monopoly can make unlimited profit: "Once its products were approved, a big drug firm such as Glaxo could sell them at almost whatever price it wanted." ("Waging Sykological Warfare," *The Economist* (January 28, 1995), pp. 61–2.)

Although AZT is critical for a person with AIDS, Glaxo cannot charge an unlimited price for the drug. Glaxo actually could set the price as high as it likes, but it cannot force people with AIDS to buy the drug. Glaxo knows that, if it sets a higher price, the quantity demanded will be lower. In 1994, the manufacturer set a wholesale price of around £1 per 100 milligram capsules and its total revenues were £207 million.

Source: Letter to shareholders, Glaxo Wellcome PLC (February 15, 1995).

Economic Inefficiency

Figure 8.1 reveals an important aspect of a monopoly's profit-maximizing production scale. At the quantity of 1.4 million units, the price is $130. Recall that the demand curve also shows the marginal benefit for every quantity of purchases. Hence, the marginal benefit at 1.4 million units is $130.

By contrast, the marginal cost at 1.4 million units is $70. Hence, the marginal benefit exceeds the marginal cost. This means that some buyers are willing to pay more than the marginal cost for the item but cannot get it. In Chapter 6, we explained that such a divergence between the marginal benefit and the marginal cost is economically inefficient.

The managerial implication of this economic inefficiency is that a profit can be made through bridging the gap to provide the item to those buyers. Since they are willing to pay more than the marginal cost, the difference is the potential profit to be made by supplying them. In Chapter 9, we discuss various pricing policies through which a seller can increase profit by bridging the inefficiency.

Changes in Demand and Cost

How should a monopoly respond to changes in demand? For instance, suppose that demand for Solar's Gamma-1 shifts outward. How should Solar adjust its price? To address this question, Figure 8.2 shows the new demand curve. From the new demand curve, we can calculate the new marginal revenue curve.

The new marginal revenue curve lies further to the right. Since the upward-sloping marginal cost curve does not change, the new marginal revenue curve crosses the marginal cost curve at a larger scale. Specifically, the two curves cross at a scale of about 1.5 million units, and the new profit-maximizing price is around $125.

Although the change was only in demand, we must consider both the new marginal revenue and the original marginal cost to obtain the new profit-maximizing sales and price.

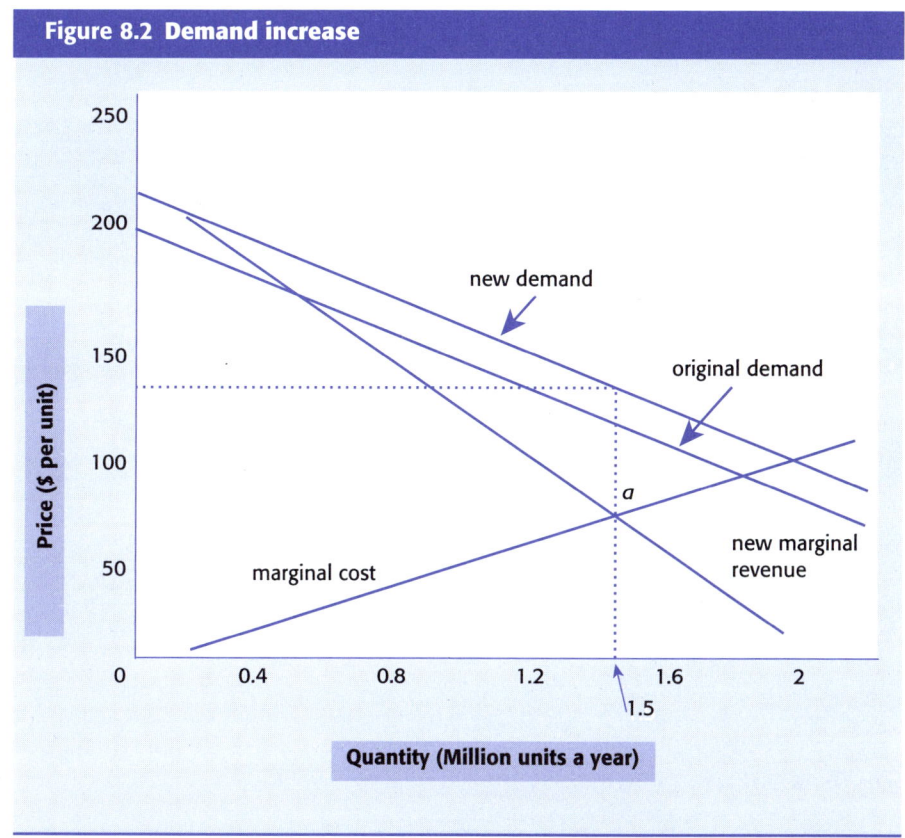

Figure 8.2 Demand increase

The new marginal revenue curve crosses the marginal cost curve at the quantity of 1.5 million units. The new profit-maximizing price is around $125.

We can use a similar approach to understand how a monopoly should respond to a change in the marginal cost. Suppose, for instance, that, relative to the data reported in Table 8.4, the marginal cost drops by half at all scales of production. Should Solar reduce the price of the drug by half as well?

To address this question, consider Figure 8.3, which shows Solar's marginal revenue and the new marginal cost. The marginal revenue and the new marginal cost cross at a quantity of about 1.7 million units. The new profit-maximizing price is around $120. Notice that Solar maximizes profits by cutting its price by about $10, which is proportionately less than the fall in the marginal cost. Further, although the change was only in the marginal cost, Solar must consider the marginal revenue as well as the new marginal cost to obtain the new profit-maximizing price and sales.

Generally, when there is a change in either demand or cost, the extent to which a monopoly should adjust its price depends on the shapes of both its marginal revenue and marginal cost curves. It should adjust the price until its marginal revenue equals its marginal cost.

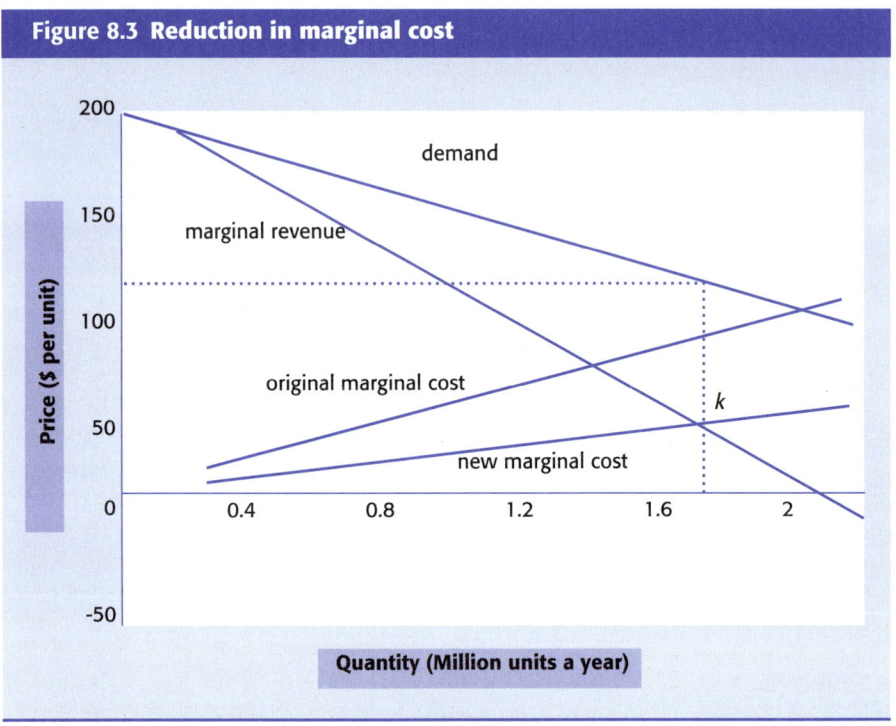

Figure 8.3 Reduction in marginal cost

The marginal revenue and the new marginal cost cross at a quantity of about 1.7 million units. The new profit-maximizing price is around $120.

Table 8.5 Increase in fixed cost

Price ($)	Sales	Total Revenue ($)	Marginal Revenue ($)	Total Cost ($)	Marginal Cost ($)	Profit ($)
200	0.0	0		90		−90
190	0.2	38	190	92	10	−54
180	0.4	72	170	96	20	−24
170	0.6	102	150	102	30	0
160	0.8	128	130	110	40	18
150	1.0	150	110	120	50	30
140	1.2	168	90	132	60	36
130	1.4	182	70	146	70	36
120	1.6	192	50	162	80	30
110	1.8	198	30	180	90	18
100	2.0	200	10	200	100	0
90	2.2	198	−10	222	110	-24

Note: Sales, total revenue, total cost, and profit in millions of dollars.

We should stress that a monopoly's profit-maximizing price and sales do not depend in any way on the fixed cost. Suppose that Solar Pharmaceutical must incur an additional fixed cost of $40 million a year to maintain its production line. In Table 8.5, we show Solar's revenues and costs with the higher fixed cost. The profit-maximizing price and sales are still $130 and 1.4 million units, respectively.

There is another way to see that the profit-maximizing price and sales do not depend on the fixed cost. Recall that a monopoly maximizes profit by operating at the scale where its marginal revenue equals its marginal cost. Changes in the fixed cost will not affect the marginal cost curve; hence, they will not affect the profit-maximizing price.

Progress Check 8C In Figure 8.1, show how the monopoly should adjust price if marginal cost increases everywhere by $10.

Progress check

Eurostar: High-Speed Rail Monopoly

Eurostar operates the only high-speed passenger through train service between London and Paris. Other rail services must connect with ferries to cross the English Channel, which separates Britain from the European continent. In July 1995, Eurostar had a capacity of 441,000 seats, and charged a fare of £220 for a first-class round trip between London and Paris.

One of Eurostar's major fixed costs is the interest on bank loans. If Eurostar renegotiated these loans, reducing the interest payments and the average cost of service, should the company cut its fares by the same amount?

The reduction in the fixed cost does not affect Eurostar's marginal cost. The profit-maximizing price depends only on the company's marginal revenue and marginal cost. It is independent of the fixed cost. Accordingly, if Eurostar succeeds in its renegotiations, it should not adjust its fares.

Source: "Eurostar: An Oncoming Train," *The Economist* (October 7, 1995), p. 85.

Short- vis-à-vis Long-Run

We have been considering how a monopoly should set price and sales. Up to this point, we have not mentioned the length of the planning horizon. Let us now emphasize that the procedure for determining the profit-maxizing price and sales is essentially the same in the short and long runs. In a short-run planning horizon, the monopoly should aim to balance short-run marginal revenue and marginal cost; in a long-run planning horizon, it should balance long-run marginal revenue and marginal cost.

4 *Advertising*

Promotion is the set of marketing activities that a business undertakes to communicate with its customers and sell its products.

A monopoly, and more generally, any seller with market power can influence the demand for its products. **Promotion** is the set of marketing activities that a business undertakes to communicate with its customers and sell its products. It encompasses advertising, sales promotion, and public relations. Let us now consider how much a business should spend on promotion. For convenience, we focus the analysis on advertising by a monopoly. The same principles apply to the other dimensions of promotion and any seller with market power.

Benefit of Advertising

How much should Solar Pharmaceutical spend on advertising its new drug, Gamma-1? Advertising can influence the market demand. Specifically, given Solar's price, expenditure on advertising can increase the quantity of sales by shifting out the demand curve as well as causing it to be less elastic. The additional sales in turn affect Solar's total revenue and variable cost and hence its contribution margin. The benefit of advertising is the change in the contribution margin.

Accordingly, the net benefit from advertising is the change in the contribution margin less the advertising expenditure. To maximize profits, Solar should advertise up to the point that the increase in the contribution margin from an additional dollar of advertising is exactly $1.

Let us understand why this rule maximizes profit. Consider a point at which the increase in the contribution margin from an additional dollar of advertising is more than $1. Then, if Solar spends an additional dollar on advertising, its contribution margin will increase by more than $1, hence Solar will increase its profit. By contrast, at a point where an additional dollar of advertising increases Solar's contribution margin by less than $1, Solar can increase profit by cutting back on advertising expenditure.

Essentially, the rule advises the seller to invest in advertising up to the point that the marginal benefit just balances the marginal cost. To keep a clear distinction between the benefits and the costs of advertising, we measure the benefits by the effect on the contribution margin.

By contrast, some marketing specialists measure the benefit of advertising by the effect on awareness and recall of the featured product or on product sales. We emphasize that it is more appropriate to consider the effect of advertising on the contribution margin generated by the product. The reason is that, ultimately, the aim of most advertisers is to increase the seller's profit rather than awareness or sales as such. Managers who focus on awareness and recall or even sales may overlook the effect on profit.

Profit-Maximizing Advertising

We have just presented a rule for advertising expenditure: To maximize profits, a monopoly should advertise up to the point that the increase in the contribution margin from an additional dollar of advertising is $1. Using the concepts of an *incremental margin* and the *advertising elasticity of demand*, we can derive a simpler version of the rule for the profit-maximizing level of advertising expenditure.

We define the **incremental margin** as the price less the marginal cost. The incremental margin is the increase in the contribution margin from selling an additional unit, holding the price constant. Recall from Chapter 3 that the advertising elasticity of demand is the percentage by which the demand will change if the seller's advertising expenditure rises by 1%, other things equal.

In the math supplement, we show that, when the marginal benefit equals the marginal cost of advertising, the advertising expenditure is the incremental margin multiplied by the advertising elasticity of demand multiplied by the sales. This provides a simpler rule for the profit-maximizing level of advertising expenditure.

We can apply this rule to determine the profit-maximizing level of advertising expenditure for Solar's new drug Gamma-1. Recall that, with the demand and costs in Table 8.4, the profit-maximizing scale of production for Gamma-1

The **incremental margin** is the price less the marginal cost (which is the increase in the contribution margin from selling an additional unit, holding the price constant).

is 1.4 million units. At that scale, the price is \$130 per unit and the marginal cost is \$70. This means that the incremental margin is \$130 − \$70 = \$60 per unit. Suppose that, at the price of \$130, the advertising elasticity of the demand is 0.05. Then the profit-maximizing level of advertising expenditure is \$130 × 0.05 × 1.4 million = \$9.1 million.

Changes in Demand and Cost

The rule for advertising expenditures implies that, if the incremental margin is higher, then the seller should spend relatively more on advertising. The reason is that each dollar of advertising produces relatively more benefit as measured by the incremental margin. Accordingly, when the incremental margin is higher, the seller should increase advertising. This means that, whenever a seller raises its price or its marginal cost falls, it should also increase advertising expenditure. By contrast, if a seller reduces its price or its marginal cost rises, it should reduce advertising expenditure.

Further, the rule for advertising expenditures implies that, if either the advertising elasticity of demand or the sales is higher, then the seller should spend relatively more on advertising. Essentially, a higher advertising elasticity of demand or sales means that the influence of advertising on buyer demand is relatively greater. In these circumstances, it makes sense to advertise more.

Progress check

Progress Check 8D Suppose that the profit-maximizing scale of production for Gamma-1 is 1.4 million units. At that scale, the price is \$140 per unit, the marginal cost is \$70, and the advertising elasticity of demand is 0.01. How much should Solar spend on advertising?

Promotion

Up to this point, we have focused on a monopoly's advertising policy. The same principles apply to promotion, which is the general set of marketing activities encompassing advertising, sales promotion, and public relations. A monopoly should promote up to the point that an additional dollar of promotion increases its contribution margin by one dollar. The profit-maximizing level of promotional expenditure is the incremental margin multiplied by the elasticity of demand with respect to an increase in promotion multiplied by the sales.

5 *Monopoly vis-à-vis Competition*

Monopoly, the case of a single seller, is one extreme of a range of market structures. At the other extreme lies perfect competition, where there are numerous sellers, each of whom is too small to affect market conditions. How do price and production depend on the competitive structure of the market? Monopoly and perfect competition are extreme cases. Knowledge of these extremes helps us understand the intermediate case, where there are several sellers who are large enough to influence market conditions.

Market Structure

To address the question of how price and production depend on the market structure, consider the following example. We take a long-run perspective. Assume that the production of oranges involves no fixed cost and the marginal cost is constant at 30 cents per unit. We will compare price and production when orange growing is perfectly competitive with the outcome when the same industry is a monopoly.

First, suppose that the orange industry is perfectly competitive. Since production requires only a constant marginal cost of 30 cents, all growers will be willing to supply unlimited quantities at 30 cents per orange. Hence, the market supply will be perfectly elastic at 30 cents per orange. Given the market demand, the supply will balance demand at a price of 30 cents. Figure 8.4(a) illustrates the market equilibrium. The sales and production will be the quantity demanded at a price of 30 cents, say, 300 million units a year. In equilibrium, each grower earns zero profit.

Next, suppose that the orange industry is a monopoly. The monopoly will produce at a scale that balances marginal revenue and the marginal cost of 30 cents. Since the marginal revenue curve lies below the demand curve, marginal revenue equals marginal cost at a quantity of less than 300 million a year. Accordingly, the monopoly will set the price above 30 cents. Suppose that the monopoly price is 60 cents and sales are 150 million units a year. Figure 8.4(b) depicts the monopoly price and sales. The monopoly will enjoy profits of $(0.60 - 0.30) \times 150 = \$45$ million a year.

The orange-growing example illustrates several general points. First, a monopoly restricts production below the competitive level, and by doing so, it can set a relatively higher price, extracting larger profit. By contrast, competition drives the market price down toward the long-run average cost and results in more production. Further, the profit of a monopoly exceeds what would be the combined profit of all the sellers if the same market were perfectly competitive.

Potential Competition

We have just seen that competition will push down the market price toward the long-run average cost. It is worth emphasizing that, under specific conditions, even *potential* competition will be sufficient to keep the market price close to the long-run average cost.

Consider a market in which sellers can enter and exit at no cost. Such a market is called **perfectly contestable**. A monopoly in a perfectly contestable market cannot raise its price substantially above its long-run average cost.

A **perfectly contestable market** is a market in which sellers can enter and exit at no cost.

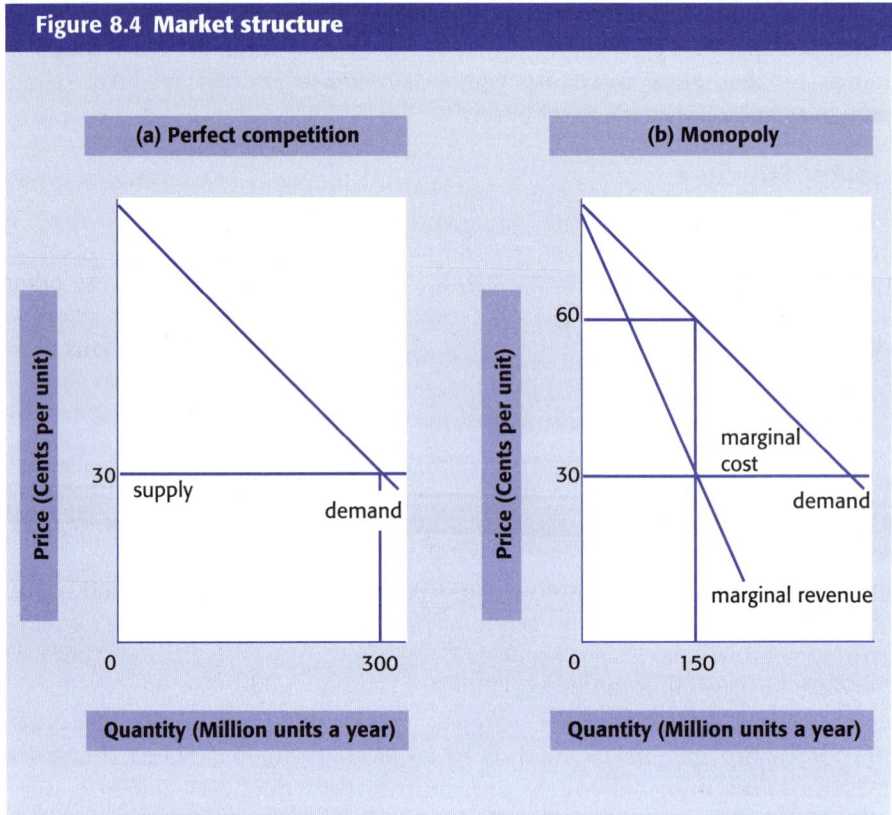

Figure 8.4 Market structure

(a) Under perfect competition, competition drives the market price down toward the long-run average cost of 30 cents. Production is 300 million units.

(b) Under a monopoly, the monopoly restricts production below the competitive level and sets a higher price of 60 cents to obtain larger profit.

To understand why, suppose that Venus Trucking is the only truck service on the coastal route and that other truckers can easily switch their trucks from other routes to the coast. Now, if Venus raises its price above the long-run average cost, other truckers can profit by entering the coastal route. They will quickly enter to compete for a share of the market. The resulting increase in supply will drive the market price back toward the long-run average cost.

We have shown that a monopoly in a perfectly contestable market cannot raise price substantially above its long-run average cost. The degree to which a market is contestable depends on the extent of barriers to entry and exit. The introduction to this chapter reviewed barriers to entry. To the extent that there are barriers to entry, it will be more difficult for competing sellers to enter and, hence, it will be easier for a monopoly to raise its price above the long-run average cost.

The degree to which a market is contestable also depends on the extent of barriers to exit. Recall that, if Venus Trucking raises its price above long-run average cost, it might attract other truckers to enter the coastal market. These other truckers are lured by the attraction of temporary profits, made possible by Venus's relatively high price. Once Venus lowers its price back toward long-run average cost, these other truckers will leave. But their brief presence in the market will have been profitable.

Now, suppose that these other truckers must incur liquidation costs to exit the coastal market. When deciding whether to enter the market, these other truckers must consider these exit costs. The higher such exit costs are, the less likely these other truckers are to enter when Venus raises its price. This illustrates how barriers to exit affect the degree to which a market is contestable.

Lerner Index

Having understood the potential effect of monopoly on price and production, it is worth considering how to measure monopoly power. One measure is the **Lerner Index,** defined as the incremental margin divided by the price (this Index was proposed by the economist Abba Lerner).

> The **Lerner Index** is the incremental margin divided by the price.

In a perfectly competitive market, every seller operates at a scale where its marginal cost equals the market price; hence, its incremental margin is 0. By contrast, a monopoly restricts sales to raise its price above its marginal cost. The more inelastic is market demand, the higher a monopoly can raise its price above its marginal cost. Accordingly, the Lerner Index focuses on the incremental margin, which is the difference between the price and the marginal cost.

The Lerner Index is defined as a ratio (incremental margin divided by price) so that it can be used to compare the degree of monopoly power in markets with different prices. For instance, the price of a floppy disk is much less than a dollar per unit, while the price of a database program may be well over a hundred dollars. It would not make sense to directly compare the incremental margins in floppy disks and database programs. Even if the market for database programs were almost perfectly competitive, the price would be a few dollars above the marginal cost. This difference would be close to the incremental margin in a floppy disk monopoly. Accordingly, to enable comparison of monopoly power in markets with different price levels, the Lerner Index is defined as a ratio.

The Lerner Index also captures the impact of potential competition. If, owing to the presence of potential competitors, a monopoly sets a price close to its marginal cost, then its Lerner Index will also be relatively low. One problem with the index, however, is that it will not detect the power that a monopoly does not exercise. Specifically, if a monopoly faces an inelastic demand but nevertheless sets a price close to its marginal cost, then the Lerner Index will be relatively low, indicating that the market is close to perfectly competitive.

Progress Check 8E Referring to Table 8.4, calculate the Lerner Index when Solar Pharmaceutical sets a price of $130.

Common Misconception

Finally, let us mention one technical difference between a monopoly and perfect competition. A common mistake is to refer to a monopoly's "supply curve." In fact, there is no such thing. Recall that, to construct a supply curve in a perfectly competitive market, we ask each seller how much it would like to supply under the assumption that it can sell an unlimited amount at the given price. For a perfectly competitive seller, its marginal cost curve is also its individual supply curve.

By definition, a monopoly is large relative to its market, so it faces a downward sloping demand curve. This means that it cannot sell an unlimited amount without affecting the market price. Accordingly, for a monopoly or, indeed, any seller with market power, we cannot construct a "supply curve."

6 *Restraining Competition*

We have just seen that a monopoly is more profitable than a competitive industry. Accordingly, rather than compete, sellers can increase profits by restraining competition among themselves. If sellers restrain competition to a sufficient degree, they can achieve the profit of a monopoly. Competing sellers can restrain competition in two ways: through agreement or by integration. We now discuss these ways of restraining competition.

Cartels

A **cartel** is an agreement to restrain competition. A seller cartel is an agreement among sellers to restrain competition in supply, while a buyer cartel is an agreement among buyers to restrain competition in demand. Typically, a seller cartel sets a maximum sales quota for each participant. By limiting each participant's sales, the cartel restricts industry supply and raises sellers' profit above the competitive level. The more effectively the cartel suppresses competition, the closer will the cartel's profit be to the monopoly level.

A seller cartel restrains sales to raise the market price above the competitive level. The higher is the price, however, the more attractive it will be for an individual seller to sell more than its quota. To the extent that any one seller exceeds its quota, the quantity supplied will increase and the market price will fall. So, to be effective, a cartel must have some way to compel each participant to abide by its quota.

*A **cartel** is an agreement to restrain competition.*

Further, if a cartel succeeds in raising the price above the competitive level, it will attract new sellers to enter the market. Hence, another issue for a cartel is how to keep out new entrants. Therefore, the key to an effective cartel, or more generally, effective restriction of competition, is enforcement against existing sellers exceeding their quotas and against the entry of new competitors.

Enforcement

The laws of most developed countries seek to encourage competition and typically do not allow cartels except for specific exemptions. Cartels that are not legal must rely on private enforcement. Generally, the effectiveness of private enforcement depends on several factors. One factor is the number of sellers in the market. Enforcement is easier when there are fewer sellers to be monitored. So, a cartel will be more effective in an industry with relatively few sellers than in a fragmented industry.

Another factor in the effectiveness of a cartel is the relation of industry capacity to market demand. If all sellers are operating near capacity, then it will be difficult for them to expand; hence, there will be little incentive to exceed the specified quotas. By contrast, a seller with substantial excess capacity will have more incentive to exceed its quota.

A third factor is the extent of sunk costs. In the short run, competitive sellers are willing to operate so long as the price covers avoidable cost. Sellers with significant sunk costs will be relatively more willing to cut the price and exceed their quotas.

A fourth factor that influences the effectiveness of a cartel is the extent of barriers to entry and exit. Suppose that all the sellers in a perfectly contestable market form a cartel. Despite their monopoly, they cannot raise the price above the long-run average cost, because that would draw new suppliers into the market, which would drive the market price back down.

Finally, the nature of the product also influences the effectiveness of a cartel. If the product is homogeneous, then each individual seller faces a relatively elastic demand, so it can easily sell more than its quota. On the other hand, if the product is homogeneous, it is easier for the cartel to monitor the various sellers. Frequently, sellers circumvent cartels by attributing increases in sales to items not covered by the cartel agreement. If the product is homogeneous, such subterfuge is no longer possible; hence, it will be easier to enforce the cartel.

Labor Unions

Labor unions are probably the most widespread cartels. Unions organize workers to negotiate with employers over wages and conditions of work. Negotiations in which workers are represented by a union are called *collective bargaining*. Unions are explicit seller cartels: Their primary purpose is to gain higher wages and better conditions than workers could obtain through individual

Government Enforcement

Some cartels have the advantage of government enforcement. For instance, the U.S. government has instituted Agricultural Marketing Orders in a number of agricultural products. Under these orders, the government regulates how much each farmer or grower may produce and, so, determines total production and the market price. In effect, these Agricultural Marketing Orders are legalized seller cartels enforced by the government.

Another market in which a seller cartel enjoys government support is international air service. International airlines need the permission of at least two governments: those at the points of departure and arrival. Many governments tightly control airline capacity, frequency, and fares through bilateral aviation agreements. Owing to these controls, an airline that cuts fares might not get government permission to expand its flights to meet the increase in quantity demanded. Hence, government regulation inhibits airlines from cutting fares. In addition, regulation also limits the entry of new airlines.

Business Triumphs over Ideology: De Beers' Central Selling Organization

Until the early 1990s, the government of South Africa practiced an official policy of racial discrimination called *apartheid*. This policy regulated many important dimensions of daily life according to race. Under apartheid, a black could not live in an area reserved for whites, a colored (mixed-race) child could not attend a school reserved for blacks, and it was even illegal for persons of different races to engage in sexual intercourse. As a result of the apartheid policy, South Africa was ostracized by the governments of many countries, including the Soviet Union.

At one time, South Africa was the world's leading producer of raw gem-quality diamonds. The De Beers group, which monopolized the South African diamond industry, established the Central Selling Organisation (CSO) to manage the international diamond market. The CSO bought diamonds when it perceived prices to be too low and sold as prices rose.

The Soviet Union's large resources of raw diamonds, however, threatened De Beers' cosy monopoly. Sensing the problem, De Beers sought a deal with Moscow. Although the Soviet government resolutely opposed South Africa's apartheid policy, it recognized the benefits of maintaining control over international diamond sales. In 1959, the Soviet government agreed to channel its diamonds through the CSO.

Over time, other countries came to dominate world production of raw diamonds. By 1992, the world's top three producers were Botswana, Russia, and Angola. While publicly hostile to South Africa, the governments of Angola and Botswana also agreed to cooperate with the CSO, so preserving the CSO's power over the diamond market.

Source: "Russian Diamonds: Disputes Are Forever," *The Economist* (September 17, 1994), pp. 71–2; "De Beers Supremo Dies at 83 Years," *South China Morning Post* (October 21, 1995), Business, p. 5.

The Brisbane Concrete Cartel

Concrete, a mixture of cement, gravel, sand, and water, is an essential input into building construction. By its very nature, concrete solidifies quickly; hence, once mixed, it cannot be transported over long distances. Suppliers must mix concrete at plants close to their customers' construction sites. Consequently, the concrete business involves a major fixed cost in the land for mixing plants. Physically, concrete is a fairly homogeneous product.

In 1989, five major suppliers—Pioneer, Boral, CSR, Goodmix/Hymix, and Rocla—accounted for about 95% of the concrete market in Brisbane, Australia. Following a price war, the big five agreed to limit competition so that each could maintain its respective historical market share. In particular, they agreed not to poach customers from one another.

The big five held regular meetings to discuss upcoming concrete sales. The meetings allocated each sale to a particular supplier and fixed the price for the sale, with the other suppliers agreeing to quote a higher price or not to quote at all. From time to time, the meetings also arranged to raise the price of concrete.

To discourage cheating, each of the big five reported information on its sales volume, prices, and raw materials costs to a firm of accountants. The accountants collated this information as the Brisbane Concrete Survey. The big five used the survey to verify their respective market shares and to check whether anyone had undercut the agreed prices.

Generally, if a cartel succeeds in raising the price above the competitive level, it will attract new entrants. In 1991, Excel Concrete entered the Brisbane market. The big five responded by targeting Excel's customers with extremely low prices. Further, Excel's concrete plants were subject to opposition in local government councils. Two years later, however, Excel was acquired by the Holderbank group of Switzerland. Once the big five saw that Excel had stronger backing, they changed tack and invited Excel to join the cartel.

After an investigation by the Australian Competition and Consumer Commission, all the big five—Pioneer, Boral, CSR, Goodmix/Hymix, and Rocla—were prosecuted and fined for colluding on prices.

Source: Letter from the Australian Competition and Consumer Commission, December 14, 1995.

---

negotiation. Developed countries have encouraged workers to form unions, and most have laws that specifically allow workers the right to form labor unions.

Recall from our earlier analysis that a monopoly restrains production to raise the price and gain larger profit. In the case of a labor union, it must restrain the amount of employment so as to raise wages above the competitive level. Accordingly, to the extent that a union succeeds in raising wages, it must restrict employment. This means that it must exclude some workers from work.

Nonunion workers present a major threat to labor unions. To prevent such competition, a union would ideally like to establish a "closed shop." A factory or other place of employment is a closed shop if the employer commits not to hire nonunion workers. A union with a closed shop has a monopoly over the labor supply. At its most extreme, a closed shop means that the employer must dismiss all nonunion workers and cannot hire nonunion workers in the future.

Another challenge to a labor union is the extent to which the employer can automate the production process or shift production overseas. Automation is the substitution of equipment for labor; moving to an overseas location is the substitution of foreign labor for domestic labor.

Progress check   **Progress Check 8F** Recall the five factors that determine the effectiveness of a cartel. How do these apply to a labor union?

The Power of Indian Banking Unions

Indian employers must apply for government permission to dismiss workers. Owing to the fear of increasing unemployment, the government seldom approves the applications. Backed by such laws, labor unions have considerable power over employers. Unions in the banking industry have used this power to block automation. In 1993, the unions forced Indian banks to agree that those with more than 500 branches would computerize at a rate not exceeding 0.5% a year, while those with fewer than 500 branches could computerize at 1% a year.

Source: "How to Keep Investors Out," *The Economist* (June 11, 1994), p. 27.

Horizontal Integration

Cartels that are illegal must rely on private enforcement to prevent sellers from exceeding their quotas. However, competing sellers can restrain competition in a way that does not raise the difficulties of enforcement. The alternative is for the competing sellers to integrate.

Consider, for instance, a combination of two sellers, each of which has 50% of a market. The combined business will have a monopoly. While it may be illegal for two independent competitors to fix prices between themselves, it is certainly legal for the two parts of the same company to agree on prices. Hence, a combination that creates a monopoly will certainly be able to set price and sales at monopoly levels, subject, of course, to the entry of potential competitors.

Horizontal integration is the combination of two entities, in the same or similar businesses, under a common ownership.

The combination of two entities, in the same or similar businesses, under a common ownership is called **horizontal integration.** This should be distinguished from **vertical integration,** which describes the combination of the assets for two successive stages of production under a common ownership.

The horizontal integration of any two businesses with market power will lead to reduction in the industry supply, and hence raise the market price and increase profits. The increase in the market price will benefit competing sellers as they will enjoy higher profits.

Vertical integration is the combination of the assets for two successive stages of production, under a common ownership.

Acquiring Market Power in Disk Drives: Seagate Technology and Conner Peripherals

Computers store data in disk drives. Until September 1995, the world's four largest manufacturers in the $17 billion disk drive industry were Seagate Technology, Quantum, Conner Peripherals, and Western Digital. Then, Seagate announced that it would acquire Conner in an exchange of shares worth over $1 billion.

Among the reasons that industry analysts cited for the acquisition was the effect on competition. The combination of Seagate and Conner commanded more than a third of the worldwide market. According to David Bunzel, of the Santa Clara Consulting Group, "It probably puts [Seagate] into a leadership role that ultimately could benefit the industry."

Seagate's announcement of the acquisition resulted in the shares of Quantum and Western Digital rising by 6.8 and 5%, respectively. These reactions were consistent with the belief that Seagate's acquisition would reduce industry competition and hence result in higher prices for all manufacturers.

Source: "Disk Drive Maker Seagate Talking Buyout with Conner," *Business Journal* [San Jose] (September 25, 1995), Section 1, p. 9; "Seagate to Acquire Conner in $1.04 Billion Stock Swap," *New York Times* (September 21, 1995), Business, pp. 1 and 6.

---

7 Monopsony

A monopoly and, more generally, any seller with market power will restrain sales to raise the price and so increase profit. Let us now consider how the behavior of a buyer with market power will differ from that of a perfectly competitive buyer. We focus on a market where there is only one buyer, that is, a *monopsony*. Since there are close parallels between monopoly and monopsony, we will briefly highlight the similarities, while focusing on the important differences.

Benefit and Expenditure

Suppose that a key input into the production of Gamma-1 is a tropical leaf that grows in South America. Solar is the only buyer of this leaf; hence, it is a monopsony. By contrast, many growers produce the leaf. Each grower is too small to affect market conditions, so the supply of the leaf is perfectly competitive.

Since the leaf is a key input into Solar's manufacturing process, it provides a benefit that can be measured as the revenue generated less the costs of other associated inputs. The leaf, however, must be bought from the South American growers. Solar's expenditure is the market price of the leaf multiplied by the quantity purchased. Accordingly, Solar's net benefit from the leaf is its benefit less expenditure. We suppose that Solar's objective is to maximize its net benefit.

Let us determine the quantity of purchases at which Solar will maximize its net benefit. Referring to Figure 8.5, Solar's benefit depends on the quantity of its purchases: We suppose that the marginal benefit of a small quantity is very high and that the marginal benefit falls with the scale of purchases.

Also referring to Figure 8.5, the supply curve shows, for every quantity, the price at which competitive sellers will provide the leaf. Equivalently, the supply curve represents the monopsony's average expenditure for every possible quantity of purchases. Since the price must be higher to induce a greater quantity of supply, the average expenditure curve slopes upward.

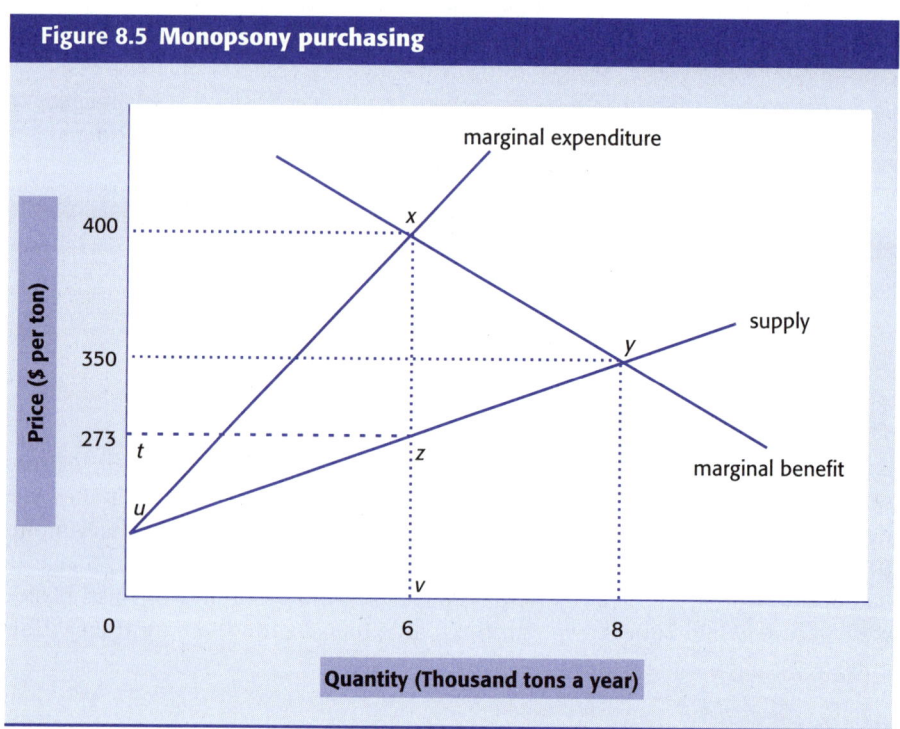

Figure 8.5 Monopsony purchasing

The marginal benefit and marginal expenditure curves cross at a quantity of 6000 tons. Reading from the supply curve, the price at that quantity is $273. The supply curve also shows the marginal cost. At 6000 tons, the marginal benefit exceeds the marginal cost.

The **marginal expenditure** is the change in expenditure resulting from an increase in purchases by one unit. For the average expenditure curve to slope upward, the marginal expenditure curve must lie above the average expenditure curve and slope upward more steeply.

The **marginal expenditure** is the change in expenditure resulting from an increase in purchases by one unit.

Maximizing Net Benefit

We can now state the following rule: A monopsony or any buyer with market power will maximize its net benefit by purchasing the quantity at which its marginal benefit equals its marginal expenditure. To explain this rule, consider a scale of purchases where Solar's marginal benefit exceeds marginal expenditure. Then, if Solar steps up purchases, its benefit will increase by more than its expenditure; hence it will obtain a larger net benefit. By contrast, if marginal benefit is less than marginal expenditure, Solar should reduce purchases: Its benefit will drop by less than its expenditure. Solar will exactly maximize net benefit when it purchases the quantity where its marginal benefit balances its marginal expenditure.

Referring to Figure 8.5, the quantity that maximizes net benefit is 6000 tons. At that quantity, the price is $273 per ton. Notice that the price of $273 per ton is less than the buyer's marginal benefit. By contrast, if the demand side was competitive and the marginal benefit curve represented the market demand, the equilibrium price would be $350 per ton and the quantity would be 8000 tons. This illustrates a general point: A monopsony restricts purchases to get a lower price and increase its net benefit above the competitive level.

Progress Check 8G In Figure 8.5, shade in an area that represents Solar's total expenditure on the tropical leaf.

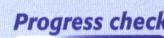

Progress check

Restraining Competition

A monopsony can use its market power to get a lower price than many small competing buyers. This provides an incentive for competing buyers to restrain purchases collectively and, so, depress the market price below the competitive level. A buyer cartel restrains each participant's purchases to a maximum quota to reduce the market price.

The lower the market price is, however, the more attractive it will be for individual buyers to purchase more than their quotas and for new buyers to enter the market. To the extent that individual buyers exceed their quotas, the quantity demanded will increase and the market price will rise. Similarly, if new buyers enter the market, they will increase the demand and raise the market price. Accordingly, the effectiveness of a buyer cartel depends on enforcement against existing buyers exceeding their quotas and against entry of new buyers.

A Monopsony over Rice

Rice is the staple diet of Japan's 120 million plus population. From World War II until 1994, the Staple Food Control Act required all domestic rice farmers to sell their output at a fixed official price to their local *nokyo*. The *nokyo* were cooperatives affiliated with the Central Union of Agricultural Cooperatives. By law, the central union had a monopsony over the wholesale market for domestic rice.

Generally, a monopsony uses its market power to restrain purchases and, so, depress the price and enhance its net benefit. Consistent with this rule, the central union did indeed fix the official purchasing price relatively low. Japanese farmers found that they could get higher prices on the black market. Consequently, farmers sold up to a quarter of annual production to the black market rather than their nokyo.

Source: "Japanese Rice: The End of an Era," *The Economist* (August 20, 1994), pp. 52–3.

The factors that determine the effectiveness of a seller cartel also apply to a buyer cartel.

Instead of forming a cartel, competing buyers can restrain competition through horizontal integration. For instance, a combination of two buyers that each have 50% of the demanded purchases will create a monopsony. The market price under a monopsony will be lower than the price with competition among buyers.

Buyer Cartel Meets Seller Cartel: Baseball

Generally, U.S. law prohibits buyers as well as sellers from cooperating to fix prices. There has been an exemption for major league baseball, however, since a decision of the U.S. Supreme Court in 1922. By virtue of this exemption, major league baseball restricts entry of new clubs, determines how clubs share revenue from ticket sales and broadcast rights, and regulates player salaries and transfers.

Until the spring of 1976, the owners of baseball teams had considerable monopsony power over baseball players. Then, the owners signed a collective bargaining agreement that allowed free agency for players with over six years' experience. Partly in consequence, the average salaries of baseball players rose from $46,000 in 1975 to over $1 million in 1992.

Alarmed by this rapid increase, the owners sought a cap on players' salaries. In August 1994, the players union rejected the salary cap and declared a strike, which led to the cancellation of the World Series for the first time since 1904.

President Clinton appointed W.J. Usery to mediate between the owners and the players. Negotiations, however, broke down in December. The owners then unilaterally imposed a salary cap, requiring the league's 21 teams to cut salaries by a total of $56 million a year.

Source: Gerald W. Scully, *The Market Structure of Sports* (Chicago: University of Chicago Press, 1995), pp. 19–40, 49–55; "Owners Cap Pay as Tax Plan Fails," *Eastern Express* (December 24–26, 1994), p. 41.

Cheating on the Cartel: The German Engineering Industry

Under Germany's system of national collective bargaining, an employer feder-ation in each industry negotiates wages and other conditions with the corre-sponding labor union. By law, the national agreement between the employers federation and the labor union binds the entire industry. The result is wages and conditions that are uniform across the industry.

In the engineering industry, the employers federation Gesamtmetall spans international giants like Daimler-Benz AG and Robert Bosch GmbH as well as small businesses such as Bauer and Haeselbarth GmbH. IG Metall, representing 3 million engineering workers, is Germany's largest union. In March 1995, negotiators for Gesamtmetall and IG Metall concluded a new collective agreement, raising wages by 3.5%, and cutting working hours from 36 to 35 a week.

Consistent with our analysis of monopsony, major employers have nego-tiated more favorable separate deals with their own workers. After Robert Bosch threatened to establish a competing factory in Scotland, its workers accepted more flexible working hours. Likewise, Daimler-Benz agreed to build a new line of compact cars in Germany only after workers conceded on wages.

The ability of large employers to reach separate deals reduces their incentive to press hard in the collective negotiations. By contrast, smaller companies have no such power. On learning of the new collective agree-ment, Bauer and Haeselbarth GmbH quit the employers federation. Manag-ing director Erhard Lenz remarked, "There's no unity among employers anymore[.]"

Source: "German Companies Sour on Centralized Bargaining," *Asian Wall Street Journal* (October 18, 1995), pp. 1 and 12.

8 Summary

A seller with market power restrains sales to raise the market price above the competitive level and extract higher profits. It maximizes profit by producing the quantity at which marginal revenue equals marginal cost. The extent to which a monopoly should adjust the price and sales in response to changes in demand or costs depends on the shapes of both the marginal revenue and the marginal cost curves. The profit-maximizing level of promotion for a seller with market power is the incremental margin multiplied by the elasticity of demand multiplied by the sales.

A buyer with market power restrains purchases to depress the price below the competitive level and raise its net benefit. Competing sellers and, likewise, competing buyers can restrain competition by forming a cartel or through horizontal integration.

Key Concepts

monopoly	perfectly contestable market
monopsony	Lerner Index
inframarginal units	cartel
contribution margin	horizontal integration
promotion	vertical integration
incremental margin	marginal expenditure

Further Reading

References on promotion include the classic by Philip Kotler, *Marketing Management*, 8th ed. (Englewood Cliffs, NJ: Prentice Hall, 1994), Chapters 22–24, and Paul R. Messinger's *Marketing Paradigm* (Cincinnati: South-Western Publishing, 1995), Chapter 8. Gerald W. Scully provides a detailed analysis of monopolistic and monopsonis-tic practices in American sports in *The Market Structure of Sports* (Chicago: University of Chicago Press, 1995). Dennis W. Carlton and Jeffrey M. Perloff provide a more detailed analysis of cartels in *Modern Industrial Organization*, 2d ed. (New York: Harper Collins, 1994), Chapter 6.

Review Questions

1. Give one example for each of the following sources of market power:
   a. A unique human or physical resource.
   b. An intellectual property.
   c. Economies of scale or scope.
   d. Regulation.
   e. Product differentiation.

2. Explain why marginal revenue is less than or equal to price. How does the difference between price and marginal revenue depend on the price elasticity of demand?

3. Luna Software has priced its new spreadsheet program such that its marginal revenue is more than its marginal cost. Advise the company how to raise its profit.

4. A monopoly restrains its sales to maximize its profit. True or false. Explain.

5. Once the patent on a product expires, others can freely manufacture the same product. Suppose that Solar Pharmaceutical's patent on the antiviral drug Beta-4 is about to expire. How will expiration of the patent affect
   a. Solar's market power over the drug?
   b. Solar's price elasticity of demand?

6. Explain why a seller must take into account both the marginal revenue and the marginal cost when considering how to adjust price following a change in costs.

7. The profit-maximizing price for Luna Software's spreadsheet program is $100. At that price, the advertising elasticity of the demand is 0.01 and sales are 500,000 units a year. The marginal cost of production is $40 per unit. How much should Luna spend on advertising?

8. Labor unions can use their market power to win higher wages and better working conditions for their members. By doing so, are they also causing unemployment?

9. A monopsony restrains its purchases to maximize its net benefit. True or false? Explain.

10. The National Collegiate Athletic Association (NCAA) restricts the amount that colleges and universities may pay their student athletes. If the U.S. government were to forbid the NCAA from such restrictive practices, what would happen to
   a. Each athlete's earnings?
   b. The number of athletes?

Discussion Questions

1. People with AIDS need zidovudine to forestall certain death. People suffering from the common cold have a wide choice of drugs to relieve their symptoms. Glaxo Wellcome PLC owns the patent to zidovudine. Bayer manufactures aspirin, which is one of the many drugs that relieve the symptoms of the common cold.
   a. Who has relatively more market power: Glaxo or Bayer?
   b. How is the difference between price and marginal revenue related to the price elasticity of demand?
   c. Compare the difference between price and marginal revenue for the two drugs, zidovudine and aspirin.

2. Table 8.4 describes the demand and costs for Solar Pharmaceutical's Gamma-1 drug. Suppose that the costs have been changed to a fixed cost of $75 million and a constant marginal cost of $50 per unit. The demand remains the same.
   a. Prepare a new table of revenues and costs according to the new data.
   b. What is the profit-maximizing price and production scale?
   c. At that production scale, what are the marginal revenue and the marginal cost?

3. The *Daily Sol* is the only newspaper in Sol City. Its price has been 25 cents a copy. A recent fall in the cost of newsprint caused the *Daily Sol's* average variable cost to fall by 2 cents per copy. The government also introduced an annual license fee of $100,000 per newspaper.
   a. Using relevant diagrams, illustrate the *Daily Sol's* profit-maximizing price before the drop in the cost of newsprint and new license fee.
   b. How should the *Daily Sol* adjust its price to take account of the 2-cent drop in the cost of newsprint?
   c. How should the newspaper adjust its price in response to the new license fee?

4. This question applies the techniques introduced in the math supplement. Suppose that Iron Music has the copyright to the latest CD of the Heavy Iron band. The market demand curve for the CD is

$$Q = 800 - 100p, \qquad (8.1)$$

where Q represents quantity demanded in thousands and p represents the price in dollars. Production requires a fixed cost of $100,000 and a constant marginal cost of $2 per unit.
   a. What price will maximize profits?
   b. At that price, what will be the sales?
   c. What is the maximum profit?
   d. Calculate the Lerner Index at the profit-maximizing scale of production.

5. The California Public Utilities Commission (PUC) regulates rates charged by the state's $2-billion-a-year trucking industry. In June 1989, a PUC official proposed to allow truckers to reduce rates by up to 10% without PUC approval. Spokespersons for the trucking industry adamantly opposed the proposal, saying that it would allow rates to fall below cost ("Truckers Oppose Rate Change," *Los Angeles Times* [June 8, 1989], Part IV, p. 2).

   a. Suppose that the trucking industry is a cartel. If individual truckers had the freedom to cut rates, what would happen to the market price?

   b. The PUC must approve all changes in rates. How does this requirement help the trucking industry?

   c. From the perspective of the trucking industry, why is it important that the PUC has the power of law?

6. Venus Shampoo has been very successful in its home market. The company has been researching the potential for its shampoo in a foreign territory. How will the following factors affect the amount that Venus should spend on advertising in the foreign market relative to the home market?

   a. The foreign demand is less elastic, so Venus will set a relatively higher incremental margin.

   b. The marginal cost is higher in the foreign market because of the cost of freight.

   c. Foreigners are more responsive to advertising; hence, they have a higher advertising elasticity of demand.

7. In Britain, cable television companies are allowed to provide local telephone service.

   a. Explain why cable television companies can provide local telephone service at relatively lower cost than other potential providers.

   b. Suppose that a company providing telephone service is proposing to merge with a cable television company. How would the two companies benefit from a merger?

8. Gesamtmetall is the federation of employers and IG Metall is the labor union in Germany's engineering industry. Under the German system of national collective bargaining, Gesamtmetall and IG Metall negotiate pay and working conditions for the entire industry.

   a. With respect to labor, does Gesamtmetall serve as a buyer cartel or seller cartel? What about IG Metall?

   b. Consider large employers such as Daimler-Benz AG and Robert Bosch GmbH. Why might they prefer to negotiate separate deals with their own workers rather than comply with the national collective agreement?

   c. If all large employers negotiate separate deals, how will this affect the wages and conditions that small companies must offer?

9. For many years, the National Basketball Association (NBA) had a monopoly over basketball and, consequently, monopsonized the market for players. This monopsony over players began to erode in 1967 with the formation of the American Basketball Association (ABA). Finally, in 1983, basketball team owners agreed to allow free agency, which removed the restrictions against players moving between teams. An analysis of earnings showed that a player who scored 10% more points would have earned 2.05% more salary between 1968 and 1975, but 3.21% more salary between 1984 and 1988 (Gerald W. Scully, *The Market Structure of Sports* [Chicago: University of Chicago Press, 1995], pp. 50–3.).

   a. Explain the connection between having a monopoly over basketball and a monopsony over basketball players.

   b. Compare the wage rate when the demand side of the market is a monopsony with the perfectly competitive wage.

c. Explain the difference in player earnings between 1968–75 as compared with 1984–88.

d. When the ABA and NBA proposed to merge, the basketball players opposed the proposal. Explain why.

10. Chrysler, Ford, and General Motors dominate American automobile production. Some automobile parts, such as batteries and tires, wear out with use and must be replaced at relatively frequent intervals. Accordingly, suppliers of these parts sell their products both as original equipment to auto manufacturers and as replacement parts to car owners. By contrast, air bags and ignition systems wear out relatively slowly. The bulk of such equipment is bought by auto manufacturers.

a. Referring to relevant sources of data, calculate the combined share of Chrysler, Ford, and General Motors in the American automobile market.

b. Assess the power of automobile manufacturers over sellers of (i) batteries and tires as compared with (ii) air bags and ignition systems.

c. For products in which auto manufacturers have monopsony power, do you expect prices to be higher in the original equipment market or the replacement market?

Chapter 8

Math Supplement

Price and marginal revenue

We first show that the marginal revenue is always less than the price, and also show how the difference depends on the price elasticity of demand. Let p represent the price of the product, and Q the scale of production. Since total revenue varies with the production scale, let us represent total revenue as a function, $R(Q)$, of Q.

By definition, total revenue is the product of price and sales, while sales is the same as the production scale,

$$R(Q) = pQ. \tag{8.2}$$

We differentiate total revenue to obtain marginal revenue,

$$\frac{dR(Q)}{dQ} = p + Q\frac{dp}{dQ}. \tag{8.3}$$

Since the demand curve slopes downward, $dp/dQ < 0$, so

$$\frac{dR(Q)}{dQ} < p. \tag{8.4}$$

This result holds at all values of Q, hence it proves that the marginal revenue is less than the price at all production scales.

Rearranging equation (8.3), the difference between the price and the marginal revenue,

$$p - \frac{dR(Q)}{dQ} = -Q\frac{dp}{dQ}. \tag{8.5}$$

By definition, the (own) price elasticity of demand,

$$e_p = \frac{p}{Q}\frac{dQ}{dp}, \tag{8.6}$$

hence

$$p - \frac{dR(Q)}{dQ} = -\frac{p}{e_p} \tag{8.7}$$

This shows that the difference between the price and the marginal revenue is inversely related to the absolute value of the price elasticity of demand.

Profit-maximizing production

Next, let us prove that a monopoly maximizes profit by producing at the scale where the marginal revenue equals the marginal cost. Since total cost and profit vary with the production scale, we represent them as functions $C(Q)$ and $P(Q)$, respectively. By definition, profit is total revenue less total cost,

$$P(Q) = R(Q) - C(Q). \tag{8.8}$$

To find the production scale that maximizes profit, we differentiate profit with respect to the production scale, and set the derivative equal to zero. This gives us

$$\frac{dR(Q)}{dQ} = \frac{dC(Q)}{dQ}, \qquad (8.9)$$

which implies that, to maximize profit, the seller must operate at a scale such that the marginal revenue just balances the marginal cost.

Let us apply this analysis to a monopoly that faces the market demand curve represented by the equation,

$$Q = 100 - 2p. \qquad (8.10)$$

This demand curve is a straight line. Suppose that production requires a fixed cost of 300 and a constant marginal cost of 10 per unit.

Rearranging equation (8.10), the price,

$$p = \frac{100 - Q}{2}, \qquad (8.11)$$

hence the total revenue,

$$R(Q) = pQ = \frac{1}{2}(100Q - Q^2). \qquad (8.12)$$

Differentiating, the marginal revenue,

$$\frac{dR(Q)}{dQ} = \frac{1}{2}(100 - 2Q). \qquad (8.13)$$

We can obtain the profit-maximizing production scale by equating the marginal revenue to the marginal cost.

$$\frac{1}{2}(100 - 2Q) = 10 \qquad (8.14)$$

Solving, the profit-maximizing production scale is $Q = 40$. By substituting $Q = 40$ into (8.11), we obtain the profit-maximizing price, $p = 30$. Hence, total revenue

$$R(Q) = p\,Q = 30 \times 40 = 1200. \qquad (8.15)$$

It was given that production requires a fixed cost of 300 and a constant marginal cost of 10 per unit. Accordingly, the total cost of producing $Q = 40$ units is

$$C(Q) = 300 + (10 \times 40) = 700. \qquad (8.16)$$

Therefore, the monopoly's maximum profit is $1200 - 700 = 500$.

Advertising

Let us prove that, to maximize profit, a seller should advertise up to the point that an additional dollar of advertising increases the contribution margin by one dollar. In this case, we must recognize that sales depend on advertising expenditure as well as the price. Let A represent the expenditure on advertising and $Q(p, A)$ the sales as a function of price and advertising.

Profit is now total revenue less production cost and less expenditure on advertising,

$$P(Q(p, A)) = pQ(p, A) - C(Q\,(p, A)) - A. \qquad (8.17)$$

To find the profit–maximizing expenditure on advertising, we take a partial derivative of P with respect to A, and set the derivative equal to zero:

$$p\,\frac{dQ}{dA} - \frac{dC(Q)}{dQ}\frac{dQ}{dA} - 1 = 0. \qquad (8.18)$$

We can rearrange this equation as

$$\left(p - \frac{dC(Q)}{dQ}\right)\frac{dQ}{dA} = 1. \qquad (8.19)$$

We call the term,

$$\left(p - \frac{dC(Q)}{dQ}\right) \qquad (8.20)$$

the *incremental margin*. It is the increase in the contribution margin from selling an additional unit, holding price constant. The other term on the left-hand side of (8.19) is dQ/dA. This is the *marginal sales response,* or the increase in sales that results from an additional dollar of advertising. (The marginal sales response is the derivative of what marketing specialists call the sales-response function.)

Accordingly, (8.19) states that, at the profit-maximizing advertising level, an additional dollar of advertising increases the contribution margin by one dollar.

We can express (8.19) in another form that applies the advertising elasticity of demand. By definition, the advertising elasticity,

$$e_a = \frac{A}{Q}\frac{dQ}{dA} \qquad (8.21)$$

Rearranging, the marginal sales response is

$$\frac{dQ}{dA} = \frac{e_a Q}{A}. \qquad (8.22)$$

Substituting this in equation (8.19), we have

$$A = \left(p - \frac{dC(Q)}{dQ}\right)e_a Q, \qquad (8.23)$$

which states that the profit-maximizing advertising expenditure is the incremental margin multiplied by the advertising elasticity and multiplied by the sales.

Monopsony

Finally, we prove that, for a buyer with market power, if the average expenditure is increasing with purchases, then the marginal expenditure curve must lie above the average expenditure curve and slope upward more steeply. Let E represent expenditure and Q represent purchases. Then the average expenditure is E/Q.

Suppose that the average expenditure is increasing with purchases,

$$\frac{d}{dQ}\left(\frac{E}{Q}\right) > 0. \qquad (8.24)$$

This implies that

$$\frac{1}{Q}\frac{dE}{dQ} - \frac{E}{Q^2} > 0, \qquad (8.25)$$

which simplifies to

$$\frac{dE}{dQ} > \frac{E}{Q}, \qquad (8.26)$$

that is, the marginal expenditure curve lies above the average expenditure curve. By differentiating again, we find that the marginal expenditure curve slopes upward more steeply than the average expenditure curve.

Pricing Policy

1 Introduction

A major issue for any business entering a foreign market is pricing. One approach to pricing in a foreign market is to add the cost of freight to the domestic price and then convert the total into the foreign currency. For instance, suppose that Mercury Bikes plans to export its top-selling racing bike from the United States to Japan. Mercury's domestic price is $350 and the freight to Japan is $30. Applying an exchange rate of ¥100 to the dollar, Mercury decides to set a price of $(350 + 30) \times 100 = ¥38,000$ in Japan. Do you agree with this approach?

In 1995, Avis Switzerland offered an Opel Vectra for weekday rental at an unlimited mileage rate of Fr 296 (Swiss francs) per day or a time and mileage rate of Fr 127 per day plus Fr 1.37 per kilometer. Under an unlimited mileage contract, the renter need not pay a mileage charge. A key factor, however, in the depreciation of a rental car is the distance through which it has been driven. The more miles on a car, the lower will be its resale value. Why then does Avis offer rentals with unlimited mileage?

In the mid-1980s, BMW of North America replaced its 320 model with the new 318 and 325. BMW designed the two new models with the same body but equipped the 318 with a 1.8 liter engine, and the 325 with a larger 2.5 liter engine. Car enthusiasts complained bitterly that the 318's engine was too small, causing the car to be underpowered. Was this a mistake on the part of BMW?

To address these issues—how to price in foreign markets, the structure of Avis Switzerland's car rental rates, and the design of BMW's 3-series—we need to understand the principles of pricing policy. In this chapter, we systematically analyze how a seller with market power should set prices to maximize profit.

We show how to apply the price elasticity of demand in setting prices. A manufacturer like Mercury Bikes that sells to foreign markets must take account of the price elasticity of the foreign demand and the marginal cost of supplying the foreign market. This approach is more profitable than a policy of simply adding freight to the domestic price and converting the total into the foreign currency.

It is very common to set the same price for every unit sold. We show that a seller can increase profit by setting prices so as to realize different margins on the various units. This depends on the extent of the seller's information about the individual buyer's demand. We consider situations where the seller has complete information as well as those where the seller has limited information. We can then explain why Avis offers unlimited mileage rates even though additional miles increase the depreciation of a rental car and also why it made sense for BMW to underpower the 318 model relative to the 325.

2 *Uniform Pricing*

Whenever managers are asked why do they not set a higher price, the most frequent response is, "Because I would lose sales." This does not, however, answer the question. Unless the demand is completely inelastic, a higher price will always result in lower sales. The real issue is how the increase in price will affect the profit of the business. As we will show, the answer depends on the price elasticity of demand and the marginal cost.

Uniform pricing is a policy where a seller charges the same price for every unit of the product.

In this section, we shall consider only policies where the seller charges the same price for every unit of the product. These are policies of **uniform pricing.** Later in this chapter, we will discuss how a seller can extract higher profit by setting prices so as to realize different margins on various units of the product.

Price Elasticity

Suppose that Mercury Bikes incurs no fixed cost in supplying the Japanese market. The only cost is a constant marginal cost of ¥30,000 per unit including production and freight. What price should Mercury set in the Japanese market? One proposal, based on the U.S. price and the freight, is a price of ¥38,000.

Recall from Chapter 3 that the own-price elasticity of demand is the percentage by which the quantity demanded will change if the price of the item rises by 1%, other things equal. (In this chapter, we will discuss only one elasticity: the own-price elasticity of demand. For brevity, we shall refer to it simply as the *price elasticity.*) When the demand is elastic, a 1% price increase causes the quantity demanded to drop by more than 1%. By contrast, when the demand is inelastic, a 1% price increase causes the quantity demanded to fall by less than 1%.

Suppose that Mercury estimates that, if it were to set the Japanese price 10% higher, at ¥41,800, then sales (which is the quantity demanded) would be 9% lower. This indicates that the demand is inelastic. Since sales fall less than proportionately with the increase in price, Mercury's total revenue will increase, specifically, by about 1%. Moreover, lower sales mean lower costs. Hence, in this example, a price increase will raise Mercury's profit. Generally, as we showed in Chapter 3, if the demand is inelastic, an increase in price will lead to a higher profit. Accordingly, a seller that faces an inelastic demand should raise the price.

Profit-Maximizing Price

We have seen that, when the demand is inelastic, a seller should raise the price. But what if the demand is elastic? More generally, what price maximizes the seller's profit? In Chapter 8, we showed that, at the profit-maximizing sales, the marginal revenue equals the marginal cost. Figure 9.1 shows the profit-maximizing price and sales for Mercury's Japanese business. Managers, however, usually do not readily have information about marginal revenue. They usually have better information about the price elasticity of demand. So, it would be more convenient to have a pricing rule based on elasticity.

Fortunately, such a rule is available. This rule applies the concept of the **incremental margin percentage,** which is the incremental margin divided

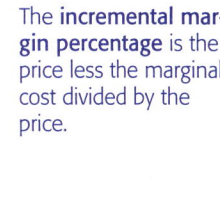

The **incremental margin percentage** is the price less the marginal cost divided by the price.

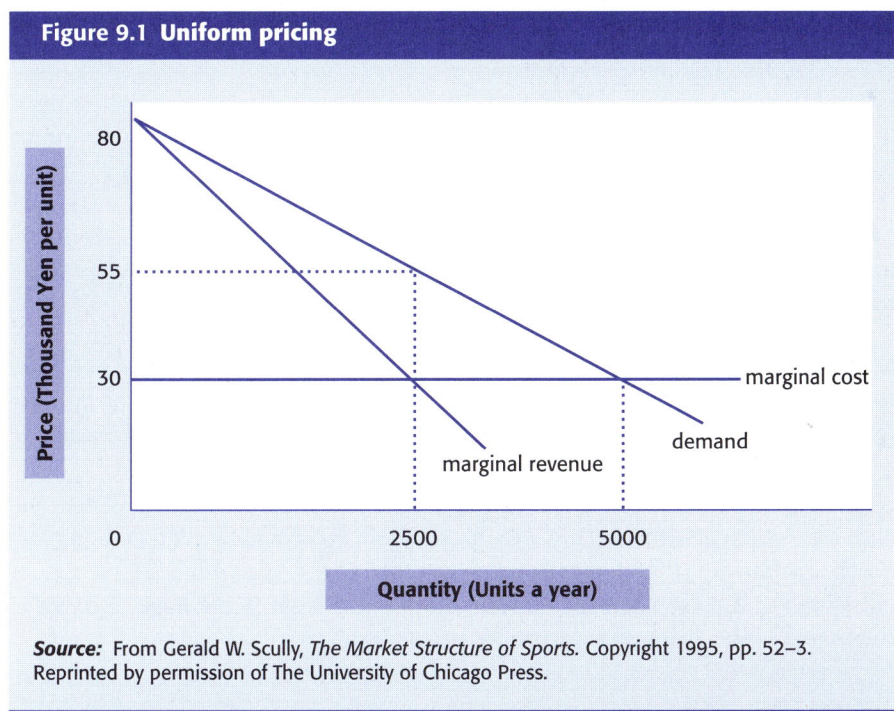

Figure 9.1 Uniform pricing

At the profit-maximizing quantity of sales, the marginal revenue equals the marginal cost. Equivalently, the incremental margin percentage equals the reciprocal of the absolute value of the price elasticity of demand.

by the price. Recall from Chapter 8 that the incremental margin is the price less the marginal cost. Hence, the incremental margin percentage is the price less the marginal cost divided by price.[1]

In the math supplement, we show that, when the marginal revenue equals the marginal cost, then the incremental margin percentage equals the reciprocal of the absolute value of the price elasticity of demand. Equivalently, a seller maximizes profit by setting a price where

$$\text{incremental margin percentage} = -\frac{1}{\text{price elasticity of demand}}. \quad (9.1)$$

The price elasticity of demand is negative; hence, the minus sign on the right-hand side of the pricing rule ensures that the entire right-hand side is positive.

Let us apply the rule to determine Mercury's price for the Japanese market. Suppose that the price elasticity of demand is –2.2. The pricing rule shows that, for Mercury to maximize its profit, the incremental margin percentage must be 1/2.2, or about 45%. Then, representing the price by p, and recalling that the marginal cost is ¥30,000, the rule implies that

$$\frac{p - 30{,}000}{p} = 0.45. \quad (9.2)$$

By solving this equation, we find that $p = 55{,}000$. Hence, the price that maximizes Mercury's profit is ¥55,000. (As Figure 9.1 shows, we get the same price if we look for the quantity where the marginal revenue equals the marginal cost.)

At the price of ¥55,000, the quantity demanded is 2500 units a year. Hence, Mercury's total revenue is $55{,}000 \times 2{,}500 = $ ¥137.5 million a year. Mercury's total cost is $30{,}000 \times 2{,}500 = $ ¥75 million; hence, its profit is $137.5 - 75 = $ ¥62.5 million.

The pricing rule highlights the importance of understanding the price elasticity of demand. In Chapter 3, we discussed the intuitive factors that underly the price elasticity. These factors include the availability of direct and indirect substitutes, buyers' prior commitments, and the cost relative to the benefit of searching for more favorable prices.

The price elasticity may vary along a demand curve. Further, the marginal cost may change with the scale of production. Accordingly, determining the profit-maximizing price typically involves a series of trials with different prices until finding a price such that the incremental margin percentage equals the reciprocal of the absolute value of the price elasticity.

---

[1] The incremental margin percentage is identical with the Lerner Index of monopoly power introduced in Chapter 8.

Changes in Demand and Cost

The pricing rule shows how a seller should adjust its price when there are changes in the price elasticity of demand or marginal cost. Consider changes in the price elasticity. If the demand is more elastic, then the price elasticity will be a larger negative number. So, according to the rule, the seller should aim for a lower incremental margin percentage. For instance, suppose that, in Mercury's case, the price elasticity is –2.5 rather than –2.2. Then, the profit-maximizing incremental margin percentage will be 1/2.5 = 40%. Letting the price be p, we have $(p - 30,000)/p = 0.40$, which implies that the profit-maximizing price is ¥50,000.

By contrast, if the demand were less elastic, say, with an elasticity of –1.5, then the profit-maximizing incremental margin percentage would be 1/1.5 = 67%. Again, representing the price by p, we would then have $(p - 30,000)/p = 0.67$, which implies that the profit-maximizing price would be ¥90,000.

Next, let us consider changes in the seller's marginal cost. In our original example, the price elasticity was –2.2, while the marginal cost was ¥30,000. Suppose that the marginal cost is ¥6,000 lower at ¥24,000. How should Mercury adjust its price for the Japanese market? Using the pricing rule, the profit-maximizing price must satisfy $(p - 24,000)/p = 1/2.2$, which implies that $p = 44,000$. Notice that, although the marginal cost is ¥6,000 lower, the profit-maximizing price is ¥11,000 lower.

Similarly, we can show that, if the marginal cost is higher, Mercury should not raise its price by the same amount. The reason is that Mercury must consider the effect of the price change on the quantity demanded.

These examples demonstrate that the way a seller should adjust its price to changes in either the price elasticity or the marginal cost depends on both the price elasticity and the marginal cost. In particular, this means that a seller should not necessarily adjust the price by the same amount as a change in marginal cost.

Progress Check 9A In the case of Mercury Bikes, suppose that the price elasticity of demand is –1.75, while the marginal cost is ¥27,000 per unit. Calculate the price that maximizes the profit.

Progress check

Common Misconceptions

The pricing rule applies the concept of incremental margin percentage. In cost accounting, the *contribution margin percentage* is defined as the revenue less variable cost divided by revenue. In the math supplement, we show that the contribution margin percentage equals the price less the average variable cost divided by the price. Accounting systems often assume that costs are proportional; in which case, the marginal cost is the same as the average variable cost.

Then, the contribution margin percentage equals what we call the *incremental margin percentage*.

Generally, however, variable production costs may be increasing or decreasing, and so, the marginal cost will not be the same as the average variable cost. In this case, it is important to keep a clear distinction between the contribution margin percentage and the incremental margin percentage. Only the latter is relevant for pricing.

A common mistake is the belief that the profit-maximizing price depends only the elasticity. According to this approach, if the demand is more elastic, the price should be lower, while if the demand is less elastic, the price should be higher. This approach considers only the demand and ignores costs. To maximize profits, however, management should take into account both the demand and costs.

To illustrate the difference between the mistaken thinking and the correct approach, consider the mini-bars that many hotels offer in their rooms. The mini-bar has considerable market power, especially in the early hours of the morning, when it would be inconvenient if not hazardous to venture out of the hotel for a beverage. Suppose that Heineken beer and Coca Cola have the same price elasticity of demand. Should the hotel set the same price for both items? Absolutely not. According to our pricing rule, the hotel should set the same incremental margin percentage on the two items. Since the marginal cost to the hotel of Heineken beer is higher than that of Coca Cola, this means that the hotel should set a higher price for Heineken.

Consumer goods retailing provides another example. Branded disposable diapers, such as Pampers and Huggies, are available at many supermarkets and drug stores. If one supermarket sets a higher price for Pampers, its customers may buy their Pampers elsewhere. So, the demand for branded diapers at any particular store may be quite elastic. By contrast, the demand for private-label diapers at the same store may be somewhat less elastic because private-label products are available only from the corresponding chain. For instance, only SavOn Drugs stores sell SavOn Drugs diapers. Then, according to our pricing rule, stores should set a higher incremental margin percentage for private-label diapers. This does not, however, necessarily mean a higher *price* for private-label diapers.

Another common mistake in pricing is to set price by marking up average cost. Cost-plus pricing poses several problems. First, in businesses with economies of scale, the average cost depends on the production scale. So, to apply cost-plus pricing, the seller must make an assumption about the scale. But the production scale depends on the price, hence cost-plus pricing leads in a circle. A related problem is how to deal with indirect costs. To allocate the indirect costs to each product, the seller must also make assumptions about the production scales of the various products.

Price Elasticity: Who Is the Customer?

Body shops repair exterior damage to automobiles. Whenever a damaged car arrives at a body shop, one of the first questions that the car owner must answer is, "Do you have insurance for the damage?" Why does the body shop care whether the owner has insurance coverage?

Automobile body repair is a case where there are two persons on the demand side: the car owner who makes the buying decision and the insurer who pays the bill. As a result of this split, the owner of a damaged car will be relatively less sensitive to the price of repairs.

Indeed, the owner may ask the body shop to repair some other outstanding damage at the insurer's expense. Realistically, however, the car owner will be concerned about the price of repairs to the extent that his or her future insurance premium or renewal of the policy depends on past claims.

Generally, demand is less sensitive to price whenever there is a split between the party that makes the buying decision and the party that pays the bill. Body shops understand and exploit this split.

A further difficulty with cost-plus pricing is that it gives no guidance as to the appropriate markup on average cost. Should a seller apply the same or different markups to different products? Suppose that a seller wants to set the markup to maximize profits. Then, the seller must go back to considering the price elasticity of demand and the marginal cost. Hence, cost-plus pricing is not so simple after all.

Cost-Plus Pricing: Wang Laboratories

In 1976, Wang Laboratories launched a word-processing machine that took the office market by storm and sales soared. Several years later, however, Apple and then IBM began marketing personal computers. The new personal computers offered a number of business applications, including word processing. Wang did consider whether to introduce a personal computer as well. Management, however, rejected the idea for fear that the new product would cut too much into its word processor sales.

Wang used a cost-plus method to set prices for its word processors. To calculate the appropriate markup, management divided overhead costs by the projected sales volume. By the mid-

1980s, personal computers were quickly eroding the demand for Wang's word processor. When Wang's sales did not meet the original projections, management had to recalculate the markup. With the same overhead costs divided by fewer sales, the result was a higher markup and higher prices. The increase in prices made Wang's machines even less attractive vis-à-vis the new personal computers and caused sales to drop even further. Eventually, Wang was forced into bankruptcy.

Source: Thomas T. Nagle and Reed K. Holden, *The Strategy and Tactics of Pricing*, 2d ed. (Englewood Cliffs, NJ: Prentice Hall, 1995), p. 3.

3 | *Complete Price Discrimination*

In the previous section, we introduced a rule for uniform pricing: The seller should set the price so that the incremental margin percentage equals the reciprocal of the absolute value of the price elasticity of demand. In Figure 9.2, we illustrate the profit-maximizing uniform price for Mercury Bikes in the Japanese market. On closer examination, however, we can show that uniform pricing does not yield the maximum possible profit. This suggests that we should look for pricing policies that are more profitable than uniform pricing.

Shortcomings of Uniform Pricing

Recall that the demand curve for a product also reflects the marginal benefits of the various buyers. At the price of ¥55,000 per unit, the benefit of a bicycle for the marginal buyer is just equal to the price. For all the other (inframarginal) buyers, who account for 2499 units, the benefit exceeds the price. Each of these inframarginal buyers is enjoying some buyer surplus. The market buyer surplus is the shaded area *abd*.

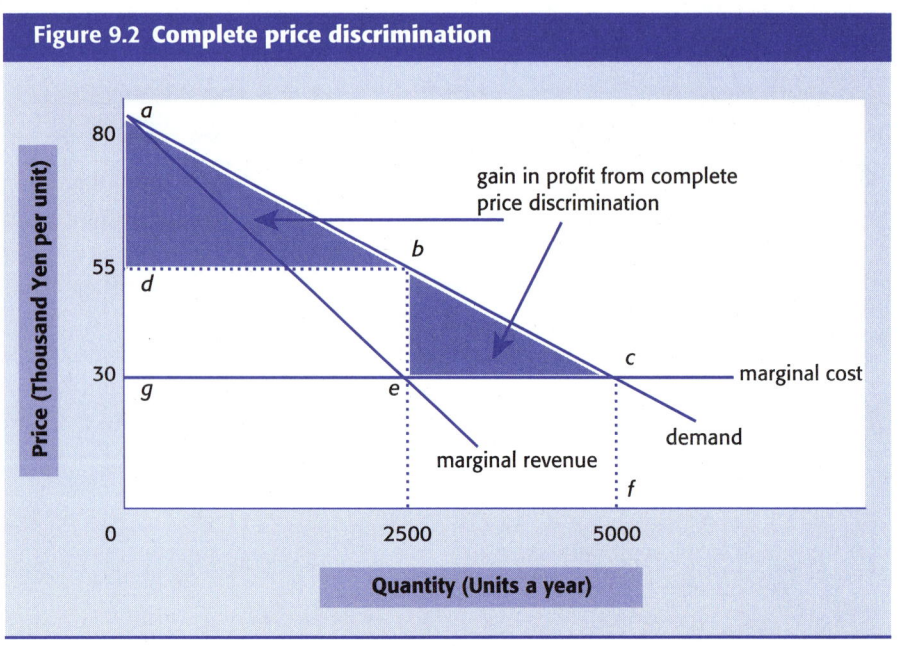

Figure 9.2 Complete price discrimination

With complete price discrimination, the seller prices each unit at the buyer's benefit and sells a quantity such that the marginal benefit equals the marginal cost. The increase in profit over uniform pricing is the shaded area *adb* plus the shaded area *bec*.

With uniform pricing, the inframarginal buyers do not pay as much as they would be willing to pay. This suggests that, by devising a way of taking some of the buyer surplus, Mercury could increase its profit.

Another shortcoming of uniform pricing is that it results in an economically inefficient quantity of sales. The marginal buyer derives a benefit of ¥55,000, while the marginal cost is only ¥30,000. This gap between the marginal benefit and the marginal cost shows that the quantity of sales is not economically efficient. By devising some way to provide the product to everyone whose marginal benefit exceeds the marginal cost, Mercury could also earn more profit.

Progress Check 9B Referring to Figure 9.2, shade in the market buyer surplus if Mercury sets a price of ¥30,000 per unit.

Progress check

Price Discrimination

Ideally, Mercury would like to sell each bike at the respective buyer's benefit. Referring to Figure 9.2, this would be like selling down the market demand curve. Then, Mercury would earn a higher incremental margin from buyers with higher benefit and a smaller margin from buyers with lower benefit. Any pricing policy under which a seller sets prices to earn different incremental margins on various units of the same or a similar product is called **price discrimination**.

We give the name **complete price discrimination** to a pricing policy where the seller prices each unit at the buyer's benefit and sells a quantity such that the marginal benefit equals the marginal cost. This policy is called *complete price discrimination* because it charges every buyer the maximum that he or she is willing to pay for each unit. Hence, the policy leaves each buyer with no surplus.

Price discrimination is a policy where a seller sets different incremental margins on various units of the same or a similar product.

Complete price discrimination is the policy where a seller prices each unit at the buyer's benefit and sells a quantity such that the marginal benefit equals the marginal cost.

To illustrate complete price discrimination, let us consider Mercury Bikes' pricing. Referring to Figure 9.2, the demand curve is a straight line with a slope of 50,000/5000 = 10. This means that the first buyer is willing to pay 80,000 – 10 = ¥79,990 for a bike; the second buyer, 80,000 – 20 = ¥79,980; and so on. Hence, under complete price discrimination, Mercury should charge ¥79,990 to the first buyer, ¥79,980 to the second buyer, and so on.

Mercury should not stop selling at the 2500th unit. The reason is that the buyer of the 2501th unit derives a benefit of 55,000 – 10 = ¥54,990, which exceeds Mercury's marginal cost of ¥30,000. This means that Mercury could increase its profit by selling a unit to that buyer.

Indeed, Mercury should sell up to the quantity where the marginal benefit just equals the marginal cost. Referring to Figure 9.2, this balance occurs at a quantity of 5000 units a year. The buyer of the 5000th unit is willing to pay exactly ¥30,000 for a bike, which is Mercury's marginal cost. If Mercury tried to sell beyond 5000 units, it would make a loss on additional units. Under complete price discrimination, the buyer of the 5000th unit is the marginal buyer.

With complete price discrimination, Mercury's total revenue will be the area 0*fca* under the demand curve from the quantity of 0 up to 5000 units a year. This area is (80,000 + 30,000)/2 × 5,000 = ¥275 million a year. As for costs, Mercury's total cost would be area 0*fcg*, which is 30,000 × 5,000 = ¥150 million a year. (Recall that Mercury incurs no fixed cost.) Hence, with complete price discrimination, Mercury's profit would be 275 − 150 = ¥125 million a year.

By contrast, in the preceding section, we showed that Mercury's maximum profit with uniform pricing is ¥62.5 million. So, Mercury's profit with complete price discrimination is higher than the profit with uniform pricing.

Comparison with Uniform Pricing

Under a policy of complete price discrimination, the seller should sell each unit for the benefit that it provides its buyer and sell the quantity where the buyer's marginal benefit just equals the marginal cost. The policy resolves the two shortcomings of uniform pricing. First, by pricing each unit at the buyer's benefit, the policy extracts all the buyer surplus. Second, the policy provides the economically efficient quantity; hence, it exploits all the opportunity for additional profit through changes in sales.

Specifically, in the case of Mercury Bikes, the policy of complete price discrimination enables Mercury to extract higher prices for the 2499 units that would be inframarginal under uniform pricing. This increase in profit is represented by the shaded area *adb* in Figure 9.2. Second, with complete price discrimination, Mercury would sell 2500 more units than with uniform pricing. These additional units raise the profit by the shaded area *bec* in Figure 9.2. The total increase in profit is the sum of the shaded areas *adb* and *bec*.

Generally, a policy of complete price discrimination yields more profit than uniform pricing. Complete price discrimination extracts a higher price from existing buyers while extending sales to new buyers who would not be served with uniform pricing.

Progress check

Progress Check 9C We can use Figure 9.2 to compare the profits from uniform pricing and complete price discrimination. The difference is areas *adb* and *bec*. Calculate the numerical values of these areas.

Discrimination by Wealth: Medical Services

Price discrimination is common in medical services. Doctors treat patients on an individual basis. A doctor's first step in treatment is always to record the patient's history. This routinely includes questions about the patient's occupation, employer, home address, and scope of insurance coverage. This information is very useful in gauging a patient's ability and willingness to pay as well as the patient's health.

To the extent that a patient is paying her or his own bill, the doctor can easily use this information to charge different prices to various patients for the same treatment. The result is close to complete price discrimination. Indeed, until the 1960s, the American Medical Association required doctors to charge lower prices to poorer patients.

Information

Under complete price discrimination, the seller charges each buyer a different price for each unit of the product. This means that a buyer who is interested in buying more than one unit of the product should be charged a different price for each unit. For instance, suppose that the Miki family is interested in two bikes. One bike is quite essential, as Mrs. Miki will use it every day when shopping for groceries. The second bike is for Grandma who uses the bike far less often. With complete price discrimination, Mercury should charge more for the first bike and less for the second.

Accordingly, to implement complete price discrimination, the seller must know each potential buyer's individual demand curve. It is not enough to know the market demand curve or the price elasticity of the individual demand curves. Rather, the seller must know the entire individual demand curve of each potential buyer. This is a tremendous requirement. In practice, most sellers will not have this amount of information, so, complete price discrimination is usually not feasible.

Since complete price discrimination requires more information than uniform pricing, we should understand when it is relatively more important to implement price discrimination. One factor is the degree to which the individual demands of potential buyers are different. The other factor is the steepness of the individual demand (marginal benefit) curves.

For instance, suppose that there are 8000 bike buyers, all of whom are identical in that they are willing to pay ¥40,000 for a bicycle and want only one unit. Then the market demand curve will be flat, as shown in Figure 9.3. In this case, with uniform pricing, Mercury should set a price of ¥40,000. Under complete price discrimination, it should set the same ¥40,000 price. The price and sales

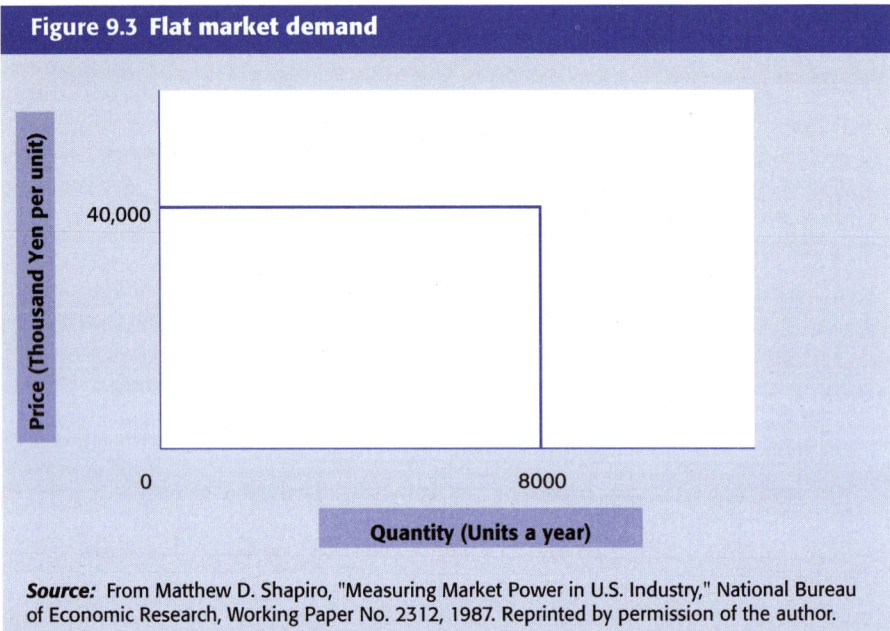

Figure 9.3 Flat market demand

Source: From Matthew D. Shapiro, "Measuring Market Power in U.S. Industry," National Bureau of Economic Research, Working Paper No. 2312, 1987. Reprinted by permission of the author.

Price, sales, and profit are identical with uniform pricing and complete price discrimination.

are identical with uniform pricing and complete price discrimination, hence Mercury's profits will be identical as well.

By contrast, if the buyers differed in their individual demand curves or individuals were willing to buy more at a lower price, then the policy of complete price discrimination would yield more profit than uniform pricing.

Price Discrimination: U.S. Treasury Bill Auctions

The U.S. government issues Treasury bills as a way to borrow funds for periods up to one year. The Treasury sells bills in a sealed-bid auction. Each participant sends in a sealed bid. After the close of bids, the Treasury opens the bids and allocates the bills for sale to the highest bidder, then to the next highest bidder, and so on until it has allocated all the bills for sale.

The Treasury has varied the rules of its auctions. At times, the Treasury has stipulated that the auction be *discriminatory* in the sense that each successful bidder must pay the amount that they bid. In a discriminatory auction, different bidders pay different prices for their Treasury bills. By using a discriminatory sealed-bid auction, the Treasury implements price discrimination.

Even though the Treasury's auction is discriminatory, it cannot implement complete price discrimination. The reason is that participating bidders generally shade their bids downward to get some buyer surplus.

4 *Direct Segment Discrimination*

To implement complete price discrimination, a seller must know the entire individual demand curve of each potential buyer. The seller, however, may not have so much information. Accordingly, we now explore other forms of price discrimination that require less information.

From the viewpoint of the seller's profit, a policy of complete price discrimination is better than uniform pricing, essentially because it sets prices on an individual basis. A seller that lacks sufficient information to price on an individual basis may still be able to discriminate among **segments** of buyers. In the language of marketing, a segment is a significant group of buyers within a larger market.

A **segment** is a significant group of buyers within a larger market.

Segment Margins

Suppose that Mercury Bikes produces men's and women's versions of its bike at the same marginal cost of ¥30,000 and that men and women buy only men's and women's bikes respectively. Then, Mercury can divide the Japanese market into two segments according to gender. It, however, does not have the information to segment the market beyond the gender of the buyer.

We give the name **direct segment discrimination** to the policy of setting different incremental margins to each identifiable segment. In Mercury's case, there are two identifiable segments: men and women. Lacking the information necessary for further discrimination, Mercury must set a uniform price within each segment. Accordingly, we can determine the profit-maximizing prices for each segment by applying the rule for uniform pricing. The prices are such that the incremental margin percentage for each segment equals the reciprocal of the absolute value of the segment's price elasticity of demand.

Direct segment discrimination is the policy where a seller charges a different incremental margin to each identifiable segment.

Let the men's and women's demands be as shown in Figure 9.4. Consider first the demand for men's bikes. Suppose that the profit-maximizing price is m. Through a process of trial and error, we find that, at the price m, the price elasticity of demand is -2.2. Accordingly, Mercury should set the price m so that the incremental margin percentage is $1/2.2 = 45\%$. This means $(m - 30,000)/m = 0.45$, hence the price of a man's bike, $m = ¥55,000$. At this price, the quantity demanded is 2500 units.

Next, we consider the demand for women's bikes. The women derive lower marginal benefits; hence, the women's demand curve is lower than that for men. Suppose that the profit-maximizing price is w. Through another process of trial and error, we find that, at the price w, the price elasticity of demand is -4. Hence, Mercury should set the price w so that the incremental margin percentage is $1/4 = 25\%$. Then, $(w - 30,000)/w = 0.25$, which implies that the price for a women's bike is $w = ¥40,000$. At this price, the quantity demanded is 1000 units.

In this example, the men's demand is less elastic. Therefore, Mercury should set a relatively higher incremental margin percentage on the men's

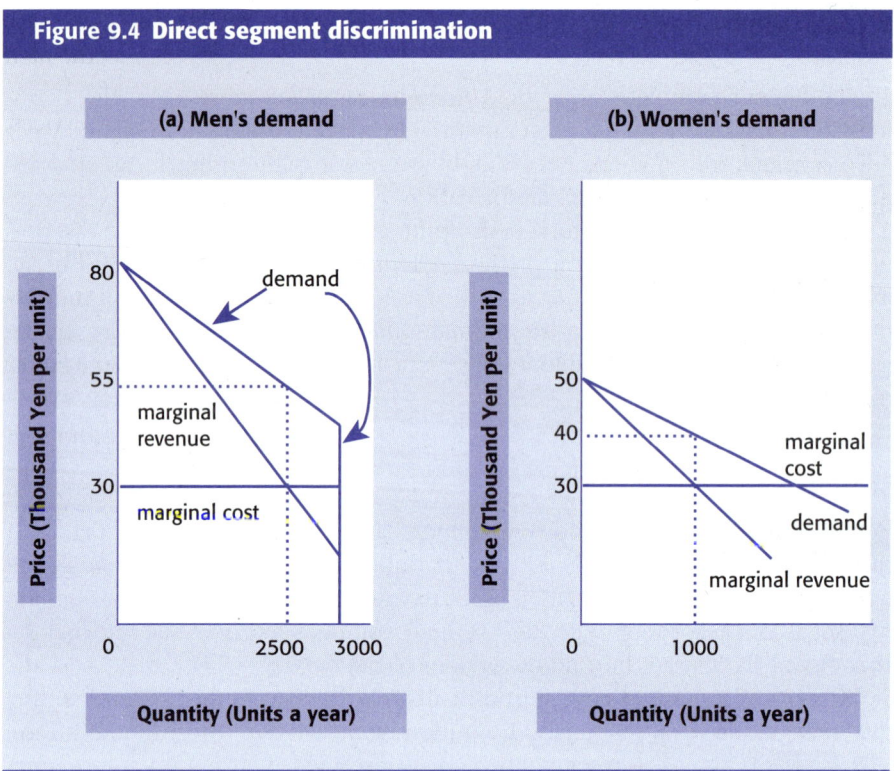

Figure 9.4 Direct segment discrimination

(a) Men's demand

(b) Women's demand

The demand for men's bikes is relatively less elastic, so the seller should set a relatively higher incremental margin percentage on men's bikes.

bikes. Mercury's profit from the men's segment is (55,000 – 30,000) × 2,500 = ¥62.5 million. Further, its profit from the women's segment is (40,000 – 30,000) × 1,000 = ¥10 million. So, its total profit with direct segment discrimination is ¥72.5 million. By contrast, its profit with complete price discrimination is ¥125 million, while its profit with uniform pricing is ¥62.5 million.

Implementation

To implement direct segment discrimination, the seller must have some way of segregating buyers into distinct segments with different demand curves. This means finding some identifiable and fixed buyer characteristic that segments the market. The characteristic must be fixed; otherwise, a buyer might switch segments to take advantage of a lower price. The seller can then base the price discrimination on this characteristic.

The second condition necessary for direct segment discrimination is that the seller must be able to prevent buyers from reselling the product among

themselves. If the segment to whom the seller sets a relatively low price could resell to other buyers, then the seller will not be able to sell anything at the high price.

Typically, it is more difficult to resell services, especially individual services, than goods. For instance, it is more difficult to resell medical treatment than pharmaceuticals, and it is more difficult to resell tax planning advice than tax preparation software. Accordingly, price discrimination is relatively more widespread in services than goods and is especially common in individual services.

The Mercury example illustrates the principles of setting prices with a policy of direct segment discrimination. The prices should be set to derive a relatively lower incremental margin percentage from the segment with the more elastic demand and a relatively higher incremental margin percentage from the segment with the less elastic demand.

In the example of Mercury Bikes, the marginal cost was a constant. By constrast, a seller that faces the constraint of a fixed capacity may have a constant marginal cost for wide ranges of output. Near to the capacity limit, however, the marginal cost is increasing. Consider, for instance, a local telephone company. Its network has a fixed capacity, and it would like to directly discriminate between the residential and business segments. How should it set prices to the two segments when the marginal cost is increasing?

The telephone company should follow the same general rule: It should set prices so that the incremental margin percentage for each segment equals the reciprocal of the absolute value of the segment's price elasticity of demand. With an increasing marginal cost, however, any change in the price for one segment that affects sales will affect the marginal cost and, hence, the incremental margin percentage for the other segment. Accordingly, when the marginal cost is increasing, the seller must conduct the trial and error search for the prices to both segments at the same time.

Profit Ranking

The Mercury example also illustrates the differences in profit from the various pricing policies. The seller's profit is highest with complete price discrimination, next with direct segment discrimination, and lowest with uniform pricing.

It is obvious that direct segment discrimination would be less profitable than complete price discrimination. Direct segment discrimination uses uniform prices within each segment; hence, it suffers from the same shortcomings as uniform pricing: Within each segment, it does not completely extract the buyer surplus and it provides economically inefficient quantities. (The exception arises when all the buyers within a segment are identical. In this case, the profit from direct segment discrimination is equal to that with complete price discrimination.)

Direct segment discrimination, however, is more profitable than uniform pricing. Through direct segmentation, the seller can reduce the margin to the segment with the more elastic demand and hence expand the quantity of sales closer to the point where the marginal benefit equals the marginal cost. Direct segmentation may also enable the seller to raise the margin to the segment with the less elastic demand and so extract more of its buyer surplus.

Progress check

Progress Check 9D Referring to Figure 9.4, suppose that the marginal cost is ¥35,000 per unit. Use the figure to illustrate the new prices for men's and women's bikes.

Heinz Ketchup: "Not for Retail Sale"

The market for ketchup consists of a retail consumer segment and an institutional segment. Institutional customers include restaurants, catering services, and airlines. The demand curves of retail and institutional customers are quite different. Institutions order larger amounts and often have professional purchasing staff who aim to secure better deals. Typically, the institutional demand is more price elastic than the retail demand.

Ketchup manufacturers supply institutional customers directly and retail consumers through distribution channels such as supermarkets and grocery stores. To the extent that manufacturers can prevent institutional customers from reselling ketchup to retail consumers, they can implement direct segment discrimination. This means setting prices for a lower incremental margin from institutional customers. It is no coincidence that every bottle of Heinz ketchup served in a restaurant is marked "Not for Retail Sale."

Discriminating by Age: Movie Theaters and Theme Parks

The demand for movies and visits to theme parks varies with such buyer characteristics as income, occupational status, and age. Movie theaters and theme parks cannot observe a customer's income, but they can check a customer's age and whether a customer is a student.

Age is a characteristic that fits the conditions for direct segment discrimination. It is easy to identify and impossible to change. A middle-aged adult cannot buy a senior citizen's ticket. Accordingly, movie theaters and theme parks set prices so as to extract lower margins from senior citizens and children. Assuming that the marginal cost of serving all patrons is the same, then the result is lower prices for senior citizens and children and higher prices for middle-aged adults.

Resale is the major hurdle to price discrimination between college students and other adults. Providers recognize this problem. Most movie theaters mark their tickets as "Not Transferable." To the extent that theaters can prevent buyers from reselling tickets, they can discriminate between college students and other adults.

Discriminating between Residential and Business Users: Local Telephone Service

The business demand for telephone service is less price elastic than the residential demand. The provider of local telephone service can raise its profit by extracting more buyer surplus from business customers. Assuming that the costs of serving the two segments are identical, a policy of direct segment discrimination would mean setting a higher price for business customers. In 1996, Singapore Telecom charged S$150 (Singapore dollars) for a business line, compared with S$100 for a residential line.

How can the telephone company prevent a business from posing as a residential subscriber to take advantage of the lower price? For fixed-line service, the telephone company can check the customer's location physically. The inspection will deter many businesses from posing as residential subscribers.

Another factor is listings in the telephone directory. A business depends on its directory listing to reach potential customers. A business that poses as a residential subscriber will not be listed in the business telephone directory. It will lose potential customers searching in the telephone directory or yellow pages.

5 Location

To the extent that a product is costly to transport and the seller can identify a buyer's location, the seller can discriminate on the basis of the buyer's location. Generally, there are two ways of pricing to buyers in different locations. One way is to set a common price to all buyers that does not include delivery. Such a price is called ex-works or **free on board (FOB).** In this case, each buyer pays the FOB price plus the cost of delivery to its respective location. With FOB pricing, the differences among the prices at various locations are exactly the differences in the costs of delivery to those locations.

The alternative way of pricing to buyers at different locations is to set prices that include delivery. This practice is called **delivered pricing**, and the price is called **cost and freight (CF).** With delivered (CF) pricing, the differences among the prices at various locations need not correspond to the differences in the cost of delivery to the respective locations.

A free on board (FOB) price does not include delivery.

Delivered pricing is the policy where a seller's price includes delivery.

A cost including freight (CF) price includes delivery.

FOB vis-à-vis CF

Let us compare FOB and CF pricing in the context of pricing to an export market. First, we illustrate FOB pricing. Suppose that Mercury Bikes sets a price of $350 in its domestic market. For its price in Japan, it plans to add the freight of

$30 and convert the total to yen. Hence, with an exchange rate of ¥100 to the dollar, Mercury's Japanese price is $380 \times 100 = ¥38,000$.

FOB pricing, however, ignores the differences between the price elasticities of demand in the various markets. The alternative is CF pricing, which can yield higher profit. In Mercury's case, assuming that it can prevent buyers in one country from reselling bicycles to the other country, it can implement direct segment discrimination across the two countries. This means setting prices so that its incremental margin percentage in each country balances the reciprocal of the absolute value of the price elasticity of demand.

If the Japanese demand is more elastic than American demand, then Mercury should set prices so that its incremental margin percentage is lower in Japan than the United States. A lower margin, however, does not necessarily mean a lower price, because Mercury's marginal cost of supplying the Japanese market includes transportation. Hence, the marginal cost in Japan will be higher than the marginal cost in the United States.

By contrast, if the Japanese demand is less elastic than American demand, then Mercury should set prices so that its incremental margin percentage is higher in Japan than the United States. Taking into account the higher marginal cost of supplying the Japanese market, this definitely means that Mercury's price in Japan should exceed that in the United States.

Thus, to the extent that Mercury can prevent buyers in one country from reselling bicycles to the other country, it can aim for different incremental margin percentages in each market. Then, it will be setting CF prices in the two markets; that is, prices including delivery, rather than FOB prices.

With CF pricing, the difference in the prices between the two markets will simply be the result of the different incremental margin percentages and the different marginal costs of supplying the two markets. In particular, the price difference need not necessarily be the cost of shipping the product from the domestic to the foreign market. Depending on the price elasticities and the marginal costs, the difference may be larger or smaller than the freight cost.

For instance, earlier, we showed that, when the price elasticity of demand in the Japanese market is –2.2 and the marginal cost of supplying the Japanese market is ¥30,000, the profit-maximing price is ¥55,000. At the exchange rate of ¥100 to $1, this price is $550. By contrast, Mercury's price in the United States was $350. The difference between the Japanese and American prices is $150, which far exceeds the $30 freight cost.

Progress check   **Progress Check 9E** Suppose that, for the Japanese market, the price elasticity of demand is –2.5 and the marginal cost including freight is ¥30,000. Calculate Mercury's CF Japanese price. If Mercury's U.S. price is $350, what is the difference between the Japanese and American prices?

Restricting Resale

If a seller is to succeed in discriminating on the basis of a buyer's location, the various buyers must not be able to adjust location to take advantage of price differences. For most goods, the seller can control only the location at which it sells the product and cannot directly monitor the buyer's location.

For instance, if Mercury sets a higher margin in Japan than the United States, some Japanese consumers may buy bikes in the United States and ship them back to Japan. Worse still, some Japanese bicycle retailers may establish a "gray market," in which they purchase large quantities of Mercury bikes in the United States for resale in Japan.

A seller of durable products can limit such reselling by restricting warranty service to the location of purchase. Mercury might refuse to provide warranty service in Japan for bikes purchased in the United States. This is a way by which a seller can ensure that consumers buy in their respective locations and not elsewhere.

Discrimination by Location: The Los Angeles Times

With a daily circulation exceeding 1 million copies, the *Los Angeles Times* is one of America's largest newspapers. In 1991, the state of California extended its sales tax to newspapers. The *Times* had to decide whether and, if so, how to adjust its price.

At the time, the *Times'* main markets were in Los Angeles and Orange Counties. Owing to the presence of strong competitors, the demand for the *Times* was relatively sensitive to price in Orange County and the San Fernando Valley of Los Angeles County. Elsewhere, however, competition was quite weak and the demand was less price sensitive.

Newspapers are sold through home delivery as well as "on the street" through machines, newsstands, and retail stores. Street sales accounted for about 30% of the *Los Angeles Times* circulation. For many years, the *Los Angeles Times* had maintained a "street" price of 25 cents for its weekday edition. The average cost of the paper was 42 cents, of which newsprint accounted for 34 cents. A tax of 6.5% on 25 cents amounted to 1.6 cents.

After studying its customer demand and competition, the management of the *Los Angeles Times* decided to raise the street price to 35 cents, except in Orange County and the San Fernando Valley, where the price was not changed. This was the first time that the *Times* had set different prices in its primary markets. The price increase was a success: It generated a substantial increase in profit.

Source: Presentation on the *Los Angeles Times* pricing policy, Anderson School, UCLA, November 1991.

6 *Indirect Segment Discrimination*

For a policy of direct segment discrimination, the seller must be able to identify some fixed buyer characteristic that divides the market into segments with different demand curves. A seller may know that specific segments have different demand curves but cannot find a fixed characteristic with which to discriminate directly. Under these circumstances, the seller may be able to apply another policy, which uses an indirect means to discriminate on price.

This policy requires the seller to analyze demand at the level of individual buyers rather than segments. Accordingly, we develop a model that focuses on the purchases of individual buyers.

Suppose that Pluto Airways operates passenger service between Toronto and Miami. Pluto has four potential customers. Maria and Tom are private bankers based in Toronto who are visiting wealthy South American clients in Miami. Robin and Leslie are traveling on vacation. Table 9.1 shows the benefit that each of these travelers will derive from air travel. Clearly, there are two segments, business persons and vacationers, with the business travelers willing to pay more. If traveling to Miami is too expensive, Robin and Leslie could take their vacation elsewhere, so, they are not willing to pay as much.

We use the information from Table 9.1 to construct the market demand curve for air travel in Figure 9.5. The market demand is discrete; hence the demand curve, as shown in Figure 9.5, is a series of steps. By contrast, Mercury Bikes' demand in Figure 9.2 is a smooth curve.

Suppose that Pluto's marginal cost is constant at $200 per seat and the airline has no other costs. Then, each potential traveler gets a benefit that exceeds the marginal cost. If Pluto could implement complete price discrimination, it would set four different fares and sell tickets to each of the four travelers.

It is not likely, however, that Pluto will be able to charge a different price to each traveler. Assuming that Pluto can directly identify business and vacation

Table 9.1 Benefits from air travel

Traveler	Segment	Benefit ($)
Maria	Business	1000
Tom	Business	900
Robin	Vacation	500
Leslie	Vacation	280

Figure 9.5 Discrete demand

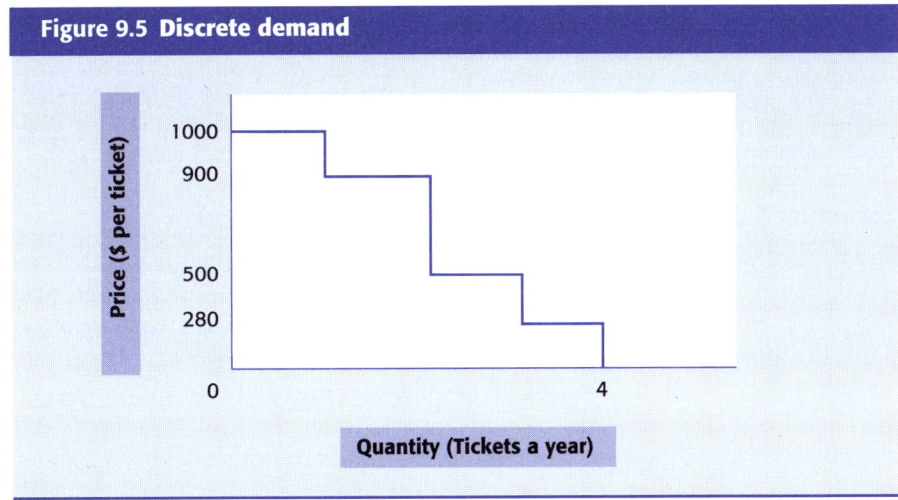

The demand curve is a series of steps.

travelers, the next best alternative is direct segment discrimination. When the segment demands are discrete, the procedure for determining the prices with direct segment discrimination is to calculate the profits from each of the possible prices as in Table 9.2. The profit-maximizing prices are a business fare of $900 and a vacation fare of $500. The airline's profit would be $1700.

We should, however, consider whether Pluto can distinguish business from vacation travelers. The airline's check-in staff might ask every traveler to declare what he or she is planning to do in Miami. Then, every passenger would

Table 9.2 Air travel, direct segment discrimination

Fare ($)	Sales	Total Revenue ($)	Marginal Revenue ($)	Marginal Cost ($)	Total Cost ($)	Profit ($)
Business segment						
1000	1	1000	1000	200	200	800
900	2	1800	800	200	400	**1400**
			Maximum segment profit			
Vacation segment						
500	1	500	500	200	200	**300**
280	2	560	60	200	400	160
			Maximum segment profit			

claim to be going on vacation. Alternatively, Pluto's staff might check whether passengers are wearing casual clothes or business attire. Then, even business travelers would dress casually to check in. Pluto might have to x-ray passengers' luggage to check for business suits and documents. Clearly, it is very difficult to discriminate directly between business and vacation travelers.

Structured Choice

Let us now consider another form of price discrimination that may be feasible when Pluto cannot directly identify business and vacation travelers. This pricing policy uses an indirect means to discriminate between the two segments. Consider the travelers' plans in more detail. Vacationers such as Robin and Leslie can book well in advance and usually want to stay through the weekend. By contrast, business travelers are less able to book early and often prefer to return home for the weekend. So, business travelers and vacationers are differentially sensitive to these features.

Suppose that Pluto offers two fares: an unrestricted fare and a fare subject to the restrictions of advance booking and weekend stay. To evaluate this policy, we must know the benefits that the various travelers get from restricted travel. Table 9.3 provides this information. All four get more benefit from unrestricted than restricted travel. The bankers, Maria and Tom, however, get relatively more benefit from unrestricted travel and relatively less benefit from restricted travel.

Note that unrestricted and restricted fares are substitutes offered by the same seller. Since Pluto cannot directly identify business and vacation travelers, each customer can choose between the two fares. This means that the demand for unrestricted travel depends on the price that Pluto sets for restricted travel. Likewise, the demand for restricted travel depends on the price of unrestricted travel.

Suppose, for instance, that Pluto sets a restricted-travel fare of $401. Table 9.3 shows that this price exceeds the benefit of every traveler from restricted

Table 9.3 Benefits from unrestricted and restricted air travel

Traveler	Segment	Unrestricted Travel ($)	Restricted Travel ($)
Maria	Business	1000	200
Tom	Business	900	180
Robin	Vacation	500	400
Leslie	Vacation	280	224

travel. This means that no one will buy the restricted fare. Hence, the demand for unrestricted travel will be the same as if no restricted fare were available. Using the data from Table 9.3, we can construct the demand for unrestricted travel when the restricted fare is $401. Figure 9.6(a) illustrates the demand curve.

Next, suppose that Pluto sets a restricted fare of $300. If Robin buys restricted travel, she will get buyer surplus of $400 – $300 = $100. So, Robin will buy unrestricted travel only if it provides her at least $100 of buyer surplus. By Table 9.3, Robin would get a benefit of $500 from unrestricted travel; hence, she will buy unrestricted travel only if the price, u, is sufficiently low that $500 – u \geq 100$, or $u \leq \$400$. Since the restricted fare of $300 exceeds the benefit of each of the other three travelers, they definitely will not buy restricted travel.

Using this information about Robin and the data from Table 9.3, we now can construct the demand for unrestricted travel when the restricted fare is $300. If the price of unrestricted travel is between $901 and $1000, only Maria will buy. If the price is between $401 and $900, both Maria and Tom will buy. If the price is between $281 and $400, then Maria, Tom, and Robin will buy.

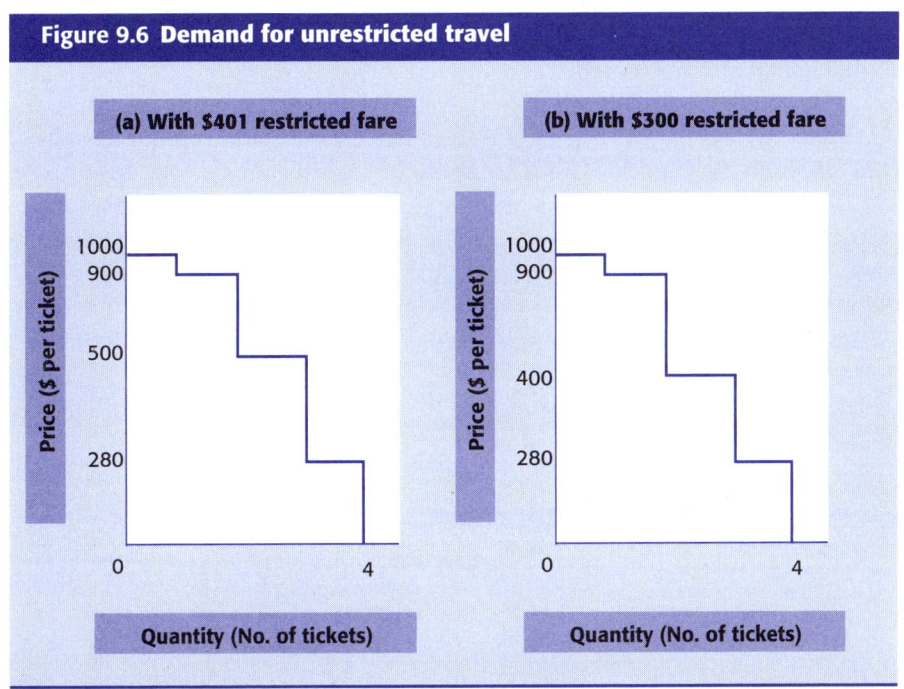

Figure 9.6 Demand for unrestricted travel

(a) With $401 restricted fare

(b) With $300 restricted fare

If the price of restricted travel is lower, then the demand curve for unrestricted travel will be lower.

Finally, if the price is less than or equal to $280, all four travelers will buy. Figure 9.6(b) illustrates the demand curve.

Comparing Figures 9.6(a) and (b), we see that the demand for unrestricted travel depends on the price of restricted travel. Generally, if the price of restricted travel is lower, then the demand curve for unrestricted travel will be lower. Accordingly, to calculate the profits from the alternative prices for restricted and unrestricted travel, we must take account of the substitution between the two products. To find the profit-maximizing prices, we must calculate the profits from every combination of unrestricted and restricted fares.

In Table 9.4, we calculate the profit from an unrestricted fare of $900 and a restricted fare of $399. With these fares, Maria would get some buyer surplus from unrestricted travel, while the restricted fare is more than her benefit. Accordingly, Maria would buy an unrestricted fare. Similarly, Tom would buy an unrestricted fare. By contrast, Robin would get some buyer surplus from restricted travel, while the unrestricted fare is more than her benefit. So, Robin would buy a restricted fare. For Leslie, both of the fares are more than the respective benefits, so she will not buy either fare. Thus, Pluto sells two unrestricted fares and one restricted fare.

With the $900 unrestricted fare and $399 restricted fare, Pluto's total revenue would be $900 × 2 + $399 = $2199. The total cost would be $200 × 3 = $600; hence its profit would be $2199 – $600 = $1599. By checking all the other combinations of unrestricted and restricted fares, we can show that this is the maximum profit.

Pluto Airways faces two segments, business travelers and vacation travelers, with different demand curves. The airline, however, has no way to directly identify the segments. Instead, it structures a choice between unrestricted and restricted travel to exploit the differential sensitivity of business and vacation travelers to restrictions on travel. Given this choice, the business travelers voluntarily choose the unrestricted fare, while one of the vacationers voluntarily chooses the restricted fare. The choice enables Pluto to discriminate indirectly between the segments.

Table 9.4 Air Travel, indirect segment discrimination

Product	Fare ($)	Sales	Total Revenue ($)	Total Cost ($)	Profit ($)
Unrestricted	900	2	1800	400	1400
Restricted	399	1	399	200	199

We give the name **indirect segment discrimination** to the policy of structuring a choice for buyers so as to earn different incremental margins from each segment.

Implementation

Two conditions are necessary for indirect segment discrimination. First, the seller must have control over some variable to which buyers in the various segments are differentially sensitive. The seller then can use this variable to structure a set of choices that will discriminate among the segments. In Pluto's case, the discriminating variable is the restriction on travel.

The other condition necessary for indirect segment discrimination is that buyers must not be able to circumvent the discriminating variable. Suppose, for instance, that Pluto allowed travelers holding restricted tickets to return without staying over the weekend. Then some business travelers might switch from unrestricted to restricted fares. Such switching will undermine the segment discrimination. Accordingly, Pluto must strictly enforce the conditions of restricted fares.

As we explain later, sellers discriminate indirectly because they cannot directly identify the customer segments. Since indirect segment discrimination means giving every buyer a choice of products, the seller obviously cannot prevent buyers from reselling the product. What is necessary for indirect segment discrimination is that buyers must not be able to circumvent the discriminating variable.

The policy of indirect segment discrimination uses product attributes to discriminate indirectly among the various buyer segments. Essentially, the product attributes are a proxy for the buyer attributes. To determine the profit-maximizing prices, the seller must consider that buyers might substitute among the various choices. Hence, the seller must analyze how changes in the price of one product affect the demand for other choices. Accordingly, the seller must not price any product in isolation. Rather, it must set the prices of all products at the same time.

Ideally, the seller should design each of the alternative product choices to maximize the difference between the buyer's benefit and the seller's cost. The difference between the benefit and the cost is the maximum available profit. It will not always be possible to attain this ideal, however. For instance, in Pluto's case, vacationer Robin chooses restricted travel. The restricted fare gives Robin less benefit than unrestricted travel, but the marginal cost of both fares is the same. If Pluto could implement complete price discrimination, it would make more profit by selling unrestricted travel to Robin. This, however, is not possible with indirect segment discrimination. In a later section of the chapter, we discuss the issue of choosing the discriminating variable in more detail.

Profit Ranking

Indirect segment discrimination uses product attributes to discriminate indirectly among the various buyer segments. By contrast, with direct segment

Indirect segment discrimination is the policy where a seller structures a choice for buyers so as to earn different incremental margins from each segment.

Table 9.5 **Ranking of pricing policies**		
Profitability	**Policy**	**Information Requirement**
Highest	Complete price discrimination	Highest
	Direct segment discrimination	
	Indirect segment discrimination	
Lowest	Uniform pricing	Lowest

discrimination, the seller can discriminate directly on the buyer's attributes. The seller can identify each buyer segment and prevent one segment from buying the product targeted at another segment. Hence, the seller can set prices without worrying about buyers switching among the products.

Direct discrimination on buyer attributes is more profitable than indirect discrimination through product attributes. One reason is that the products under indirect discrimination may provide less benefit than those with direct discrimination. For instance, with indirect discrimination, Pluto must sell restricted travel to the vacationers, which provides less benefit than the unrestricted travel. By contrast, with direct discrimination, Pluto can sell unrestricted travel to all the passengers and so earn a higher profit.

Another reason why indirect discrimination is less profitable is that it may involve relatively higher costs. The next case explains how consumer products manufacturers use cents-off coupons to indirectly discriminate among consumers with different price elasticity. Coupons impose costs on both the issuers and users.

Finally, indirect discrimination relies on the various segments voluntarily identifying themselves through the structured choice. This may not always work perfectly: Consumers in one segment may buy the item aimed at the other segment. Such leakage will also reduce the profitability of indirect discrimination.

Table 9.5 ranks the various pricing policies in decreasing order of profitability. The most profitable is complete price discrimination, with direct segment discrimination second, indirect segment discrimination third, and uniform pricing as least profitable.

Progress check

Progress Check 9F Referring to Table 9.3, suppose that the value of Maria and Tom's benefits from restricted travel change to $600 and $500, respectively. With these changes, can Pluto implement indirect segment discrimination?

Cents-off Coupons: Consumer Time and Price Elasticity of Demand

In 1995, American businesses distributed 292 billion coupons with a face value of almost $200 billion. Of these, consumers redeemed only 5.8 billion coupons with a face value of about $4 billion. An intriguing marketing issue is why sellers do not directly cut product prices. Considering that the redemption rate of coupons is a low 2%, direct price cuts would seem to be a more cost-effective way of promoting product sales.

From the consumer's viewpoint, a major difference between direct price cuts and coupons is the time and effort needed to redeem a coupon. The more valuable a consumer's time, the higher the cost of redeeming a coupon will be.

Consumers differ in their price elasticity of demand. Ideally, a seller would like to set prices so as to achieve lower margins from consumers whose demand is more elastic and higher margins from those with less elastic demand. To the extent that consumers whose time is more valuable are also those whose demand is less elastic, sellers can use coupons to implement indirect segment discrimination. Buyers whose time is more valuable will tend not to redeem coupons. Only those whose time is relatively cheap will use coupons.

By issuing coupons, a seller can target a discount at the consumer segment that is relatively more price elastic. In contrast, a direct price cut will benefit all buyers, regardless of their price elasticity. Hence, a direct price cut will be less profitable than the policy of issuing coupons.

Source: "P&G Bets on Low Prices 'Every Day' to Cut Out Need for Company Coupons," *Wall Street Journal* (January 8, 1996), p. A11B.

7 Bundling

Indirect segment discrimination usually involves a structured choice that persuades the various buyer segments to identify themselves through their choices. One method of indirect segment discrimination, however, deliberately restricts buyer choices. This is **bundling,** which is the combination of two or more products into one package with a single price.

> **Bundling** is the combination of two or more products into one package with a single price.

Pure Bundling

Cable television providers make extensive use of bundling in their pricing. To illustrate this pricing policy, suppose that Venus Cable has an educational channel and a music video channel. There are two segments among the viewer population: conservatives and a middle-of-the-road segment. Table 9.6 shows the segment sizes and their monthly benefits from the two channels. Venus Cable incurs a fixed cost of $100,000 a month, while the marginal cost of providing each channel is nothing.

Suppose that Venus Cable can implement direct segment discrimination. This means setting prices so as to obtain a different margin for each channel from each segment. Since the marginal cost is nothing, Venus should provide both channels to both segments. It should set the prices equal to the segment's benefits. For instance,

Table 9.6 Benefits from cable television

Segment	Population	Educational Channel ($)	Music Channel ($)	Bundle ($)
Conservatives	4000	20	2	22
Middle-of-the-road segment	6000	11	11	22

the prices of the educational and music channels to the conservative segment should be $20 and $2 per month, respectively. The contribution margin will be ($20 × 4,000) + ($2 × 4,000) = $88,000. For the middle-of-the-road segment, both channels should be priced at $11, yielding a contribution margin of ($11 × 6,000) + ($11 × 6,000) = $132,000. Venus's profit would be $88,000 + $132,000 – $100,000 = $120,000.

What if Venus lacks sufficient information to implement direct segment discrimination? Another way to set prices yields an equally large profit. Let Venus offer the two channels as a bundle. Table 9.6 also shows the benefits provided by the bundle. Both segments value the bundle at the same amount of $22 a month. If Venus offers the bundle at a uniform price of $22, then everyone will buy the bundle. The profit will be $22 × (4,000 + 6,000) – $100,000 = $120,000.

In this example, the seller offered only a bundle of the two channels. A pricing policy that offers only a bundle and does not allow the alternative of buying the individual products is called *pure bundling*. Next, we will consider policies that do offer the alternative of the individual products.

With bundled pricing, Venus earns the same profits as from direct segment discrimination. Generally, the bundling strategy will be more profitable than uniform pricing, but less profitable than direct segment discrimination.

Mixed Bundling

In the preceding example, the seller offered only a bundle. Typically, however, the seller can make more profit by allowing buyers a choice between the bundle and the individual products. To illustrate, suppose that Venus incurs a marginal cost of $5 per channel for each customer. The fixed cost remains $100,000 and Table 9.6 still represents the buyers' benefits.

Suppose that Venus Cable can implement direct segment discrimination. Consider the prices Venus should set to the conservative segment. Venus should not provide these viewers with the music channel as their benefit of $2 is less than the $5 marginal cost. They should be sold only the educational channel at a price of $20. Venus will earn a contribution margin of $(20 – 5) × 4,000 = $60,000. As for the middle-of-the-road segment, the benefit to these viewers for each channel exceeds the marginal cost. Hence, they should be provided both channels at a price of $11 each, yielding a contribution margin of $(11 – 5) × 6,000 + $(11 – 5) × 6,000 = $72,000. Venus's profit would be $60,000 + $72,000 – $100,000 = $32,000.

Now suppose that Venus Cable lacks sufficient information to implement direct segment discrimination. Pure bundling at a $22 price would be economically inefficient because it would provide both channels to the conservatives. This means that the conservatives would get the music channel, for which their benefit is less than the marginal cost. If it could avoid this inefficiency, Venus could earn a higher profit.

The economic inefficiency can be resolved through mixed bundling, which offers buyers a structured choice between the bundle and the individual products. Let Venus offer the bundle at a price of $22, and the educational channel separately at just under $20. What will the conservatives buy? If they buy the bundle, they will get no buyer surplus. If, however, they buy only the educational channel, they will get a little buyer surplus. Hence, they will choose the educational channel, and Venus will earn a contribution margin of just under $(20 - 5) \times 4,000 = $60,000$.

As for the middle-of-the-road viewers, they will get no buyer surplus from the bundle. Since the price of the educational channel exceeds the benefit, they will not buy the educational channel. Hence, they will choose the bundle, and Venus will earn a contribution margin of $(22 - 5 - 5) \times 6,000 = $72,000$. Venus's total profit would be just under $60,000 + $72,000 - $100,000 = $32,000$. This is only a little less than the profit with direct segment discrimination.

Mixed bundling is a form of indirect segment discrimination. In this example, the conservatives and the middle-of-the-road segments are differentially sensitive to the product structure. The conservatives benefit relatively more from the educational channel, while the middle-of-the-road segment benefits relatively more from the music channel. Through mixed bundling, Venus attracts only the middle-of-the-road segment to choose the bundle, and persuades the conservatives to choose the educational channel.

Application

Bundling is relatively more useful under three conditions: where there is substantial disparity among the segments in their benefits from the separate products, where the benefits of the segments are negatively correlated in the sense that a product that is extremely beneficial to one segment provides relatively little benefit to another, and where the marginal cost of providing the product is low.

With the first and second conditions, the benefit from the bundle will be relatively less disparate across the segments than the benefits from the separate products. The third condition means that relatively little economic inefficiency will accrue from providing the bundle to all buyers.

In the Venus Cable example, each channel provides widely disparate benefits to each of the two segments. The bundle, however, provides exactly the same benefit of $22 to both segments. Accordingly, it is easy to set a price for the bundle.

When provision of the product involves a substantial marginal cost, a seller should consider mixed bundling. This is essentially a form of indirect segment discrimination. By structuring a choice among the bundle and the separate products, the seller can persuade the various segments to identify themselves through their product choice. In this way, the seller can avoid the economic inefficiency of providing a product for which the marginal cost is less than the buyer's benefit.

As already mentioned, bundling is ubiquitous in cable television. Another example of bundling is packaged holidays. A package consisting of airline travel and rooms in a beach resort will be relatively more attractive to vacationers than business travelers. Given a choice of airline travel and a package holiday at a somewhat higher price, business travelers are relatively more likely to choose the separate airline travel, while vacationers will prefer the package.

Progress check   **Progress Check 9G** Referring to Table 9.6, suppose that the conservatives derive a benefit of $19 from the educational channel, and $1 from the music channel. The marginal cost of providing each channel is $5. What prices should Venus set with mixed bundling?

Avis Switzerland: Bundling Unlimited Mileage

The market for car rentals, like that for airline services, consists of business and vacation segments. To the extent that employers or clients pay for business rentals, the demand of business drivers is relatively less elastic. A challenge for car rental agencies is how to discriminate between business and vacation drivers. Since rental agencies cannot discriminate directly, they need some variable with which to discriminate indirectly.

Suppose that vacationers tend to drive long distances, while business renters drive relatively shorter distances. Accordingly, these segments are differentially sensitive to mileage charges. Then, a rental agency can use mileage charges to discriminate between business and vacation drivers. Specifically, it should structure two choices. One choice combines a relatively high daily charge with a low mileage charge to draw vacationers. In the extreme, this could offer unlimited mileage. The other choice should have a lower daily charge with a higher mileage charge to attract business drivers.

Essentially, the unlimited mileage rate is a bundle of two products: the car and unlimited usage. The time and mileage rate sets separate prices for the two products.

In 1995, Avis Switzerland offered an Opel Vectra for weekday rental at an unlimited mileage rate of Fr 296 (Swiss francs) per day or a time and mileage rate of Fr 127 per day plus Fr 1.37 per kilometer. The break-even mileage at which the unlimited mileage rate became cheaper than the time and mileage rate was 123 kilometers. Provided that most business renters drive less than 123 kilometers a day, the Avis pricing policy would succeed in indirect segment discrimination.

8 *Selecting the Discriminating Variable*[2]

We have discussed how a seller can discriminate even when it cannot directly identify the various buyer segments. Indirect segment discrimination proceeds by offering buyers a choice of several alternatives, structured so that each segment makes a different choice. One issue that we have not yet considered is how to select the discriminating variable. For instance, should an airline require 7, 14, or 21 days' advance purchase for a restricted fare?

We now address this issue, and for simplicity, we do so in a context where the seller can choose among many different levels of the discriminating variable.

Suppose that Jupiter Suds has identified two segments in the market for its laundry detergent. There are 100,000 singles and 100,000 families. Figure 9.7(a) shows a single's demand for detergent, while Figure 9.7(b) shows a family's demand for detergent. Families need more detergent than singles, hence have a higher demand curve. Jupiter's marginal cost of laundry detergent is constant at 10 cents per ounce and there are no other costs.

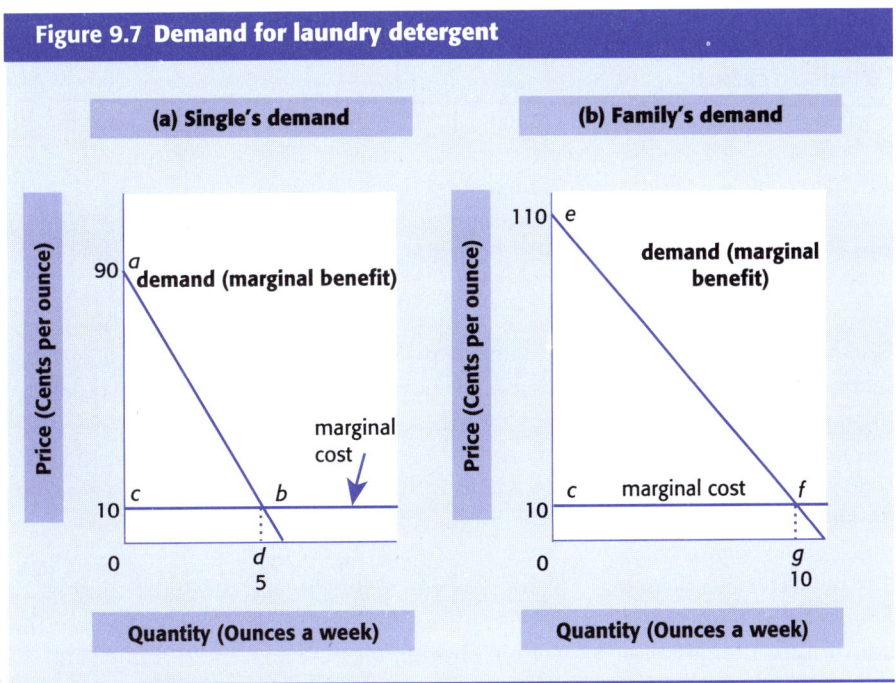

Figure 9.7 Demand for laundry detergent

(a) Single's demand

(b) Family's demand

With direct segment discrimination, Jupiter would sell a 5-ounce bottle to singles and a 10-ounce bottle to families. The singles would pay area *aOdb* = $2.50 per bottle, and families would pay area *eOgf* = $6.00 per bottle

---

[2] This section is more advanced. It may be omitted without loss of continuity.

Consider the singles market. If Jupiter could directly identify single buyers, it would manufacture a bottle of the size at which a single person's marginal benefit equals the marginal cost. By Figure 9.7(a), this size is 5 ounces. A single person's benefit from a 5-ounce bottle is the area $a0db$, under the demand curve up to 5 ounces. This area is $1/2 \times (10 + 90) \times 5 = \$2.50$. Hence, if Jupiter charges \$2.50 for a 5-ounce bottle, every single will buy one bottle and get zero buyer surplus.

The cost of the 5-ounce bottle is $5 \times 10 = \$0.50$, hence the incremental margin from each bottle is $\$2.50 - 0.50 = \$2.00$. Since there are 100,000 singles and no other costs, the profit is $\$2.00 \times 100,000 = \$200,000$.

Similarly for families, if Jupiter could directly identify the families, it would manufacture a size that balances a family's marginal benefit with the marginal cost. By Figure 9.7(b), this size is 10 ounces, and a family would pay up to area $e0gf$, or $1/2 \times (10 + 110) \times 10 = \$6.00$ for a 10-ounce bottle.

The cost of the 10-ounce bottle is $10 \times 10 = \$1.00$; hence, the incremental margin from each bottle is $\$6.00 - \$1.00 = \$5.00$. Since there are 100,000 families and no other costs, the profit is $\$5.00 \times 100,000 = \$500,000$. Therefore, with direct segment discrimination, Jupiter's total profit would be $\$200,000 + \$500,000 = \$700,000$.

Cannibalization

Consider, however, a family's choice if Jupiter allowed it to choose between the 5- and 10-ounce bottles at prices of \$2.50 and \$6.00, respectively. A family would get zero buyer surplus from a large bottle at \$6.00.

What if it were to buy the small bottle? Figure 9.8 shows both the family's and a single's demand curves. If it bought a 5-ounce bottle at \$2.50, the family would get buyer surplus equal to the area $e0dh$, under the family's demand curve up to 5 ounces, minus \$2.50. The area $e0dh$ is $1/2 \times (110 + 60) \times 5 = \$4.25$, hence the family's buyer surplus would be $\$4.25 - \$2.50 = \$1.75$. This exceeds the buyer surplus from a large bottle; hence, every family would buy the 5-ounce bottle.

Graphically, referring to Figure 9.8, the area $a0db$ is \$2.50. Since the area $e0dh$ represents the family's benefit from the 5-ounce bottle, we can represent the family's buyer surplus from the 5-ounce bottle by the shaded area $eabh$. The shaded area $eabh$ is \$1.75.

In marketing language, if Jupiter offers the 5- and 10-ounce bottles at prices of \$2.50 and \$6.00, respectively, the small bottle would **cannibalize** the demand for the large bottle. Cannibalization occurs when sales of one product reduce the demand for another product with a higher incremental margin.

Cannibalization occurs when the sales of one product reduce the demand for another product with a higher incremental margin.

The fundamental reason for cannibalization is that Jupiter has no way to distinguish families from singles directly; hence, it cannot prevent families from buying the bottle aimed for the singles segment. Accordingly, Jupiter must fall back on indirect segment discrimination. This means designing and pricing the two bottles so that families voluntarily choose the large bottle.

Suppose that Jupiter offers the 5-ounce bottle at $2.50. Then, as we have calculated already, every family will derive buyer surplus of $1.75 from the 5-ounce bottle. So, Jupiter must ensure that a family will get buyer surplus of slightly more than $1.75 from the 10-ounce bottle. Let p represent the price of the 10-ounce bottle. Referring to Figure 9.8, if a family buys the 10-ounce bottle, its benefit will be area $e0gf$, which is $6.00; hence, its buyer surplus will be $6.00 − p$.

For a family to get buyer surplus of slightly more than $1.75 from the 10-ounce bottle, the price that Jupiter charges must satisfy $6.00 − p > 1.75$. Thus, the maximum price is $p = 4.24. Graphically, referring to Figure 9.8, the maximum that Jupiter can charge for the 10-ounce bottle is slightly less than area $e0gf$, under a family's demand curve up to 10 ounces, less the shaded area $eabh$, the buyer surplus that a family would get from the 5-ounce bottle.

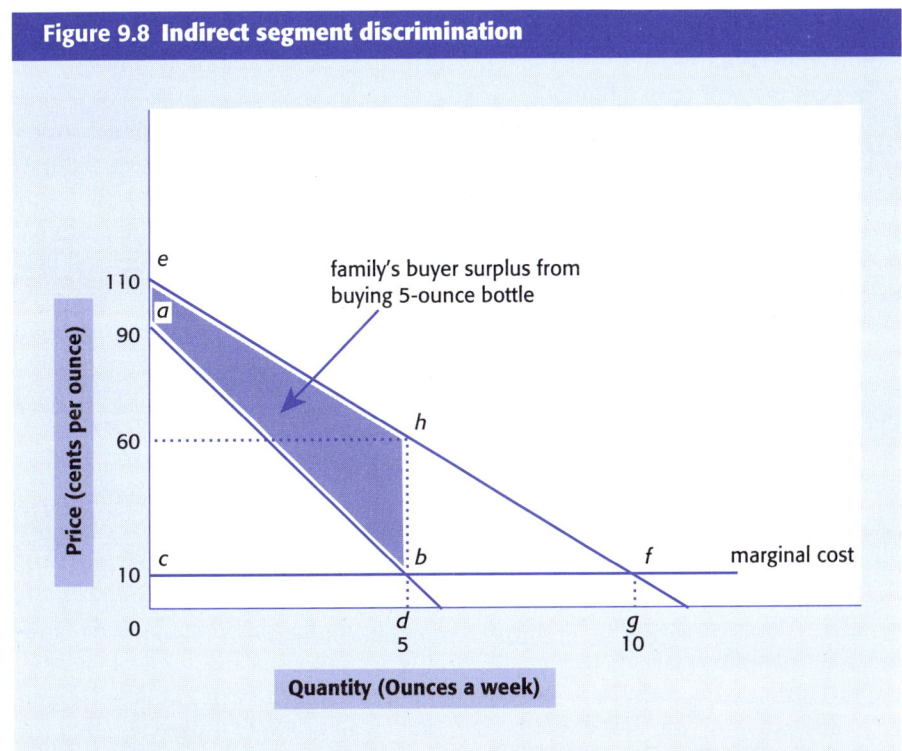

Figure 9.8 Indirect segment discrimination

For a family to voluntarily choose the 10-ounce bottle, the maximum that it can be charged is slightly less than area $e0gf$, under a family's demand curve up to 10 ounces, less the shaded area $eabh$, the buyer surplus that a family would get from the 5-ounce bottle.

Accordingly, if Jupiter offered a 5-ounce bottle at $2.50 and a 10-ounce bottle at $4.24, singles would buy the 5-ounce bottle, while families would buy the 10-ounce bottle. With these prices, Jupiter could discriminate between singles and families.

Let us calculate Jupiter's profit. The cost of the 5-ounce bottle is $5 \times 10 = 0.50; hence, the incremental margin from each bottle is $2.50 − $0.50 = 2.00. The cost of the 10-ounce bottle is $10 \times 10 = 1.00, hence the incremental margin from each bottle is $4.24 − $1.00 = 3.24. Since there are 100,000 singles and 100,000 families and no other costs, Jupiter's profit is ($2.00 \times 100,000$) + ($3.24 \times 100,000$) = $524,000$.

Progress check   **Progress Check 9H** With indirect segment discrimination, if Jupiter reduces the price of the 5-ounce bottle to $2.00, how much can it charge families for the 10-ounce bottle?

Degrading Quality

So far, we have assumed that Jupiter offers a 5-ounce bottle at $2.50. Notice from Figure 9.9 that, at every quantity, a single person's marginal benefit from detergent is lower than a family's marginal benefit.

Suppose that Jupiter were to reduce the small bottle by 0.1 ounce to 4.9 ounces. Then, it must reduce the price of the small bottle by the marginal benefit to a single perosn of the 4.9th ounce. According to Figure 9.9, this marginal benefit is area *bkjd*, or $(11.6 + 10)/2 \times 0.1 = 1.08$ cents. Recall that the marginal cost of detergent is 10 cents per ounce. So, by cutting the size of the small bottle, Jupiter will reduce its cost by $10 \times 0.1 = 1$ cent per bottle. Thus, the incremental margin from the 4.9-ounce bottle will be $(1.08 − 1) = 0.08$ cent less than from the original 5-ounce bottle.

With the small bottle reduced to 4.9 ounces, a family's buyer surplus from the small bottle will fall by area *hmkb*, or $(49.4 + 50)/2 \times 0.1 = 0.497$ cent. Hence, Jupiter can raise the price of the 10-ounce bottle and still attract families to buy the 10-ounce bottle. Specifically, Jupiter can raise the price by 0.497 cent, which increases its margin by 0.497 cents.

The net effect of these changes is to raise Jupiter's profit by a total of ($0.497 \times 100,000$) − ($0.08 \times 100,000$) = 417. Accordingly, Jupiter can increase its profit by downgrading the smaller bottle. Essentially, this downgrading mitigates the extent to which the smaller bottle cannibalizes the demand for the larger bottle and, so, allows Jupiter to extract more profit from families.

Generally, Jupiter should downgrade the small bottle to a size such that the marginal reduction in profit from singles equals the marginal gain in profit from families. This balance depends on the single relative to the family demand and the number of singles relative to families. In the extreme case, if the demand from singles is very low and there are very few singles, Jupiter may decide to sell only a large bottle and cater only to families.

Figure 9.9 Mitigating cannibalization

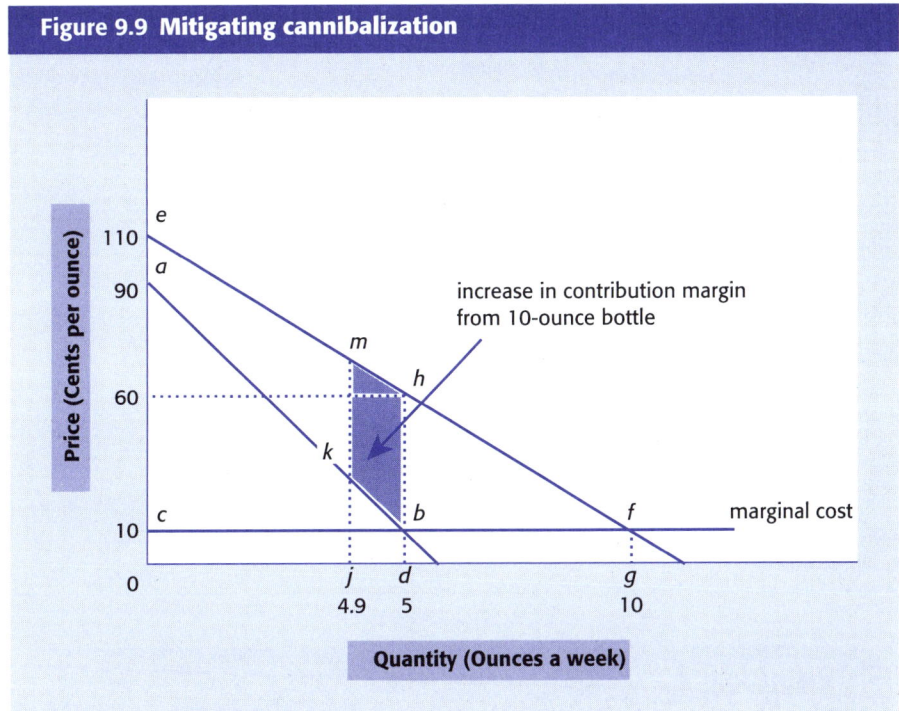

A 0.1-ounce reduction of the smaller bottle mitigates the extent to which it cannibalizes the demand for the 10-ounce bottle. Hence, the seller can extract the shaded area *mkbh* in additional contribution margin from buyers of the 10-ounce bottle.

Cellular Telephone Service: How Many Choices to Offer

Indirect segment discrimination is widespread in cellular telephone service. Table 9.7 reports Cellular One/Boston's 1995 price schedule. The company offered a choice of five plans, differing in the monthly basic charge, the quantity of free airtime, and the rates for additional airtime.

To decide how many alternatives to offer buyers, a seller should consider the number of segments in the market. Generally, the number of alternatives should not exceed the number of segments. Owing to the problem of cannibalization, however, it may not be profitable to discriminate among all segments. In this case, a seller may choose to provide buyers with fewer alternatives and so allow some market segments to choose the same product.

Table 9.7 Cellular One/Boston price schedule, 1995

Plan	Monthly Fee ($)	Inclusive Airtime (Minutes)	Additional Airtime ($ per minute)
Assurance Choice Plus	19.95	10 minutes peak 10 minutes off peak	0.45 peak $0.29 off peak
Smart Choice Plus	29.95	30 minutes peak 30 minutes off peak	$0.42 peak $0.29 off peak
Weekend Choice Plus	39.95	Unlimited off peak	$0.42 (7 am–8 pm) $0.19 (8–10 pm) free off peak
Performance Choice Plus	65.95	150 minutes peak 30 minutes off peak	$0.35 peak $0.26 off peak
Business Choice Plus	95.95	300 minutes peak	$0.27 peak $0.17 off peak

Source: Cellular One/Boston.

Mitigating Cannibalization: Underpowering the BMW 318

In the mid-1980s, BMW of North America introduced new 318 and 325 models, using a common body, differentiated through engine size. BMW equipped the 318 with a 1.8 liter engine and the 325 with a larger, 2.5 liter engine. Car enthusiasts, however, complained bitterly that the 318 was underpowered.

From the standpoint of maximizing overall profits, it may have been very sensible to underpower the 318. Since the two models shared the same body, the 318 might cannibalize sales of the more expensive 325. By underpowering the 318, the manufacturer was limiting the degree of cannibalization.

We have emphasized that a necessary condition for indirect segment discrimination is that buyers must not be able to circumvent the discriminating variable. BMW can easily satisfy this condition. It is quite inconceivable to combine two 318s to make a high-end 325!

9 Summary

The simplest way to set price is through uniform pricing. At the profit-maximizing uniform price, the incremental margin percentage equals the reciprocal of the absolute value of the price elasticity of demand. The most profitable pricing policy is complete price discrimination, where each unit is priced at the benefit that the unit provides to its buyer. To implement this policy, however, the seller must know each potential buyer's individual demand curve and be able to set different prices for every unit of the product.

The next most profitable pricing policy is direct segment discrimination. For this policy, the seller must be able to directly identify the various segments. The third most profitable policy is indirect segment discrimination. This involves structuring a set of choices around some variable to which the various segments are differentially sensitive. A commonly used method of indirect segment discrimination is bundling. Uniform pricing is the least profitable way to set a price.

Key Concepts

uniform pricing
incremental margin percentage
price discrimination
complete price discrimination
segment
direct segment discrimination

free on board (FOB)
delivered pricing
cost including freight (CF)
indirect segment discrimination
bundling
cannibalization

Further Reading

Thomas T. Nagle and Reed K. Holden provide a comprehensive economic analysis of pricing in *The Strategy and Tactics of Pricing*, 2d ed. (Englewood Cliffs, NJ: Prentice Hall, 1995).

Review Questions

1. Many supermarkets sell both branded and private-label merchandise. Suppose that some supermarket estimates that the demand for its private-label cola is less elastic than the demand for Coca Cola. Does this mean that it should set a higher price for private-label cola?

2. Sol Electric manufactures 60-Watt long-life light bulbs. The marginal production cost is 50 cents per unit. Sol estimates that the price elasticity of demand is –1.25. Assuming that Sol will set a uniform price, what is the profit-maximizing price?

3. Sol's Technical Department has found a way to reduce the marginal cost of a 60-Watt light bulb from 50 to 40 cents. Should Sol reduce the selling price of a light bulb by 10 cents?

4. Give an example of direct segment discrimination. Discuss whether the product meets the conditions for such discrimination.

5. Some department stores offer free delivery service. For stores that provide free delivery, is the FOB price of goods less than, equal to, or greater than the CF price?

6. Sol Electric is planning to export light bulbs to Germany and South Africa. The marginal production cost is 50 cents per unit. The cost of shipping is 5 cents to Germany and 10 cents to South Africa. The price elasticity of demand is –1.2 in Germany and –1.5 in South Africa. What prices should Sol set in the two export markets?

7. On which of the following products would it be easier to discriminate by the buyer's location (choose a or b)? Explain your answer.

   For publications,
   a. Newspapers.
   b. Scientific journals.

   For building materials,
   a. Bricks.
   b. High-quality ceramic tiles.

8. Give an example of indirect segment discrimination. Discuss whether the example meets the conditions for such discrimination.

9. Some restaurants offer a choice between a la carte and all-you-can-eat self-service buffets.

Explain how this choice will indirectly discriminate between consumers with small and big appetites.

10. Venus Airways offers two classes of service: business class and economy class. The airline is evaluating a proposal to upgrade its economy class service. Which of the following factors should the airline consider in deciding how much to invest in upgrading:
    a. The effect on sales of business class fares.
    b. The effect on sales of economy class fares.

Discussion Questions

1. Most international airlines offer special excursion fares, which are subject to restrictions such as a minimum three night's stay at the destination. Regular economy class fares carry no such restrictions. A study of North Atlantic airline services found that the price elasticity of demand was –1.30 for regular economy class and –1.83 for excursion fares (J. Cigliano, "Price and Income Elasticities for Airline Travel: The North Atlantic Market," *Business Economics* [September 1980]).
   a. Explain why the demand for regular economy class is less elastic than the demand for excursion fares.
   b. Assume that one airline has a monopoly over the North Atlantic routes and that travelers cannot substitute between regular economy and excursion fares. How can it use the data on price elasticities to set the two fares?
   c. In reality, travelers can substitute between regular economy and excursion fares. Explain how the demand for one product depends on the price of the other.

2. Major industrial corporations often borrow money through loans that are syndicated among multiple banks. The managers of the syndicated loan may specify the interest rate as the London Interbank Offer Rate (LIBOR) plus a "spread" to account for the riskiness of the borrower. Most banks prefer to source funds from savings and time deposits as the rates on these deposits are usually lower than the London Interbank market.
   a. Does LIBOR reflect a typical bank's average or marginal cost of funds?
   b. For purposes of pricing, which is relevant—average or marginal cost?
   c. In addition to the riskiness of the borrower, should banks consider the borrower's price elasticity of demand when setting spreads on syndicated loans?

3. Doctors routinely ask patients about their occupation, employer, home address, and scope of insurance coverage. How do the following factors affect the scope for price discrimination in medical services?

   a. Characteristics such as occupation and home address are quite fixed.

   b. It is physically impossible to transfer medical treatment from one person to another.

   c. Doctors treat patients on an individual basis.

4. Referring to Figure 9.1, suppose that Mercury Bikes' marginal revenue and demand curves cross the marginal cost curve at quantities of 3000 and 6000 units a year, respectively. All other data remain the same.

   a. Calculate the profit under policies of (i) uniform pricing, and (ii) complete price discrimination.

   b. Suppose that Mercury is implementing complete price discrimination. Explain why it should sell up to the quantity where the buyer's marginal benefit equals Mercury's marginal cost.

   c. Explain why Mercury's profit is higher with complete price discrimination than with uniform pricing.

5. Some publishers of personal computer software offer their products at special discounts to students. Others have developed special "student" editions of their software that have fewer features than the regular packages.

   a. Why do publishers offer discounts to students?

   b. What is the purpose of developing less powerful "student" editions?

   c. Should software publishers also offer discounts to senior citizens or develop "senior citizen" editions?

6. A Japanese manufacturer of big-screen TVs is planning to introduce its product in Hong Kong. Its market research shows that other Japanese consumer electronics manufacturers set higher prices in Tokyo than in Hong Kong. This, however, has created a "gray market" through which Japanese retailers buy cheap products in Hong Kong and ship them back to the Japanese market.

   a. Explain why some Japanese consumer electronics manufacturers set higher prices in Tokyo than in Hong Kong.

   b. Explain why the gray market presents a problem.

   c. Compare the gray market problem for big-screen TVs relative to cosmetics.

7. Magazines are distributed through both newsstands and subscriptions. Advertising accounts for up to 50% of the revenues of titles like *Time* and *Sports Illustrated*.

   a. The larger a title's circulation, the more its publisher can charge for advertising. How should a publisher take account of this factor in setting the cover price of a magazine?

   b. From the reader's standpoint, what are the differences between buying at a newsstand and through subscription? How should a publisher price subscriptions relative to newsstand sales?

   c. Generally, newsstand sales vary more than subscriptions. Advertisers prefer the stability of subscription sales. How should a publisher take account of this factor in pricing subscriptions relative to newsstand sales?

8. Each year, consumer products manufacturers spend millions of dollars to distribute cents-off coupons to consumers. An intriguing marketing issue is why manufacturers do not directly cut the wholesale prices of the products. A direct price cut would be much cheaper to administer than coupons.

    a. Some say that retailers would absorb a direct wholesale price cut instead of passing it on to consumers. They argue that, by contrast, retailers cannot absorb the value of coupons. Suppose that the retail sector is perfectly competitive. Compare the demand-supply equilibrium in the retail market with (i) a wholesale price cut of 50 cents and (ii) widespread distribution of 50-cent coupons. For this part, you may assume that all consumers use coupons.

    b. Would there be any difference between the wholesale price cut and using coupons if the retailer were a monopoly? (Continue to assume that all consumers use coupons.)

    c. Explain how coupons may be used to discriminate among consumers on price.

9. When marketing prerecorded videotapes, movie studios must choose between selling at a relatively high price for the rental market and selling at a lower price for "sell-through" to consumers. The buyers of rental tapes are video-rental stores.

    a. Under U.S. law, a movie studio cannot prevent the buyer of a videotape from renting the tape to other parties. If studios could prohibit renting, would they wish to do so?

    b. Even if a studio sets a low price for a tape, there will still be some demand to rent the tape. How do rental rates affect consumers' demand to buy a tape as opposed to renting it?

    c. Studios use cheaper, lower-quality materials for "sell-through" tapes than for tapes that they intend to be rented. Explain this practice.

    d. How does "sell-through" pricing affect the business of video pirates who illegally reproduce films?

10. Refer to the example of Jupiter Suds. Suppose that Jupiter's marginal cost is 5 cents per ounce, while the demands of singles and families remain unchanged.

    a. Calculate the profit-maximizing bottle sizes and prices with direct segment discrimination.

    b. Suppose that Jupiter offers the bottle sizes and prices in (a). How much buyer surplus would a family get from buying the small bottle?

    c. Suppose that Jupiter offers the bottle sizes in (a) and sets the price of the small bottle as in (a). What is the maximum that Jupiter could charge a family for the large bottle?

Math Supplement

Uniform Pricing: Profit-Maximizing Price

Let us prove the rule for a profit–maximizing price in terms of the price elasticity of demand: The incremental margin percentage equals the reciprocal of the absolute value of the price elasticity. Let Q represent sales, and $R(Q)$ and $C(Q)$ represent total revenue and total cost, respectively. Then, a seller's profit is total revenue less total cost:

$$P = R(Q) - C(Q). \tag{9.3}$$

From Chapter 9, we know that, at the profit-maximizing amount of sales, the marginal revenue equals the marginal cost:

$$\frac{dR(Q)}{dQ} = \frac{dC(Q)}{dQ} \tag{9.4}$$

Now the marginal revenue is

$$\frac{dR(Q)}{dQ} = \frac{d}{dQ}(p \times Q) = p + Q\frac{dp}{dQ}. \tag{9.5}$$

Substituting in (9.4), we have

$$p + Q\frac{dp}{dQ} = \frac{dC(Q)}{dQ}. \tag{9.6}$$

By the definition of the price elasticity of demand,

$$e_p = \frac{p}{Q}\frac{dQ}{dp}; \tag{9.7}$$

hence,

$$Q\frac{dp}{dQ} = \frac{p}{e_p}. \tag{9.8}$$

Substituting in (9.6), we have

$$\frac{p - dC(Q)/Q}{p} = -\frac{1}{e_p} \tag{9.9}$$

This states that, at the profit-maximizing price, the incremental margin percentage equals the reciprocal of the absolute value of the price elasticity.

Contribution Margin Percentage

Next, we prove that the contribution margin percentage is equal to the price less the average variable cost divided by the price. In cost accounting, the contribution margin percentage is defined as total revenue less variable cost divided by total revenue, or

$$CM\% = \frac{R(Q) - V(Q)}{R(Q)}. \tag{9.10}$$

Dividing both the numerator and the denominator by sales (or the quantity demanded), we have

$$CM\% = \frac{R(Q)/Q - V(Q)/Q}{R(Q)/Q}. \tag{9.11}$$

Consider the first term in the numerator and the same term in the denominator:

$$\frac{R(Q)}{Q} = \frac{P \times Q}{Q} = P \qquad (9.12)$$

Hence, the contribution margin percentage simplifies to

$$CM\% = \frac{P - V(Q)/Q}{P}, \qquad (9.13)$$

which is the price less the average variable cost divided by the price.

Chapter 10

Strategic Thinking

1 Introduction

The Organization of Petroleum Exporting Countries (OPEC) is an international cartel including many of the world's major oil-exporting countries. In November 1994, the members of OPEC met to plan their oil production in the following year. After some discussion, they agreed to limit total production to 24.52 million barrels per day. Within this overall limit, Iran and Venezuela received quotas of 3.6 and 2.359 million barrels per day, respectively. After the meeting, Iran's Oil Minister Gholamreza Aqazadeh remarked, "it will be very good for the market ... prices will be stronger than now. I hope everybody will agree to the quota without any violations in the next year."[1] Should Mr Aqazadeh be optimistic?

Lithography is a process by which an artist creates a stone or metal plate, then treats the plate with ink, and prints pictures. Most lithographers specify the number of copies that they will print from each plate and mark each print with a serial number. For instance, the mark "5/30" means the 5th of 30 copies. Some lithographers destroy their plates after printing the specified number of copies. Why do lithographers engage in such practices?

Dean Witter, Discover & Co. is a financial services group, encompassing consumer credit and securities businesses.[2] In April 1995, the company adopted a shareholder rights plan that created one right for every outstanding

---

[1] "Producers Maintain Oil Output Ceilings," *South China Morning Post* (November 23, 1994), Business Post, p. 14.
[2] In February 1997, Dean Witter, Discover announced that it would merge with the investment bank Morgan Stanley.

common share of the company. Under the plan, the acquisition by any party of 15% or more of Dean Witter, Discover's common shares could activate the rights. Then each right could be exercised to buy additional shares of the company at a 50% discount to their value. Any rights owned by the party whose acquisition activated the rights, however, would be canceled and could not be exercised. How does a shareholder rights plan, such as that established by Dean Witter, Discover, affect the likelihood of a hostile takeover of the company?

By joining in labor unions, workers can gain market power and secure improvements in wages and conditions of work. A major weapon of unions when negotiating with employers is the threat of a strike. The frequency of strikes varies among various industries. Why are strikes particularly rare in professional American football?

A **strategy** is a plan for action in a situation where the parties actively consider the interactions with one another in making decisions.

OPEC oil ministers, lithographers, takeover bidders, and union leaders are making *strategic* decisions. A **strategy** is a plan for action in a situation where the parties actively consider the interactions with one another in making decisions.

Consider an OPEC member's decision whether to abide by its production quota or produce more than its quota. Its choice will affect the oil market. In making such a decision, it would surely consider the reactions of other OPEC members. The OPEC member is making a strategic decision. Contrast an OPEC member with a small Brazilian gold mine that is deciding whether to increase production from 10,000 to 15,000 ounces a year. The mine is too small to affect the gold market; hence, it need not consider the reactions of other gold producers. The mine's production decision is not strategic.

A party deciding whether to launch a takeover bid for a company should consider the reaction of the target's management and shareholders. In particular, the potential bidder should consider whether its takeover will trigger the company's shareholder rights plan and how that will affect the cost of a takeover. Accordingly, a takeover bidder's decisions are strategic.

In this chapter, we consider how to organize thinking about strategic decisions, choose among alternative strategies, and make better strategic decisions. This chapter is based on a set of ideas and principles to guide strategic thinking called **game theory.** Game theory can provide guidance to an OPEC member whether to abide by its oil production quotas. The theory explains why lithographers number each copy that they make, and some even destroy their plates after printing the specified number of copies.

Game theory is a set of ideas and principles that guides strategic thinking.

Corporate financiers have made substantial use of strategic thinking in takeover bidding. We will apply game theory to analyze how a shareholder rights plan affects the cost and likelihood of a hostile takeover. Our analysis will explain why stock analysts have given the name *poison pill* to such rights plans.

We will also apply the ideas and principles of game theory to analyze the circumstances under which workers should strike against their employers.

Game theory can explain why strikes are relatively infrequent in professional football.

Before going further, we should note that a decision-maker always has the option of acting nonstrategically. An OPEC member could ignore the actions of other oil producers in deciding on its production. Similarly, a potential takeover bidder could make an offer without considering how the management of the target company will respond. Obviously, there will be situations where the cost of strategic thinking outweighs the benefit. In this chapter, however, we shall focus on situations where it is worthwhile to act strategically.

Progress Check 10A Explain why the decisions of a union leader are strategic.

Progress check

2 *Nash Equilibrium*

Jupiter Elevator has recently entered the European elevator market. Jupiter has learned that Merkur Engineering, a long-established German elevator manufacturer, is about to finalize large orders with several English and German clients in the next week. Jupiter's president plans to call on Merkur's clients to win some of the pending orders by offering a special price and full technical support.

Jupiter's president has time to cover either England or Germany but not both. She must decide which country to target. She knows that Merkur's chief executive will defend his territory by visiting the same clients. Merkur's chief executive also has time to visit only one country.

The dilemma for Jupiter's president is that her best decision depends on what she believes Merkur would do. If both Jupiter and Merkur go to England, then Jupiter will win two orders. If Jupiter goes to Germany but Merkur visits England, then Jupiter will win three orders. If Jupiter goes to England but Merkur covers Germany, then Jupiter will win two orders. Finally, if both companies visit Germany, which is Merkur's home base, then Jupiter will win only one order.

Ideally, Jupiter would like to visit the country that Merkur is not covering. If Merkur is covering England, Jupiter would prefer to visit Germany, while, if Merkur is covering Germany, Jupiter would want to visit England. Jupiter's best choice depends on which country Merkur would cover, but Jupiter cannot expect Merkur to reveal its decision. How should Jupiter decide?

Strategic Form

The battle for the new orders is clearly a strategic situation. Jupiter's dilemma is that its best decision depends on what it believes Merkur would do. Jupiter might place itself in Merkur's shoes to figure out which country Merkur would cover. But Merkur might be doing the same. Jupiter is faced with a problem of *infinite regress:* Its best decision depends on how it expects Merkur to act, which in turn depends on how Merkur expects Jupiter to act, and so on.

Let us try to clarify Jupiter's position in the following way. Recall that a strategy is a plan for action in a situation where the parties actively consider interactions with one another in making decisions. Jupiter must decide on a strategy. Jupiter has a choice of two alternative strategies, visit England or Germany, and likewise, Merkur has a choice of two strategies, cover England or Germany.

Accordingly, there are four possible outcomes: Jupiter visits England while Merkur covers England, Jupiter visits Germany while Merkur covers England, Jupiter visits England while Merkur covers Germany, and Jupiter visits Germany while Merkur covers Germany. For each of these outcomes, we know the number of orders that Jupiter will win from Merkur.

Next, we gather this information in Table 10.1 as follows. We mark Jupiter's alternative strategies along the rows, and Merkur's strategies along the columns. The columns and rows delineate four cells, each representing one of the four possible outcomes. In each cell, we record the consequences for Jupiter and Merkur, respectively. For instance, in the cell where Jupiter visits England and Merkur covers Germany, we mark 2 to represent the two orders that Jupiter would win and then –2 to represent the two orders that Merkur would lose.

Table 10.1 is called a **game in strategic form.** It is a very useful way to organize thinking about strategic decisions that parties must take simultaneously. Let us use the game in strategic form to consider how Jupiter should move. First, look at the situation from Merkur's position. If Jupiter visits England, then Merkur gets –2 whether it covers England or Germany. If Jupiter visits Germany, then Merkur is better off covering Germany than England (getting –1 rather than –3). So, regardless of Jupiter's move, Merkur should

A **game in strategic form** is a tabular representation of a strategic situation, showing one party's strategies along the rows, the other party's strategies along the columns, and the consequences for the parties in the corresponding cells.

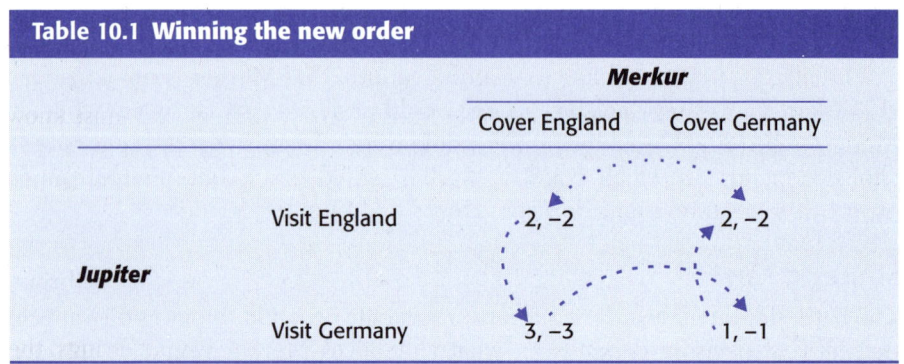

Table 10.1 Winning the new order

		Merkur	
		Cover England	Cover Germany
Jupiter	Visit England	2, –2	2, –2
	Visit Germany	3, –3	1, –1

cover Germany. For Merkur, the strategy of covering England is **dominated** by the strategy of covering Germany.

A *dominated strategy* is a strategy that generates worse consequences than some other strategy, regardless of the choices of the other parties.

A strategy is *dominated* if it generates worse consequences than some other strategy, regardless of the other parties' choices. It makes no sense to adopt a dominated strategy.

For Merkur, to cover England is a dominated strategy. Accordingly, Jupiter can figure out that Merkur will cover Germany. Given that Merkur covers Germany, Jupiter must choose between visiting England and getting 2 or visiting Germany and getting 1. Thus, having reasoned that Merkur would cover Germany, Jupiter should visit England.

Progress Check 10B Check whether any of Jupiter's strategies in Table 10.1 is dominated.

Progress check

Definition

The pair of strategies—Jupiter visits England and Merkur covers Germany—is the obvious way for the two companies to act. Moreover, this pair of strategies is a stable situation in the following sense. Even if Merkur knows that Jupiter will visit England, Merkur will be indifferent between covering England and Germany, so will still cover Germany. Likewise, even if Jupiter knows that Merkur will cover Germany, Jupiter will still visit England.

In a strategic situation, a **Nash equilibrium** is a set of strategies such that, given that the other parties choose their Nash equilibrium strategies, each party prefers its own Nash equilibrium strategy. In the battle for the new orders, the pair of strategies in which Jupiter visits England and Merkur covers Germany is a Nash equilibrium. As we have just shown, even if Merkur knows that Jupiter will visit England, Merkur will still cover Germany, even if Jupiter knows that Merkur will cover Germany, Jupiter will still visit England.

A *Nash equilibrium* is a set of strategies such that, given that the other players choose their Nash equilibrium strategies, each party prefers its own Nash equilibrium strategy.

What justifies a Nash equilibrium as a reasonable way for the relevant parties to act? One reason is that a Nash equilibrium provides a logically consistent solution to the problem of infinite regress that strategic decisions present.

Recall that, in the battle for the new orders, Jupiter could have placed itself in Merkur's shoes to guess Merkur's strategy, but at the same time, Merkur could also put itself in Jupiter's shoes to guess Jupiter's strategy. The result is a problem of infinite regress: To identify Merkur's best strategy, we must know Jupiter's strategy, but to identify Jupiter's strategy, we must know Merkur's strategy. The Nash equilibrium provides a logically consistent solution to this problem of infinite regress.

Another reason to act according to Nash equilibrium strategies is that, in many typical strategic situations that we analyze later, the Nash equilibrium strategies seem like the most reasonable and obvious way to behave. By extension, this provides ground for believing that, in other, less familiar settings, the relevant parties should also act according to Nash equilibrium strategies. Accordingly, the Nash equilibrium strategies provide a focal point for strategic decision making.

Solving the Equilibrium

The formal way to find a Nash equilibrium is, first, to rule out dominated strategies and, next, to check all the remaining strategies, one at a time.

A simple, informal method of finding a Nash equilibrium is to draw arrows between the cells as follows.[3] Supposing that Merkur covers England, then Jupiter prefers to visit Germany; draw an arrow from 2 in the top left-hand cell pointing toward 3 in the bottom left-hand cell. Next, supposing that Merkur covers Germany, then Jupiter prefers to visit England; draw an arrow from 1 in the bottom right-hand cell pointing toward 2 in the top right-hand cell.

Now, supposing that Jupiter visits England; Merkur is indifferent between covering England and Germany; so draw a double-pointed arrow linking –2 in the top left-hand cell with –2 in the top right-hand cell. Finally, supposing that Jupiter visits Germany, Merkur prefers to cover Germany; so draw an arrow from –3 in the bottom left-hand cell pointing toward –1 in the bottom right-hand cell.

Using this "arrow" technique, we can easily see if a strategy is dominated. A strategy is dominated if the row or column corresponding to the strategy has all the arrows pointing out. From Table 10.1, Merkur's strategy of covering England is dominated. The arrow technique also easily identifies an equilibrium. If there is a cell with all arrows leading in, then the strategies marking that cell are a Nash equilibrium.

Game Theory at War: The Battle of the Bismarck Sea

In late February 1943, Japanese commander Rear-Admiral Kimura had assembled a convoy of sixteen transport ships and destroyers at the port of Rabaul. Admiral Kimura's mission was to bring the convoy to Lae, on the mainland of New Guinea. American Lieutenant-General Kenney, commander of Allied Air Forces in the area, was ordered to intercept and destroy the Japanese convoy.

Admiral Kimura had to choose between sailing along a northern route through the Bismarck Sea and a southern route. Meteorologists forecasted that there would be rain on the northern route, which would reduce visibility. Weather on the southern route, however, would be fine.

---

[3] This method was presented by a UCLA management student.

General Kenney had to decide the direction in which to concentrate his reconnaissance aircraft. Once his aircraft spotted the Japanese convoy, Kenney would dispatch his bombers. The dilemma for Kenney was that his best decision depended on what he believed Kimura would do.

Table 10.2 represents the Battle of the Bismarck Sea in strategic form. In each cell, the first entry represents the number of days of bombing that Kenney could inflict on the Japanese, while the second entry represents the number of days of bombing that Kimura would suffer.

Using the arrow technique, we can solve the Nash equilibrium, which is for Kenney to fly north and Kimura to sail north. Indeed, on February 28, Admiral Kimura set out on the northern route. General Kenney's reconnaissance planes discovered the Japanese convoy on March 2. In two days of massive aerial raids, Kenney's bombers destroyed the Japanese convoy.

Source: O.G. Haywood, "Military Decision and Game Theory," *Journal of the Operations Research Society of America* 2, no. 4 (November 1954): pp. 365–85; Eric Rasmusen, *Games and Information*, 2d ed. (Cambridge, MA: Basil Blackwell, 1994), Chapter 1; and J. Rohwer and G. Hummelchen, *Chronology of the War at Sea, 1939–45*, vol. 2, trans. Derek Masters (London: Ian Allan, 1974), p. 306.

Table 10.2 Battle of the Bismarck Sea

		Kimura	
		North	South
Kenney	North	2, –2	2, –2
	South	1, –1	3, –3

A Cartel's Dilemma

A particularly useful application of game theory is to analyze the behavior of participants in a cartel. Recall from Chapter 8 that competing sellers can raise their profit by organizing a cartel. A cartel agreement restricts the sales of each individual seller to a specific quota. The total quota is set below the quantity that a competitive market would supply; hence, the cartel can increase its profit above the competitive level.

Suppose, for instance, that Hilda, Inc., and Sharon Corporation dominate the market for truck rentals. The managements of the two companies have discussed a cartel agreement limiting each company to a specific quota of truck rentals a year. The quotas have been set to maintain the price at the monopoly level.

Table 10.3 A cartel's dilemma

		Sharon	
		Follow quota	Produce more
Hilda	Follow quota	15, 10	10, 13
	Produce more	19, 5	12, 8

This discussion of cartels, however, has ignored the incentives of the individual sellers. Each seller makes an independent decision on its sales. Accordingly, it is important to ask, will the individual sellers comply with their quotas?

To address this question, suppose that Hilda and Sharon each have two alternatives: either follow the quota or produce more. Table 10.3 is a game in strategic form that describes the cartel comprising Hilda and Sharon. In each cell, the first entry is Hilda's annual profit in millions of dollars and the second entry is Sharon's profit.

Consider Hilda's decision. Assume that Sharon follows its quota. Then, if Hilda follows its quota, its profit will be $15 million, while if it produces more than its quota, its profit will be $19 million. Hence, if Sharon follows its quota, Hilda should produce more than its quota. Similarly, if Sharon produces more than its quota, Hilda should also produce more than its quota. From Hilda's standpoint, following its quota is a dominated strategy. No matter what Sharon does, the best strategy for Hilda is to exceed its quota.

Similarly for Sharon, following its quota is a dominated strategy. Hence, for both companies, the Nash equilibrium strategy is to produce more than the quota.

We call this situation a *cartel's dilemma* because both companies know that, if they can cooperate, then they can increase their profit. The snag, however, is that when each individual company acts independently, it will decide to exceed its quota. The final outcome is that the two companies produce at a competitive rather than monopoly level.

Progress check   **Progress Check 10C** Referring to Table 10.3, use the arrow technique to identify the Nash equilibrium strategies.

Nonequilibrium Strategies

We have explained how to analyze a strategic situation using the concept of a Nash equilibrium. Given that the other players choose their Nash equilibrium strategies, each party's best choice is its own Nash equilibrium strategy. But, what if some party does not follow its Nash equilibrium strategy? Then the other parties may find it better to deviate from their respective Nash equilibrium strategies.

For example, refer to Table 10.1, which describes the strategic situation between Merkur Engineering and Jupiter Elevator. Jupiter's Nash equilibrium strategy is to visit England, while Merkur's Nash equilibrium strategy is to cover Germany. Suppose, however, that Merkur decides, for some reason, to cover England and that Jupiter has this information. Then, Jupiter can win more orders by visiting Germany rather than England.

Accordingly, in the battle for the new orders, if one party does not follow its Nash equilibrium strategy, then it may be better for the other party to choose a strategy that is not a Nash equilibrium strategy.

In other situations, however, it may be better for a party to stick to its Nash equilibrium strategy even if the other does not follow its Nash equilibrium strategy. These are cases where the other strategies are dominated.

Consider, for instance, the cartel's dilemma in Table 10.3. Suppose that Sharon decides to follow its quota. Hilda should still produce more than its quota. The alternative strategy—following the quota—is dominated.

OPEC: Dilemma of an Oil Cartel

Like any other cartel, OPEC suffers from the problem that individual members prefer to exceed their quotas. No matter what the other members do, the best strategy for each member is to cheat. This explains the concern of Iran's oil minister Gholamreza Aqazadeh at the November 1994 meeting: "I hope everybody will agree to the quota without any violations in the next year."

The actual behavior of OPEC members in 1995 was consistent with our game theory analysis. By November 1995, it was estimated that OPEC was exceeding its total quota by 900,000 barrels per day, with Venezuela accounting for one-third of the excess production.

Source: "Producers Maintain Oil Output Ceilings," *South China Morning Post* (November 23, 1994), Business Post, p. 14; "OPEC Fears Quota Cheats May Hurt Price," *South China Morning Post* (November 23, 1995), Business Post, p. 9.

The Prisoners' Dilemma

The cartel's dilemma is just one concrete application of a general strategic situation called the *prisoners' dilemma*. Greg and Susan stole a handbag and have been apprehended by the police. The police do not have sufficient evidence to convict them of theft. The only witnesses to the theft are the two suspects.

The chief of police has put Greg and Susan into separate interview rooms. In each room, the police interrogator is offering the suspect a deal: "If the other suspect doesn't confess, but you do, we'll give you a reward of $1000." Each suspect knows that if neither confesses, they will be let off. If one confesses while the other does not, then the confessing suspect will receive the $1000 reward, while the other will be fined $2000 for theft. If both confess, each will be fined $1000.

Each suspect must choose between confessing and not confessing. Table 10.4 represents the game in strategic form.

For Greg, the strategy of not confessing is dominated by the strategy of confessing. The same is true for Susan. The Nash equilibrium is for both suspects to confess—even though both would be better off if they did not confess.

Source: A.W. Tucker, "A Two-Person Dilemma," mimeo, Stanford University, May 1950.

Table 10.4 Prisoners' dilemma

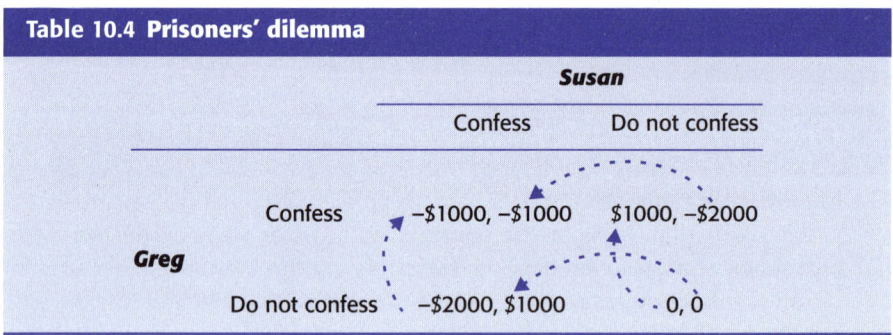

	Susan	
	Confess	Do not confess
Greg Confess	−$1000, −$1000	$1000, −$2000
Do not confess	−$2000, $1000	0, 0

3 Randomized Strategies[4]

When the various parties act strategically, it seems reasonable for them to choose Nash equilibrium strategies. In some situations, however, there is no Nash equilibrium of the type that we have been considering. To illustrate, let us

---

[4]This section is more advanced. It may be omitted without loss of continuity.

Table 10.5 Modified battle for new orders

		Merkur	
		Cover England	Cover Germany
Jupiter	Visit England	2, −2	3, −3
	Visit Germany	3, −3	2, −2

modify the situation between Jupiter Elevator and Merkur Engineering. Suppose that Table 10.5 represents the game in strategic form.

For Merkur, covering England no longer is dominated by covering Germany. Specifically, if Jupiter visits England, then Merkur would prefer to cover England, while, if Jupiter visits Germany, then Merkur would prefer to cover Germany.

By applying the arrow technique to Table 10.5, we can see that there is no Nash equilibrium in "pure strategies": No cell has all the arrows leading inward. A *pure strategy* is one that does not involve randomization. In Table 10.5, Jupiter has two pure strategies, visit England or Germany, and Merkur also has two pure strategies, cover England or Germany.

Although there is no Nash equilibrium in pure strategies, there is another way for Jupiter and Merkur to act. Essentially, Jupiter does not want Merkur to know or predict which country it will visit. One way by which Jupiter can keep Merkur in the dark is to randomize the choice between visiting England and Germany. If Jupiter randomizes its choice, the company itself will not know whether it will be visiting England or Germany. Then, of course, Merkur will not know either.

Similarly, Merkur does not want Jupiter to know or predict which country it will cover. If Merkur randomizes its decision, Jupiter cannot guess or learn which country Merkur will cover.

Under a **randomized strategy,** the party specifies a probability for each of the alternative pure strategies and chooses a pure strategy randomly according to the probabilities. The various probabilities must add up to 1.

A randomized strategy is a strategy for choosing among the alternative pure strategies in accordance with specified probabilities.

Nash Equilibrium in Randomized Strategies

Suppose that Jupiter adopts the following randomized strategy: visit England with probability 1/2 and Germany with probability 1/2. To implement this strategy, Jupiter's president marks a coin with "England" on one side and "Germany" on the other side, then gives the coin to her sales manager. She then orders the sales manager to toss the coin and fix the visit schedule according to which side of the coin faces up.

Given that Jupiter has chosen this randomized strategy, how should Merkur act? Referring to Table 10.5, let us calculate the expected consequence for Merkur from covering England. It will lose two orders if Jupiter visits England or three orders if Jupiter visits Germany. Hence, Merkur's expected return from covering England is $(-2 \times 1/2) + (-3 \times 1/2) = -5/2$, that is, a loss of 5/2 orders. Simlarly, we can calculate the expected consequence to Merkur of covering Germany. It is $(-3 \times 1/2) + (-2 \times 1/2) = -5/2$ orders, which is identical to the expected consequence of covering England.

What should Merkur do? Since it gets the same expected consequence from its two pure strategies, it is indifferent to the two. Accordingly, it would be willing to randomize between the two strategies. Specifically, suppose that Merkur covers England with probability 1/2.

Then, we must consider how Jupiter will act. If Jupiter visits England, its expected consequence is $(2 \times 1/2) + (3 \times 1/2) = 5/2$, meaning that it will win 5/2 orders. If Jupiter visits Germany, its expected consequence is $(3 \times 1/2) + (2 \times 1/2) = 5/2$, which is identical to the expected consequence of visiting England. Therefore, given Merkur's strategy, Jupiter is indifferent to visiting England or Germany.

A Nash equilibrium in randomized strategies is like a Nash equilibrium in pure strategies: Given that the other players choose their Nash equilibrium strategies, each party's best choice is its own Nash equilibrium strategy. The following randomized strategies constitute a Nash equilibrium in the modified battle for the new orders: Jupiter visits England with probability 1/2 and Merkur covers England with probability 1/2.

Suppose that Jupiter has adopted the Nash equilibrium strategy of visiting England with probability 1/2. Suppose further that Merkur has learned Jupiter's strategy through a spy. How can Merkur exploit this information? The answer is that it cannot—as we have calculated earlier, whether Merkur covers England or Germany, it will lose 5/2 orders. Generally, whenever a party adopts a Nash equilibrium strategy, the other parties cannot benefit from learning the strategy.

By contrast, suppose that Jupiter decides to visit England with certainty, which is not a Nash equilibrium strategy. Then, if Merkur learns this strategy, Merkur will cover England with certainty, thus reducing the number of orders that Jupiter wins to two. For Jupiter, this is worse than the 5/2 orders that it would get from the Nash equilibrium with randomized strategies.

We should emphasize that the advantage of randomization comes from being unpredictable. To implement the randomized strategy, Jupiter must leave the direction of its visit to the coin toss. Jupiter must not make any conscious decision on the choice of country. If it chooses the country in a conscious way, Merkur may be able to guess or learn Jupiter's direction and cover the countries accordingly.

Progress Check 10D Referring to Table 10.5, suppose that Jupiter visits England with probability 2/5. Calculate the expected consequences for Merkur if it covers (1) England and (2) Germany.

Progress check

Solving the Equilibrium

Having understood the usefulness of randomization, we must learn how to determine the Nash equilibrium probabilities. We can do so by using Figure 10.1, where the horizontal axis shows the probability with which Jupiter will visit England, and the vertical axis shows Merkur's loss of orders.

We draw two lines in Figure 10.1. The downward-sloping line shows Merkur's loss of orders from covering Germany as a function of the probability with which Jupiter visits England. The higher the probability that Jupiter visits England, the more orders Merkur will lose from covering Germany. The upward-sloping line shows Merkur's loss of orders from covering England as a function of the probability with which Jupiter visits England.

At the crossing point of the downward- and upward-sloping lines, Merkur will suffer the same loss of orders whether it covers England or Germany. That point marks Jupiter's Nash equilibrium probability of 1/2. We can draw a similar diagram for Merkur to find its equilibrium probability, which is also 1/2.[5]

Figure 10.1 Randomization

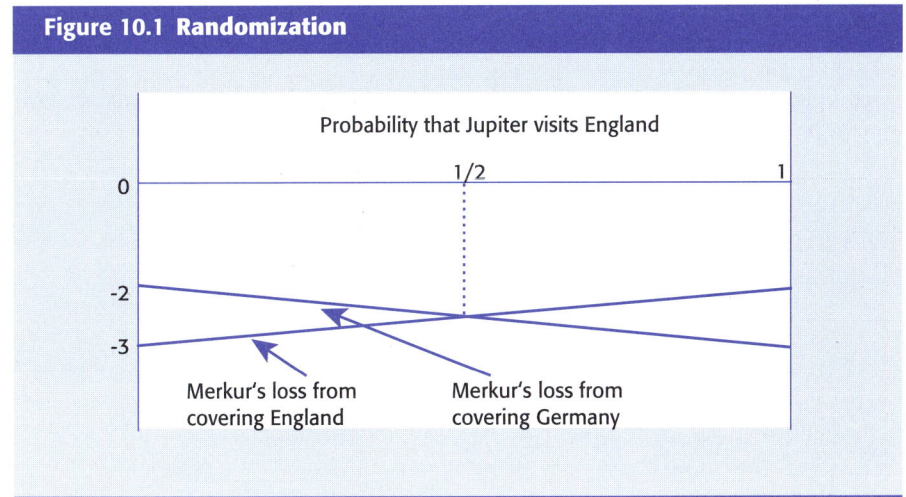

If Jupiter visits England with probability 1/2, then Merkur will receive the same consequences whether it covers England or Germany.

---

[5] This technique is based on Avinash Dixit and Barry Nalefuff, *Thinking Strategically: The Competitive Edge in Business, Politics, and Everyday Life* (New York: W.W. Norton, 1991), Chapter 7.

Another way to find the Nash equilibrium probabilities is to use algebra. In equilibrium, both Merkur and Jupiter must randomize. Suppose that Jupiter visits England with probability q. For Merkur to be willing to randomize, it must be indifferent between its alternative pure strategies: England and Germany. Given Jupiter's strategy, this means that Merkur must receive the same expected return from covering England and Germany.

To calculate Merkur's expected return from covering England, we refer to Table 10.5. If Merkur covers England, it will receive –2 if Jupiter visits England, which occurs with probability q, while Merkur will receive –3 if Jupiter visits Germany, which occurs with probability $1 - q$. Hence, Merkur's expected return is $-2(q) - 3(1 - q) = q - 3$. Similarly, we can calculate Merkur's expected return from covering Germany as $-3(q) - 2(1 - q) = -q - 2$. Equating these expected returns, we have $q - 3 = -q - 2$ and hence $q = 1/2$.

Likewise, we can determine Merkur's Nash equilibrium strategy. Suppose that Merkur covers England with probability p. For Jupiter to be indifferent to its alternative pure strategies, it must receive the same expected gain in orders from visiting England and Germany. This means that $2p + 3(1 - p) = 3(p) + 2(1 - p)$, or $p = 1/2$.

Price Promotions: Randomization in Retailing

For retailers such as supermarkets, a major competitive challenge is how to attract price-sensitive customers without sacrificing profit from the less price-sensitive segment. The typical retailer has two alternative pure strategies: maintain a high price or offer a discount price.

Consider the high-price strategy. This may extract the buyer surplus of the less price-sensitive customers but fails to attract the price-sensitive customers. Further, it exposes the retailer to a competitor setting a discount price. By contrast, if the retailer chooses the alternative discount-price strategy, it will attract price-sensitive customers but must forgo the full buyer surplus of the less price-sensitive customers.

There is an intermediate alternative: randomize between the high price and the discount price. When a retailer adopts a randomized pricing strategy, its pricing will not be predictable. It then will be more difficult for competitors to take away potential customers. In retailing, a strategy of randomization is an effective way of mitigating the intensity of competition.

Note that the retailer should discount its price at random and not in a predictable way. Suppose, for instance, that Safeway Supermarket announces that it will cut the price of Huggies diapers by 10% in the first week of every month. Competing stores can then respond with even lower prices in the first week of each month, thus, undermining Safeway's discount. This example shows that price discounts must be random and not predictable.

4 *Competition vis-à-vis Coordination*

In the original battle for the new orders (Table 10.1), if we add the consequences for Jupiter and Merkur in each cell, we get a sum of 0 in every cell. The situation is a *zero-sum game*. Similarly, the modified battle for the new orders (Table 10.5) is also a zero-sum game.

A **zero-sum game** is a strategic situation where one party can become better off only if another is made worse off. A zero-sum game is the extreme of competition: There is no way for all parties to become better off. Note that a strategic situation can be a zero-sum game even if the consequences for the various parties do not add up to 0 in every cell of the game in strategic form. If the consequences for the various parties add up to the same constant in every cell of the game in strategic form, then one party can become better off only if another is made worse off. Accordingly, such a strategic situation is also a zero-sum game.

> A **zero-sum game** is a strategic situation where one party can become better off only if another is made worse off.

Coordination

Many strategic situations are not zero-sum games. Consider the following example. Suppose that there are two different technologies for a database program: Orange and Green. From the user's viewpoint, the two technologies are equally effective. It would be beneficial if all users adopt the same software, however. This would facilitate the sharing and exchange of databases. By contrast, users adopting different technologies would have more difficulty in sharing and exchanging databases.

This example of database software illustrates a **network effect.** There is a *network effect* in the demand for a product if the benefit to one user depends on the total number of other users.

> A **network effect** arises when the benefit from a good or service depends on the total number of other users.

Table 10.6 presents a game in strategic form that describes the situation facing two potential users, Venus, Inc., and Sol Corporation. Each must choose between the Orange and Green database programs. In Table 10.6, each cell shows the consequences for Venus and Sol, respectively. Recall that the two users will benefit if they both adopt the same software. Hence, we represent the benefit to Venus and Sol by 1.5 each when they both choose the Orange

Table 10.6 Adopting database software

		Sol Corp.	
		Orange	Green
Venus, Inc.	Orange	1.5, 1.5	1, 1
	Green	1, 1	1.5, 1.5

program. If they choose different programs, then each will get a benefit of 1. The two programs are equally effective; hence, if both companies choose the Green program, their benefits are also 1.5 each.

A **positive-sum game** is a strategic situation where one party can become better off without another being made worse off.

Let us check whether the strategic situation facing Venus, Inc., and Sol Corporation is a zero-sum game. If both choose the Orange program, their total benefit is 1.5 + 1.5 = 3 units. If they choose different programs, their total benefit is 1 + 1 = 2 units. If they both choose the Green program, their total benefit is 1.5 + 1.5 = 3 units. Accordingly, Venus and Sol do not face a zero-sum game. Rather, their situation is a **positive-sum game**. In a *positive-sum game,* one party can become better off without another being made worse off.

As Table 10.6 suggests, the situation of Venus and Sol is essentially one of coordination rather than competition. If the two users can coordinate on the same software, both will benefit. If, however, they fail to coordinate, both will suffer. Strategic situations involving coordination are positive-sum games.

Let us apply the arrow technique to analyze the Nash equilibria in Table 10.6. There are two Nash equilibria in pure strategies. In one, both users choose the Orange program; in the other equilibrium, both users choose the Green program.[6]

Progress check

Progress Check 10E Check whether the cartel's dilemma (Table 10.3) is a zero-sum game.

Focal Point

Previously, we discussed why it is reasonable to adopt a Nash equilibrium strategy. In situations of coordination, there is an additional reason to adopt a Nash equilibrium strategy. Suppose that the various parties are able to talk to one another before making their choices and they agree on how to act. Then, a Nash equilibrium is a good basis for discussion because, by definition, Nash equilibrium strategies are self-enforcing in the sense that, if one party expects the others to follow their Nash equilibrium strategies, then its best choice is its own Nash equilibrium strategy.

For instance, in the situation facing Venus, Inc., and Sol Corporation, there are two Nash equilibria in pure strategies. This presents the companies with the question of which strategy to adopt. Since the essential issue is coordination between the two companies, it is reasonable that they meet to agree on one choice.

If Venus and Sol discuss their choices, they might easily agree on one program, say, the Orange software. Then, when they make their purchases, if each expects the other to buy the Orange software, its own best choice is also the

[6] In addition to the two Nash equilibria in pure strategies, there is also a Nash equilibrium where both parties randomize with probability 1/2.

Credit Cards: Coordinating Consumers and Merchants

Until the mid-1980s, the American market for general-purpose credit cards was dominated by MasterCard and Visa. The profitability of the industry attracted two new entrants. American Express introduced Optima, while Sears launched the Discover Card. This presented consumers and merchants with the issue of which, if any, of these new cards to patronize.

For simplicity, let us ignore MasterCard and Visa and focus on the choice, for consumers and merchants, between Optima and Discover. The major considerations for an individual choosing between the two credit cards are the annual fee, interest rate, and how widely the cards can be used. For a merchant deciding whether to accept a credit card, two important factors are the cardholder base and the percentage fee that the merchant must pay on each transaction.

Suppose that, other things equal, consumers and merchants consider that American Express and Sears provide equally good service, making the two credit cards equivalent. Then the situation is purely one of coordination: Consumers and merchants want to adopt the same card. If consumers and merchants choose different cards, neither group receives any benefit. If both consumers and merchants choose the same card, both groups receive a benefit, which we represent by the number 1 in Table 10.7. The entries in the cells are the benefits of consumers and merchants, respectively.

There are two Nash equilibria in pure strategies: Both groups choose Discover or both groups choose Optima. Obviously, Sears, which owned the Discover Card, preferred the equilibrium where consumers and merchants choose Discover. The question for Sears was how to push the market to that equilibrium.

Sears moved on two fronts. While other credit-card issuers charged annual fees of $20 or more, Sears pulled in consumers by not charging an annual fee for the Discover Card. It also offered cardholders a novel cash rebate based on the value of their annual purchases. In addition, Sears attracted merchants by offering lower transaction fees.

Once Discover Card gained a critical mass of cardholders and merchants, the choices of cardholders and merchants became self-reinforcing. As more consumers subscribed, more merchants accepted the card, leading still more consumers to subscribe. By 1993, within seven years of its launch, the Discover Card had secured 40 million cardholders and 1.88 million merchants, becoming the United States' largest single issuer of general purpose credit cards

Source: Dean Witter, Discover & Co, *1993 Annual Report*, pp. 10–1.

Table 10.7 Discover versus Optima

		Merchants	
		Discover	Optima
Consumers	Discover	1, 1	0, 0
	Optima	0, 0	1, 1

Orange software. In this way, a Nash equilibrium provides a focal point for discussion and action by the two parties.

Competition and Coordination

Some situations involve elements of both competition and coordination. Consider a city with two TV stations, Channel Zeta and Channel Delta. Market research shows that the demand for a news program peaks at 8:00 PM, so both stations want to schedule their evening news at 8:00 PM. If, however, both stations broadcast their news at the same time, they will both be worse off than if one broadcasts at 8:00 PM and the other at 7:30 PM.

We construct the strategic form of this situation in Table 10.8. Each station has two pure strategies: broadcast at 7:30 PM or at 8:00 PM. In each cell, we present the profits to Channels Zeta and Delta, respectively. If both stations broadcast their news at 7:30 PM, then they will get a profit of $1 million a month each. If one broadcasts at 7:30 PM while the other takes the 8:00 PM slot, then the station with the 7:30 PM slot will earn $3 million, while the station with the 8:00 PM slot will earn $4 million. Finally, if both stations broadcast their news at 8:00 PM, then they will get a profit of $2.5 million each.

By adding the profits of the two TV stations in each cell of Table 10.8, we see that the situation is a positive-sum game. The total profit of the two TV stations is not a constant. It is largest when they take different time slots. The next highest total profit arises when both stations broadcast at 8:00 PM. The total profit is lowest when both stations broadcast at 7:30 PM. The two TV stations need to coordinate and avoid scheduling their evening news at the same time.

While the battle for the evening news involves coordination, it also has an element of competition. Both stations will be better off if they schedule their news at different times. But one station will benefit relatively more—the station that gets the 8:00 PM slot. Accordingly, there are elements of competition as well as coordination.

Applying the arrows technique, we can find the Nash equilibria. As in the situation of choosing the database software, there are two Nash equilibria in

Table 10.8 Battle for the evening news

		Channel Delta	
		7:30 PM	8:00 PM
Channel Zeta	7:30 PM	1, 1	3, 4
	8:00 PM	4, 3	2.5, 2.5

pure strategies: Channel Zeta gets the 8 o'clock slot and Channel Delta takes 7:30 PM, or Delta gets the 8 o'clock slot and Zeta takes 7:30 PM.[7]

Maximin: An Alternative Approach to Strategic Decisions

We have focused on choosing strategies according to the concept of a Nash equilibrium. Another way of making strategic decisions is the very conservative **maximin** approach. This assesses each strategy according to the worst that could happen: the minimum gain. It advocates choosing the strategy that provides the largest possible minimum gain.

To illustrate, consider the original battle for the new orders (Table 10.1). For Jupiter, if it visits England, the worst that could happen is that Merkur covers England, giving Jupiter only two orders. If Jupiter visits Germany, the worst that could happen is that Merkur covers Germany, giving Jupiter only one order. So, between Germany and England, Jupiter's maximin strategy is to visit England.

As for Merkur, if it covers England, the worst that could happen is that Jupiter visits Germany, causing a loss of three orders. If Merkur covers Germany, the worst that could happen is that Jupiter visits England, resulting in a loss of two orders. So, Merkur's maximin strategy is to cover Germany.

Notice that the strategies where Jupiter visits England and Merkur covers Germany are not a Nash equilibrium. Generally, the maximin approach need not coincide with a Nash equilibrium.

A **maximin** approach assesses each strategy according to the worst that could happen (the minimum gain), choosing the strategy that provides the largest possible minimum gain.

5 Sequencing

So far, we have focused on situations where the various parties move simultaneously. However, in many business situations, the parties move one at a time. We shall see that the best strategy may be quite different if the parties move in sequence. To organize thinking about a strategic situation in which the various

---

[7]There is also an equilibrium strategies randomized, where each station chooses 7:30 PM with probability 1/7 and 8:00 PM with probability 6/7.

parties act in sequence, we use the **game in extensive form.** An *extensive form* explicitly shows the sequence of moves and the corresponding outcomes. It consists of nodes and branches: A node represents a point at which a party must choose a move, while the branches leading from a node represent the possible choices at the node.

Let us apply this concept to the battle for the evening news where Channel Zeta can schedule its news before Delta. Figure 10.2 is a game in extensive form that represents the situation of the two TV stations. The first node, A, is on the extreme left. At that node, Channel Zeta must choose between 7:30 PM (the upper branch) and 8:00 PM (the lower branch). Channel Delta has the next move. Delta's node depends on Zeta's choice. If Zeta has chosen 7:30 PM, then Delta will be at node B and must decide between the two branches of 7:30 PM and 8:00 PM. If Zeta has chosen 8:00 PM, then Delta will be at node C and must decide between the two branches of 7:30 PM and 8:00 PM.

The consequences for Channel Delta of 7:30 PM or 8:00 PM depend on Zeta's choice. At the end of each branch, we mark the profits to Zeta and Delta, respectively. If Zeta chooses 7:30 PM and Delta also chooses 7:30 PM, they both receive $1 million profit. If Zeta chooses 7:30 PM while Delta chooses 8:00 PM, then Zeta makes $3 million and Delta earns $4 million. If Zeta chooses 8:00 PM while Delta chooses 7:30 PM, then Zeta makes $4 million and Delta earns $3 million. Finally, if both stations choose the peak time of 8:00 PM, they both earn $2.5 million.

Figure 10.2 Battle for the evening news: Extensive form

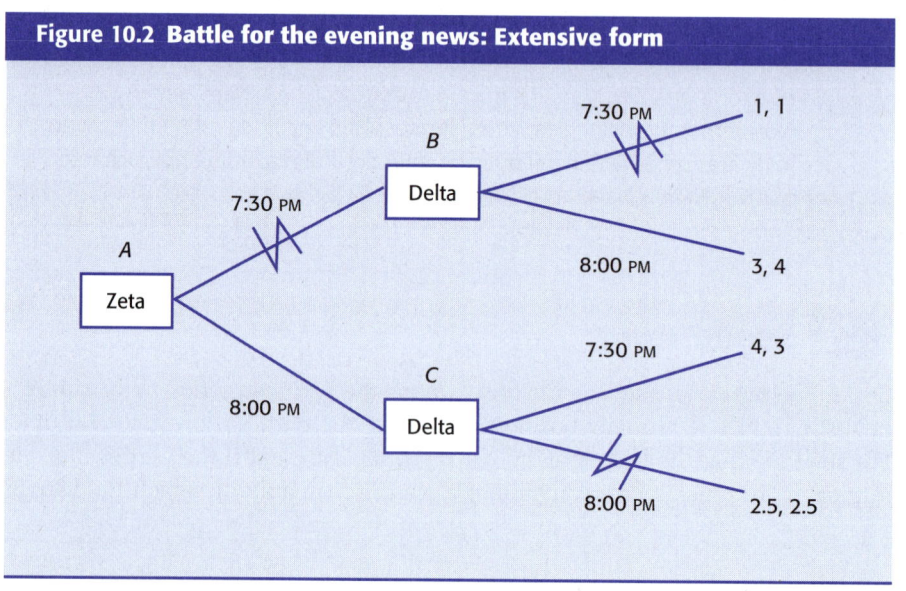

At node B, Delta will choose 8:00 PM. At node C, Delta will choose 7:30 PM. By backward induction, at node A, Zeta will choose 8:00 PM.

Backward Induction

How should the two stations act? We solve the extensive form by **backward induction,** which means looking forward to the final nodes and reasoning backward toward the initial node. We can use this procedure to identify the best strategies for the two stations. There are two final nodes: B and C. At node B, Channel Delta can choose 7:30 PM, which yields $1 million, or it could choose 8:00 PM, which yields $4 million. Clearly, at node B, Delta would choose 8:00 PM. Accordingly, we cancel the 7:30 PM branch. Now, consider node C. Here, Delta must choose between 7:30 PM, which yields $3 million, or 8:00 PM, which yields $2.5 million. It will choose 7:30 PM, so we cancel the 8:00 PM branch.

Having determined how Channel Delta will act at each of its two possible nodes, B and C, we work back to consider the initial node, A. At node A, if Zeta chooses 7:30 PM, it can foresee that Delta will choose 8:00 PM, so Zeta will earn $3 million. On the other hand, if Zeta chooses 8:00 PM, it can foresee that Delta will choose 7:30 PM, so Zeta will earn $4 million. Therefore, Zeta should choose 8:00 PM. Accordingly, in the battle for the evening news, when Zeta can move first, it will choose the 8:00 PM slot, while Delta will take the 7:30 PM time.

Equilibrium Strategy

In a game in extensive form, a party's **equilibrium strategy** consists of a sequence of its best actions, where each action is decided at the corresponding node. In the battle for the evening news, when Channel Zeta can move first, Zeta's equilibrium strategy is to choose the 8:00 PM slot, while Channel Delta's equilibrium strategy is take the 7:30 PM time.

We have assumed that Channel Zeta could move before Channel Delta. If Delta can move first, then the game in extensive form will be like Figure 10.2, except that Delta would schedule its broadcast time at node A, and Zeta would schedule its broadcast time at node B or C. Then, Delta's equilibrium strategy would be to take the 8:00 PM slot, and Zeta's equilibrium strategy would be to settle for 7:30 PM.

To decide on a strategy in a situation where the parties move in sequence, the basic principle is to look forward and anticipate the other parties' responses. So, when Channel Delta can set its schedule before its competitor, Delta must look forward and anticipate how Zeta will respond to each of Delta's choices. In this way, Delta anticipates that, if it chooses 7:30 PM, then Zeta would choose 8:00 PM, while if it chooses 8:00 PM, then Zeta would choose 7:30 PM. By this procedure of backward induction, Delta and Zeta can determine their equilibrium strategies.

The concept of equilibrium strategy in a game in extensive form is different from that of the Nash equilibrium strategy in a game in strategic form. In a strategic form, the parties act simultaneously, and a party's Nash equilibrium strategy is the best strategy given that the other parties adopt their respective Nash equilibrium strategies. By contrast, in an extensive form, the parties move in sequence, and a party's equilibrium strategy is the sequence of the best actions for that party, where each action is decided at the corresponding node.

In the battle for the evening news, we have shown that, when the two stations move simultaneously, there are three Nash equilibria. But when the stations move in sequence, there is only one equilibrium. In the battle for the evening news, the equilibrium in the extensive form is also a Nash equilibrium in the corresponding strategic form. In other cases, however, the equilibrium in the extensive form may not be a Nash equilibrium in the corresponding strategic form. Accordingly, when analyzing a strategic situation, it is important to consider carefully the structure of the moves: Do the parties move simultaneously or sequentially?

Progress check

Progress Check 10G Suppose that Channel Delta can set its schedule before Zeta. Using a suitable game in extensive form, illustrate this sequence of moves and analyze the two stations' equilibrium strategies.

Who Takes Care of the Baby?

A major issue among professional couples is who, husband or wife, stays at home to care for the baby. Elena and Frank are both equally successful in their professional careers and are equally proficient in caregiving. Then, there are two possible Nash equilibria in pure strategies. In one equilibrium, Frank stays at home to look after the baby while Elena continues her professional career. In the other equilibrium, the roles are reversed.

What if Elena and Frank work for the same organization and they have a choice between four weeks' paid maternity or paternity leave? Who should take the leave? Let us see how the decision on taking the leave may determine who stays at home to look after the baby in the long term as well.

If Elena takes four weeks' paid maternity leave, then by end of the leave, she will be relatively more attached to the baby and more proficient at caregiving. Hence, it is more likely that she will become the long-term caregiver. By contrast, if Frank took four weeks' paid paternity leave, he would be more likely to stay at home in the long term.

As this example shows, where husband and wife have similar professional prospects and proficiency in caregiving, the long-term issue of who stays at home to look after the baby may turn on such minor points as whether they choose maternity or paternity leave.

Source: Rhona Mahony, *Kidding Ourselves: Breadwinning, Babies, and Bargaining Power* (New York: Basic Books, 1995), pp. 193–6.

6 *Strategic Moves*

In the introduction, we asked why most lithographers number all the copies they make from a plate and why some lithographers destroy their plates after printing a specified number of copies. Let us consider lithography from the customer's standpoint. The value of a lithograph, like any other work of art or indeed any product in general, depends on the supply. In the case of a lithograph, the supply is the number of copies that the artist has printed or will print.

Lithography is a business with significant economies of scale. Once the cost of preparing the plate has been incurred, the lithographer can generate more prints for the minor cost of ink and paper. So, after producing an initial 30 prints, the lithographer may consider selling another 30 at a lower price. Provided that the marginal revenue covers the marginal cost, the lithographer will earn additional profits. Indeed, having sold the second batch of 30, the lithographer may produce a third batch. Generally, the lithographer always has an incentive to continue producing more prints so long as the marginal revenue covers the marginal cost.

We can represent the lithographer's actions by a game in extensive form, Figure 10.3. To analyze the situation, we must look forward to the final nodes and reason backward toward the initial node. At node C, the lithographer considers whether the marginal revenue of additional sales will cover the marginal cost. If so, she will then generate more prints. Working back to node B, consumers will decide not to buy: They would rather wait for the lithographer to cut the price at node C.

The lithographer needs some way to convince potential buyers that she will not keep producing more prints. One way is to specify the total number of prints and number each copy; for instance, "5/30" means the 5th of 30 copies.

Figure 10.3 Lithographer's incentive

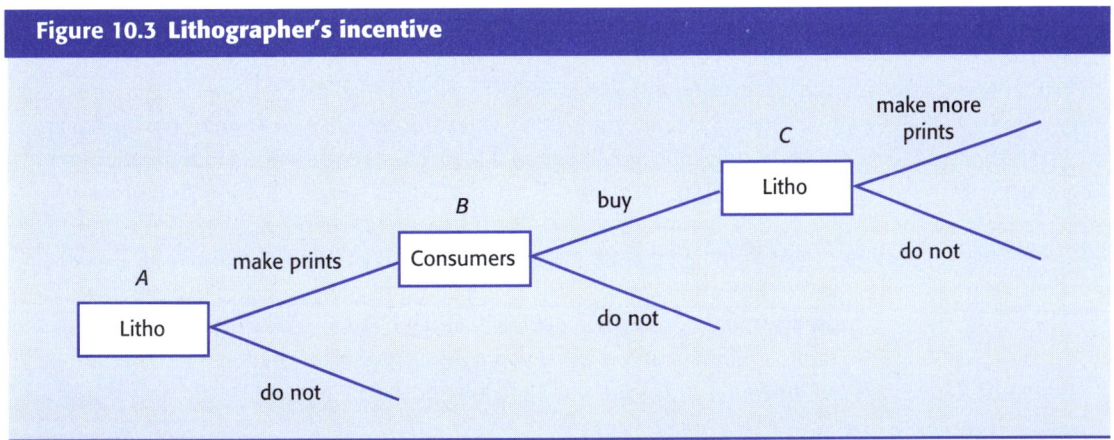

At node C, the lithographer will generate more prints. By backward induction, at node B, consumers will choose not to buy.

Numbering the prints, however, does not affect the lithographer's incentive to produce more copies in the future, so potential buyers may still be wary.

A definitive way to resolve this problem is for the lithographer to destroy the plates after printing the initial set of copies. Then, buyers can be confident that there will be no further prints, and they will be more willing to purchase.

A **strategic move** is an action to influence the beliefs or actions of other parties in a favorable way.

The lithographer's destruction of her plates is an example of a **strategic move.** A *strategic move* is an action to influence the beliefs or actions of other parties in a favorable way. Typically, a strategic move requires the party making the move to deliberately restrict its own freedom of action. For instance, by destroying her plates, the lithographer prevents herself from producing more prints in the future. This self-imposed restriction is a way to assure collectors that the supply will be limited.

Notice that the lithographer's strategic move involves a real cost. Once the plates have been destroyed, it will not be possible to produce more prints even if all the initial buyers want to have more.

Strategic Move: Airbus Product Line

One of an airline's major costs is maintenance and repair. This involves keeping stocks of specialized tools, equipment, and spare parts as well as having personnel trained on the relevant aircraft. To the extent that different aircraft from a single manufacturer share common parts and technology, an airline can reduce the costs of maintenance and repair if it buys all its aircraft from the same manufacturer.

Airbus and Boeing, the world's leading manufacturers of international civil jet transports, aim to produce a full line of aircraft. A full product line, covering all the major segments as defined by capacity and operating range, will block opportunities for potential competitors to enter the market.

Suppose, instead, that a leading manufacturer leaves out some segment, say, jets to carry more than 500 passengers. This gap will present an entry point for a potential competitor. Once the potential competitor has sold this plane to an airline, the airline must invest in the specialized tools, equipment, spare parts, and personnel. Then, that airline will be relatively more amenable to buying other types of aircraft from the competitor.

Accordingly, a key element in the strategy of Airbus is to produce a full line of planes. Plugging a gap in the line is a strategic move. In assessing the profits from introducing a new aircraft type, the manufacturer should consider the impact on potential competitors as well as the marginal revenue and marginal cost from that particular aircraft.

Source: "Airbus 'must bag half of world market in 5 years'," *Straits Times* (February 15, 1997), p. 34.

Credibility

The battle for the evening news is another setting where strategic moves are possible. By Table 10.8, if both stations move simultaneously, then there are two possible Nash equilibria in pure strategies: One station (either Channel Delta or Channel Zeta) gets the 8:00 PM slot and the competitor settles for 7:30 PM. By contrast, if one station can set its schedule before the other, then it can secure the lucrative 8:00 PM slot.

Suppose that Delta announces that it wants the 8:00 PM slot. Is this sufficient to persuade Zeta to settle for 7:30 PM? Probably not. Delta's announcement may prompt Zeta to make its own announcement that it is scheduling its news at 8:00 PM. A strategic move must be credible to influence the beliefs or actions of other parties. A mere announcement is not very credible.

For a strategic move to be credible, it must involve sufficient commitment to persuade other parties to change their beliefs or actions. Suppose that Delta contracts with several major advertisers to broadcast their advertisements during the 8:00 PM news. Further, the contracts provide that Delta must pay several million dollars in compensation if the station changes the time of the evening news. Then, these advertising contracts are a commitment and may be enough to persuade Channel Zeta to take the 7:30 PM slot.

Let us consider another possible setting for strategic moves. Suppose that Agua Luna and Moonlight Water dominate the market for bottled water. Their products are differentiated: Agua Luna is natural spring water, while Moonlight produces distilled water. Each manufacturer must decide whether to produce 1 or 2 million bottles a year. Table 10.9 presents the game in strategic form. If both manufacturers produce 1 million bottles a year, they will get a profit of $750,000 a year each. If one manufacturer produces 2 million bottles while the other produces 1 million, then the larger producer will earn $1.1 million, while the smaller producer will earn $700,000. Finally, if both manufacturers produce 2 million bottles a year, then each will get a profit of $600,000.

Table 10.9 Competing on production capacity

		Moonlight Water	
		Produce 1 million bottles	Produce 2 million bottles
Agua Luna	Produce 1 million bottles	$750,000 $750,000	$700,000 $1,100,000
	Produce 2 million bottles	$1,100,000 $700,000	$600,000 $600,000

Assuming that the two manufacturers decide on production simultaneously, there are two Nash equilibria in pure strategies: Agua Luna produces 2 million bottles a year and Moonlight Water produces 1 million or Moonlight produces 2 million and Luna produces 1 million.

Now suppose that Agua Luna can set its production before Moonlight Water. By analyzing the game in extensive form, we can show that, in equilibrium, Agua Luna will produce 2 million bottles a year, while Moonlight Water will produce 1 million. By contrast, if Moonlight can move first, it will produce 2 million bottles a year, while Agua Luna will produce 1 million.

Moonlight would like to produce 2 million bottles a year and persuade Agua Luna to produce only 1 million. As in the battle for the evening news, a mere announcement would not be credible. A credible commitment would be for Moonlight to sign contracts with major buyers, such as catering services and supermarkets, committing it to supply 2 million bottles a year.

Let us consider another strategic move that might persuade Agua Luna to produce 1 million bottles a year. Manufacturing bottled water requires the construction of a production facility and acquiring materials, labor, and utilities. Suppose that the production facility is a large proportion of the total cost and that Moonlight builds a 2-million bottle a year facility. Will this convince the competing manufacturer, Agua Luna, to produce 1 million bottles a year?

The answer depends on the extent to which Moonlight's facility is a *sunk* cost of the bottled water business. Recall from Chapter 7 that *sunk* costs are costs that have been committed and cannot be avoided. If the entire facility cost is sunk, Agua Luna will understand that Moonlight is committed to producing 2 million bottles a year. Then, Agua Luna is likely to acquiesce. By contrast, if Moonlight also intends to expand its beer business and could easily convert the facility from water to beer, then the facility cost will not be so much sunk to the bottled water business. In this case, construction of the facility is not such a strong commitment to producing 2 million bottles of water a year.

Progress check   **Progress Check 10H** Suppose that Agua Luna can set its production before Moonlight Water. By analyzing the game in extensive form, identify the equilibrium strategies.

First Mover Advantage

In the battle for the evening news, the station that is first to commit its schedule will make the larger profit. Similarly, in the bottled water example, the manufacturer that is first to commit its production will make the larger profit.

In these settings, the first mover has the advantage. There is **first mover advantage** in any strategic situation where the party that moves first has an advantage over parties that move later. To identify whether a strategic situation involves first mover advantage, it is necessary to analyze the game in extensive form.

The first mover advantage is a concept that corporate strategists emphasize a great deal. Note, however, that the first mover advantage is not a universal rule in business or other strategic situations. In some circumstances, the follower has an advantage. For instance, in retail pricing, if one store sets its price first, then its competitors will have the opportunity to undercut it with lower prices. Similarly, in military confrontations, the party that moves first may reveal its strategy and the other side can take advantage of that information.

In the introduction of a new product category, later movers have some advantage over earlier movers. A business introducing a new product category must make considerable investments in advertising and promoting the new category as distinct from its own particular product. These expenditures on advertising and promotion of the new category will benefit all businesses introducing new products in the same category. Hence, later movers can piggyback on the advertising and promotion expenditures of the pioneer.

> A **first mover advantage** gives the party that moves first an advantage over parties that move later.

Marketing Jack Nicholson: First and Second Mover Advantage

In situations where the first mover has an advantage, the various parties will compete to move first. By contrast, where later movers have an advantage, the various parties will jockey and maneuver for the opportunity to move later. Two movies starring Jack Nicholson provide a vivid example.

The six-week Christmas season is a prime time for the movie exhibition industry. In 1992, two major studios, Columbia and Fox, both planned to release movies starring Jack Nicholson. Columbia had scheduled to release *A Few Good Men* on December 18. When Fox announced that it planned to open *Hoffa* on December 11, Columbia then advanced the release of *A Few Good Men* by one week from December 18 to December 11.

Finally, Fox postponed the opening of *Hoffa* by two weeks to December 25. The studio's executive vice-president, Tom Sherak, explained, "If *A Few Good Men* is as strong as we think it'll be, we'll get a lot of publicity for our own very good Jack Nicholson film[.]"

Source: "Yule Laugh, Yule Cry," *Business Week* (November 2, 1992).

7 *Conditional Strategic Moves*

A **conditional strategic move** is an action under specified conditions to influence the beliefs or actions of other parties in a favorable way.

Destroying plates is a costly way for a lithographer to convince art collectors that she will not make more prints in the future. In some situations, it is possible to influence the actions or beliefs of others at lower cost through **conditional strategic moves.** There are two types of conditional strategic moves: threats and promises. A **threat** is a strategic move that imposes costs under specified conditions to change the beliefs or actions of other parties. By contrast, a **promise** is a strategic move that conveys benefits under specified conditions to change the beliefs or actions of other parties.

To the extent that a threatened or promised action need not actually be carried out, the conditional strategic move has no cost. A more accurate name for an action like destroying the plates is an *unconditional strategic move* because the party taking the action does not condition it on any eventuality. An unconditional strategic move usually involves a cost under all circumstances.

A **threat** imposes costs under specified conditions to change the beliefs or actions of other parties.

A **promise** conveys benefits under specified conditions to change the beliefs or actions of other parties.

Threats

To understand threats, let us consider how companies can fend off hostile takeovers. An effective way of deterring a hostile takeover is the so-called scorched earth defense, which means destroying the company. The scorched earth defense is a very costly strategic move. Clever bankers and lawyers have devised more sophisticated defenses that are much less costly. One example is the shareholder rights plan, which has also been called the *poison pill*. As we will explain, this plan is a conditional strategic move: It comes into action only in the event of a hostile takeover.

In the introduction, we asked how a shareholder rights plan would affect the cost and hence the likelihood of a hostile takeover. Let us now address this question. Suppose that Sharon Corporation has 1 million shares, with a value of $2 each, hence, a total value of $2 million. The company has adopted a shareholder rights plan that created one right for every share of the company. Under the plan, if any party acquires 100,000 or more of Sharon's shares, then Sharon's management can activate the rights. Each right could be exercised to buy additional shares of the company at a half their value. Any rights owned by the party whose acquisition activated the rights, however, would be canceled.

Hilda, Inc., is potentially interested in taking over Sharon Corporation. Let us construct a game in extensive form to analyze the strategic interaction between Hilda and Sharon. Referring to Figure 10.4, at node *A*, Hilda must decide whether to acquire 100,000 Sharon shares with the attached rights. At node *B*, Sharon's management must choose whether to activate the rights.

Suppose that, at node *B*, Sharon's management activates the rights. This cancels Hilda's 100,000 rights. The holders of the remaining 900,000 rights will

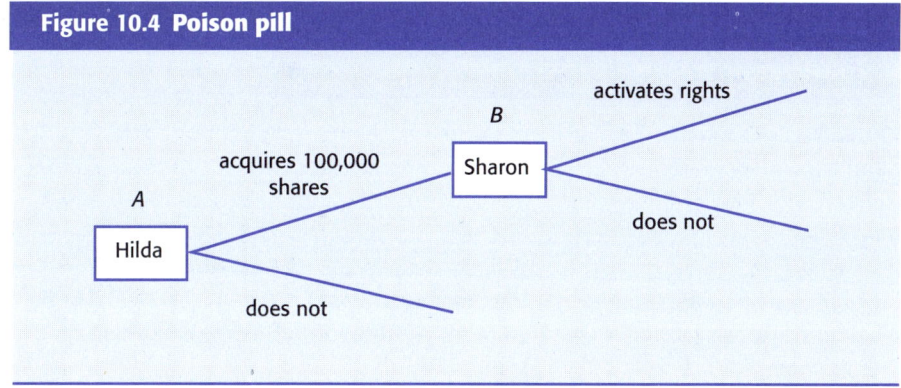

Figure 10.4 Poison pill

At node *B*, Sharon will activate the rights. By backward induction, at node *A*, Hilda will choose not to acquire the 100,000 shares.

now buy an additional 900,000 shares at half their value. The activation increases the number of shares by 900,000 to 1.9 million and also draws more money into Sharon as the holders of the 900,000 rights pay for their additional shares. The number of shares, however, increases proportionately more than the value of the company; hence, the value of each share will fall. Specifically, in the math supplement, we show that the activation reduces the value of each share to $1.38.

The activation has two implications for Hilda. First, it raises the cost to Hilda of acquiring 100% of Sharon. If Sharon's management does not activate the rights, there are 900,000 remaining shares and Hilda must pay $2 × 900,000 = $1.8 million to buy them. By contrast, if Sharon's management does activate the rights, there will be 1,900,000 remaining shares, and Hilda must pay $1.38 × 1,900,000 = $2.622 million.

Second, the activation of the rights causes a reduction in the value of Hilda's 100,000 shares from $2 × 100,000 = $200,000 to $1.38 × 100,000 = $138,000. So, Hilda will suffer a 31% loss on its investment. It is no wonder that such shareholder rights plans have been given the nickname of a *poison pill*.

In the case of Sharon Corporation, a potential bidder will look ahead from node *A* and see how Sharon's management could raise the costs of a takeover bid. Accordingly, the establishment of a shareholder rights plan significantly reduces the likelihood of a hostile takeover. If the plan succeeds in discouraging hostile takeovers, the rights need never be activated.

Threats are frequently used in negotiations. In negotiations with employers, unions may threaten a strike. For instance, a union may say, "If you don't agree to raise wages by at least 7%, we will strike." Employers fear the disruption to

Threats in Corporate Finance: The Two-Tier Takeover

In December 1994, Williams Companies, a natural gas producer and pipeline operator, announced a two-tier bid for Transco Energy Co. Williams's first tier offered to buy up to 60% of Transco's common shares for $17.50 in cash. The first-tier cash offer expired within one month and was conditional on Williams securing at least 51% of Transco's shares.

The second tier of the takeover bid would come into effect if Williams received 51% or more of Transco's shares through the cash offer. In the second tier, Williams would exercise its majority control to convert all remaining Transco shares into 5/8ths of a Williams common share. After Williams announced its takeover bid, the price of its shares dropped to $24 on the New York Stock Exchange. At this price, the value of the second tier was $5/8 \times 24 = \$15$ for each Transco share.[8]

The two-tier structure implies a threat: A Transco shareholder who does not sell his or her shares in the first tier would be squeezed out for a lower price in the second tier.

Suppose that Sally owns one share of Transco. How should she respond to Williams's first-tier offer? Figure 10.5 presents the game in extensive form between Williams and Sally. For brevity, the Figure shows only the outcomes for Sally at the ends of the final branches.

Suppose that, at node B, Sally accepts the $17.50 first-tier offer. At node C, we draw a circle to indicate that the ensuing consequences depend on the decisions of the other shareholders. (Neither Williams nor Sally makes a move at node C.) If Williams gets 51% or more of the shares, hence, gains control over Transco, then it would proceed to the second-tier squeeze out. Since Sally accepted the first-tier offer, she would have $17.50. If, however, Williams fails to secure 51% of the shares in the first tier, it would return all the shares and Sally would be back to holding one share of Transco.

Suppose, instead, that, at node B, Sally rejects the $17.50 first-tier offer. At node D, we again draw a circle to indicate that the ensuing consequences depend on the decisions of the other shareholders. If Williams wins control over Transco, then Williams would proceed to the second-tier squeeze out. Since Sally rejected the first-tier offer, she would be squeezed out in the second tier and end up with $15. If, however, Williams fails to win control in the first tier, it would return all the shares and Sally would continue to hold one share of Transco.

Looking forward from node B, not to accept the first-tier offer is a dominated strategy for Sally. However the other shareholders act, Sally will be no worse off by accepting the first-tier offer. Accordingly, Sally should accept the first-tier offer. Indeed, all the shareholders of Transco should accept the first-tier offer. Through a two-tier offer, Williams can be assured of winning control of Transco.

[8]"Williams to Buy Transco Energy for $3 Billion," *Asian Wall Street Journal* (December 13, 1994), p. 2.

operations resulting from a strike. The threat of a strike may persuade an employer to concede on wages. The occurrence of strikes, however, varies with

Figure 10.5 Two-tier takeover bid

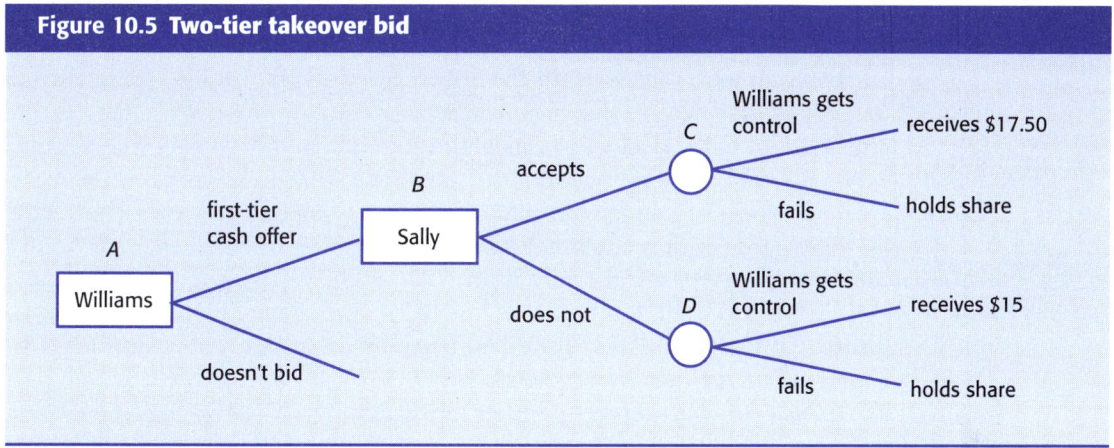

The outcomes at nodes *C* and *D* are uncertain, depending on the decisions of the various shareholders. By backward induction, at node *B*, for Sally, the outcomes if she does not accept are dominated by the outcomes if she accepts, so she will accept. At node *A*, Williams will make the first-tier cash offer.

the industry. In the introduction, we asked why strikes are so rare in professional American football.

To address this question, we analyze whether a union's threat of a strike is credible. Credibility is an issue because a strike also imposes costs on the workers themselves. During a strike, the workers must forgo part or all of their wages. In Figure 10.6, at the node B, where the union decides whether to proceed with a

Figure 10.6 Strike

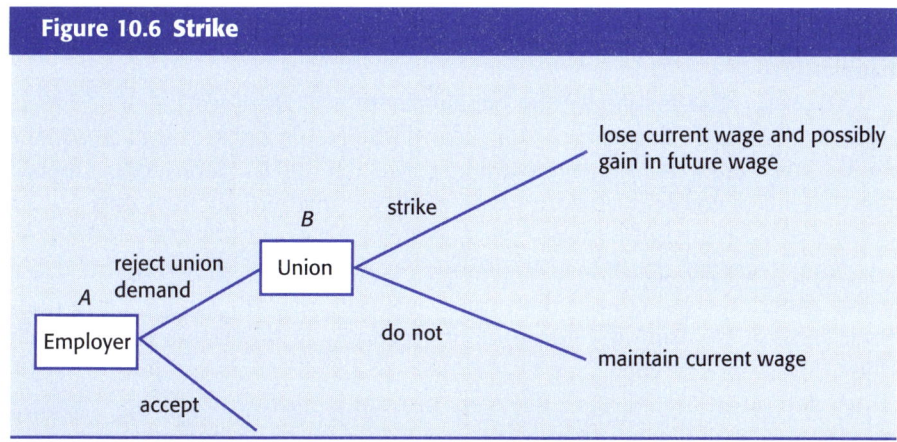

If the workers' union strikes, it will lose current wages and possibly gain higher wages in the future. If it does not strike, then it will maintain the current wage.

strike, the union must compare the consequences of a strike with those from no strike.

If the union proceeds with the strike, the workers will lose some current wages, and they may be able to convince their employer to increase their future wages. If the union decides to cancel the strike, then the workers will continue to receive their current wage. For the threat of a strike to be credible, the workers must expect to gain more from a strike than by continuing to work normally.

Compared with many other workers, the career of a professional American football player is relatively short. Like other workers, if football players strike, they are trading off current loss of income against higher wages in the future. As football players have short careers, they are not so attracted by higher wages in the future. Accordingly, football players are relatively less likely to strike than workers in other industries.

Promises

By contrast to threats, the other type of conditional strategic move is promises. For an outstanding example of a promise, we turn to banking. Most governments are concerned about the stability of their banking systems. Banks take deposits in checking and savings accounts and lend the funds to short- and long-term borrowers. This means that, generally, banks do not have enough cash at hand to repay all their depositors on short notice.

Consider a typical depositor. Every day, she must choose between maintaining her savings account with a bank and withdrawing the deposit to get cash. Cash, of course, is the safest possible investment. It, however, yields no interest. Other things equal, the depositor would rather keep the money in the savings account. If, however, she hears a rumor that the bank is in trouble, she will rush to withdraw her deposit. As all depositors rush to withdraw, the bank may run short of funds. So, rumors can bring down even financially sound banks.

To ensure the stability of the banking system, many governments provide deposit insurance. This means that, if a participating bank cannot repay the money deposited, then the government will pay all its depositors. Deposit insurance is a conditional strategic move: The government pays only in the event that the bank cannot repay.

Now, consider the effect of deposit insurance. The depositor need not worry about rumors. Even if the rumors are true, she will still get her money back, in this case, from the government. Accordingly, depositors will not withdraw their deposits when they hear rumors that their banks are in difficulties. Thus, deposit insurance can effectively prevent bank runs. If the government insures only sound banks, then government need never pay out any compensation. That is the beauty of a conditional strategic move.

8 *Repetition*

So far, we have considered strategic interactions that take place only once. Many strategic interactions, however, are repeated. Generally, the range of possible strategies is much wider in repeated interactions than in one-shot scenarios. In situations that involve coordination, the wider range of strategies may enable the various parties to achieve better outcomes than in the one-shot scenarios. Let us see how repetition can improve the outcome in two situations.

Consider the battle for the evening news. With simultaneous moves on a one-shot basis, each station will jockey and manuever for the first-mover advantage. Suppose, however, that the stations look at their situation as a repeated interaction. Then other strategies become possible. In particular, a station could adopt a strategy under which its schedule is conditioned on some independent variable.

For instance, Channel Delta could condition its news schedule on the month: broadcast at 8:00 PM in odd months and at 7:30 PM in even months. Likewise, one of Channel Zeta's strategies is to broadcast at 7:30 PM in odd months and at 8:00 PM in even months. These two strategies are an equilibrium in the repeated battle for the evening news.

Essentially, the stations alternate between the two time slots. By alternating, the stations can ensure that they achieve the efficient outcome where one station broadcasts at 8:00 PM and the other broadcasts at 7:30 PM. Each will have an equal share of the premium 8:00 PM slot. The alternating strategy will be better than fighting over the 8:00 PM slot on a one-shot basis, which might result in both stations broadcasting their news at the same time.

A cartel is another situation where repetition widens the range of possible strategies as compared with one-shot interactions. Every member of a cartel knows that, if all sellers cooperate in restricting production, they will collectively be able to increase their profits. In one-shot cartels, however, individual members have an overwhelming incentive to exceed their quotas. Table 10.3 shows the game in strategic form: Following the quota is a dominated strategy.

Let us now consider a repeated cartel, that is, a cartel that continues over an extended period of time. In a repeated cartel, a seller can adopt a strategy under which it conditions its production on the actions of another party at a earlier time. One such strategy is tit for tat: I will begin with following my quota and will continue until you exceed your quota, in which case, I shall produce more than my quota in the following month, and thereafter, I will follow your move.

A tit-for-tat strategy combines a promise with a threat. The promise is to abide by quota if the other seller follows its quota. When all sellers abide by their quotas, they can achieve profits above the competitive level. The threat is to produce more than one's quota if the other seller exceeds its quota. Whenever a seller exceeds its quota, it will depress the market price and, hence, reduce the profits of other sellers.

In a repeated cartel, the tit-for-tat strategy is an equilibrium strategy. In the tit-for-tat equilibrium, every individual seller will restrict production. Thus, when competing sellers interact over an extended period of time, it is possible to maintain a cartel and achieve profit above the competitive level.

A cartel can further improve the likelihood that individual sellers will restrict production if it extends agreement to several different markets. In a cartel that covers several markets, a seller can condition its production on the preceding actions of another party in all the markets.

For instance, in a cartel that encompasses the markets for equipment leasing and truck rentals, a seller could adopt the following tit-for-tat strategy: I will begin with abiding by my quota and will continue until you exceed your quota in any market, in which case, I shall produce more than my quota in both markets; and thereafter, I will follow your move in both markets.

The tit-for-tat strategy is an equilibrium strategy. In a cartel that extends to several markets, the tit-for-tat strategy promises a greater benefit: increased profit in all the markets if sellers restrict production. Moreover, the tit-for-tat strategy threatens a greater punishment: reduced profit in all the markets if sellers exceed their quotas.

9 *Summary*

In strategic situations, when the parties move simultaneously, there are several useful principles to follow: Avoid using dominated strategies, focus on Nash equilibrium strategies, and consider randomizing. When the parties move

Restricting Competition in Building Materials

Boral, CSR, and Pioneer International are leading manufacturers of building materials with operations throughout Australia. In 1989, the three corporations, together with Goodmix/Hymix and Rocla, supplied 95% of the market for ready-mix concrete in Brisbane. The five companies formed a cartel and agreed not to poach customers from one another. They held regular meetings to allocate sales and fix prices. The Brisbane concrete cartel continued until mid-1994.

Boral, CSR, and Pioneer were also involved in cartelizing other markets for building materials elsewhere in Australia. The three corporations fixed the prices of ready-mix concrete in Melbourne in 1978–79, as well as roof tiles in Adelaide. The geographical and product spread of the cartel would have helped to increase the incentive of individual members to abide by their quotas in each market.

Sources: "CSR, Pioneer, Boral Are Fined for Price-Fixing," *Asian Wall Street Journal* (December 5, 1995), p. 5; letter from James Lambie, Australian Competition and Consumer Commission (December 14, 1995).

sequentially, a strategy should be worked out by looking forward to the final nodes and reasoning back to the initial node.

Through conditional or unconditional strategic moves, it may be possible to influence the beliefs or actions of other parties. In some settings, the first mover has the advantage; in others, the first mover is at a disadvantage. Finally, it is important to consider whether the situation will be played just once or repeated. The range of possible strategies is wider in a repeated situation.

In a zero-sum game, one party can become better off only if another is made worse off. In a positive-sum game, one party can become better off without another being made worse off.

Key Concepts

strategy
game theory
game in strategic form
dominated strategy
Nash equilibrium
randomized strategy
zero-sum game
network effect
positive-sum game

maximin
game in extensive form
backward induction
equilibrium strategy in a game in extensive form
strategic move
first mover advantage
conditional strategic move
threat
promise

Further Reading

Two entertaining and very readable books on strategic thinking are Avinash Dixit and Barry Nalefuff's best seller, *Thinking Strategically: The Competitive Edge in Business, Politics, and Everyday Life* (New York: W.W. Norton, 1991), and Thomas C. Schelling's classic, *The Strategy of* *Conflict* (Cambridge, MA: Harvard University Press, 1980). Eric Rasmusen's *Games and Information*, 2d ed. (Cambridge, MA: Basil Blackwell, 1994), Chapters 1–6, provides a more formal yet approachable review of game theory.

Review Questions

1. Speedy Snaps is a small public company in the perfectly competitive fastener industry. Which of the following choices by Speedy are strategic?
   a. Switching deposits from Citibank to Chase Manhattan Bank.
   b. Hiring another worker for the night shift.
   c. Adopting a poison pill.

2. Explain the following concepts:
   a. Dominated strategy.
   b. Nash equilibrium.

3. Which of the following are reasons to adopt a Nash equilibrium strategy?
   a. I can minimize my expected loss.
   b. I can guarantee a minimum level of payoff.
   c. Even if the other party knows my strategy, it cannot take advantage of that information.

4. This question relies on the randomized strategies section. Referring to Table 10.6, calculate the Nash equilibrium in randomized strategies.

5. This question relies on the randomized strategies section. Some right-handed boxers also train themselves to box with their left hands. Which of the following strategies will be more effective?
   a. Throw a left-hand punch after every three right-handers.

   b. Box mainly with the right hand and throw a left-hand punch at random.

6. Referring to Table 10.1, suppose that Jupiter's visit will also generate new orders from clients who are not negotiating with Merkur. Increase Jupiter's return by 1 in every cell. Is the situation a zero-sum game?

7. Recall the choices of Venus and Sol between the Orange and Green database software (please refer to Table 10.6). Suppose that Venus can move first. Using an extensive form, analyze the equilibrium.

8. Explain the following:
   a. A strategic move.
   b. A promise.
   c. A threat.

9. Compare the following actions by a lithographer to assure her buyers. Which is more credible?
   a. She announces that she will print only 30 copies.
   b. She destroys the plates after printing 30 copies.

10. Brian has a $50,000 savings deposit at a local bank. The deposit is fully insured by the FDIC and pays 6% interest while other banks pay only 5%. Brian has just heard a rumor that the bank is in trouble. Should he withdraw his money?

Discussion Questions

1. The National Collegiate Athletic Association (NCAA) restricts the amount that colleges and universities may pay their student athletes. Suppose that there are just two colleges in the NCAA: Ivy and State. Each must choose between paying athletes according to NCAA rules or paying more.
   a. Construct a game in strategic form to analyze the choices of Ivy and State.
   b. Identify the equilibrium or equilibria.
   c. The NCAA rules have government backing. How will this affect the equilibrium or equilibria?

2. For most new films, the demand at movie theaters is highest in the first few days after opening, then tapers off. Accordingly, studios must time new releases very carefully. Two key factors affecting potential demand are the season (the Summer and Christmas vacation periods are the best times) and the timing of other releases. Suppose that both Studio Luna and Moonlight Movies are producing major action movies.
   a. The two studios simultaneously must choose between release on December 11 or 18. If both films open on December 11, each will sell 200,000 tickets. If one opens on December 11 and the other on December 18, then the early release will sell 350,000 tickets, while the later release will sell 150,000. If both open on December 18, each will sell 100,000 tickets. Construct a game in strategic form to illustrate the situation and identify the equilibrium or equilibria.
   b. The payoffs in (a) assumed that the two films were competitors. Now suppose that the publicity surrounding one movie will increase the demand for the other film. So, the total number of tickets for the two movies will be largest if both open on the same day. Adjust the data in (a) according to this new information. How does this affect the equilibrium or equilibria?

3. Automobile traffic between the mainland and Pleasant Island can cross either by ferry or through a tunnel. For simplicity, assume that total demand is 27,200 car round-trips (54,400 one-way trips) per day, and that total demand does not respond to changes in price. The tunnel charges $10 per one-way crossing and is operating near capacity. It serves 48,000 one-way crossings a day. The tunnel's costs are $480,000 a year, which do not vary with demand.

   The ferry service is slower and charges a price of $5 per crossing. Each of four ferries makes two round-trips (four trips total) a day carrying 40 cars. Annual costs are $240,000 per boat. The ferry company has several vessels on reserve.

   If the tunnel were to cut its fare to $9, it would only draw an additional 960 one-way crossings. If the ferry company were to cut its fare to $4.70, however, it could generate an additional 3200 one-way trips. If both tunnel and ferry cut prices, there would be no change in sales.
   a. Construct the following game in strategic form. Show the tunnel's strategies along the left-hand side of the strategic form, and the ferry company's strategies along the top of the strategic form. Calculate the profits of the tunnel and the ferry company for each pair of strategies on a monthly basis. Assume that there are 30 days in a month.
   b. Identify the equilibrium or equilibria.
   c. How might the equilibrium or equilibria change if the tunnel were not constrained by capacity?

4. Eastern Airways and Aero Este dominate the route to the east coast. Suppose that both airlines charge $400 for a round-trip economy class fare and that, presently, each airline has an equal share of the market. Each airline believes that, if it cuts its price by 10% while the other airline maintains its price, the elasticity of demand will be –4.0. Half of the additional customers will be new flyers, while the other half will switch from the higher-priced airline. If both airlines cut their prices by 10%, then each will have a demand elasticity of –2.0. In this case, all of the additional customers will be new flyers. Let the unit cost of each seat be constant at $200 for both airlines.

    a. Use a game in strategic form to analyze this situation. For each airline, the possible strategies are to maintain its price or to cut its price 10%. What will be the equilibrium?

    b. Suppose now that the two airlines form a revenue pool. Under this arrangement, they will contribute all their revenues to a common pool and each will get a half share of the pooled revenues. Each, however, must pay its own costs. Use a game in strategic form to analyze this revised situation. For each airline, the possible strategies are the same as in (a). What will be the equilibrium?

5. The Spanish conquistador Hernando Cortés led an expedition from the island of Cuba to conquer Mexico on the Central American mainland. The Spanish were outnumbered by the Mexican armies, and after landing in Mexico, some of Cortés's followers tried to escape back to Cuba. Cortés, however, believed that, if every knight and soldier in his expedition fought with complete determination, they would succeed in conquering Mexico. He also knew that, without total commitment, they would lose.

    In a historic move, Cortés ordered his carpenters to dismantle all their ships, and to use the timber and metal in the landward expedition. Using a game in extensive form, explain Cortés's decision (Bernal Diaz del Castillo, *The Discovery and Conquest of Mexico, 1517–1521*, trans. A.P. Maudslay [New York: Harper & Brothers, 1928], pp. 168–9).

6. A common issue among couples is what to do on the weekend. A woman may wish to go shopping, while a man would rather attend a football match. Other things equal, both would rather be together. So, the consequences if the two persons attend separate activities are relatively poor. Game theorists call this situation the *battle of the sexes*.

    a. Construct the following game in strategic form. Show the man's strategies along the left-hand side of the strategic form, and the woman's strategies along the top of the strategic form. Calculate the consequences for the man and the woman from each pair of strategies.

    b. Identify the equilibrium or equilibria.

    c. How might the equilibrium or equilibria change if the woman could move first?

7. In 1995, Apple Computer launched its new MacOS operating system. Apple faced two major challenges: persuading end users to buy computers with the new operating system and inducing independent software publishers to develop applications software based on the new MacOS.

    a. Identify the interactions between end-users' decisions whether to adopt MacOS and independent software publishers' decisions whether to develop MacOS applications.

    b. Using a suitable strategic form, identify the possible equilibria of the decisions of end-users and independent software publishers.

    c. How can Apple influence the equilibrium in its own favor?

8. In December 1994, the Williams Companies made a two-tier bid for the common shares of Transco Energy. In the first tier, Williams offered $17.50 per share in cash; in the second tier, Williams offered stock worth $15. Before the bid was announced, Transco shares were trading at $12.625. Williams conditioned its first-tier cash offer on receiving 51% or more of Transco's shares. Only if Williams gained control through the first-tier cash offer would it be able to effect the second-tier squeeze-out.

   a. Using a suitable extensive form, analyze how a Transco shareholder should respond to the cash offer.

   b. Suppose, instead, that Williams's first-tier cash offer had been unconditional. How should a Transco shareholder respond under the following conditions:

      i. She believes that Williams will get control through the first-tier cash offer.

      ii. She believes that Williams will not get control through the first-tier cash offer.

9. Lithograph collectors fear that the lithographer will use the same plates to produce more prints in the future.

   a. Explain why some lithographers destroy their plates after making a specified number of prints.

   b. Suppose a lithographer promises to buy back his prints at any time at the original sale price. Explain how this buyback offer affects the lithographer's incentive to produce additional prints in the future.

   c. Compare the strategic moves in (a) and (b) as ways of assuring art collectors that the lithographer will not use the same plates to produce more prints in the future.

10. Explain whether it will be relatively easy or difficult to maintain a cartel in the following industries:

   a. Semiconductors, where the pace of technological progress is so fast that the effective selling life of each new model is 50% shorter than that of the preceding generation.

   b. Rice, where the crop is grown throughout the world and there is a high turnover among producers.

   c. Refined oil, where the industry is relatively stable with the same producers dominating the market for many years.

Math Supplement

Let us analyze the effect of Sharon Corporation's shareholder rights plan on the value of the company's shares in the event of activation. We show that, if Sharon's management activates the rights, it will reduce the value of each share to $1.38.

Suppose that Sharon's management activates the rights and cancels Hilda's 100,000 rights. Let the value of each share become v. The holders of the remaining 900,000 rights will now buy an additional 900,000 shares at $0.5v$ each. Their payments for these shares will increase the value of the company by $0.5v \times 900,000$ to $2 million + $0.5v \times 900,000$.

Since the activation increases the number of shares by 900,000 to 1.9 million, the value of each share is the value of the company divided by the number of shares,

$$\$v = \$(2,000,000 + 0.5v \times 900,000)/1,900,000. \quad (10.1)$$

Solving, we have $2,000,000 = 1,450,000v$, which implies that $v = 1.38$.

Part III

Managing in Imperfect Markets

Chapter 11

Externalities

1 Introduction

The Walt Disney Company manages theme parks throughout the world, including Disneyland in California, Disney World in Florida, Tokyo Disneyland, and Euro-Disney near Paris. These parks attract thousands of visitors a day. In addition to spending money within the theme park, the visitors patronize nearby shops, hotels, restaurants, and transport services. In the late 1980s, the Walt Disney Company planned a large program of investments to upgrade Disneyland. Before commencing the investments, the company purchased much of the property around the theme park, including the Disneyland Hotel. Why did the company buy the surrounding property before upgrading the theme park?

Intel is the world's leading manufacturer of microprocessors for IBM-compatible personal computers. To foster consumer recognition, Intel has encouraged personal computer manufacturers to add an "Intel Inside" label to their products. Typically, Intel will share the cost of manufacturer advertising that features the "Intel Inside" label. This practice is called *cooperative advertising*. Why does Intel offer cooperative advertising?

The Internet is a global computer network based on the communications protocol transmission control protocol/internet protocol (TCP/IP). TCP/IP provides a common basis for communication among independent computer networks that use different technologies such as AppleTalk, DECnet, and Netware. In 1985, the Internet linked 200 networks with 1000 end-user computers. By April 1994, it had grown to over 30,000 networks with over 2 million end-user computers. Apparently, the more users join the Internet, the more others want to join. What explains the spiraling growth of the Internet?

Every Fourth of July, in cities all over the United States, millions of Americans gather to watch Independence Day fireworks. The fireworks attract more people than top baseball and football teams. Similarly, in Britain, thousands watch fireworks on Guy Fawkes Night. Clearly, there is a huge untapped demand for fireworks all over the world. Why don't some entrepreneurs provide this form of entertainment on a commercial basis?

An **externality** arises when the actions of one party affect others directly rather than through a market. There is no market through which Disneyland can collect a fee from nearby shops, hotels, and restaurants for its investments in new attractions. Accordingly, Disneyland's investments generate an externality for neighboring businesses.

An **externality** arises when the actions of one party affect others directly rather than through a market.

A personal computer manufacturer that advertises Intel microprocessors will generate more sales for itself as well as other manufacturers using Intel chips. There is no market through which personal computer manufacturers pay those who advertise Intel microprocessors, however. Without such a market, a computer manufacturer that advertises Intel is generating an externality for other manufacturers using Intel chips.

In this chapter, we analyze externalities and consider how they can be resolved. We will apply this analysis to explain why the Walt Disney Company bought property around Disneyland before upgrading its theme park. We will also explain why Intel offers cooperative advertising. By doing so, Intel resolves the externality from one computer manufacturer's advertisements to other manufacturers.

One type of externality worth special attention is the network externality. This explains why the Internet has been growing at an accelerating rate. Finally, we introduce the concept of a public good to explain why fireworks cannot be provided on a commercial basis.

2 *Benchmark*

An externality arises when the actions of one party affect other parties directly rather than through a market. Suppose that Luna, a major department store, is opening a 50,000-square-foot store on Main Street. To obtain the site, Luna had to outbid several other major chains. The bidding has raised the general level of rents along Main Street. The increase in rents affects other stores in the area, but this increase is not an externality because it passes through the real estate market.

Luna's new store affects other retailers in another way. Specialty retailers sell smaller ranges of products, for instance, casual wear, flowers, or shoes. Luna's new store will draw more shoppers to Main Street and, hence, generate more business for nearby specialty retailers. There is no market through which specialty retailers pay Luna for the additional business, however. Accordingly, the additional business is an externality from Luna to the specialty retailers.

Alternatively, Luna's new store may take customers away from other department stores on Main Street. The cut in business does not pass through any market; hence, it is an externality from Luna to other department stores.

A **positive externality** is a benefit to other parties that is conveyed directly rather than through a market.

A **negative externality** is a cost for other parties that is imposed directly rather than through a market.

Externalities can be positive or negative. An externality is positive if it conveys a benefit to other parties. The additional business that Luna generates for specialty retailers is a **positive externality.** By contrast, a **negative externality** imposes a cost on other parties. The business that Luna's new store takes away from other department stores along Main Street is a negative externality.

As the Luna example suggests, there are significant positive externalities in real estate. In Britain, leading banks, insurers, and other financial institutions congregate in the one square mile City of London to benefit from positive externalities among themselves. The same is true in many other countries: Financial institutions and associated professionals such as lawyers and accountants tend to cluster in the same area.

Construction of transportation facilities provides another example of externalities in real estate. Whenever the government builds a mass transportation system, it generates externalities for the owners of nearby property. For instance, construction of a subway will raise the value of retail businesses such as grocery stores and restaurants located close to the subway stations. By improving access, a subway may also raise the value of residential property.

Positive Externalities

By definition, an externality conveys a benefit or cost directly rather than through a market. So, in deciding on the levels of externalities, the source considers only the benefits and costs to itself, while ignoring the benefits and costs to others.

In the case of Luna's investment in its new Main Street store, Luna will consider its own benefit and cost and ignore the benefits and costs to other stores. Let us assume that Luna aims to maximize the profit from its investment. Our analysis will be easier if we segregate the cost of sales from the cost of the investment in the following way. Luna's profit is the difference between its benefit (revenues less the cost of sales) and the cost of the investment. To maximize profit, Luna should invest up to the point that the marginal benefit from an additional dollar in investment equals the marginal cost.

At this level of investment, however, Luna may be ignoring opportunities for additional profit from positive externalities. To understand this point, let us change our earlier setting. Suppose now that the Luna department store belongs to Group Luna and the group also owns a florist shop and a shoe store already on Main Street. Then, when deciding on the level of its investment, the group will consider the benefits and the costs to all of its stores.

Externalities in Talent: Silicon Valley

There is an exceptional concentration of computer, electronics, and related businesses in the peninsula between the San Francisco Bay and the Pacific Ocean. The area, aptly nicknamed *Silicon Valley,* is home to high-technology leaders such as Apple Computer, Hewlett-Packard, Sun Microsystems, and Varian Associates.

Two institutions, Stanford University and the Xerox Palo Alto Research Center (PARC), played key roles in fostering the development of Silicon Valley. Basic and applied research at the two institutions has provided the foundation for many successful high-tech products.

A local area network links separate personal computers over short distances. Robert Metcalfe and David Boggs invented the Ethernet local area network at the Xerox PARC. In 1979, Metcalfe left the Xerox PARC to found 3Com (the three "coms" being computer, communication, and compatibility) to serve the Ethernet compatible marketplace. 3Com has since grown to become the world's second largest manufacturer of data networking systems.

Stanford University staff and students personally established several of the most successful Silicon Valley businesses. Routers are devices that link computer networks in different locations that may use different protocols. Sandy Lerner and Len Bosack started Cisco Systems while working at Stanford University. In 1986, they left the university to run Cisco full time. The company has grown to become the world's largest manufacturer of routers and other data-networking systems.

In April 1994, two graduate students in Stanford's electrical engineering department, David Filo and Jeff Yang, started an index to the Internet. Their hobby quickly grew into Yahoo!, one of the most popular guides to the Internet's multimedia World Wide Web.

Sources: Douglas K. Smith and Robert C. Alexander, *Fumbling the Future* (New York: William Morrow, 1988), pp. 95–103; letter from Robert Metcalfe (July 16, 1996); letter from Cisco Systems (May 23, 1996); World Wide Web pages www.cisco.com and www.3com.com (May 22, 1996), www.yahoo.com (June 25, 1996).

The total benefit from Luna's investment is the sum of the benefits to every store in the group, including the new store. The group's marginal benefit from investment in the new store is the increase in benefit to the group resulting from an additional dollar of investment in the new store. The additional dollar of investment will generate benefits for all the stores. Accordingly, the group's marginal benefit is the sum of the individual marginal benefits to each of the stores.

In Figure 11.1, we illustrate the marginal benefits from investment in the new store for the new store and the two other stores. Note that each store may receive a different marginal benefit. For instance, if the florist is nearer to the new store than the shoe store, it will benefit relatively more. The stronger the positive externality, the higher the recipient's marginal benefit curve will be.

Graphically, the group's marginal benefit is the *vertical sum* of the individual marginal benefits. A vertical sum means that, at every quantity of investment, we add the corresponding heights on each of the individual marginal benefit curves. For instance, referring to Figure 11.1, if Luna invests $100,000, the florist's marginal benefit is $360,000, the shoe store's marginal benefit is $80,000, and Luna's own marginal benefit is $900,000. Hence, the sum of the marginal benefits is $1,340,000, which marks the corresponding point on the group marginal benefit curve.

In Figure 11.1, we also draw the marginal cost of investment in the new store. If Luna considers only the benefit and the cost for the new store, it would maximize profit where the store's marginal benefit equals the marginal cost, which is at an investment of $900,000. This, however, ignores the positive externalities. If Luna considers the benefits and the costs for the entire group, then it would maximize profit at the level of investment where the group marginal benefit equals the marginal cost. Referring to Figure 11.1, the profit-maximizing investment would be $929,000.

As this example shows, when the source of a positive externality considers only the benefit and the cost for itself, it overlooks an opportunity for additional profit. Referring to Figure 11.1, by increasing its investment from $900,000 to $929,000, the group can gain the shaded area in additional profit.

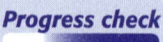
Progress check

Progress Check 11A Referring to the preceding discussion and to Chapter 2, explain the difference between the following: (1) the horizontal sum of individual demand curves is the market demand curve and (2) the vertical sum of individual marginal benefit curves is the group marginal benefit curve.

Negative Externalities

Having considered positive externalities, we next consider how to take account of negative externalities. Recall that Luna's new store will take away business from other Main Street department stores. Changing our earlier setting, let us now suppose that the Group Luna owns two department stores, the Luna as

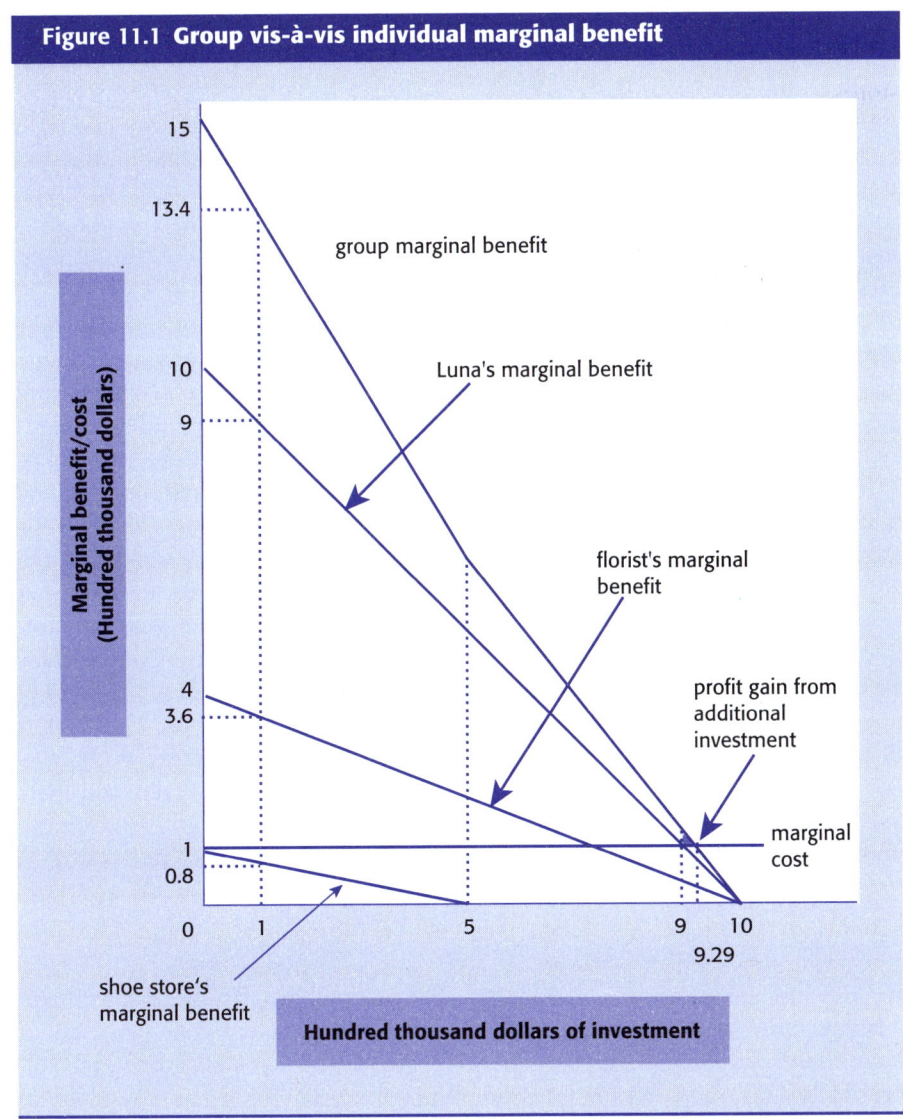

Figure 11.1 Group vis-à-vis individual marginal benefit

The group's marginal benefit is the vertical sum of the individual marginal benefits. At every quantity of investment, we add the corresponding heights on each of the individual marginal benefit curves. The group maximizes profit at an investment of $929,000, where the group marginal benefit equals the marginal cost. If Luna considers only the benefit and the cost for itself, it would invest only $900,000. By increasing its investment to $929,000, the group could gain the shaded area in additional profit.

well as the existing Sol store on Main Street, but does not own any specialty retailers. When deciding on its investment in the new Luna store, the group should consider the benefits and the costs to both department stores.

The total cost of investment in the new Luna store is the sum of the costs to both stores in the group. Accordingly, the group's marginal cost of investment in the new store is the increase in cost to the group resulting from an additional dollar of investment in the new store. This group marginal cost is the sum of the individual marginal costs for each store from an additional dollar of investment in the new store. For the new store, the marginal cost of an additional dollar of investment is just $1. For the existing store, the marginal cost is the reduction in profit arising from an additional dollar of investment in the new store.

In Figure 11.2, we illustrate the marginal costs from investment in the new store for the new store itself and the existing store. Graphically, the group's marginal cost is the vertical sum of the individual marginal costs. A vertical sum means that, at every quantity of investment, we add the corresponding heights on each of the individual marginal cost curves. For instance, at an investment of $500,000, the marginal cost for the Luna store is $100,000, while the marginal cost for the Sol store is $100,000; hence, the group marginal cost is $200,000.

In Figure 11.2, we also draw the marginal benefit from investment in the new store. If Luna considers only the benefit and the cost for the new store, it would maximize profit where the marginal benefit equals Luna's marginal cost, which is at an investment of $900,000. If, however, Luna considers the benefits and the costs for the entire group, then it would maximize profit at the level of investment where the group marginal benefit equals the marginal cost. Referring to Figure 11.2, the profit-maximizing investment is $750,000.

As this example shows, when the source of a negative externality considers only the benefit and the cost for itself, its profit will be less than the maximum possible. By Figure 11.2, if the group would reduce its investment from $900,000 to $750,000, it could increase its profit by the shaded area *abc*.

Externalities in General

If one member of a group generates positive externalities, the group maximizes profit where the sum of the marginal benefits equals the marginal cost of investment. Similarly, if one member of a group generates negative externalities, then the group maximizes profit where the marginal benefit equals the sum of the marginal costs of investment. Generally, if a group has a member that generates positive as well as negative externalities, then the group maximizes profit where the sum of the marginal benefits equals the sum of the marginal costs.

So far, we have considered externalities that affect the revenues and costs of the recipients, which can be measured directly in terms of dollars and cents. The benefits and costs of some externalities, however, are not in monetary form. For instance, suppose that there is a large church on Main Street. The church expects Sunday attendance to fall as people are attracted to Luna's new department store. The negative externality that Luna imposes on the church is

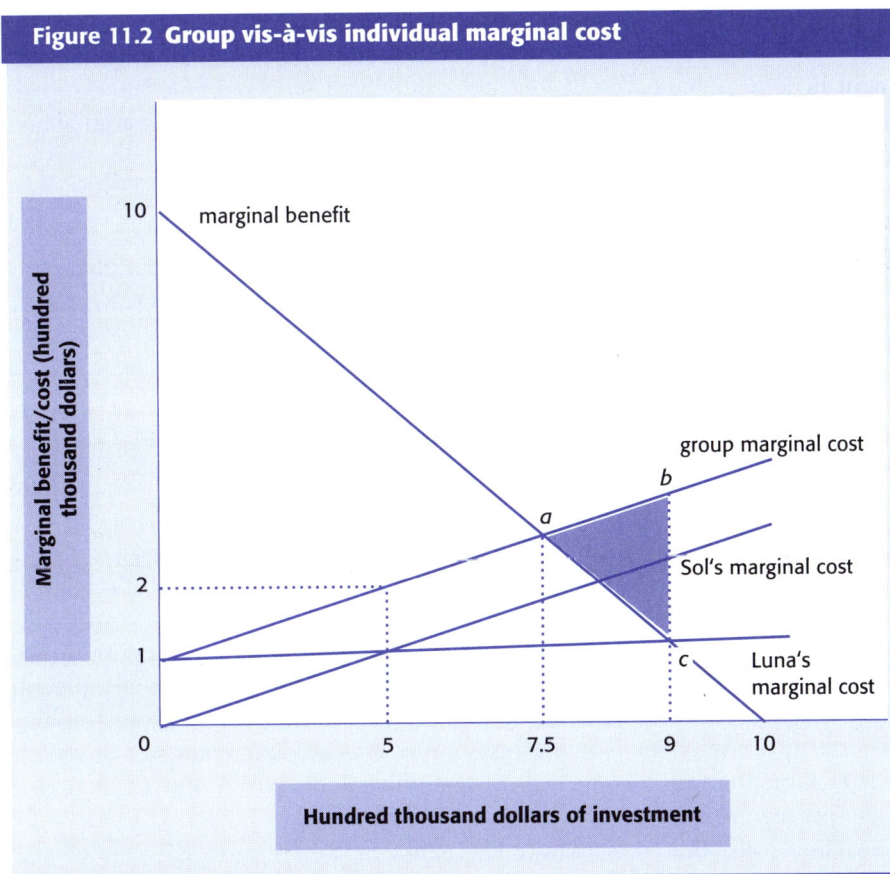

Figure 11.2 Group vis-à-vis individual marginal cost

The group's marginal cost is the vertical sum of the individual marginal costs. The group maximizes profit at an investment of $750,000, where the group marginal benefit equals the marginal cost. If Luna considers only the benefit and the cost for itself, it would invest $900,000. By reducing its investment to $750,000, the group could gain the shaded area *abc* in additional profit.

not only monetary. Similarly, the new Luna store may generate positive externalities that are not monetary.

To take account of externalities in nonmonetary form, we require only that the recipients be able to measure the benefits and costs in terms of money. We suppose that, rather than maximizing profit, these recipients aim to maximize their net benefit, which is the benefit less the cost. Where all externalities are in monetary form, the net benefit simplifies to the profit.

A group that has a member that generates positive as well as negative externalities maximizes net benefit at the the following benchmark: where the sum of the marginal benefits equals the sum of the marginal costs. Recall from

An **externality is resolved** when the sum of the marginal benefits equals the sum of the marginal costs.

Chapter 6 that this balance also defines the economically efficient level of the activity generating the externalities. Thus, another way to define the benchmark is the economically efficient level of the activity generating the externalities. We say that an **externality is resolved** when the sum of the marginal benefits equals the sum of the marginal costs.

Progress check

Progress Check 11B Referring to Figure 11.2, suppose that the negative externality to the Sol store is stronger. How will this affect (1) Sol's marginal cost curve and (2) the level of investment that maximizes the group profit?

In developing the benchmark, we took the viewpoint of a group that included the source as well as recipients of the externalities. We next show that the same benchmark applies when the source is separate from the recipients.

Consider a positive externality and suppose that the sum of its marginal benefits exceeds the marginal cost. Then, if the source increases the externality, the marginal benefits will be greater than the marginal cost; hence, there will be a net benefit. This is a profit opportunity for an intermediary, which could collect fees from the recipients to pay the source to increase the externality. The set of transactions is feasible since the intermediary could set the fee to each recipient at less than its marginal benefit and the payment to the source to cover its marginal cost.

There will be an opportunity for such a profit whenever the sum of marginal benefits exceeds the marginal cost. Accordingly, the intermediary will pay the source to increase the externality up to the point where the sum of the marginal benefits equals the marginal cost, which defines the economically efficient level of the activity generating the positive externality. At that point, the externality is resolved.

Having considered positive externalities, we next explain why the benchmark also applies to negative externalities when the source is separate from the recipients. If the marginal benefit is less than the sum of the marginal costs, an intermediary could make a profit by collecting fees from the recipients to pay the source to reduce the externality. This set of transactions is feasible, since the intermediary could set the fees from the recipients at less than their marginal costs and the payment to the source to cover its marginal benefit.

The intermediary can profitably pay the source to reduce the externality up to the point where the marginal benefit of the source equals the sum of the marginal costs. At that point, the activity generating the negative externality will be at the economically efficient level.

Thus, for positive as well as negative externalities, an intermediary maximizes profit when it arranges for the source to resolve the externality, that is, choose the economically efficient level of the activity generating the externality. At that point, the intermediary maximizes profit. Accordingly, the benchmark of economic efficiency applies whether the source of the externality is separate or integrated with the recipients.

3 *Resolving Externalities*

We have identified the benchmark for an externality as the economically efficient level. In Chapter 6, we showed that, in a perfectly competitive market, the invisible hand ensures economic efficiency. By definition, however, externalities do not pass through markets. Hence, externalities will be resolved only through deliberate action. We now turn to consider practical ways to resolve externalities.

In the case of Luna's new store, we saw that, when a single entity owns all the stores along Main Street, it considers all the benefits and costs of its investments; hence, will invest up to the economically efficient level. This suggests how to resolve an externality: The source and the recipient of the externality should combine into a single entity.

Combining the source and the recipient of the externality into a single entity is a unilateral approach to resolving an externality. We discuss the alternative—joint action—later in this section.

Unilateral Action

Unilateral action can be implemented in one of three ways. Either the recipient of the externality acquires the source, the source of the externality acquires the recipient, or a third party acquires both the source and the recipient. In the case of Luna's new store, either the existing Main Street retailers should acquire Luna, Luna should buy all the retailers presently on Main Street, or Luna and the existing retailers should all sell out to a third party.

From the viewpoint of resolving externalities, it does not matter who buys whom. Once the source and the recipient of the externality are combined, the single entity will take account of all the benefits and the costs of its investments and will invest up to the economically efficient level.

Let us justify this claim for Luna's positive externalities. First, suppose that the existing florist and shoe store on Main Street acquire the Luna department store to form the Main Street group. Then, the total benefit of the group consists of the benefit from the three stores. To maximize profit, the group should invest up to the point that the group marginal benefit equals the marginal cost. The group marginal benefit is the sum of the marginal benefits from the three stores. Hence, referring to Figure 11.1, the profit-maximizing investment level is $929,000.

Next, suppose Luna buys the two specialty retailers to form Group Luna. Again, the total benefit of the group consists of the benefit from the three stores. To maximize the group profit, it should invest up to the point that the sum of the marginal benefits from the three stores equals the marginal cost. Again, referring to Figure 11.1, the profit-maximizing investment level is $929,000.

Finally, suppose that Luna and the two specialty retailers all sell out to a third party, Moonlight Holdings. In this case, Moonlight Holdings owns the three stores. As in the two previous cases, the owner of the three stores will maximize profit by investing $929,000, the point where the sum of the marginal benefits from the three stores equals the marginal cost.

We have shown that, for a positive externality, the level of investment will be economically efficient if the source and the recipient of the externality are combined. It does not matter how the combination takes place. The same is true for a negative externality and, generally, for an activity that generates both positive and negative externalities. Regardless of how the source and the recipient of the externality are combined, the combined entity will choose an economically efficient level of investment.

Mickey Mouse Externalities

The Walt Disney Company owns and manages Disneyland in Anaheim, California. This theme park is surrounded by hundreds of businesses, including motels, restaurants, souvenir stores, and transportation services. Disneyland visitors are the major source of income for these neighboring businesses. In the late 1980s, the Walt Disney Company decided to embark on a large program of investments to upgrade Disneyland. Before commencing construction, the company bought much of the property around the theme park. The company paid $200 million for the Disneyland Hotel.

By purchasing the surrounding property, the Walt Disney Company ensured that it would capture relatively more of the benefits from new attractions. Consequently, the company had a greater incentive to make the economically efficient level of investment in new attractions at the theme park.

The Walt Disney Company has continued to buy real estate around Disneyland. In December 1995, it acquired the Pan Pacific Hotel, which has been renamed the Disneyland Pacific Hotel.

Source: Gary Wilson, chief financial officer, The Disney Company, speech at the Anderson School, UCLA, March 15, 1989; "Walt Disney Co.," *Asian Wall Street Journal* (December 13, 1995), p. 22.

Academic Externalities: A Free Campus

In May 1995, the regents of the University of California met to choose the location for its proposed San Joaquin campus, to be the 10th branch of the university. The regents considered two alternatives: a site at Lake Yosemite on 2000 acres offered free of charge by the Virginia Smith Trust and another site at Table Mountain, near the city of Fresno, that would be purchased. Swayed in part by the free land, the regents voted for Lake Yosemite.

The Virginia Smith Trust owned 7000 acres of land by Lake Yosemite. When the trust made the offer to the university, its land was used to graze cattle. The trust projected that, with establishment of the new campus, it could earn $350 million from development of the remaining 5000 acres of real estate.

The positive externalities generated by the new campus were sufficient to justify the "gift" of 2000 acres to the University of California.

Source: "Lake Yosemite Selected for Proposed Campus," *UC Focus* [Office of the President, University of California] 9, no. 5 (June–July 1995), pp. 1 and 7.

Joint Action

We have seen how the affected parties can resolve externalities through unilateral action. Unilateral action, however, is not always feasible. For instance, recall the negative externality that Luna's new department store would impose on the church. Unilateral action to resolve this negative externality would mean combining the church and the Luna store under a common ownership. Such a combination may not be feasible.

Accordingly, it is important to explore the alternative approach to resolving an externality: joint action. To resolve an externality through joint action, the source and the recipient of the externality must negotiate and agree on how to resolve the externality. Joint action is a feasible way to resolve the negative externality from Luna's new store to the church. For instance, the church may offer Luna the use of its parking area if Luna agrees not to open on Sunday mornings. Such a deal is a way of jointly resolving the negative externality.

Joint action is also a way by which the positive externalities from Luna to the specialty retailers can be resolved. Since Luna's investment increases the revenues of the florist and the shoe store, the two specialty retailers would like Luna to increase its investment.

Cooperative Advertising: Resolving "Intel Inside"

Compaq is one of the world's leading manufacturers of IBM-compatible personal computers. Intel is the dominant manufacturer of IBM-compatible microprocessors. Compaq spends millions of dollars each year on advertising. Many of these advertisements feature "Intel Inside," the mark that a computer is powered by an Intel microprocessor. By publicizing Intel, these advertisements boost the demand for the products of other manufacturers using Intel microprocessors.

From Intel's standpoint, the economically efficient amount of "Intel Inside" advertising by Compaq balances the marginal benefit to all manufacturers with the marginal cost to Compaq. In planning its advertising, however, Compaq might ignore the positive externalities to other manufacturers.

Intel resolves these externalities through cooperative advertising: The microprocessor manufacturer shares the cost of advertising by personal computer makers that features "Intel Inside." This subsidy encourages producers of personal computers to invest the appropriate amount of resources in advertising Intel microprocessors.

Source: "Compaq and Intel Renew Old Alliance," *South China Morning Post* (January 23, 1996), Technology, p. 6.

Suppose that the florist pays Luna a contribution equal to its marginal benefit from Luna's investment and that the shoe store does likewise. Then Luna's total benefit will be the benefit from its own store plus the contributions from the two specialty retailers. Luna's profit will be its total benefit less the cost of the investment. Therefore, it will maximize profit by choosing the level of investment where the sum of the marginal benefits equals the marginal cost. Referring to Figure 11.1, that level of investment is $929,000. Accordingly, joint action can give Luna sufficient incentive to look beyond its own benefits and costs and resolve its positive externalities.

With joint action, the source and the recipient of the externality remain separate entities. Joint action to resolve an externality requires two steps. First, the affected parties must agree on how to resolve the externality. This step involves collecting information about the benefits and costs to the various parties, and then planning the level of the activity that generates the externality. The second step is to enforce compliance with the agreed plan. Enforcement includes monitoring the source of the externality and applying incentives to ensure that the source complies with the planned level of the externality-generating activity.

Hurdles to Resolution

Externalities can be resolved through unilateral or joint action. There are some hurdles, however, that may prevent the resolution. Let us discuss these hurdles in the context of Luna's positive externalities. Suppose that Luna and the two specialty retailers aim to resolve the externalities through joint action. Then the three parties must agree on the marginal benefit that Luna's investment will generate for the florist. This will determine the florist's contribution to Luna's investment.

To reduce its contribution, the florist may claim that its marginal benefit from Luna's investment is low. Since the florist will probably have better information than the other two parties about its own marginal benefit, it may be difficult for the other two parties to know whether the florist is bluffing. The result may be that the parties cannot agree and the positive externality would not be resolved.

Similarly, differences in information about the shoe store's marginal benefit from Luna's investment might also prevent resolution of the externality to the shoe store. As these examples show, differences in information may prevent the affected parties from reaching an agreement on how to resolve an externality.

Differences in information can be compounded in the following way. It is difficult for Luna to exclude the florist from receiving the positive externality. Hence, the florist can still benefit from Luna's investments even if it contributes less than its marginal benefit. When the florist considers its contribution from a purely selfish viewpoint, it will maximize its own profit by underreporting its marginal benefit.

In this example, the florist is taking a free ride on Luna's investment. Generally, a **free rider** understates its benefit from an externality and contributes less than its marginal benefit to resolution of the externality. In the extreme, the free rider claims that it derives no benefit and avoids all contribution. The incentive to take a free ride arises whenever it is costly to exclude particular individuals from receiving an externality.

The incentive to take a free ride is stronger when the externality affects many recipients and these recipients differ widely in their marginal benefits. When an externality affects many recipients, the contribution of any particular recipient is relatively small. Hence, the other recipients may resolve the externality even if some recipients take a free ride. When the recipients of the externality differ widely in their marginal benefits, there is relatively more scope for an individual recipient to claim a low marginal benefit.

A **free rider** contributes less than its marginal benefit to the resolution of an externality.

Fisheries I: Joint Action

There are significant negative externalities among producers in the fisheries industry. The more that one fisher catches, the less there will be available for others. Fishers, however, may engage in practices that are privately beneficial but are not economically efficient. Such practices include indiscriminate fishing methods that catch young as well as mature fish. As a result of overfishing, many marine resources are being exhausted.

The fisheries industry also provides an example where some of the affected producers have resolved the negative externalities through joint action. The American state of Maine is famous for its lobsters. Lobster catchers in some areas organized to restrict catching with very dramatic results. In the restricted areas, the number of lobsters per trap was 60% higher than in unrestricted areas and the average weight of caught lobsters was 67% higher.

Source: James A. Wilson, "A Test of the Tragedy of the Commons," in *Managing the Commons*, ed. Garrett Hardin and John Baden (San Francisco: W.H. Freeman & Co., 1977), pp. 96–111.

Fisheries II: The Limits to Joint Action

International waters are marine areas beyond the jurisdiction of a single country. Marine resources in international waters attract fishers from all over the world. Consequently, joint action to resolve negative externalities among fishers can be problematic. Even if the parties involved can agree on how much to catch, it may be difficult to enforce compliance.

Turbot, also known as Greenland halibut, found in the Grand Banks off Newfoundland, attract trawlers from Canada, Portugal, Spain, and other countries. The Northwest Atlantic Fisheries Organization (NAFO) regulates the fishing for turbot in the Grand Banks. In September 1994, the organization set a quota of 16,200 metric tons for Canada and 3,400 tons for the European Union. Despite the quotas, there have been serious disagreements among the NAFO member countries. Canada, for instance, has accused Spanish trawlers of flouting the quotas. In March 1995, the dispute escalated when Canadian Navy ships fired warning shots to force the Spanish trawler Estai into the Canadian port of St John's.

The Antarctic provides another example. The International Whaling Commission has banned commercial hunting of whales in the Antarctic since December 1994. Nevertheless, Japan has exploited a loophole to catch several hundred whales for "scientific purposes." Caught in the name of science, these whales provide meat to Japanese restaurants for sale at $160 a pound.

Sources: "Spanish Vessel Seized," *South China Morning Post* (March 11, 1995), p. 14; "Hunters Defy Ban on Killing Minke Whales," *South China Morning Post* (February 16, 1995), p. 14.

4 *Potential Externalities*

So far, we have considered externalities that will definitely arise, and discussed how they can be resolved through unilateral and joint action. In other instances, the challenge is to resolve potential externalities that can be realized only with some deliberate action.

Consider the following example. Suppose that the Lakeside Hotel in Lucerne, Switzerland, provides an efficient service at a reasonable price. Many guests have been so pleased with the service that they have asked for recommendations of similar hotels in Geneva, Zurich, and other Swiss cities. The goodwill generated by Lakeside's service is a potential positive externality.

Lakeside's goodwill is only a *potential* positive externality. If it takes appropriate action to realize the externality, it can generate additional customers for hotels in other Swiss cities. If, however, Lakeside does not take some deliberate action, there will be no externality. There will simply be a large number of satisfied guests searching for similar hotels elsewhere in Switzerland.

An obvious way to realize the potential positive externality is to establish a chain of Lakeside hotels. The Lakeside name on these other hotels will surely attract many of the travelers who appreciated the Lakeside service in Lucerne. By setting up a chain of hotels, Lakeside can realize and resolve the potential positive externality. Good service at the Lakeside in Lucerne will increase the demand at Lakeside Hotels in other Swiss cities.

A chain should aim to assure a consistent standard of service and price at all member hotels. Different chains may choose different standards, according to their target markets; for instance, five-star hotels cater to wealthy travelers, while budget hotels target students and young people. Whatever the niche, it is crucial that the standard of service and price be consistent across the entire chain.

If standards are not consistent across a chain, then travelers will not be sure what to expect from each individual hotel. For instance, suppose that service and price vary randomly among the different Lakeside Hotels. Then, reasonably priced, efficient service at the Lakeside in Lucerne may not tell a traveler anything about the standards at other Lakeside Hotels. In this case, the positive externality will not be realized.

Furthermore, there is potential for negative externalities within a chain of hotels. If one hotel drops its standards, it will hurt not only its own business but also the image and business of the entire chain. This is a negative externality because the hotel that lowers standards does not compensate the other members of the chain. To maintain consistency, a chain must spend considerable effort to monitor the standards of service at the member hotels.

Although we have presented this story in the context of hotels, the same principles apply to any good or service whose customers travel from one place to another. Examples include car rental, fast food, and gasoline. In each of these markets, service providers can build up goodwill among customers. This goodwill is a potential positive externality that can be realized by establishing a chain spanning the places to which customers may travel. To realize the potential externality, the chain must ensure a consistent standard of service and price at all retail locations.

The scope for realizing potential externalities in customer goodwill depends on customer mobility. The more mobile the customers are, the greater the scope. This explains why chains predominate in locations that attract traveling customers disproportionately. By contrast, chains have a smaller presence in locations that cater mainly to local customers. For instance, in the car rental business, chains have a larger share at airports than in city centers. In gasoline, chains have a larger share along highways than in suburban areas.

Realizing Potential Externalities: Holiday Inn

In August 1952, Kemmons Wilson opened the first Holiday Inn in Memphis, Tennessee. By 1995, the chain had grown to become the world's largest, with over 2000 hotels in Asia and the Pacific, Europe, and North America. About 85% of Holiday Inns are owned and operated by independent parties or franchisees with contracts to use the Holiday Inn business format. The chain continues to open new hotels at the rate of 120–140 a year.

Industry analysts have credited Holiday Inn with standardization of service quality and room rates over a dispersed international network. A major factor in the consistency of service is the Holiday Inn University, which was established in 1959. The university trains Holiday Inn employees and franchisees in management, housekeeping, and labor relations. This training helps to maintain uniform standards in Holiday Inns all across the world.

Sources: International Directory of Company Histories, vol. 3, ed. Adele Hast, (Chicago: St James Press, 1991), pp. 94–5; "Gains Seen at Water Firm and Giant Brewers," *South China Morning Post* (December 4, 1995), Business, p. 8.

5 Network Externalities

The Internet is a global computer network based on the communications protocol, TCP/IP. The most popular Internet services include electronic mail, file transfer, and the World Wide Web. In the introduction, we noted an unusual aspect of the demand for Internet connections: The more users join, the more others want to join. As a result, the Internet has been growing at an accelerating rate. The essential reason for the accelerating growth is a *network externality*.

A **network externality** arises if the actions of one user affect other users directly rather than through a market and the effect depends on the total number of users. To understand the meaning of a network externality, suppose that Hilda is the only user connected to the Internet. To whom could she send electronic mail? When Hilda is the only subscriber, Internet electronic mail service is worthless.

Suppose, by contrast, that there are 20 million other users on the Internet. Then, Hilda could use electronic mail to communicate with 20 million other persons. The benefit of Internet electronic mail to Hilda depends on the total number of other users, regardless of how close or distant they may be. The adjective *network* emphasizes that the externality is generated by the entire network of users.

In Chapter 2, we discussed the factors—including price, buyer income, and prices of related products—that affect demand for a good or service. The demand for a product that generates network externalities depends on one additional factor, which is the total number of other users. In the case of the Internet, the more users join, the greater will be the benefit that an Internet connection provides to each user or, equivalently, the higher will be each individual's demand curve. The Internet's network externalities explain why connections have grown at an accelerating rate.

> A **network externality** arises when the actions of one user affect other users directly rather than through a market and the effect depends on the total number of users.

Network Effects

We should distinguish network externalities from *network effects*, in general. As we explained in Chapter 10, a *network effect* arises whenever the benefit from a good or service depends on the total number of other users. A network externality is the special case of a network effect that is transmitted directly rather than through a market.

To illustrate a network effect, consider telephone service. The benefit that one subscriber derives from telephone service definitely depends on the total number of other subscribers. Hence, connections to telephone service generate network effects. Are these effects also network externalities? Note that there is a market for telephone service: The service provider can increase its profits by resolving the effect from one subscriber's connection to the benefit of other subscribers. Thus, connections to telephone service generate network externalities only to the extent that they are not resolved by the service provider.

Progress Check 11C Which of the following are network externalities?
   a. An increase in the number of people speaking French benefits existing French speakers.
   b. An increase in the number of merchants accepting a new credit card benefits existing cardholders.

Progress check

Impact on Demand and Competition

The **critical mass** is the number of users at which the quantity demanded becomes positive.

The presence of network externalities has several implications for the character of demand and product competition. First, the quantity demanded of the product will be 0 unless the total number of users exceeds a **critical mass**. The *critical mass* is the number of users at which the quantity demanded becomes positive. For instance, in the case of the Internet, there is some number of users below which the quantity demanded will be 0. Supposing that the number is 100, then the critical mass for Internet is 100 users. This means that there will be a positive demand for the Internet only when the price or other factors are sufficient to attract 100 users.

The second implication is that the market demand for a product that generates network externalities will be relatively elastic. Recall that the price elasticity of demand is the percentage by which the quantity demanded will change if the price of the product rises by 1%, holding all other factors unchanged. In the case of a product that generates network externalities, if the price rises by 1%, then the total number of users will fall, which feeds back to reduce the market demand even further. Hence, the network externality tends to amplify the effect of a price increase, causing the quantity demanded to fall relatively more.

Similarly, the presence of a network externality tends to amplify the effect of a price cut, causing the quantity demanded to increase relatively more. By amplifying the effect of price changes on the quantity demanded, the network externality causes the market demand to be relatively more elastic.

Tipping is the tendency for the market demand to shift toward a product that has gained a small initial lead.

The third implication concerns the character of competition among products that generate network externalities. A small increase in the user base of one product can *tip* the market demand toward that product. **Tipping** is the tendency for the market demand to shift toward a product that has gained a small initial lead. (For the origin of the metaphor, consider a seesaw that is just balanced. The addition of even a very small weight to one side will tip the seesaw to that side.)

To illustrate the phenomenon of tipping, suppose that there are two global computer networks, the Internet and the Total-Net, each with 100 users. The two networks are incompatible; hence, Internet subscribers cannot communicate with Total-Net subscribers and vice versa.

Now, suppose that 10 users decide to switch from the Internet to the Total-Net. Then, the Internet will have 90 subscribers, while the Total-Net will have 110 subscribers. Consider Max, a typical Internet subscriber: With 10 users switching, he can now communicate with only 89 other people. Hence, the number of Internet users has dropped below the critical mass. So, Max switches from the Internet to the Total-Net. Every other Internet user also switches. Ultimately, the initial switch by 10 users tips everyone toward the Total-Net.

In a market for competing products that generate network externalities, the likelihood of tipping means that one product will eventually dominate the market. Any slight movement in demand toward one product will tip all the users to that product. Consequently, it is unlikely that several competing products will coexist for an extended period of time.

World Wide Web Consortium

The World Wide Web is a set of Internet standards that provides access to multimedia resources. Tim Berners-Lee developed the Web at CERN, the European laboratory for research in particle physics. The prototype of the Web was launched in 1990–1991, and within a few years, the Web became one of the most popular services of the Internet.

CERN handed over responsibility for development of the Web to the World Wide Web Consortium (W3C). The W3C includes American, European, and Japanese computer hardware and software manufacturers and communications and content providers. With dual bases at the MIT Laboratory of Computer Science, Cambridge, Massachusetts, and the Institut National de Recherche en Informatique et en Automatique in France, the W3C aims to develop and promote a set of common standards for the Web.

The W3C engaged Tim Berners-Lee as director. One of the consortium's most successful projects has been the Platform for Internet Content Selection (PICS), a standard for labeling and rating Web content. Other projects include protocols for active objects, security, and replication and caching.

Sources: World Wide Web pages: www.w3.org, www.inria.fr, and www.cern.ch, (March 29, 1996).

---

6 *Public Goods*

In the introduction to this chapter, we observed that open-air fireworks are extremely popular all over the world and asked why they are not provided on a commercial basis. To address this issue, we must explain the concept of a **public good**. A *public good* is an item that provides **nonrival** consumption or usage. Consumption or usage is *nonrival* if one person's increase in consumption or usage does not reduce the quantity available to others.

Open-air fireworks are an example of a public good. For instance, if Joy comes to watch a show of open-air fireworks, she does not reduce the quantity available for other people. Hence, open-air fireworks provide nonrival consumption and are a public good.

Consumption or usage is **nonrival** if one person's increase in that consumption or usage does not reduce the quantity available to others.

A **public good** provides nonrival consumption or usage.

Another way of understanding nonrival consumption or usage is through the concept of scale economies. Given that open-air fireworks are being provided to one viewer, the marginal cost of providing the same display to additional viewers is nothing. There is an extreme economy of scale in providing a public good: Provision involves only a fixed cost and the marginal cost of serving additional consumers or users is 0.

As suggested by the question of why there is little or no commercial provision of open-air fireworks, the provision of public goods is a complicated issue. To lay the foundation for an answer, we first discuss the differences between public and private goods, and then consider the economically efficient provision of a public good.

Rivalness

Public goods lie at one end of a spectrum of rivalness, with **private goods** at the other extreme (Figure 11.3). A *private good* is an item that provides **rival** consumption or usage. Consumption or usage is *rival* if one person's increase in consumption or usage by some quantity reduces the total available to others by the same quantity.

Food and clothing, for instance, are private goods. If Lucas eats a four-ounce frozen yogurt, then there will be four ounces less for other consumers. If Max is wearing a new polo shirt, no one else can wear it at the same time. Industrial and engineering materials are also private goods: If one technician is using some solder and wire, there will be that much less for other technicians.

Some items are neither public nor private. An example are items that provide **congestible** consumption or usage. This means that one person's increase in consumption or usage by some quantity reduces the total available to others but by less than that quantity. Congestible items are public goods when consumption or usage is low but are private goods when consumption or usage is high.

> A **private good** provides rival consumption or usage.
>
> Consumption or usage is **rival** if one person's increase in consumption or usage by some quantity reduces the total available to others by the same quantity.
>
> Consumption or usage is **congestible** if one person's increase in consumption or usage by some quantity reduces the total available to others but by less than that quantity.

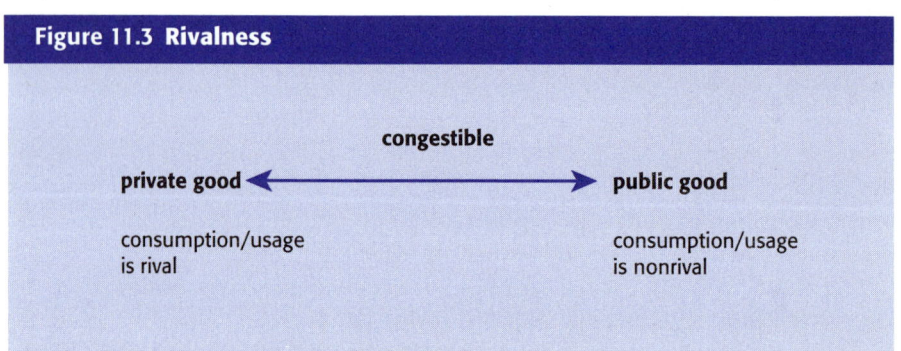

Figure 11.3 Rivalness

A private good provides rival consumption or usage. At the other extreme, a public good provides nonrival consumption or usage.

For instance, entertainment by a juggler is congestible: Several people can comfortably watch a juggler, but after some number, additional viewers will get in the way and reduce the quantity of entertainment available to other viewers. The Internet is also congestible. At off-peak times, an increase in usage by one person will not reduce the service to others. At peak times, however, the more users connect to the Internet, the slower will be the service for others.

Progress Check 11D On the spectrum of Figure 11.3, mark the following items: (1) services of a mainframe computer, (2) computer monitor, (3) technique for coronary bypass operation, (4) cardiac (heart) surgeon's services, and (5) bottled oxygen.

Progress check

Content vis-à-vis Delivery

To understand the degree of rivalness, it is important to distinguish between content and delivery. Consider, for instance, television programming, which can be broadcast in a number of ways: over the air from land-based transmission towers, directly to receivers from orbiting satellites, or by cable.

Regardless of the method of delivery, the content of broadcast television is nonrival. If Maria switches on her television to watch the evening news, she does not affect the quantity of the evening news available to other people. This is true whether the signal comes over the air or by cable.

The method of delivery, however, may be a public or private good. Delivery by over-the-air transmission is a public good. The same signal can serve any number of television sets within the transmission range. Delivery by cable, however, is a private good. One cable serves only one television set.

Scientific knowledge provides another illustration of the distinction between content and delivery. Consider, for instance, this textbook on managerial economics. The intellectual content of this book is a public good. If one more person understands the principles of managerial economics, she or he does not reduce the quantity available to other people.

On the other hand, the principles of managerial economics are delivered through the medium of a textbook. The textbook is a private good: If one person is using a copy of this book, that copy is unavailable to others.

As we shall discuss later in this chapter, the distinction between content and delivery is important for commercial provision of public goods. The basis of commercial provision of many public goods is to deliver them in the format of private goods.

Economic Efficiency

Previously, we showed that, when an externality is at an economically efficient level, there are no further opportunities to profit from adjusting the activity generating the externality. Let us now show the same for a public good. Suppose that there are three viewers of open-air fireworks—Alan, Mary, and Peter—with marginal benefits as shown in Figure 11.4. The figure also shows the marginal cost of open-air fireworks, which we suppose to be a constant $5.60 per minute.

Consider the provision of one minute of fireworks. Since fireworks are a public good, there will be 1 minute for each of the three viewers. Accordingly, each would be willing to pay her or his marginal benefit for that minute. By Figure 11.4, the sum of the marginal benefits to the three viewers is $0.80 + $3.60

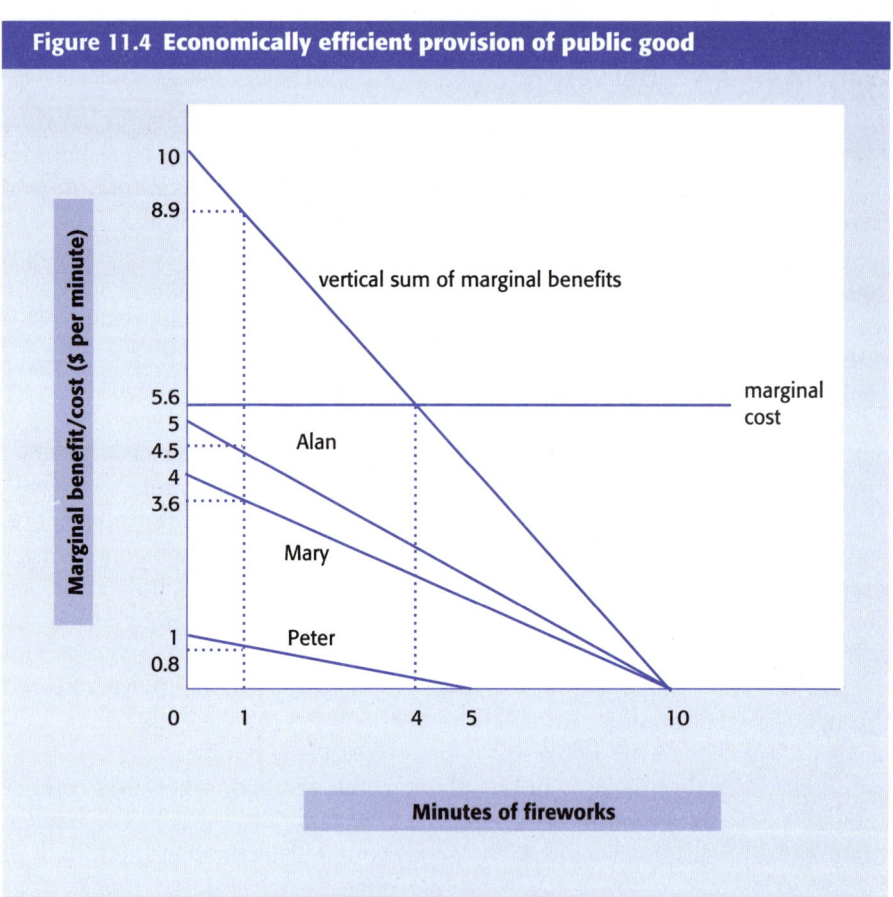

Figure 11.4 Economically efficient provision of public good

At the economically efficient quantity of a public good, the sum of the individual marginal benefits equals the marginal cost. Every individual marginal benefit curve lies below the marginal cost of $5.60; hence, no individual person would be willing to buy even one minute of fireworks. If each individual tries to get a free ride, it might not be possible to provide even one minute of fireworks on a commercial basis.

+ \$4.50 = \$8.90. The cost of one minute is \$5.60, hence there is an opportunity to make a profit by providing one minute of fireworks. This same argument applies for additional quantities up to four minutes.

At four minutes of fireworks, the sum of the individual marginal benefits equals the marginal cost. Can someone make money by increasing provision to five minutes? By Figure 11.4, the fifth minute provides an additional benefit to Alan and Mary only. The sum of their marginal benefits is \$2.00 + \$2.50 = \$4.50. Since the cost of each minute is \$5.60, providing the fifth minute would result in a loss.

We have shown that opportunities for profit are exhausted at the point where the vertical sum of the individual marginal benefits equals the marginal cost. By the definition in Chapter 6, this is the economically efficient quantity of the public good. Accordingly, at the economically efficient quantity, there are no further opportunities to profit from adjusting the provision of the public good.

In Figure 11.4, notice that each of the individual marginal benefit curves lies below the marginal cost of \$5.60. Hence, no individual person would be willing to buy even one minute of fireworks. The sum of the individual marginal benefit curves, however, lies above the marginal cost curve at quantities of between zero and four minutes. Since a public good provides nonrival consumption, the three persons' willingness to pay is given by the vertical sum of the individual marginal benefit curves. While no single person would buy even one minute of fireworks, they collectively would be willing to pay for four minutes.

Managing Congestion: Waiting Times and the Price of Gasoline

The pumps at a gasoline station are a congestible facility. At off-peak times, an increase in usage by one driver will not reduce the service to others. At peak times, however, the more drivers are filling up, the slower will be the service for others.

Gasoline stations resolve the congestion through pricing. For many years, at the corner of Le Conte and Gayley Avenues in Westwood, Los Angeles, a Chevron station charged lower prices than the Shell station across the street. A station that sets higher prices will draw fewer customers; hence, it implicitly offers faster service. One estimate shows that, on average, drivers are willing to pay a 1% higher price for a 6% reduction in congestion.

Source: I.P.L. Png and David Reitman, "Service Time Competition," *RAND Journal of Economics* 25, no. 4 (Winter 1994), pp. 619–34.

7 *Excludability*

Having discussed the nature of public goods and their economically efficient provision, we are now ready to address the issue of how public goods can actually be provided. Many private goods are provided on a commercial basis. There is a fundamental condition for commercial provision of any product that is easy to overlook. That condition is that, to sell a product, the seller must be able to exclude those who do not pay. The condition is crucial in the commercial provision of public goods.

Consumption or usage is **excludable** if the seller can exclude particular consumers or users. Excludability is a fundamental requirement for commercial provision of any item.

> Consumption or usage is **excludable** if the seller can exclude particular consumers or users.

When consumption or usage of an item is not excludable, commercial provision will be difficult. To illustrate the problem, let us suppose that Luna Entertainment wants to provide one minute of open-air fireworks to Alan, Mary, and Peter. Referring to Figure 11.4, Luna knows that, at that quantity, the individual marginal benefits of Alan, Mary, and Peter are $4.50, $3.60, and $0.80 respectively. If Luna charges each person a price equal to her or his marginal benefit, then Luna will collect $4.50 + $3.60 + $0.80 = $8.90 from Alan, Mary, and Peter. Luna's cost of providing one minute of fireworks is $5.60; hence, it will realize a profit of $3.30.

Peter, however, might reason that if he refuses to pay, while Alan and Mary do pay, then Luna would collect $4.50 + $3.60 = $8.10, which would be enough to cover the cost of $5.60. Then, Luna would provide the one minute of fireworks and, since viewing open-air fireworks is not excludable, Peter would enjoy a free show. Alan and Mary, however, might also think in similar ways. If everyone tries to get a free show, Luna will incur a loss from the fireworks. Hence, in the extreme, the incentive to get a free show prevents the provision of even one minute of fireworks on a commercial basis.

The basic problem is that, whenever consumption or usage of some item is non-excludable, individual consumers or users will have an incentive to take a free ride. Free riding will cut into the seller's revenues and, so, reduce the seller's profit and hamper commercial provision of the item.

Many public goods provide consumption or usage that is not excludable. Accordingly, to understand the scope for commercial provision of public goods, we must consider the degree of excludability. This depends on two factors: law and technology.

Law

In the previous section, we explained that scientific knowledge is a public good. An example of scientific knowledge is the formula for an antiviral drug. If Luna

Pharmaceuticals uses the formula to manufacture the drug, it will not affect the availability of the formula for other users. Hence, the formula is a public good. Similarly, the formulas for other drugs and chemical processes are public goods.

Through the concept of a **patent**, however, the law has made the use of many scientific formulas excludable. A *patent* is a legal, exclusive right to the product or process covered by the terms of the patent. It is illegal to manufacture a product or use a process covered by a patent without the permission of the patent owner. Such illegal activity is called *infringement*. The owner of a patent can sue infringers for a court order to stop the infringement as well as an award of damages.

With legal authority, the owner of a patented antiviral drug can exclude those who do not pay from getting the drug. Accordingly, commercial production is feasible. Indeed, by virtue of the patent, the owner will have a monopoly over the drug and can price it above the competitive level.

Patents provide the basis for the commercial provision of scientific knowledge in the chemicals, electrical and electronic equipment, and pharmaceutical industries. The development of a new pharmaceutical, for instance, can take a decade and cost several hundred million dollars. Private enterprises are willing to invest large amounts in research and development only because of the profits that are possible with patent protection. Past scientific discoveries that have been covered by patents include aspirin, the light bulb, and the transistor. More recently, patented products include AZT and the Pentium microprocessor.

Like scientific knowledge, artistic, literary, and musical compositions are also public goods. The content of the *Oxford English Dictionary* may be used any number of times without affecting its availability to other users. Similarly, the content of Mozart's piano concertos, Madonna's songs, the movie *Pulp Fiction*, and computer software is also nonrival.

The law, however, has made the use of artistic, literary, and musical expression excludable through the concept of **copyright**. A *copyright* is a legal, exclusive right to an artistic, literary, or musical expression. It is illegal to reproduce a copyrighted expression without the permission of the copyright owner. The owner of a copyright can sue infringers for a court order to stop the infringement as well as an award of damages.

Copyright gives the owner a legal monopoly over the copyrighted material. Hence, the owner will have authority to exclude those who do not pay from using the material and charge a monopoly price for usage. Commercial provision of literary and musical compositions and computer software is possible only with copyright law. For instance, if there were no copyright protection for personal computer software, all users could freely copy the products and the business of software development would not be commercially viable.

Patent and copyright are two forms of rights over intellectual property, which is the legal concept for ownership of ideas. By providing an exclusive right, a

> A **patent** is a legal, exclusive right to the product or process covered by the terms of the patent.

> A **copyright** is a legal, exclusive right to an artistic, literary, or musical expression.

patent or copyright creates a monopoly. The law deliberately creates this monopoly to encourage investment in creating new scientific knowledge, literary and musical compositions, and computer software.

Patents and copyrights are limited to specific periods of time. Once the patent on a product or process has expired, the owner loses the exclusive right and anyone can freely imitate the item. Similarly, after the expiration of the copyright on a literary or musical work, anyone is free to copy or use the work. For instance, the copyright on Mozart's piano concertos expired long ago, hence advertising agencies and movie studios can freely use Mozart's works.

The law can establish excludability through intellectual property. The effectiveness of exclusion, however, depends on enforcement. Consider, for instance, the process for distilling water: Heat the water to its boiling point, recover the steam, and then cool the steam and collect the condensate. Even if the law allowed a patent on this process, the right would be nearly impossible to enforce. Imagine trying to exclude particular high-school students, engineers, or household cooks from using the process to distill water.

By contrast, a patent on the formula for an antiviral drug is quite enforceable. The only potential commercial users of the formula are pharmaceutical manufacturers. To make money from the drug, a manufacturer must produce it on a large scale and sell it on the open market. This means that use of the formula will be relatively easy to detect. Accordingly, the owner of the patent can effectively exclude particular persons from usage.

Computer software provides another example of the distinction between establishing and enforcing intellectual property. Millions of people have personal computers and use spreadsheet and word-processing programs. Any one can quite easily copy personal computer software. By contrast, the number of mainframe computers is relatively small, which in turn limits the demand for mainframe software. Accordingly, it is much easier to enforce intellectual property over software for mainframe computers than personal computers.

Technology

In addition to the law, the other factor affecting excludability is technology. Recall Luna Entertainment's difficulty in marketing an open-air fireworks show: It could not exclude particular persons, so some if not all of the viewers might refuse to pay. Suppose, however, that Luna could produce fireworks that could be seen only through a special set of viewing glasses. Then, it could charge a price for the special glasses. In this example, a change of technology transforms the consumption of the product from being nonexcludable to excludable.

We have mentioned that the content of television programming is a public good. Whether, however, consumption of broadcast television is excludable depends on the technology of delivery. Consumption of free-to-the-air televi-

> ### Patents: Seventeen Years Was Not Long Enough for the Real Thing
>
> Coca Cola, one of the world's most famous products, has not been patented, and deliberately so. The reason is that the applicant for a patent must submit a detailed description of the product or process for which it seeks protection. This information becomes part of the public record, so that others can avoid infringing the patent. Potential competitors, however, can refer to the public records for details of the product or process. Once the patent expires, they are free to imitate the product or process.
>
> If Coca Cola had filed for a patent, it would have enjoyed only 17 years of protection. (Beginning in 1995, U.S. patents were extended to 20 years.) Then, on the expiration of the patent, anyone—even Coca Cola's arch-rival, Pepsi—could manufacture the "real thing." The Coca Cola Company decided not to obtain a patent and chose instead to keep its formula a trade secret. Over 100 years later, the company continues to have a monopoly over the real thing.

sion is not excludable. The station cannot prevent particular individuals from watching a broadcast.

With scrambling technology, however, the consumption of over-the-air television can be made excludable. If a station scrambles its signal, only viewers who pay for decoding equipment can watch the programs. In this case, scrambling technology has transformed the medium of delivery from being nonexcludable to excludable.

Consumption of television programming that is broadcast by cable is very easily excludable. A cable television station simply disconnects viewers who do not pay.

Software provides another example. The intellectual content of a new computer program is a public good. Suppose that the publisher distributes the program through the Internet. Whether the delivery is excludable depends on the technology implemented by the publisher. If access is open, then anyone can go to the publisher's site and download the program. On the other hand, the publisher could restrict access to users with an authorized password. Then the delivery would be excludable.

Commercial Provision

Generally, the commercial provision of a public good depends on the extent to which the seller can exclude those who do not pay from consumption or usage. In Figure 11.5, we present a spectrum of excludability, with items

Commercial Provision without Exclusion? Free-to-the-Air TV

We have claimed that commercial provision of a public good is difficult when consumption or usage is nonexcludable. Consumption of free-to-the-air television is nonexcludable. In America, however, four major networks provide free-to-the-air television on a commercial basis. Far from limping along, the business has flourished. What is the television networks' secret?

Commercial television networks such as Fox and NBC get no revenues directly from their viewers. Their primary source of revenues is advertising. In 1996, NBC sold 30-second spots during the prime-time Summer Olympics for up to $400,000. While viewers of Fox and NBC do not directly pay for television, they do pay indirectly. They pay by increasing their purchases of the products advertised on television. If television advertising had no effect on consumer demand, would Anheuser-Busch, General Motors, and Visa spend millions of dollars each year on advertising? Obviously not.

whose consumption or usage is excludable at one extreme and those whose consumption or usage is nonexcludable at the other extreme.

Considering scientific knowledge, the formula for an antiviral drug is at the excludable end, while the process for distilling water is at the nonexcludable end. With regard to broadcast television, cable television is excludable, while free-to-the-air television is nonexcludable.

We have discussed how excludability depends on law and technology. Neither of these factors, however, is fixed. Like technology, the law can change with time, and so a public good may change from being excludable to nonex-

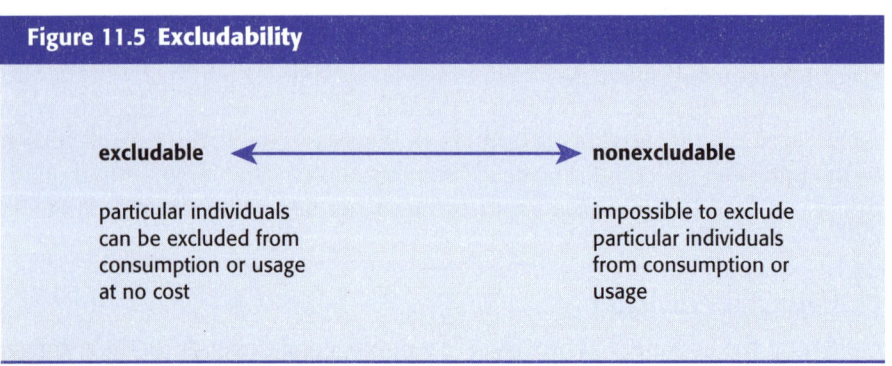

Figure 11.5 Excludability

excludable ⟵—————————————⟶ nonexcludable

particular individuals
can be excluded from
consumption or usage
at no cost

impossible to exclude
particular individuals
from consumption or
usage

Consumption or usage ranges from being excludable at one extreme to being nonexcludable at the other extreme.

cludable or vice versa. Moreover, the scope of intellectual property differs among legal jurisdictions. For instance, discoveries that can be patented in one country may not get protection elsewhere. Accordingly, it is important to pay attention to differences in law and technology over time and place.

Progress Check 11E Using the spectrum of Figure 11.5, mark the following items: (1) mainframe computer services; (2) Ohm's Law, which relates electric voltage, current, and resistance; (3) a technique for a coronary bypass operation; and (4) a cardiac (heart) surgeon's services.

Progress check

8 *Summary*

An externality arises when the actions of one party impose a benefit or cost directly on others, rather than through a market. Two particular externalities worth a special note are goodwill and network externalities. A public good is an item that provides nonrival consumption or usage.

The benchmark for externalities and public goods is economic efficiency. At that point, all parties maximize their net benefits. Externalities can be resolved through unilateral or joint action, but resolution may be hampered by differences in information and free riding. Similarly, the commercial provision of a public good depends on being able to exclude free riders. Excludability depends on law and technology.

Key Concepts

externality
positive externality
negative externality
externality is resolved
free rider
network externality

critical mass
tipping
nonrival
public good
private good

rival
congestible
excludable
patent
copyright

Further Reading

A symposium in the *Journal of Economic Perspectives* (8, no. 2, [Spring 1994]: pp. 93–150) reviews network effects and externalities. Arthur R. Miller and Michael H. Davis provide a simple and useful guide to intellectual property in *Intellectual Property—Patents, Trademarks and Copyright in a Nutshell*, 2d ed. (St. Paul, MN: West Publishing, 1990).

Review Questions

1. Give one example each of
   a. A negative externality.
   b. A positive externality.

2. When the sum of the marginal costs from a negative externality is greater than the marginal benefit to the source, an intermediary could collect fees from the recipients to pay the source to cut back on the externality. Please explain.

3. The subway system is planning to build a new line to the southern part of the city. Will this generate positive or negative externalities for
   a. The owners of high-class residential property?
   b. The owners of low-income residential property?
   c. The owners of businesses and commercial property?

4. Which of the following actions will help to resolve the externalities generated by the new southern subway line?
   a. The subway system buys the property around the new stations.
   b. The owners of property near the new stations buy shares in the subway system.
   c. The subway system buys the bus company that operates from the city center to the southern district.

5. Luna City lies two miles off Interstate Highway 105. Several of the city's leading property owners have proposed to build an exit from the interstate to attract traffic into the city. Moonlight Properties, which owns several motels, has refused to contribute any money for the new exit.
   a. How will the new exit affect Moonlight's business?
   b. Use this example to explain the "free rider incentive."

6. Explain the externalities among fishers. In which of the following cases will it be more difficult to resolve the externalities (choose a or b)?
   a. Trout in a small lake within an Indian tribal reservation.
   b. Tuna in the Pacific Ocean.

7. Give an example of a network externality. Explain the concepts of a critical mass and tipping.

8. Give an example of a public good. Explain how the use of the good is nonrival.

9. Which of the following services is excludable?
   a. Cable television.
   b. Free-to-the-air television.
   c. Wireless telephone service.
   d. A page on the World Wide Web.

10. Give examples of public goods that have been made excludable through
    a. Copyright law.
    b. Patent law.

Discussion Questions

1. Suppose that Jupiter Airlines is planning to increase evening service from Chicago's O'Hare Airport to the West Coast. These additional flights will depart after 6 PM Central Standard Time and are scheduled to arrive on the West Coast at around 9 PM. Which of the following effects is a negative externality?
   a. To provide the additional flights, Jupiter must hire more pilots and flight attendants. The additional demand will raise the wages of aircrew, thus affecting the labor costs of other airlines.

b. O'Hare has a limited capacity. Suppose that, to make room for the additional Jupiter flights, the airport manager must reschedule the flights of some smaller airlines.

c. Jupiter's additional flights will increase nighttime noise levels around West Coast airports.

2. Most local telephone service providers publish Yellow Page telephone directories. They distribute these directories free of charge to all telephone subscribers. As the Yellow Pages are an effective way of attracting customers, businesses are willing to pay for listings. The Yellow Pages provide local telephone companies with a lucrative source of revenue.

a. How does one telephone subscriber's acquisition of telephone service affect other subscribers?

b. How should a telephone company adjust the price of Yellow Page listings according to the circulation of the directory?

c. Compare two telephone companies. Southern Telephone publishes Yellow Pages, while Northern Telephone does not. Which operator has a higher marginal revenue from telephone service?

d. Assuming that Southern Telephone and Northern Telephone face the same marginal cost of providing telephone service, which will operate on a larger scale?

3. Throughout the world, shopping malls are taking an expanding share of the retail market at the expense of traditional main street stores. Let us compare the development of a new shopping mall with the same quantity of retail space along a main street.

a. A new retail development will draw more customers for nearby stores. Which development will capture more of such positive externalities for itself?

b. In which development can negative externalities such as street people and traffic congestion be more easily controlled?

4. With populations growing, an increasing number of people are choosing to live in multifamily dwellings such as condominiums. Condominiums have rules that specify the rights and the obligations of the owners and residents.

a. By considering the demand and supply of land, explain why condominiums are becoming relatively more popular.

b. Give examples of negative externalities that condominium residents can generate for one another.

c. Should the law require the residents of a condominium to comply with the condominium rules?

d. Some residents in a condominium are annoyed by the barking of other residents' dogs. How could they jointly resolve this externality?

5. The management of Venus Inn has divided the world into a number of territories with an area manager for each territory. A major responsibility of area managers is to monitor the quality of service at the hotels within the area.

a. Suppose that Venus Inn's manager for Israel has slackened on monitoring his territory. What might happen to the quality of service?

b. Leah Zuckerman owns a Venus Inn in Haifa, Israel. Should she report the area manager to the world headquarters?

6. From an economic and technical standpoint, there is an optimal rate at which to extract oil from a field. Consider an oil field that straddles the British-Norway international boundary. Hilda Oil has the drilling rights on the British side, while Sharon Oil has the rights on the Norwegian side.
   a. What are the externalities between the production of the two oil companies?
   b. Suppose that the two companies decide to negotiate an agreement. Should they aim to increase or reduce production?
   c. Assess the likelihood that the externality can be resolved through joint action.

7. With the growth of international trade and travel, more and more people are learning English. For instance, a number of major European companies have adopted English as a common language. English is also the standard language for communication among aircraft pilots and air-traffic controllers. In France, however, legislators have been so alarmed that they passed a law to restrict the use of English.
   a. Is there a network externality among people when they choose which language to learn?
   b. Does the growth of English generate a positive or negative externality for (i) people who are already fluent in English and (ii) people who do not speak English?
   c. What are the prospects for French as an international language?

8. Salmon breed inland, then travel to mature in the open seas. Once mature, they travel thousands of miles to breed in their respective birthplaces, thus renewing the cycle. Fly fishing of salmon along streams and rivers has grown into a major business. In Scotland, a single salmon can generate £500–2000 in rents, tackle purchases, gillies' wages, and hotel bills. Fishing rights may cost as much as £5000. The demand for fly fishing, however, has been growing faster than the limited number of fish. Fly fishers also blame commercial fishers for depleting supplies.

Owing to success in salmon farming and commercial fishing at sea, the wholesale price of wild salmon has dropped to about £20. Consequently, Britain's farm minister remarked that "wild salmon…should be treated not as a food resource but as a leisure resource" ("Poetic Fisherman," *The Economist* [November 28, 1992], p. 105).
   a. From the viewpoint of fly fishers, are salmon a public good?
   b. Fly fishers must pay for the right to fish on Scottish streams and rivers. How do these rights help to resolve negative externalities among fishers?
   c. If the wholesale price of wild salmon is dropping, will commercial fishermen increase or reduce the catching of salmon in the open seas?

9. Cheryl and Zak were close friends in high school. Cheryl now lives in London, while Zak lives in Brooklyn. They agreed to meet in Manhattan one weekend. As Cheryl was leaving her London apartment, she collected her camera bag. Her boyfriend remarked that they need not bring a camera since Zak surely would. Suppose that the cost of carrying a camera is 1/2 and that the benefit to each party, if there is at least one camera, is 1. Additional cameras do not increase anyone's benefit.
   a. Using a suitable game in strategic form, analyze the situation between the two friends.
   b. Identify the equilibrium or equilibria of the situation.
   c. What should Cheryl do?
   d. How would your answer to (c) change if, just before leaving London, Cheryl could leave a message for Zak to tell him whether she would bring a camera?

10. The United States and most other developed countries provide copyright protection for personal computer software such as Microsoft Word and Lotus Notes.

    a. Compare the demand for software that can be copied and used by many persons in a local area network with the demand for software that cannot be copied and can be used only on a single machine.

    b. By comparing the prices under the two scenarios in (a), explain why some publishers do not copy-protect or limit the multiple usage of their software.

    c. The effectiveness of copyright protection varies among countries. From the standpoint of maximizing profits, should a software publisher charge a higher or lower price in a country where copyright protection is relatively weak?

Math Supplement

Let us first show how to obtain the group marginal benefit curve from individual marginal benefit curves. Let b represent marginal benefit and q the amount of Luna's investment in the new Main Street store. Suppose that the investment generates marginal benefits, $b = 10 - q$ for Luna, $b = 4 - 0.4q$ for the florist, and $b = 1 - 0.2q$ for the shoe store.

We draw these marginal benefit curves in Figure 11.1. Notice that Luna's marginal benefit is positive for q in the interval [0, 10], the florist's marginal benefit is positive for q in the interval [0, 10], while the shoe store's marginal benefit is positive for q in the interval [0, 5].

Over the interval [5, 10], the vertical sum of the individual marginal benefits is

$$b = (10 - q) + (4 - 0.4q) + (1 - 0.2q) = 15 - 1.6q. \quad (11.1)$$

Over the interval [5, 10], the vertical sum of the individual marginal benefits is

$$b = (10 - q) + (4 - 0.4q) = 14 - 1.4q. \quad (11.2)$$

Accordingly, the group marginal benefit is

$$b = 15 - 1.6q \quad (11.3)$$

for q in the interval [0, 5], and

$$b = 14 - 1.4q \quad (11.4)$$

for q in the interval [5, 10]. We draw this in Figure 11.1.

Next, given the marginal cost of 1, let us calculate the economically efficient quantity. By Figure 11.1, the group marginal benefit will cross the marginal cost with investment in the interval [5, 10]. In that interval, the group marginal benefit is

$$b = 14 - 1.4q. \quad (11.5)$$

Equating this to the marginal cost of 1, we have

$$q = 13/1.4 = 9.29. \quad (11.6)$$

Accordingly, the efficient amount of investment is $929,000.

Similarly, we can derive the group marginal cost as the vertical sum of the individual marginal cost curves and calculate the economically efficient investment. We do not elaborate, as the procedure is similar to that for marginal benefits.

Chapter 12

Asymmetric Information

1 Introduction

Amy: "My husband and I are planning to buy a house. We're here to get a mortgage."

Loan Officer: "Sure, we can arrange a loan for you. What's your after-tax pay?"

Amy: "After tax, I make $35,000 a year and my husband about $25,000. That's a total of $60,000. How much can we borrow?"

Loan Officer (entering the numbers into a calculator): "We can lend you up to three times your combined after-tax income. In your case, that's three times $60,000, or $180,000. Presently, fixed rate loans are going at 8.25%."

Amy: "Oh ..., we're thinking of something in Scarsdale, near my parents. We need more like $200,000. What if we offer you a higher interest rate?"

Loan Officer: "I'm sorry, perhaps you don't understand. We can't lend you more than three times your combined after-tax income. That's it. No matter what the interest rate."

Many financial institutions apply a simple rule to determine how much they will lend for a residential mortgage. The maximum loan is some multiple of the borrower's annual after-tax income. No matter how much a borrower is willing to pay in interest, the lender will not lend more. Indeed, if a potential borrower presses too hard for a larger loan, the lender may well get suspicious and refuse to lend anything at all.

Founded in 1875, the Prudential Insurance Company is the largest insurer in the United States, with policies in effect serving over 7 million households. Prudential requires every applicant for life insurance policies above specific limits to undergo a medical examination. The company will not provide insurance to applicants who refuse the examination.

Business practices in the markets for lending and insurance differ from those in other services such as housing and transportation. Providers of housing and transportation rarely limit the quantity that each customer may buy. Moreover, a customer can often get a larger quantity by offering a higher price. Further, providers of housing and transportation never require customers to undergo personal examinations.

When there is **asymmetric information** between two parties, one party has better information than the other.

Why do lenders and insurers behave so differently from providers of other services? The essential reason is that, in lending and insurance, the buyers and sellers have **asymmetric information**. This means that one party has better information than the other.

Recall from Chapter 5 that a condition for perfect competition is that buyers and sellers have equal information. Hence, a market where information is asymmetric cannot be perfectly competitive. In this chapter, we analyze situations where buyers and sellers have asymmetric information. Generally, the better-informed party will seek to take advantage of its superior information. This will lead the less-informed party to take precautions, resulting in economic inefficiency. We discuss how the affected parties can profitably resolve the asymmetries of information and economic inefficiency.

Our analysis applies to any market where buyers and sellers have asymmetric information. We will explain why business practices in such markets differ from those in perfectly competitive markets. Essentially, these practices are ways to resolve information asymmetries and hence increase profit. In particular, we will explain why lenders set limits to the amount that a person can borrow and why insurers like Prudential require applicants for life insurance to undergo a medical examination.

2 *Risk*

Imperfect information is the absence of certain knowledge.

Before analyzing situations of asymmetric information, we should understand the concept of **imperfect information**. To have *imperfect information* about something means not having certain knowledge about that thing. Most people have imperfect information about future events such as next Monday's Standard and Poors 500 Index, the severity of the coming winter, and the next year's growth in employment. It is also possible to have imperfect information about things in the present or past. For instance, do you know precisely the height above sea level of Mount Kilimanjaro or the distance between Berlin and Kansas City?

Imperfect vis-à-vis Asymmetric Information

A single person can have imperfect information. By contrast, asymmetric information involves two or more parties, one of whom has better information than the other or others. Asymmetric information will always be associated with imperfect information, because the party with poorer information definitely will have imperfect information. For instance, if the seller of an antique knows whether the item is genuine or fake but a potential buyer does not, then the buyer has imperfect information. The item could be a genuine antique or a fake, but the buyer does not know which for sure.

Although the concepts of asymmetric and imperfect information are related, it is important to remember the difference between the two. The reason is that a market can be perfectly competitive even when buyers and sellers have imperfect information, so long as they all have the same (imperfect) information. In a perfectly competitive market, the forces of demand and supply will channel resources into economically efficient uses; hence, no further profitable transactions are possible.

For instance, the current demand for heating oil depends on expectations about temperatures in the coming winter. Buyers and sellers have equal access to meteorological forecasts. Based on these forecasts, each buyer determines its demand for heating oil. In a market equilibrium, the quantity demanded equals the quantity supplied and the marginal benefit equals the marginal cost. Hence, any further sales would be unprofitable.

By contrast, a market where information is asymmetric cannot be perfectly competitive. This means that, if buyers and sellers can resolve the information asymmetries, they can increase their benefits by more than their costs.

Risk Defined

When information is imperfect, there is risk. To understand the meaning of *risk*, let us consider the following example. Hilda knows, with probability 1.5%, that someone will steal her $20,000 car within the next 12 months. If that were to happen, Hilda would lose $20,000. If Hilda's car is not stolen, however, Hilda would lose nothing. The probability that her car will not be stolen is 100 – 1.5 = 98.5%.

Hilda has imperfect information about her future losses, because she does not know for sure whether her car will be stolen. Hilda bears a **risk:** Either she will lose $20,000 with probability of 1.5% or she will lose nothing with probability of 98.5%. *Risk* is uncertainty about benefits or costs and arises whenever there is imperfect information about something that affects benefits or costs.

Risk is uncertainty about benefits or costs due to imperfect information.

If Hilda knew for sure that her car would not be stolen within the next 12 months, then she would not bear any risk. Similarly, if she knew for sure that her car would be stolen, she would also not bear any risk. It is because her information is imperfect that she faces risk.

To explain the distinction between risk and imperfect information, consider Max, who is unrelated to Hilda. Max also has imperfect information about whether Hilda's car will be stolen. But the fate of Hilda's car does not affect Max's benefits or costs. Hence, Max does not bear any risk with regard to Hilda's car.

Risk Aversion

A **risk averse** person prefers a certain amount to risky amounts with the same expected value.

A **risk neutral** person is indifferent between a certain amount and risky amounts with the same expected value.

How a person responds to situations involving risk depends on the extent to which he or she is **risk averse**. A person is *risk averse* if she or he prefers a certain amount to risky amounts with the same expected value. A person is **risk neutral** if she or he is indifferent between a certain amount and risky amounts with the same expected value.

Given Hilda's possible losses and the probabilities, her expected loss is ($20,000 × 0.015) + ($0 × 0.985) = $300. If Hilda is risk averse, she will prefer to lose $300 for certain than to lose $20,000 with probability of 1.5%, or lose nothing with probability of 98.5%. If Hilda is risk neutral, she will be indifferent between losing $300 for certain and the risk of losing $20,000 with probability of 1.5%, or losing nothing with probability of 98.5%.

Insurance is the business of taking certain payments in exchange for eliminating risk.

Risk-averse persons will pay to avoid risk. **Insurance** is the business of taking certain payments in exchange for eliminating risk. Suppose that an insurer offers Hilda an insurance policy that pays her $20,000 if her car is stolen but pays nothing if her car is not stolen. If Hilda has the policy and her car is stolen, she loses the car but receives $20,000, so on balance, she gains and loses nothing. If her car is not stolen, the insurer will not pay her anything, so she gains and loses nothing. Thus, the insurance policy eliminates the risk that Hilda must otherwise bear. Recall that, without insurance, Hilda's expected loss is $300. Hence, if she is risk averse, she would pay at least $300 for the insurance policy.

How much risk-averse persons are willing to pay for insurance depends on their degree of risk aversion in that situation. A more risk-averse person will be willing to pay a larger amount to avoid risk. By contrast, a risk-neutral person will not pay anything to avoid risk. For instance, suppose that Sharon faces the same situation as Hilda. If Sharon is risk neutral, she would pay no more than $300 for the insurance policy.

It is important to understand the meaning of risk and risk aversion because, whenever information is asymmetric, the less-informed party has imperfect information. To the extent that this means uncertainty about benefits or costs, the less-informed party faces risk.

Progress check

Progress Check 12A Suppose that Hilda buys the insurance policy that pays her $20,000 if her car is stolen but pays nothing if her car is not stolen. Who of the following has imperfect information and who faces risk: (1) Hilda; (2) the insurer?

3 *Adverse Selection*

The cost of producing a fake antique can often be very low compared to the value of the genuine article. If fakes are sufficiently convincing, they present a serious problem for the legitimate market. Under such circumstances, potential buyers will be concerned whether they are getting a fake or the genuine article. By contrast, sellers will be much better informed about the true provenance of what they are selling. In these circumstances, information is asymmetric.

Let us use the antiques example to understand the implications of asymmetric information. Specifically, we will consider the nature of market equilibrium and the effect of price changes on the quantity demanded and supplied.

Market Equilibrium

Initially, suppose that sellers offer only genuine antiques. The stock of antiques is fixed (or almost fixed, since a small number are always being discovered). The supply for sale at any one time, however, is more elastic: It depends on existing owners' willingness to sell. In Figure 12.1, we show the supply and the demand for genuine antiques. In equilibrium at point b, the price would be $500 per unit and 3000 units of antiques would be sold each month.

Now suppose that forgers produce a quantity of 1000 fakes at no marginal cost. In principle, there could be two markets: one for fakes and another for genuine antiques. Suppose, however, that potential buyers cannot distinguish genuine antiques from fakes. Then, there will be only one market. In that single market, fakes trade alongside genuine antiques, so the supply of genuine antiques and fakes is combined.

Graphically, in Figure 12.1, since forgers produce 1000 fakes at no marginal cost, the combined supply of genuine antiques and fakes begins with 1000 fakes at no cost, and then, at that quantity, the supply curve jumps up and runs parallel to the supply of genuine antiques.[1]

What about the demand side of the market? Each individual buyer has a marginal benefit curve for genuine antiques. Buyers, however, know that they might get fakes. Suppose that all buyers derive no marginal benefit from a fake. So, taking into account the probability of getting a fake, the actual marginal benefit is lower than the marginal benefit from a genuine antique.

Suppose that all buyers are risk neutral and that they purchase a total of Q thousand pieces, of which 1000 are fake. Then each buyer has a probability $1/Q$ of getting a fake and a probability $(Q-1)/Q$ of getting a genuine antique. Since all buyers are risk neutral, each buyer's actual marginal benefit is only $(Q-1)/Q$ of the marginal benefit for genuine antiques. So, a buyer's actual marginal benefit

---

[1] This model is adapted from B. Peter Pashigian, *Price Theory and Applications* [New York: McGraw-Hill, 1995], pp. 520–6.

Figure 12.1 Market with adverse selection

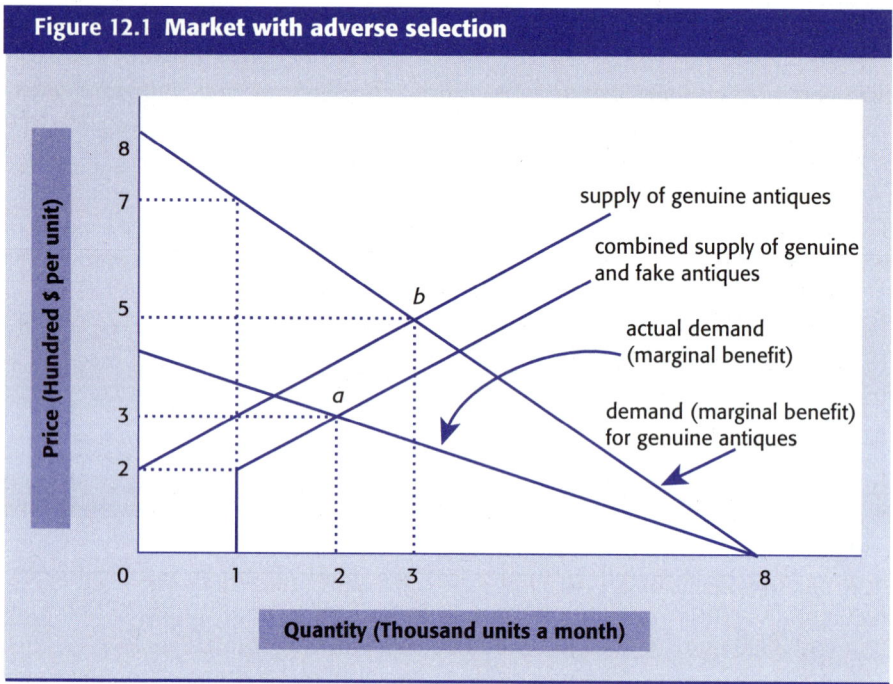

The supply and demand for genuine antiques is in equilibrium at point *b*, with a price of $500 per unit and a quantity of 3000 units. The combined supply of genuine antiques and fakes begins with 1000 fakes at no cost, then jumps up and runs parallel to the supply of genuine antiques. The actual demand, which reflects the probability of getting a fake, is the demand curve for genuine antiques shifted down by the proportion 1/Q. The actual demand and the combined supply cross at point *a*, where the price is $300 per unit and quantity is 2000 units a month.

curve, which reflects the probability of getting a fake, is his or her marginal benefit curve for genuine antiques, shifted down by the proportion 1/Q at every quantity.

Accordingly, the actual demand for antiques, which reflects the probability of getting a fake, is the demand curve for genuine antiques shifted down by the proportion 1/Q. Equivalently, at every possible quantity, the buyers' actual willingness to pay is only a fraction (Q − 1)/Q of their willingness to pay for the same of quantity of antiques that are definitely genuine.

Having laid out the demand and the supply, we can study the equilibrium. The actual demand and the combined supply cross at point *a*, where the price is $300 per unit and the quantity is Q = 2000 units a month. Hence, the probability that a buyer gets a fake is 1000/2000 = 50% and the probability of getting a genuine antique is 50%.

What if the quantity of fakes were different? If, for instance, there are 500 fakes, then the actual demand will be higher and the combined supply of genuine antiques and fakes will be further to the left. Then, the equilibrium will have a higher price. The equilibrium quantity, however, may be higher or lower: The demand is higher, but supply is further to the left.

By contrast, if the quantity of fakes is larger, then the actual demand will be lower and the combined supply will be further to the right. Hence, the market price will be lower. Again, sales may be higher or lower, depending on the balance between demand and supply.

Let us consider the effect of a price reduction on the antiques market. The marginal cost curves of legitimate sellers slope upward. So, when the market price is lower, each of them supplies a smaller quantity. By contrast, a drop in the market price does not affect the quantity of fakes supplied. Hence, the drop in the market price increases the proportion of fakes, leaving buyers with an **adverse selection**.

The problem of an *adverse selection* arises in situations of asymmetric information: The party with relatively poor information will draw a selection with relatively less attractive characteristics. In the antiques case, the buyers have less information and draw a mixture of fakes and genuine antiques, which is an adverse selection of items.

> In an **adverse selection**, the party with relatively poor information draws a selection with relatively less attractive characteristics.

Progress Check 12B Using Figure 12.1, illustrate the market equilibrium with 500 fakes. Will the market price be higher or lower than when there are 1000 fakes?

Progress check

Economic Inefficiency

How does the introduction of fakes affect buyer and seller surplus? Buyer surplus falls as some buyers receive fakes. On the other hand, buyer surplus rises to the extent that the market price falls. Buyer surplus may also increase if sales are higher. Accordingly, the effect on buyers is ambiguous. As for sellers, we must distinguish those who sell fakes from those who sell genuine antiques. Legitimate sellers definitely are worse off: They get a lower price and they sell fewer units (as genuine antiques get crowded out by lower-cost fakes). Sellers of fakes are the only group that are definitely better off from the entry of fakes into the antiques market.

Is the market equilibrium with fakes economically efficient? Each buyer purchases up to the point that its actual marginal benefit (adjusted for the probability of getting a fake) balances the market price. Similarly, each legitimate seller supplies up to the point that its marginal cost balances the market price. Since fakes provide no marginal benefit, in equilibrium, buyers who get fakes will have a marginal benefit less than the legitimate sellers' marginal cost. On the other hand, buyers who get genuine antiques will have a marginal benefit higher than the legitimate sellers' marginal cost. Accordingly, the equilibrium is not economically efficient.

Specifically, referring to Figure 12.1, if sellers offered only genuine antiques, then in equilibrium, the price would be $500 per unit and 3000 units would be sold. At this quantity, the marginal benefit and the marginal cost are both $500.

When the supply includes 1000 fakes, however, the price falls to $300 per unit and the equilibrium quantity drops to 2000 units. The equilibrium quantity of genuine antiques is 2000 – 1000 = 1000 units. The supply curve for genuine antiques shows that the marginal cost of the 1000th unit is $300. The demand curve for genuine antiques shows that the marginal benefit of the 1000th unit is $700. Hence, in equilibrium, the marginal benefit exceeds the marginal cost, so the quantity traded is not economically efficient.

If, somehow, another genuine antique could be sold, then there would be a buyer willing to pay almost $700 for that item and there would be a seller willing to provide it for a little above $300. Accordingly, there is potential gain of just under $400.

We can relate this analysis to Chapter 11 on externalities. Sellers of fakes impose a negative externality on sellers of genuine antiques and buyers. From our study of externalities, we know that, unless it is resolved, there will be too much of a negative externality relative to the economically efficient level. This means that a profit can be made by resolving the externality, which in this case, means resolving the information asymmetry.

Market Failure

Before considering how to resolve an asymmetry of information, let us look at an extreme possibility in the antiques example. Suppose that there are F fakes. Referring to Figure 12.2, the combined supply of genuine antiques and fakes has a kink at point c. Now suppose that the number of fakes is so large that the actual demand crosses the combined supply at some point d below the kink. In this case, there will be no supply of genuine antiques and the entire supply will be fakes. Then, a buyer's probability of getting a genuine antique is 0. This means that the actual marginal benefit and the actual demand curve must coincide with the horizontal axis. Thus, the initial supposition that the actual demand crosses the combined supply at some point d is not valid.

This discussion shows that there cannot be an equilibrium with the actual demand curve crossing the combined supply below the kink. Indeed, the same logic also shows that there cannot be an equilibrium with the actual demand curve crossing the combined supply above but close to the kink. If there cannot

Figure 12.2 Market failure

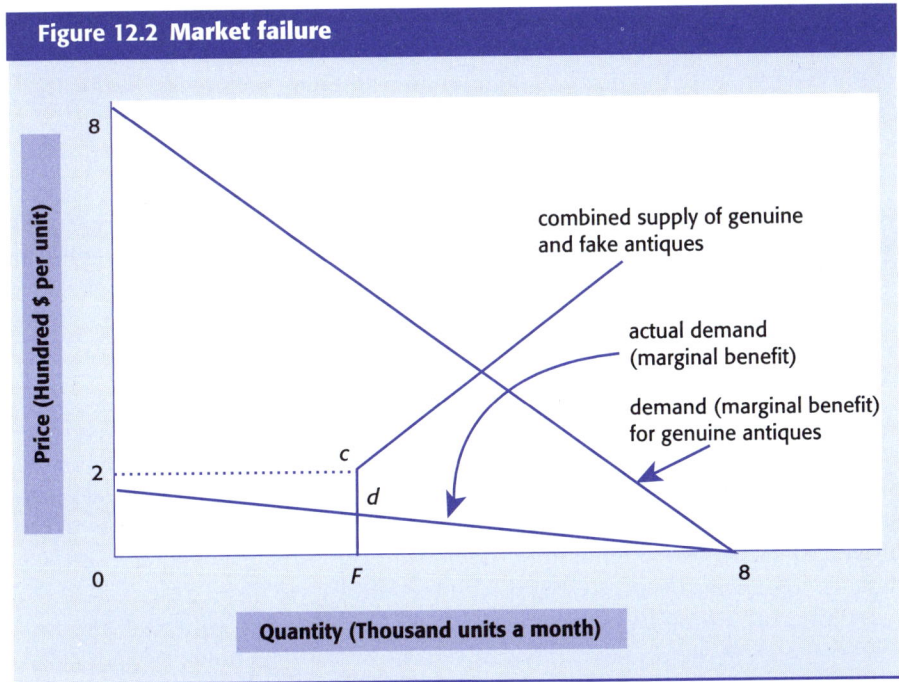

Supposing that the actual demand crosses the combined supply at point *d,* then the entire supply will be fakes. The actual demand curve must coincide with the horizontal axis, so the actual demand cannot cross the combined supply at point *d.* Generally, there cannot be an equilibrium with the actual demand curve crossing the combined supply above but close to the kink.

be an equilibrium, then buyers and sellers cannot trade. This means that the intrusion of fakes has caused the entire market to fail!

Let us view the market failure from another perspective. We will show that a change in price has very different effects in a perfectly competitive market as compared with a market subject to adverse selection. Suppose that, in a perfectly competitive market, the quantity supplied exceeds the quantity demanded. Then, a price reduction will reduce the quantity supplied and raise the quantity demanded. A sufficient reduction of the market price will restore equilibrium.

By contrast, suppose that the antiques and fakes market is out of equilibrium, with the quantity supplied greater than the quantity demanded. Consider a reduction in the price. This will cause some genuine sellers to withdraw, hence increasing the proportion of fakes. Thus, buyers will face a worse adverse selection and their willingness to pay and the demand curve will drop. Reducing the price cuts the demand as well as the quantity of supply, so it will not necessarily restore the equilibrium. In the extreme, if the price is sufficiently low, the actual demand curve will drop down to 0 and there will be no sales at all. In this case, the fakes have destroyed the market completely.

Generally, the market equilibrium will belong to one of two classes. In one class, the number of fakes is sufficiently small that the actual demand will balance the upward sloping portion of the combined supply well above the kink at point c. Then, in an equilibrium, the supply consists of both fakes and genuine antiques. In the other class, so many fakes have flooded the market that the actual demand curve will drop down to 0 and the market will fail.

Lending and Insurance

In the antiques market, sellers have better information about their own characteristics than buyers. In other markets, buyers have better information about their own characteristics than sellers. Consider the market for residential mortgages. One question is at the forefront of any lender's mind: If the value of the property falls below the amount of the outstanding principal, will the borrower default? To *default* means to stop paying the interest and principal.

When the property value is less than the outstanding principal, the borrower's equity in the property is negative. If he or she then defaults on the loan, the borrower is effectively selling the property to the lender for the outstanding principal. Some borrowers will not hesitate to default, while others will continue to make payments, even when they have negative equity.

To the extent that borrowers have better information about their personal willingness to default, there is asymmetric information between borrowers and lenders. Generally, a lender will have some chance of lending to a (bad) borrower who would readily default and some chance of lending to a (good) borrower who would be reluctant to default. If the lender raises the interest rate, it will draw an adverse selection of borrowers: The higher the interest rate, the fewer good borrowers will want loans and the higher will be the proportion of bad borrowers. This explains why a bank will not necessarily agree to lend more if a borrower offers a higher interest rate.

Insurance is another market where buyers have better information about their own characteristics than do sellers. Life insurance is insurance against the possibility of death. (It would be more accurate, but much less appealing, to call it *death insurance*.) The likelihood that a person will die within the next 12 months depends on her or his state of health and style of life. For instance, the probability of death is higher among people with heart trouble, those who engage in rock climbing and scuba diving, and those who have unprotected sex with many different partners.

It is difficult for an insurer to obtain all the relevant information about an applicant's state of health and style of life, however. Hence, there is asymmetric information between insurers and applicants for insurance.

The price that an insurer charges for an insurance policy is called a *premium*. Life insurers face an adverse selection problem: If an insurer charges a high premium, it is likely to draw applicants who know that they are in relatively poor health or who maintain risky lifestyles. Life insurers need some way to resolve the asymmetry of information.

Progress Check 12C Suppose that a life insurer presently has a high percentage of high-risk policyholders. If the insurer reduces its premiums, what will be the effect on the percentage of high-risk policyholders?

Progress check

Resolving Adverse Selection: Disallowing Choice

Many workers receive life and medical insurance through a group policy purchased by their employer. On a per capita basis, life and medical insurers generally charge lower premiums for group as compared with individual insurance policies. Generally, if the same persons were to apply for insurance on an individual basis, they must pay much higher premiums.

One reason for the difference in premiums for group vis-à-vis individual policies is the savings in administrative costs. Another reason is that a group policy can resolve adverse selection. Consider a policy that covers all employees of a company. Since individuals cannot choose whether or not to participate, the insurer can be sure of getting people with the whole distribution of characteristics. Accordingly, the insurer can avoid the problem of adverse selection.

By contrast, when offering individual policies, the insurer encounters the problem of attracting an adverse selection of applicants.

4 Appraisal

Our discussion of fakes in the antiques market illustrates that, when information is asymmetric, the market outcome will not be economically efficient. Generally, if the information asymmetry can be resolved, then benefits will increase by more than costs and, hence, there is room to make a profit.

The most obvious way to overcome asymmetric information is to obtain the information directly. In the antiques market, a collector could engage an expert to appraise a potential purchase. Referring to Figure 12.1, in the equilibrium at point *a*, the marginal benefit of a genuine antique is $700, while the market price is $300. For that marginal buyer, there is a potential gain of almost $400 by identifying a genuine antique. Provided that an appraisal costs less than the potential gain, then the buyer will purchase the appraisal.

This argument applies to all buyers for whom the marginal benefit of a genuine antique exceeds the market price by more than the cost of appraisal. To the extent that buyers obtain appraisals, there will be a separate market for genuine antiques. In that market, buyers and sellers will have equal information and, so, perfect competition will lead to economic efficiency. The buyers, however, must pay the cost of appraisals. (Recall from Chapter 5 the distinction between paying and bearing a cost. Who bears the cost of appraisals depends on the elasticities of demand and supply.)

There are some buyers whose marginal benefit from a genuine antique is relatively low, however, so that the difference between their marginal benefit and the market price does not cover the cost of appraisal. These buyers will choose not to get appraisals; hence, they cannot distinguish genuine antiques from fakes. The information asymmetry means that they will suffer from an adverse selection.

For an information asymmetry to be resolved directly, the asymmetry must satisfy two conditions. First, the characteristic about which information is asymmetric must be objectively verifiable. If an expert cannot objectively distinguish genuine antiques from fakes, then appraisals will not resolve the information asymmetry between buyers and sellers. The verification must be objective: If different appraisers give different opinions, then buyers' and sellers' information will still be asymmetric.

The second condition is that the potential gain from resolving the asymmetric information must cover the cost of appraisal. The maximum potential gain is the difference between the marginal benefit and the marginal cost. Buyers, however, focus on the difference between the marginal benefit and the market price, which is a smaller difference. Sellers focus on the difference between the market price and their marginal cost. Generally, if the potential gain is too small, then the information asymmetry will not be resolved.

Progress check   **Progress Check 12D** Will appraisals be more common in the market for cheap or more expensive antiques?

Procuring the Appraisal

In the antiques example, we supposed that the buyers procured expert appraisals to resolve the information asymmetry. Recall that the intrusion of fakes hurts sellers of genuine antiques. Hence, sellers of genuine antiques may pay for expert appraisals to distinguish themselves from sellers of fakes.

Indeed, it is more economical for sellers to procure the appraisals. The seller of an item can obtain one appraisal and present the results to many potential buyers. The appraisal is a public good: Any number of potential buyers can use the same information. Hence, it is less costly for the seller to get an appraisal than for every potential buyer to procure an appraisal of the same item.

Under what circumstances should a seller rather than potential buyers obtain the appraisal? One factor is the number of potential buyers. If there is only one potential buyer, then the expenditure will be the same whether the seller or the buyer procures the appraisal. By contrast, if there are many potential buyers, then there will be a relatively greater saving if the seller procures the appraisal.

Another factor is the extent to which the various potential buyers seek the same information about the item. If different potential buyers have different considerations, then it may be difficult for the seller's appraisal to provide all the required information. In this case, each potential buyer might prefer to obtain an individual appraisal.

Appraising Borrowers

In the market for loans, borrowers have better information about their ability and willingness to repay than potential lenders. To guard against adverse selection, lenders can also appraise applicants for loans. One input into the appraisal is a credit check. This shows the applicant's outstanding debts and record in repaying loans and other forms of credit. A credit check provides information about a borrower's ability and willingness to repay. Many lenders will also check a loan applicant's employment record, which is another indicator of ability to repay.

Credit checks and employment reports can help borrowers with some history to resolve their asymmetry of information with lenders. What about borrowers such as new immigrants and graduating students who have little prior credit history or employment record? They may have no way to directly resolve the information asymmetry.

5   *Screening*

We have discussed how asymmetric information can be directly resolved through appraisal. Since appraisal is costly and not always feasible, however, it

Moody's: Appraising Debt

Private and public corporations, municipalities, sovereign governments, and international organizations raise funds through issuance of debt obligations such as commercial paper and bonds. These debt obligations may be sold to numerous investors, dispersed all over the world. A major concern for investors is the possibility that the issuer will default. Issuers, however, have better information about their own financial condition and likelihood of default.

Issuers can address this asymmetry by obtaining an independent rating of their debt. Moody's Investors Service was founded in 1909 to rate railway bonds. At the request of an issuer, Moody's will rate a debt obligation. The issuer can then provide the rating to potential investors.

The validity of the ratings system has been confirmed through empirical studies that show that issuers with lower Moody's ratings have been systematically more likely to default. By the end of 1994, Moody's had outstanding ratings on 98,000 corporate and municipal debt obligations.

Sources: "Rating the Rating Agencies," *The Economist* (July 15, 1995), pp. 61–2; Moody's Investors Service, Inc., *Global CD Report on Dun & Bradstreet Corp.,* 1995.

How's Your Health? Getting a Piece of the Rock

Applicants for life insurance have better information about their health and lifestyles than potential insurers. Life insurers are aware of this information asymmetry and the associated problem of adverse selection. The Prudential Insurance Company, American's largest insurer, requires some applicants for life insurance to undergo a medical examination. The company will not provide insurance to applicants who refuse the examination.

The practice of the life insurance industry is to require more stringent and comprehensive physicals for applicants who are older and seek larger policies. Both factors help guard against adverse selection. From the insurer's perspective, a medical examination helps to weed out applicants who are in relatively poor health.

The insurer's benefit from this weeding is greater for older applicants because there is greater variation in health among older than younger people. Further, the insurer's benefit from the physical is greater for larger policies. The cost of the medical examination, however, does not vary with the applicant's age and policy amount. Accordingly, life insurers typically require more stringent and comprehensive physicals for applicants who are older and seek larger policies.

is important to consider indirect alternatives. Generally, asymmetric information can be resolved in three indirect ways. We discuss one in this section, and the others in later sections.

In a situation where one party has better information about its own characteristics, the less-informed party may be able to elicit another party's characteristics indirectly through **screening.** *Screening* is an initiative of a less-informed party to indirectly elicit the other party's characteristics. It exploits the sensitivity of the better-informed party to some variable that the less-informed can control. The less-informed party must design choices around that variable to induce **self-selection**, meaning that parties with different characteristics choose different alternatives.

Screening is an initiative of a less-informed party to indirectly elicit the other party's characteristics.

In **self-selection**, parties with different characteristics choose different alternatives.

The ancient Jewish king Solomon provided the classic example of screening. Two women came before him, one holding a dead boy and the other a living boy. Each woman claimed the living boy to be her son. Solomon had to decide:

> [T]he king said, "Bring me a sword... Divide the living child in two, and give half to the one, and half to the other." Then the woman whose son was alive said to the king, because her heart yearned for her son, "Oh, my lord, give her the living child, and by no means slay it." But the other said, "It shall be neither mine nor yours; divide it." Then the king answered and said, "Give the living child to the first woman, and by no means slay it; she is the mother." (1 Kings 3.16–27 RSV)

In this famous case, Solomon was the less-informed party: He did not know which woman was truly the mother of the living boy. He did know, however, that the true mother would not allow her son to be killed, while the false mother might be indifferent. The two women were differentially sensitive to Solomon's proposal to divide the boy. The king exploited this differential to good effect. The true mother and the false mother quickly identified themselves.

If, however, both women had been indifferent to cutting the boy, then Solomon's proposal would have failed to induce self-selection between the two women. Screening is possible only if the less-informed party can control some variable to which the better-informed parties are *differentially* sensitive. By contrast with direct appraisal, screening elicits the characteristics of the better-informed party indirectly. Screening is an indirect way of resolving an information asymmetry.

Screening Home Mortgage Borrowers: "Points"

In the United States, financial institutions making residential mortgage loans face borrowers with different horizons. Some borrowers plan to repay within a short time, while others intend to keep their loans for a longer period. The longer the period, the more profit the lender will earn from the loan.

Lenders, however, cannot directly distinguish borrowers with different horizons. They do so indirectly through an up-front charge called *points*. The charge is set as a percentage of the principal. So, for instance, the charge on a $100,000 loan that bears 1.5 points is $1,500.

Lenders typically offer borrowers a choice among loans with different interest rates and points. Loans with lower interest rates bear higher points. For instance, in the *Los Angeles Times* of June 8, 1995, the DiTech Funding Corporation advertised 30-year fixed interest loans of less than $203,150 as follows: a rate of 7.00% with 2.0 points, a rate of 7.25% with 1.0 point, and a rate of 7.50% with no points.

By offering these alternatives, lenders can screen among borrowers according to how long they plan to hold their loans. A borrower who plans to repay his or her loan within a short time horizon will prefer a loan with low points. Such a borrower would rather pay a higher interest rate for a relatively short period of time. By contrast, a borrower who plans to hold the loan for a long time will prefer a loan with a lower interest rate and higher points. The savings on interest will make up for the higher up-front charge in points.

Accordingly, the choice between high points or a high interest rate effects self-selection among the borrowers. Loans with high points and low interest rates draw longer-term borrowers, while those with lower points and higher interest rates attract borrowers with shorter horizons.

Indirect Segment Discrimination

One of the key business applications of screening is to pricing policy. In Chapter 9, "Pricing Policy," we gave the name *indirect segment discrimination* to pricing policies that apply screening to induce self-selection among buyers with different characteristics. Generally, to effect indirect segment discrimination, the seller must identify some variable to which the segments are differentially sensitive and then structure a set of alternatives that will induce self-selection.

Airlines offer a choice between unrestricted and restricted fares to screen between business and leisure travelers. Business travelers cannot book far in advance and do not wish to stay away for the weekend. Airlines charge a higher price for fares that do not require advance booking or weekend overstay and a lower price for restricted fares. The unrestricted fares attract business travelers, while the restricted fares draw leisure travelers.

Similarly, consumer products manufacturers also engage in indirect segment discrimination. They use cents-off coupons to screen between customers with higher and lower price elasticity of demand. The customers with more elastic demand are more likely to use the coupons and hence get a lower price. The customers with inelastic demand are less likely to use the coupons and hence pay a higher price.

Cable television providers also engage in indirect segment discrimination. They apply bundling to screen between customers with different preferences. Bundled channels attract viewers with relatively middle-of-the-road preferences, while separate channels draw viewers with more extreme tastes.

Differentiating Variable

In some instances, the less-informed party may have the choice of several differentiating variables. Ideally, the less-informed party should structure the choice that drives the biggest possible wedge between the better-informed parties with the different characteristics.

The less-informed party must consider the effectiveness of each differentiating variable in driving a wedge between the various segments. This means comparing the differential sensitivity of the segments to each variable. The less-informed party should place relatively more emphasis on the more effective variable.

For instance, airlines could use clothing as a differentiating variable, offering a lower fare to travelers wearing casual clothing and a higher fare to travelers in business attire. Business travelers could easily circumvent this differentiating variable; hence, it is not effective. By contrast, airlines have found advance booking and weekend stayover to be effective differentiating variables.

The most effective screening may involve a combination of the differentiating variables. For instance, airlines use a combination of restrictions, advance booking and weekend stayover, and a separation between first class and coach to screen leisure from business travelers.

Multiple Unobservable Characteristics

In some cases, the information asymmetry between two parties concerns not just one but several characteristics. Then, if the less-informed party screens on a single differentiating variable, the resulting choices may not resolve the asymmetry.

Consider the following example. Comprehensive automobile insurance covers loss or damage to a car arising from all causes, including fire and theft. The likelihood of loss or damage depends on the driver's behavior. It is lower for a careful driver who parks in secure, well-lighted places and uses a steering lock and car alarm. By contrast, the likelihood of loss or damage is higher for less careful drivers.

The demand for comprehensive insurance arises from risk-averse drivers: They would rather pay a fixed premium than face the risk of loss or damage. The insurer, however, cannot directly observe either the driver's carefulness or degree of risk aversion.

Many automobile insurers offer comprehensive insurance with a choice of several deductibles, where the insurer compensates loss or damage only in excess of the specified deductible. Insurers charge relatively higher premiums for policies with lower deductibles.

The choice of deductible can screen drivers by their carefulness. Careful drivers will select cheaper policies that carry higher deductibles. Less careful drivers will prefer expensive policies with low deductibles. The choice of deductibles, however, also screens drivers by their degree of risk aversion. Less risk-averse drivers will prefer cheaper policies with high deductibles, while more risk-averse drivers will prefer policies with lower deductibles.

The choice of deductibles screens two characteristics: carefulness and risk aversion. A single variable, the deductible, cannot resolve the asymmetry of information over two characteristics. For instance, the insurer will not know whether those choosing the high-deductible policies are more careful drivers or less risk averse.

Generally, to resolve information asymmetries through screening, the less-informed party needs as many differentiating variables as there are characteristics that it cannot observe.

Progress check

Progress Check 12E Collateral is property that a borrower provides to a lender as a security for a loan. If the borrower defaults on the loan, the lender can seize the collateral. Explain how a lender can use requirements for collateral to screen among borrowers with different willingness to repay.

Screening Not Permitted: The Right to Remain Silent

Criminal trials provide a clear example of asymmetric information. The defendant knows much more about his or her past conduct than does the prosecuting lawyer, the judge, or the jury. In American and English criminal courts, every person who takes the witness stand may be examined by the lawyers for the prosecution as well as the defense. If a defendant were to testify, then she or he might be subject to cross-examination by the prosecution. So, a defendant with something to hide would rather not take the witness stand.

This suggests a very obvious screening mechanism: Every defendant should be permitted to choose whether to take the witness stand, but the court can draw a negative inference about one who elects not to testify. This policy should induce self-selection among defendants according to whether they are concealing evidence of their own guilt.

American and English criminal courts, however, allow every defendant the right to remain silent and prohibit the court from inferring anything from the defendant's decision. This right nullifies what would otherwise be a very effective screening procedure.

6 Auctions[2]

We have discussed how businesses can apply screening to discriminate among buyers who are willing to pay different prices. Let us now discuss auctions, a pricing technique that screens by exploiting strategic interaction among potential buyers.

Consider the following example. Venus Paper wants to sell a tract of British Columbia forest. There are many potential buyers and Venus wants to get the highest possible price. In this case, it does not seem feasible to apply indirect segment discrimination: What set of choices would induce self-selection? One feasible approach is to negotiate with all the possible buyers on an individual basis. Individual negotiation, however, would take a lot of time. An alternative is for Venus to conduct an auction.

An auction applies competitive pressure to the participating bidders. Each bidder must act strategically since its best bid depends on the competing bids: If the other bids are low, then a bidder can win with a relatively low bid, while, if the other bids are high, then a bidder must bid relatively high to win. Each bidder faces a fundamental trade-off. By bidding more aggressively, it will improve its chances of winning the auction. On the other hand, if it bids more aggressively, it will get a smaller profit from winning the auction.

The differentiating variable in an auction is the probability of winning. A bidder with a higher value for the item will gain relatively more from winning the auction and hence will pay relatively more for a higher probability of winning. Thus, the auction induces self-selection among the participants according to their respective values for the item.

Auction Methods

There are various methods of conducting an auction. The bidding could be open or sealed. The seller may or may not specify a **reserve price**, below which it refuses to sell the item. In an auction for multiple items, each winning bidder could be required to pay the price that she or he bid or the price bid by the marginal winning bidder.

How the method of auction affects bidding depends on various factors, including the extent to which bidders share the same value for the item on sale, the bidders' uncertainty about the true value, and bidders' risk aversion. Rather than investigate all of these factors in detail, we discuss some implications that apply generally.

Auction houses such as Christie's and Sotheby's use open auctions to sell jewelry, real estate, and works of art. The auctioneer calls out prices in an ascending sequence, and the bidders indicate whether or not they wish to continue

> The **reserve price** is the price below which the seller will not sell the item.

---

[2]This section is more advanced. It may be omitted without loss of continuity.

participating. By contrast, other auctions allow only sealed bids. One factor in the choice between open and sealed-bid auctions is the potential for collusion among the bidders. As we discussed in Chapter 8, competing buyers can increase their net benefit by colluding to depress the price. This principle applies to auctions as well: Competing bidders can benefit by agreeing on a low price.

The bidders in an open auction can see each other's behavior. This means that colluding bidders can observe whether they are each abiding by their collusive agreement. If one bidder cheats by bidding above the agreed price, another bidder can raise the price and prevent the cheater from winning the auction. By contrast, in a sealed-bid auction, a bidder can easily cheat on the collusive agreement with a bid exceeding the agreed price. The other bidders will learn about the cheating only when the seller announces the result of the auction. At that time, it would be too late to rein in the cheater.

Another difference between open and sealed-bid auctions concerns the character of information revealed during bidding in an open auction. We consider this difference later in this section.

We have discussed how open auctions are more vulnerable to collusion among bidders than sealed-bid auctions. The seller in open auction, however, can counteract collusion by applying a reserve price. A bidder must exceed the reserve price to get the item. The major reason for a seller to set a reserve price is to defeat collusion among the bidders. A reserve price forces bidders to bid higher or face the prospect of not getting the item.

The downside of a reserve price is that all the bids may fall below the reserve price. In this case, the sale will fail and the seller gets no revenue. Accordingly, in setting a reserve price, the seller must balance the increased revenue from a sale against the probability of no sale. A factor in this trade-off is the number of bidders: When there are many bidders, it is more likely that at least one bidder will exceed the reserve price.

In a **discriminatory auction,** each winning bidder pays the price that she or he bid.

In a **nondiscriminatory auction**, each winning bidder pays the price bid by the marginal winning bidder.

In a **discriminatory auction,** each winning bidder pays the price that she or he bid. By contrast, in a **nondiscriminatory auction,** each winning bidder pays the price bid by the marginal winning bidder. Since a winning bidder at a nondiscriminatory auction pays the price of the marginal winning bidder, a bidder at a nondiscriminatory auction should bid relatively higher than at a discriminatory auction.

This, however, does not necessarily imply that the seller will get higher revenue from a nondiscriminatory auction. Although bidders make relatively higher bids, the seller collects only the price bid by the marginal bidder for each item sold. Whether a seller gets a higher revenue from a discriminatory or nondiscriminatory auction depends on the balance between the two factors.

Winner's Curse

In addition to not knowing their competitors' strategies, the bidders participating in an auction may also be uncertain about the value of the item for sale. For instance, in the example of Venus Paper, the various bidders may be unsure about the quantity of wood pulp that the trees will yield. Let us see how this uncertainty can affect the outcome of bidding.

Suppose that Joy is one of four bidders at the auction and that her estimate of the yield is 4000 tons of pulp a year, while the other bidders have lower estimates. Then, Joy will probably make the highest bid and win the auction. On the basis of the information of all four bidders, however, Joy probably has over-estimated the true yield. It is even possible that Joy's estimate is so high that her bid exceeds the true yield, so that she will incur a loss on the deal.

Joy's example illustrates the **winner's curse**. The *winner's curse* arises in an auction where the various bidders are uncertain about some common element in the value of the item for sale. A bidder whose estimate of that common element is about right will probably not win the auction. On the other hand, a bidder whose estimate is too high has a higher probability of winning. Hence, on average, the winning bidder is one who has overestimated the true value of the item.

A bidder should take account of the possibility of the winner's curse by bidding more conservatively, that is, aiming for a larger margin between her estimate of the value of the item and her bid. By bidding conservatively, she can reduce the likelihood of overbidding for the item.

> The **winner's curse** is that the winning bidder overestimates the true value of the item for sale.

The winner's curse is more severe when the number of bidders is larger, when the true value of the item is more uncertain, and in a sealed-bid compared with an open auction. If there are 20 bidders, then the winner will probably be one whose estimate is higher than 19 other estimates. By contrast, if there are four bidders, then the winner's estimate is probably higher than three other estimates. An estimate that is higher than 19 others is more likely to exceed the true value than an estimate that is higher than three others.

If the true value of the item is more uncertain, then the probability that the highest estimate exceeds the true value will be higher. Consider, for instance, an ounce of gold. There is no uncertainty about the true value of an ounce of gold. Every bidder would know the value to be the prevailing market price, and hence all their estimates and bids would be the same. The winner's curse arises only when there is uncertainty about the true value of the item for sale. The greater the uncertainty about the true value, then the greater will be the extent of the winner's curse.

In an open auction, bidders with relatively low values for the item will drop out progressively as the price ascends. Since the record of bidding is open, the remaining bidders can see the prices at which the various bidders drop out. The price at which a bidder drops out reveals information about her or his estimate of the true value of the item. The remaining bidders can use this additional information to refine their estimate of the true value. Hence, open bidding mitigates the winner's curse.

We have discussed three factors that affect the extent of the winner's curse. Whenever the winner's curse is relatively more severe, a bidder should adjust by bidding more conservatively.

Progress check

Progress Check 12F Venus Paper has procured an independent appraisal of the tract that it is selling by auction.

    a.   Should it provide this information to the bidders?
    b.   How will this affect the extent of the winner's curse?

Winner's Curse: The Los Angeles Metro

Governments frequently use auctions to procure goods and services. The principles of an auction to buy are exactly the same as for an auction to sell. In an auction where the bidders are competing to supply an item and they are uncertain about some common cost element, the winner's curse is the prospect of bidding *less* than the true cost. The following example illustrates the winner's curse in a procurement auction.

In late 1987, the Southern California Rapid Transit District (RTD) called tenders to build an underground Los Angeles Metro station at the intersection of Seventh and Flower Streets. There were eight bids for this project, ranging from $37.8 to $58.1 million, with an average bid of $46.6 million (see Table 12.1).

The RTD awarded the contract to the Granite-Marmolejo joint venture, which bid $42.5 million. Four years later, on completing the project, Granite-Marmolejo filed a claim for an additional $27 million, which amounted to 64% of its original price. The contractor claimed that it had incurred the extra costs to deal with unforeseen difficulties that the RTD had not disclosed during the tender. These difficulties included unmarked utility lines, unstable soil, and underground obstacles.

Source: "Metro Rail 64% over Budget, Builder Says," *Los Angeles Times* (February 4, 1992), p. B1.

Table 12.1 Bids to build LA Metro Seventh/Flower station

Bidder	Price ($ million)
Fru-Con & Bilfinger + Berger	37.8
Granite-Marmolejo	42.5
Tutor-Saliba-Perini J.V.	44.0
M-K / Healy	46.2
Guy F. Atkinson	47.6
Kiewit Pacific Company / Kajima	48.0
Homer J. Olsen, Inc.	49.0
J. F. Shea Company, Inc.	58.1
Average	*46.6*

Source: Southern California Rapid Transit District.

7 *Signaling*

In a situation where information is asymmetric, the marginal benefit does not equal the marginal cost; hence, a profit can be made by resolving the asymmetry. We have considered two ways of resolving information asymmetries. One is direct appraisal of the unknown characteristics. An indirect way is screening, an initiative of the less-informed party to elicit the characteristics of the better-informed party.

Another indirect way of resolving an information asymmetry is through the initiative of the better-informed party. **Signaling** is an action by the better-informed party to communicate its characteristics in a credible way to the less-informed party.

Signaling is an action by the better-informed party to communicate its characteristics in a credible way to the less-informed party.

To illustrate the concept of signaling, let us consider again a market where buyers of antiques cannot distinguish between genuine items and fakes. In this market, the unknown characteristic is the true nature of an item. With the intrusion of fakes, the market outcome is not economically efficient. Since sellers of genuine antiques clearly suffer from the fakes, they may take the initiative to resolve the asymmetry of information.

Suppose that an antiques dealer guarantees to buy back anything that it sells at the original sale price at any time. To assure potential customers that the offer is legitimate, the dealer posts a sufficiently large bond with a reputable bank. Can this buyback offer effectively signal that the dealer is indeed selling a genuine antique? Equivalently, is the buyback offer a credible signal?

The answer depends on whether the seller of a fake will also make such a buyback offer. Assuming that buyers of fakes eventually discover the truth, a dealer who sells fakes and makes the buyback offer would eventually have to buy back all the fakes that it has sold. Accordingly, sellers of fakes would prefer not to make buyback offers. The buyback offer makes sense only for sellers of genuine antiques. Thus, it credibly distinguishes sellers of genuine antiques from sellers of fakes.

By contrast with direct appraisal, signaling communicates the characteristics of the better-informed party indirectly. Signaling is an indirect way of resolving an information asymmetry. For instance, the antiques dealer does not directly declare its item to be genuine. Rather, the dealer makes a commitment that indirectly and credibly communicates that it is selling a genuine item. Because sellers of fakes would not make the same commitment, the buyback offer is a credible signal.

Credibility

To be credible, a signal must induce self-selection among the better-informed parties. Specifically, the cost of the signal must be sufficiently lower for parties with superior characteristics than for parties with inferior characteristics. Then, only those with superior characteristics will offer the signal. For instance, in the case of the antique dealers, if buyers of fakes eventually discover the truth, then the cost of the buyback offer is lower for sellers of genuine antiques than for sellers of fakes. This cost difference drives the self-selection among the various sellers.

Suppose that Mercury Antiques posts a sign "All genuine" outside its store. Will this be a credible signal? The answer depends on whether it is relatively more costly for the seller of a fake to post the sign. The cost of posting an "All genuine" sign is the same for sellers of genuine antiques and fakes. Hence, such a sign alone will not induce self-selection among sellers and cannot be a credible signal.

Advertising and Reputation

We have just claimed that an "All genuine" sign cannot be a credible signal that a seller is offering genuine antiques. Let us next consider a somewhat different proposal. Suppose that Mercury Antiques spends several thousand dollars to advertise that it deals only in genuine articles. If, however, Mercury pushes out fakes, then buyers will discover the subterfuge and the word will spread. If the word spreads quickly enough, Mercury will not recover the investment in its advertising. In this case, the advertising expenditure is an investment that pays off only if Mercury does indeed deliver genuine antiques.

A sunk investment that pays off only if the seller does indeed deliver good quality can be a credible signal. This signaling depends on three conditions. First, the investment must be sunk. If the advertising expenditure is reversible, then a seller of low quality can also make the same investment, pass out inferior products, and get its money back. A reversible investment would not be a credible signal.

Second, buyers must be able to detect poor quality fairly quickly. If a seller can fool buyers for a long time, then even one offering poor quality can afford the sunk investment. Many car owners purchase rust treatment: It is almost impossible for any individual driver to tell whether the treatment is effective. Automobile rust treatment is a product for which a sunk investment may not be a credible signal.

The third condition is that word of poor quality must spread and cut into the seller's future business. A one-time seller can afford to pass off poor quality because it will never face the punishment of losing repeat business. Fast-food restaurants along highways serve many customers on a one-time basis. If a restaurant provides poor quality, its customers may notice but they might never pass the same way again, so the restaurant does not lose.

Any investment that meets these three conditions can be a credible signal of good product quality. Two candidates are advertising and reputation. An "All genuine" sign may not be meaningful for a seller with a short time horizon. By contrast, a seller who has been in business for many years can build up a reputation. This is a sunk investment that would not make sense for a seller offering inferior quality.

Progress Check 12G Explain the difference between screening and signaling.   *Progress check*

Branding: Signaling Service Station Quality

Service stations market a variety of products ranging from hot dogs to gasoline and repair service. The seller's reputation is a potentially credible signal of good product quality. But, it would be credible only to customers who are likely to come back. What about one-time customers?

The asymmetry of information can be resolved through branding. A brand attaches its reputation to many service stations, all over the country. Hence, if one station provides poor service, it affects the reputation of the entire brand, and customers will cut back their patronage of all the stations with the same brand. The owner of the brand will invest effort in monitoring the various stations to maintain quality, and so avert a brandwide drop in business.

Service stations along highways have a higher proportion of one-time relative to repeat customers. Hence, they have greater need for branding as a way to assure customers of product quality. An empirical study of service stations in eastern Massachusetts showed that stations along highways were 19% more likely to be affiliated with a major brand than stations off highways.

Source: I.P.L. Png and David Reitman, "Why Are Some Products Branded and Others Not?" *Journal of Law and Economics* 38, no. 1 (April 1995): pp. 207–24.

8 *Contingent Payments*

A **contingent payment** is a payment made if a specific event occurs.

We have discussed two ways of indirectly resolving an information asymmetry: screening and signaling. Let us now consider a third indirect approach, which is to use a **contingent payment**. A *contingent payment* is a payment made if a specific event occurs. Bets are contingent payments: You get a dollar from me if the coin turns up heads, while I will get a dollar from you if it turns up tails. In this bet, the specific event is the side of the coin that faces up after the toss.

All insurance policies make use of contingent payments. A life insurance policy makes a payment in the contingency of death, a health insurance policy makes payments in the contingency of illness, and a driver's liability policy makes a payment in the contingency of an automobile accident.

Buyback offers also make use of contingent payments. An antique dealer's offer to buy back items is essentially a payment contingent on the customer not being satisfied with her or his purchase. As the buyback offer suggests, contingent payments can be very useful in signaling information.

Let us consider a more subtle example. Recall Venus Paper's auction of a tract of British Columbia forest. Suppose that Venus knows that these trees will yield an exceptional quantity of wood pulp, say, 6000 tons a year. It, however, has no independent appraisal or other information that would directly convince potential buyers.

What if Venus were to specify that it would sell the tract for a share of the pulp production rather than a straight cash payment? By asking for a share, Venus is taking a payment that is contingent on the yield from the tract. If the tract produces a high yield, then Venus will get a higher payment, while if it produces a low yield, then Venus's payment will be low.

Selling the tract for a share of the production is a way by which Venus can signal its information to potential buyers. Other things equal, sellers of average or relatively low-yielding trees would prefer to sell for straight cash. Hence, those selling relatively better trees can distinguish themselves by selling for a share of the production. Accordingly, the share induces self-selection among sellers offering products of different quality.

Contingent payments can be used to screen as well as signal. In the example of Venus's trees, the seller can retain a share of the production as a way of signaling its information. On the other hand, a potential buyer could take the initiative of offering the seller a choice between payment in a share of the production or straight cash. A seller who chooses straight cash is implicitly admitting that the production will be relatively low.

Buyback in International Investment

Many developing countries want to boost their exports of manufactured products. With this aim, they actively promote the acquisition of production technology and equipment from foreign suppliers. The developing countries use these to produce manufactured items for export to the world market.

The developing countries, however, suffer from an information asymmetry. Specifically, compared with large multinational companies, the developing countries have relatively poor information about current technology and world market conditions. They worry that foreign suppliers are palming off some old write-offs rather than providing the most cost-effective technology and equipment. They also worry that the foreign suppliers may exaggerate the market potential for the manufactured product.

One way to resolve these information asymmetries is to require the foreign supplier of production technology and equipment to buy back a specified quantity of future production of the manufactured item. This forces the foreign supplier to sell the product on the world market. The sales will depend on the quality of production technology and facilities that it had supplied to the developing country. The sales will also depend on the world market conditions.

Through the arrangement, the payment to the foreign supplier becomes contingent on the quality of production technology and equipment supplied and the supplier's estimate of world market conditions. The foreign supplier will then have a strong incentive to supply the most cost-effective technology and equipment and provide a realistic projection of the market potential for the manufactured product.

Source: Jean Francois Hennart, "The Transaction-Cost Rationale for Countertrade," *Journal of Law, Economics, and Organization* 5, no. 1 (Spring 1989): pp. 127–53.

9 *Balancing the Alternatives*

In situations of asymmetric information, the allocation of resources will not be economically efficient; hence, the marginal benefit will diverge from the marginal cost. A profit can be made by resolving this divergence. We have discussed four general ways to resolve information asymmetries. The direct approach is appraisal, while there are three indirect approaches: screening, signaling, and contingent payments.

Each approach may involve costs of implementation, and they may differ in the extent to which they can reduce the divergence between the marginal benefit and the marginal cost. For instance, screening, signaling, and contingent payments may differ in their effectiveness in inducing self-selection.

Accordingly, the relevant parties should aim to balance the several approaches. In any particular situation, the appropriate balance among appraisal, screening, signaling, and contingent payments depends on the relative cost-effectiveness of the alternative ways to resolve the information asymmetry.

While clear in principle, the distinction among appraisal, screening, signaling, and contingent payments may not be so obvious in practice. For instance, an antiques dealer could offer an independent appraisal as a way to signal that it is selling genuine items. Similarly, a potential buyer could require sellers to provide independent appraisals as way of screening out sellers of fakes.

Some business practices can serve to both screen and signal. In the market for residential mortgages, borrowers have better information about their ability and willingness to repay than potential lenders. A borrower can resolve this asymmetry of information by making a larger down payment. If the down payment is larger, the value of the property will be less likely fall below the outstanding principal of the loan, and hence the likelihood of negative equity will be lower.

A good borrower, who would not default when she or he has negative equity, will not be concerned about the likelihood of negative equity being lower. A bad borrower, however, the type who would take advantage of negative equity to default, would be more concerned. Hence, by offering a larger down payment, a good borrower can signal her or his superior characteristics to potential lenders. The larger down payment induces self-selection.

By the very same logic, a lender can insist on a large down payment as a way to screen between good and bad borrowers. Just as the larger down payment induces self-selection and effects signaling, it can also effect screening. Either way, it helps to resolve the information asymmetry.

10 *Summary*

In situations of asymmetric information, the allocation of resources will not be economically efficient. The asymmetry can be resolved directly through appraisal or indirectly through screening, signaling, or contingent payments. The indirect methods depend on inducing self-selection among parties with different characteristics. When information is asymmetric, some parties may bear risk. This may conflict with self-selection on other characteristics.

A key business application of screening is indirect segment discrimination in pricing. A related application is auctions, which exploit strategic interaction among competing bidders to force bidders with higher values to pay higher prices.

Key concepts

asymmetric information
imperfect information
risk
risk averse
risk neutral
insurance

adverse selection
screening
self-selection
reserve price
discriminatory
   auction

nondiscriminatory auction
winner's curse
signaling
contingent payment

Further Reading

For more on the economics of asymmetric information generally, see Michael L. Katz and Harvey Rosen, *Microeconomics* (Homewood, IL: Irwin, 1994), Chapter 16, and Eric Rasmusen, *Games and Information* (Cambridge, MA: Basil Black-well, 1994). Paul Milgrom and John Roberts apply the economics of asymmetric information to corporate finance in Chapter 15 of *Economics, Organization, and Management* (Englewood Cliffs, NJ: Prentice-Hall, 1992).

Review Questions

1. In the following situations, explain the asymmetry of information, if any.
   a. Investors cannot perfectly predict the next day's Standard and Poors 500 Index.
   b. Acquirer is planning a takeover bid for Target at a price of $50 a share, which is 25% above the current market price of $40 a share. The directors of Acquirer are secretly buying shares of Target for their personal accounts.
   c. Henry tosses a fair coin. He bets heads, while James bets on tails.
   d. Henry has chosen a coin that is loaded in favor of heads. Henry bets heads, while James bets on tails.

2. Using relevant examples, explain the following:
   a. Asymmetric information.
   b. Imperfect information.
   c. Risk.

3. True or false?
   a. Where there is asymmetric information, there will be imperfect information.
   b. Whenever people face risk, they will seek insurance.

4. Bohemian Clothing, a manufacturer of women's fashions, pays its production workers through a piece rate. The Human Resources manager has proposed to offer workers the alternative of a fixed salary. Will this alternative draw an adverse selection of workers?

5. Toshi is about to buy a secondhand Nissan. The seller is offering a below-market price. The seller has assured Toshi that the car is in perfect mechanical condition. Explain why Toshi should get an expert to evaluate the car.

6. Give an example of screening. Explain
   a. The asymmetry of information.
   b. How screening works through self-selection.

7. This question relies on the auctions section. Explain the impact of the following on collusion among bidders at an auction:
    a. Using open bidding vis-à-vis sealed bids.
    b. Setting a reserve price.

8. This question relies on the auctions section. In which of the following auctions for the rights to extract oil will the winner's curse be more serious?
    a. The seller provides all available geological information to the bidders.

b. The seller has made a geological study but is keeping it secret.

9. Give an example of signaling. Explain
    a. The asymmetry of information.
    b. How signaling works.

10. Intuit, the publisher of Quicken, a financial management program, once offered full refunds to any dissatisfied purchaser. Is the refund policy a credible signal of product quality?

Discussion Questions

1. Pedro farms wheat in Argentina. Each season, he sells his crop of 100,000 bushels to a general trading company which exports the wheat to Asia.
    a. Explain how the future price of wheat will affect Pedro's sales. For simplicity, suppose that the future price of wheat will be either $4 or $5 per bushel with equal probability.
    b. Assuming that Pedro has imperfect information about the future price of wheat, what risk does he bear?
    c. Pedro is averse to risk. The trading company has offered to buy Pedro's crop in advance at a fixed price of $4.45 per bushel. Explain how this will eliminate Pedro's risk.

2. This question applies the technique for deriving a market equilibrium with adverse selection presented in the math supplement. Suppose that the demand for genuine antiques is $D = 4 - p$ and the supply is $S = p - 2$, where D and S are in thousands of units a month and p represents price in hundreds of dollars. In addition, some sellers produce 500 fakes at no marginal cost.
    a. In a market of purely genuine antiques, what will be (i) the buyers' marginal ben-

efit from a quantity Q, (ii) the sellers' marginal cost of providing a quantity Q, and (iii) the market equilibrium price and quantity.
    b. In a market including both genuine antiques and fakes, what will be (i) the buyers' marginal benefit from a quantity Q, (ii) the sellers' marginal cost of providing a quantity Q, and (iii) the market equilibrium price and quantity.

3. A life insurance policy provides a payment in case of death of the insured party. Some life insurers require applicants to undergo a medical examination, while other insurers offer life insurance with no medical examination.
    a. Why do some life insurers require applicants to undergo a medical examination?
    b. Explain the adverse selection problem that will arise from offers of life insurance with no medical examination.
    c. How will the premiums for insurance with no medical examination (per dollar of coverage) compare with those of insurers that require a medical examination?

4. Medical insurance covers the cost of the treatment and prescriptions necessary for the insured party to recover from an illness or accident. Some medical insurance policies also cover medical expenses associated with pregnancy.

   a. Explain the asymmetry of information between the insurer and insured party.

   b. Why do some insurers require a minimum deductible no matter how much an applicant is willing to pay?

   c. Unlike falling sick or meeting with accidents, in many cases, women voluntarily enter into pregnancy. If a medical insurer covers pregnancy, will it encounter an adverse selection?

   d. Suppose that an insurer decides to cover pregnancy. Should it offer pregnancy coverage as an option or as part of the basic coverage?

5. Many countries have a consumers association that assesses the quality and prices of consumer goods and services. Consumers pay for most of these assessments. Some countries also have institutions that test products according to specified standards. Testing institutions include the British Standards Institute, the TUV in Germany, and the Underwriters' Laboratory in the United States. Typically, manufacturers pay for their products to be tested.

   a. Identify the consumers association and testing institution in your country.

   b. Which are relatively more subjective: (i) product assessments by a consumer association or (ii) tests by a testing institution?

   c. Based on your answer to (b), can you explain why consumers pay for most product assessments by consumer associations, while manufacturers pay for most tests by testing institutions?

6. Market research has shown that a major factor in top business executives' choice among hotels is the bathroom. They are willing to pay for large, well-equipped bathrooms. Top business executives are not very concerned about price. By contrast, vacationers care much less about bathrooms and more about price.

   a. Explain the asymmetry of information between hotels and their customers.

   b. How can a hotel screen between top executives and vacationers?

7. The final examination aims to assess students' understanding of the whole course. It is difficult, however, for an instructor to cover the entire course in a limited number of questions. After some research, your instructor has developed the following grading scheme. At the final examination, there will be a choice between Exam E (Easy) and Exam D (Difficult). Students must choose between E and D without seeing either in advance.

   Exam E is straightforward and the average student may expect to answer it correctly. Exam D is trickier: Only those who have understood the relevant topics very well will be able to answer it correctly. Students with only an average understanding can expect lower marks on Exam D than Exam E. The maximum possible score on Exam E, however, is less than the maximum possible on Exam D. For a student to earn a final course grade of A- or higher, it will be necessary to answer Exam D successfully.

   a. Explain what information the instructor is hoping to learn from the student's choice between E and D.

   b. How might strong differences in students' degree of risk aversion affect the result of this choice?

   c. Will the screening work if students are allowed to look at E and D before making their choice?

8. This question relies on the auctions section. Suppose that the government is selling the rights to mine silver from a tract of federal land by sealed-bid auction. Luna Mining's geologists estimated that the tract would yield 2.2 million ounces of silver. Luna, however, has learned that a competitor's estimate of the recoverable silver is 2.5 million ounces.
    a. Explain the winner's curse in the context of this example.
    b. How should Luna adjust its estimate of the recoverable silver in light of the competitor's estimate?
    c. If the government switches to an open auction, should Luna bid more or less aggressively?

9. American automobile manufacturers are very keen to persuade consumers that their cars are of high quality. Explain which of the following actions by a manufacturer will credibly signal superior quality of its car.
    a. Requiring all employees to buy the car.
    b. Offering a longer product warranty.
    c. TV commercials showing a typical American family endorsing the car.

10. Automobile repair is a service that most consumers purchase relatively infrequently. It is also difficult for a consumer to assess the quality of a repair: Did the car break down because of a poor repair or because it was in bad shape anyway?
    a. Explain the asymmetry of information between buyers and sellers of automobile repair service.
    b. How can sellers resolve this asymmetry through reputation and branding?
    c. Explain how buyers can resolve this asymmetry by getting an independent opinion.
    d. Will the unresolved divergence between the buyer's marginal benefit and the seller's marginal cost be larger or smaller for major as compared with minor repairs?

Math Supplement

In an early section of the chapter, we presented a market equilibrium with adverse selection. Let us now derive the equilibrium precisely using algebra. Suppose that the demand for genuine antiques is

$$D = 8 - p \qquad (12.1)$$

and the supply is

$$S = p - 2, \qquad (12.2)$$

where D and S are in thousands of units a month and p represents price in hundreds of dollars.

Since the demand for genuine antiques is $D = 8 - p$, the buyers' marginal benefit from a quantity Q of genuine antiques is $(8 - Q)$. Since the supply of genuine antiques is $S = p - 2$, the sellers' marginal cost of providing a quantity Q of genuine antiques is $(2 + Q)$.

In a market of purely genuine antiques, the market equilibrium will be at the price where $D = S$; that is,

$$8 - p = p - 2, \qquad (12.3)$$

or $p = 5$. At this price, $D = S = 3$.

Now, suppose that some sellers produce 1000 fakes at no marginal cost. The market equilibrium includes both genuine antiques and fakes. Suppose that the equilibrium quantity is Q (in thousands of units a month). Then, a buyer's probability of getting a genuine antique is

$$(Q - 1)/Q. \qquad (12.4)$$

We have shown the buyers' marginal benefit from a quantity Q of genuine antiques is $(8 - Q)$. Hence, with the fakes, the buyers' actual marginal benefit is

$$(Q - 1)/Q \times (8 - Q). \qquad (12.5)$$

On the other side, the market supply consists of 1000 fakes plus the genuine supply. Referring to Figure 12.1, for any quantity Q, the marginal cost of the genuine and fake antiques is $2 + (Q - 1)$.

At the market equilibrium, the buyers' actual marginal benefit equals the sellers' marginal cost, which in turn is the market price:

$$(Q - 1)/Q \times (8 - Q) = 2 + (Q - 1), \qquad (12.6)$$

or

$$2Q^2 - 8Q + 8 = 0, \qquad (12.7)$$

which implies that $Q = 2$. By (12.5), the buyers' actual marginal benefit, and the market price, is $1/2 \times 6 = 3$.

Thus, the market equilibrium with both genuine antiques and fakes is at a price of $300 per unit and quantity of 2000 units a month.

Previously, we also showed that the antiques market will fail if the quantity of fakes is too large. We can illustrate this with the mathematical model. Suppose that, in the preceding scenario, there are 2000 rather than 1000 fakes. Then, the buyers' actual marginal benefit will be

$$(Q - 2)/Q \times (8 - Q). \tag{12.8}$$

The sellers' marginal cost will become $2 + (Q - 2) = Q$.

In equilibrium, the buyers' actual marginal benefit equals the sellers' marginal cost:

$$(Q - 2)/Q \times (8 - Q) = Q, \tag{12.9}$$

or

$$2Q^2 - 10Q + 16 = 0. \tag{12.10}$$

This equation has no real roots, which implies that there is no equilibrium. In intuitive terms, the market has failed.

Chapter 13

Incentives and Organization

1 Introduction

Stanford University doctors performed America's first heart transplant in 1968. Achievements in cardiac surgery and molecular biology helped to establish Stanford's hospital as a leading center for premium quality specialized and primary medical care. Beginning in the late 1980s, however, the hospital came under increasing pressure from major customers to reduce charges. To address these concerns, Stanford undertook a major reorganization. One key measure was to tie doctors' earnings to the hospital's profit. Why would such a measure help to reduce the costs of medical treatment?

In Hong Kong, traffic wardens perform static traffic control and enforcement against illegal parking and unpaid parking meters. The government Audit Department monitored a random sample of traffic wardens to check their performance. The auditors found that wardens who were monitored issued 69 to 215% more parking citations than the average. Based on this observation, the Audit Department proposed that each traffic warden be assigned a daily quota of citations. Do you agree with the proposal?

In developing countries throughout the world, economic growth is increasing the demand for electric power. Electric power plants can cost several hundred million dollars. Investments in developing countries, however, are subject to political and economic risks. Owing to these risks, it is difficult for suppliers of power plants to secure financing for construction in developing countries. Smith Cogeneration International avoided these difficulties in a contract for a power plant in the Dominican Republic by mounting the plant on a barge. How does a floating plant mitigate the political and economic risks of investment?

To address these questions, we apply the economics of incentives and organization. First, we present the problems that arise when one party relies on the services of another. The problems include how to motivate effort, ameliorate risk, ensure a balance of attention to multiple responsibilities, and avoid opportunistic behavior. Then, we consider how two general forms of incentives—performance incentives and ownership—can mitigate the problems.[1]

The analysis of incentives for effort will explain how tying doctors' earnings to the profit of Stanford's hospital can help to reduce the cost of medical treatment. The link to the hospital's profit increases the doctors' incentive to prescribe economically efficient treatment and medicines.

Our analysis also applies to the Hong Kong government's decision whether to set each traffic warden a quota of parking citations. This depends on the desired balance among the wardens' attention to multiple responsibilities, including enforcement of parking regulations as well as other tasks.

Further, we analyze opportunistic behavior and the precautions that may be taken to guard against such actions. These explain how a floating plant can mitigate the political and economic risks of supplying a power plant in a developing country. A floating plant can be removed in the event of unfavorable political or economic occurrences. Investors in a floating plant are less vulnerable to losses from such occurrences than those who invest in a plant that is permanently fixed in the host country.

Finally, we tie together the various threads of analysis to construct a framework within which businesses can address a fundamental question of organization: Should an item be produced internally or acquired from an external source? We explain the trade-off between managing an internal employee vis-à-vis managing an external source.

2 *Moral Hazard*

Suppose that Luna Supermarket acquires a fleet of trucks and hires personnel to establish a delivery department. Mary is a delivery person in the afternoon shift. By the very nature of her job, a delivery person operates independently. Hence, it is difficult for Luna to monitor Mary's work. She alone decides how fast to drive and where to park; she alone determines how quickly to move goods from her truck into a customer's home.

Another feature of Mary's job is that she and her employer may disagree over how hard she should work. Luna wants her to exert the maximum effort and deliver the goods as quickly as possible. For instance, this may mean carrying goods up a staircase rather than waiting for an elevator. Mary, however, prefers to take the day at a more leisurely pace.

---

[1] This chapter draws extensively from Chapters 5–7, 9, and 16 of Paul Milgrom and John Roberts's *Economics, Organization, and Management* (Englewood Cliffs, NJ: Prentice Hall, 1992).

In this example, Mary is subject to **moral hazard**. A party is subject to moral hazard if its actions affect but are not observed by another party with whom it has a conflict of interest. Mary's actions certainly affect Luna Supermarket. Luna, however, does not monitor her throughout the day. There is a conflict of interest between Mary and her employer over her level of effort since she prefers less effort while her employer prefers her to exert more.

Sales representatives provide another example of moral hazard. They must work independently. It is difficult enough for an employer to monitor a salesperson's hours, for instance, whether he or she began sales calls at 8:00 AM or 9:00 AM. It is even more difficult to monitor how much effort a salesperson puts into his or her work. Further, there is a conflict of interest between the salesperson and the employer: The salesperson bears the entire cost of effort, but the profit from additional sales accrues to the employer.

Moral hazard also arises in large publicly listed corporations. A large publicly-listed company may have many diverse shareholders ranging from pension funds with million-dollar holdings to individuals with several hundred shares. Few shareholders consider it worthwhile to monitor the managers of the company. Further, there may also be a conflict of interest between shareholders and management. While shareholders are primarily concerned about the value of their shares, senior managers may have other objectives such as building a large corporate empire or hobnobbing with fashionable artists.

Asymmetric Information about Actions

If Mary's employer could freely monitor her at all times, then it could direct her to use staircases rather than wait for elevators, take shortcuts rather than the easier but slower route, and the like. Then Mary would not be subject to moral hazard. As this discussion shows, moral hazard arises because information is asymmetric. The employer depends on the worker's effort but cannot observe it.

In Chapter 12, we discussed asymmetric information in situations such as buying and selling antiques where the buyer is uncertain about the true provenance of an item, an application for life insurance where the applicant has better information about his or her health, and an application for a loan where the borrower has better information about his or her ability and willingness to repay. In all of these cases, the asymmetry of information concerned some individual characteristic of the better-informed party.

By contrast, in the example of Mary and Luna Supermarket, the delivery person has better information about her future actions. In this case, the asymmetry of information concerns some future action of the better-informed party. This information asymmetry is a necessary condition for there to be moral hazard.

Economic Inefficiency

Let us analyze the example of Mary and Luna Supermarket to understand the effect of moral hazard on the relevant parties. The degree of effort that a delivery person exerts at work affects the employer's revenues and costs and, hence, profit. Let us separate the wages and other incentives that the employer pays to the worker from the employer's other costs. We call the employer's revenue less the other costs, the employer's benefit. Then the employer's profit is its benefit less the wages and other incentives paid to the worker.

For the worker, her net benefit is these wages and incentives less the cost of her effort. Considering the worker and the employer as a group, the group's net benefit from the worker's effort is the employer's benefit less the worker's cost of effort.

If a delivery person increases her effort, the resulting change in the employer's profit is its marginal benefit from the worker's effort. The additional cost required to increase effort is the worker's marginal cost of effort. In Figure 13.1, we draw the employer's marginal benefit from the delivery person's effort and the worker's marginal cost of effort.

From the perspective of maximizing the group's net benefit, the worker should put in the amount of effort that balances the employer's marginal benefit with the worker's marginal cost. By the definition in Chapter 6, this also characterizes the economically efficient level of effort. Referring to Figure 13.1, the employer's marginal benefit equals the worker's marginal cost at an effort of 120 units. There, the employer's marginal benefit is 60 cents per unit of effort, which equals the worker's marginal cost of 60 cents per unit of effort.

Recall, however, that the worker acts independently. Hence, the worker does not consider the employer's marginal benefit but rather her personal marginal benefit from effort. Her personal marginal benefit depends on the structure of her wages and other incentives. In Figure 13.1, we also draw the worker's personal marginal benefit from effort. The worker chooses the level of effort that balances her personal marginal benefit with her marginal cost. This is the level of effort that will actually be realized.

Referring to Figure 13.1, the worker's marginal benefit equals her marginal cost at an effort of 100 units. At that level, the worker's marginal benefit and marginal cost are both equal to 50 cents. At 100 units of effort by the worker, however, the employer's marginal benefit is 65 cents. This exceeds the worker's marginal cost of 50 cents.

Generally, a party that is subject to moral hazard will choose to act according to its own marginal benefit and marginal cost. As a result, its behavior will diverge from the economically efficient choice.

Suppose that the worker could be induced to increase her effort to 120 units. Then the additional benefit to the employer would be the area *cdea* under the employer's marginal benefit curve, between 100 and 120 units of effort. The additional cost to the worker would be the area *bdea* under the worker's marginal cost curve, between 100 and 120 units of effort. Hence, the additional benefit to the employer would exceed the additional cost to the

Figure 13.1 Economically efficient effort

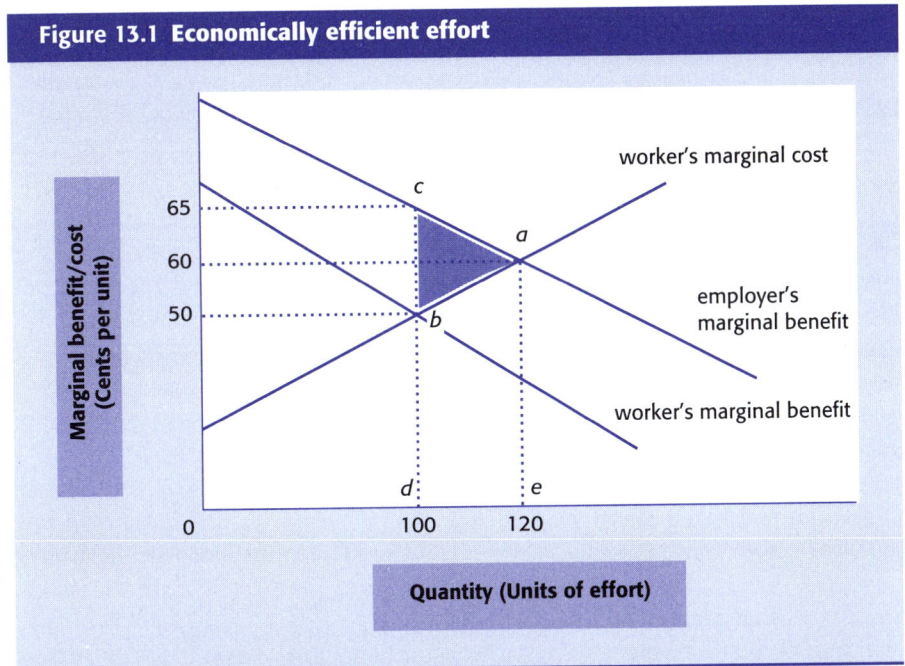

The economically efficient level of effort, 120 units, balances the employer's marginal benefit with the worker's marginal cost. Mary, the worker, chooses 100 units of effort, which balances her personal marginal benefit with her marginal cost. The lower is the worker's marginal benefit relative to the employer's marginal benefit, the lower will be the effort that the worker chooses relative to the economically efficient level.

worker by the shaded area acb. This represents the amount of profit that can be earned by resolving the worker's moral hazard. The challenge then is how to resolve the moral hazard.

Degree of Moral Hazard

Suppose that there were no conflict of interest between Mary and Luna Supermarket. This means that the worker's marginal benefit from effort would coincide exactly with the employer's marginal benefit from effort. Then, the worker would choose the economically efficient level of effort. Under these conditions, there will be no moral hazard.

Referring to Figure 13.1, the lower the worker's marginal benefit relative to the employer's marginal benefit, the lower will be the effort that the worker chooses relative to the economically efficient level.

This example suggests that we can measure the degree of moral hazard by the difference between the economically efficient action and the action chosen by the party subject to moral hazard. The larger this difference, the greater will be the degree of moral hazard and the gain in net benefit that can be realized by resolving the moral hazard.

Progress check

Progress Check 13A Suppose that the worker's marginal cost of effort in Figure 13.1 were higher. Draw the new marginal cost curve. How does this affect (1) the economically efficient level of effort and (2) the effort that the worker actually chooses?

Moral Hazard at the Top

American Express, listed on the New York Stock Exchange, is a global provider of travel and financial services. In December 1992, following pressure from major shareholders, the company announced that its long-time chairman and chief executive James Robinson would step down. Within a day of the announcement, the price of the company's common shares jumped 6%, increasing the market value of American Express by $667 million.

Under Robinson, American Express had expanded into credit cards by launching the Optima card and into investment banking through the acquisition of Shearson Lehman Brothers. Robinson's successor, Harvey Golub, chose a strategy that Wall Street much preferred. He spun off the investment bank and refocused the company on its travel-related and charge card businesses.

Sources: Corporate Governance and Pension Plans, Wharton impact conference, University of Pennsylvania (May 5, 1995); World Wide Web page, www.kiplinger.com/magazine/jul96/dow10k2.html (October 30, 1996).

Moral Hazard in Medicine: What Did the Doctor Order?

Patients rely on doctors for advice and, often, get treatment from the doctor providing the advice. Consequently, the doctor is subject to moral hazard. The more treatment a doctor recommends, the more he or she will earn.

Obstetricians are doctors who specialize in treating pregnant women and delivering babies. Babies can be delivered either naturally through the vagina or by cesarean section. Obstetricians earn higher fees from cesarean sections. In 1989, the average charge for a cesarean section was $2053, or 28% more than that for a vaginal delivery. Obstetricians also prefer cesarean sections because these can be scheduled in advance and may take less time than vaginal deliveries.

The demand for obstetric services depends crucially on the rate at which women become pregnant. Between 1970 and 1982, the U.S. fertility rate fell by 13.5% from 1.84 to 1.59 per hundred population. This decline in fertility would have substantially cut obstetricians' incomes. By a happy coincidence, however, the proportion of deliveries by cesarean section increased by 240% over the same period.

A study by the National Bureau of Economic Research found that the increase in cesarean sections was not such a coincidence. Obstetricians exploited their informational advantage and substituted cesarean sections for vaginal deliveries. In this way, the obstetricians could maintain their incomes even as fertility declined.

Source: Jonathan Gruber and Maria Owings, "Physician Financial Incentives and Cesarean Section Delivery," *RAND Journal of Economics* 27, no. 1 (1996): pp. 99–123.

3 *Incentives*

We have identified the potential gains from resolving moral hazard. Generally, there are two complementary approaches to resolve moral hazard. One is to invest in monitoring, surveillance, and other methods of collecting information about the behavior of the party subject to moral hazard. The other approach is to align the incentives of the party subject to moral hazard with those of the less-informed party.

These two approaches are complementary because all incentives must be based on behavior that can be observed, so the better is the available information, the wider will be the choice of incentive schemes. Ideally, the relevant parties would like to completely resolve the moral hazard, so that the better-informed party will make the economically efficient choice. For instance, in the case of Mary and Luna Supermarket, the ideal effort by Mary is 120 units (Figure 13.1). Let us now discuss how to resolve the moral hazard of a worker relative to her employer.

Monitoring

The simplest monitoring system focuses on objective measures of performance. Most employers require workers to punch a card to record the time at which they arrive and depart work. The time clock is a basic and almost universal monitoring system. In the case of a delivery person, another simple monitoring system is a vehicle log, in which the worker records every point of collection and delivery. The employer can compare the log with the mileage on the truck's meter.

Hours on the job, however, is distinct from effort. A worker can arrive at 8:00 AM and leave at 5:00 PM, but do nothing during that time. Accordingly, employers need monitoring systems that provide more than basic objective information.

One method that employers frequently use to collect information is to hire supervisors. It is not cost effective for supervisors to monitor workers all the time, however. Hence, supervisors should make only random checks. In Chapter 10, we discussed the advantages of randomization. The same principle applies to supervision: The supervisor should check workers at random, rather than according to some regular pattern.

Employers can also enlist customers to monitor worker performance. Customers have a natural advantage in monitoring workers, such as delivery persons and sales representatives, who spend more time with customers rather than at the employer's location. Employers can encourage customers to report worker performance and then follow up by investigating reports of especially poor or good performance.

Performance Pay

The counterpart to monitoring systems is incentive schemes. Incentive schemes resolve the moral hazard by tying payments to some measure of performance.

The schemes depend on a link between the unobservable action and some observable measure of performance. Generally, the scope of incentive schemes depends on what indicators of the unobservable action are available.

An employer can use the information provided by monitoring systems to structure incentives for its workers. For instance, in the case of Luna Supermarket, the employer cannot observe Mary's effort. But it can monitor the number of deliveries. Then it could base incentives on the number of deliveries.

One common incentive scheme is **performance pay**, which bases a worker's pay on some measure of performance. Let us consider performance pay in the example of the Luna Supermarket. Suppose first that Luna pays Mary a fixed daily wage of $50 and that Luna does not monitor Mary at all, not even using a time clock or vehicle log. Then, Mary cannot affect her earnings in any way, whether she starts early or late and whether she works quickly or slowly. Her personal marginal benefit from effort will be 0. In Figure 13.2, the

Performance pay is an incentive scheme that bases pay on some measure of performance.

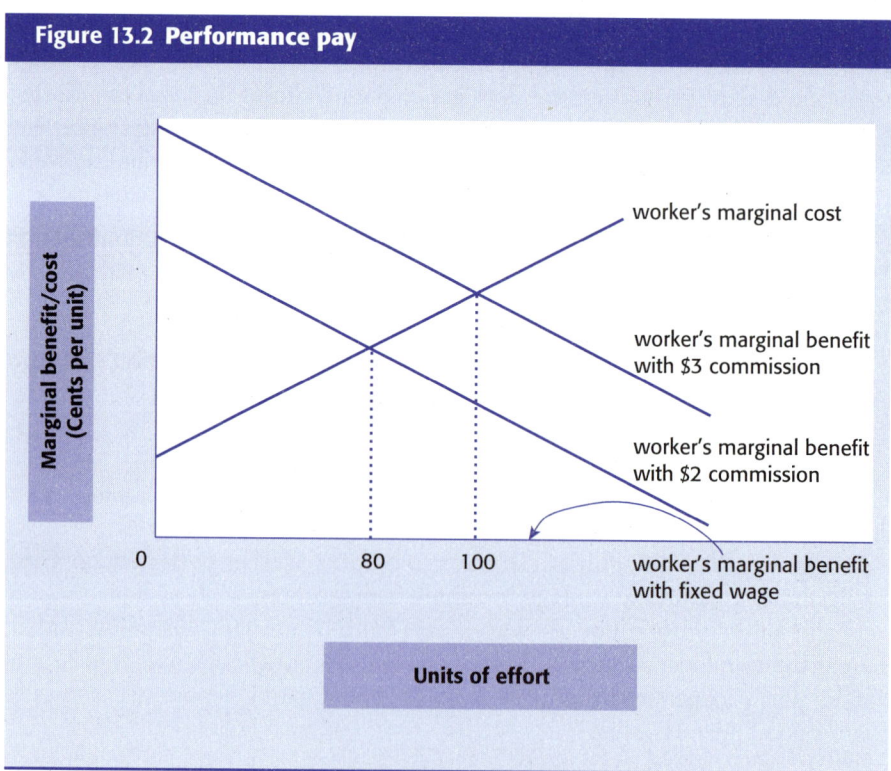

Figure 13.2 Performance pay

worker's marginal cost

worker's marginal benefit with $3 commission

worker's marginal benefit with $2 commission

worker's marginal benefit with fixed wage

Marginal benefit/cost (Cents per unit)

Units of effort

0   80   100

With a fixed daily wage, the worker's personal marginal benefit is the horizontal axis. A commission of $3 leads the worker to choose more effort than a $2 commission.

worker's personal marginal benefit with a fixed daily wage is the horizontal axis. This is lower than the worker's marginal cost at all levels of effort. Hence, with a fixed daily wage, the worker chooses no effort.

Now, suppose that Luna pays Mary $2 for each delivery that she makes. This is an example of payment based on performance. The more deliveries that Mary makes, the more she will earn. With this incentive scheme, her personal marginal benefit from effort will be positive. The height and slope of the personal marginal benefit curve depend on how the worker's effort affects the number of deliveries.

In Figure 13.2, we also show the worker's personal marginal benefit with a commission of $2 per delivery. This crosses her marginal cost at an effort of 80 units. With a commission of $2 per delivery, the worker chooses effort of 80 units. Accordingly, the commission helps to resolve the worker's moral hazard.

An incentive scheme is relatively "stronger" if it provides a higher personal marginal benefit for effort. Suppose that the employer strengthens the incentive scheme by raising the commission to $3 per delivery. Then the worker's personal marginal benefit curve would be higher, and it would cross the marginal cost curve at a higher level of effort, say, at 100 units of effort. This shows that, the stronger is the incentive scheme, the higher will be the worker's effort.

Progress Check 13B Using Figure 13.2, draw a personal marginal benefit curve such that the worker would choose the economically efficient level of effort.   *Progress check*

Performance Quotas

In the case of Mary and Luna Supermarket, if Luna paid a large enough commission, Mary's personal marginal benefit would be sufficiently high that she would choose the economically efficient 120 units of effort. This, however, may mean paying a large sum of money in commissions.

Let us explore another way to induce a worker to choose the economically efficient level of effort. Suppose that Luna establishes the following incentive scheme for Mary: Luna will pay a fixed daily wage provided that Mary performs a specified quota of deliveries each day; otherwise, she will be dismissed. A **performance quota** is a minimum standard of performance, below which a worker is subject to penalties. The penalties could include deferral of promotion, reduction in pay, or even dismissal.

A **performance quota** is a minimum standard of performance, below which penalties apply.

Figure 13.3 Performance quota

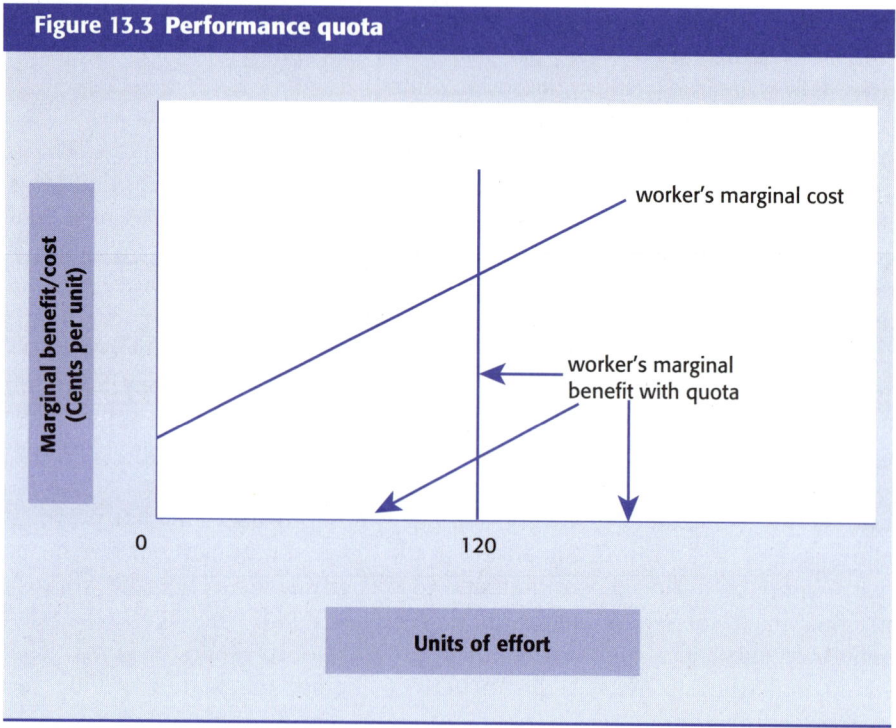

With a quota of 20 deliveries a day, the worker's personal marginal benefit curve has three parts, and the worker chooses 120 units of effort.

To apply a performance quota, Luna Supermarket must identify the number of deliveries that would result if Mary chose the economically efficient 120 units of effort. Suppose that 120 units of effort would generate 20 deliveries a day. Then the employer should set the performance quota at 20 deliveries a day. In Figure 13.3, we show the worker's personal marginal benefit curve with a quota of 20 deliveries a day.

The worker's personal marginal benefit curve has three parts. Recall that the employer pays the worker a fixed daily wage provided that he or she meets the quota; otherwise that worker will be dismissed. At 119 units of effort and below, the worker will be dismissed. Additional effort does not affect her earnings; hence, her personal marginal benefit is 0.

The incentive scheme pays the worker no extra for additional effort above 120 units. Accordingly, at 121 units of effort and above, the worker's personal marginal benefit also is 0. The personal marginal benefit, however, is very high at exactly 120 units of effort. An increase in effort from 119 to 120 units is just enough to satisfy the quota and hence allows worker to get the daily wage and retain her job.

Thus, the worker's personal marginal benefit curve follows the horizontal axis from 0 to 119 units of effort, spikes up at 120 units, and then follows the horizontal axis again at 121 units of effort and above. Therefore, the personal marginal benefit curve crosses the marginal cost at 120 units of effort. Accordingly, the worker chooses 120 units of effort.

A performance quota is a cost-effective way of inducing the worker to choose the economically efficient level of effort. It is cost efficient because it does not reward effort below the economically efficient level. It focuses the incentive at the economically efficient level of effort.

Progress Check 13C Suppose that 100 units of effort would generate 18 deliveries a day. Using Figure 13.3, illustrate the worker's marginal benefit if the employer specifies a quota of 18 deliveries a day.

Progress check

Smog Check: "Don't Pass, Don't Pay"

To reduce lead emissions, the state of California requires all new automobiles to be equipped with catalytic converters and to use unleaded gasoline. Where leaded gasoline is cheaper than unleaded, many drivers are tempted to fuel their cars with leaded gasoline. To deter such switching, the state government requires each car to undergo a smog check every two years.

The California Bureau of Automotive Repair licenses service stations to conduct the smog checks. It also conducts random roadside inspections of cars. The bureau's records show that 5% of all cars failed the biennial smog check. By contrast, 25% of cars checked in the roadside inspections had defective emissions control equipment.

Who was responsible for this disparity? The obvious suspects were the mechanics and service stations that performed the smog checks. They have an incentive to pass their customers. Some stations even go so far as to advertise "Smog Check: Don't Pass, Don't Pay."

Source: "Smog Checks to Get in Gear with Air Act," *Los Angeles Times* (February 28, 1991), pp. A3 and A31.

Stanford University Hospital: Paying Doctors More to Do Less

Patients rely on doctors for advice and treatment. For various reasons, doctors may have an incentive to prescribe excessive tests, treatment, and drugs. To the extent that a patient's medical costs are covered by insurance or a managed health care plan, he or she will not be sensitive to the cost of excessive care. After all, a third party pays the bills.

Large third-party payers including the federal government, managed health care plans, and medical insurers have reacted to the doctors' moral hazard. The federal Medicare program for elderly patients instituted a fixed price for each case, regardless of actual treatment costs. Likewise, many providers of managed health care are pressing doctors and hospitals to accept a fixed fee per patient.

Stanford University Hospital has been caught between major customers who want to cut costs and doctors who prescribe premium care. For instance, HealthNet, a major provider of medical benefits, warned Stanford that it might withdraw its business unless the hospital could reduce its costs.

Stanford responded to these pressures by merging the medical faculty with the hospital to form Stanford Health Services. The new organization ties the doctor's pay more closely to the hospital's profit. University administrators believe that this tie will give doctors a stronger incentive to consider the cost of tests, treatment, and drugs to the hospital and so find ways to reduce the cost of medical care.

For instance, through careful re-examination of its procedures, the Department of Cardiothoracic Surgery has been able to cut the price of heart transplants by over 20%. Other doctors are researching standard patterns of treatment for common illnesses such as asthma. Such standard procedures will help to cut the cost of treating such illnesses.

Source: George Anders, "Prescription for Change: Stanford Hospital Confronts the Cost-Conscious '90s," *Stanford Magazine* 23, no. 1 (March 1995), pp. 36–41.

4 *Risk*

Incentive schemes resolve moral hazard by tying payments to some observable indicator of the unobservable action. But, what if the indicator is affected by factors other than the unobservable action? Then, the payments will depend on these other factors. A party who is subject to moral hazard and has imperfect information about these factors will face risk.[2]

For instance, in the example of Luna Supermarket, the supermarket may base Mary's incentives on the number of deliveries a day. The number of deliveries, however, may also depend on other factors such as customers' orders, traffic congestion, and the weather. An incentive scheme based on the number of deliveries will impose a risk on Mary. Specifically, it is possible that, even when she puts in a great deal of effort, her deliveries will be hindered by traffic congestion or bad weather.

Risk is the second major issue that arises when one party relies on the services of another. It arises whenever incentives are based on an indicator that depends on extraneous factors and the party subject to the moral hazard has imperfect information about those factors. The incentive scheme that maximizes net benefit, that is, the economically efficient scheme, must take account of the cost of risk.

Costs of Risk

The cost imposed by risk depends on three factors. The first is the structure of the incentive scheme. Generally, as we showed in the preceding section, a stronger incentive scheme would induce the worker to increase her effort. A stronger incentive scheme, however, would impose a heavier burden of risk on the party subject to moral hazard.

For example, in Figure 13.2, if the commission per delivery were raised from $2 to $3, the worker would increases the effort from 80 to 100 units. With the larger commission, however, a bigger part of worker's income will depend on the number of deliveries. This means that the worker will bear more risk.

The second factor that affects the risk-bearing cost is the degree of risk aversion in the party subject to moral hazard. If the party is risk neutral, then the risk imposes no cost. Risk imposes a cost only if the party is risk averse. The more risk averse that the party is, then the larger will be the cost imposed by risk.

The third factor is the influence of the uncertain factors on the indicator that forms the basis for the incentive scheme. The strength of this influence depends on the way in which the indicator depends on these factors and the extent to which these factors can vary. For instance, if the indicator were sensitive to these factors and the factors were subject to wide swings, then the risk would be relatively large. By contrast, if the indicator were insensitive to these factors or the factors would not vary much, then the risk would be relatively smaller.

---

[2] The reader may wish to refer to the section on risk in Chapter 12.

Generally, the incentive scheme should be stronger if the party subject to moral hazard is relatively less risk averse and the extraneous factors are weaker. Conversely, the incentives should be weaker if the risk aversion is higher and extraneous factors have a stronger influence.

Progress check

Progress Check 13D Alan and Mary are delivery persons for Luna Supermarket. Alan is more risk averse than Mary. Whose incentive scheme should be stronger?

Comprehensive Auto Insurance: Balancing Moral Hazard and Risk

Comprehensive automobile insurance covers loss or damage to a car arising from all causes, including fire and theft. The likelihood of theft depends on the driver's behavior: taking care to park in secure, well-lighted places; using a steering lock; and activating the car alarm. Short of hiring a full-time private detective, it is difficult for an insurer to monitor the driver's behavior completely.

A driver who has comprehensive automobile insurance, however, may take fewer precautions. For instance, the driver may sometimes neglect to engage the steering lock or, in a pinch, park in dark alley. While the driver personally bears all the costs of precautions, a large part of the benefit in terms of reduced likelihood of theft accrues to the insurer.

Many insurers offer comprehensive automobile insurance only with a minimum deductible. Such policies provide compensation only to the extent that the loss exceeds the deductible. A driver will benefit from precautions against loss to the extent of her or his deductible. Accordingly, the deductible helps to resolve the driver's moral hazard.

The deductible, however, imposes risk on the driver. Drivers buy insurance because they are averse to risk. Ironically, the insurer must limit the extent of insurance to resolve the problem of moral hazard.

Relative Performance Incentives

In some situations, the moral hazard can be resolved in a very natural way without imposing risk. Suppose that Mary is just one of many delivery persons working for Luna Supermarket. Then Luna could adopt the following incentive scheme, which is based on *relative* performance. Using records of the deliveries made by the various workers, Luna can calculate the average number of deliveries. It can then pay Mary a fixed daily wage plus a \$2 commission for each delivery that she performs in excess of the average for all delivery personnel.

Luna's incentive scheme will not penalize Mary for an extraneous factor like bad weather. Suppose that the weather is bad. This will hamper all delivery persons and cut the average number of deliveries. If Mary exerts relatively more effort, she will still achieve more deliveries than the average and hence will earn the \$2 commission.

By gauging performance on a relative basis, the incentive scheme cancels out the effect of extraneous factors to the extent that they affect all workers equally. This reduces the risk due to extraneous factors.

Even with a relative incentive scheme, however, a worker must continue to bear the risk due to idiosyncratic factors that do not affect the average worker to the same extent. For instance, if Mary's territory is relatively more prone to traffic congestion, she will suffer relatively more risk from this factor.

Generally, an incentive scheme based on relative performance will eliminate the risk due to extraneous factors that affect all parties equally. Relative incentive schemes are most useful where common extraneous factors are important.

Evaluating Managerial Performance

A common way of evaluating the performance of company management is through the stock price. H.J. Heinz is a leading international manufacturer of food products. Heinz common shares rose by 156% between 1990 and 1995. Should investors cheer?

Not if they consider their alternatives. Figure 13.4 shows the cumulative total shareholder returns from investments in Heinz shares as compared with the Standard and Poors Foods Group, which is an index of shares of major food manufacturers. An investment in the Foods Group would have been much more profitable.

This example suggests that a more reasonable way of evaluating managers is to measure their performance against that of other companies in the same industry. Relative performance evaluation cancels out background factors over which managers have no control. This yields a more accurate measure of management's performance.

Source: H.J. Heinz, proxy statement pursuant to Section 14A of the Securities Exchange Act of 1934 (August 3, 1995), p. 18.

Relative Performance in Sports: The Olympic Games

The Olympics reward relative not absolute performance: The gold medal goes to the athlete who runs fastest, jumps highest, or throws the farthest. Suppose that the Olympics were restructured to evaluate performance on an absolute basis. For instance, in the 100 meters flat event, the rule could be that every person who finishes in less than 10 seconds will get a gold medal. Under this rule, however, in 1968, when the Summer Olympics were held in Mexico City, at an altitude of 7,700 feet, there would have been little incentive for any athlete to bother with the race.

By giving the gold medal to the fastest runner, no matter how slow, the Olympics generates an incentive to compete hard under any conditions. This makes especially good sense for an athletic competition that is held outdoors and in a different location each time.

Figure 13.4 Heinz relative performance

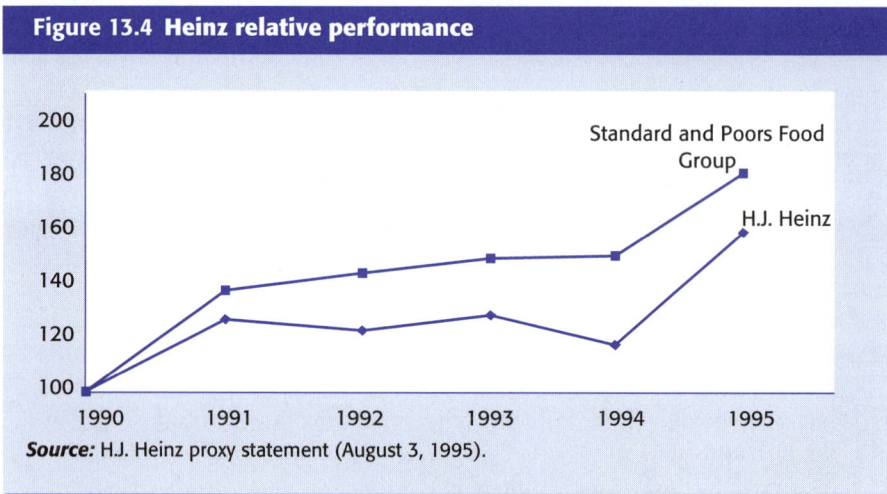

Source: H.J. Heinz proxy statement (August 3, 1995).

Between 1990 and 1995, the cumulative total shareholder return from investments in Heinz shares was less than the return from the Standard and Poors Foods Group.

5 | Multiple Responsibilities

Until this point, we have focused on situations where the moral hazard concerns a single action or responsibility. In many cases, however, the party subject to the moral hazard has multiple responsibilities. For instance, a supermarket may want delivery persons to carry out their work quickly as well as in a polite and friendly way that will encourage repeat customers. In a department store, a salesclerk may be required to make new sales, process returns, as well as look out for shoplifters.

Consider situations where the moral hazard concerns multiple responsibilities. This means that the party subject to moral hazard takes multiple actions that affect but are not observed by another party with whom it has a conflict of interest.

Balancing multiple responsibilities is the third major issue that arises when one party relies on the services of another. Ideally, an incentive scheme should aim to balance the multiple responsibilities. This means that there should be some investment in monitoring each of the unobservable actions and incentives based on the corresponding indicators.

Balancing multiple responsibilities becomes harder when it is more difficult to measure performance for some responsibilities than others. An incentive scheme may focus on a particular responsibility because that dimension is relatively easier to monitor. As we emphasized previously, the scope of an incentive scheme depends on the available indicators of the unobservable action.

Suppose, however, that the incentive scheme focuses on just one responsibility. Then, it will induce better performance on that dimension but have the side effect of aggravating the moral hazard with regard to the other responsibilities.

For instance, Luna Supermarket wants Mary to carry out deliveries quickly and in a polite and friendly way. Performance in politeness and friendliness, however, is much more difficult to measure than the number of deliveries. If Luna adopts a strong incentive scheme for the number of deliveries, Mary will speed up her work, but this will undercut the goal of polite and friendly service.

Incentive schemes focus on actions for which there are reliable measures of performance. If, however, there are important responsibilities for which it is difficult to measure performance, then it will be better to adopt relatively weak performance incentives. A deliberate use of weak incentives is a way to achieve a balance among multiple responsibilities.

Progress Check 13E Suppose that a department store has switched its salesclerks from a straight salary to a salary plus a commission on sales. How will this affect the salesclerks' incentive to process returns?

Progress check

Balancing Multiple Responsibilities: Hong Kong's Traffic Wardens

In Hong Kong, traffic wardens have two responsibilities: static traffic control duty and enforcement against illegal parking and unpaid use of parking meters. For the individual traffic warden, strict enforcement of parking regulations means intensive patrolling and possibly receiving verbal or other abuse from drivers. By avoiding enforcement, a traffic warden can pass the day quietly and peacefully.

When the government Audit Department monitored a random sample of traffic wardens, it discovered that those who were monitored issued 69 to 215% more parking citations than the average traffic warden. The Audit Department proposed to resolve the moral hazard problem by assigning each traffic warden a quota of citations.

The proposed quota would surely induce traffic wardens to put more effort into enforcement of parking regulations. The Audit Department, however, overlooked an important side effect of its proposal. Traffic wardens are also responsible for static traffic control duty. The quotas on parking citations would induce traffic wardens to reduce their attention to traffic control. Overall, the quotas would improve parking regulation enforcement but lead to worse traffic control.

Source: Hong Kong, Director of Audit, Report No. 23, *The Royal Hong Kong Police Force*, Chapter 7, "The Performance of the Traffic Warden Corps," (Hong Kong: Audit Department, 1994).

6 Holdup

To understand the meaning of a *holdup*, suppose that Luna Supermarket engages Speedy, a contractor that specializes in deliveries, to deliver grocery orders. According to their contract, Speedy makes two rounds of deliveries a day, one beginning at 12:00 noon and another at 4:00 PM. One day, however, Luna received so many delivery orders that it asked Speedy to make a third round of deliveries. Sensing that Luna was in a desperate situation, Speedy refused to make the additional delivery unless Luna paid twice the usual price.

A **holdup** is an action to exploit another party's dependence.

In this example, Speedy took advantage of Luna's special need to *hold up* the supermarket. A **holdup** is an action to exploit another party's dependence. A holdup is distinct from moral hazard in that it does not require asymmetric information. For example, when Luna requested the extra delivery, Speedy openly refused. Luna could clearly observe Speedy's action: hence, there was no asymmetry of information. A holdup is similar to moral hazard in that it arises only when there is a conflict of interest between the parties.

Speedy's holdup has implications beyond the exceptional price that Luna paid on that one occasion. The prospect of a holdup in the future will lead Luna to take precautions and avoid depending too much on Speedy. For instance, Luna might warn customers that delivery cannot be assured on the same day, it might limit the number of orders for delivery each day, or it might establish its own delivery service.

Limiting the number of orders for delivery each day will reduce Luna's benefit from Speedy's service. Establishing its own delivery service will add to Luna's costs. Luna's precautions either reduce its benefit from Speedy's service or increase its own costs.

Generally, whenever there is the prospect that someone will engage in a holdup, other parties will take precautions to avoid dependence. These precautions either reduce the benefit from the relationship or increase costs. Thus, the potential for a holdup reduces the group's net benefit.

Specific Investments

One particular type of precaution against a holdup is not so obvious and, hence, should be highlighted. Suppose that, to optimize delivery time and fuel, Speedy has installed a computerized route planning system on every truck. To use this system, every package must be marked with a bar code strip. Then, the driver scans the packages so that the onboard computer can prepare the optimal delivery route.

Luna must prepare a delivery order for each package. The easiest way of preparing the route planning bar codes is to generate them with the delivery orders. This, however, requires Luna to integrate Speedy's bar codes with its delivery system. Integration will make Luna relatively more dependent on Speedy and, hence, more vulnerable to a hold up. Accordingly, Luna will be reluctant to invest in such integration.

In this example, integrating the bar codes is an investment by Luna that is specific to its relationship with Speedy. The **specificity** of an investment in an asset is the percentage that will be lost if the asset is switched to another use.

Specificity is the percentage of the investment that will be lost if the asset is switched to another use.

For instance, suppose that Luna must spend $5000 to integrate Speedy's bar codes with its delivery system. Of the $5000 investment, $2000 is for a bar-code printer, while the remaining $3000 pays for tailor-made software specified by Speedy. If Luna switches to another delivery contractor, it will lose the $3000 specialized investment. Hence, the integrated bar-code system is 3000/5000 = 60% specific to the relationship with Speedy.

By contrast, suppose that Luna buys several mobile phones to contact delivery persons when they are on the road. The same phones, however, can be used by any delivery contractor. Hence, these are nonspecific assets. The prospect that Speedy might act opportunistically will have relatively little impact on Luna's investments in such non-specific assets.

Specific assets can be physical; for instance, plant and equipment. Specific assets also encompass human capital. Many businesses provide new recruits with introductory training. Through on-the-job training programs, employees are making investments in specific human capital. The prospect of a hold up will deter investments in all forms of specific assets.

Progress check

Progress Check 13F Which of the following requires you to invest relatively more in specific human capital: a university degree program or on-the-job training?

Incomplete Contracts

A **complete contract** specifies what each party must do and the corresponding payments under every possible contingency.

Suppose that the contract between Luna and Speedy had specified conditions under which Luna could request an additional delivery and the corresponding price. Then, Speedy would not have been able to hold up Luna. Generally, the scope for a holdup depends on the extent to which a contract is incomplete. A **complete contract** specifies what each party must do and the corresponding payments under every possible contingency. By contrast, a contract is incomplete if it does not specify duties or payment in some contingency.

It would be extremely costly for Luna and Speedy to prepare and agree on a complete contract. A huge number of contingencies would have to be covered: The need for a fourth delivery, the possibility that Speedy's truck may break down, and the possibility of an earthquake are just a few. Rather than consider every such detail, the two parties will probably agree on an incomplete contract.

As this example suggests, in practice, all contracts are incomplete, and deliberately so. The issue then is how incomplete the contract should be. Generally, the answer depends on two factors: the potential benefits and costs at stake and the extent of the possible contingencies.

Let us consider the first factor: the potential benefits and costs at stake. The larger are the stakes, the more the parties should invest in preparing the contract. Compare, for instance, Luna's purchases of sundry hardware and dairy products. Sundry hardware such as nails and screws is a minor item in Luna's sales. By contrast, dairy products account for a large part of Luna's sales and are much more important. Accordingly, Luna might not need a contract with its supplier of sundry hardware, but it will need a detailed contract with its supplier of dairy products.

The second factor in the incompleteness of the contract is the extent of the possible contingencies. Consider again Luna's purchases of sundry hardware and dairy products. Hardware is a durable item with relatively slow sales. Since dairy products are perishable and sold in high volume, Luna needs frequent supply. The supply of dairy products is relatively more vulnerable to disruptions by bad weather, transportation problems, and labor disputes. Accordingly, Luna will seek relatively more assurance about the supply of dairy products. This means a relatively more detailed contract.

Gains from Resolution

In general, contracts are deliberately incomplete. This incompleteness gives rise to the possibility of a holdup. In turn, this leads the affected parties to take precautions such as avoiding investments in specific assets. These precautions reduce the net benefit of the various parties from the relationship. If, however, the potential for holdup can be resolved, then the additional benefit will exceed the additional cost. Accordingly, a profit can be made by resolving the potential for holdup.

An obvious way to resolve the potential for holdup is for the relevant parties to specify contracts in greater detail. We have already discussed the factors to consider when deciding on the degree of contractual incompleteness.

Another way to resolve holdup is through changing the ownership of the relevant assets. We consider how changes in ownership will affect the incentives for a holdup in the next section.

Specificity in Electric Power Investments: Floating Power Plants

Smith Cogeneration International of Oklahoma City manufactures electric power plants. When the company was invited to supply a power plant in the Dominican Republic, it learned that over 20 other potential suppliers had refused to bid. Owing to the political and economic risks of investment, the other suppliers could not secure the several hundred million dollars of financing necessary for construction.

Taking inspiration from sailboat racing, company president Donald Smith contracted to supply a *floating* plant. The company built a gas turbine plant on a barge at a yard in Beaumont, Texas, and then towed it across the Caribbean Sea to the Dominican Republic.

The barge had two advantages over a conventional land-based plant. First, in the event of default by the host governemnt, Smith could actually float the plant away. The extent of its specific investment was much lower than with a land-based plant. The second advantage was faster delivery. Smith did not have to send personnel to the Dominican Republic and thus saved six months in construction time.

Source: "Power Plants Atop Barges Will Make Waves in Asia," *Asian Wall Street Journal* (May 23, 1996), pp. 1 and 6.

7 *Ownership*

Ownership means the rights to residual control.

The rights to **residual control** are those rights that have not been contracted away.

In the preceding section, we mentioned that one way to resolve a holdup is through changing the ownership of the relevant assets. Let us now consider the implications of changes in ownership. **Ownership** means the rights to **residual control,** which are those rights that have not been contracted away.

To explain the meaning of *residual control*, suppose that Moonlight Properties borrowed $5 million from a bank to develop a supermarket, which it has rented to Luna on a five-year lease. The bank has a mortgage against the building. This means that, if Moonlight fails to make the loan payments on time, the bank will have the legal right to take possession of the building. This is a right that Moonlight contracted away to get the loan.

Moonlight has also entered into a five-year lease with Luna Supermarket. Through the lease, Luna has the right to use the property for five years. This is another right that Moonlight has contracted away.

As owner, Moonlight has residual control. This means that it has all rights except those contracted away. For instance, it may have the right to enter into a second mortgage on the building, and it has the right to use the building after the expiration of Luna's lease.

A transfer of ownership means shifting the rights of residual control to another party. Suppose that Luna buys ownership of the supermarket building from Moonlight. Then, Moonlight no longer will have the right to enter into a mortgage on the building. Such rights now belong to the new owner, Luna.

Residual Income

Residual income is the income remaining after payment of all other claims.

One dimension of residual control particularly is worth emphasizing. The owner of an asset also has the right to receive the **residual income** from the asset, which is the income remaining after payment of all other claims.

To illustrate, suppose that Moonlight collects $100,000 a month in rent from Luna. Moonlight's expenses include $50,000 in interest and principal to the bank as well as $20,000 in taxes and other expenses. As owner of the building, Moonlight receives the residual income of $100,000 – $50,000 – $20,000 = $30,000.

As the recipient of the residual income, the owner gets the full benefit of changes in income and costs. For instance, if Moonlight can raise the rent by $5,000 to $105,000, then its profit will increase by $5,000 to $35,000. Similarly, if Moonlight can reduce expenses by $2,000, then its profit will increase by $2,000 to $32,000. On the other hand, if Moonlight's expenses increase by $5,000, then its profit would fall by $5,000 to $25,000.

As we shall explain later, the right to receive the residual income gives the owner a strong incentive to make economically efficient use of the asset.

Holdup

First, let us consider how the problem of a holdup can be resolved by changing the ownership of the relevant assets. Recall that, when Luna requested an additional delivery on short notice, Speedy extracted double the usual price for the service. What if Luna had an in-house delivery service? To make the additional delivery, it might have to order a driver to work overtime. The driver could respond by striking to demand a special overtime payment. By doing so, however, the driver runs the risk that Luna may replace her with another worker.

If the driver strikes, the cost imposed on Luna is the cost of hiring a replacement driver on short notice. This will be lower than the cost of hiring a replacement truck and driver which would be necessary if Speedy should withhold its services.

As this example suggests, an employee is less likely than an external contractor to engage in a holdup and would impose lower costs if it did so. The reason is that the external contractor owns the assets necessary to provide the service. Residual control of an asset includes the right to withhold its services. Hence, an external contractor has the power to withhold the services of its assets. By contrast, an employee has no such power since the assets on which she works belong to the employer. With its smaller power, the employee is less likely to behave opportunistically and engage in a holdup and would impose lower cost if it did so.

The potential for holdup can be mitigated through vertical integration into the relevant stage of production. *Vertical integration* occurs when the assets for two successive stages of production are combined under a common ownership. In Luna's case, it could reduce the potential for a holdup by vertical integration into delivery service.

Vertical integration is downstream or upstream, depending on whether it involves the acquisition of assets for a stage of production nearer to or further from the final consumer. Suppose, for instance, that a food manufacturer acquires a supermarket. Since the supermarket operates a stage of production nearer to the final consumer, this is an example of downstream vertical integration. By contrast, if the food manufacturer were to acquire a grower of fresh fruit, it would be vertically integrating upstream. Table 13.1 lists some recent examples of vertical integration.

We emphasize that vertical integration can mitigate the potential for a holdup but may not resolve it completely. Even an employee can engage in a holdup. As we have argued, however, an employee is less likely than an outside contractor to engage in a holdup and would impose lower costs if it did so.

Progress Check 13G Referring to Table 13.1, identify the examples as upstream or downstream vertical integration.  *Progress check*

Table 13.1 Vertical integration

Acquirer		Target		Source
Company	**Business**	**Company**	**Business**	
Walt Disney Co.	Production of films and television programming	CapCities/ABC	Television broadcasting	a
Seagate Technology	Manufacturing of disk drives	Conner Peripherals	Manufacturing of disk media (component of disk drive)	b
Broken Hill Proprietary Co.	Copper mining	Magma Copper	Copper smelting	c
Loral Space & Communications	Manufacturing of satellites	Space Systems/ Loral	Satellite communications services	d

Sources:
[a] "Disney's Kingdom," *Business Week*, (August 15, 1995), p. 33.
[b] "Seagate, Conner to Merge," *EE Times Interactive*, no. 867 (September 25, 1995), p. 16.
[c] "Broken Hill Proprietary Sets Perpetual Growth Plan," *Wall Street Journal* (January 10, 1996), p. B4.
[d] "Loral Space Posts Net, Seeks Control of Unit,"*Asian Wall Street Journal* (October 30, 1996), p. 11.

Moral Hazard

We have discussed how a change in the ownership of an asset can affect the likelihood and cost of a holdup. A change in ownership will have other important effects. One is the incentive to make economically efficient use of the asset.

Earlier, we considered the moral hazard of an employee relative to the employer. Generally, the employer's marginal benefit diverges from the worker's personal marginal benefit. Since the worker chooses effort according to the personal marginal benefit, she chooses less than the economically efficient level of effort.

By contrast, suppose that the employee owns the business. In this case, the worker receives the residual income of the business. Hence, if the worker exerts an additional unit of effort, she will receive the entire marginal benefit. By contrast, if the worker did not completely own the business, she would receive only a part of the marginal benefit.

Likewise, a worker who reduces effort by one unit will suffer the entire reduction in the marginal benefit. Thus, when balancing her marginal benefit with the marginal cost, the worker will choose the economically efficient level of effort. Giving ownership to the worker will resolve the moral hazard.

Generally, since the owner of an asset receives its residual income, it will aim to maximize the net benefit, which means using the asset in an economically efficient way. This explains why many businesses pay senior managers through shares and stock options. To the extent that these managers have a share of ownership, their interests will be more closely aligned with those of the business, which reduces the degree of the moral hazard.

How does this analysis apply to Luna's in-house delivery service? It implies that Mary's moral hazard will be relatively low if she owned the service. The delivery person's moral hazard would be higher if the service were owned by the supermarket. So, if Luna vertically integrates into the delivery business, it will increase the delivery person's degree of moral hazard.

Vertical integration changes ownership: It transforms a supplier of a service from an owner into an employee. An employee is subject to relatively greater moral hazard than an owner. Accordingly, vertical integration increases the degree of moral hazard. This is a major cost of vertical integration.

The Risk of Ownership: Wal-Mart's Employee Stock Ownership Plan

Wal-Mart, the world's largest retailer, firmly believes in motivating employees through stock ownership. The company encourages workers to participate in the company's Employee Stock Ownership Plan (ESOP) by offering shares at a 15% discount. As of early 1996, the plan had invested over 80% of its assets in Wal-Mart shares. Wal-Mart's ESOP was the stuff of legends, such as the employee whose $1,200 investment had grown to $138,000 over 17 years.

At the time of writing, however, the decline in Wal-Mart's share price in recent years had made its employees realize the risks of having a high proportion of their investments tied to their employer. After peaking at over $34 in February 1993, Wal-Mart's shares dropped to below $20 in early 1996.

While share ownership can be an effective way of motivating employees, it subjects them to increased risk as the share price can fall as well as rise. In Wal-Mart's case, some elderly employees were forced to postpone retirement as their investments declined in value.

Source: "Wal-Mart's Slipping Stock Cuts into Worker's Morale," *Asian Wall Street Journal* (January 5, 1996), pp. 1 and 20.

Internal Monopoly

Another cost of vertical integration is that the internal provider may acquire monopoly power. If Luna establishes its own delivery service, it will prefer using its own delivery service to engaging an external contractor. This is a reasonable policy to the extent that some of the costs of the in-house delivery service are sunk.

The preference in favor of an internal provider, however, means creating an internal monopoly. In Chapter 8, we showed that a seller with market power will restrict production and raise price. An internal provider may also use its market power to raise its price. Then, the organization as a whole will find that the cost of internal provision may rise above the price charged by external contractors. This higher cost must be borne by the organization.

One way of resolving the problem of an internal monopoly is to outsource whenever the internal provider's cost exceeds that of external sources. *Outsourcing* is the purchase of services or supplies from external sources. It subjects internal providers to the discipline of market competition and, so, limits the extent to which the cost of internal provision diverges from the competitive level.

Economies of Scale

Finally, a decision on vertical integration into some stage of production should also take account of scale economies. Recall from Chapter 7 that, if there are economies of scale, then the average cost of provision will be lower with a larger scale. Typically, an internal provider will operate at a smaller scale than an external contractor. It then is necessary to consider how the average cost varies with the operating scale.

For instance, in Luna's case, the supermarket's deliveries may occupy a truck and driver for only four hours a day. If Luna were to set up its own delivery service, its utilization of the assets and human resources would be relatively low. By contrast, an external delivery contractor may get 10 or 12 hours a day of work from its equipment and personnel. The external contractor would have better capacity utilization and hence a lower average cost. To this extent, it would be less costly to purchase the service from the external contractor.

We can also illustrate the significance of scale economies by comparing a supermarket's need for delivery service with that for armored truck service to convey cash and checks. While some supermarkets have their own delivery service, almost none have their own armored trucks. A major reason for this difference is economies of scale. It hardly would be efficient for a supermarket to buy an armored truck that makes one daily trip to the bank.

Figure 13.5 Vertical integration

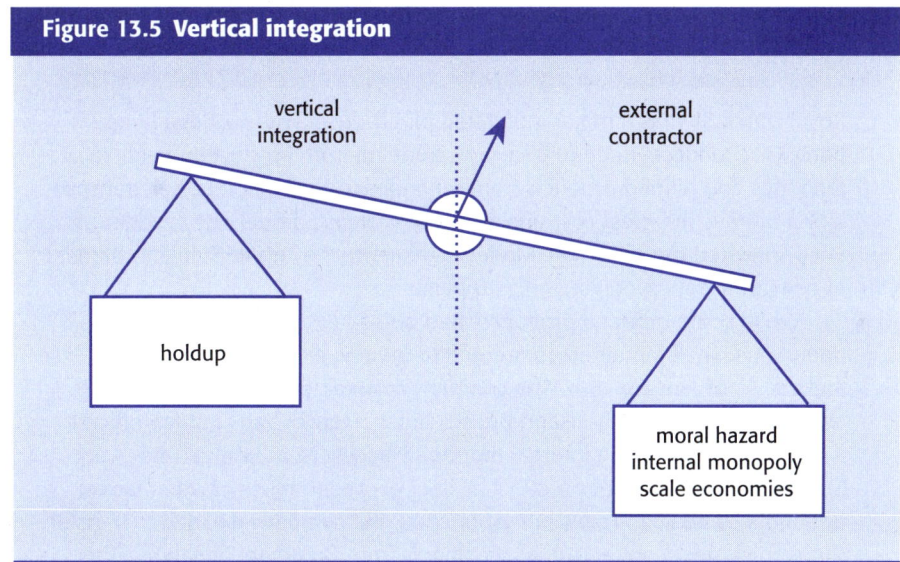

The scope for a holdup weighs in favor of vertical integration, while the degree of moral hazard, internal monopoly power, and the extent of economies of scale weigh against it.

Balance

The decision whether to vertically integrate into some stage of production depends on a balance among all the factors that we have discussed: the scope for holdup, the degree of moral hazard, internal monopoly power, and the extent of economies of scale (see Figure 13.5). Further, it also depends on other ways to resolve these issues. Specifically, holdup can be resolved through investment in more detailed contracts, moral hazard can be resolved through performance incentives, and internal monopoly power can be resolved through outsourcing. Generally, the economically efficient solution will involve a mix of all policies.

Progress Check 13H Jupiter Bank has 1 million credit card accounts, while Mercury Bank has only 1000 accounts. Explain why Jupiter chooses to own and operate its own credit card processing, while Mercury contracts out for that service.

Progress check

Royal Dutch Shell: The Costs of Internal Provision

Royal Dutch Shell is a major integrated oil producer with worldwide operations. Oil producers need to transport crude oil from production fields to refineries and refined products from refineries to final markets. Sea transportation often is the most cost-effective way. Marcus Samuel, the founder of Shell, invented the oil tanker. Modern tankers convey up to 3 million barrels of oil with a crew averaging only 20 persons.

While some other oil producers had outsourced their transportation operations, Shell remained committed to owning and managing its own tankers. As of January 1996, the company maintained a fleet of 54 tankers and employed over a thousand British, Dutch, French, and German officers.

Consistent with the internal monopoly arising from vertical integration, Shell found that the labor costs of its fleet exceeded those of other tanker operators by 40%. To reduce its labor costs, the company decided to transfer the employment contracts of all its officers from Britain to Singapore. The transfer enabled savings on British social security contributions and working conditions, as well as cuts in pay.

Sources: World Wide Web page, www.shellus.com (June 28, 1996); "Shell to Move Seamen's Contracts to Singapore," *Financial Times* (January 18, 1996), p. 8.

8 Summary

This chapter considered a general issue of organization: Should an item be provided internally or purchased from an external source? Internal provision means dealing with employees, while external provision requires managing suppliers. In either case, management must resolve the issues of moral hazard, risk, balancing multiple responsibilities, and holdup. Generally, resolving these difficulties involves a balance among performance incentives, more detailed contracts, outsourcing, and ownership.

Strong performance incentives resolve moral hazard but may impose the cost of risk and redirect attention from other responsibilities that are less easy to monitor. A holdup can be resolved through either more detailed contracts or vertical integration. Vertical integration, however, may increase moral hazard, create an internal monopoly, and result in an inefficient scale of operations.

Key concepts

moral hazard   relative performance   complete contract
performance pay   holdup   ownership
performance quota   specificity   residual control
    residual income

Further Reading

The key reference is Paul Milgrom and John Roberts's *Economics, Organization, and Management* (Englewood Cliffs, NJ: Prentice Hall, 1992). Professors Milgrom and Roberts apply state-of-the-art scholarship to the issues of incentives and organization. See especially their Chapters 5–7, 9, and 16.

Review Questions

1. Explain the asymmetry of information and the conflict of interest in the following situation. Leah has just bought comprehensive insurance on her car. This covers loss and damage for any reason including theft. Her insurer is concerned that she may take fewer precautions against theft.

2. By considering benefits and costs to the various parties, explain why a profit can be made by resolving moral hazard.

3. Compare the following ways of paying a lawyer in terms of the incentive for effort.
   a. Hourly rate, in which the lawyer receives a fixed dollar amount for each hour of work on the case.
   b. Contingency fee, in which the lawyer receives a portion of the amount that the client recovers. If the client loses the legal action, the lawyer gets nothing.

4. A department store employs both sales staff and delivery drivers. Explain how incentives based on relative performance can be structured to achieve the following objectives:
   a. Motivating salespersons to promote merchandise.
   b. Motivating drivers to maintain their vehicles carefully and avoid breakdowns.

5. A secretary's job includes typing letters, answering telephone calls, and handling visitors as well as other responsibilities. Comment on a proposal to pay a secretary according to the number of letters that he types.

6. For each of the following investment funds, suggest an appropriate benchmark against which the performance of the fund might be measured:
   a. A fund specializing in small stocks.
   b. A U.S. Government bond fund.
   c. A Japanese stock fund.

7. Maria is a pilot. Which of the following investments is the relatively more specific?
   a. An executive MBA program for middle managers.
   b. Training on an Airbus A-340 simulator.

8. Give an example of a holdup. Explain how this will induce the affected parties to avoid specific investments.

9. Explain the difference between vertical and horizontal integration.

10. A property management business is considering whether to replace an outside contractor with its own cleaning service. What are the arguments for and against this proposal?

Discussion Questions

1. Alan is a sales representative for a cellular telephone manufacturer. He must operate independently, calling on clients. Some of his clients are difficult and troublesome, while others are pleasant and easygoing. Spending one hour with a difficult client requires much more effort than four hours with an easy client.

    a. Is Alan subject to moral hazard?

    b. From the company's perspective, how much effort should Alan put into promoting sales?

    c. Comment on a proposal to pay sales representatives by the number of hours that they spend with clients.

2. In April 1996, the Aetna Life and Casualty Company announced that it would acquire U.S. Healthcare for $8.8 billion. At the time, Aetna was a leading provider of medical insurance. Medical insurance allows the insured party a relatively free choice of doctors and treatment centers. By contrast, U.S. Healthcare specialized in managed health care, under which covered patients could get treatment only from specific doctors and at specified facilities ("Aetna to Buy U.S. Healthcare in Big Move to Managed Care," *New York Times* [April 2, 1996], p. A1).

    a. A medical insurer pays the bills, while a doctor decides on tests, treatment, and prescriptions. Explain the moral hazard between doctors and medical insurers.

    b. A managed health care plan may restrict coverage to treatment by the plan's own employees and facilities. Compare the extent of a doctor's moral hazard under managed health care relative to medical insurance.

    c. Using your answer to (b), explain why managed health care is less costly than medical insurance.

3. The market for rental apartments includes both unfurnished and furnished units. Landlords of furnished units must make allowance for depreciation of the appliances and furniture.

    a. Explain how the depreciation of appliances and furniture depends on the behavior of the tenants.

    b. Which of the following items is relatively more sensitive to misuse by tenants: a sofa or a TV set?

    c. Explain why furnished apartments usually include sofas but not TV sets.

4. In 1986, the shares of Ralston-Purina, a manufacturer of foods and animal feeds, were trading at around $60. The company's Board of Directors established the following incentive scheme for senior management. Salaries were set below those at other major food producers. Managers, however, could get 491,000 free shares if the shares of Ralston-Purina traded above $100 for 10 consecutive days. In February 1991, the target was achieved and chief executive officer William P. Stiritz received 160,000 shares valued at $16.2 million ("Stock's Performance Pays off in Shares for Ralston Managers," *Wall Street Journal* [February 25, 1991], p. 21).

    a. Referring to relevant sources, calculate the percentage change in a relevant stock market index between January 1986 and January 1991. Compare this to the percentage change in the price of Ralston-Purina shares.

    b. Suggest an incentive scheme based on relative performance and compare it with Ralston-Purina's scheme.

5. Hong Kong traffic wardens prefer a quiet peaceful day to vigorous enforcement against illegal parking and unpaid parking meters. The government Audit Department proposed to resolve the moral hazard by assigning each traffic warden a quota of parking citations.

Table 13.2 Traffic warden vs. driver

		Driver	
		Parks illegally	Does not
Traffic warden	Enforces	2, –1	–1, 0
	Does not	0, 1	0, 0

a. The extent of illegal parking varies by the time of day and day of the week. What risk will the quota impose on traffic wardens?

b. Please suggest how an incentive scheme based on relative performance can resolve the problem in (a).

c. Construct the following game in strategic form. A traffic warden must choose between enforcing or not enforcing, while a driver must choose between parking illegally or legally. Table 13.2 shows the net benefits of the two parties. Show that there is no equilibrium in pure strategies.

6. The Sol Department Store pays large commissions to its sales staff. Salespersons, however, have other duties in addition to promoting merchandise. These include answering customers' telephone enquiries and processing returns.

a. Recently, a Sol customer complained that a salesperson did not attend to her when she asked to return several items. Explain how the salesperson's behavior is related to the company's policy of paying large commissions on sales.

b. Should Sol pay a commission to salespersons for processing returns as well?

c. Comment on the alternative solution of centralizing returns in the customer service section, where the staff do not receive commissions.

7. Mars Power has built an electric power generating plant next to the Mercury coal mine. Mars has tailored its plant to the grade of Mercury's coal. The other customers for Mercury's coal are relatively distant.

a. Use this example to explain specific assets.

b. How can Mars take advantage of Mercury? How can Mercury take advantage of Mars?

c. If Mars acquires the coal mine, how will that affect (i) the potential for holdup and (ii) unobservable efforts by Mercury managers?

8. On July 31, 1995, Chairman Michael D. Eisner announced that the Walt Disney Company would acquire Capital Cities/ABC Inc. for $19 billion. Through the acquisition, the Disney Company, which produces films and television shows, gained ownership of a major customer, the ABC television network. *Business Week* remarked that the deal would give Disney "a guaranteed platform for its first-run syndication programs–shows that might otherwise die on the vine" ("Disney's Kingdom," *Business Week* [August 15, 1995], p. 33).

a. Use this example to explain the meaning of downstream vis-à-vis upstream vertical integration.

b. Considering the ABC television network as a division of the Walt Disney Company, explain the meaning of outsourcing.

c. From the perspective of maximizing the company's overall profit, does it make sense for Disney to force ABC to broadcast programs that "might otherwise die on the vine"?

9. One disadvantage of vertical integration is that the in-house provider may be too small to achieve an the efficient scale. To what extent does this factor explain the following differences?

    a. Building contractors usually employ their own bricklayers and carpenters but hire subcontractors for electrical work and elevators.

    b. Large commercial buildings have their own teams of cleaners but hire external contractors for maintenance of heating, ventilation, and air-conditioning equipment.

10. General Motors and Toyota are two of the world's largest automobile manufacturers. The two companies differ significantly in the degree of vertical integration. While General Motors produces many components itself, Toyota tends to buy components from external suppliers.

    a. A consultant has measured labor productivity among automobile manufacturers by the number of cars produced per employee. On this measure, labor productivity is much lower at General Motors than Toyota. Comment on this measure.

    b. External subcontractors may be able to achieve a more efficient scale than an internal provider. Does this factor apply to Toyota?

    c. One reason for producing components in-house is to avoid a holdup by external suppliers. Suppose that, owing to long-term relationships, Toyota's suppliers are relatively less opportunistic. How does this affect Toyota's degree of vertical integration?

Regulation

1 Introduction

The Potomac Electric Power Co. has a monopoly over the distribution of electricity in Washington, DC. Similarly, Midlands Electricity and the Southeast Queensland Electricity Board have monopolies over electricity distribution in their respective territories. In Chapter 8, we showed that monopolies restrict competition to raise market prices. Why then do governments assign legal monopolies for electricity distribution?

In 1995, the South African mines of Gencor and Lonrho produced 22 and 12%, respectively, of the world platinum supply. When the two companies proposed to merge their platinum businesses, the European Commission, the executive arm of the European Union, blocked the plan. Why did the merger of two South African mining businesses concern the European Commission?

To practice in California, a lawyer must have a license from the state bar association. The bar subjects lawyers to a number of restrictions. For instance, the bar restricts how lawyers may advertise and prohibits them from practicing as limited companies. Further, legal practices must be separate from other professions such as accounting. Why are lawyers subject to these regulations?

The development of a new pharmaceutical may take 12 years and require an investment of $400 million. Developers of new drugs can apply for a patent that gives the owner an exclusive right. No one may manufacture a patented product or use a patented process without permission. Most governments, however, limit patent protection to 20 years. Once a patent has expired, anyone may freely imitate the product or process. Since patents are a critical incentive for investment in research and development, why are they limited to 20 years?

This chapter considers situations where the invisible hand fails. Buyers and sellers, acting independently and selfishly, do not equalize marginal benefit and marginal cost; hence, the allocation of resources is not economically efficient. The root of the inefficiency may be market power, asymmetric information, externalities, or public goods.

If the resource allocation is economically inefficient and private action fails to resolve the inefficiency, then there may be a role for government action. The government can act through regulation. If government regulation can resolve the divergence between the marginal benefit and the marginal cost, then it will increase net benefit for society.

To understand the role of government regulation, we consider the various sources of economic inefficiency: market power, asymmetric information, externalities, and public goods. In each case, we then analyze the conditions under which the government should intervene and the appropriate form of regulation.

In our analysis of economic inefficiency due to market power, we explain why a government may award legal monopolies for businesses with significant economies of scale relative to demand. One example is electricity distribution. In a global market, any restriction of competition among suppliers will affect users all over the world. This explains why the merger of two South African mining businesses concerned the European Commission.

In our analysis of economic inefficiency due to asymmetric information, we show how restrictions on the conduct of parties with better information can resolve asymmetric information. This can explain why Californian lawyers are restricted in advertising and prohibited from merging with accountants. Finally, the analysis of economic inefficiency in externalities and the provision of public goods will explain why patents are limited to 20 years.

2 *Natural Monopoly*

Recall from Chapter 8 that a monopoly will restrict sales to a quantity where the price exceeds the marginal cost. If buyers have no market power, they each purchase a quantity where the price equals the marginal benefit. Hence, at the monopoly price, some buyers will be willing to pay more than the seller's marginal cost but cannot get the product. This outcome is not economically efficient.

If monopolies cause economic inefficiency, why have governments all over the world awarded exclusive franchises to electricity distributors? To address this question, we must consider the technology of the business and, specifically, the presence of substantial economies of scale or scope.

Electricity is distributed through a network of cables running from a central source to every user. Consider a town in which there are two separate electricity distributors. Then, two sets of cables would run into every home, office, and factory. In the electricity distribution business, having more than one provider could mean wasteful duplication.

A market is a **natural monopoly** if the average cost of production is minimized with a single supplier. Examples of natural monopolies include distribution of electricity, gas, and water, and collection of sewage. In all of these markets, the economies of scale may be large relative to the market demand. Consequently, the average cost of production is lowest when there is only one supplier. Similarly, in a market with economies of scope that are large relative to the market demand, the average cost of production will be minimized with a single supplier.

If a market is a natural monopoly, the government should prohibit competition and award an exclusive franchise to a single supplier. This will establish the conditions for production at the lowest average cost.

The monopoly, however, might exploit its exclusive right to raise its price at the expense of its customers. The increase in the price will force the marginal benefit above the marginal cost. Accordingly, to ensure economic efficiency, the government must establish controls on the monopoly.

A monopoly can be controlled in two ways: The government itself can own and operate the business, or a monopoly franchise could be awarded to a commercial enterprise that would be subjected to government regulation. Historically, government ownership of natural monopolies was relatively more common in Europe and developing countries, while private ownership subject to government regulation was more common in the United States. Since the 1980s, however, there has been a worldwide trend to privatize government enterprises and adopt the American model.

Government Ownership

The major reason for privatization is that government-owned enterprises tend to be relatively inefficient. One problem is that they are more prone to be coopted by employees, so that the enterprise serves its employees rather than its customers. Some symptoms of employee control are high wages and overstaffing, both of which inflate the cost of production.

Another problem for government-owned enterprises is their dependence on the government for investment funds. The national government budget must finance everything from social welfare to military equipment. A government-owned enterprise must compete with other priorities for an allocation from the budget. Unlike a commercial enterprise, a government-owned enterprise cannot borrow or raise capital independently. The reason is that lenders cannot prevent the government from spending the funds on military equipment or other purposes. By contrast, a privately owned enterprise can commit to invest borrowed funds or capital in its own business.

A **natural monopoly** is a market where the average cost of production is minimized with a single supplier.

Privatization is the transfer of ownership from the government to the private sector.

Owing to these problems, government-owned natural monopolies may fall far short of resolving economic inefficiency in their respective markets. We have mentioned that there has been a worldwide trend toward privatization. **Privatization** means transfering ownership from the government to the private sector. It does not necessarily mean allowing competition. Indeed many privatized enterprises continue to have exclusive franchises in their respective businesses.

Government vis-à-vis Private Ownership: Telmex

For many years, the Mexican government owned most of the national telecommunications carrier, Telefonos de Mexico (Telmex). Owing to the government's fiscal difficulties, Telmex lacked funds to keep up with customer demand. The carrier provided only 5.5 lines per 100 residents, well below the world average of 9 lines per 100 residents. Moreover, the service was notoriously poor: The waiting list for telephone lines was 1.5 million long, the system did not complete a high percentage of calls, and fewer than 20% of lines were digital.

In December 1990, the government sold control of Telmex to a consortium of Mexican investors, Southwestern Bell, and France Telecom. The next year, Telmex was listed on the New York Stock Exchange. The company retained its monopoly over local, long-distance, and international services. The government allowed competition in cellular services, however.

Following privatization, Telmex embarked on a $11 billion program of investment. By 1995, its provision reached almost 9 lines per 100 residents, the call-completion rate was much higher, and over 50% of lines were digital. Between 1989 and 1995, earnings per share rose six times from 39 cents to $2.40.

Sources: "Slim Competition," *The Economist* (April 27, 1996), p. 81; *Value Line Survey,* Telefonos de Mexico (April 12, 1996), p. 797; "Market: The Mexican Model," *Ericsson Connexion,* no. 1 (March 1994).

Price Regulation

If the government awards an exclusive franchise for a natural monopoly to a commercial enterprise, then the government must regulate the monopoly. How should the government carry out the regulation?

Recall from Chapter 6 that the provision of any good or service will be economically efficient at the level where the marginal benefit equals the marginal cost. Suppose that the government awards an exclusive franchise for gas distribution to Pluto Gas. Pluto's costs include a fixed cost and a constant marginal cost of 15 cents per cubic foot. Figure 14.1 shows the distribution cost and the demand for gas.

Suppose that the government requires the franchise holder to set its price equal to its marginal cost and to meet the quantity demanded. Then, referring to Figure 14.1, at every possible quantity, the price will be the marginal cost. In effect, the government's policy forces the franchise holder to behave like a perfectly competitive supplier. This policy is called **marginal cost pricing.**

Marginal cost pricing is the policy in which the price is set equal to the marginal cost and the provider must supply the quantity demanded.

The demand curve crosses the marginal cost curve at point *a*. If Pluto sets a price of 15 cents a cubic foot, the market quantity demanded will be 9 million cubic feet. Under the regulation, Pluto must meet the quantity demanded; hence, it must produce 9 million cubic feet. Recall that each customer buys the quantity that balances the marginal benefit with the price. Thus, the marginal benefit equals the marginal cost, which is the condition for economic efficiency.

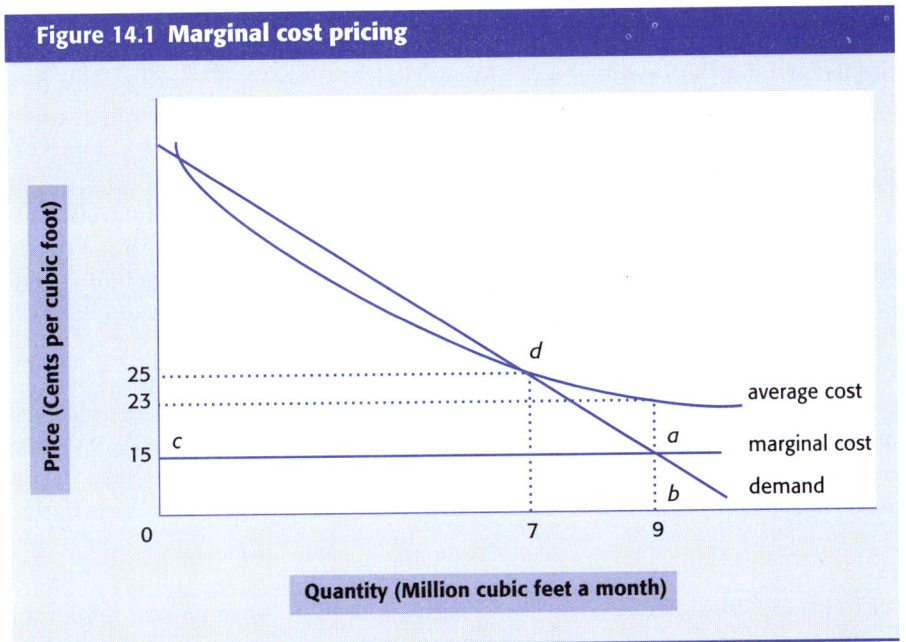

Figure 14.1 Marginal cost pricing

The demand curve crosses the marginal cost curve at point *a*. Under marginal cost pricing, the provider sets a price of 15 cents per cubic foot and the market quantity demanded is 9 million cubic feet a month. The demand curve crosses the average cost curve at point *d*. Under average cost pricing, the provider sets a price of 25 cents and the market quantity demanded is 7 million.

Pluto's revenue is represented by area 0*bac*, which is $0.15 × 9 million = $1.35 million a month. The average cost at the 9 million production rate is 23 cents per cubic foot, which means that the total cost of production is $0.23 × 9 million = $2.07 million. Accordingly, the government must provide a subsidy of $2.07 − $1.35 million = $720,000 a month to ensure that the franchise is financially viable. In this case, the subsidy is necessary to achieve economic efficiency.

Average cost pricing is the policy in which the price is set equal to the average cost and the provider must supply the quantity demanded.

How should the government regulate Pluto if it does not wish to provide a subsidy? In this case, the regulation must allow the franchise holder to break even. This can be achieved by requiring the franchise holder to implement **average cost pricing**, which means setting the price equal to average cost and meeting the quantity demanded. With average cost pricing, the franchise holder will exactly cover its costs.

Let us illustrate average cost pricing in the case of Pluto Gas. In Figure 14.1, the demand curve crosses the average cost curve at point *d*. If Pluto set a price of 25 cents a cubic foot, the market quantity demanded would be 7 million cubic feet. Under the regulation, Pluto must meet the quantity demanded: It must produce 7 million cubic feet. Its total revenue would exactly balance its total cost; hence, it would break even.

Where there are economies of scale in production, the average cost curve will be higher than the marginal cost curve. Then, average cost pricing leads to a lower level of provision than marginal cost pricing. Pluto Gas illustrates such a situation. With average cost pricing, it would produce 7 million cubic feet, while it would produce 9 million with marginal cost pricing.

Generally, the provision under average cost pricing is not economically efficient. The reason is that, with this regulation, buyers purchase up to the quantity where their marginal benefit equals the price. The franchise holder's price is set so that the price equals the average cost. Hence, the quantity of provision is such that the marginal benefit equals the average cost and not the marginal cost.

In Pluto's case, with average cost pricing, the franchise holder produces a quantity of 7 million cubic feet. At this quantity, the marginal benefit is 25 cents per cubic foot, while the marginal cost is 15 cents. Hence, the provision is not economically efficient.

Let us note a major difficulty in the implementation of price regulation based on the franchise holder's costs: Such regulation gives the franchise holder an incentive to persuade the regulator that its costs are higher than they actually are. Then the regulator will allow the franchise holder to set a higher price, closer to the monopoly level, which means a higher profit.

Note that the incentive is for the franchise holder to exaggerate its reported costs. Since the regulated price is fixed, the franchise holder will not try to inflate its actual costs. An increase in the franchise holder's actual costs would cut into its own profit.

Progress Check 14A Referring to Figure 14.1, suppose that the franchise holder is subject to average cost pricing. It reports to the regulator that its average cost curve is 10% higher than the true curve. Draw the new regulated price and show the franchise holder's profit.

Progress check

Rate of Return Regulation

To implement price regulation, the regulator needs information about the franchise holder's costs. We have seen that this gives the franchise holder an incentive to exaggerate its reported costs. The alternative to price regulation is rate of return regulation. This avoids the issue of costs by focusing on the franchise holder's profit. The regulator allows the franchise holder to set prices freely, provided that it does not exceed the maximum allowed profit.

Under rate of return regulation, the regulator specifies the franchise holder's maximum allowed profit in terms of a maximum rate of return on the value of the **rate base,** which is the assets to which the regulation applies. Whenever the franchise holder's rate of return exceeds the specified maximum, it will be required to reduce its prices.

The **rate base** is the the assets to which the rate of return regulation applies.

Suppose, for instance, that Pluto Gas is subject to rate of return regulation with a maximum 12% rate of return, and the rate base consists of all plant and equipment used for producing and distributing gas. The value of this plant and equipment is $1 billion. Then, Pluto's maximum allowed profit will be $0.12 \times \$1$ billion = $120 million a year.

Rate of return regulation presents three major difficulties for the regulator. The first is determining the maximum permissible rate of return. Since the rate base is typically a very large number, a small difference in the allowed rate of return will translate into a large sum of money. There is considerable room for dispute over the appropriate rate of return because the franchise holder is a monopoly, which means that there will be few comparable investments.

The second problem is that there will be disputes over what assets are needed to provide the regulated service and, hence, should be counted in the rate base. The franchise holder will seek the widest possible definition to increase its profit.

The third problem with rate of return regulation is that it creates an incentive for the franchise holder to invest beyond the economically efficient level. Specifically, if the franchise holder enlarges its rate base, the allowed rate of return will be applied to a larger base; hence, the franchise holder can earn a larger profit.

For example, the demand for electric power varies over time: The peak demand from commercial and industrial customers occurs during working hours, while the peak demand from residential customers occurs in the early morning and late evening. Suppose that there are two neighboring electric power utilities, one catering to mainly commercial and industrial demand and the other serving mainly residential users. It would be efficient for the two utilities to share generating capacity to meet differences in their peak demands. However, if they are subject to rate of return regulation, each may prefer to build more generating plants to increase its rate base.

A Free Gift from Your Local Power Company

China Light and Power holds a monopoly franchise for electricity supply in the two most heavily populated regions of Hong Kong. The government subjects China Light to a maximum 15% rate of return on a rate base that consists of the plant and equipment used to produce and distribute electricity. The electrical risers contained within residential buildings can be included in China Light's rate base.

A result of the regulatory structure is that China Light provides free electric water heaters to developers of new residential projects. In return, the developers transfer the electrical risers within their buildings to the power company. These risers are added to China Light's rate base and, hence, increase its future allowed profit.

Source: Hong Kong Consumer Council, Assessing Competition in the Domestic Water Heating and Cooking Fuel Market, 1995, p.30.

3 *Potentially Competitive Market*

By contrast with a natural monopoly, a potentially competitive market is one where economies of scale or scope are small relative to market demand. A market can switch from a natural monopoly to potentially competitive or *vice versa* with changes in demand or technology. The mathematical supplement gives one example of such a change.

If perfect competition prevails over a potentially competitive market, the invisible hand will ensure economic efficiency. Some potentially competitive markets, however, have government protection through exclusive franchises or restrictions against foreign imports. From the standpoint of economic efficiency, these markets should be opened to competition.

In most jurisdictions, the policy regarding competition depends on whether the industry is subject to government regulation. (A jurisdiction could be a state, country, or collection of countries.) Unregulated industries are subject to general competition law, while regulated industries are further subject to laws specific to the industry.

Competition Laws

Table 14.1 lists the key laws regarding competition in Australia, Canada, the European Union, and the United States. In addition to these laws, individual countries within the European Union and individual American states may have their own competition laws. Table 14.1 also lists the agencies responsible for enforcing competition laws in the various jurisdictions.

Generally, the competition laws prohibit competitors from colluding on price and prohibit mergers or acquisitions that would create monopolies or monopsonies. In addition, the laws may prohibit or restrict specific anticompetitive business practices such as control over resale prices and exclusive agreements. What exactly is prohibited varies from one jurisdiction to another.

The role of the competition agency is to enforce the competition laws. Enforcement involves two dimensions. One is prosecution against those who violate the laws. The competition agency will prosecute competing sellers or competing buyers that engage in price collusion. The agency is also responsible for prosecuting anyone involved in anticompetitive practices.

The other major dimension of enforcement is to review proposals for mergers and acquisitions. Each jurisdiction has its own set of criteria regarding mergers and acquisitions. The competition agency must ensure that all proposals meet the criteria. The agency may approve a merger or acquisition subject to specific conditions. For instance, the agency may require divestment of particular businesses to mitigate the anticompetitive impact of a merger or acquisition.

Table 14.1 Competition laws

Jurisdiction	Law	Enforcement Agency
Australia	Trade Practices Act, 1974 Competition Law Reform Act, 1995	Australian Competition and Consumer Commission
Canada	Competition Act, 1976	Bureau of Competition Policy
European Union	Treaty of Rome, 1957, Article 87	European Commission
United Kingdom	Fair Trading Act, 1973 Resale Prices Act, 1976 Restrictive Trade Practices Act, 1976	Office of Fair Trading Monopolies and Mergers Commission
United States of America	Sherman Act, 1890 Clayton Act, 1914 Robinson-Patman Act, 1938 Federal Trade Commission Act, 1915	U.S. Department of Justice Federal Trade Commission

In addition to government enforcement, the competition laws may provide for persons affected by anticompetitive behavior to sue in civil court. Under American laws, for instance, plaintiffs in civil actions can recover three times the damages they suffered. Further, civil plaintiffs can petition the courts for an order to stop anticompetitive conduct.

Platinum and the European Commission

Platinum is an inert metal that is resistant to corrosion and has a high electrical resistance. It is mainly used as a chemical catalyst for electrical contacts and in laboratory apparatus. The market for platinum is global. The world supply of platinum is highly concentrated, with just three companies—Anglo-American Platinum, Gencor, and Lonrho—accounting for 72% of total production (see Table 14.2). The members of the European Union account for a large portion of the demand for platinum.

When Gencor and Lonrho proposed to merge their platinum businesses, the European Commission blocked the merger. The commission found that Lonrho had played a major role in lowering the price of platinum and that the merger would have reduced competition in a highly concentrated industry.

The reduction in competition would therefore have harmed European users of platinum. That is why a merger of two South African companies motivated the European Commission to act.

Source: "Lonrho-Gencor Platinum Merger Is Rebuffed by EU Commission," *Asian Wall Street Journal* (April 25, 1996), p. 2.

Table 14.2 World platinum production, 1995

Producer	Market Share
Anglo American Platinum Corp.	38%
Impala Platinum Holdings (controlled by Gencor, Ltd)	22%
Lonrho, PLC	12%
Russia	27%

Source: "Lonrho-Gencor Platinum Merger Is Rebuffed by EU Commission," *Asian Wall Street Journal* (April 25, 1996), p. 2.

A Multinational Marriage: Kleenex and Viva

A merger that creates substantial market power within a jurisdiction may require government approval. By the same token, a merger that spans several jurisdictions may require the approval of all the relevant competition agencies. Each agency will apply its own criteria and specify its own set of conditions for approval.

Kimberly-Clark is a leading manufacturer of synthetic and natural fiber products whose most famous product is Kleenex tissues. In July 1995, Kimberly-Clark announced that it would acquire the Scott Paper Company. At the time, Scott was the world's largest manufacturer of beauty and bathroom tissues with operations in 22 countries. Scott's brands included Andrex, Cottonelle, Scott, and Viva.

To secure approval of the acquisition by the U.S. Department of Justice, Kimberly-Clark agreed to divest its Scott Baby Fresh Wipes and Scotties facial tissues businesses, as well as three tissue mills in the United States. For approval of the European Commission, Kimberly-Clark had to sell the Kleenex Velvet bathroom tissue businesses in the United Kingdom and Ireland and one English bathroom tissue mill. In addition, Kimberly-Clark also sought clearance from the Canadian Bureau of Competition Policy and the Federal Competition Commission in Mexico.

Source: Kimberly-Clark Corporation, Form 10-K, fiscal year ending December 31, 1995.

Structural Regulation

The fact that one market is a natural monopoly does not necessarily mean that related upstream or downstream markets are also natural monopolies. In natural gas, for instance, production may be potentially competitive even while distribution is a natural monopoly. Likewise, distribution of water may be a natural monopoly, while production is potentially competitive.

Under such circumstances, the government must consider how to preserve the benefits of monopoly in one market while fostering competition in the other. A special challenge to the regulator arises when the monopoly franchise holder also participates in the potentially competitive market.

To illustrate the issues, suppose that the government awarded a monopoly franchise for water distribution to Agua Fresca, while allowing competition in production of water. Since Fresca has a monopoly over distribution, it has a monopsony over the purchase of water. Hence, the government must regulate Fresca's monopoly over water distribution as well as its monopsony over water purchases.

Now, suppose that Fresca has vertically integrated upstream into the production of water. Then, Fresca may have an incentive to extend its monopoly upstream by discriminating against external water producers. An external source of water might offer a lower price with slightly different technical specifications. It may not be easy for the regulator to distinguish legitimate engineering reasons against the outside source of water from spurious arguments. Hence, external sources may be at a disadvantage.

This particular problem arises when the monopoly and the potentially competitive market occupy successive stages of production. One solution is structural regulation to separate the natural monopoly from the potentially competitive market. Applied to the example of Agua Fresca, the regulator may require Fresca to separate its water distribution and production businesses. An extreme form of structural regulation would be to require that Fresca divest itself of the production business.

Progress check

Progress Check 14B Suppose that the production of natural gas is potentially competitive and its distribution is a natural monopoly. Explain how structural regulation can ensure economic efficiency in the two markets.

Lights Off:
Structural Regulation of British Electricity

For many years, the government-owned Central Electricity Generating Board (CEGB) had a monopoly over generation, transmission, and distribution of electric power in England and Wales. Then, in March 1990, the government of Prime Minister Margaret Thatcher dismantled the CEGB and privatized the individual businesses.

Considering the distribution of electricity to be a natural monopoly, the British government awarded exclusive franchises for distribution to 12 regional electricity companies. The government established the Office of the Electricity Regulator (Offer) to regulate the regional companies. Offer imposed a long-term price regulation under which the regional companies could raise prices by no more than the increase in the retail price index less a productivity factor, the so-called RPI − X formula.

The British government, however, deemed generation to be a competitive business. It formed two companies, National Power and PowerGen, to take over the CEGB's generation businesses. At the same time, it opened generation to free competition and specifically allowed the regional electricity companies to buy electric power from any source.

Source: "How Britain Changed from Public to Private Power—Overnight," *Power Engineering* 95, no. 6 (June 1991): pp. 42–3.

4 *Asymmetric Information*

The second situation in which the invisible hand may fail is where there is asymmetric information about some characteristic or future action. Then, from Chapters 12 and 13, we know that, if the information asymmetry is not resolved, the marginal benefit will diverge from the marginal cost and the allocation of resources will not be economically efficient.

Consider, for instance, the market for medical services. Patients rely on doctors for advice as well as treatment. Owing to the asymmetry of information between doctor and patient, the doctors are subject to moral hazard. Specifically, doctors can overprescribe treatment and so increase their incomes.

Figure 14.2 illustrates the market equilibrium. The true demand reflects the patients' marginal benefit if they and their doctors had equal information. The inflated demand is the demand that is actually realized and reflects the asymmetry of information. The inflated demand is higher than the true demand to the extent that doctors induce patients to get excessive treatment.

Figure 14.2 Moral hazard in medical services

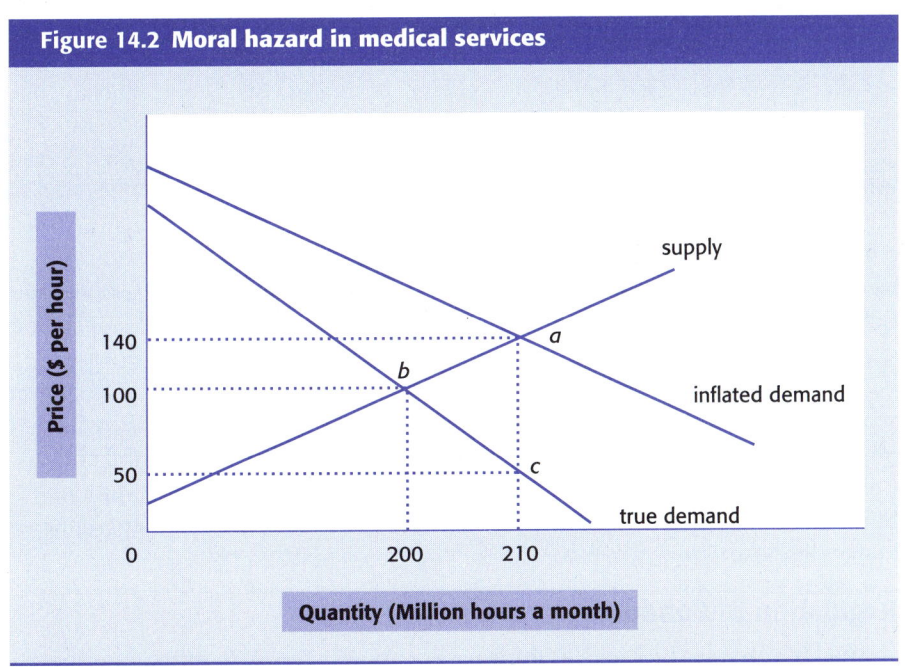

The inflated demand is higher than the true demand. The market equilibrium lies at point *a*, where the inflated demand crosses the supply. The price is $140 per hour and the quantity is 210 million hours a month. If the moral hazard can be resolved, the inflated demand will shift down to the true demand and the equilibrium will be at point *b*, where the true marginal benefit equals the marginal cost.

The inflated demand crosses the supply of medical services at point *a*. In the market equilibrium, the price is $140 per hour and the quantity of treatment is 210 million hours a month. At that quantity, the true marginal benefit of medical services is $50, which is the height of the true demand curve. The marginal cost of medical services is $140, the height of the supply curve at the equilibrium quantity. In equilibrium, the marginal cost exceeds the true marginal benefit by $90. This economic inefficiency is the result of the asymmetry of information between doctors and patients.

Supposing that doctors and patients could not privately resolve the information asymmetry, how can regulation help? In markets with asymmetric information, the regulator can resolve the asymmetry in three ways. First, the regulator can require the better-informed party to disclose its information. Second, it can regulate the conduct of the party with better information. Third, it can impose regulations on the business structure of the better-informed party.

Disclosure

The most obvious way to resolve asymmetric information is to require the better-informed party to disclose its information truthfully. In an unregulated market, parties may supply false information. For instance, dealers in fake antiques may falsely claim to be selling the genuine item, a service station may pass off regular low-octane gasoline as high-octane premium, or an obstetrician may exaggerate a pregnant woman's need for a cesarean section.

A regulatory requirement for disclosure will be meaningful only if the information can be objectively verified. Of the three examples mentioned—fake antiques, substituted gasoline, and an unnecessary cesarean section—disclosure works best for the substituted gasoline. The regulator can require service stations to mark each pump with the octane content of the gasoline and randomly inspect the pumps to ensure that the gasoline matches the specified octane level.

Whether disclosure can resolve the asymmetry of information between sellers and buyers of antiques depends on whether fakes can be distinguished objectively from genuine antiques. Disclosure will not be so helpful if the distinction between fakes and genuine antiques depends on individual judgment. Similarly, the need for a cesarean section is a matter of professional judgment; hence, disclosure may not resolve the information asymmetry.

Regulation of Conduct

Instead of directly resolving an information asymmetry, an alternative is to regulate the conduct of the better-informed party and limit the extent to which he or she can exploit the informational advantage. If parties with better information cannot exploit their advantage, then they are more likely to assist in resolving the asymmetry.

For example, in the market for medical services, a regulation may prohibit doctors from advertising. This may help to prevent further inflation of demand. Another possible regulation is a requirement that doctors recommending major procedures must advise their patients to get a second opinion. The second opinion provides a check against excessive treatment. Doctors could also be required to give patients a minimum time during which to decide on a major procedure. To the extent that these checks are effective, the inflated demand in Figure 14.2 will shift down toward the true demand and the equilibrium will be closer to point b, where the true marginal benefit equals the marginal cost.

Another example of asymmetric information arises in the market for real estate. Typically, a seller will have better information about her or his property than potential buyers. A seller may use this advantage to pressure a potential buyer. For instance, the seller may say, "Ten other people came this morning, and three of them are making offers. You'd better move fast or you'll lose this house." A regulator can restrict such high-pressure sales tactics by stipulating a minimum waiting period during which a buyer can cancel a purchase at no cost.

Another way by which to ensure proper conduct in real estate transactions is to require that all agreements be in writing and witnessed. This will restrict the scope for a seller to provide misleading information and rush potential buyers into a purchase.

Structural Regulation

In addition to regulating conduct, a way to limit the extent to which a better-informed party can exploit an informational advantage is structural regulation. By enforcing separation of different businesses, a regulator may reduce the opportunities for exploiting superior information.

The market for medical services provides one example of structural regulation. Doctors providing medical advice will have much less incentive to overprescribe if the treatment is provided by others. Hence, a structural regulation requiring doctors to specialize in either providing advice or providing treatment would mitigate the moral hazard problem. While reducing the demand for medical services, this mandatory specialization would increase the cost of the services actually provided. Accordingly, the benefit of the specialization would have to be weighed against the cost.

Mandatory specialization is not as outlandish as might be thought. In some parts of the world, doctors are allowed to sell medicines and medical supplies in their clinics. Under these circumstances, the doctors will have an incentive to overprescribe these items. In other countries, doctors are prohibited from selling medicines and medical supplies. This regulation effectively separates medical services from retailing of medicines and medical supplies and dissuades doctors from excessive prescriptions.

Another example of structural regulation arises in the market for real estate transactions. Suppose that one agent represents both the seller and the buyer of some real estate. Then, the agent will suffer a conflict of interest between the seller and the buyer. The agent, for instance, may learn how much the buyer is willing to pay and convey that information to the seller. Such conflicts of interest can be prevented by a regulation requiring that the seller and the buyer must have separate representation.

Self-Regulation

> **Self-regulation** is the regulation of practitioners by a professional organization.

To forestall direct government regulation, some professions subject themselves to **self-regulation**. This means that a professional organization licenses all practitioners. The organization sets conditions for licensing and rules of conduct. The licensing conditions may include specific preparatory education and training, and examinations.

The professional organization may also regulate conduct such as advertising, pricing, and business structure. For instance, some professional organizations prohibit their members from incorporating with limited liability. Other organizations publish set prices and restrict advertising. Some professional organizations require that members undergo continuing education.

Typically, as a quid pro quo for self-regulation, the government gives the professional organization an exclusive right to license practitioners. Accordingly, one important issue is whether professional organizations use self-regulation as a cover to limit competition. Some rules may have anticompetitive effects. For instance, restrictive admission standards may pose a barrier to entry of new professionals. Further, guidelines on pricing and limits on advertising may also restrict competition among professionals.

Regulating the American Securities Markets

Following the great stock market crash of 1929, the United States established the Securities Exchange Commission (SEC). The SEC makes wide use of disclosure in regulating the securities markets. For instance, it requires the underwriters of a new share issue to publish a prospectus explaining the business purpose of the issue and possible risks. The SEC also requires publicly listed companies to provide quarterly and annual reports to their shareholders.

The SEC also regulates the conduct of participants in securities markets. For instance, the securities laws prohibit insider trading and market manipulation. The laws also specify rules of conduct for broker-dealers with regard to segregation of customer funds, financial responsibility, and minimum net capital.

Finally, the securities markets are also subject to structural regulation. Under the Glass-Steagall Act, commercial banks may not underwrite, sell, or distribute securities, while securities brokers and dealers may not take deposits. The act imposed a statutory wall between the banking and securities industries.

Source: William A. Lovett, *Banking and Financial Institutions Law in a Nutshell* (St. Paul, MN: West Publishing Co., 1992).

Self-Regulation of Lawyers: The State Bar of California

The state Bar Association of California is the self-regulatory authority for lawyers in California. The bar's admission requirements include a specified number of years of law school and a membership examination. The bar regulates advertising by lawyers. This may be a way to prevent lawyers from inflating the demand for their services. It has not prevented ambulance chasers from promoting their services on late-night television, however.

The bar also prohibits lawyers from forming partnerships with accountants. This restriction is a structural regulation to ensure that clients receive independent opinions on legal and financial issues.

The California Bar Association will not automatically grant admission to lawyers from other states. Each state bar sets its own standards of admission. The differences in these standards hinder lawyers from crossing between states, hence, constitute a barrier to competition.

5 Externalities

Externalities arise when the markets for some costs or benefits fail to exist. Absent a market, the invisible hand cannot work. In Chapter 11, we considered how externalities can be resolved through private action. Some externalities, for instance, aircraft noise and automobile emissions, involve hundreds if not thousands of parties. In these cases, the difficulty of organizing all the sources and the affected parties means that private action will probably fail to resolve the externality. Government regulation may be the only solution.

To analyze how to regulate such widespread externalities, let us consider the emissions that create smog. Smog results from a complicated chemical reaction between nitrogen oxides and volatile organic compounds (VOCs). Chapter 6 showed that, for an economically efficient allocation of resources, every good or service must be provided up to the level that the marginal benefit balances the marginal cost. Although emissions are bad, the same principle applies: The economically efficient quantity of emissions balances the marginal benefit of emissions with the marginal cost, taking into account both private benefits and costs and external benefits and costs.

The major benefit of emissions is that the sources can avoid the cost of technologies that generate fewer emissions. Fixed sources of VOCs include petroleum refineries, chemical plants, and furniture manufacturers, while mobile sources include cars, trucks, buses, boats, and lawn mowers. Furniture makers, for instance, could switch to less volatile paints and varnishes, automobiles could use cleaner fuels such as methanol, and buses could switch to electric power.

The cost of smog is chest pain and the increased risk of asthma attacks among people and damage to crops. Smog is ambient: It affects victims over a wide area and each victim suffers to an equal degree. For example, if a delivery service adds a new truck, the additional emissions affect all neighboring residents to the same extent. If one victim increases his or her exposure to the emissions, this does not mean that another would be affected less. Accordingly, the marginal cost to society is the sum of the marginal costs to the various victims.

As depicted in Figure 14.3, the economically efficient rate of emissions is 8000 tons a year, where the marginal benefit equals the marginal cost to society. Having identified the economically efficient rate of emissions, the remaining issue is how to achieve it. Generally, there are two approaches. One aims to mimic Adam Smith's invisible hand: Allow all sources to emit as much as they like provided that they pay a set fee. The other approach is to control emissions directly through standards.

Emission Fee

Referring to Figure 14.3, at the economically efficient rate of emissions, the marginal cost to society is $35 per ton. Suppose that the regulator sets an emis-

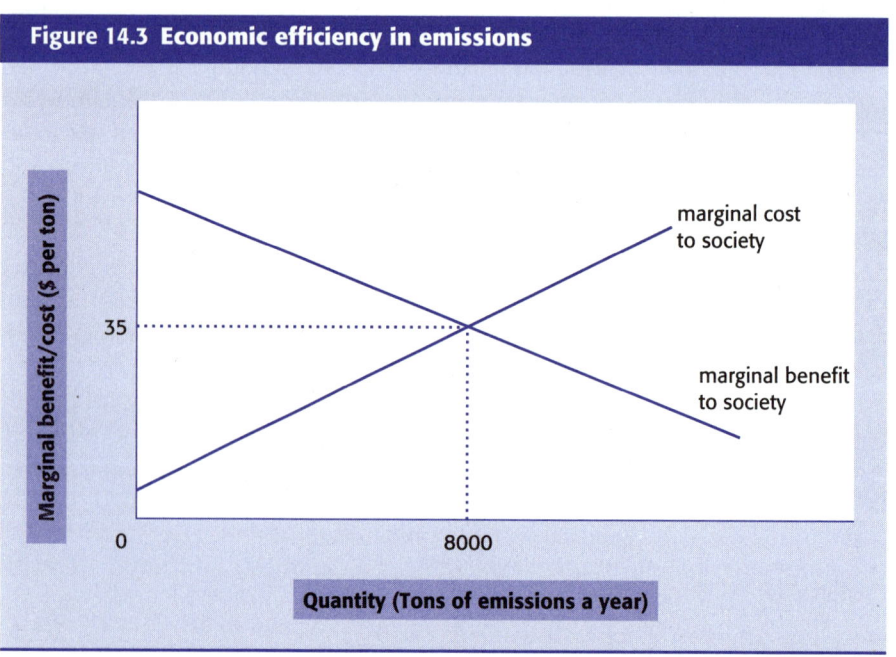

Figure 14.3 Economic efficiency in emissions

marginal cost to society

marginal benefit to society

35

Marginal benefit/cost ($ per ton)

0   8000

Quantity (Tons of emissions a year)

The economically efficient rate of emissions is 8000 tons a year, where the marginal benefit and the marginal cost to society are both equal to $35 per ton.

sions fee of $35 per ton and allows every source to buy as many emissions as it would like at that price.

Consider an oil refinery that emits pollutants. To maximize profits, the refinery should buy emissions up to the rate where the marginal benefit of emissions balances the $35 fee. Suppose that, as shown in Figure 14.4, the refinery's marginal benefit balances the $35 fee at an emissions rate of 500 tons a year.

To see why 500 tons maximizes profit, consider emissions of less than 500 tons a year, say, 400 tons. Then, as Figure 14.4 shows, the marginal benefit will be $45, which exceeds the $35 fee; so, by increasing emissions, the refinery can increase profits. Consider, instead, emissions of more than 500 tons a year, say, 600 tons. Then, the marginal benefit will be $25, which is less than the $35 fee; so the refinery should cut back on emissions. Accordingly, the refinery maximizes profit at the emissions rate where its marginal benefit equals the fee.

Other sources of emissions such as dry cleaners and furniture manufacturers will make the same calculation: Each will emit up to the point that its marginal benefit equals $35. Since the regulator charges the same $35 fee to all sources, the marginal benefits of all sources will be equal.

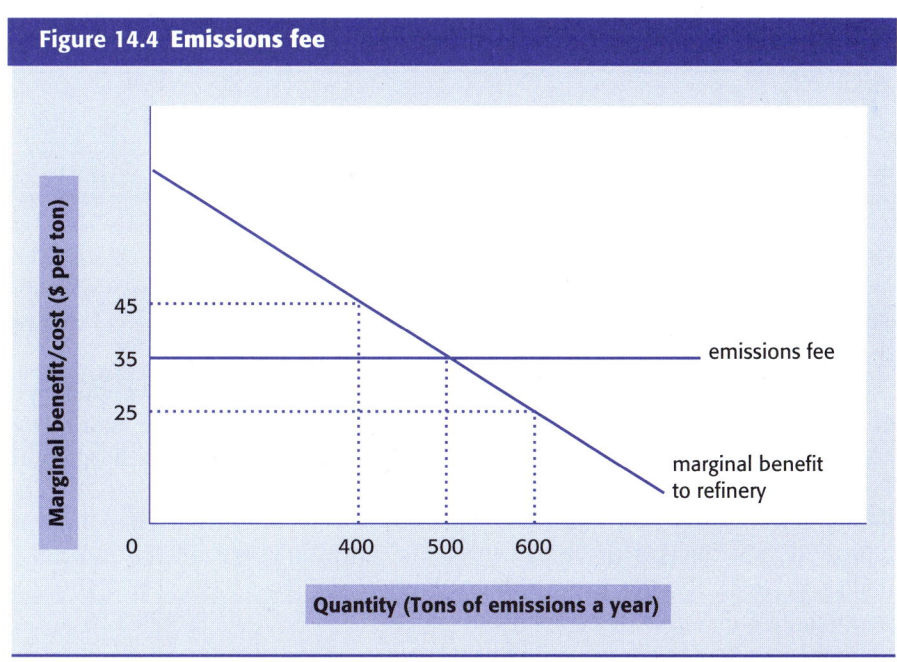

Figure 14.4 Emissions fee

The refinery's marginal benefit equals the $35 fee at an emissions rate of 500 tons a year. If the refinery emitted 400 tons, the marginal benefit would be $45, which exceeds the $35 fee, so by increasing emissions, the refinery could increase profits. If the refinery emitted 600 tons, then the marginal benefit would be $25, which is less than the $35 fee, so the refinery should cut back on emissions.

Since the regulator set the fee at the social marginal cost of emissions, it balances the marginal benefit with the marginal cost of emissions to society. Accordingly, the emissions fee achieves the economically efficient rate of emissions.

Fees in Action: Gasoline Taxes

Most governments levy excise taxes on gasoline sales. In addition to raising revenue, a gasoline tax serves as an implicit fee for automobile emissions. In 1994, a Royal Commission on Environmental Pollution recommended that the British government increase fuel taxes by 100% to reduce emissions from cars.

Taxes on fuel can also be used to reflect differences in the external cost of different types of fuel. For instance, the Singapore government levies a lower excise tax on unleaded gasoline than on leaded gasoline. The difference in tax rates is effectively the fee for lead emissions.

Source: Royal Commission on Environmental Pollution, "Transport and the Environment" (London: HMSO, 1994).

Standards

The alternative to charging a fee for emissions is to regulate directly through standards. From Figure 14.3, the economically efficient emissions rate is 8000 tons a year, which is the appropriate standard. There are many sources of emissions, however. How should the regulator allocate the 8000 tons a year among the various sources?

The answer depends on the cost of monitoring. Suppose that the emissions of all sources can be monitored at relatively low cost. The regulator could issue licenses for 8000 tons of emissions a year and sell them through public auction. Potential sources of emissions will provide the demand for the licenses. The demand of each source for licenses will be the same as its marginal benefit from emissions. The market demand will be the horizontal sum of the individual demand curves. So, the market demand curve will be identical to the social marginal benefit curve in Figure 14.3.

The supply of licenses would be perfectly inelastic at 8000. In equilibrium, the market demand will balance the supply at a quantity of 8000 licenses a year. Now, by Figure 14.3, the marginal benefit of the 8000th ton of emissions is $35. Thus, the equilibrium price of a license will be $35. Each source will buy licenses up to the point that its marginal benefit balances the price of $35. As a result, each source's emissions will be economically efficient and the total emissions will be at the economically efficient rate of 8000 tons a year.

By selling emissions licenses, the regulator is effectively charging an emissions fee that is determined by a competitive market. The license scheme, however, may be difficult to implement for small mobile sources such as powerboats and lawn mowers. It will be relatively expensive to monitor emissions from these sources. In such cases, it may be better for the regulator to specify directly the type and size of engine and fuel.

Trading in Emissions Licenses: Curbing Acid Rain

At the time of writing, the General James M. Gavin power plant was the largest in Ohio, generating over 12.5 billion kilowatt-hours of electricity. Together with other midwest coal-fired power plants, the Gavin accounted for two-thirds of all American emissions of sulfur dioxide.

Emissions of sulfur dioxide cause acid rain. The Clean Air Act requires the United States to reduce its annual sulfur dioxide emissions by 10 million tons. Beginning in 1977, the Clean Air Act required all new power plants to install flue-gas desulfurization equipment ("scrubbers"). The problem was how to reduce sulfur dioxide emissions from existing power plants. It did not seem economical to require scrubbers in older plants.

Congress decided to allow existing plants to reduce emissions by any means including installing scrubbers, switching to low-sulfur coal, and paying other sources to reduce their emissions by more than their own requirement. The latter option has created a market in emissions rights. This approach is estimated to have reduced emissions $2–3 billion more cheaply than if all existing plants had been required to retrofit with scrubbers.

Sources: "Polluting Rights," *Scientific American* (November 1989), pp. 76–9; "The Greening of the Invisible Hand," *The Economist* (December 24, 1988), pp. 105–6; Paul R. Portney, "Economics and the Clean Air Act," *Journal of Economic Perspectives* (Fall 1990): pp. 133–81.

Fees vis-à-vis Standards

Fees and standards are two alternative ways of regulating a negative externality such as emissions. How should a regulator choose between these two approaches? A frequent argument is that fees work like Adam Smith's invisible hand, so the regulator need not spend resources to collect detailed information about each source's marginal benefit and each victim's marginal cost or to monitor the actions of sources and victims.

This common argument is quite wrong. There is a crucial difference between a competitive market and setting a fee for a negative externality. In a competitive market, the equilibrium price is determined by buyers and sellers acting independently. By contrast, a regulator must set the fee for a negative externality. To determine the economically efficient fee, the regulator must collect information about each source's marginal benefit and each victim's marginal cost. The regulator needs exactly the same information to set the economically efficient standard.

Moreover, in a competitive market, sellers collect money from buyers. A regulator that sets a fee for a negative externality must collect the fee. So, the regulator must monitor each source to know how much to charge. Hence, to implement an emissions fee, the regulator must monitor the various sources as closely as it must to regulate through standards.

Accordingly, the common argument that fees are generally better than standards is flawed. There are reasonable grounds, however, for choosing between fees and standards. These are the robustness of fees relative to standards when the regulator is uncertain about the marginal benefit.

To compare fees with standards, let us reconsider the regulation of emissions. Referring to Figure 14.5, suppose that the regulator knows the true marginal cost of emissions to society but is uncertain about the true marginal benefit to society. Specifically, the regulator mistakenly believes the marginal benefit is higher than the true marginal benefit.

Suppose that, under the mistaken belief, the regulator sets an emissions fee of $45, the level at which the marginal cost equals the mistaken marginal benefit. At that price, according to their true marginal benefit, the sources would emit 7000 tons a year. This is less than the economically efficient rate of 8000 tons. The $45 fee causes a deadweight loss of the shaded area *cda* relative to the economically efficient emissions rate.

Suppose, instead, that the regulator imposes a standard of 10,000 tons a year, which is the emissions rate where the marginal cost equals the mistaken marginal benefit. Then, sources would emit 10,000 tons a year, which exceeds the economically efficient rate of 8,000 tons. The 10,000-ton standard causes a deadweight loss of the shaded area *aeb* relative to the economically efficient emissions rate.

Thus, both the fee and the standard cause deadweight losses. In Figure 14.5, where the marginal benefit is relatively steeper than the marginal cost, the shaded area *cda* is smaller than the shaded area *aeb*. Hence, the fee causes a smaller deadweight loss than the standard, and so the regulator should use a fee.

Figure 14.5 Fee better than standard

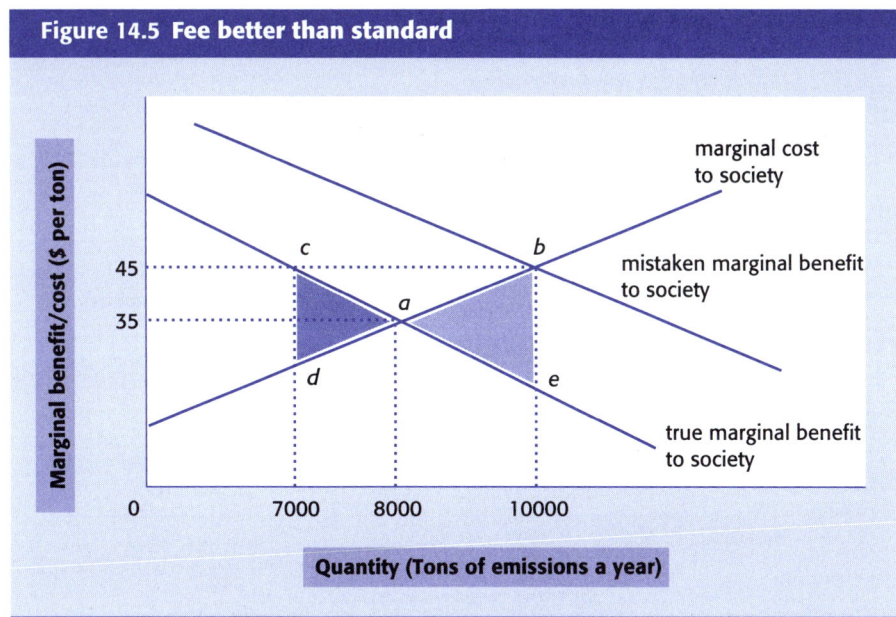

If, following the mistaken marginal benefit, the regulator sets an emissions fee of $45, then emissions would be 7000 tons a year. This would cause a deadweight loss of the shaded area *cda* relative to the economically efficient emissions. If, following the mistaken marginal benefit, the regulator sets a standard of 10,000 tons a year, then this would cause a deadweight loss of the shaded area *aeb*. The shaded area *cda* is smaller than the shaded area *aeb*; hence, the fee is better than the standard.

So far, we have considered the case where the marginal benefit to society is relatively steeper than the marginal cost to society. Let us now consider the alternative case. In Figure 14.6, the marginal benefit is relatively gentler than the marginal cost. If, based on the mistaken marginal benefit, the regulator sets a $40 emissions fee, the deadweight loss would be the shaded area *cda*. If, however, the regulator sets a 9000-ton a year standard, the deadweight loss would be the shaded area *aeb*. In this case, the shaded area *cda* is larger than the shaded area *aeb*. Hence, the regulator should apply a standard rather than a fee.

Accordingly, when the regulator is uncertain about the true social marginal benefit, neither a fee nor a standard generally is better than the other. Which policy to apply depends on whether the marginal benefit is relatively steeper or gentler than the marginal cost. Although our analysis supposed that the mistaken marginal benefit was greater than the true marginal benefit, the same principles apply when the mistaken marginal benefit is less than the true marginal benefit.

Figure 14.6 Standard better than fee

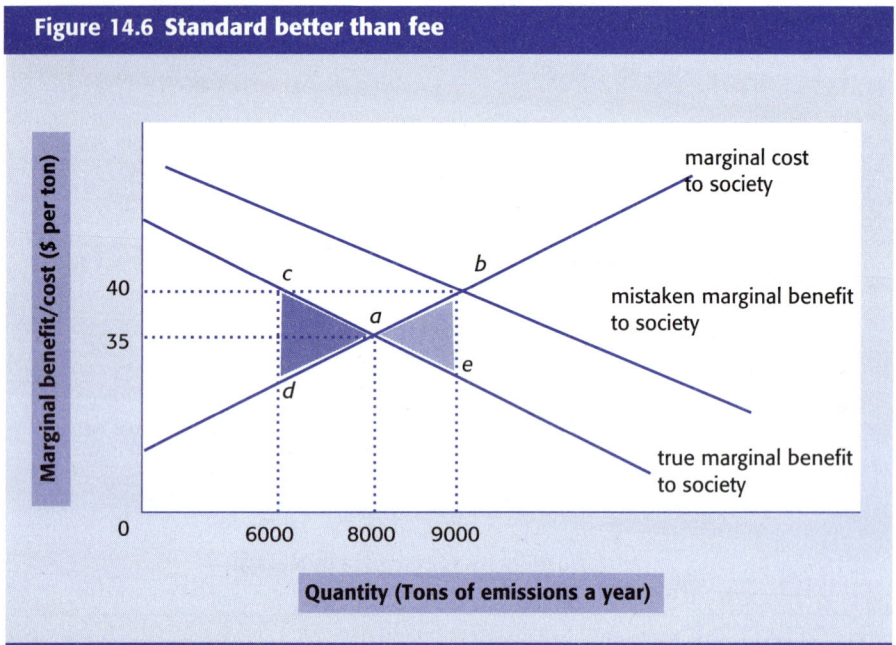

If, following the mistaken marginal benefit, the regulator sets an emissions fee of $40, then emissions would be 6000 tons a year. This would cause a deadweight loss of the shaded area *cda* relative to the economically efficient emissions. If, following the mistaken marginal benefit, the regulator sets a standard of 9000 tons a year, then this would cause a deadweight loss of the shaded area *aeb*. The area *cda* is larger than the shaded area *aeb*; hence, the standard is better than the fee.

So far, we have supposed that the regulator knows the marginal cost but is uncertain about the marginal benefit. What if the regulator knows the marginal benefit to society but is uncertain about the marginal cost to society? Figure 14.7 illustrates this situation. If the regulator sets a fee of $40, where the marginal benefit equals the mistaken marginal cost, the sources would emit 6000 tons a year. This is less than the economically efficient rate and there will be a deadweight loss of the shaded area *hmk*.

If the regulator sets a standard of 6000 tons a year, the emissions rate at which the marginal benefit equals the mistaken marginal cost, the sources would emit up to that rate. Hence, the resulting deadweight loss will also be the shaded area *hmk*. Thus, if the regulator knows the marginal benefit but is uncertain about the marginal cost, both the fee and the standard lead sources to choose the same level of emissions, so, the two policies are equivalent. Accordingly, fees and standards have different implications only when the regulator is uncertain about the marginal benefit of emissions.

Figure 14.7 Equivalent policies

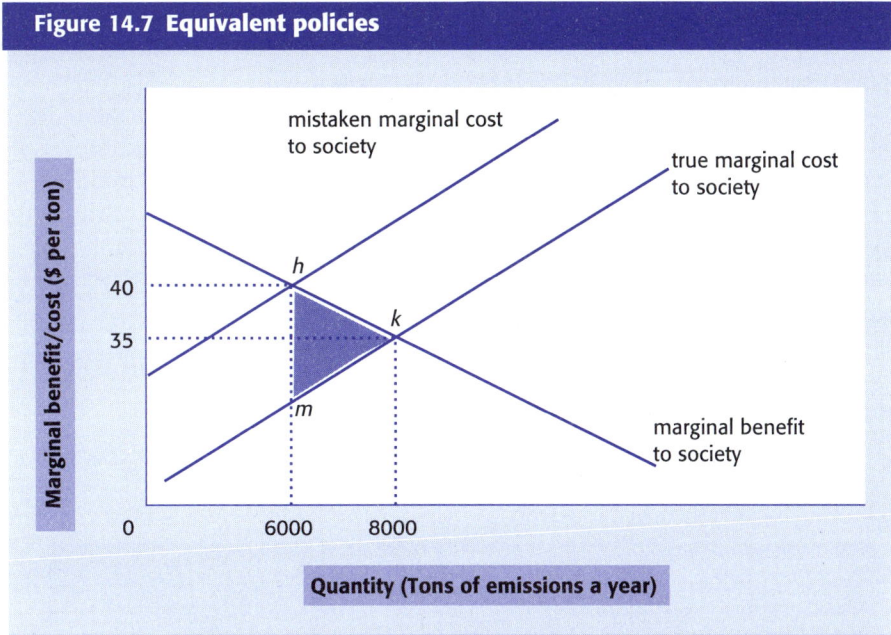

Quantity (Tons of emissions a year)

If, following the mistaken marginal cost, the regulator sets an emissions fee of $40, then emissions would be 6000 tons a year. This is the same as if the regulator sets a standard of 6000 tons a year. Both policies lead to the same deadweight loss of the shaded area *hmk*.

Progress Check 14C Referring to Figure 14.6, compare the deadweight losses that would arise from a fee vis-à-vis a standard if the regulator underestimated the marginal benefit.   *Progress check*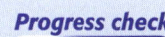

Regional and Temporal Differences

The efficient degree of an externality balances the marginal benefit with the marginal cost. Many externalities that need regulatory action are regional problems. For instance, smog above Los Angeles does not affect Chicago. Further, the marginal benefit and the marginal cost of an externality may vary from one place to another.

If the benefits and costs of an externality are confined to a region, then it is economically efficient to allow each region to determine its own degree of the externality. Uniform national standards may result in economic inefficiency.

National or international standards, however, are necessary for externalities that cross boundaries. For instance, sulfur dioxide emitted by coal-fired electric power plants in the American Midwest causes acid rain in the Northeast and Canada. Chlorofluorocarbons from all over the world damage the ozone layer in the atmosphere. Federal regulation is necessary to resolve externalities among states, and international regulation for externalities among countries.

If the marginal benefit and the marginal cost of an externality vary over time, then the efficient degree of the externality will also vary with time. This is most obvious with noise. Society may be relatively more willing to tolerate noise during working hours than at night or on weekends. The same principle also applies over longer periods of time. As victims become more sensitive to air pollution or new technologies to reduce emissions become available, the economically efficient rate of emissions will fall.

Clean Air Act: Federal vis-à-vis State Standards

The Clean Air Act, passed by the U.S. Congress in 1970, imposes uniform federal standards for air quality throughout the United States. The Act has substantially enhanced the American quality of air. By 1995, emissions of lead had been cut by over 95%, and smog-forming organic compounds had been reduced by almost 25%.

The federal Environmental Protection Agency (EPA) has specified controls on petroleum refineries, chemical plants, and even dry cleaners. Further, in several especially polluted areas, the EPA has required gasoline stations to sell only reformulated gasoline, which causes less pollution but also provides lower mileage.

The annual cost of complying with the Clean Air Act, however, exceeded $30 billion in 1990 and was estimated to reach $60 billion by 2005. The costs of compliance are leading some states to seek novel solutions. For instance, in Wisconsin, small engines generate 11% of emissions. The state offered to buy old outboard motors in exchange for credits toward new motors. In southern California, the oil company Unocal was required to cut emissions from its marine terminal. The conventional approach would have been to install a vapor-recovery system. Instead, Unocal bought and destroyed 350 old cars, so reducing emissions by the required amount at much lower cost.

Sources: National Air Quality and Emissions Trends Report, EPA-450/4-90-002, U.S. Environmental Protection Agency (March 1990); "Clean Air (1)," *The Economist* (March 4, 1995), p. 36.

Accidents

As discussed earlier, private action may fail to resolve externalities that involve large numbers of parties. A specific class of such externalities is accidents. When Joy drives out of her house onto the main road, she joins an anonymous stream of other cars, buses, and trucks. She has no way of knowing the other drivers, let alone negotiating and agreeing with them on how to deal with an accident.

Yet each driver influences the likelihood and severity of accident by the care that he or she takes in driving. The economically efficient degree of care balances the marginal benefit to society (in terms of the reduced expected damage from accidents) with the marginal cost of care to the driver. We illustrate this balance in Figure 14.8.

Private action, however, may fail to resolve the externality imposed by one driver on another. It is difficult for every driver to negotiate with every other driver about their respective degrees of care in driving and even more difficult to enforce compliance. Accordingly, government intervention is necessary to balance the marginal benefit and the marginal cost.

Figure 14.8 Care

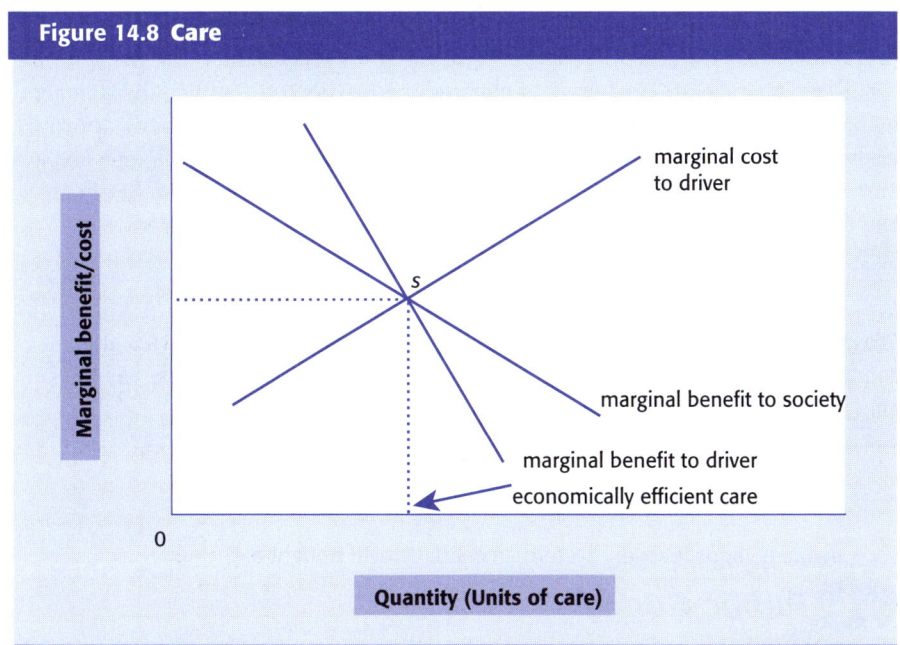

At the economically efficient degree of care, the marginal benefit to society equals the marginal cost of care to the driver. If the marginal benefit of care to the driver balanced the marginal cost at the economically efficient level, then the driver would choose the economically efficient degree of care.

The **law of torts** is the law governing interactions between parties that have no contractual relationship.

Typically, the government does not intervene directly. Rather, the government establishes a legal framework to deal with accidents. The legal framework consists of laws and the court system. The **law of torts** governs interactions between parties that have no contractual relationship. The court system provides the mechanism by which the victim of an accident can enforce her or his legal rights.

The law of torts specifies the **liability** of the parties to an accident. Liability is the set of conditions under which one party must pay damages to another party. The law regarding liability varies from one jurisdiction to another. For instance, in some jurisdictions, the injurer is liable only if he or she was negligent, and in other jurisdictions, the injurer is not liable if the victim contributed to the occurrence of the accident.

Liability is the set of conditions under which one party must pay damages to another party.

The law of torts also specifies the amount that the injurer must pay in damages to the victim. Generally, the damages include compensation for the victim's loss, including medical expenses and lost earnings. Again, the precise rules on damages vary among jurisdictions.

In effect, by specifying liability and damages, the law of torts establishes a price for causing an accident or, equivalently, a price for failing to take care. Unlike prices in competitive markets, the price for an accident is paid only after the event. This legal framework is less costly than requiring every potential injurer to negotiate and agree with every potential victim in advance.

Within this framework, each potential injurer will balance the private marginal benefit of care (in terms of the reduced expected liability for damages) against the marginal cost. If the law specifies liability and damages appropriately, then the potential injurer will choose the economically efficient level of care. Referring to Figure 14.8, this will happen if the marginal benefit of care to the driver balances the marginal cost at the economically efficient level.

Progress check

Progress Check 14D Suppose that, relative to the situation in Figure 14.8, the courts double the damages that injurers must pay accident victims. How will this affect a driver's choice of care?

6 *Public Goods*

A public good provides nonrival consumption or use. Private enterprises provide many public goods, including free-to-the-air television, literary and musical works, and software on a commercial basis. Usually, a public good can be provided commercially only if the consumption or use of the item is excludable.

If a provider could not exclude free riders, then it would be very difficult to sell the item. As we discussed in Chapter 11, excludability depends on law and technology.

Here, we discuss the legal framework for excludability and show that regulators must balance two factors: that excludability is necessary for private provision and that private provision may result in less than the economically efficient level of provision. We then discuss the alternative to private provision, which is provision by charity or the government.

Legal Framework

In Chapter 11, we considered two forms of intellectual property—copyright and patent—that make the use of scientific knowledge excludable. A copyright is a legal, exclusive right to an artistic, literary, or musical expression. The concept extends protection to software. Similarly, a patent is a legal, exclusive right to a product or process.

The owner of a copyright has a legal monopoly over the copyrighted material, while the owner of a patent has a legal monopoly over the corresponding product or process. Suppose that the owner aims to maximize profit and applies uniform pricing. Each individual user will purchase the quantity where the marginal benefit equals the price. Hence, the marginal benefit equals the price. But the profit-maximizing uniform price exceeds the marginal cost. This means that each user's marginal benefit will exceed the marginal cost and the use will be less than the economically efficient level.

For economic efficiency, a public good should be provided up to the quantity that the marginal benefit equals the marginal cost. A public good provides nonrival use; hence, the marginal cost of additional provision is nothing. Thus, the public good should be provided up to the quantity that the marginal benefit is zero for each user. A profit-maximizing owner applying uniform pricing will not achieve this level of provision.

We have just shown that copyright and patent protection may result in use at less than the economically efficient level. On the other hand, without such protection, there would be little incentive for commercial creation of scientific knowledge. Accordingly, society faces a trade-off between the incentive to create scientific knowledge and inefficient use.

This trade-off explains why copyrights and patents have limited lives. Under U.S. law, copyrights last for the life of the creator plus 50 years, while patents are valid for 20 years. On the expiration of a copyright, anyone can freely copy or use the material. Similarly, once a patent has expired, anyone can freely imitate or use the product or process.

The expiration of a copyright or patent allows free use of the formerly protected scientific knowledge. Usage will extend to the point where the marginal benefit equals zero, which is the economically efficient level. During the life of a copyright or patent, however, the owner has a monopoly and society bears the cost of less than efficient usage.

Progress check   **Progress Check 14E** If society wants to increase the usage of existing scientific knowledge, should it reduce or extend the validity of copyrights and patents?

Public Provision

For some public goods, it would be difficult or impossible to exclude people who do not pay. For instance, if the air circulating above Houston becomes cleaner, it would be difficult to exclude specific persons from enjoying the cleaner air. The same is true of national defense: During an enemy bomb raid, anti-aircraft batteries cannot protect some people without protecting everyone else in the neighborhood.

For other public goods, exclusion may be possible but only against some users. Consider the process for distilling water. Suppose that the law allowed a patent on this process. The owner of the patent could probably enforce it on large-scale users such as commercial suppliers of distilled water. It would be nearly impossible to exclude high-school students or household cooks from using the process, however.

Typically, if use of a public good is nonexcludable or difficult to exclude, it can be provided only by charities or the government. Some of the public goods provided by charities are medical and scientific research, public health, and free-to-the-air radio and television. The public goods that are provided by government include civil laws, environmental protection, and national defense. Table 14.3 lists some providers of scientific research.

Table 14.3 **Funding for scientific research**		
Jurisdiction	**Organization**	**Research Area**
Australia	CSIRO	Science and technology
Japan	Science and Technology Agency	Science and technology
United Kingdom	Medical Research Council Science Research Council Wellcome Foundation	Medicine Science Medicine
United States	National Institutes of Health National Science Foundation	Medicine Science and technology

In addition to the issue of excludability, there is another reason for charitable or government provision of a public good. To the extent that these providers do not charge a price for the use of the good, it will be used up to the quantity where the marginal benefit equals zero. Hence, the use will be economically efficient.

It is important to distinguish public goods from goods provided by the government, however. Not all items provided by the government sector are public goods. Compare, for instance, public health programs such as the eradication of communicable diseases with medical treatment. The eradication of communicable diseases such as tuberculosis is a public good. Once tuberculosis is wiped out, everyone benefits to an equal degree. By contrast, medical treatment is a private good: A doctor that spends more time treating one patient will have less time for other patients.

Governments provide many private goods such as food, education, housing, and medical services. By providing these private goods, the government may be aiming to equalize the distribution of wealth and provide equal opportunity for future generations.

Home Copying U2

Polygram is a major recording company that owns labels such as A&M, Hollywood, Island and Polydor. The company publishes music by a diverse range of artists, including ABBA, P.M. Dawn, Lionel Richie and U2. Polygram earns revenues from sales of the recorded music and, in addition, receives royalties from radio stations that play recordings over the air. Some listeners, however, tape record music from over-the-air radio broadcasts. These recordings impose a negative externality on the publisher's sales of recorded music.

In 1986, the government of France imposed a levy of Fr 1.50 (French francs) per hour of playing time on all sales of blank audiotapes. These levies serve as a general license for home copying, and the government distributes the revenues to the recording industry. The Recording Industry Association of America has proposed a similar levy in the United States but, at the time of this writing, the federal government had not given approval.

Sources: Web Page www.polygram.com (May 10, 1996); U.S. Congress, Office of Technology Assessment, Copyright and Home Copying: Technology Challenges the Law, OTA-CIT-422 (Washington, DC: U.S. Government Printing Office, October 1989).

Congestible Facilities

The use of facilities such as tunnels is excludable. Such facilities often have a capacity that is relatively large compared with demand, causing them to be natural monopolies. Hence, for economically efficient usage, they must be prevented from exercising monopoly power. In principle, these facilities could be provided by a commercial operator subject to regulation. Some, however, are provided by the government.

The demand for such facilities usually varies with time. Outside of peak hours, the facility provides nonrival use. By contrast, during peak hours, each additional user adds to congestion, the costs of which include delays, additional fuel, and an increase in accidents; hence, usage is a private good.

Consider a tunnel that can smoothly convey up to 30 vehicles a minute. When 30 vehicles a minute already are entering the tunnel, however, additional drivers will cause congestion. From the standpoint of economic efficiency, traffic through the tunnel should be managed so that the marginal benefit of each user balances the marginal cost. When there are fewer than 30 vehicles a minute, the marginal cost of a crossing is nothing. So, the tunnel should not exclude any driver.

When, however, 30 vehicles per minute are in the tunnel, the marginal cost becomes positive. For economic efficiency, the tunnel should set a toll equal to the marginal cost. This will ensure that the only drivers who enter the tunnel are those whose benefit exceeds the marginal cost.

What if the tunnel does not charge a toll? Consider the decision of a marginal driver (the 31st) whether to enter the tunnel or wait until there is less traffic. If the driver enters immediately, she will save some time. In making the decision, that driver compares her private benefit from crossing at that time with her private cost and ignores the additional costs on other drivers. Owing to this negative externality, the number of drivers entering the tunnel tends to exceed the economically efficient number. The solution is for the tunnel to charge a toll equal to the marginal cost of a crossing.

Generally, for economic efficiency, congestible facilities should levy a price, set equal to the marginal cost of use, where the cost includes the externalities imposed on other users. As the marginal cost varies with the time of day, so should the price. This pricing would ensure economically efficient usage of facilities such as bridges, tunnels, roads, and subways.

Progress check

Progress Check 14F Suppose that a local telephone services provider sets the same price for local calls at all times of the day. Would this lead to economically efficient usage?

Congestion in Space

Satellites provide a convenient platform for transmission of electromagnetic signals over long distances, especially in relatively undeveloped regions. In recent years, the rapid growth of international broadcasting and telecommunication has boosted the demand for satellite transmission.

To operate effectively, a communications satellite must remain within the line of sight of all its corresponding earth stations. For this, the satellite should be positioned at a height of 35,784 kilometers, so that it will remain stationary relative to its position over the earth. This position is called a *geosynchronous orbit.*

Since transmissions from one satellite can interfere with those of another, it is important that there be adequate spacing between satellites. Consequently, there is a limit to the number of geosynchronous positions.

The International Telecommunications Union regulates the positioning of communications satellites. It stipulates a 3–4° angular spacing between satellites, depending on the frequencies at which the satellites are transmitting.

In July 1994, a Chinese consortium launched and positioned its Apstar 1 at 131° East, with only a 1° spacing from the Japanese Sakura satellite at 132° East and the Russian Rimsat at 130° East. Predictably, the Apstar 1 interfered with the Sakura's communications.

The Japanese Government protested vigorously. Eventually, the Chinese consortium moved the Apstar 138° East.

Sources: William Stallings and Richard Van Slyke, *Business Data Communications*, 2d ed. (New York: Macmillan, 1994), pp. 110–8; "Chinese Satellite Launch Condemned by Japan," *New Straits Times* (July 23, 1994), p. 19.

7 *Summary*

The marginal benefit of an item may diverge from the marginal cost for three basic reasons: market power, asymmetric information, and externalities and public goods. This divergence results in economic inefficiency. Government regulation may help where private action fails to resolve the economic inefficiency.

Generally, the government can regulate conduct, information, and structure. Specifically, the conduct of a franchised monopoly may be regulated directly through price or indirectly through the rate of return. Competition law regulates the conduct and structure of businesses in general. In situations of asymmetric information, mandatory disclosure is one form of regulation.

Externalities may be regulated through fees or standards. The appropriate choice between these policies depends on the regulator's information. The government can help to resolve inefficiency in accidents and public goods by providing an appropriate legal framework. The laws regarding copyrights and patents must balance the incentive for new research against inefficient use of existing knowledge.

Key Concepts

natural monopoly	rate base
privatization	self-regulation
marginal cost pricing	law of torts
average cost pricing	liability

Further Reading

West Publishing publishes simple and useful guides to many areas of United States law and regulation. Relevant titles include Ernest Gellhorn and William Kovacic's *Antitrust Law and Economics in a Nutshell*, 4th ed. (1994); Roger W. Findley and Daniel A. Farber's *Environmental Law in a Nutshell*, 3d ed. (1992); and Arthur R. Miller and Michael H. Davis's *Intellectual Property—Patents, Trademarks and Copyright in a Nutshell*, 2d ed. (1990).

Review Questions

1. Using relevant examples, explain the following concepts:
   a. A natural monopoly.
   b. A rate base.
   c. Self-regulation.

2. Name one franchised monopoly from which you buy services. Is the monopoly subject to regulation on any of the following?
   a. Price.
   b. Rate of return.
   c. Structure.

3. Why do competition laws generally restrict mergers and acquisitions that create monopolies or monopsonies?

4. Explain the differences between
   a. Privatization.
   b. Allowing competition.

5. Name one self-regulated monopoly in your market. Does it regulate disclosure, conduct, or structure?

6. At one time, U.S. law prohibited movie producers from owning theaters. Use this example to explain
   a. Vertical integration.
   b. Structural regulation.

7. True or false? Mandatory disclosure is always the best way to resolve asymmetric information.

8. Explain how the following policies can be used to control noise pollution by construction equipment:
   a. Fee.
   b. Standard.

9. A charitable foundation sponsored the development of a drug that cures bone-marrow cancer. The foundation has patented the drug and is selling it on a commercial basis. Will the use of the drug be economically efficient?

10. Which of the following situations involves random externalities?
    a. The workers in a factory may injure themselves on the production equipment.
    b. Two ships may collide while passing through a narrow channel at night.

Discussion Questions

1. This question applies the mathematical technique for analyzing a natural monopoly presented in the math supplement. The demand for electric power in Sol Province is $p = 20 - 20q$, where p and q represent the price in thousands of dollars and the quantity in megawatt-hours, respectively. Suppose that an electricity plant generates power at a constant marginal cost of $1000 per megawatt-hour up to a capacity of 10 megawatt-hours. Suppose that Sol Province requires the plant to implement marginal cost pricing.
    a. Illustrate the price and quantity with marginal cost pricing.
    b. Suppose that demand grows to $p = 20 - 0.1q$. At a price of $1000 per megawatt-hour, what is the minimum number of plants needed to produce the quantity demanded?

2. Moonlight City's Water Authority produces water under conditions of increasing marginal cost. The marginal cost of the least costly water is $0 per acre-foot (an acre-foot is the volume that covers an acre to the depth of 1 foot). The Water Authority practices marginal-cost pricing. Presently, the price of water is $224 per acre-foot and the quantity demanded is 679,000 acre-feet a year.
    a. Illustrate the current price and quantity on an appropriate diagram.
    b. Central Valley farmers have government rights to buy water at $20 per acre-foot. Suppose that Moonlight's Water Authority acquires the rights to 1000 acre-feet of water. On your diagram, show how

this acquisition will affect the authority's marginal cost of water.
    c. Assume that the Water Authority continues to practice marginal cost pricing. On your diagram, show the increase in buyer and seller surplus that Moonshine City as a whole will achieve from the acquisition of the water rights to 1000 acre-feet.

3. An alternative to marginal cost pricing is requiring a monopoly franchise holder to price at average cost. This ensures that the business covers variable and fixed operating expenses as well as the cost of its initial investment.
    a. Compare the level of service under marginal cost pricing with that under average cost pricing.
    b. Using an appropriate diagram, explain which pricing scheme maximizes the sum of buyer and seller surplus.

4. Which of the following practices are illegal under the competition laws of your jurisdiction?
    a. The suppliers of 95% of the ready-mix concrete market organize a cartel to limit sales and raise prices above the competitive level.
    b. An electronics store offers different prices to different customers.
    c. A pharmaceutical manufacturer's contracts with retailers provide that the retailers must set prices above a specified minimum, failing which the manufacturer will stop further shipments.

5. In the United States, all stockbrokers must insure customer accounts up to a minimum level with the Securities Investor Protection Corporation (SIPC). This insurance covers customers against default by the broker.
   a. What is the minimum required level of SIPC insurance?
   b. Can you explain this requirement in terms of asymmetric information between brokers and investors?
   c. Many brokers purchase private insurance to cover losses that exceed the minimum SIPC cover. Please explain this practice as a way by which brokers can signal their financial reliability.

6. Consider the following practices of the Hong Kong medical profession. Do they serve to resolve economic inefficiency or limit competition?
   a. Doctors are not allowed to advertise.
   b. Doctors can sell medicines from their clinics. Until recently, they could dispense drugs in unmarked containers without indicating the medicine. At the time of writing, they were not required to mark the expiration date of the medicine.
   c. Doctors admitted in Ireland can practice freely in Hong Kong, but graduates of Harvard Medical School who are qualified in an American state must undergo special training and a rigorous examination.

7. Leaded gasoline is a major source of lead emissions. Compare these two alternative ways of reducing lead emissions:
   a. Requiring all new automobiles to be equipped with catalytic converters so that they can operate on unleaded gasoline. The catalytic converter will be damaged if it is used with leaded gasoline.

   The requirement does not apply to older cars.
   b. Setting a lower excise tax on unleaded gasoline than on leaded gasoline so that unleaded is cheaper at the pump.

8. Marine traffic through the Luna Straits is very heavy, and especially at night, there is a significant risk of collision between passing vessels.
   a. Using a suitable diagram, analyze the marginal benefit and marginal cost of care to society in navigation through the Luna Straits.
   b. Suppose that the law of torts provides that any ship's master who fails to take due care must bear liability for accidents. Using the diagram in (a), explain how a typical ship's master will choose care.
   c. Suppose that the courts reduce the damages that masters must pay to victims of accidents. How will this change affect masters in their degree of care in the straits?

9. The U.S. Federal Aviation Administration (FAA) classifies all civil transport aircraft according to noise. The categories range from Stage 1, which is the noisiest, to Stage 3, which is the quietest category.
   a. If one airport prohibits landings by Stage 1 and 2 aircraft, will it impose externalities on other airports?
   b. Who should regulate aircraft noise, the federal government or local airport authorities?
   c. Suppose that an airport has specified standards for aircraft noise. Some airlines operate older, noisier aircraft than others. Should the airport create permits for aircraft noise and allow airlines to trade these permits?

10. Prentice Hall, Inc., owns the copyright to Professor Philip Kotler's best-selling textbook, *Marketing Management*. Prentice Hall earns revenues from sales to students and libraries.

   a. Explain the sense in which the content of Professor Kotler's book is a public good.

   b. Students who photocopy a library copy of the book are breaching Prentice Hall's copyright. Compare the following proposals in terms of rewarding authors and administrative cost: (i) The government imposes a levy on all copies made on library photcopying machines. It distributes the revenues from the levy to authors. (ii) The government bans photocopying machines from libraries.

Chapter 14

Math Supplement

Let us apply a numerical example to see how a natural monopoly can evolve into a potentially competitive market. Suppose that the demand for electric power is

$$p = 10 - q, \qquad (14.1)$$

where p and q represent price in thousand dollars and quantity in megawatt-hours, respectively. All generating plants have a capacity of 10 megawatt-hours. Generation involves a fixed cost of $50,000 and a constant marginal cost of $1,000 per megawatt-hour.

Figure 14.9 depicts the demand and costs. The demand curve intersects the marginal cost at the quantity where

$$1 = 10 - q \qquad (14.2)$$

or $q = 9$.

Hence, at the intersection, the quantity demanded is 9 megawatt-hours. A single plant can produce this quantity at a total cost of $50,000 + $1000 × 9 = $59,000, or an average cost of $59,000/9 = $6,556 per megawatt-hour. If, however, two plants were generating, then each would incur the fixed cost of $50,000, hence the total cost would be $109,000, implying an average cost of $109,000/9 = $12,111 per megawatt-hour. In this case, generation is a natural monopoly.

Now, suppose that the demand grows to $p = 10 - 0.05q$. This new demand curve will cross the marginal cost at a quantity of $1 = 10 - 0.05q$, or $q = 9/0.05 = 180$. If every plant operates at full capacity, 18 plants would be needed to meet this quantity demanded. The economies of scale are now small relative to the market demand. The market is no longer a natural monopoly but is close to being potentially competitive.

Figure 14.9 Demand and market structure

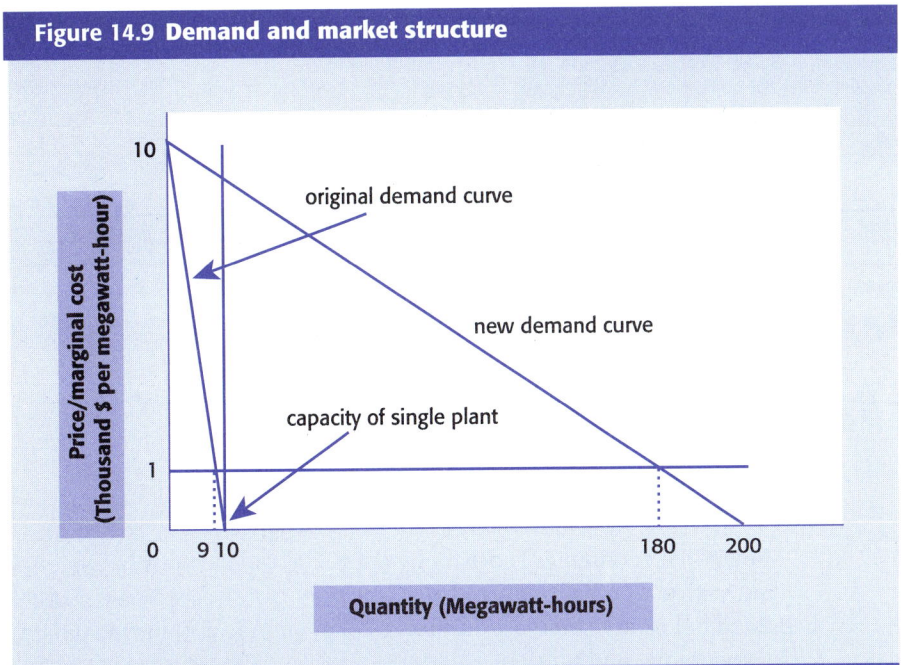

With the original demand curve, generation is a natural monopoly. With the new demand curve, the economies of scale are now small relative to the market demand; hence, the market is close to being potentially competitive.

Guide to Data Sources

Managerial economics is driven by data: The theory must be systematically verified with empirical data, and the concepts can be applied to actual numbers. Listed below are some useful sources of economic and financial data, organized by geography and product.

1 Global Economics and Finance

The *Financial Times*, *New York Times*, and *Wall Street Journal* daily provide stock, bond, commodities, and derivatives prices; exchange rates; interest rates; and other financial information.

Lexis-Nexis is a comprehensive on-line electronic database that provides business, legal, and general information in full text.

International Marketing Data and Statistics (London: Euromonitor, annually) provides information on the market share of suppliers for a wide range of industrial and consumer products.

International Financial Statistics (Washington, DC: International Monetary Fund, monthly) provides records of exchange rates, interest rates, and other financial series for all member states of the International Monetary Fund.

World Development Report (New York: Oxford University Press, annually) provides statistics on income, education, nutrition, and other variables relevant to economic and human development.

United States

Economic Report of the President (Washington, DC: United States Government Printing Office, annually) describes current government economic policies and reviews the economy. The report also provides a comprehensive set of macroeconomic and financial statistics.

Statistical Abstract of the United States (Washington, DC: United States Government Printing Office, annually) provides a wide range of demographic, economic, government, and social statistics. It is a good starting point from which to find sources of more detailed information.

Federal Reserve Bulletin (Washington, DC: Board of Governors of the Federal Reserve System, monthly) reports on the Federal Reserve's monetary policy, foreign exchange operations, and decisions on applications for acquisition and reorganization by banks. The bulletin also provides statistics on the banking and financial system.

Other Countries

The Economist Intelligence Unit's Country Profiles (London: Economist Intelligence Unit, periodically) provide general reviews of individual countries, political as well as economic information.

Companies and Industries

Securities and Exchange Commission 10-K, annually provides the detailed financial and business information that every company publicly traded in the United States must file with the Securities and Exchange Commission. It is available through the World Wide Web at www.sec.gov by using the EDGAR archive.

Moody's, Standard and Poors, and Value Line publish periodic reports on specific companies and industries. The reports are aimed at investors in stocks and bonds.

In addition to these general sources, a number of specialized publications focus on particular markets. These include the following:

Automotive News Market Data Book (Detroit: Crain Automotive Group, annually).

Knight-Ridder Financial/Commodity Research Bureau, *CRB Commodity Yearbook* (New York: John Wiley & Sons, annually).

FAO Production (New York: United Nations Food and Agriculture Organization, annually).

Monthly Energy Review (Washington, DC: U.S. Energy Information Administration, monthly).

Energy Statistics Sourcebook (Tulsa, OK: PennWell Publishing Co., periodically).

Oil and Gas Journal Data Book (Tulsa, OK: PennWell Publishing Co., periodically).

Gale Directory of Publications and Broadcast Media (Detroit: Gale Research, annually).

National Transportation Statistics (Washington, DC: U.S. Department of Transportation, annually).

Answers to Progress Checks and Selected Review Questions

Chapter 1 Introduction to Managerial Economics

2. No, models must be less than completely realistic to be useful.

3. (a) Average price per minute = $(360 + 210 \times 4)/5$ = ¥240 per minute.
   (b) Price of marginal minute = ¥210.

4. (a) Flow.
   (b) Stock.
   (c) Stock.

5. (a) The electricity market includes buyers and sellers.
   (b) The electricity industry consists of sellers only.

6. (a) False.
   (b) False.

7. (a) Intel.

8. (b).

9. (a) and (b).

10. Competitive markets have large numbers of buyers and sellers, none of which can influence market conditions. By contrast, a buyer or seller with market power can influence market conditions. A market is imperfect if the choices of one party affect others directly rather than through a price or if one party has better information than another.

Chapter 2   Demand

2A.   The theater must cut its price by $3 from $7.50 to $2.50.

2B.   (1) It slopes downward because of diminishing marginal benefit.

   (2) Assuming that black-and-white TVs are an inferior product, the drop in the consumer's income will cause the demand curve to shift to the right.

2C.   Video rentals are a substitute for movies. A fall in the price of video rentals will cause the demand curve for movies to shift to the left.

2D.   An increase in the price of a complement would cause the market demand to shift to the left.

2E.   If the price of movies is $5, Joy's buyer surplus would be the area *dcba*.

2F.   It can increase its profit by reducing labor to 1000 worker-hours.

3.   Introduction of the female condom will
   (a) Reduce the demand for male condoms.
   (b) Increase the demand for lingerie.

4.   Foreign soft drink manufacturers will use relatively more sugar and less corn syrup.

5.   (a) Shift in the demand for corn syrup.
   (b) Movement along the demand for corn syrup.
   (c) Shift in the demand for corn syrup.

6.   (a) Overstates

7.   (a) The demand for Marriott rooms will increase.
   (b) Assuming that Motel 6 rooms are an inferior product, the demand for Motel 6 rooms will decrease.

8.   For writing instruments, Mont Blanc fountain pens are a luxury item and more sensitive to income distribution. For watches, Rolex watches are a luxury item and more sensitive to income distribution.

9.   (a), (b), and (c).

10.   The carrier should set the price so that the consumer has no buyer surplus.

Chapter 3   Quantitative Demand Analysis

3A.   The residential demand for water is relatively less elastic than the industrial demand.

3B.   The demand curve is a straight line. At a price of $11,000, the quantity demanded would be 14,000 while at a price of $12,000, the quantity demanded would be 12,000. Accordingly, the proportionate change in the quantity demanded is –2,000/13,000 and the proportionate change in the price is 1,000/11,500. Hence, by the arc approach, the own-price elasticity of demand is –1.77.

3C. The demand for liquor is relatively more income elastic than the demand for cigarettes.

3D. For a durable, the short-run demand could be more or less elastic than the long-run demand.

3E. The advertising elasticity of demand is $0.03 \times 446.67/88.93 = 0.15$.

1. For a campus bookstore, the demand for (b) is relatively more elastic; for consumer products, the demand for (b) is relatively more elastic; and for downtown restaurants the demand for (b) is relatively more elastic.

3. Rise.

5. (a) True.
    (b) True.

6. (b) Complements.

7. The increase in quantity demanded would be $1.3 \times 5 = 6.5\%$.

8. Advertising by one particular brand will draw customers from customers of other brands as well as increase the demand for beer in general. Advertising of beer in general can only increase the market demand.

9. More elastic in the long run.

10. A cross section records all the data at one time, while a time series records changes over time.

Chapter 4 Supply

4A. The total cost curve would be higher but the variable cost curve would not change.

4B. The marginal and average variable cost curves would not change, but the average cost curve would be lower.

4C. To maximize profit, Luna must produce at the rate where marginal cost equals 75 cents. Please refer to Figure 4C.

4D. If the market price of eggs is $1.31, Luna should produce 8000 dozen eggs a week and its revenue would be $1.31 \times 8000 = \$10,840$, hence its profit would be $\$10,480 - \$7,232 = \$3,248$.

4E. See Figure 4E.

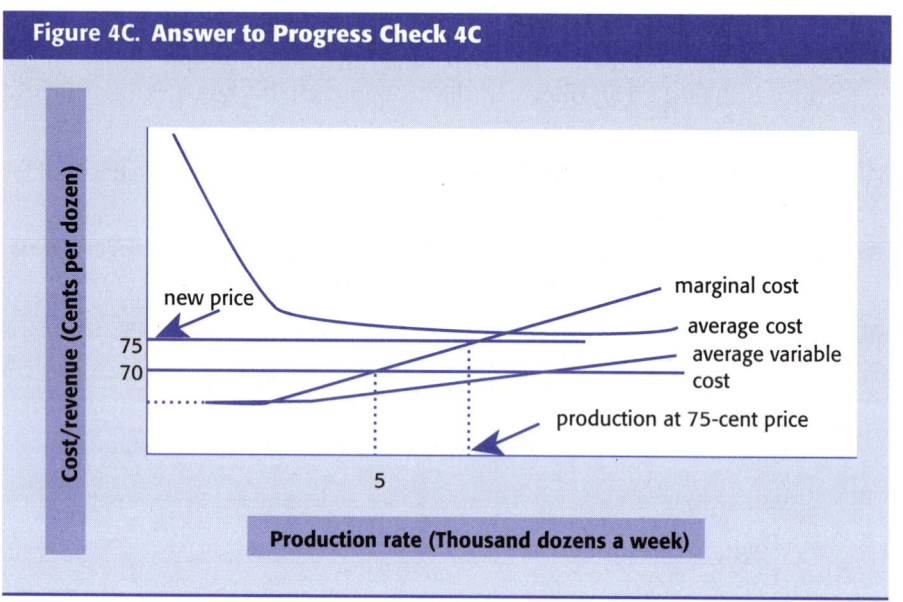

Figure 4C. Answer to Progress Check 4C

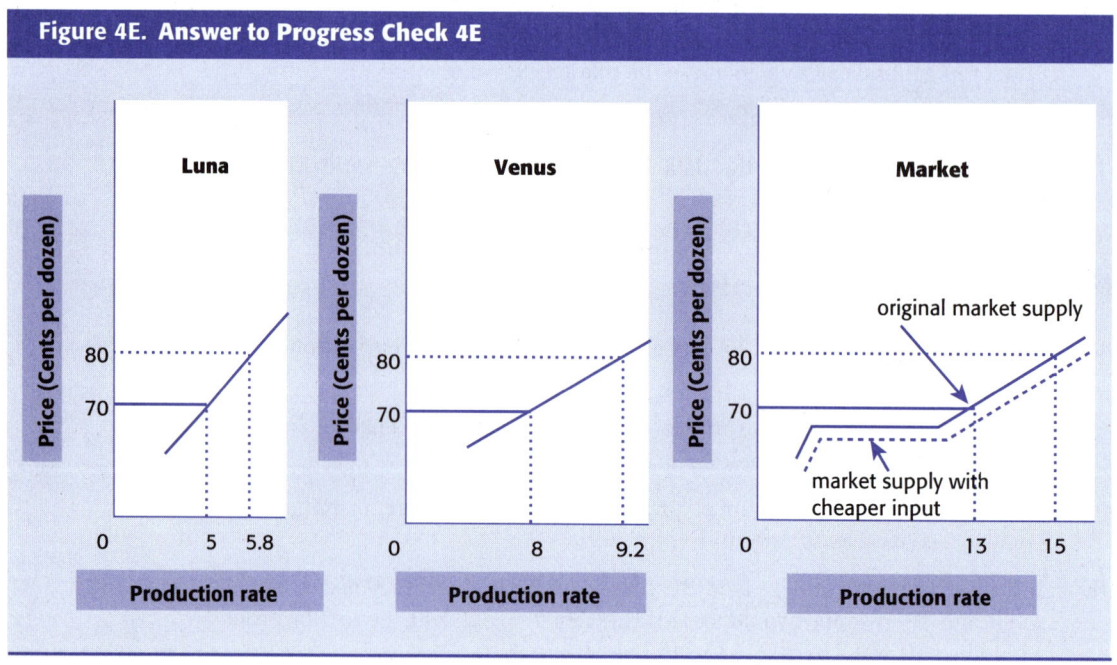

Figure 4E. Answer to Progress Check 4E

4F.   See Figure 4F.

4G.   Proportionate change in quantity = (6500 – 5800)/6150 = 11%. Proportionate change in price = (90 – 80)/85 = 12%. Hence, the price elasticity = 11/
12 = 0.9.

1.   The short run is a time horizon within which a seller cannot adjust at least
one input. By contrast, the long run is a time horizon long enough that the
seller can adjust all inputs. Assuming that all fixed costs are also sunk, while
all variable costs are not sunk, then there are fixed costs only in the short run,
while all costs are variable in the long run.

2.   This statement confuses average with marginal cost. The average cost is $2.
The marginal cost may be greater than, equal to, or less than $2, depending
on the production technology.

3.   Since the price of Mercury's output is less than the marginal cost, Mercury
can raise profit by reducing production.

4.   The analysis underestimates the increase in profit: It considers only the
increase in profit on the existing production, and ignores the increase in
profit resulting from an increase in production.

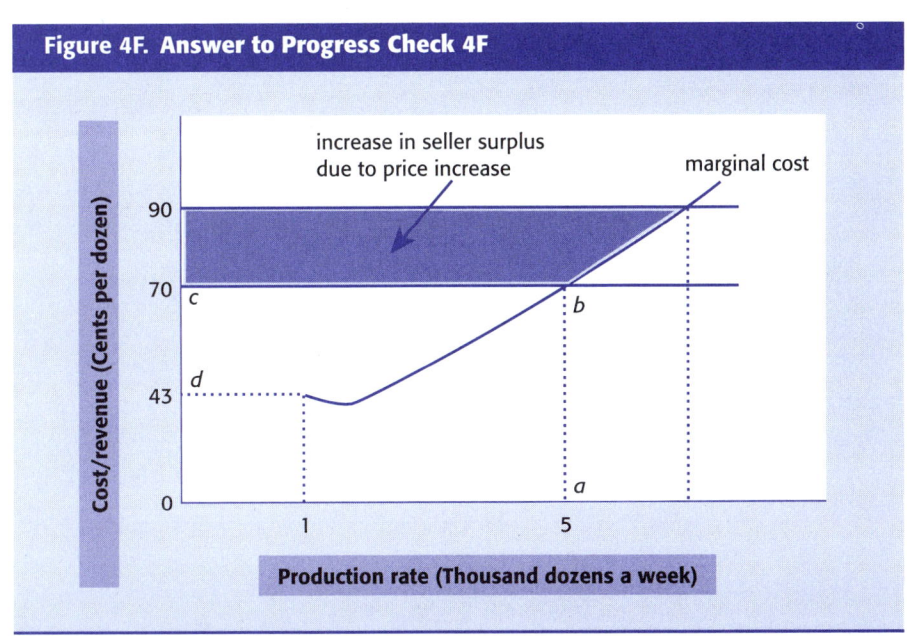

Figure 4F. Answer to Progress Check 4F

5. (a) Increases both average and marginal cost curves.
    (b) No effect.
    (c) Reduces both average and marginal cost curves.

6. (a) Movement along the market supply curve.
    (b) Shift of the entire market supply curve.
    (c) Shift of the entire market supply curve.

7. The buyer should design its order to leave the seller with zero seller surplus.

8. (a) False.
    (b) True.

10. The supply will be relatively more elastic in the long run.

Chapter 5   Competitive Markets

5A. If some sellers have market power and get lower prices, then different buyers pay different prices. Moreover, a seller with market power could affect the selling price; hence, it could not answer the question, "How much would you sell, assuming that you could sell as much as you would like at the going price?" Thus, it is not possible to construct a market supply curve.

5B. See Figure 5B.

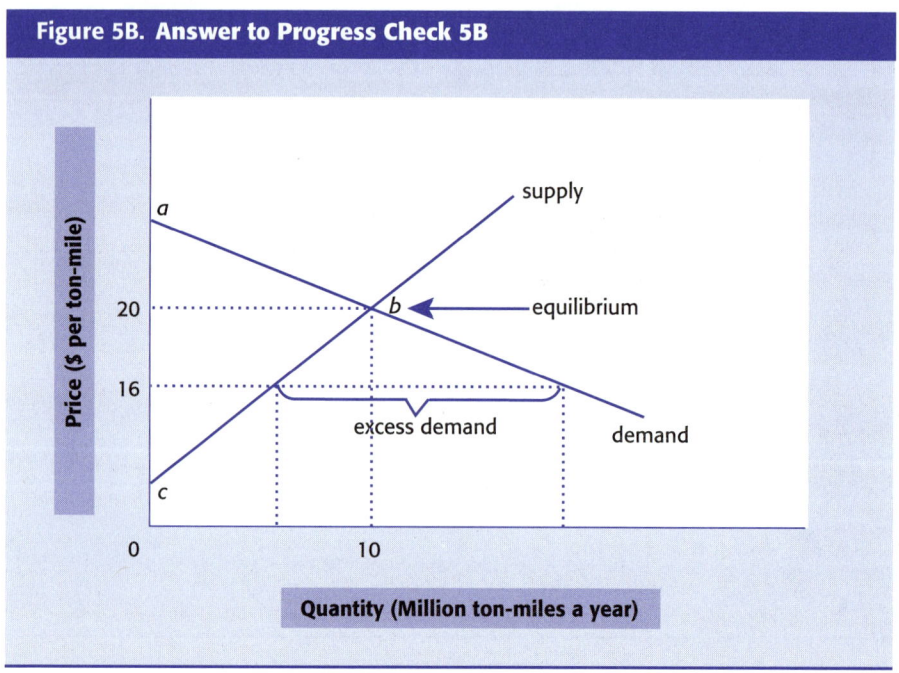

Figure 5B. Answer to Progress Check 5B

5C.   (1) False.
      (2) True.

5D.   See Figure 5D.

5E.   See Figure 5E.

5F.   The price will be 1.33% lower at $19.73, and the quantity will be 2.66% higher at 10.27 million.

5G.   See Figure 5G.

5H.   See Figure 5H.

1.   In entertainment, the market that better fits the model of perfect competition is (b), while for energy, it is (b), and for investments it is (a).

2.   True.

3.   (b) The quantity supplied will exceed the quantity demanded.

4.   (a) Reduce the supply.
      (b) Increase the supply.
      (c) Increase the demand.
      (d) Increase the demand.
      (e) No effect.

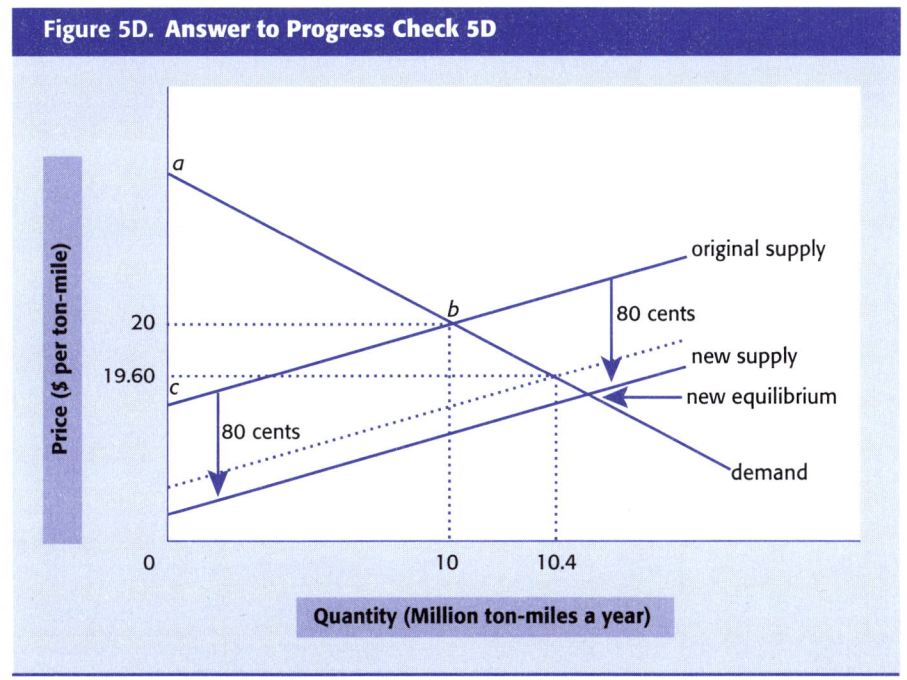

Figure 5D. Answer to Progress Check 5D

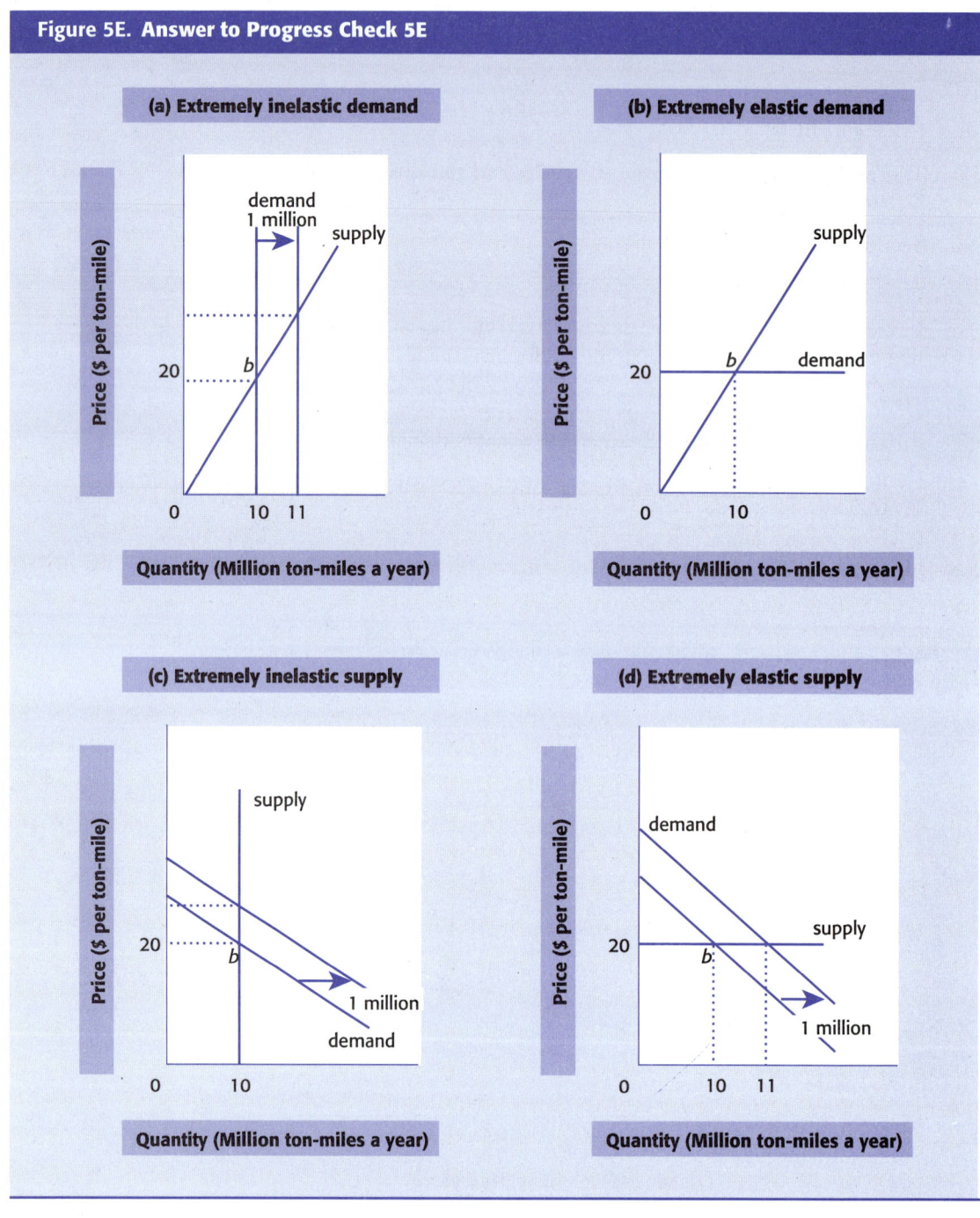

Figure 5E. Answer to Progress Check 5E

Figure 5G. Answer to Progress Check 5G

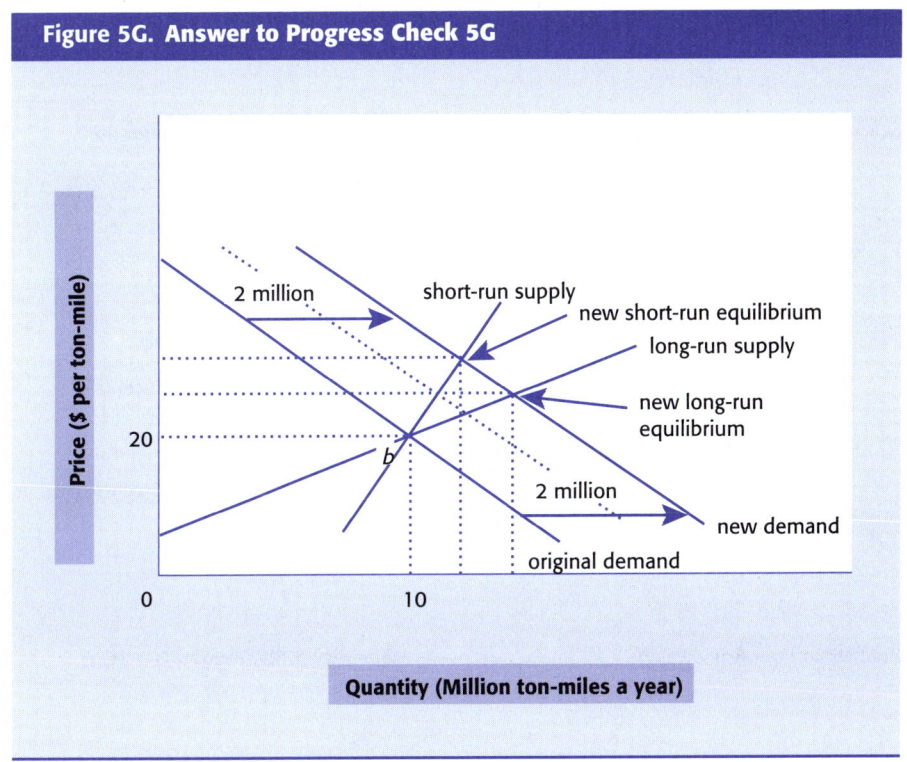

5. If the demand is extremely elastic or the supply is extremely elastic.

6. (c).

7. The market price would rise by 1.44/0.94 = 1.5%.

8. The supply of new housing is more elastic in the long run than the short run. Hence, the price will rise further in the short run than the long run, while the quantity will increase more in the long run than the short run.

9. False. If sunk costs are substantial, sellers will quit production only if the price drops by a large amount. Hence, prices will be more volatile.

10. The retailers receive the wholesale price cut. In a competitive retail market, however, the wholesale price cut will increase the supply. The new equilibrium will have a lower retail price. Consumers benefit from a lower retail price, so part of the wholesale price cut will be incident on consumers.

Figure 5H. Answer to Progress Check 5H

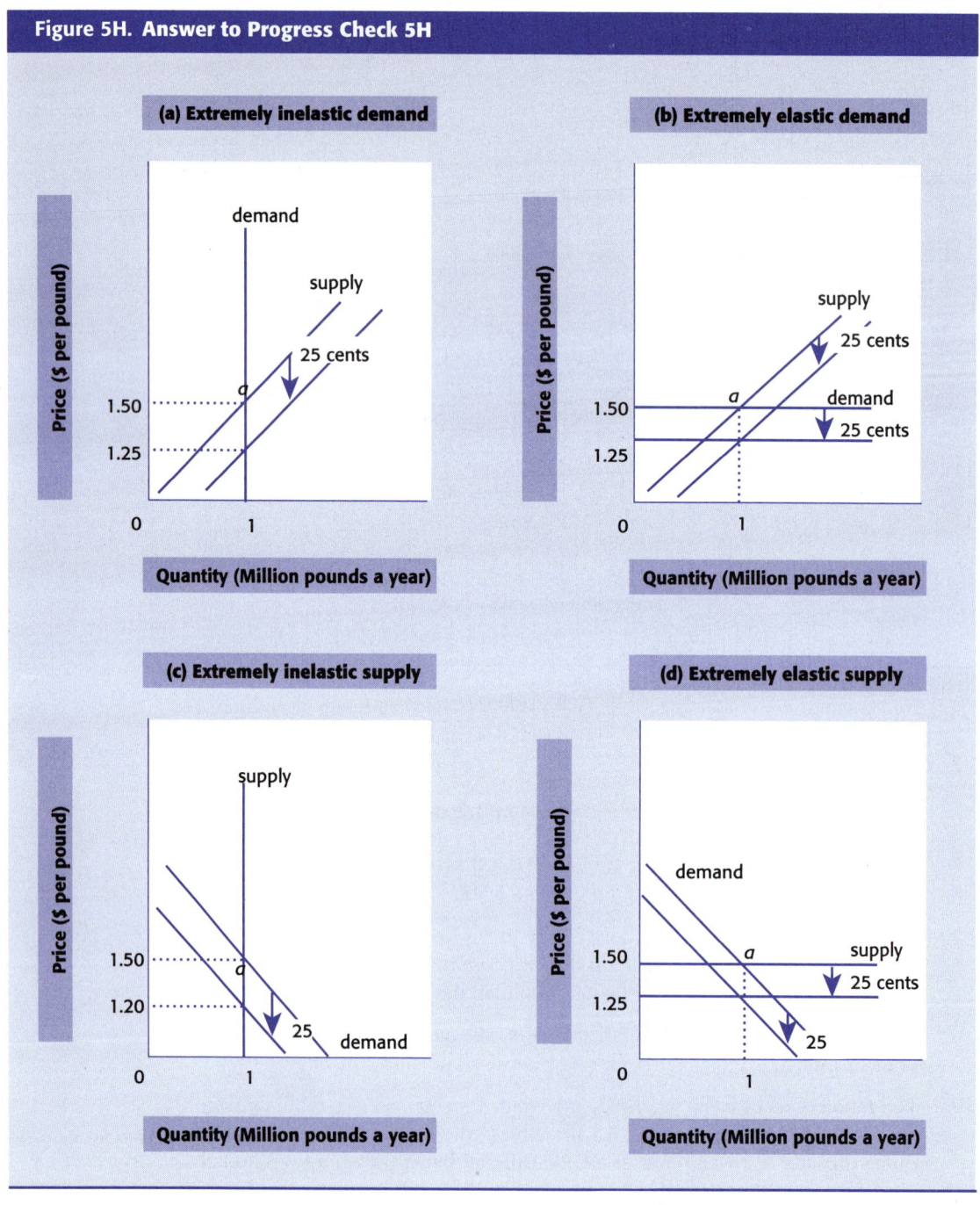

Chapter 6 Economic Efficiency

6A.   In the oil market, technical efficiency means providing oil at the minimum possible cost, while economic efficiency requires providing the quantities such that all users have the same marginal benefit, all producers operate at the same marginal cost, and the marginal benefit equals the marginal cost.

6B.   The invisible hand will drive up the price of grain, which will encourage consumers to conserve and producers to grow more.

6C.   With decentralization, the bank should set the transfer price equal to the market price of funds. Then, both divisions will use funds up to the point where marginal benefit equals the transfer price. This will ensure economic efficiency.

6D.   No. If the marginal cost of steel exceeded the marginal benefit, then the high production rate was not efficient.

6E.   See Figure 6E. The new deadweight loss is area *mnb*.

6F.   The deadweight loss is increased by area *mnhe*. See Figure 6F.

Figure 6E. Answer to Progress Check 6E

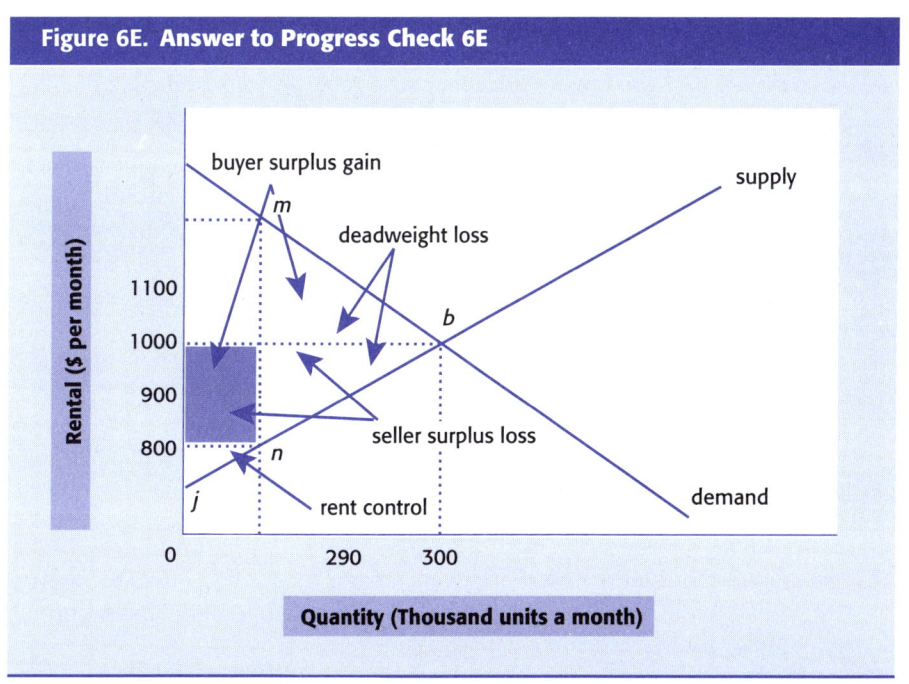

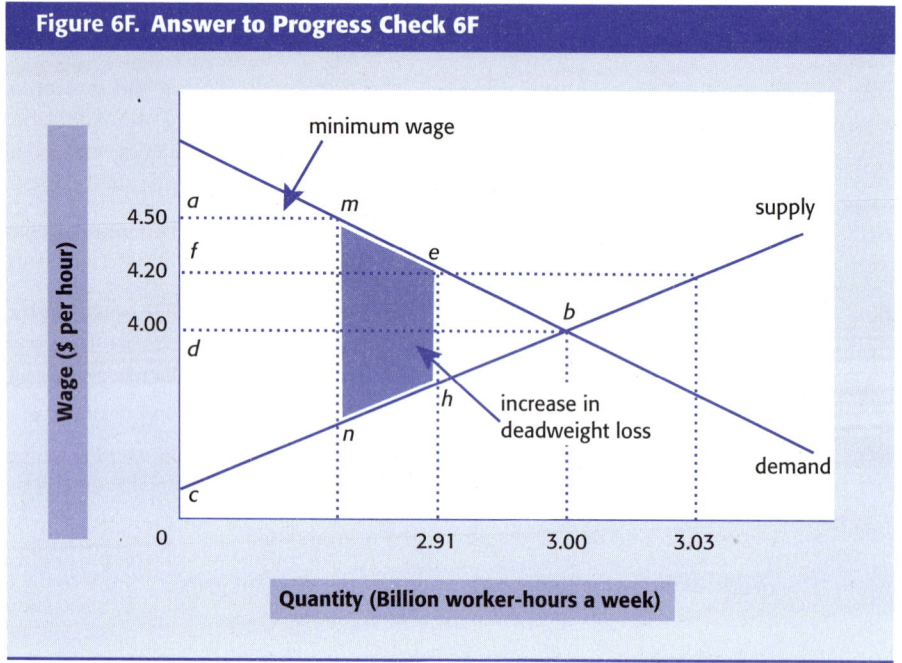

Figure 6F. Answer to Progress Check 6F

6G. See Figure 6G. The buyer's price increases relatively more. Hence, the incidence of the tax on travelers will be relatively higher.

1. Children were using bread (in sport) up to the point that the marginal benefit equaled the very low price. This price was less than the marginal cost. Hence, the marginal benefit of use was less than the marginal cost and not economically efficient.

2. The condition that all users receive the same marginal benefit.

3. In a competitive labor market, all buyers (employers) purchase up to the quantity where the marginal benefit equals the wage, and all sellers (workers) supply up to the quantity where the marginal cost equals the wage. Buyers and sellers face the same wage; hence, the allocation of labor is economically efficient.

5. Country B has higher barriers to exit.

7. (a) If demand is more inelastic, renters are less sensitive to price. So, a given reduction in the quantity will cause larger reduction in the buyer surplus among those who cannot get apartments.

   (b) If supply is more elastic, landlords are more sensitive to price. So, a given reduction in rent will induce a larger reduction in the quantity supplied.

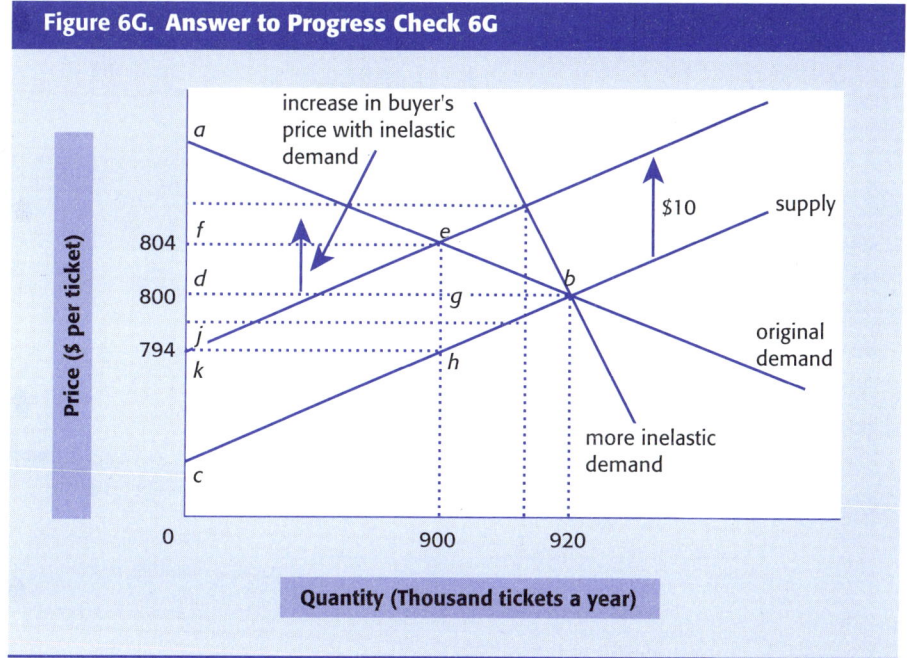

Figure 6G. Answer to Progress Check 6G

8. In services, the effect will be greater among janitors. In manufacturing, the effect will be greater for rubber shoes.

9. Employers buy labor up to the quantity where the marginal benefit equals the buyer's wage. Workers supply up to the quantity where the marginal cost equals the seller's wage. With an income tax, the buyer's wage exceeds the seller's wage; hence, the allocation is not economically efficient.

10. Since demand is inelastic and supply is very elastic, the tax will be incident mostly on the demand side. Manufacturers would not be much affected.

Chapter 7   Costs

7A. See Figure 7A.

7B. Neither economies nor diseconomies of scope.

7C. The revenue from a shutdown in Table 7.5 would become $460,000 and the opportunity cost in Table 7.6 would become $680,000. Eleanor should continue in the warehouse business.

7D. In Table 7.7, the columns for "Cancel Launch" would have zero in every cell. In Table 7.8, the graphics consultant cost would be $50,000, the *Road Runner*

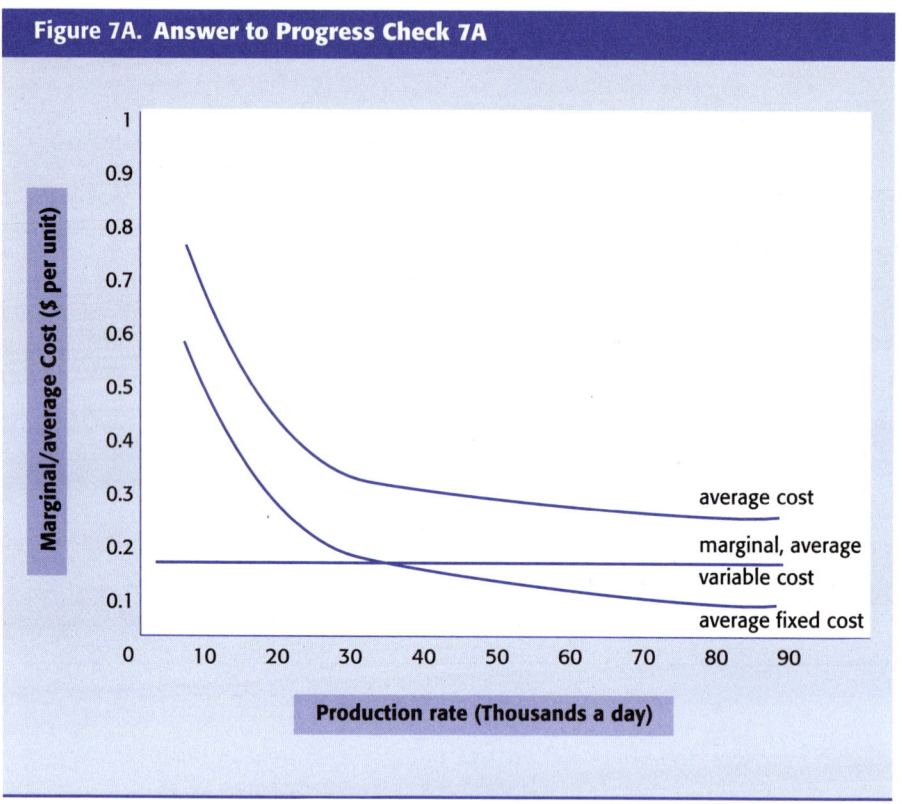

Figure 7A. Answer to Progress Check 7A

would charge $60,000, and the *Daily Globe* would charge $200,000. Sol should cancel the launch.

7E.   The average cost of both models would be identical at $104.50.

2.   Southern Power's average fixed cost will rise.

3.   For automobiles, economies of scale are more significant in (b), while for restaurants, they are more significant in (a).

4.   No.

5.   Economies of scope.

6.   Diseconomies of scope.

7.   (a).

8.   (a).

9.   Direct labor and materials may not be the drivers of the indirect costs. Allocating indirect costs according to direct labor and materials may result in misleading cost calculations.

10. (a) The marginal benefit of identifying some expenses as direct costs may outweigh the marginal benefit; hence, these are classified as indirect costs.
     (b) The marginal benefit of identifying some expenses as fixed costs may outweigh the marginal benefit; hence, these are classified as variable costs.

Chapter 8   Monopoly

8A. No difference: The price would be identical to the marginal revenue.

8B. It should raise price, so reducing sales up to the quantity where its marginal cost equals its marginal revenue.

8C. See Figure 8C.

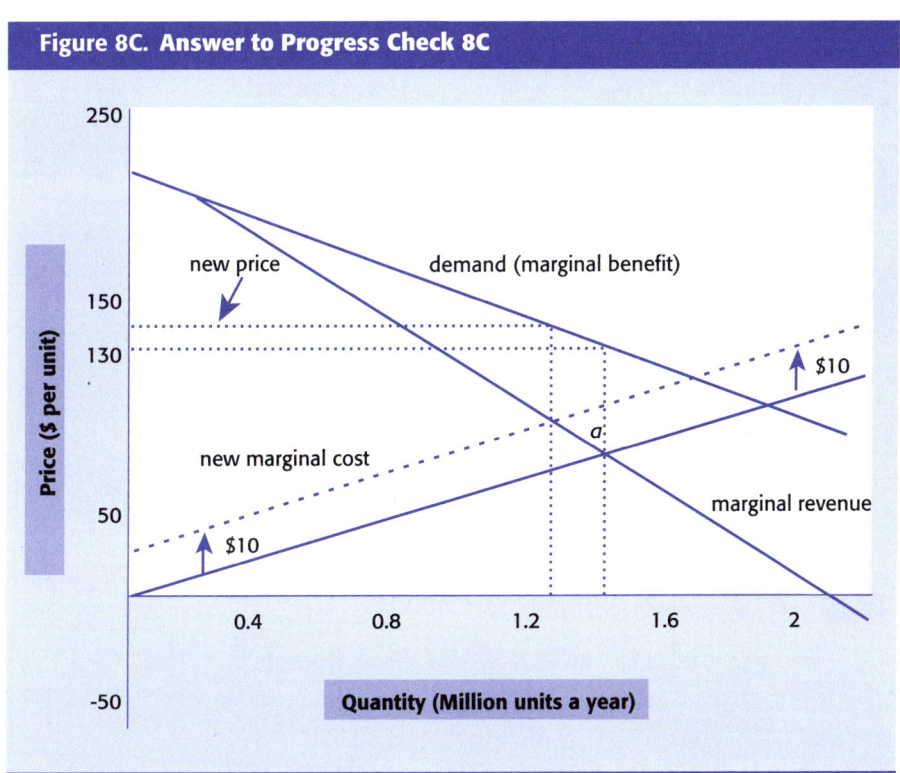

Figure 8C. Answer to Progress Check 8C

8D.   The advertising expenditure should be $(140 – 70) \times 0.01 \times 1.4 = \$0.98$ million.

8E.   Lerner Index = $(130 – 70)/130 = 0.46$.

8F.   A union will be relatively more effective in a market with relatively few workers, if all workers are working full time, if workers have few commitments to employers, and if there are significant barriers to entry and exit. The fifth factor is ambiguous.

8G.   Solar's total expenditure is represented by either the area *u0vx* under the marginal expenditure curve from a quantity of 0 to 6,000 tons or the rectangle *t0vz*.

2.   To sell additional units, a seller must reduce its price. So, when increasing sales by one unit, the seller will gain the price of the marginal unit but lose revenue on the inframarginal units. Hence, the marginal revenue is less than or equal to the price. If the demand is very elastic, then the marginal revenue will be close to the price. If, however, the demand is very inelastic, then the marginal revenue will be much lower than the price.

3.   Reduce the price, and so increase sales.

4.   True.

5.   Expiration of the patent will
(a) Reduce Solar's market power.
(b) Raise the price elasticity of demand.

6.   The profit-maximizing quantity is such that the marginal revenue equals the marginal cost. Hence, after a change in costs, the seller should look for the quantity where the marginal revenue equals the new marginal cost. So, it must consider both the marginal revenue and the marginal cost.

7.   Advertising expenditure = $(100 – 40) \times 0.01 \times 500,000 = \$0.3$ million.

8.   Yes.

9.   True.

10.   If the U.S. government were to forbid the NCAA from restrictive practices,
(a) Athletes' earnings would rise.
(b) The number of athletes would increase.

▌ *Chapter 9   Pricing Policy*

9A.   The profit-maximizing price is ¥63,000.

9B.   The market buyer surplus is the area *agc*.

9C.   Area *adb* = ¥31.25 million. Area *bec* = ¥31.25 million.

9D.   See Figure 9D.

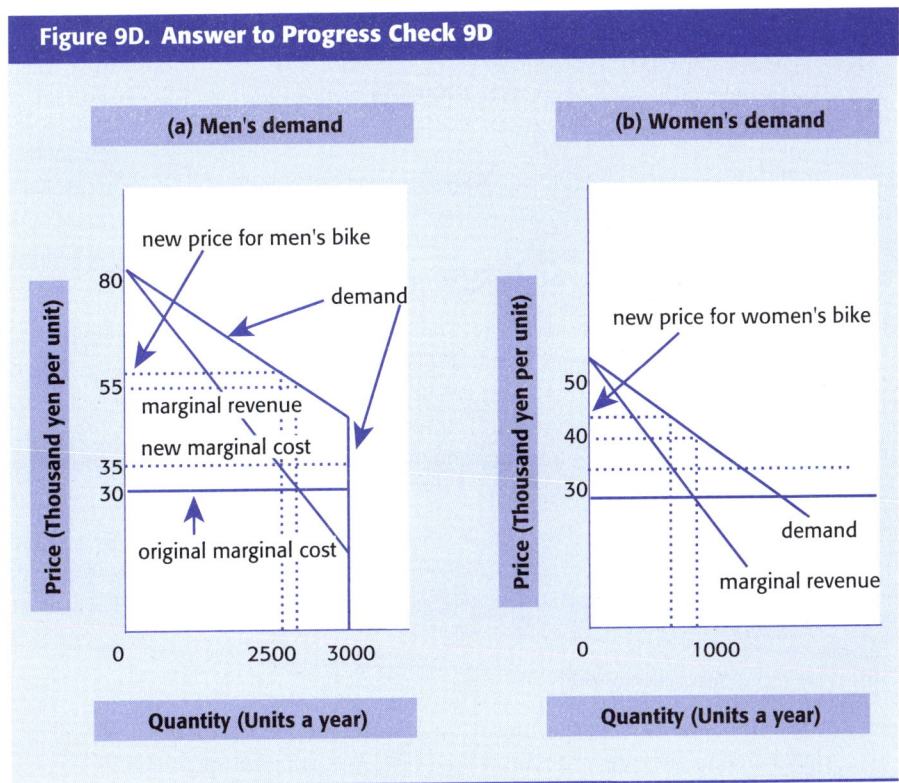

Figure 9D. Answer to Progress Check 9D

(a) Men's demand

new price for men's bike

80

demand

Price (Thousand yen per unit)

55

marginal revenue

new marginal cost

35
30

original marginal cost

0   2500   3000

Quantity (Units a year)

(b) Women's demand

new price for women's bike

Price (Thousand yen per unit)

50

40

30

demand

marginal revenue

0   1000

Quantity (Units a year)

9E.   CF with the Japanese price = ¥50,000 = $500. The difference with the American price = $150.

9F.   No, the two segments will not be differentially sensitive.

9G.   Price the bundle at $22 and the educational channel at $19.

9H.   The maximum price of the large bottle = $3.74.

1.   Not necessarily. The price also depends on the marginal cost.

2.   The profit-maximizing price = $2.50.

3.   No.

5.   Equal.

6.   The price in Germany = $3.30; the price in South Africa = $1.80.

7.   For publications, it would be easier to discriminate against newspapers because they have time value and are priced low relative to transportation

cost. For building materials, it would be easier to discriminate against bricks because they are priced low relative to transportation cost.

9. Consumers with small appetites prefer a la carte to buffets; big eaters prefer the buffets. The result is indirect segment discrimination.

10. (a) and (b).

Chapter 10   Strategic Thinking

10A. A union leader must consider how employers will react to her or his decisions. Accordingly, these decisions are strategic.

10B. Neither is dominated.

10C. The Nash equilibrium is for both comanies to produce more. Please refer to Table 10C.

10D. (1) If Merkur covers England, its expected return would be $(-2 \times 2/5) + (-3 \times 3/5) = -13/5$.
(2) If Merkur covers Germany, its expected return would be $(-3 \times 2/5) + (-2 \times 3/5) = -12/5$.

10E. It is not a zero-sum game.

10F. If the two stations take different time slots, their combined profit will be higher than if they take the same time slot. Accordingly, the situation is not a zero-sum game.

10G. Delta would choose 8:00 PM and Zeta would choose 7:30 PM.

10H. Agua Luna would produce 2 million bottles, and Moonlight would produce 1 million bottles. See Figure 10H.

1. (c).

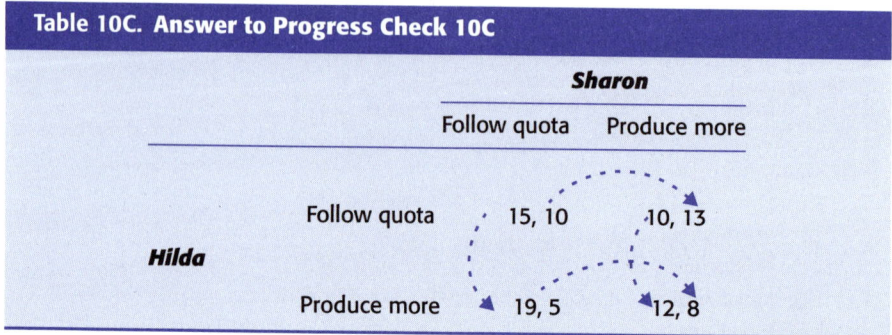

Table 10C. Answer to Progress Check 10C

		Sharon	
		Follow quota	Produce more
Hilda	Follow quota	15, 10	10, 13
	Produce more	19, 5	12, 8

Figure 10H. Answer to Progress Check 10H

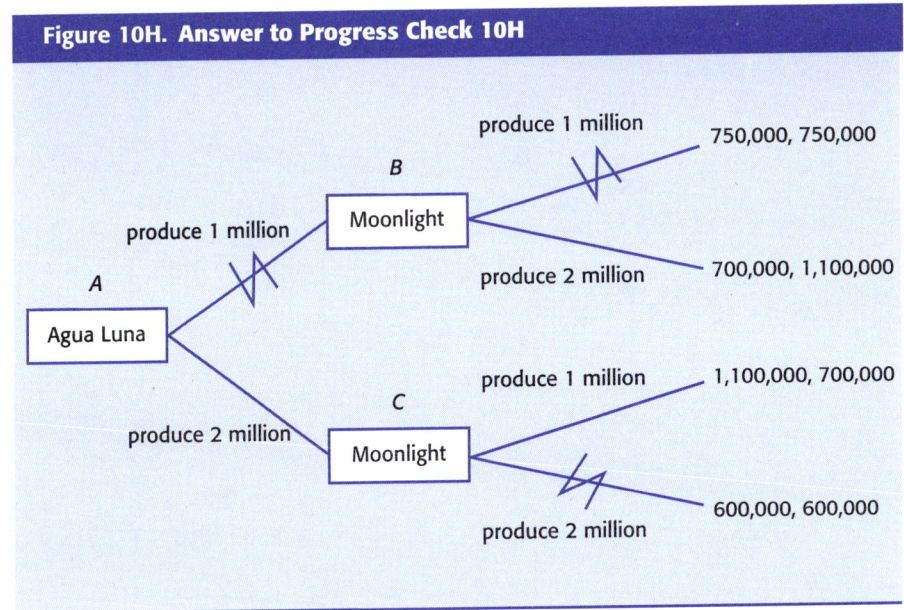

2. (a) A dominated strategy generates worse consequences than some other strategy, regardless of the other parties' choices. It makes no sense to adopt a dominated strategy.
   (b) Given that the other parties choose their Nash equilibrium strategies, each party prefers its own Nash equilibrium strategy. It is a logically consistent solution to the problem of infinite regress. It also provides a focal point for strategic decision making.

3. (c).

4. Venus chooses Orange with probability 0.5 and chooses Green with probability 0.5; and Sol does the same.

5. (b).

6. Yes, because the returns in each cell add up to the same number, in this case, 1.

7. Venus will choose either Orange or Green—either way, it will receive 1.5. Please refer to Figure RQ7.

8. (a) A strategic move is an action to influence the beliefs or actions of other parties in a favorable way. Typically, the move involves a deliberate restriction of the party's freedom of action.
   (b) A promise conveys benefits under specified conditions to change the beliefs or actions of other parties. It is effective only if it is credible.
   (c) A threat imposes costs under specified conditions to change the beliefs or actions of other parties. It is effective only if it is credible.

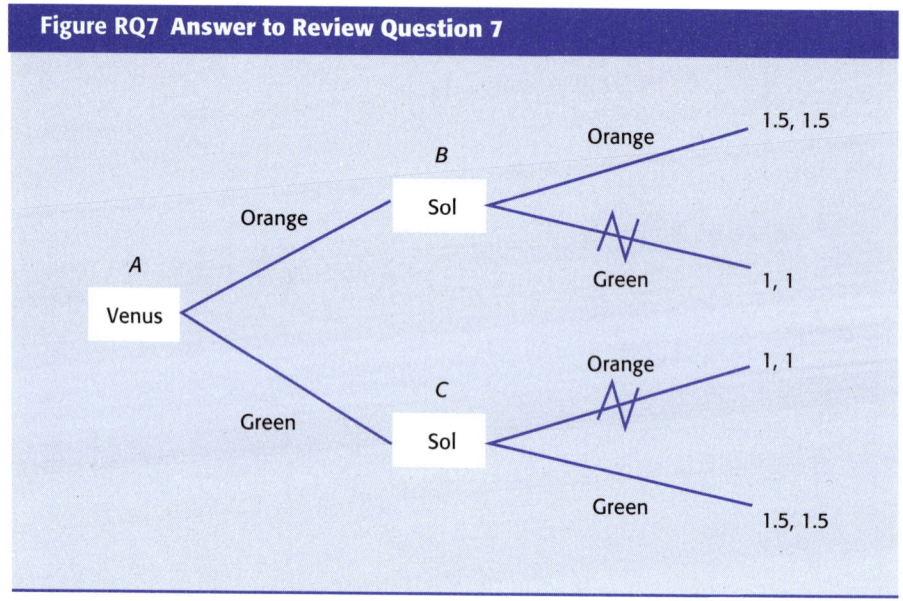

Figure RQ7 Answer to Review Question 7

9. Strategy (b) is more credible.

10. No. He gets higher interest from the bank and the deposit is guaranteed by the FDIC. To withdraw would provide a lower return.

Chapter 11   Externalities

11A. (1) The horizontal sum of individual demand curves is the market demand curve: At every price, we add the *quantities* demanded by the individuals to get the market quantity. The curves are added in a horizontal direction.

(2) The vertical sum of individual marginal benefit curves is the group marginal benefit curve: At every quantity, we add the *marginal benefits* of the individuals to get the group marginal benefit. The curves are added in a vertical direction.

11B. (1) Sol's marginal cost curve will be higher, and (2) the level of investment that maximizes the group profit will be lower. Please refer to Figure 11B.

11C. (a) is a network externality;
(b) is a network effect.

11D. See Figure 11D.

Figure 11B. Answer to Progress Check 11B

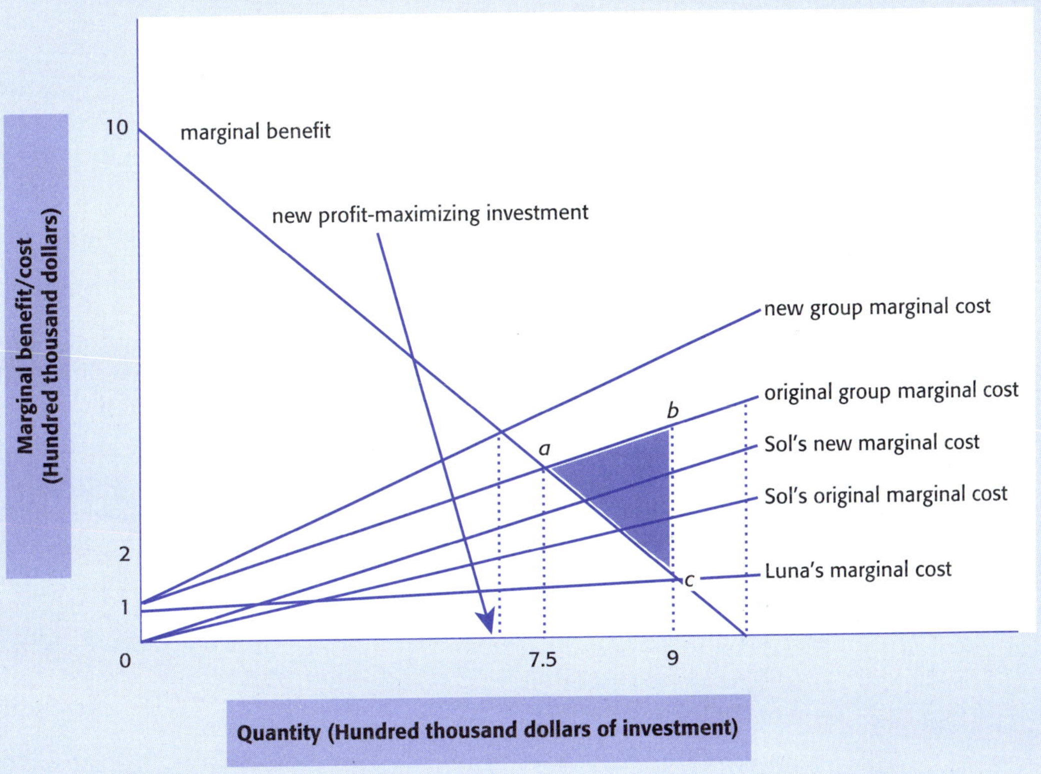

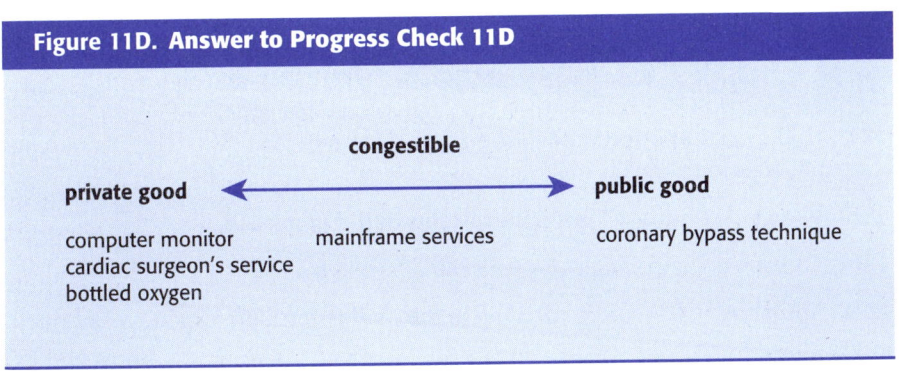

Marginal benefit/cost (Hundred thousand dollars)

Quantity (Hundred thousand dollars of investment)

10 — marginal benefit

new profit-maximizing investment

new group marginal cost

original group marginal cost

Sol's new marginal cost

Sol's original marginal cost

Luna's marginal cost

a

b

c

2

1

0

7.5

9

Figure 11D. Answer to Progress Check 11D

congestible

private good ←————————→ public good

computer monitor   mainframe services   coronary bypass technique
cardiac surgeon's service
bottled oxygen

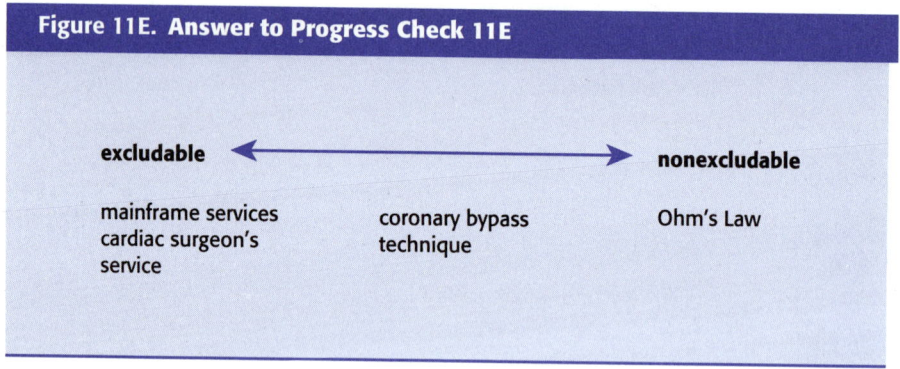

Figure 11E. Answer to Progress Check 11E

excludable ←——————————————————→ nonexcludable

mainframe services   coronary bypass   Ohm's Law
cardiac surgeon's   technique
service

11E. There are only a few users of techniques for coronary bypass, hence, usage is relatively easy to monitor. See Figure 11E.

2. The amount that the recipients of the negative externality are willing to pay for a marginal reduction is less than or equal to the marginal cost. The amount that the source is willing to accept for a marginal reduction is greater than or equal to the marginal benefit. Since the sum of the marginal costs exceeds the marginal revenue, the intermediary could make money.

3. (a) Negative externalities.
   (b) Positive externalities.
   (c) Positive externalities.

4. (a) and (b).

5. (a) The new exit will increase Moonlight's business.
   (b) Moonlight is taking a free ride on the investments by the other property owners.

6. (b).

9. (a), (c), and (d).

Chapter 12   Asymmetric Information

12A. Hilda has imperfect information but does not face risk. The insurer has imperfect information and faces risk.

12B. The market price will be higher, as shown in Figure 12B.

12C. The percentage of high-risk policyholders will fall.

12D. Appraisals will be more common in the market for more expensive antiques.

12E. Borrowers who are more willing to repay will be relatively more likely to post collateral.

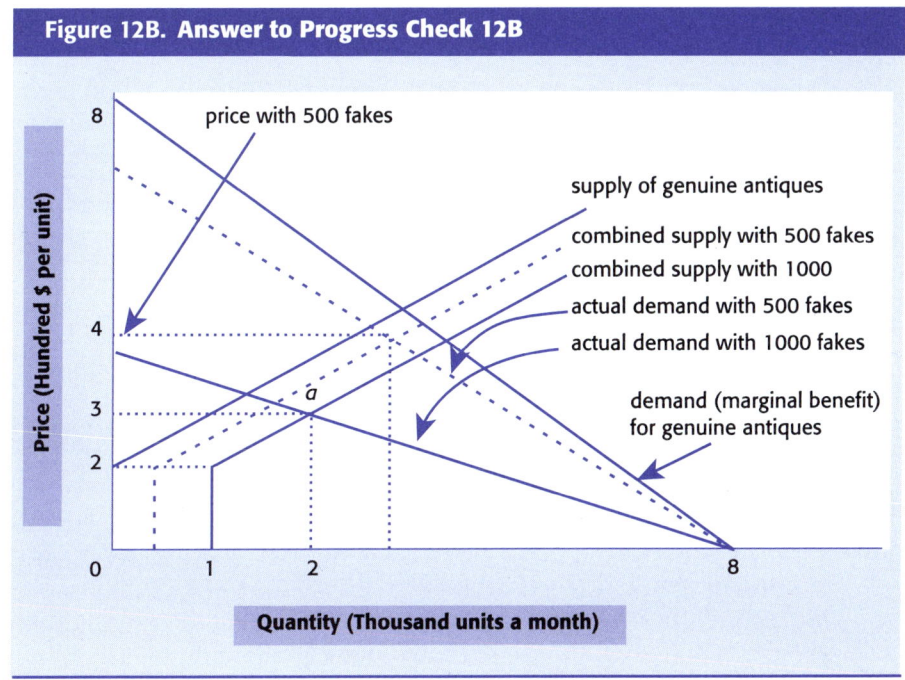

Figure 12B. Answer to Progress Check 12B

price with 500 fakes

supply of genuine antiques

combined supply with 500 fakes

combined supply with 1000

actual demand with 500 fakes

actual demand with 1000 fakes

demand (marginal benefit)
for genuine antiques

Price (Hundred $ per unit)

Quantity (Thousand units a month)

12F. (a) It should provide the information to the bidders.
(b) This information will reduce the extent of the winner's curse.

12G. Screening is an initiative of the less-informed party, while signaling is an initiative of the better-informed party.

1. (a) No asymmetry.
(b) The directors of Acquirer have better information than the general investor.
(c) No asymmetry.
(d) Henry has better information than James.

3. (a) True.
(b) False. Risk neutral persons will not want insurance.

4. Yes, this will draw relatively less hardworking persons.

5. The seller has an interest not to reveal negative information about the car.

7. (a) Open bidding allows the participants to observe the bids of others. This
supports collusion.
(b) Setting a reserve price will put a limit to collusion.

8. (b).

10. Yes.

Chapter 13   Incentives and Organization

13A. The new marginal cost curve lies above the original. Please refer to Figure 13A.
(1) The economically efficient effort will be lower.
(2) The effort that the worker actually chooses will be lower.

13B. Draw any personal marginal benefit curve that crosses the marginal cost curve at 120 units of effort.

13C. See Figure 13C.

13D. Mary's incentive scheme should be stronger.

13E. The salesclerk's incentive to process returns will be reduced.

13F. On-the-job training.

13G. Walt Disney integrated downstream; Seagate integrated upstream; Broken Hill integrated downstream; Loral integrated downstream.

13H. There are scale economies in processing credit card transactions. Mercury is too small to operate the service efficiently.

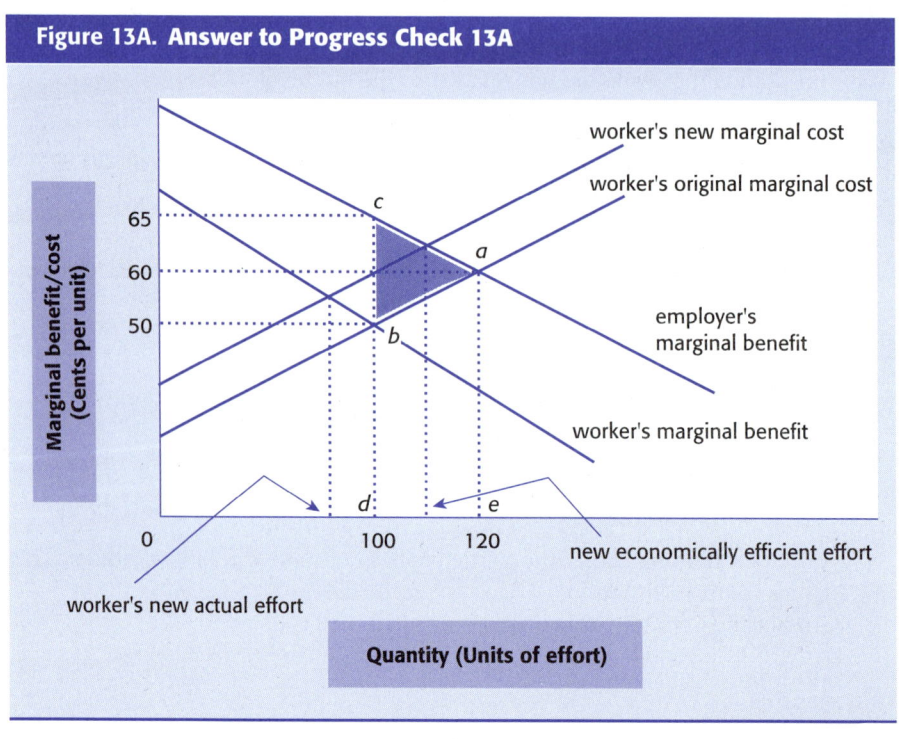

Figure 13A. Answer to Progress Check 13A

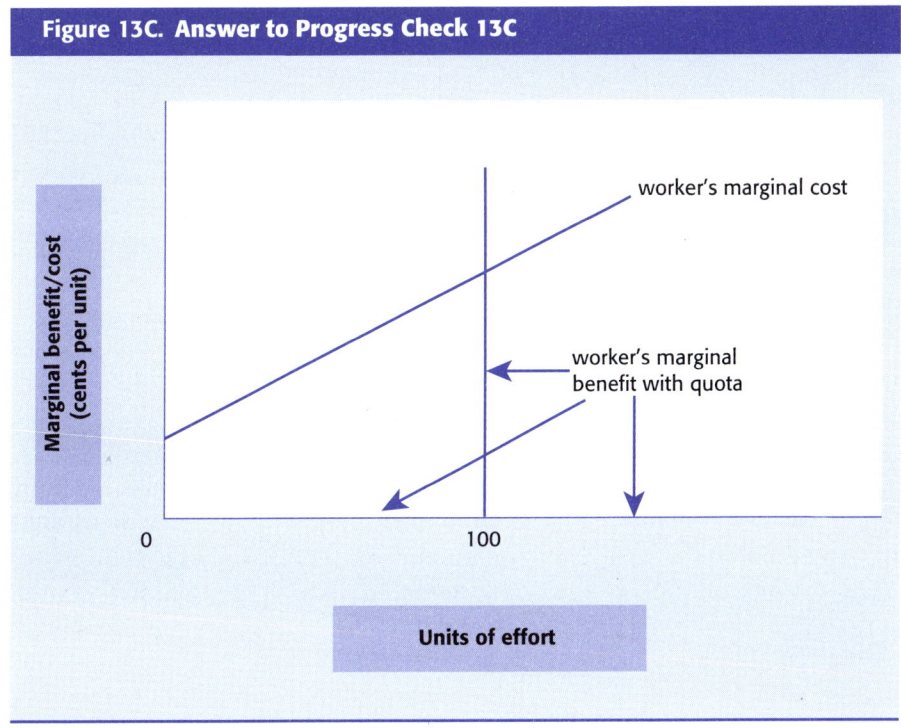

Figure 13C. Answer to Progress Check 13C

worker's marginal cost

worker's marginal benefit with quota

Marginal benefit/cost (cents per unit)

0   100

Units of effort

1. Regarding asymmetry, it is costly for the insurer to monitor Leah's precautions. There is a conflict of interest because, with insurance, Leah bears the cost of precautions but receives only part of the benefit.

2. With moral hazard, the marginal benefit of effort exceeds the marginal cost. By resolving the moral hazard, the potential profit is the marginal benefit less the marginal cost.

3. Method (b) provides more incentive to the lawyer.

4. (a) Pay or quotas based on sales relative to the average.
   (b) Rewards or quotas based on the number of accidents or breakdowns relative to average.

5. The scheme will reduce the secretary's incentive for effort in the other tasks.

6. (a) Index of small stocks.
   (b) Index of U.S. government bonds.
   (c) Index of Japanese stocks.

7. (b)

9. Vertical integration involves combining assets for the two successive stages of production under common ownership. Horizontal integration involves combining assets for the same stage of production under common ownership.

10. For: reduces potential for hold up. Against: increases moral hazard, creates internal monopoly, does not benefit from scale economies.

Chapter 14   Regulation

14A. See Figure 14A.

14B. One operator should be given a monopoly franchise for distribution of gas. It should be either not allowed to produce natural gas or required to separate its distribution and production businesses.

14C. See Figure 14C. The mistaken fee would be $30; hence, the emissions would be 8500 tons, causing a deadweight loss of area *aeb*. The mistaken standard would be 7000 tons, causing a deadweight loss of area *cda*. Area *cda* is larger than area *aeb*.

14D. See Figure 14D. The new care would exceed the economically efficient level.

14E. Reduce.

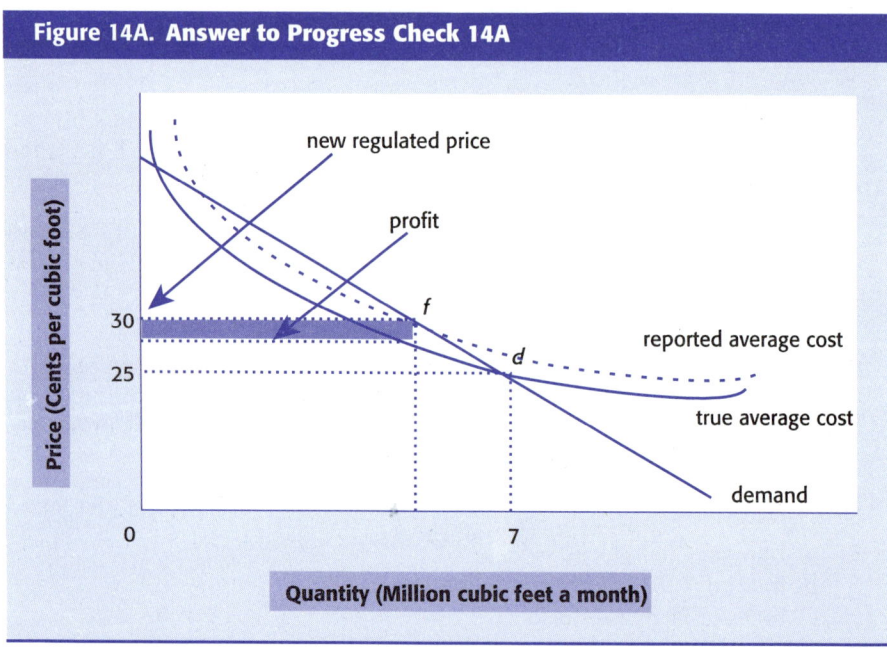

Figure 14A. Answer to Progress Check 14A

new regulated price

profit

f

reported average cost

30

25

d

true average cost

demand

Price (Cents per cubic foot)

0   7

Quantity (Million cubic feet a month)

Figure 14C. Answer to Progress Check 14C

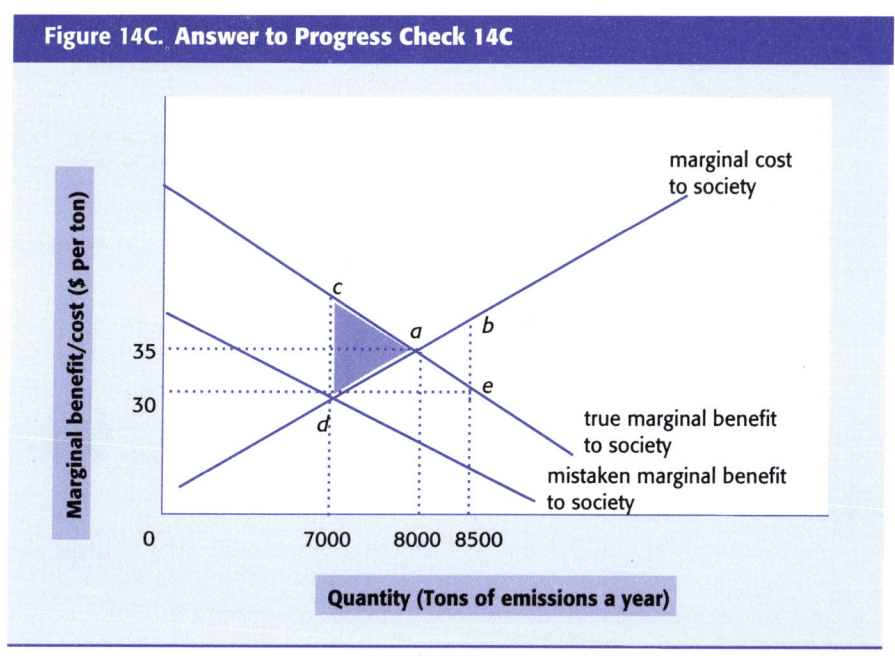

Quantity (Tons of emissions a year)

Figure 14D. Answer to Progress Check 14D

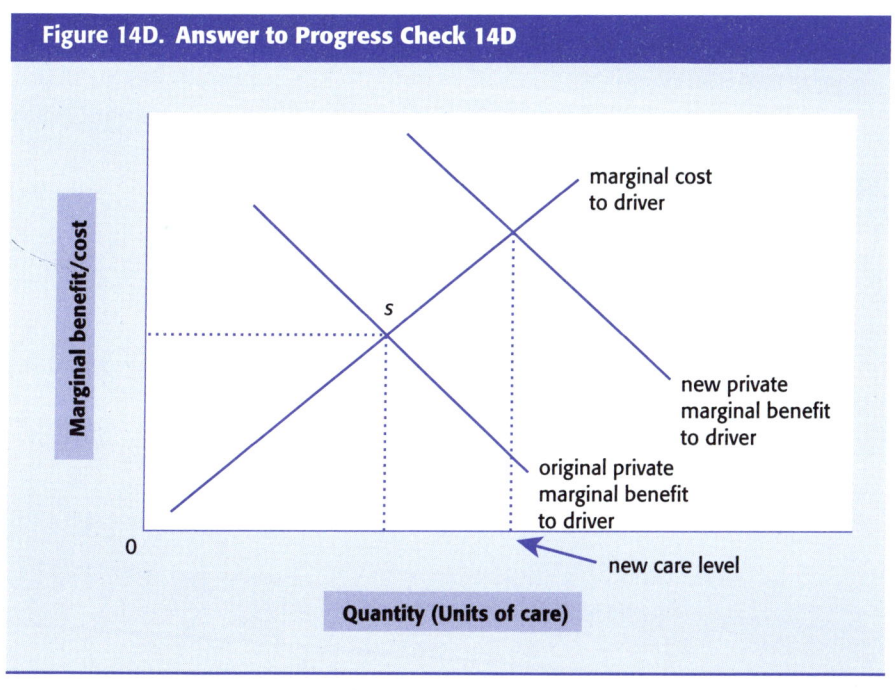

Quantity (Units of care)

14F. Assuming that demand varies over the day, the marginal cost of usage will also vary. Economically efficient usage requires the price to vary with the marginal cost.

3. Monopolies restrict provision to raise the price, while monopsonies restrict purchases to reduce the price. In both cases, the outcome is not economically efficient.

4. Privatization means transferring ownership from the public to the private sector. Allowing competition means removing an exclusive right.

6. (a) A movie producer that owns a theater is vertically integrated into the downstream stage of production.
   (b) The law that prohibited movie producers from owning theaters is a structural regulation to separate the movie production and exhibition businesses.

7. False.

8. (a) The regulator could charge a fee for noise generated by the construction equipment.
   (b) The regulator could set a standard and make it illegal for construction equipment to generate noise exceeding the standard.

9. No.

10. (a) Not an externality because all the parties belong to the market for production workers.
    (b) This is an externality.

Index of Companies and Organizations

Author Index

Subject Index